BURIED

GENEALOGICAL DATA

A Complete List of Addressed Letters Left
in the Post Offices of Philadelphia,
Chester, Lancaster, Trenton,
New Castle & Wilmington
Between 1748 and 1780

Abstracted from
The Pennsylvania Gazette

Edited By

KENNETH SCOTT

&

KENN STRYKER-RODDA

CLEARFIELD

Reprinted for
Clearfield Company, Inc. by
Genealogical Publishing Co., Inc.
Baltimore, Maryland
1998

Library of Congress Catalogue Card Number 77-82335
International Standard Book Number 0-8063-0782-X

Made in the United States of America

INTRODUCTION

Postmaster General Spotswood in 1737 removed William Bradford from the office of Postmaster of Philadelphia and appointed in his stead Benjamin Franklin. Up to that time letters were held at a post office until called for, but Franklin, desirous of improving the system, began the publication of names of persons for whom unclaimed letters were in the office under his jurisdiction. The first list appeared in Franklin's *Pennsylvania Gazette* of 21 March 1738 and, as a result, addressees, their friends or messengers, picked up much of the mail.*

These lists, which were printed from time to time throughout the Colonial Period, with occasional lapses, provide a wealth of genealogical information by locating thousands of individuals at various times and, upon occasion, identifying their trade, profession, or military rank. Sometimes the *Gazette* published lists from other towns than Philadelphia, specifically Chester, Lancaster, Trenton, New Castle, and Wilmington. It should be noted that after Benjamin Franklin and William Hunter were appointed Deputy Postmasters General in August of 1753 the publication of lists of unclaimed letters was undertaken in other newspapers in the Colonies.

The present volume contains the names of persons whose letters were in the post offices of Philadelphia, Chester, Lancaster, Trenton, New Castle, and Wilmington. All lists printed in the *Gazette* from 1748 throughout the Colonial Period are here published, with the names arranged alphabetically. Lists previous to 1748 appear in *Abstracts from Ben Franklin's Pennsylvania Gazette, 1728-1748* (Baltimore: Genealogical Publishing Co., Inc., 1975). It is hoped that this book will be of value for genealogical research. Certainly it would have delighted Benjamin Franklin to have his innovation in the postal service become a tool for tracing ancestors, a pursuit which gave him "pleasure" and led him to make a journey to Northamptonshire, where the Franklins had lived in the same village for three hundred years and more.

The capital letter designations P, C, L, T, N, W following the addressee's name signify respectively the post offices in Philadelphia, Chester, Lancaster, Trenton, New Castle, and Wilmington in which letters lay unclaimed. In instances where a specific locality is given, it is understood that the letters were so addressed. The dates which complete each entry indicate the day of publication in the *Gazette*.

*See Ruth Lapham Butler, *Doctor Franklin, Postmaster General* (Garden City, N.Y.: Doubleday, Doran & Co., Inc., 1928), p. 55.

A--ORN
Robert P: Phila 19 Jy 80
AAIR
William L: Shearman's Valley
2 Mar 74
ABBOTT?ABBOT
Anne P: Chester Co 1 May 76
Henry P: Phila 30 May 54
Joseph B. P: Phila 31 Dec 61
ABEIT
Mons. P: Phila 19 Jy 80
ABELL
Daniel P: Gloucester 24 Feb
63
ABERCROMBIE/ABERCRUMBY
James P: Phila 9 Ag 59
William L: Cumberland Co
2 Mar 74
ABERDEEN
Mrs. P: Phila 18 Mar 62
ABERNATHY/ABERNETHY/ABERNERTHY
James P: Bristol 12 Ja 58
John L: Tyrone, York Co 29
Jy 72. P: Phila 27 Dec 53
William L: Carlisle, Cumber-
land Co 19 Dec 71. P: Car-
lisle 3 Ja 60, 13 Oct 63
ABEY
Mrs. P: Maryland 2 Ag 70
ABLE
Henry P: Phila 3 Ja 60
ACKLEY
Mary P: Phila 19 Ja 69
ACKO
Sarah P: Phila 27 Ja 73
ACKROYD/AKROYD
John P: Phila 19 Jy 80
Joseph P: Phila 21 Dec 58,
8 Jy 62
ACRELIUS
Israel P: Christine 30 May
54
ACTON
John P: Phila 30 Ja 66
ADAIR/ADEAR/ADAJR
Alexander P: Phila 6 Jy 58,
27 Jy 58, 9 Ag 59, 18 Mar
62
Barney P: Phila 27 Oct 73
David P: Hopewell Twp 31 Dec
61. T: Hopewell 4 Nov 72
Edward P: Bristol 3 Sep 61
James P: Lancaster Co 13
Ja 63
John P: N. Castle Co 5 Ag 62;
Pa 2 Feb 64
Joseph P: Lancaster Co 3 Ja
60; Phila 4 Feb 68, 28 Ap
68, 2 Oct 69
Robert P: Phila 18 Mar 62,
4 Ag 63
William L: Lancaster Co 29
Jy 72. P: Newcastle Co
28 Nov 54, 4 Ag 63; Shear-
man's Valley 16 Jy 72

ADAM
Thomas P: Little Canabaga
19 Jy 80
ADAMS
Mr. P: Phila 25 Ap 71
Widow P: Pa 15 Mar 64
Alexander P: Phila 21 Dec 58,
2 Sep 62; Shrewsbury 9 Ag
59
Athlannah P: Wilmington 9 Ag
59
Charles P: Phila 28 Oct 62.
T: Boundbrook 17 Oct 54
Christopher P: Phila 2 May
65
David P: Pa 12 Ja 58
Deidamia P: Marcus Hook 13
Ja 63
Dunlap P: Phila 24 Feb 63
George P: New Castle Co 9
May 54, 2 Feb 64; Christine/
Christine Bridge 11 Sep 56,
21 Dec 58, 3 Dec 61, 8 Jy
62
George N: 29 Nov 64; Fan
Twp, see BEAN, Daniel
James L: 11 Ap 65. P: Bucks
Co 24 Jy 76; Christeen 13
Ja 63; Pa 4 Ag 63; North-
hampton, Bucks Co 27 Ja 73
Jane P: Phila 20 Jy 69
Jean P: Phila 15 Mar 64
John L: Marsh-creek Settle-
ment 19 Dec 71. P: German-
town 2 May 65, 25 Jy 65;
Pa 12 Ja 58, 18 Mar 62;
Phila 9 May 54, 11 Sep 55,
24 Feb 63
Jonathan P: Phila 8 Jy 62,
13 Oct 63, 21 Jy 68, 20 Oct
68, 19 Ja 69; Schuylkill 1
Nov 70
Joseph P: Phila 5 Ag 62, 26
Jy 64, 25 Jy 65, 30 Ja 66,
21 Jy 68, 25 Ap 71, 27 Oct
73
Josias P: Phila 13 Oct 63
Levi P: Phila 19 Jy 80
Mary P: Dorchester Co 9 Ag
59
Matthew P: Phila 4 Ag 63,
27 Oct 73
Nathan P: Kent Co 1 May 76
Ralph P: Phila 27 Oct 73
Ro. P: Desartmartin 9 Ag 59
Robert P: Phila 3 Ja 76
Sarah P: Phila 8 Jy 62, 27
Oct 73
Susannah T: Trenton 10 Ag 58
Thomas P: Whiteclay Creek
24 Feb 63
William L: c/o John Finley,
York Co 19 Dec 71. P: Kent
Co 8 Jy 62; Phila 4 Ap 54,
11 Sep 55, 1 Jy 56, 27 Jy

58, 8 Jy 62 (Capt), 4 Feb
68
ADAMSON
  Joseph   P: Phila 24 Oct 54
  Capt. William   P: Phila 27
  Oct 73
ADDEM
  Samuel   P: Pa 15 Mar 64
ADDISON
  Margaret   P: Phila 6 Jy 58
  William   P: New Londonderry
  27 Jy 58
ADGAR
  Polly   P: Phila 3 Ja 76
ADLOM
  Elizabeth   T: Trenton 3 Oct
  65
ADOLF
  John   P: Phila 22 Nov 53
ADONECHEY
  Patrick   P: Pa 15 Mar 64
ADWARD
  George   P: Phila 21 Jy 68
ADWELL/ADUDDELL/ADUDLE/ADIDDELL
  James   L: Lebanon Twp 20 Ja
  73 (2).   P: Merion Twp 31
  Dec 61; Phila 30 Ja 66
AFARCKUS
  John   P: Pa 2 Feb 64
AFFEY
  Mrs.   P: Phila 25 Jy 65
AGAR
  Thomas   P: Cumberland Co 28
  Oct 62
  Rev. William   P: Pa 20 Oct 68
AGILTAN
  Hugh   P: Phila 26 Oct 69
AGNEW
  David   P: Phila 13 Oct 63
  Florence   P: America 9 Ag 59;
  Pa 3 Ja 60, 18 Mar 62;
  Phila 21 Dec 58 (Mrs. Flor.)
  George   P: Phila 13 Oct 63
  James   P: York Co 13 Oct 63
  John   P: Carlisle 12 Feb 61,
  8 Jy 62, 31 Mar 63, 19 May
  63; Cumberland 2 Feb 64;
  Phila 5 Ag 62, 15 Mar 64
  Peter   P: New-Castle Co 3 Ja
  60, 13 Ja 63
  William   P: Pa 3 Ja 60; Phila
  8 Jy 62, 28 Oct 62, 2 Ag 70
AHEHURST
  George   T: Trenton 3 Oct 65
AHIER
  Philip   P: Phila 9 Ag 59
AICHISON
  John   P: Phila 27 Oct 73
AIKMAN/AKMAN
  Adam   P: Phila 12 Feb 61, 4
  Ag 63
  Robert   P: New-Castle 3 Sep
  61
AINIES
  Brice   P: Phila 30 Oct 76

AIR
  William   P: Abington 1 Nov 53
AIREY/AREY
  John   P: Phila 28 Ap 68
  Joseph   P: Phila 9 May 54
AIRTH
  Alexander   P: Phila 4 Ag 63
AITKEN/AITKIN
  John   P: Phila 26 Oct 69
  (Capt.)   W: near Christiana
  Bridge 27 Ag 77
  Matthew   P: Phila 2 Ag 70
AKEN/AKIN/AIKINE/AIKON/AIKIN
  Widow   P: Phila 13 Oct 63,
  3 Ja 65
  Alexander   P: New-Castle Co
  19 May 63
  James   P: Pennsylvania 4 Feb
  68
  John   P: Phila 10 Oct 65;
  Pincado 2 Ag 70
  Robert   P: N. Castle Co 8 Jy
  62; Phila 31 Jy 60, 28 Oct
  62
  Samuel   P: Chester 19 May 63
  William   P: Bucks Co 18 Mar
  62; Phila 1 Nov 70
AKENHEAD
  Andrew   P: Pa 3 Ja 60; Phila
  11 Sep 55
AKINS
  Timothy   P: East Jersey 31 Jy
  60
ALBERTSON
  Ricloff/Rickliff/R.   P: Phila
  16 Jy 77; 13 Ja 63 (Capt.),
  23 Oct 66 (Capt.)
  Thomas   P: Phila 18 Ag 57
ALBERTY
  Philip   P: Phila 19 Ja 69
ALBMAN
  Dorothy   P: Lancaster Co 28
  Oct 62
ALBON
  John   P: Chester Co 18 Mar 62
ALBRO
  Capt. Layton/Laton   P: Phila
  3 May 70, 2 Ag 70
ALBURY
  Matthew   P: Phila 20 Ag 54
ALCORN
  John   P: Cheater Co 28 Oct 62
ALDOR
  George F.   P: Phila 5 Ag 62
ALDRICH/ALDRICKS; see also
  ALRICKS/ALDRAGE/ALDRIGE
  Freades   P: New Castle Co 18
  Feb 55
  Joseph   P: Phila 4 Ag 63
  Richard   P: Carlisle 3 Ja 60
  (Esq); Cumberland Co 9 Ag 59
ALEA
  Thomas   P: Phila 26 Oct 69
ALECKS
  Robert   P: Cumberland Co 2

Feb 64

ALEXANDER

Capt. P: Phila 30 Ap 77

Mrs. P: Phila 2 Sep 62

Adam P: Chester Co 18 Ag 57

Alexander P: Phila 11 Sep 55, 12 Ja 58, 6 Jy 58, 27 Jy 58, 9 Ag 59, 31 Jy 60, 4 Ag 63, 3 Ja 65, 16 Jy 67

Amos P: Newcastle Co 24 Oct 54

Arthur P: Sasquehannah 4 Ag 63

Capt. Charles P: Phila 23 Oct 66

David P: Phila 1 Nov 53

Eleanor P: Phila 20 Oct 68

George P: Phila 28 Oct 62; Wilmington 9 Ag 59

Hugh L: Shearman's Valley 20 Ja 73. P: Phila 6 Jy 58, 27 Jy 58, 9 Ag 59

Dr. J. P: New Munster 11 Sep 55

Jacob P: Pa 28 Oct 62

James P: Buckingham, Bucks Co 26 Oct 69; Chester Co 31 Dec 61; Goshen 5 Ag 56; Norrington 26 Oct 69; Phila 4 Ap 54, 24 Feb 63

John P: Coecil Co 31 Jy 60; Norrington 19 May 63, 13 Oct 63; Phila 27 Ja 63

Joseph L: 29 Ja 67. P: Phila 6 Jy 58, 30 Ap 67, 26 Oct 69, 1 Feb 70, 2 Ag 70, 27 Oct 73, 3 Ja 76

Matthew, soldier in 18th Regt. P: Phila 3 May 70

Patrick P: Lancaster Co 1 Nov 53

Robert C: Chester, Little Britain 30 Oct 66. P: Fogs Manor 31 Dec 61

Thomas P: Harris's Ferry 27 Jy 58; Paxton 28 Nov 54; Phila 30 Ja 66, 27 Ja 73

William P: Perkeomen 1 Jy 56; Phila 20 Oct 68

William M. P: Pa 2 Feb 64

ALEY

John P: Phila 31 Ja 76

ALFONTZ

R̄ev. P: Germantown 10 Oct 65

ALFORD/ALLFORD

Catherine P: Bucks Co 31 Dec 61

Samuel P: Phila 13 Oct 63

ALLAIRE

Alexander P: Phila 11 Sep 55, 10 Ap 66

ALLCOCK

George P: Phila 5 Ag 56

ALLEN/ALLANN/ALLIN/ALLON

Messieurs Allen and Dennis P:

Somerset Co 19 May 63

Mrs. P: Phila 18 Mar 62

Widow T: Allentown 17 Oct 54

Ann T: Allens-town 17 Oct 54

Charles C: Cheater 30 Jy 77. P: Phila 28 Oct 62

David P: Fog's Manor 24 Oct 54, 18 Ag 57

El. P: Fairfield 15 Mar 64

Eleanor P: Phila 31 Dec 61

Elizabeth P: Phila 3 Sep 61, 27 Ja 73

George P: Lancaster Co 1 Nov 53, 5 Feb 54; Phila 30 Ap 67; West Jersey 12 Feb 61

Henry C: at Francis Keys, in Charlestown, Md. 30 Oct 66

James L: 11 Ap 65. P: 12 Ja 58 (Lt. in army); Marcus Hook 31 Mar 63; Phila 2 Sep 62 & 31 Mar 63 (Capt), 30 Ap 77; Sadsbury 12 Ja 58

Jane P: Fog's Manor 24 Oct 54; Pa 18 Mar 62, 24 Feb 63

Jenny P: Phila 27 Ja 73

John P: Phila 27 Jy 58, 12 Feb 61, 15 Mar 64; N.J. 1 Feb 70

John and Peter L: Octerara 29 Jy 72

Jonathan C: Chester 30 Jy 77

Joseph P: Chester Co 3 Ja 60; Phila 5 Ag 62, 13 Oct 63, 2 Feb 64, 15 Mar 64, 16 Jy 72; Shrewsbury 30 Oct 76

Malcum P: Lancaster Co 22 Nov 53

Mary P: Phila 30 Ja 66

Capt. Moses P: Phila 13 Ja 63

Capt. Nathaniel P: Phila 30 Ap 67, 16 Jy 67

Peter P: Phila 4 Feb 68, 1 May 76; see also John & Peter

Robert L: Chestnut-Level 31 Ja 71. P: Phila 19 May 63

Samuel P: N. Castle Co 31 Dec 61; Phila 19 May 63

Susannah P: Phila 3 Ja 60

Thomas P: Bucks Co 13 Ja 63, 15 Mar 64; Lancaster Co 24 Oct 54; Phila 31 Dec 61, 28 Oct 62, 15 Mar 64, 28 Ap 68, 3 Ja 76

W. P: Pa 12 Ja 58

William P: Lancaster Co 24 Oct 54; Pa 12 Feb 61, 31 Dec 61; Phila 18 Ag 57, 20 Oct 68; Snow Hill 19 May 63

ALLEND

William P: Elk River 9 Ag 59

ALLET
  Benjamin P: Chester Co 28
    Oct 62
ALLEUT
  Mr. P: Phila 21 Jy 68
ALLIBONE/ALLOBON
  Capt. John P: Phila 19 Jy 80
  Capt. W. P: Phila 15 Mar 64
  William P: Phila 8 Jy 62
ALLISON/ALLASON/ALISON/ALLIASON
  Alexander P: Phila 3 Ja 76
  Capt. Benjamin Ashley P:
    Phila 30 Ap 67
  Rev. Francis P: Phila 20 Oct
    68
  Hannah P: Phila 19 Jy 80
  Rev. Hector P: Pa 31 Dec 61
  James P: Forks of Delaware
    9 Ag 59, 26 Oct 69
  John L: Little Britain 14
    May 72, 2 Mar 74. P: Bucks
    Co 26 Jy 64; Cumberland Co
    9 Ag 59; Donegall 13 May 56,
    31 Jy 60; Lancaster Co 27
    Jy 58 & 3 Ja 60 (Esq)
  Justice P: Donegall 15 Mar
    64
  Matthew P: Great Swamp 8 Jy
    62
  Moses P: Fogs Manor 31 Dec
    61; Lancaster Co 12 Feb 61
  Patrick P: Phila 23 Oct 66
  Robert P: Donegall 3 Sep 61;
    Phila 13 Ja 63, 19 May 63
  Samuel L: Conegocheague 20
    Ja 73
  Sarah P: Wilmington 1 Jy 56
  Capt. W. P: Phila 2 Sep 62
ALMOND
  John P: New-Castle Co 15 Mar
    64
ALRICKS; see also ALDRICKS
  Wessel P: Reedy-Island 18
    Mar 62
ALSENTZ
  Rev. P: Phila 21 Dec 58
ALSOP
  Robert C: Charles-town; see
    BAKER, Francis
ALSTON
  John P: Phila 20 Jy 69
ALTENIZ
  Rev. J.G. P: Germantown 18
    Mar 62
ALTER/ALTAR
  Frederick P: Reading Town 10
    Ap 66; Phila 2 Feb 64
  Jacob P: Reading 19 Jy 80
ALTIMUS
  Frederick P: Phila 24 Jy 76
ALVEY
  John P: Phila 31 Jy 60
AMBELEAR
  Capt. Nathaniel P: Phila 18
    Mar 62

AMBORN
  Jacob P: Pa 4 Ag 63; Pa Co
    15 Mar 64
AMBRAY
  Joshua P: Phila 27 Ja 73
AMERSON/AMMERSON
  Lambert P: Phila 31 Jy 60
  Mary P: Phila 21 Dec 58
AMHURST
  William P: Providence, Phila
    Co 20 Ap 69
AMIEL/AMIELL
  Otho P: Phila 1 May 76
  Capt. Philip P: Phila 19 Jy
    80
AMONNET
  John P: Phila 30 May 54
AMORY
  John P: Phila 11 Sep 55, 4
    Feb 68 (Capt)
  Capt. William P: Phila 28
    Oct 62
ANCRUM
  Capt. George P: Phila 27 Oct
    73
ANDERSON
  ... P: Phila 13 May 56
  Capt. T: near Trenton; see
    LEE, Mrs. Mary
  Mrs. P: Phila 25 Jy 65
  Mr. P: Phila 31 Jy 60, 31
    Dec 61, 3 Dec
  Andreas T: Long-bridge 17
    Oct 54
  Archibald P: near Phila 1
    Feb 70
  Arthur P: Phila 28 Oct 62
  Barbara P: Phila 25 Ap 71
  Catharine P: Phila 1 May 76
  Charles P: Phila 3 May 65
  David N: c/o James Anderson
    Newark 4 Dec 66. P: Phila
    30 Oct 76
  Dinah P: Phila 20 Ap 69
  Elizabeth P: Phila 23 Oct 66,
    19 Jy 80
  Capt. Enoch P: Phila 30 Ap
    77
  Ephraim P: Phila 13 Oct 63
  Francis P: New Castle Co 7
    Ap 57
  George P: Cumberland Co 18
    Ag 57; in the army, Capt.
    21 Dec 58
  Hezekiah P: Bucks Co 13 Ja
    63
  Hugh P: Phila Co 7 Ap 57
  Isabella/Isabel P: Phila 27
    Oct 73. T: Amwell 6 Dec 64
  Ensign J. P: Maidenhead 24
    Feb 63
  James P: Phila 3 Ja 65; N.J.
    4 Feb 68; Phila 15 Mar 64,
    16 Jy 72, 1 May 76. T:
    Colesnake 4 Nov 72

Jane   P: Chester Co 27 Jy 58,
  31 Jy 60, 12 Feb 61
John   L: Pequea 31 Ja 71;
  Raphoe Twp 19 Dec 71;
  Salisbury 29 Jy 72. P: 3
  Ja 65; Cumberland Co 2 Feb
  64; Lancaster Co 31 Dec 61;
  Octorara 12 Ja 58; Pa 2 Feb
  64; Phila 30 May 54, 28 Nov
  54, 5 Ag 62, 2 Sep 62, 23
  Oct 66; York Co 24 Oct 54
  T: Maidenhead 17 Oct 54
  (Capt.); near Trenton 6
  Dec 64; Trenton 4 Nov 72
Joshua   L: Middle Octarara,
  Chestnut Level 19 Dec 71
Margaret   P: New Castle Co 7
  Ap 57
Mary   P: Phila 31 Jy 60;
  Whitemarsh 18 Ag 57. T:
  Trenton 10 Ag 58
Nancy   P: Phila Co 3 Ja 60
Richard   P: Phila 1 Nov 70,
  25 Ap 71
Robert   P: Phila 27 Jy 58,
  24 Feb 63, 19 May 63, 16
  Jy 72, 19 Jy 80
Roger   P: Lancaster Co 13
  Oct 63
Samuel   P: Bucks Co 9 Ag 59,
  2 Ag 70; Cumberland Co 3
  Sep 61, 5 Ag 62
Sarah   P: Lancaster Co 24
  Oct 54
Tasable   T: Amwell 15 Mar 64
Thomas   C: Marlborough 30 Oct
  66. P: N.J. 4 Ag 63
Walter   P: Phila 2 Ag 70
William   L: near Shearman's
  Valley 19 Dec 71. P:
  Chester Co 31 Jy 60;
  Chestnut Level 18 Mar 62;
  Phila 18 Feb 55, 18 Mar 62,
  4 Ag 63, 4 Feb 68, 19 Ja 69;
  Radaor 9 Ag 59; Whitemarsh
  28 Ap 68. T: Hopewell 4
  Nov 72
ANDERTON
  Mary   P: Phila 11 Sep 55
  Thomas   P: Phila 25 Jy 65
ANDOVER
  Joseph   P: Phila 12 Ja 58, 31
  Jy 60
  Prudence   P: Phila 31 Dec 61
ANDREW
  James   P: Phila 25 Jy 65, 10
  Ap 66, 23 Oct 66, 30 Ap 67
  Moses   P: Lancaster Co 24 Feb
  63
  Nicholas   P: Germantown 1 Feb
  70
  Robert   P: Chester Co 18 Mar
  62
ANDREWS
  Benjamin   P: Phila 8 Jy 62

John   C: West Nottingham,
  Chester Co 18 Jy 65. P:
  East-Jersey 31 Jy 60; Pa
  28 Oct 62; & Co., Phila 27
  Ja 73
Robert   P: Phila 19 Ja 69
Sarah   P: Pa 2 Feb 64
Thomas   P: Phila 2 Ag 70, 27
  Ja 73
William   P: Phila 1 Nov 53
ANGEVINE
  Margaret   P: Scarsdale 15 Mar
  64
ANNAN
  Rev. Robert   P: Marsh Creek
  30 Ap 67
ANNELY
  Edward   P: Phila 29 Ag 54
ANNEND
  David   P: Phila 7 Ap 57
ANNESLY
  Thomas   P: Phila 3 Ja 76
ANSLEY
  John (soldier)   P: Phila 21
  Dec 58
ANSON
  J.   P: Phila 31 Jy 60
ANTHONY
  Dr. Christian   P: Phila 4 Feb
  68
  George Mich.   P: Phila 6 Sep
  53
  Johannah   P: Phila 16 Jy 72
  Capt. Joseph   P: Phila 23 Oct
  66
ANTIS
  Henry   P: Chestnut Hill 3 May
  70
APLEY
  John   P: Northampton Co 3 Ja
  60
APPLEBEE/APLEBY
  William   P: Phila 6 Jy 58, 26
  Jy 64; Sr. 23 Oct 66
APPLEGATE
  William   T: Cranberry 10 Ag
  58
APPLETON
  Josiah   P: New Jersey 20 Ap
  69
  Nicholas   P: Phila 18 Ag 57
  Samuel   P: Phila 4 Ap 54
APPOWEN
  Capt. Samuel   P: Phila 2 Sep
  62
APTIE
  Thomas   P: Phila 31 Dec 61
ARBUCKLER
  James   P: Lancaster Co 28 Oct
  62
ARCHER
  George   P: Chester Co 13 May
  56
  James   P: Phila 31 Dec 61
  Joseph   L: Carlisle 2 Mar 74

ARCHIBALD/ARCHBOLD
  David P: Oxford 10 Oct 65
  Lt. George P: in the army
    12 Ja 58
  Robert P: Norrington 10 Ap
    66; Pa 15 Mar 64
  William P: Phila 3 Ja 76
ARECOT
  Mons. P: Phila 19 Jy 80
ARKLEY/ARKLEYS
  Thomas P: Phila 18 Mar 62,
    4 Feb 68
ARMANDS
  John P: Bound-Brook 24 Feb
    63
ARMBRUSTER/AMBRUSTER
  Anthony P: Phila 23 Oct 66,
    25 Ap 71
ARMER
  William N: at Deep Water
    Side, near New-Castle 29
    Nov 64
ARMITAGE
  Benjamin P: Phila 30 May 54
  Caleb P: Bristol Twp 24 Jy
    76
  James P: Phila 1 Nov 70, 16
    Jy 72
  Samuel P: Abington, B.C. 20
    Ap 69; Bucks Co 9 Ag 59
ARMITS
  John P: Phila 12 Feb 61
ARMITT
  & DAWSON, Messieurs P: Phila
    30 Ap 67
ARMOUR/ARMOR
  Jane P: New-Castle 21 Dec 58
  William P: New-Castle Co 3
    Ja 60, 8 Jy 62
ARMSTRONG
  Aaron P: Pa 5 Ag 62
  Andrew P: Carlisle 24 Feb
    63; Cumberland Co 18 Mar 62;
    Phila 30 Ja 66
  Ann P: Plymouth 20 Oct 68
  Archibald P: New-Castle Co
    12 Ja 58, 3 Ja 60
  Francis L: Peach Bottom 20
    Ja 73. P: Little Britain
    13 May 56, 4 Ag 63
  George L: Carlisle 14 May
    72. P: Cumberland Co 18
    Mar 62; Phila 30 Ap 67
  Henry P: Lancaster Co 13 Ja
    63
  Col. J. P: Carlisle 31 Dec
    61
  James L: Peach Bottom 2 Mar
    74. P: Baltimore Co 31 Mar
    63; Cumberland Co 3 Sep 61;
    Phila 16 Jy 72; Whiteland
    Twp 12 Ja 58
  John L: 31 Ja 71 (Col.);
    student, Pequea 2 Mar 74.
    N: 12 Feb 67; c/o Rev.

M'Cannon, Mill Creek Hun-
    dred 4 Dec 66
  John P: Conegocheague 3 Ja
    60; Cumberland Co 18 Mar
    62, 18 Mar 62 (Col,); N.
    Castle Co 13 Ja 63; Pa 19
    May 63, 13 Oct 63
  Josiah P: Phila-Gaz. 3 Ja 76
  Martin T: Somerset Court
    House 1 Sep 68
  Robert P: Pa 2 Feb 64; Phila
    20 Oct 68
  Samuel P: Phila 26 Jy 53
  Thomas P: Carlisle 13 Ja 63,
    24 Feb 63; Cumberland Co
    15 Mar 64; Forks of the
    Delaware 18 Mar 62; New
    Castle Co 31 Mar 63; Pa 28
    Oct 62, 2 Feb 64; Phila 16
    Jy 67, 30 Ap 77; W: Wilming-
    ton 13 Oct 63
  W. P: New-Castle Co 12 Ja 58
  William L: Carlisle 29 Jy 72;
    Juniata, Cumberland Co 31
    Ja 71, 19 Dec 71. N: 29
    Nov 64. P: Delaware Forks
    24 Oct 54, 12 Feb 61; New
    Castle 3 Sep 61; Paxton 4
    Feb 68
ARNETT/ARNET/ARNETTS
  James P: Bucks Co 8 Jy 62
  John C: c/o John Hays Oxford
    Twp 30 Oct 66
  Joseph C: Cross Roads 18 Jy
    65
ARNEY
  Ann P: Phila 5 Ag 56
ARNOLD/ARNOLDS
  Martha P: Phila 28 Ap 68
  Robert P: Phila 28 Oct 62, 2
    May 65
ARNOTT
  Capt. John P: Phila 30 Ap 67
ARRIL
  Catharine P: Phila 9 Ag 59
ARTHUR
  John N: Kent Co 12 Feb 67
  Mary P: Pa 4 Ag 63
  Patrick P: Phila 21 Dec 58
  Peter P: Phila 27 Jy 58, 5
    Ag 62, 15 Ja 63, 15 Mar 64,
    3 Ja 76
  Robert P: Bucks Co 27 Ja 73;
    Pa 31 Dec 61, 24 Feb 63
  William N: Kent Co 12 Feb 67
ARVENN
  William P: New Castle Co 7
    Ap 57
ARWIN
  James P: Phila 24 Feb 63
ASBURY
  Francis P: Phila 31 Ja 76
ASGILL
  Mr. P: Phila 21 Jy 68
ASH/ASHE

Mr.   P: Sheptown 3 Ja 76
John   P: Chester Co 13 Ja 63
L.   P: Phila 18 Mar 62
Lawrence   P: Phila 3 Ja 65, 2
    Ag 70
Norman   P: Phila 18 Mar 62,
    31 Mar 63, 2 Feb 64, 15
    Mar 64, 26 Jy 64, 30 Ap 67
    (Capt)
William   P: Phila 18 Feb 55
ASHBRIDGE
Aaron   P: Pa 3 Sep 61
George   C: Willistown; see
    RANDAL, William
ASHBURN
Elizabeth   P: Phila 22 Nov
    53
Martin   P: Phila 24 Oct 54,
    18 Ag 57
ASHBURNER
Capt. W.   P: Phila 28 Nov 54
ASHBURY, see BAGNALL &
ASHCRAFT
Elizabeth   P: Pa 12 Ja 58
ASHERALT
Edward   P: Northampton Co 27
    Oct 73
ASHERON
John   P: Salem Co 23 Oct 66
ASHLEY
William   P: Bethlehem 9 Ag
    59; Phila 23 Oct 66
ASHMED
Samuel   P: Germantown 31 Dec
    61
ASHMIT
Samuel   P: Germantown 10 Oct
    65
ASHTON
Dr.   P: Phila 5 Ag 62
Charles   P: Warrington 2 Ag
    70
George   P: Phila 31 Dec 61
James   P: Phila 31 Ja 76;
    Whiteland 5 Ag 62 (Esq.)
Joseph   P: Phila 1 Nov 53
William   P: Bucks Co 2 May
    65; Phila 10 Oct 65
ASHUR
Isaac   P: Phila 25 Jy 65
ASK
Ann P: Chester Co 1 Nov 53
ASKEL/ASKELL
Mr.   P: Phila 31 Ja 76
James   P: Phila 27 Ja 73
ASKEN
Michael   P: at E. Nottingham
    28 Nov 54
ASKEW
William   P: Chester Co 13 May
    56
ASKEY
Thomas   P: Cumberland Co 15
    Mar 64
ASKING

Michael   P: East Nottingham
    13 May 56
ASKINS
John   P: Phila 30 Ap 77
ASKWITH
Samuel   P: Pa 18 Ag 57; Phila
    12 Ja 58
ASPDEN
Matthias   P: Phila 30 Ap 77
ASPINWALL
Dr. William   P: Phila 20 Jy
    69
ASPLE
John   P: Phila-Gaz. 3 Ja 76
ASTON/ASTIN
Daniel   P: Bucks Co 15 Mar 64;
    Wrights Town 12 Feb 61
Peter   P: Phila 26 Jy 64
Thomas   P: Phila 9 Ag 59
ATCHISON; see also AICHISON
Thomas   P: Phila 20 Ap 69
ATHERTON
Thomas   P: Chester Co 18 Mar
    62
ATKIN/ATKINS
Edmond, Esq.   P: Phila 7 Ap
    57
Ekins   P: Phila-Gaz. 3 Ja 76
George   P: Phila 20 Ap 69
Henry   P: Phila 4 Ag 63, 2
    Feb 64
Robert   P: Phila 10 Oct 65
Samuel   P: Phila 21 Dec 58
Sellius   P: Phila 4 Feb 68
ATKINSON
and PARKER   P: Phila 2 May 65
Capt.   P: Phila 6 Sep 53
Edward   P: Pa 28 Oct 62
Elizabeth   P: Snowhill 12 Ja
    58
George   P: Phila 6 Jy 58, 8
    Jy 62, 15 Mar 64, 26 Oct 69
John   P: Lancaster Co 9 Ag 59
Robert   P: Phila 21 Dec 58
Thomas   P: Falls of Delaware
    20 Jy 69; Phila 7 Ap 57
William   P: 3 Ja 65; Phila 3
    Ja 76
ATLAY
Mr.   P: Phila-Gaz. 3 Ja 76
ATLEE
Samuel J.   P: Lancaster-Gaz.
    19 Jy 80
William   P: Lancaster 9 Ag 59
ATLETT
Thomas   P: Pa 13 May 56
ATWOOD/ATTWOOD
Isaac   W: near Wilmington 27
    Ag 77
Richard   L: Campobellow, Amer-
    ica 19 Dec 71
Thomas   P: Phila 13 Oct 63
AUBLE
Mr.   P: Phila 30 Ap 77
AUGHSTIN

William   P: Goshen 12 Ja 58
AULD
  Robert   P: Phila 27 Jy 58, 6
    Jy 58
  William   P: Phila 27 Oct 73
AULL
  Jacob   P: Harris's Ferry 24
    Feb 63
  John   P: Phila 28 Nov 54
AUSTIN; see also AUGHSTIN
  Miss   P: Phila 1 May 76
  Benjamin   P: Abington B.C.
    28 Ap 68, 20 Ap 69
  Charles   P: Phila 11 Sep 55
  James   P: Pa 4 Ag 63
  Nicholas   P: Phila 18 Ag 57
  Thomas   P: Phila 6 Jy 58
AVERY
  Molly   P: Phila 31 Jy 60
  Peter   P: St. Georges 12 Ja
    58
AVIS
  George   P: Gloucester Co 20
    Jy 69
AX
  J. Frederick   P: Germantown
    27 Jy 58
AYLITT
  William   P: Phila 30 Oct 76
AYRES/AYRE
  John   P: Phila 3 Ja 65, 9 Ag
    59 (Capt.)
  Martha   T: Burlington 17 Oct
    54
  William   P: Phila 7 Ap 57

J.F.B.
  c/o J.F. and S. Richard
    Banks   P: Phila 30 Ap 67
B_TNER, illegible
  ⁻Elias   P: Phila-Gaz. 19 Jy 80
B_ _ _ _, illegible
  ⁻Francis   P: Pa 12 Ja 58
B_LE, /?/
  ⁻William   P: Phila 24 Feb 63
B_LOWIE, illegible
  ⁻Mr.   P: Phila 31 Mar 63
B___RICK, illegible
  ⁻Richard   P: Phila 31 Mar 63
BABE
  Hinsent   P: Phila 13 May 56
BACHE
  Richard   P: Phila 10 Oct 65
BACKER/or BARKER?/
  Arthur   P: Phila 12 Feb 61
BACKET
  W.   P: Phila 31 Dec 61
BACKHOUSE/BACKHOUS
  Capt.   P: Phila 3 Sep 61
  Capt. John   P: Phila 24 Oct
    54
BACKOVEN
  George Germantown 5 Ap 76-
    Gaz. 1 May

BACON
  David   P: Phila 18 Feb 55
  Henry   P: Kent Co 16 Jy 72
BADGER, see DONALDSON &
  Capt.   P: Phila 20 Oct 68
  Bernard   P: Phila 6 Jy 58
  Daniel   P: Phila 16 Jy 67, 25
    Ap 71 (Capt)
BADLAM
  Ezra   P: Phila 5 Ap 77-Gaz.
    30 Ap 77
BADMAN
  Thomas   P: Whitemarsh 3 Ja 65,
    30 Ja 66
BAGLEY
  Thomas   P: Phila 4 Ap 54
BAGNALL/BAGNEL
  and ASHBURY   P: Phila 16 Jy 72
  John   L: Carlisle 2 Mar 74
BAILEY/BAILIE/BAILLIE/BAYLEY/
  BAYLY/BAILE/BEALEY
  Alexander   P: Phila 26 Jy 64
  Caleb   L: Marlborough Town
    15 Ap 56
  Charles   P: in the army 12
    Ja 58; (Capt.) Phila 19 Ja
    69
  Christian   P: Phila 12 Ja 58
  David   N: 12 Feb 67; York Co
    4 Dec 66
  Eliz.   P: Phila 21 Dec 58
  Henry   P: Phila-Gaz. 3 Ja 76.
    T: 4 Nov 72
  James   P: Pa 15 Mar 64
  John   P: Cumberland Co 7 Ap
    57; Haddonfield 9 May 54;
    Kent Co 20 Oct 68; Phila 28
    Oct 62, 13 Ja 63, 16 Jy 72
  Joel   P: Chester Co 15 Mar 64
  Nath.   P: Phila 2 Ag 70
  Peter   P: Pa 3 Ja 60, 31 Dec
    61 (2); Phila 3 Ja 60, 4
    Ag 63
  Robert   P: Pa 18 Mar 62; Phila
    13 Oct 63, 27 Oct 73
  Thomas   P: Phila 1 Jy 56
  Lt. W.   P: in the army 12 Ja
    58
  William   P: Great Valley 19
    May 63; Phila 31 Jy 60, 2
    Sep 62, 28 Ap 68
BAIN/BAINS; see also BAYN
  Daniel   P: Phila 28 Ap 68
  John   P: Brandywine 3 Sep 61;
    Phila Co 31 Dec 61
  Joshua   P: Great Valley 12 Ja
    58
  Robert   T: Freehold 7 May 67
BAIRD
  Archibald   P: Phila 26 Jy 53
  Hugh   P: Charlestown 31 Dec
    61; Chester Co 28 Nov 54
  James   P: Phila 10 Ap 66, 4
    Feb 68
  John   P: York Co 13 Ja 63

Robert   P: N.Castle Co 3 Sep
   61
William   P: Phila 30 Ap 77
BAITE
Robert   P: Phila 3 Ja 65
BAKER
   Mr.   P: Phila 10 Ap 66
   Aaron   P: Chester Co 4 Ap 54
   Bartel   P: Phila 4 Feb 68
   Benjamin   P: Phila 20 Ap 69
   Bowman   P: Phila 21 Jy 68
   Elizabeth   P: Chester Co 31
      Mar 63
   Francis   C: c/o Robert Alsop
      Charles-Town 22 Ja 67
   Frederick   P: Phila 19 May
      63, 13 Oct 63
   George   P: Phila 30 Ap.67
   Ignatius   P: Phila 10 Oct 65
   James   P: Phila 10 Oct 65
   Jer./Jeremiah   P: Salem 18
      Ag 57, 12 Ja 58
   John   P: Chester Co 31 Jy 60;
      Phila 15 Mar 64, 23 Oct 66,
      30 Ap 77. T: 7 May 67
   Joseph   Phila 1 May 76, 24
      Jy 76, 30 Oct 76
   Margaret   P: Bucks Co 12 Ja
      58; Phila 30 Ap 67
   Mary   P: Phila 12 Ja 58
   Rachel   P: Pa 4 Ag 63
   Rebecca   P: Phila 27 Ja 73
   Richard   P: Bradford Twp 31
      Dec 61
   Robert   P: Pa 28 Oct 62, 13
      Ja 63
   Timothy   T: Maidenhead 10 Ag
      58
   William   T: Pa 31 Ja 71
BARD
   Mary   P: Phila 9 Ag 59
   Peter   P: Phila 25 Jy 65
   William   P: Phila 21 Dec 58,
      6 Jy 58, 5 Ag 62
BARDEWISES
   Vincent Germantown 5 Oct 76
      Gaz. 30 Oct 76
BARE
   David   P: Welch-Tract 3 Sep
      61
   Hugh   P: Manor of Moreland
      18 Ag 57
BARECROFT
   Ambrose   P: Bucks 28 Nov 54
BARKER
   James   P: Phila 21 Dec 58,
      31 Ja 76
BALANCE/BALLANCE
   Robert   L: Rapho Twp 14 May
      72, 29 Jy 72
BALBERRY
   Jane   P: Pa 13 Ja 63
BALDERSON
   John   P: Bucks 18 Feb 55, 18
      Mar 62, 8 Jy 62, 20 Oct 68,

   28 Ap 71
BALDESQUI
   Capt.   P: Phila 5 Jy 80 Gaz.
      19 Jy 80
BALDRIDGE
   James   P: Phila 25 Jy 65
   William   P: Lancaster Co 31
      Jy 60
BALDWIN/BALDWINE/BAULDIN
   Anthony   C: 30 Jy 77
   Dr. Cornelius Phila 16 Jy 77
   John   C: Kennet, see TAGART,
      Jacob. P: Bristol Twp 7
      Ap 57; Newport 7 Ap 57;
      Phila 28 Nov 54, 19 May 63,
      26 Jy 64 (2)
BALENTINE
   Ann P: Phila 13 May 56
BALFOUR
   Edward   P: Phila 25 Jy 65
BALL
   David   P: Baltimore Co 31 Mar
      63
   Edward   P: Phila 9 May 54
   James   P: Kingsessing 2 Ag 70
   John   P: Phila 16 Jy 77
   Michael   P: Phila 25 Ap 71
   Richard   P: Phila 2 Ag 70
   William   P: Phila 6 Jy 58.
      T: Maidenhead 6 Dec 64
BALLARD/BALLAD
   Dr. T: Elizabethtown 17 Oct
      54
   Dr. John   T: Trenton 17 Oct
      54; Hopewell 10 Ag 58
   Peter   P: Phila 26 Jy 64, 3
      Ja 65
   William   P: Phila 30 Ja 66
BALLINGTON
   Henry   P: Phila 26 Oct 69
BALMAN
   Elizabeth   P: Cohansey 26 Jy
      53
BALON
   Mary   P: Phila 26 Jy 64
BALTEMORE
   Mr. L: 29 Ja 67
BAMBER
   James   P: Whitemarsh 31 Jy 60
BAMBERGER
   Mr.   P: Phila 23 Oct 66
BAMFORD
   ....., woollen weaver   L: 2
      Mar 74
BAMPTON
   Edith   P: Phila 19 Ja 69
   William/Will.   P: Phila 15
      Mar 64, 26 Jy 64, 20 Ap 69
BANCKER
   Ann P: Phila 5 Ag 62
BANCROFT
   Dr. Daniel   P: Phila 5 Jy 76
      Gaz. 24 Jy 76
BAND
   Samuel, near Darby 30 Ap 77

BANDELER
  Peter, c/o Justice Cole T:
    New Germantown 1 Sep 68
BANESTER
  Thomas C: Naaman's Creek,
    Chester Co 18 Jy 65
BANFIELD
  John P: Phila 2 May 65
BANFORD
  Francis T: Hopewell 10 Ag
    58
BANKHEAD
  Hugh P: Md. 13 Oct 63; New
    Castle Co 13 Oct 63
  James P: Md. 13 Oct 63
  William P: Coecil Co 18 Mar
    62
BANKS
  James P: Phila 25 Jy 65, 10
    Oct 65
  John P: Phila 13 Oct 63
  Richard P: Phila 31 Dec 61
  S. Richard P: Phila 30 Ap
    67
  Thomas P: Phila 3 May 70
  William P: Phila 16 Jy 72
BANKSON
  Richard P: Phila 10 Oct 65
BANN
  John P: Phila 21 Jy 68
BANNERMAN
  Benjamin P: Phila 3 Ja 76
BANNET/BANNOT
  John P: Phila 13 Oct 63
  Peter P: Phila-Gaz. 27 Oct
    73
BANSON
  Thomas P: Phila 26 Jy 64
BAR, see BARR
BARAS
  David P: Phila 10 Oct 65
BARBER
  Mr. P: Phila 1 Nov 70
  Miles P: Lancaster Co 28
    Oct 62
  Patrick P: N.J. 2 Feb 64
  Thomas-Mary-Ann /?/ L: Fur-
    nace 2 Mar 74
BARBERNIE
  Frances P: Phila 2 Ag 70
BARCH
  Jacob P: Phila 3 Ja 65, 2
    May 65
BARCLAY/BARCLY
  & Hay, Messieurs P: Phila
    30 Ap 67, 21 Jy 68, 20 Oct
    68
  George P: Pa 8 Jy 62
  James N: near New Castle 29
    Nov 64
  John W: Christiana Bridge
    27 Ag 77
  Mary P: Phila 2 Feb 64
  Rebecca P: Phila 26 Jy 64
BARCROFT

John P: Salesbury 5 Ag 56
BARD
  Mrs. P: Phila 31 Jy 60
  Elizabeth P: Phila 7 Ap 57
  John P: Wilmington 18 Ag 57
BARKER
  Peter P: Phila 2 Ag 70, 27
    Oct 73
  William P: Phila 3 Ja 60
BARKLEY/BARKLY; see also BARCLAY
  Alexander P: Manor Moreland
    19 Ja 69
  Hugh P: Neshaminy 10 Ap 66
  James P: Newport 9 Ag 59
BARLIFF
  William P: Phila 3 Ja 65
BARLOW
  Francis P: Phila 1 Feb 70
  Sarah P: Phila 27 Jy 58
  Thomas P: B.Co. 20 Jy 69
BARLOY
  John P: Cross Roads 13 Oct
    63
BARM
  John P: Phila 20 Jy 69
BARNER
  John P: Phila 7 Ap 57
BARNES/BARNS
  Miss P: Phila 25 Jy 65
  Mrs. P: Phila 25 Jy 65
  David P: Phila 6 Jy 58
  Isaac P: Bucks Co 19 Jy 80
  Capt. James P: Phila 31 Dec
    61
  John P: Kent Co 31 Dec 61;
    Phila 25 Jy 65; near York
    Town 24 Oct 54; York Co 12
    Ja 58, 9 Ag 59
  Capt. W. P: Phila 24 Feb 63
  William P: Phila 3 Ja 65;
    Capt., Phila 3 Sep 61, 2
    Feb 64, 26 Jy 64
BARNET/BARNETT
  Ann P: Phila 8 Jy 62
  Benjamin P: Sussex Co 27 Jy
    58
  George P: New Castle Co 13
    Oct 63
  James P: New Castle Co 9 Ag
    59
  John P: Chester Co 24 Feb
    63; New Castle Co 9 Ag 59;
    Phila 1 Feb 70
  Mark P: Phila 15 Mar 64
  Robert P: Lancaster Co 3 Sep
    61
  Sarah P: Phila 2 Feb 64
  William P: Chester Co 24 Feb
    63
BARNEY
  James P: Phila 21 Dec 58
  Joshua P: Phila 30 Oct 76
BARNFORD
  Estimah P: Marcus H/ook/ 12
    Ja 58

BARNHILL
  John   P: Neshaminy 12 Ja 58;
    Phila 1 Nov 70
  William   P: Bucks Co 12 Feb
    61, 15 Mar 64, 3 Ja 65;
    Cumberland Co 21 Dec 58,
    12 Ja 58
BARNSLY
  Capt.   P: Bristol 23 Oct 66
  Lt.   P: in the army 12 Ja 58
BARNWELL
  Peter   P: Phila 9 Ag 59
BARO
  Patty   P: Phila 19 May 63
BARON
  John   P: Phila 31 Mar 63, 4
    Ag 63
BARR/BAR
  Mr.   P: Phila 3 Sep 61
  Hans   P: Lancaster 7 Ap 57
  John   P: Lancaster Co 13 Oct
    63, 26 Jy 64; Pequea 18
    Mar 62; Phila 3 Sep 61, 18
    Mar 62, 5 Ag 62, 2 Sep 62,
    28 Oct 62
  Robert   C: Kennet Twp 30 Oct
    66. L: Pequea 20 Ja 73.
    P: Mount Joy 13 Oct 63;
    New Castle 24 Oct 54;
    Pequea 9 Ag 59, 8 Jy 62,
    19 May 63; near Phila 31
    Jy 60
  Thomas   P: Horsham Twp 28 Oct
    62; Worcester Co 12 Ja 58
  William   P: Fogs Manor 1 Nov
    53
BARRA
  David   C: Christine Bridge
    18 Jy 65
BARREE
  James   P: Phila 27 Ja 73
BARREL/BARRELL
  Rev.   P: Wilmington 31 Dec
    61
  Henry   P: Busseltown 1 Nov 70
  John   P: Phila 10 Ap 66
BARRETT/BARRET/BARRITT/BARROT/
  BARROTT
  Mr.   P: Phila-Gaz. 27 Oct 73
  Catharine   P: Phila 31 Jy 60
  Edmond   P: Phila 30 Ap 67
  Henry   -Eastown 30 Oct 76
  James   P: Phila 3 May 70
  John   P: Phila 5 Ag 62, 2
    Feb 64 (2), 15 Mar 64, 26
    Jy 64, 10 Ap 66, 20 Oct 68,
    28 Oct 69, 3 Ja 76
  Judith   P: Phila-Gaz. 3 Ja 76
  Mary   P: Phila 19 Ja 69
  Timothy   P: Phila 19 Jy 80
  William   P: Phila 13 Ja 63,
    2 May 65
BARRINGTON
  Robert   P: Phila 11 Sep 55
BARRITE

  Judah   P: Phila 13 Oct 63,
    3 Ja 65
BARRON
  John   P: Phila 24 Feb 63
  Samuel   P: near Phila 3 Sep
    61
BARROW
  Francis   P: Phila 26 Oct 69
  John   P: Manor of Moreland
    18 Ag 57
BARRY/BARY
  Charles   P: Phila 31 Dec 61,
    16 Jy 72
  Edward   P: Phila 5 Ag 62
  George   P: Phila 27 Jy 58, 21
    Dec 58, 9 Ag 59
  John   P: Phila 5 Jy 80; Gaz.
    19 Jy 80
  Mary Ann   P: Phila 15 Mar 64
  Richard   P: Phila 16 Jy 77
BARSING
  Conrad   P: Phila 3 Ja 65
BARTHOLOMEW
  Austin   P: Phila 13 Ja 63
  George   P: Phila 3 Ja 65
  John Great Valley 30 Ap 77;
    Phila 21 Dec 58
  Thomas   P: Phila 1 Jy 56
BARTLE
  Sarah   P: Phila 12 Feb 61
BARTLET/BARTLETT/BARTLITT
  Mr.   P: Phila 2 May 65
  Bayley   P: Phila 5 Oct 76;
    Gaz. 30 Oct 76
  Elizabeth   P: Phila 31 Dec 61
  Henry   P: Phila 13 Oct 63
  John   P: Phila 3 Ja 60, 18
    Mar 62
  Sarah   P: Phila 9 Ag 59, 31
    Jy 60, 31 Dec 61
BARTLEY
  John   P: Phila 3 Ja 76
BARTON/BARTIN
  Edward   L: York Co 14 May 72
  Elias   P: Phila 20 Oct 68, 3
    May 70
  Joseph   N: Mill Creek Hundred,
    see RICHARDSON, James
  Mary   P: Phila-Gaz. 3 Ja 76
  Stephen   T: Hopewell 10 Ag 58
  Susanna   P: Phila 5 Jy 80;
    Gaz. 19 Jy 80
  Thomas   P: Chester Co 12 Ja
    58, 8 Jy 62; Phila 11 Jy 54,
    24 Oct 54; York Co 21 Dec
    58 (Rev)
  William   P: Lancaster Co 13
    Oct 63
BARTRAM
  William   P: Phila 2 Ag 70, 25
    Ap 71
BARWATER
  William   P: Phila 7 Ap 57
BASDEN
  Daniel   P: Phila 28 Oct 62

BASHFORD
  Moses P: Phila 28 Ap 68
  William L: c/o John Magee
    Carlisle 20 Ja 73
BASKE
  Richard P: Phila 23 Oct 66
BASKILL
  John P: Phila 13 Ja 63
BASS
  George P: Phila 5 Ag 56;
    West Jersey 12 Ja 58
  Nathaniel P: Phila 3 Sep 61
  Robert P: in the army 27 Jy
    58 (Dr.); Phila 13 Oct 63,
    3 Ja 65
BASSET/BASSETT
  Ann-Dover 30 Ap 77
  David P: Greenwich 2 Ag 70;
    Phila 31 Mar 63
  Francis P: Phila 13 Oct 63.
    T: Burlington 6 Dec 64
  Richard-Dover 16 Jy 77
  Thomas, Esq. P: in the army
    27 Jy 58
BASTER
  Mons. Hendrie P: Phila 12 Ja
    58
BASTICK
  Henry P: Phila 3 Ja 65
BASTON
  Henry P: Phila 4 Ag 63
BATCHELDER
  Capt. Josiah P: Phila 8 Jy
    62
BATE
  Mr. P: Phila 15 Mar 64
  Conrad P: Phila 3 Sep 61
  William P: Bethlehem 20 Oct
    68; Kingwood, N.J. 20 Jy 69
BATES
  Capt. David P: Phila 4 Feb
    68
  Elizabeth P: Greenwich Twp
    10 Ap 66
  Thomas P: Phila 3 Ja 65
BATEW
  Ignatius P: Phila 30 Ja 66
BATH
  George P: Phila 7 Nov 53
BATHER
  William P: N.Castle 27 Jy 58
BATHKEEL
  William P: Phila-Gaz. 3 Ja
    76
BATHO
  Charles P: Phila 1 Feb 70
BATLOW
  Catharine P: Phila 18 Mar 62
BATSON
  Thomas P: Phila 24 Oct 54
BATT
  James P: Phila-Gaz. 27 Oct
    73
  Thomas P: Phila 1 Feb 70
BATTEN

  James C: Chester Co 28 Nov
    65. P: Chester Co 3 May
    54; Phila 3 Ja 76
BATTERSLEY
  Thomas P: Phila 27 Oct 73
BATTERSON
  Walter P: Phila 23 Oct 66
BATTES
  Mary P: Phila 25 Ap 71
BAUMAN/BAUGHMAN
  George Christian P: Phila
    19 Ja 69
  Michael L: 29 Ja 67
BAUNE
  Sarah P: Phila 3 Sep 61
BAVERS
  Thomas (soldier) P: 21 Dec
    58
BAVINGTON
  Jonathan P: Phila 16 Jy 67
BAXTER/BACKSTER
  Elizabeth P: Phila 3 May 70
  James (soldier) P: 21 Dec
    58; Phila 3 Ja 76
  John P: Phila 27 Ja 73, 1
    May 76
  Jonathan P: Phila 5 Ap 77;
    Gaz. 30 Ap 77
  Robert P: Phila 3 Ja 76
  Thomas (sailor) P: Phila 21
    Dec 58
  William P: Bucks Co 27 Ja
    73; Pa 26 Jy 64; Phila 15
    Mar 64, 3 Ja 65
BAY
  Rev. Andrew P: Deer Creek 13
    Ja 63
BAYARD
  Capt. P: Phila 1 May 76
  James P: Phila 10 Oct 65
  John B. P: Phila-Gaz. 27 Oct
    73
BAYE
  Jacob-Germantown /?/ 1 May 76
BAYERLAI /?/
  Jacob P: Phila 25 Jy 65
BAYLIFF
  Edward P: Chester Co 4 Ap 54,
    18 Mar 62
  Thomas P: Chester Co 9 Ag 59
BAYN/BAYNE/BAYNES; see also
  BAIN
  Miss P: Phila-Gaz. 27 Oct 73
  James P: Phila 1 Feb 70
  Kennet P: Phila 25 Ap 71
  Mary P: Phila 18 Feb 55
  Nathaniel/Nat. P: Phila 13
    May 56, 31 Mar 63
BAZIN
  Capt. Thomas P: Phila 6 Sep
    53
BEACH
  Capt. James P: Phila 20 Oct
    68
BEACOCK

Michael P: Phila 1 Nov 70
BEACON
  Capt. William P: Phila 2 Feb
    64
BEAK
  Nat. P: Phila 5 Ag 62
BEAKER
  John P: Phila 30 Ap 67
  Joseph P: Pa 12 Feb 61
BEAKS
  Abraham P: Crosswicks 15 Mar
    64
  Joseph P: Phila 15 Mar 64,
    10 Ap 66
BEAL/BEALE/BEALL·
  Gen. P: Phila 24 Feb 63
  Innocent P: Phila 18 Mar 62
  John P: Phila 5 Feb 54
BEALES
  George P: Phila 12 Feb 61
BEALHER
  Mary P: Phila 24 Oct 54
BEAM
  Philip P: Phila 13 Ja 63
BEAMMER
  Peter P: Phila 25 Ap 71
BEAMS
  William P: Phila 21 Jy 68
BEAN/BEEN
  Daniel N: 12 Feb 67; Fan
    Twp, c/o George Adams,
    Christeen Bridge 4 Dec 66
  John P: Phila 3 May 70
  Mat. P: Chester Co 13 Ja 63
  Robert L: Conigojig 14 May
    72
  William P: Chester Co 18 Mar
    62
BEAR
  James P: Phila 25 Ap 71
  John P: Lancaster 19 May 63
BEARCROFT
  Elizabeth P: Lancaster Co
    31 Jy 60
BEARD
  James P: Phila 10 Oct 65
  John P: Elk River 27 Jy 58;
    Phila 24 Jy 76
  Rev. John C: Nottingham 22
    Ja 67; see also MORRISON,
    Robert, and SHERER, Hugh.
    L: 14 May 72
  Rebecca P: Kingsess-Gaz. 3
    Ja 76
  Rose P: Phila 30 Ja 66
  Dr. Thomas P: near Phila 3
    Sep 61
BEARDS
  Jacob P: Phila 15 Mar 64
BEATH
  Patt. P: Phila 3 May 70
BEATTY/BEATY/BETTY/BETEY; see
  also BETTY
  Rev. P: Neshaminey 7 Ap 57
  Andrew P: Phila 9 Ag 59, 8

Jy 62
  Arthur P: Phila 3 Ja 65
  Bell C: c/o Thomas Charls-
    town, Fogs Manor 18 Jy 65,
    28 Nov 65
  Rev. C. P: Neshaminy 11 Sep
    55
  Rev. Charles P: Phila 5 May
    70; Shaminey 30 Ja 66;
    Warminster 25 Ap 71
  David P: York Co 13 Oct 63
  Hannah P: Phila 18 Ag 57
  Hugh P: Phila 30 Ap 67
  James P: Neshaminey 18 Mar
    62 (Rev); Phila 26 Oct 69
  John P: Christine Bridge 21
    Dec 58
  Joseph C: West Fallowfield
    30 Oct 66
  Samuel C: New London 22 Ja
    67
  William P: Chester Co 3 Sep
    61; Phila 2 Feb 64, 3 Ja 65
BEAUCANNON
  George P: Phila 24 Oct 54
BEAUMONT
  John P: Bucks 11 Sep 55, 12
    Ja 58, 31 Jy 60
BEAVIN/BEAVEN
  Capt. David P: Phila 3 Ja 60
  Wm. P: Phila 19 Ja 69
BECHAM
  John T: Bordentown 17 Oct 54
BECHELS
  Richard P: Phila 12 Feb 61
BECK/BEK
  Asa P: Phila 10 Oct 65
  John P: Phila 3 Ja 76
  Mary P: Phila 26 Jy 64
  Shoemaker P: Phila 30 Ap 67
BECKER
  Anna Margaretta P: Phila 1
    Jy 56
  Bartholomew P: Phila 3 Ja 65
  Capt. F. P: Phila 24 Feb 63
BECKETT/BECKET
  Lawrence P: Phila 28 Nov 54
  Peter P: Phila 26 Oct 69
BECKLES
  Richard P: Phila 31 Dec 61
BECKMAN
  David P: Phila 4 Feb 68
  James P: Phila 9 Ag 59
BEDFORD/BETFORD
  Edward P: Phila 2 Feb 63
  Grosvenor P: Phila 9 Ag 59
BEEBE/BEBBEE/BEEBY
  Stephen P: Phila 30 Ja 66
  William P: Phila 18 Mar 62
  Zaccheus P: Bucks Co 5 Ag 56,
    3 Ja 60, 31 Dec 61, 8 Jy 62.
    T: Hopewell 17 Oct 54;
    Trenton 1 Sep 68
BEEK
  Edward P: Bucks Co 18 Ag 57

BEEKMAN and GOOLD
  P: Shrewsbury 30 Ap 77
BEEL
  Joseph   P: Phila 21 Dec 58
BEETH
  Isabella   P: Phila 3 May 70
BEGER
  John   P: Phila 19 Ja 69
BEGERLE
  Jacob   P: Phila 5 Ag 55
BEGGS/BEGS
  Alexander   P: Pequea 7 Ap 57,
    2 May 65
  Andrew   P: Phila 30 Ja 66
  James   P: Phila 30 Ja 66
BEGWELL
  John   P: Sussex Co 23 Oct 66
/BEIDELL/BEIDELL
  John   P: Phila 31 Dec 61
BELCHER
  Hannah   P: Northampton Co
    27 Jy 58
  Lt. James   P: in the army 12
    Ja 58
  Jane   P: Phila 9 Ag 59
BELEW
  Daniel   P: Chester Co 18 Mar
    62
  Patrick/Pat.   P: Phila 2 Feb
    64, 25 Jy 65
BELFIELD
  John   P: Phila 5 Ap 77-Gaz.
    30 Ap 77
BELFORD
  Ann   P: Phila 1 Nov 70
  Edward   P: Phila 31 Dec 61
BELIEF/BEALIFF
  Robert   P: Phila 13 Oct 63
  William   P: Chester Co 3 Sep
    61; Pa 12 Feb 61
BELL
  ....   P: Phila 3 May 70
  & DRINKER   P: Phila 13 Ja 63
  Mr.   P: Phila 30 Ja 66
  Alexander   P: Norington 20
    Ap 69, 3 May 70; Pa 21 Dec
    58; Phila 18 Ag 57, 30 Ap
    67
  Baisobymy   P: Phila 12 Feb 61
  Charles   P: Phila 29 Ag 54
  Edmond   P: Bucks Co 2 Feb 64
  (alias HAMPTON), Elizabeth
    P: Phila 26 Oct 69
  George   P: Phila 26 Oct 69
  Henry   P: Phila 3 Ja 76
  James   P: Christine Bridge
    28 Nov 54; Kingsess 20 Oct
    68; Phila 5 Ag 56, 6 Jy 58,
    27 Jy 58, 31 Jy 60 (Capt),
    4 Feb 68
  Jean   P: Chester Co 3 Sep 61
  John   P: East-Town 8 Jy 62;
    Forks of Delaware 10 Ap 66;
    Phila 21 Dec 58, 13 Oct 63,

    2 Feb 64, 19 Ja 69
  Jonathan   P: Phila 30 Ap 67
  Joseph   P: Phila 27 Jy 58, 3
    Ja 65, 30 Ja 66
  Magnus (sailor)   P: Phila 21
    Dec 58
  Mary   P: Phila 31 Jy 60
  Robert   P: Pa 18 Ag 57, 12 Ja
    58; Phila 18 Ag 57, 27 Oct
    73
  Samuel   P: Phila 27 Jy 58, 21
    Dec 58
  Sarah   P: Paxton Twp 31 Mar 63
  Thomas   L: 29 Ja 67.   P: Phila
    10 Oct 65, 3 Ja 76
  William   L: Lancaster, see
    RICHARDSON, William.   P:
    Paxton 7 Ap 57, 4 Ag 63;
    Phila 2 Feb 64, 27 Oct 73,
    30 Oct 76
  William, Jr.   P: Vincent Twp
    5 Ag 56
BELLAMY
  Rev.   P: Bethlehem 18 Ag 57
  David   P: Bethlehem-Gaz. 27
    Oct 73
  Rev. Joseph   P: Bethlehem 20
    Ap 69
  William   P: Phila 1 Nov 70
BELLAS
  Alexander   P: Pa 12 Feb 61
BELLEW/BELYEW
  Daniel   P: Pa 9 Ag 59
BELLYS
  Matthew   L: supposed to be in
    Lancaster Co 19 Dec 71
BELZONA
  Mr.   P: Phila 5 Jy 80-Gaz. 19
    Jy 80
BEMER
  Frederick   P: Phila 25 Ap 71
BENDER
  Jacob   P: Phila 31 Dec 61
BENEZEL
  Rebecca   P: Phila 31 Jy 60
BENEZET
  James   P: Phila 6 Jy 58, 27
    Jy 58
  Samuel   P: Phila 23 Oct 66
BENN/BEN
  Capt. J.   P: Phila 18 Mar 62
  John   P: Phila 19 Ja 69, 3
    May 70
BENNETT/BENNET
  Andrew   P: Phila 25 Jy 65
  Daniel   P: Phila 9 May 54
  George   P: 11 Sep 55
  Jacob   P: Wilmington 26 Jy 64
  James   P: Phila 9 Ag 59
  Jer.   P: West New Jersey 18
    Ag 59
  Joseph   P: Kennet Twp 4 Ag 63;
    Phila 1 Jy 56; Wilmington
    13 Ja 63

Joshua   P: Lower Smithfield
   16 Jy 72
Mary   P: Lancaster 27 Jy 58
Philip   P: Phila 30 Oct 76
Richard   T: N.J. 15 Jy 56
Samuel   P: Phila 12 Ja 58
William   P: Chester Co 12 Feb
   61; Phila 26 Oct 69
BENNIBLE
   Robert   P: Phila 24 Oct 54
BENNING/BENING
   Jacob   P: Easton 3 Ja 76
   William   P: Phila 13 Ja 63
BENNY
   Thomas   P: Phila 10 Ap 66
BENSON
   Edward   P: Phila 28 Ap 68
   Martin   P: Phila 19 Jy 80
   Thomas   P: Phila 13 Oct 63,
      3 Ja 65
BENSTED
   Alexander   P: Phila 1 Nov 70
BENT
   Thomas   P: Phila 4 Feb 68
   William   P: Phila 24 Jy 76
BENZEL
   Lt. Adolphus   P: in the army
      21 Dec 58
   Rebecca   P: Wilmington 1 Jy
      56
BERAT
   Charles   P: Phila 3 Ja 76
BERCHALL
   James   P: Phila-Gaz. 27 Oct
      73
BERGE
   Mons.   P: Phila 19 Jy 80
BERGEN
   Jacob   T: Rockeyhill 15 Jy 56
BERGMAN/BERGMANN
   Mr.   P: Phila 23 Oct 66
   John G.   P: Germantown 21 Jy
      68
BERIN
   John   P: Phila 8 Jy 62
BERIT
   Mary   P: Phila 18 Mar 62
BERN
   Henry   P: Germantown 27 Ja 73
BERNARD
   Charles, Esq.   P: Phila 30 Ja
      66
   David, Esq.   P: Phila 23 Oct
      66
   Hiacinthe   P: Phila 19 Jy 80
BERNETT
   Ann   P: Phila 2 May 65
BERNEY
   Peter   P: Phila 26 Oct 69
BERRELL
   Henry   P: Bucks Co 3 Sep 61
BERRIEN
   John   P: Kingston 18 Mar 62
BERRIMAN
   James   P: Phila 3 Sep 61

BERRY
   Charles   P: Phila 18 Mar 62
   Hugh   P: near Phila 3 Sep 61
   Jane   P: Manor Morel 12 Ja 58
   John   P: CrossRoads 13 Ja 63;
      New London 12 Ja 58; Pa 28
      Oct 62
   Standish   P: New-Castle Co 5
      Ag 56
BERWICK
   James   P: Phila 25 Ap 71
BESSEE
   Joseph   P: Phila 21 Dec 58
BESSONET/BASONETT
   John   P: Pa 31 Dec 61; Union
      Works 12 Ja 58
   John, Jr.   P: Pa 12 Feb 61
BEST
   David   P: Phila 30 Ja 66
   Isabella   P: Phila 13 Oct 63
   John   P: Phila 18 Mar 62; W.
      Nottingham 13 Oct 63
   William   L: 29 Ja 67
BETAGH
   Francis   P: Phila 27 Ja 73
BETHEL/BETHIL
   Nathaniel   P: Phila 31 Dec 61
   Robert   P: Phila 16 Jy 77
   William (sailor)   P: Phila 21
      Dec 58 (2)
BETHESON
   Anne   P: Phila 24 Jy 76
BETTY/BETTIE; see also BEATTY
   Charles   P: Neshaminy 20 Jy
      69 (Rev); Shaminy 5 Ag 56
   James   P: Brandywine 7 Ap 57;
      Chester Co 31 Dec 61
   Walter   P: York Co 18 Mar 62
   William   P: Pa 28 Oct 62;
      Phila 26 Jy 64
BEUNBO
   Mary   P: Phila 15 Mar 64
BEVAN/BEVEN
   Aubrey   P: Chester 27 Jy 58
   David   P: Chester 18 Mar 62;
      Phila 9 Ag 59
   Edward   P: Phila 8 Jy 62
   Dr. George   P: Phila 27 Jy 58
   Richard   P: Phila 10 Ap 66,
      23 Oct 66
BEVERIDGE
   David   P: Phila 19 May 63, 4
      Ag 63, 13 Oct 63, 2 Feb 64
   Capt. John   P: Phila 3 Sep 61
BEW
   Daniel   P: Phila 28 Ap 68
BEWES
   Ensign Geo.   L: 18th Regt. 31
      Ja 71
BEWGIN
   John   P: West New Jersey 18
      Ag 57
BEWHENAS
   David   P: Chester Co 31 Jy 60
BEWLE

Nathan   P: Phila 31 Jy 60
BEY
Preston   P: Kent Co 3 Sep 61
BEZER
John   P: Phila 23 Oct 66
BIBBY
Jane   P: Phila 1 Nov 70
BIBERG
Ann   P: Phila 24 Oct 54
BICHRINGS
John   P: Phila 3 Ja 65
BICKEN
Jonathan   P: Pa 28 Oct 62
BICKERDIKE
Esther   P: Phila 10 Oct 65
BICKERING
John   P: Phila 26 Jy 64
BICKERTON
Henry   P: near Dover 24 Oct
54
BICKET
Abraham   P: Phila 16 Jy 67
John   P: Phila 20 Oct 68
BICKHAM
Francis   P: Newcastle Co 12
Ja 58
James   L: 25 Dec 66.   P: Lan-
caster 8 Jy 62
Nancy   L: Middle Octerara 29
Jy 72
BIDDLE
Clayton   P: Chester Co 18 Ag
57
Mary   P: Hempstead 8 Jy 62
BIDGLEY
Nicholas   P: near Dover 28
Nov 54
BIEN
William   P: near Phila 3 Sep
61
BIGART/BIGARD/BIGGERT
James   P: Donegall 31 Dec 61
John   P: Phila 20 Oct 68, 27
Ja 73
BIGGENS/BIGGINS
John   P: Phila 15 Mar 64 (2),
26 Jy 64
BIGGS
Mrs.   P: Mountholly 19 Ja 69;
Phila 25 Ap 71
Ephraim   P: Phila 13 Ja 63,
25 Ap 71
BIGHAM
Hugh   P: Octerara 13 Oct 63
John   P: Lancaster Co 3 Ja 60,
28 Oct 62
BILBY
Joseph   P: Phila 10 Ap 66
BILES
Jonathan   P: Phila 19 Ja 69
BILL
John   P: Phila 31 Dec 61
BILLS
William   P: Phila 31 Dec 61

BILLSLAN
Henry   P: Phila 1 Feb 70
BILSLAN
Henry   P: Phila 2 May 65
John   P: Phila-Gaz. 27 Oct 73
BIME
Alice   P: Phila 30 Ja 66
BINES
Dr.   P: Newcastle 18 Mar 62
Robert   P: New-Castle Co 9
Ag 59; Phila 3 Ja 56; Dr.
New-Castle Co 3 Ja 60, 31
Jy 60, 13 Oct 63; Dr.
Whiteclay-creek 27 Jy 58
BINET
Capt. G.   P: Phila 1 Nov 70
BINGHAM
John   P: Lancaster Co 31 Jy
60
Robert   P: Phila-Gaz. 27 Oct
73
BINNEY
Capt. Benjamin   P: Phila 18
Ag 57
BIOREN
Benjamin   P: Phila 24 Jy 76
BIRCH/BIRSH; see also BURCH
Caleb   P: Phila 28 Oct 62
Thomas   P: Phila 24 Feb 63,
19 May 63, 13 Oct 63
BIRD; see also BURD
Empson   P: New Castle Co 11
Sep 55
Henry   T: Kingwood 15 Jy 56
Jonathan   P: Phila 28 Ap 68
Martha   P: Phila 30 Ap 77
Richard   P: Phila 27 Oct 73
William   P: Amity Iron Works
28 Nov 54; Berks Co 12 Ja
58, 9 Ag 59, 12 Feb 61(Esq)
BIRK
Mrs.   P: Phila 12 Ja 58
BIRKIT
William   P: Phila 2 Ag 70
BIRMINGHAM
William   L: Lancaster Co 20
Jan 73
BIRNEL
Hugh   P: Phila 10 Oct 65
BIRNEY/BIRNIE
Arthur   P: Bucks 28 Nov 54;
Pa 27 Jy 58, 31 Dec 61 (Dr)
Hugh   L: Winchester, Virginia
25 Dec 66.   P: Phila 30 Ja
66
Peter   P: Phila 1 Feb 70, 3
Ja 76
BIRSTELL
Capt. John   P: Kings-Town 24
Feb 63
BIRTH
Thomas   P: Phila 3 Ja 65
BISBY
Benjamin   P: Phila-Gaz. 27 Oct
73

BISHOP
  Ann P: Lancaster Road 27 Jy
    58
  Edward P: Phila 26 Jy 64
    (Capt), 3 Ja 65
  Joseph P: West Caln 9 Ag 59
  Thomas P: Phila 26 Jy 64
BLACK
  Mr. P: Germantown-Gaz. 27
    Oct 73; brass founder, Phila
    3 Ja 65
  Ann P: Phila 30 Ap 67, 21 Jy
    68, 1 May 76
  Archibald P: Phila 28 Ap 68
  Donald, soldier P: prob. in
    Pittsburgh 15 Mar 64; Fort
    Pitt 26 Jy 64
  Ezra P: Bordentown 19 May 63
  George P: Little Britain 12
    Ja 58; Phila 1 Jy 56, 10 Oct
    65
  Hugh L: Derry Twp 15 Ap 56
  James P: in the army 12 Ja
    58; N.J. 18 Mar 62; Lan-
    caster Co 13 Oct 63; Pa 26
    Jy 64; Phila 3 Sep 61, 26
    Jy 64, 3 Ja 65, 26 Oct 69,
    31 Ja 76
  John P: Fogs Manor 18 Ag 57;
    Phila 1 Nov 53, 3 Ja 60, 25
    Jy 65
  Joseph L: York Co 19 Dec 71
  Nancy P: Christine Bridge 31
    Jy 60
  Peter P: Phila 21 Jy 68
  Robert P: New Castle 7 Ap 57
    (a smieth); Nottingham 24
    Oct 54; Phila 27 Jy 58;
    York Co 13 Oct 63
  Samuel P: Bucks Co 20 Oct 68
  Thomas L: Leacock Twp 19 Dec
    71. P: Lancaster Co 31 Jy
    60; Pa 12 Feb 61. W: near
    Christiana Bridge 27 Ag 77
  William P: Phila 8 Jy 62, 3
    Ja 76
BLACKBURN/BLACKBORN/BLACKBOURN
  Andrew P: Pa 13 Ja 63
  Hilton P: Phila 16 Jy 72
  John P: Phila 15 Mar 64
  Thomas L: York Co 31 Ja 71.
    P: 31 Jy 60, 12 Feb 61, 31
    Dec 61; York Co 23 Oct 66
  William P: N. Castle 24 Feb
    63
BLACKENY, see BLAKENY
BLACKFORD
  Garret P: Phila 1 Jy 56, 21
    Jy 68
BLACKHAM
  Richard P: Phila 1 Nov 53
BLACKISTON
  Mr. P: Phila 19 Jy 80
  Michael P: Talbot Co 13 Oct
    63

BLACKLEY
  Ab. P: Phila 2 Feb 64
BLACKLIDGE/BLACKLEDGE
  Thomas P: Bucks Co 9 Ag 59,
    2 Feb 64
BLACKSTON
  Priscilla P: Phila 2 Ag 70
BLACKUM
  William P: New-Castle Co 9
    Ag 59
BLACKWOOD
  Capt. John P: Phila 19 May
    63
  Samuel P: Woodbury, New Jer-
    sey 21 Jy 68
BLADWELL
  John P: Phila 19 Ja 69
BLAIN/BLAINE
  Daniel P: York Co 31 Dec 61
  John P: Phila 2 May 65
  Robert P: Chester Co 13 Oct
    63
BLAINCHER
  Margaret P: Phila 31 Ja 76
BLAIR/BLARE
  Rev C: Fogs Manor, see HILL,
    William
  Alexander P: Phila 25 Jy 65
  Jane P: Pa 31 Dec 61
  John L: c/o Charles Blair,
    Bucks Co 19 Dec 71; near
    Mill Creek 15 Ap 56. Bucks
    Co 7 Ap 57; Foggs Manor 3
    Ja 65; Lancaster Co 18 Mar
    62; N.J. 13 Ja 63; Pa 18 Ag
    57, 9 Ag 59, 12 Feb 61, 15
    Mar 64, 26 Jy 64; Phila 24
    Oct 54 (Rev), 16 Jy 72;
    West Jersey 3 Ja 76; York
    Co 18 Mar 62. T: Peepack
    17 Oct 54
  Nancy P: Phila 4 Ag 63
  Nancy Ann P: Octerara 13 Oct
    63
  Robert P: Pa 18 Ag 57
  Rev. Sa. L: 13 Jn 65
  Samuel L: 11 Ap 65
  Thomas P: Cumberland Co 12
    Ja 58 (Dr); Pequea 5 Ag 56;
    Phila 2 Feb 64 (Capt), 26
    Jy 64 (Capt), 3 Ja 65
  William P: Newcastle 24 Oct
    54, 11 Sep 55
BLAKE
  George P: Phila 2 Feb 64, 26
    Jy 64
  John P: Jersey 13 May 56
  Robert P: Phila 27 Jy 58, 21
    Dec 58
  Roger P: Phila 13 Oct 63
BLAKELY, see BLEAKLEY
BLAKENY/BLACKENY/BLAKNEY/BLACK-
  NEY
  Gabriel L: 14 May 72
  George P: Bucks Co 8 Jy 62,

3 Ja 60; Pa 3 Ja 60
John   P: Phila 6 Jy 58
BLAKES
James   P: Phila 3 Ja 60
BLAN
William   P: Phila 12 Feb 61
BLANCA
John   P: Phila 31 Dec 61
BLAND
Thomas   P: Phila 20 Oct 68
BLANEY
James   N: near Red Lion 12
Feb 67
BLANGE
Isaac   P: Egg-Harbour 31 Jy
60
BLANKLEY/BLANKELY/BLANKNEY
John   P: Phila Co 24 Feb 63,
4 Ag 63, 15 Mar 64
BLAY
John   P: N. Providence 11
Sep 55
BLAYLOCK/BLELOCK
James   P: Chester Co 3 Sep
61; Wilmington 3 Sep 61
BLEACK
Theophilus   P: Brandywine 28
Oct 62
BLEAKLY/BLEAKELY/BLEAKLEY/
BLAKELY/BLECKLEY
George   P: Bucks Co 31 Dec 61
John   P: Pa 31 Dec 61; Phila
20 Jy 69, 19 Jy 80
Robert   P: Phila 30 Ja 66, 27
Oct 73
William   P: Phila 2 Feb 64,
26 Oct 69
BLEAR
John   P: Phila-Gaz. 27 Oct 73
BLEIN
Thomas   P: Newcastle 28 Nov
54
BLESSING
Jacob   P: Pa 12 Feb 61
BLEWER
Joseph   P: 18 Mar 62 (Capt),
20 Ap 69
BLEZARD
Conway   P: Phila 8 Jy 62
BLISS
John   P: Phila 26 Jy 64, 30
Ja 66
Mary   P: Phila 5 Ag 62
BLOODWORTH
Rebecca   P: Phila 8 Jy 62
BLOOM
John   P: Lancaster Co 22 Nov
53
BLOONFIELD
Joseph   P: Phila 30 Ap 77
BLOWET
Francis   P: Phila 27 Ja 73
BLUCKER
John   P: Bucks Co 3 Ja 60
BLUER

Joseph   P: Phila 13 Oct 63
BLUMER
Abraham   P: Bucks Co 27 Ja 73
(Rev); Northampton Co 30
Oct 76 (Monsieur)
BLUNT
Stephen   Phila 5 Ap 76-Gaz. 1
May 76
BLYDEN
Peter   P: Phila 18 Mar 62
BLYTH
Benjamin   P: Pequay 1 Nov 53
James   P: Phila 23 Oct 66
Joseph   P: Pa 28 Oct 62; Phila
18 Mar 62
Patrick   P: Phila 4 Ap 54
Samuel   P: Cumberland Co 29
Ag 54; Pequay 1 Nov 53
William   P: Cumberland Co 15
Mar 64; Phila 3 Ja 65, 28
Ap 68, 27 Oct 73
BO_DLEY
Matthew   P: Phila 5 Jy 80-Gaz.
19 Jy 80
BOAKE/BOAKS
Amos   P: Chester 13 May 56;
Phila 7 Ap 57
BOAL
Robert   L: c/o Robert Cree,
Lancaster Co 19 Dec 71
BOARDLEY
John   P: Chester Town Mary-
land 7 Ap 57
BOARDMAN
George   P: Phila 9 Ag 59
BOCHIUS
John   P: Germantown-Gaz. 3 Ja
76
BODEKER
William   P: Durham 1 Jy 56
BODEN
Abijah   P: Phila 19 May 63
BODILL/BODDIELL
John   P: Bucks 27 Dec 53,19
Ja 69
BODINGHAM
John   C: c/o William Bunton,
Oxford 22 Ja 67
BODLY
Elizabeth   P: Northampton Co
31 Dec 61
BODY
Capt. William   P: Phila 6 Sep
53
BOFFIN/or BOSSIN/
Holddrich   P: Phila-Gaz. 27
Oct 73
BOGGS/BOGS
Mrs.   P: N.Castle 31 Dec 61
Edward   P: Phila 28 Oct 62
Elizabeth   P: New-Castle Co
11 Sep 55, 27 Jy 58
Ezekiel   P: Newcastle 18 Mar
62
Henry   P: Phila 27 Ja 73

Dr. James   P: Phila 26 Jy 64
John   P: Chester Co 1 Jy 56,
   26 Jy 64
Mary   P: Phila 2 May 65
Richard   P: Chester Co 27 Jy
   58
Samuel   P: Pa 12 Feb 61
William   P: Phila 28 Nov 54,
   18 Mar 62
BOGINGHAM
John   Phila 16 Jy 77
BOGLE/BOGALL
James   C: East Bradford 22 Ja
   67
Joseph   P: Phila 12 Feb 61
Malcolm   P: Foggs Manor 9 Ag
   59
BOHANNON
Mary   P: Pa 12 Ja 58
BOHTT
John Henry   P: York 13 May 56
BOIG
Alexander   P: Phila 30 Ap 67
BOLAND
James   P: Phila 18 Ag 57
Thomas   L: Cumberland Co 29
   Jy 72
BOLARD
Catherine   P: Phila 3 May 70
BOLDERSON
John   P: Bucks Co 3 May 70
BOLDING
Elizabeth   P: Phila 10 Oct 65
BOLDS
Ann   P: Phila 27 Jy 58
BOLITHO
Capt. John   P: Phila 5 Ag 62
BOLL
John   P: Phila 5 Ag 56
Richard   P: Phila 13 Oct 63
BOLT
John   P: Phila 24 Feb 63
BOLTON
James (sailor)   P: Phila 21
   Dec 58
John   P: Newcastle 24 Oct 54;
   Phila 16 Jy 77
Sarah   P: Bucks 11 Sep 55
BOMBERGER
Henry   P: Germantown 31 Dec
   61
BOND
Mrs.   P: Phila 28 Ap 68
Andrew   P: Phila 30 Ap 67, 16
   Jy 67
Benjamin   P: Phila 16 Jy 67
John   P: Baltimore Co 31 Mar
   63
Samuel   L: Great Valley 15 Ap
   56. P: Phila 10 Ap 66
Wille   P: Phila 23 Oct 66
BONDFIELD
Acklam   Phila 16 Jy 77
BONE
John   P: Phila 7 Ap 57

Thomas   P: Phila 1 Nov 70
BONES
Samuel   P: Phila 26 Oct 69
BONHAM
Malakiah   T: Kingwood 6 Dec
   64
BONN/BON
Janett   P: Lancaster 24 Oct
   54
John   P: Phila 24 Oct 54
BONNELL/BONNILL; see also
   THOMPSON & BONNELL
Henry   T: Falls Twp 10 Ag 58
Samuel   P: Phila 31 Dec 61
Sarah   Phila 31 Ja 76
BONNEMY
Nicholas   P: Phila 4 Ag 63
BONNEN
James   P: Byberry Twp 19 Ja
   69
BONNER
James   P: Byberry 1 Nov 70
John   P: Phila 3 Sep 61
BONNEY
Andrew   P: Phila 25 Ap 71
BONSELL/BONSALL/BONSOLL
Joseph   P: Chester Co 3 Sep
   61; Darby 27 Dec 53, 21 Dec
   58, 9 Ag 59, 31 Jy 60
Richard   L: at Potomack, or
   Fort Augusta 31 Ja 71
BONUTON
Henry   P: Phila 1 Feb 70
BOON/BOONE
Andrew   P: Chester Co 30 May
   54
Eve   Berks Co 30 Oct 76
James   P: Bucks Co 12 Ja 58
John   P: Berks Co 31 Dec 61;
   Phila 13 May 56
Rose   P: Chester Co 31 Jy 60
William   P: Phila 31 Mar 63
BOORE
Thomas   P: West New Jersey 18
   Ag 57
BOORS
William   P: Kent Co 9 Ag 59
BOOTH
Catharine   P: Phila 10 Oct 65
George   P: Phila 9 Ag 59
John   P: Manington 2 Ag 70
William   C: Ridley 30 Oct 66
BORALBY
Thomas   P: Point-no-Point 8
   Jy 62
BORDLY/BORDLEY
William   P: Phila 5 Ag 62 (2)
BORIM
Jacob   P: St. George's Hundred
   7 Ap 57
BORLAND/BORELAND
James   P: Chester Co 15 Mar 64
John   P: Chester Co 3 Sep 61;
   Pa 18 Mar 62
BORTZ

Jacob   P: Phila 29 Ag 54
BOSS
  John   P: Bucks Co 3 May 70
BOSSIN, see BOFFIN
BOSSWELL
  William   Phila 31 Ja 76
BOSTICK
  John   P: Phila 28 Ap 68
BOSTWICK
  Nathan   P: Phila 1 Jy 56
BOTHELL
  W.   P: Phila 31 Dec 61
BOTTLEMOREGER
  .....   P: Lancaster 24 Oct 54
BOTTOMLEY
  John   P: Phila 31 Dec 61
BOUCHELL
  Dr.   P: Md. 24 Feb 63
BOUCHER
  Francis   P: Phila 2 Feb 64
  James   P: Phila 30 Ap 67
  W.   P: Lewes To. 12 Ja 58
  William   P: Sussex Co 18 Ag
    57
BOUCHET
  Remy   P: Phila-Gaz. 27 Oct 73
BOUCHLER
  Francis   P: Phila 1 Feb 70
BOUDE/BOUD
  John   P: Phila 12 Ja 58
  Joseph   P: Phila 20 Oct 68
  Thomas   P: Phila 26 Oct 69
BOUND
  Capt. Cornelius   P: Phila 3
    Sep 61
  Joseph   P: Phila 5 Feb 54
  Sarah   P: Phila 30 May 54
BOUNEING, see WALTON & BOUNEING
BOURD
  Paul   P: Phila 19 May 63
BOURG/BLANC
  Mademoiselle Pegue   Phila 16
    Jy 77
BOURK/BOURKE; see also BURKE
  Bridget   P: Phila 2 Ag 70
  Dr. Francis   P: Phila 19 Ja
    69
  Capt. James   P: Phila 15 Mar
    64
BOURNE
  Mary   P: Abington 19 May 63
  Capt. T.   P: Phila 19 May 63
  Thomas   P: Abington 2 Feb 64,
    10 Ap 66
BOURTREE
  Walter   N: in Cecil Co, Mary-
    land 29 Nov 64
BOUSFIELD
  Joseph   P: Phila 20 Oct 68,
    20 Jy 69
BOWD
  Capt. F.   P: Phila 2 Sep 62
  Capt. Ferdinando   P: Phila 19
    May 63
  Sarah   P: Phila 4 Feb 68

BOWDEN
  Hannah   P: Phila 8 Jy 62
  John   P: Phila 10 Oct 65
  Mary   P: Phila 19 Ja 69
BOWDITCH
  Thomas   P: Phila 28 Ap 68
BOWEIS
  James   P: Lancaster Co 1 Nov
    53
BOWEN
  Benjamin   P: Phila 25 Jy 65
  Jonathan, Esq.   P: Cumberland
    Co, N.J. 4 Feb 68
  Noah   T: Salem Co 10 Ag 58
  Thomas   P: Salem 3 Sep 61
BOWERS
  Harvey   P: Phila 9 Ag 59
BOWES
  Hugh   P: Pa 13 Ja 63; Capt.;
    Phila 6 Jy 58, 27 Jy 58
BOWIE
  Daniel   Phila 30 Oct 76
BOWLAND
  Michael   P: Bucks Co 16 Jy 67
BOWLBY
  Thomas   P: Phila 2 Feb 64, 30
    Oct 76; Point-no-Point 24
    Feb 63
BOWLES/BOWLS/BOWELLS
  Capt. John   P: Phila 4 Feb 68
  Thomas   N: near New-Castle
    29 Nov 64.   P: 28 Nov 54,
    2 Feb 64
  William   P: Pa 26 Jy 64
BOWMAN/BOMAN
  Charles   P: Phila 12 Feb 61
  James   P: Delaware Forks 24
    Oct 54
  John   P: Phila 4 Ag 63, 16 Jy
    72
  Rev. Joseph   P: Sasquehannah
    4 Ag 63
  Mary   P: Germantown 5 Ag 62
  Roger   P: Phila 28 Oct 62
  William   P: Bucks Co 31 Dec
    61, 16 Jy 72
BOWNE; see also BOUND
  James   Phila 31 Oct 76
  James, Jr.   Phila 30 Ap 77
  Obadiah   P: N.J. 18 Mar 62
  Samuel   P: Phila 8 Jy 62
BOWNES
  Benjamin   P: Pottsgrove 30
    Ja 66
BOWYMAN
  John (soldier)   P: 21 Dec 58
BOX
  Thomas   P: Phila 31 Jy 60
BOYCE
  Robert   P: Chester Co 13 Ja
    63; New-Castle Co 13 Ja 63;
    Newgarden 9 Ag 59
BOYD/BOID/BOYDE, see WILLIAMS,
  John
  Dr.   L: Lancaster

Mr. T: Trenton 17 Oct 54
Rev. Mr. C: Octarara, see
  LEVINGSTON, Sarah
A. P: Middle Octarara 11
  Sep 55
Adam P: Chester Co 1 Nov 53;
  Octarara 24 Oct 54; Rev.
  Adam: Chester Co 30 May 54,
  27 Jy 58; Octarara 12 Ja
  58; Pa 3 Ja 60
Agnes P: Phila 27 Ja 73, 27
  Oct 73
Andrew C: 30 Jy 77. P: New-
  Castle Co 9 Ag 59; Marsh
  Creek 3 Ja 60; Pa 12 Feb 61
Archibald P: Pa 12 Ja 58
Benjamin P: Phila 3 Ja 76.
  T: Trenton 10 Ag 58
Daniel P: Sussex Co 23 Oct
  66
Elizabeth P: Forks Delaware
  1 Feb 70
George L: living betwixt
  Phila and Lancaster 19 Dec
  71
Hector P: Phila 9 Ag 59, 8
  Jy 62
Hugh P: Abington 1 Feb 70
Ja. L: at the Gap Tavern 14
  May 72
James P: Brandywine 3 May 70;
  Great Valley 21 Dec 58;
  Lancaster Rd 21 Dec 58; New
  Castle Co 13 Oct 63; Phila
  24 Oct 54, 3 Ja 65, 19 Ja
  69; Sadsbury 27 Jy 58;
  Strait Gap 15 Mar 64;
  Whiteclay Creek 4 Ag 63
John P: Newcastle Co 12 Ja
  58; Pa 15 Mar 64; Phila 3
  Sep 61, 28 Oct 62, 10 Ap 66,
  27 Ja 73, 3 Ja 76; Salem Co
  26 Jy 64
Joseph P: Forks of Delaware
  4 Feb 68
Mary P: Chester Co 3 Sep 61
Patrick P: Phila 13 May 56,
  19 Ja 69
Phoebe P: Phila 30 Ja 66
Robert P: Phila 18 Feb 55,
  6 Jy 58
Samuel P: Drummore 24 Feb 63;
  Lancaster Co 28 Nov 54, 13
  Ja 63; Phila 29 Ag 54, 12
  Ja 58, 30 Ja 66
Thomas C: Chestnut Level 18
  Jy 65
William P: Augusta Co near
  Phila 1 Sep 68; Chester Co
  13 Oct 63, 2 Feb 64; Dover
  31 Jy 60; Forks of Delaware
  24 Feb 63, 1 Feb 70; K.J.
  18 Mar 62; Phila 12 Feb 61,
  26 Jy 64, 16 Jy 67, 3 May

70. L: Fogs Manor 15 Ap
  56
BOYER
  Christopher P: Phila 11 Jy
  54
BOYLE/BOYELL/BOYL
  Charles P: Gloucester Co 26
  Jy 64
  Daniel P: Phila 23 Oct 66
  Edward P: Phila-Gaz. 27 Oct
  73
  Hugh L: Lancaster Co 15 Ap
  56
  James L: Cumberland Co 2
  Mar 74. P: near Newcastle
  28 Nov 54; Phila 24 Oct 54,
  18 Mar 62, 1 Feb 70
  John P: Deep Run 18 Mar 62;
  Lancaster Co 2 Feb 64;
  Phila 8 Jy 62, 28 Oct 62,
  31 Ja 76
  Patrick P: Phila 1 Nov 70
  Robert L: c/o John Rankin
  Lancaster 29 Jy 72
  Thomas P: Baskinridge 13 Ja
  63
BOYLES
  John P: Bucks Co 2 Feb 64
BRACE
  Alexander P: Phila 1 Jy 56
BRACKEN
  Thomas L: 3 Oct 65
BRACKENRIDGE/BRAKENRIGG/BRIKEN-
  RIDGE/BRAKANRIG
  George P: Phila 20 Oct 68,
  19 Ja 69
  John P: Chester Co 31 Dec 61;
  Fogs Manor 31 Dec 61; Pa 3
  Ja 60, 2 Feb 64
BRACKNELL
  James P: Phila 13 Oct 63
BRADFIELD
  John, Jr. P: Bucks 1 Nov 53
BRADFORD/BRATFORD
  Andrew P: Phila 3 May 70
  Henry P: Phila 4 Ag 63
  James P: Caecil Co 31 Dec 61;
  Phila 19 Jy 80
  Capt. John P: Phila 4 Ag 63
  Joseph P: Phila 13 May 56
  Robert P: Pa 15 Mar 64
  Sa. L: Rapho Twp/?/ 14 May 72
  Samuel P: New Castle 7 Ap 57,
  3 Sep 61
  William P: Phila 3 Sep 61
  William, Jr. P: Phila 19 Jy
  80
BRADLEY; see also BREADLY
  Mary Tinicum Island 24 Jy 76
  Richard L: at Curtis Gruff's
  Iron Works 20 Ja 73
  Susannah P: Phila 27 Jy 58,
  12 Feb 61
  Terence P: Phila 3 May 70

Thomas P: Forks of Delaware
  28 Ap 68
William P: Chester Co 18 Mar
  62
BRADON
  Eleanor P: Carlisle 31 Dec
  61
BRADY/BRADEY; see also BREADY
  Dorothy P: Chester Co 29 Ag
  54
  James P: Phila 8 Jy 62, 25
  Jy 65
  John P: Cumberland Co 13 Oct
  63
  Peter P: Phila 13 Oct 63
BRAGG
  Henry P: Phila 28 Oct 62, 13
  Ja 63
BRAIDEN
  John P: Lancaster 27 Jy 58;
  Pa 4 Ag 63
BRAIM/BRAME
  John P: Phila 25 Ap 71
  William P: Phila 25 Jy 65
BRAINER
  Petrus P: West New Jersey 18
  Ag 57
BRAISLE
  Mr. P: Phila 18 Mar 62
BRALLEY
  John P: Pa 12 Feb 61
BRAMWELL
  William P: Phila 19 Jy 80
BRAND
  John Phila 1 May 76
  Martin P: Baltimore Co 31
  Mar 63
  Mary P: Phila 25 Jy 65
BRANDON
  Elenora P: Carlisle 12 Feb
  61
  Elizabeth P: Pa 26 Jy 64;
  Phila 3 Ja 65
  James P: Carlisle 9 Ag 59
BRANDWOOD
  Andrew P: Marsh Creek 21 Dec
  58, 27 Jy 58, 3 Sep 61
BRANNAN/BRANNEN/BRANNON
  Benjamin P: Darby 20 Oct 68
  Elizabeth P: Carlisle 31 Dec
  61
  John P: Darby 31 Dec 61
  Martin P: Phila 13 Oct 63
  Nolah P: Phila 31 Dec 61
BRANSDELL
  Valentine P: Phila 31 Dec 61
BRANSON
  Day P: Phila 1 Nov 53
BRANT
  Lawrence P: Manor Moreland
  19 Ja 69
BRANTON
  John C: 30 Jy 77
BRARTY /?/
  James P: Pa 13 Ja 63

BRASHER
  Abraham P: Phila 27 Jy 58
BRATEHY
  Robert P: Lancaster Co 28
  Nov 54
BRATNEY
  Alexander P: Phila 3 Ja 65
BRATT
  Daniel P: Bucks 22 Nov 53
BRATTAN/BRATTEN/BRATTON/BRATTAIN
  Adam L: Cumberland Co 20 Ja
  73
  Horace P: York Co 28 Oct 62
  James P: Chester Co 15 Mar
  64; Phila 27 Ja 73
  John P: Chester Co 9 Ag 59
  William P: Phila 28 Oct 62,
  30 Ja 66
BRATTY/or BRATTS?/
  Andrew P: Phila 3 Sep 61
BRAYOR
  Alexander P: N.J. 27 Dec 53
BREADLY; see also BRADLEY
  John P: Kingsess 27 Jy 58
  Neal P: Phila 27 Jy 58
BREADY/BREDY; see also BRADY
  John P: Cumberland Co 31 Dec
  61; Capt, Phila 31 Dec 61
  Neal P: Phila 2 May 65
  Owen P: Md. 24 Feb 63
  Robert P: Bucks Co 27 Ja 73;
  Neshaminey 16 Jy 72
BREAKLEY
  Andrew P: Phila 24 Feb 63
BREAKSING
  Barbara P: Phila 21 Jy 68
BREASTON
  Manace C: c/o James Wilcocks
  Providence 22 Ja 67
BRECHELL
  Andrew P: Phila 11 Sep 55
BREDEN/BREDON/BREADEN
  James P: Pa 3 Ja 60, 8 Jy 62
  Joseph P: Upper Freehold-
  Gaz. 27 Oct 73
  Robert P: Phila 12 Feb 61, 2
  Feb 64 (2), 15 Mar 64, 26
  Jy 64
  William P: Octarara 8 Jy 62
BREEMSTEAD
  Jeremiah P: Phila 4 Feb 68
BREEZE
  Sydney P: Phila 13 May 56
BREHCOT
  Elizabeth P: Phila 30 Oct 76
BREHELL
  Andreas P: Phila 18 Feb 55
BREINTNALL
  George P: Phila 1 May 76
BRENISBAR
  Alexander P: Phila 3 Ja 60
BRENNAN/BRENNON
  John P: Phila 24 Feb 63, 19
  May 63, 4 Ag 63
BRENNER

BRENNER
Simeon T: Allen's Town 1 Sep 68
BRENNOCK
James P: Phila 20 Ap 69
BRESLIM
Neil P: Phila 2 May 65
BRESON
Hugh P: Phila 30 Ja 66
BRETT
Robert P: Phila 3 Ja 76
BRETZELL
Johann-Daniel P: Phila 7 Ap 57
BREWER
Hannah P: Jersey 7 Ap 57
BREWNING
Elizabeth P: Phila 6 Sep 53
BREWSTEN
Hannah P: Pilesgrove-Gaz. 27 Oct 73
BREWSTER/BROUSTER/BRUSTER
Samuel P: Phila 3 Ja 65
Thomas P: Phila 18 Mar 62, 2 Sep 62
BREWTON
Capt. B P: Phila 3 Ja 60, 13 Ja 63
Robert P: Wilmington 19 May 63, 2 Feb 64
BRIAN, see BRYAN
BRICE; see also BRYCE
Alexander P: Phila 6 Jy 58
James P: Lancaster Co 9 May 54; Rapho Twp 18 Ag 57
Thomas P: Phila 31 Mar 63
BRICK
Josiah P: Salem 31 Dec 61
Thomas P: Phila 5 Ag 56
BRICKELL
Mary P: Phila 5 Ag 62
BRICKLAND
Capt. Philip P: Phila 5 Ag 62
BRIDDEN
Robert P: Phila 3 Ja 65
BRIDE
John P: Phila 29 Ag 54
BRIDENBOUGH
John P: Phila 10 Oct 65
BRIDGES
..... P: Phila 3 May 70
George P: Phila 12 Feb 61
Mary P: Phila 27 Jy 58
BRIER
David P: Pa 15 Mar 64
BRIERLY; see also BRYERLY
Robert P: Phila 18 Feb 55
BRIGGS/BRIGS
Anna P: Brandywine 31 Dec 61
George P: Phila 9 May 54 (Capt), 3 Ja 60
John P: Phila 18 Mar 62
Richard P: Chester Co 18 Feb 55

BRIGHT
John P: West New Jersey 25 Ap 71
BRIMIGUM
M. P: Phila 20 Jy 69
BRINE
Isabella P: Phila 27 Ja 73
BRINGEMAN
Mr. =P: Phila 10 Oct 65
BRINGHURST
John P: Germantown 13 May 56, 28 Ap 68; Phila 13 Ja 63
BRINICH
Mark L: 25 Dec 66
BRINK
Isaac P: Phila 12 Ja 58
Sarah P: Delaware 31,Dec 61
BRINTON
Edward P: Chester Co 13 Oct 63
Moses P: Lancaster Co 9 May 54
BRISBANE/BRISBAN/BRISBIN/BRIS-BEN
Jo. L: Mill-creek 14 May 72
John P: Phila 2 Ag 70
Sam./Samuel Chester Co 27 Dec 53, 31 Jy 60, 3 Sep 61, 2 Feb 64; Nottingham 24 Oct 54
Wm. P: Chester Co 27 Dec 53, 3 Sep 61; Nottingham 24 Oct 54
BRISON/BRISSON/BRYSON
Capt. Francis P: Phila 30 Ap 67
George P: Phila 4 Feb 68
Hugh P: Chester Co 2 Feb 64; Lancaster Co 28 Oct 62; Pa 24 Feb 63
John L: Cumberland Co 2 Mar 74. P: Pa 18 Mar 62
William P: Cumberland Co 13 Oct 63
BRISS
John P: Phila 2 Feb 64
BRITAIN
Widow T: Trenton 3 Oct 65
BRITCH
Thomas P: Phila 31 Dec 61
BRITT
John P: Phila 3 Ja 60
BRITTEN/BRITTIN/BRITTON
Daniel P: Phila 27 Ja 73
George P: Phila 27 Ja 73
John P: Pa 4 Ag 63
William P: Phila 25 Jy 65
BRITTLE
Joseph Phil 31 Ja 76
BROAD
John P: Phila 28 Ap 68, 27 Ja 73
BROADES
Peter P: Phila 11 Sep 55
William P: Phila 11 Sep 55

BROADFIELD
  Edward   P: Phila 30 May 54,
    31 Dec 61. T: near Trenton
    3 Oct 65
BROBSON
  William   P: New-Castle Co 3
    Ja 60
BROC
  Alexis (French Neutral)   P:
    13 May 56
BROCKINGTON
  Capt. J.   P: Phila 19 May 63
  James   P: Phila 13 May 56, 9
    Ag 59, 4 Ag 63 (Capt)
BRODDLEY
  John   P: Pa 31 Dec 61
BRODEN
  William_ Phila 30 Oct 76
BRODERG /or BRODERA?/
  John   P: Phila 1 Jy 56
BRODRECK/BROADRICK
  Charles   P: Phila 12 Feb 61,
    3 Sep 61
BROIZER
  Mrs.   P: Phila 24 Feb 63
BROMFIELD
  Samuel   P: Phila 13 Oct 63
  Thomas   P: Phila 12 Feb 61
BROMLEY
  Mrs.   P: Germantown 20 Jy 69.
    T: 7 May 67
BROMWELL
  Jacob   P: Phila 7 Ap 57, 18
    Ag 57 (Capt), 12 Ja 58
BROMWICH
  William   P: Phila 24 Feb 63
BROOK/BROOKE
  Rev.   P: New Castle 7 Ap 57
  Clement   P: New-Castle Co 5
    Ag 56
  Philip   P: Phila 3 Ja 76
BROOKHOUSE
  Samuel   P: Phila 10 Ap 66, 2
    Ag 70
BROOKIE
  John   P: Phila 27 Ja 73
BROOKS/BROOKES
  Andrew   P: Phila 3 Sep 61, 18
    Mar 62, 5 Ag 62
  Ann P: Pa 24 Feb 63
  Benjamin   P: Phila 3 Ja 76
  Charles   P: Phila 8 Jy 62
  David   P: Merion Twp 18 Ag 57
  Henry   N: Capt., near Notting-
    ham, Md 4 Dec 66, 12 Feb 67.
    P: Phila 2 Ag 70
  James   P: Phila 24 Oct 54;
    Schuylkill 18 Mar 62
  John   P: Providence Twp 27
    Ja 73
  Joseph   P: Phila 4 Feb 68
  Nicholas   P: Phila 15 Mar 64
  Richard   P: Milford 15 Mar 64
  Robert   Phila 24 Jy 76
  Thomas   P: Phila 13 Ja 63, 30

    Ap 67. T: Hackets-Town 31
    Ja 71
  William   P: New-Castle Co 5
    Ag 56
BROOKSBY
  Thomas   P: Phila 8 Jy 62 (2)
BROOMFIELD
  Mr. Phila 1 May 76
BROTHERTON
  John, soldier   P: Phila 1 Feb
    70
BROW
  Ann   P: Phila 27 Ja 73
  Charles   P: Phila 12 Ja 58
  Daniel   P: Phila 12 Ja 58
  John   P: Phila 21 Jy 68
BROWMAN
  Margaret   P: Germantown 27
    Jy 58
BROWN/BROWNE
  ....   P: Phila 1 Jy 56
  & GORDON   P: Phila 3 May 70
  Lt. in the army   P: 12 Ja 58
  Mr.   P: Phila 31 Dec 61
  Abraham   P: Phila 2 May 65
  Alexander   P: Phila 28 Nov
    54, 21 Dec 58; near Phila
    3 Sep 61; York Co 9 Ag 59
  Andrew   P: Phila 20 Jy 69, 3
    May 70
  Benjamin   P: Phila 21 Dec 58
  Charles   P: New Jersey 13 Ja
    63; Phila 28 Ap 68
  Charlotte   P: Phila 1 Jy 56
  Christian   P: Phila 2 Ag 70
  Cornelius/Cor.   P: Phila-Gaz.
    27 Oct 73, 15 Mar 64
  Daniel   P: near Phila 27 Jy
    58; Phila 27 Dec 53, 19 Jy
    80 (Lt. of the Holker)
  David   P: Pequea 9 Ag 59;
    Phila 5 Feb 54, 2 Sep 62,
    20 Oct 68 (Capt)
  Edmund   P: Phila 20 Jy 69
  Edward   P: Bush River 21 Dec
    58; Phila 28 Oct 62, 3 Ja
    65, 27 Ja 73 (Dr)
  Elijah   P: Phila 5 Ag 62
  Elisha   Phila 31 Ja 76
  Elizabeth   P: Phila 1 Feb 70,
    19 Jy 80
  Everardus   P: Phila 23 Oct 66
  George   C: 30 Jy 77. L: at
    the Big Spring, Cumberland
    Co 31 Ja 71
  George   P: Cumberland Co 31
    Dec 61, 15 Mar 64; Lancaster
    Co 12 Feb 61; Pequea 13 Ja
    63, 3 Ja 65; Pa 26 Jy 64;
    Phila 30 Ja 66, 23 Oct 66,
    4 Feb 68; York 1 Jy 56
  Gustavus   P: Phila 30 Ja 66
  Hannah   P: Phila 4 Feb 68
  Henry   P: Phila 6 Sep 53
    (Capt), 31 Dec 61, 25 Ap 71

Hubbard P: Moreland 27 Ja 73
Hugh L: Marsh Creek 2 Mar 74.
   P: Phila 19 Ja 69, 27 Oct 73
   (Capt)
Jacob P: Phila 5 Ag 62
James P: Baskinridge 15 Mar
   64; Bucks Co 2 Feb 64, 30
   Ja 66, 27 Ja 73; Chester Co
   9 Ag 59, 3 Sep 61; Forks of
   Delaware 13 Ja 63; Goshen
   21 Dec 58; Lancaster Co 3
   Sep 61; New-London 27 Jy 58;
   Oxford Twps 5 Ag 56; Pa 3
   Ja 60; Phila 13 May 56, 21
   Dec 58, 31 Jy 60, 30 Ja 66,
   20 Jy 69, 1 Feb 70, 27 Oct
   73, 3 Ja 76, 24 Jy 76;
   Schuylkill 12 Ja 58; Wilming-
   ton 3 Ja 60
Jane P: Phila 23 Oct 66
Jeremiah P: Chester Co 31 Dec
   61, West Nottingham 7 Ap 57
Jo. L: 3 Oct 65
John L: Carlisle 2 Mar 74
   (student). P: Brandiwine
   18 Mar 62; Buckingham, Bucks
   Co 26 Oct 69; Bucks Co 16 Jy
   72; near Newcastle 28 Nov 54;
   Pa 3 Ja 60; Phila 9 May 54,
   12 Ja 58, 3 Ja 60, 8 Jy 62,
   2 Sep 62, 4 Ag 63, 30 Ja 66,
   1 Feb 70, 3 May 70, 25 Ap 71,
   31 Ja 76 (2), 30 Ap 76; Rox-
   borough 3 May 70. T: Cross-
   wicks 10 Ag 58
Jos./Joseph P: Huntington Co,
   West Jersey 26 Oct 69;
   Phila 4 Ap 54, 18 Feb 55,
   27 Jy 58, 18 Mar 62, 23 Oct
   66
Joshua L: York Co 19 Dec 71
Judith Phila 31 Ja 76
Justus Phila 30 Ap 77
Lawrence P: Bucks Co 12 Ja
   58; Pa 18 Ag 57
Magnes/Magness P: Phila 13
   Oct 63, 3 Ja 65
Margaret P: Abington 13 Oct
   63; Phila 19 May 63, 2 Ag
   70
Mary P: Phila 5 Ag 62, 13
   Ja 63, 13 Oct 63, 15 Mar
   64, 3 Ja 65, 21 Jy 68
Nancy P: Phila 28 Oct 62
Nathan P: Pa 8 Jy 62
Nathaniel L: Sturgeon's Mill
   2 Mar 74. P: Phila 24 Jy
   76
Neal P: Phila 26 Jy 64
Patrick P: Chester Co 26 Jy
   64; N.J. 31 Dec 61; Phila
   29 Ag 54
Peter P: Phila-Gaz. 27 Oct
   73
Preserve T: Nottingham 10 Ag

58
Richard L: York Co 2 Mar 74
   (Esq). P: Phila 27 Ja 73;
   Salem, New Jersey 26 Oct 69;
   York Co 31 Dec 61 (Esq)
Robert P: East New Jersey 12
   Feb 61; New Jersey 13 Ja 63;
   Pa 4 Ag 63; Phila 10 Oct 65,
   16 Jy 67, 19 Ja 69, 20 Ap
   69, 27 Ja 73. T: Morris-
   Town 15 Nov 64, 6 Dec 64
Robert, Jr. P: Phila 30 Ja
   66
Rolin P: Phila 27 Jy 58
Samuel P: Norrington 2 Feb
   64, 15 Mar 64; Pa 28 Oct 62;
   Phila 12 Ja 58, 5 Ag 62, 24
   Feb 63, 15 Mar 64, 10 Oct
   65; Phila Co 28 Ap 68
Sar./Sarah L: 13 Jn 65. P:
   15 Mar 64
Standford P: Phila 20 Oct 68
Stephen P: Phila 12 Feb 61,
   18 Mar 62, 26 Jy 64
Thomas C: Fogs Manor, Chester
   Co 30 Oct 66. L: near Car-
   lisle 2 Mar 74. P: 3 Ja
   65; Chester Co 28 Nov 54;
   Chestnut Level 12 Ja 58;
   Fogs Manor 31 Dec 61; Pa 28
   Oct 62, 24 Feb 63; Phila 6
   Jy 58, 3 Sep 61, 31 Dec 61
   (2), 18 Mar 62, 2 Sep 62, 2
   Feb 64, 26 Jy 64, 3 Ja 76,
   24 Jy 76
Thomasine P: Phila 11 Sep 55
Ensign Waram P: in the army
   27 Jy 58
William P: Abington 7 Ap 57;
   Abington Twp 3 Ja 60; East-
   land Twp 5 Ap 76; at the
   Gap, Lancaster Co 7 Ap 57;
   Pa 18 Mar 62, 13 Ja 63;
   Phila 28 Nov 54, 11 Sep 55,
   12 Ja 58, 6 Jy 58, 3 Ja 60,
   31 Jy 60, 18 Mar 62, 13 Ja
   63, 25 Jy 65, 10 Oct 65,
   26 Oct 69, 16 Jy 72, 30 Ap
   77 (Dr), 19 Jy 80
William B. P: Salem 4 Ag 63
Windsor P: Phila 21 Jy 68,
   25 Ap 71
BROWNELL
   Ab. P: Phila 18 Mar 62
BROWNFIELD
   John P: Bethlehem 22 Nov 53
BROWNING
   Abigail P: Phila 13 May 56
   Joseph P: Phila 3 Ja 76
   William P: Phila 1 Nov 53,
   24 Oct 54
BROWNLEE/BROWNLIE/BROUNLIE
   Arch. P: Mount Mebo 18 Ag 57;
   Octarara 12 Ja 58
   John L: Mount Nebo 15 Ap 56.

P: Lancaster Co 27 Dec 53
BROWNLOW
  John   P: Phila 3 Ja 65
BROWNSON
  Richard   L: 13 Jn 65. P:
    surgeon in army, Fort Pitt
    26 Jy 64
BROXTON
  Nicholas   P: Lancaster Co 2
    Ap 57
BRUCE
  Alexander   P: Phila 27 Jy 58
  John   P: East New Jersey 12
    Feb 61; Phila 25 Jy 65
  Thomas   P: Pa 2 Feb 64
BRUFF
  James   P: Talbot Co 13 Oct 63
  Joseph   P: Talbot Co 13 Oct 63
  Thomas   P: Talbot Co 13 Oct 63
  William   P: Phila 27 Ja 73;
    Talbot Co 13 Oct 63
BRUINGTON
  Robert   P: Phila 27 Ja 73
BRUMFIELD
  Philip   P: Phila 5 Ja 76-Gaz.
    31 Ja
BRUNING/BRUNEING
  Caroline   P: Phila 3 Ja 65
  Carvin   P: Phila 2 Feb 64
  Cornelia   P: Phila 13 Oct 63
  William   P: Phila 31 Mar 63
BRUNOR
  George   P: Point-no-Point 18
    Ag 57
BRUNTIN
  Thomas   P: Phila 3 Ja 76
BRUSH
  Craen   P: Phila 2 May 65
BRUSTIN
  Mrs.   P: Phila 12 Feb 61
BRUSTRUM
  James   Phila 1 May 76
BRYAN/BRIAN/BRIEN
  Christopher   Phila 19 May 63
  Donogh   Phila 26 Jy 64
  Elizabeth   P: Phila 16 Jy 67
  Hugh   P: Pa 13 Ja 63
  James   P: Pa 4 Ag 63
  John   P: Phila 3 Sep 61, 10
    Oct 65; Sardoine 2 May 65
  Margaret   P: Phila 28 Oct 62,
    31 Mar 63
  Patrick   P: Marcus-Hook 13 Oct
    63; New Castle 22 Nov 53;
    Phila 30 Ja 66, 20 Oct 68
  Peter   P: Burlington 27 Jy 58
  Robert   P: New Castle 31 Dec
    61; Pa 12 Feb 61; Phila 31
    Dec 61
  Samuel   P: Phila 20 Ap 69, 27
    Oct 73
  Timothy   P: Phila 2 Feb 64, 3
    Ja 65
  William/Will.   P: Bucks Co 9
    Ag 59, 16 Jy 72; Josehion,

Bucks Co 21 Jy 68; Phila 21
    Jy 68, 20 Ap 69
BRYANT/BREYANT
  Henry   P: Phila 2 Feb 64, 26
    Jy 64
  John   P: Phila 20 Ap 69
BRYCE; see also BRICE
  John   Phila 1 May 76
  Nicoll   Phila 1 May 76
  Robert   Phila 1 May 76
BRYERLY; see also BRIERLY
  Hugh   P: Baltimore Co 9 Ag 59
BRYNER
  Jacob   L: Reading 14 May 72
BRYSON, see BRISON
BUB
  Joseph   P: Phila 27 Jy 58
BUBIER
  John   P: Phila 20 Jy 69
BUCHAN
  Robert   P: Phila 3 Ja 65
BUCHANAN; see also BEAUCANNON/
    BOHANNAN
  Andrew   P: Chester Co 2 Feb 64
  Archibald   P: New Jersey 18
    Mar 62
  David   P: Chester Co 27 Jy 58;
    West Fallowfield 13 Ja 63
  James   P: Pa 31 Dec 61; Phila
    2 Ag 70
  John   P: Phila 31 Jy 60, 28
    Oct 62
  Robert   P: Phila 28 Ap 68
  Thomas   P: Phila 21 Jy 68
  William   C: see HOOK,William.
    L: Donegall, Lancaster Co
    31 Ja 71. P: Phila 25 Ap
    71; West Nottingham 18 Ag
    57
BUCK
  Asa   P: Phila /?/ 20 Ap 69
  Elizabeth   P: Phila 30 Ap 67
  Capt. H.   P: Phila 18 Mar 62
  Hendric   P: Phila 20 Ap 69
  Henry   P: Phila 28 Oct 62, 31
    Mar 63 (Capt)
  James   P: Phila 20 Ap 69
  Thomas   P: Phila 4 Feb 68, 20
    Ap 69
BUCKERFIELD
  Thomas   P: Phila 27 Ja 73
BUCKINGHAM
  Elizabeth   P: Phila 16 Jy 67
BUCKLEY
  Adam   P: Upper Dublin 20 Oct
    68
  Cornel.   P: Phila 18 Mar 62
  George   P: Phila 5 Ag 62, 27
    Oct 73
  Phineas   P: Phila 13 Oct 63
  William   P: Bucks Co 9 Ag 59
BUCKWALDER
  John   L: Lancaster Co 14 May
    72
BUDD

John   P: Phila 21 Jy 68;
  Salem 5 Ag 56; Salem Co 9
  Ag 59. T: Roxbury 17 Oct
  54
Thomas   P: Phila 26 Jy 64, 3
  Ja 65; Salem 1 Nov 70
BUDDEN
  Capt. P: Phila 9 Ag 59
  Isaac   Phila 30 Ap 77
  Mary   P: Phila 1 Nov 70
  Capt. Richard   P: Phila 6 Jy
    58
  William   P: Phila 18 Mar 62
BUDDING
  Ann   Phila 31 Ja 76
BUDDRA
  Francis   P: Phila 27 Ja 73
BUFFIN
  John   P: Phila 30 Ap 67
BUFFINGTON
  Jane   P: Phila 12 Ja 58
BUGLESS
  Mary   L: 13 Jn 65; c/o Sam-
    uel Lefever, Strasborg Twp
    19 Dec 71
BUHLER
  James   P: Phila 21 Jy 68
BUHN
  Mrs.   P: Phila 21 Jy 68
BUIND
  Mr.   P: Phila 19 May 63
BULDERBACK
  Hans Adam   P: Phila 29 Ag 54
BULGER
  David   P: Phila 19 Ja 69
BULKELEY
  John   P: Phila 13 May 56
  Capt. Richard   P: Phila 28
    Ap 68
BULL
  Caleb   Phila 30 Oct 76
  Capt. John   P: Phila Co 24
    Feb 63
  Joseph   P: Byberry 2 Ag 70
BULLARD
  John   Phila 16 Jy 77
  William   P: Pa 21 Dec 58;
    Phila 21 Dec 58 (sailor)
BULLEY
  Robert   P: Phila 25 Jy 65
BULLOCK
  George   P: Phila 21 Dec 58
  John   C: c/o Jacob Taggart
    18 Jy 65
  Joseph   P: Phila 16 Jy 72
  Margaret   P: Chester Co 21
    Dec 58
BUNALL
  Jonathan   P: Phila 19 Jy 80
BUNN
  Surriah   P: Phila 9 Ag 59
BUNTING
  Samuel   P: Phila 9 Ag 59, 13
    Oct 63
BUNTON

William   C: Oxford, see
  BODINGHAM, John
BURBRIDGE
  Thomas   P: Phila 20 Ap 69
BURCH; see also BIRCH
  Ann   P: Octarara 25 Ap 71
  Edward   P: Phila 9 Ag 59
  Elizabeth   P: Lancaster Co 5
    Ag 62
  Joseph   P: Phila 1 Nov 70
  Thomas   P: Phila 31 Dec 61
BURCHALL
  Robert   P: Phila 3 Ja 76
BURCHAN/BURCHEM
  Robert   P: Phila 12 Ja 58, 5
    Ag 62, 2 May 65
BURD
  James   P: Phila 5 Ag 62 (Col),
    10 Oct 65
BURDICK
  Jonathan   P: Phila 5 Ag 62
BURGE
  John   P: Phila 3 Ja 76
BURGER
  Elias   P: Phila 4 Ap 54
BURGESS/BURGES/BURDGESS
  Gervase/Jarvess/Gervas/Gervass
    P: Phila 11 Sep 55, 13 May
    56, 7 Ap 57, 12 Feb 61, 18
    Mar 62, 8 Jy 62, 4 Ag 63, 15
    Mar 64, 25 Jy 65, 10 Oct 65,
    30 Ap 67
  Henry   P: Phila 10 Jy 72
  John   L: Whiteclay Creek 15
    Ap 56
  Joseph   P: Bucks Co 8 Jy 62
BURGIN
  John   P: West Jersey 7 Ap 57
BURGOIN
  Joseph   P: East New Jersey 8
    Jy 62
BURGWIN
  John   P: Phila 21 Jy 68
BURK/BURKE/BOWRKE
  Mr.   P: Phila 24 Feb 63
  Catharine   P: Phila 5 Ag 62
  Eleanor   P: Phila 4 Ap 54
  Elizabeth   P: Phila 27 Jy 58,
    16 Jy 67
  Francis (or Frances?)   L:
    York Co 2 Mar 74
  James   P: Phila 8 Jy 62
  John   P: Bucks Co 3 Ja 60;
    Phila 20 Ap 69, 2 Ag 70 (2)
  Michael   P: Phila 3 May 70, 2
    Ag 70
  Patrick   P: near Phila 3 Sep
    61
  Paul   P: Phila 19 May 63
  Ruth   P: Phila 3 Ja 65, 2 May
    65
  Susannah   P: Phila 2 May 65
  Thomas   P: Phila 28 Ap 68
  William   P: Phila 19 Ja 69, 3
    Ja 76

BURKELOW/BURRELOE
  Mr.   P: Phila 13 Ja 63
  Samuel   P: Phila 27 Jy 58
BURKLEE
  Samuel   P: Phila 18 Feb 55
BURKLORE
  Samuel   P: Phila 5 Ag 56
BURLEY
  John   P: Bucks Co 3 May 70
BURLING
  Deborah   P: Phila 4 Feb 68
BURLT
  Eleanor   P: Phila 27 Dec 53
BURM
  William   P: Chester Co 3 Sep
  61
BURN
  Andrew   P: Phila 4 Ag 63
  Garrett   P: Lower Dublin 13
  Ja 63
  James   P: Phila 4 Ap 54, 24
  Oct 54, 18 Mar 62
  John   P: Phila 6 Sep 53
  Robert   P: Phila 28 Oct 62
  Thomas   P: Lancaster Co 22
  Nov 53
BURNEL
  Margaret   P: Phila 31 Jy 60
BURNER
  William   P: Phila 2 Ag 70
BURNET
  James   P: Phila 25 Jy 65
BURNEY
  John   P: Nottingham 3 Ja 60
BURNS
  Ann   P: Bethlehem Twp 5 Ag 62
  Hugh   P: Pa 2 Feb 64; Phila 2
  Feb 64
  Joseph   Phila 16 Jy 77
  Joshua   P: Middle-Ferry 31
  Dec 61
  Sarah   P: Pa 12 Ja 58
  Thomas   P: Phila 27 Oct 73
BURNSIDE
  David   P: Phila 3 May 70
  John   P: Lancaster Co 1 Nov 53
  Mathew/Mat   P: Pa 13 Ja 63;
  Shaminey 15 Mar 64; York Co
  7 Ap 57
  Thomas   P: Pa 4 Ag 63; Phila
  19 May 63 (2)
  William   P: Pa 26 Jy 64; Phila
  10 Ap 66
BURR/BUR
  Elizabeth   P: Phila 28 Ap 68
  John   P: Phila 12 Ja 58
  Peter   P: Piles Grove 24 Oct
  54
  Thadd, Esq.   T: Fairfield 17
  Oct 54
BURRAGE
  John   P: Phila 27 Ja 73
BURREES
  Peter   P: Phila 24 Oct 54
BURROUGH

  Forster   P: Hopewell 28 Oct
  62
BURROUGHS/BURROWS
  Mrs.   P: Frederick-Town 4 Ag
  63
  Capt. Arthur   P: Phila 19 May
  63
  Isabella   P: Kent Co 18 Ag 59
  John   P: Phila 11 Sep 55, 5
  Ag 62, 19 Ja 69. T: 7 May
  67; Middletown 3 Ja 71;
  Pa 31 Ja 71
  Thomas   T: Hopewell 17 Oct 54
  William   P: Phila 21 Dec 58
  (sailor), 9 Ag 59
BURT
  James   P: Phila 3 Ja 65
  Thomas   P: Phila 12 Ja 58
BURTIS
  Francis   P: New Jersey 31 Jy
  60
  Sarah   T: Penington 10 Ag 58
BURTLEY
  James   P: Phila 28 Oct 62
BURTON
  Agnes   P: Bucks Co 9 Ag 59
  Francis   P: Phila 31 Jy 60,
  3 May 65
  Henry   C: 30 Jy 77
  James   P: Phila 8 Jy 62
  John   P: Phila 1 Feb 70
  John Maalten   P: Indian River
  16 Jy 67
  Joshua   P: Indian River 12 Ja
  58
  Stratton   P: Phila 19 May 63
  Thomas   P: Phila 1 Nov 70,
  25 Ap 71
BURTZ
  Elizabeth   P: Phila 9 Ag 59
BUSH
  David   P: New Castle 21 Dec
  58, 3 Ja 60 (Esq), 2 Feb 64;
  Wilmington 3 Sep 61, 18 Mar
  62 (Esq)
  Philip   P: Schuylkill 31 Mar
  63
BUSHELL
  John   P: Phila 1 Nov 70
BUSS
  John   P: Phila 28 Oct 62
BUSTEED
  Morgan   P: Phila 3 May 70
BUTCHER
  George   P: Lancaster 26 Jy 64
  Walter   P: near Phila 27 Jy 58
BUTLER
  Capt.   P: Phila 2 Feb 64, 26
  Jy 64
  Andrew   P: Phila 2 Ag 70
  Anthony   P: Phila 27 Oct 73
  Charles   P: Phila 18 Mar 62
  Capt. E.   P: Phila 5 Ag 62
  Capt. Edward   P: Phila 26 Jy
  64

Eleanor P: Phila 31 Dec 61
Henry P: Phila 26 Oct 69
James P: Phila 8 Jy 62, 31
  Mar 63
Capt. John P: Phila 28 Oct
  62, 27 Ja 73; Salem 31 Dec
  61
Margaret P: Phila 31 Mar 63
Mary P: Phila 1 Feb 70
Nicholas P: Pa 4 Ag 63
Philip(sailor) P: Phila 21
  Dec 58
Richard P: Dover 2 Ag 70
Samuel P: Phila 26 Jy 64
Simon P: Bucks Co 12 Ja 58,
  9 Ag 59
Thomas L: Lancaster Co 15
  Ap 56. P: Lancaster Co 1
  Nov 53, 28 Nov 54, 12 Ja
  58; Phila 10 Oct 65
BUTT
  Matthew P: Phila 1 Nov 53
BUTTAN
  Edward P: Phila 4 Feb 68
BUTTERWOOD
  John (soldier) P: 21 Dec 58
BUXTON
  Daniel P: Phila 20 Jy 69
BUZAGLO
  Moses P: 5 Jy 58, 27 Jy 58
BUZBY
  Thomas P: Oxford 7 Ap 57
BYBERT
  Ann P: Phila 28 Nov 54
BYE
  James P: Phila 31 Jy 60, 5
  Ag 62, 13 Ja 63
  Joseph P: Phila 18 Mar 62
BYERLY
  Jacob P: Phila 4 Ap 54, 3
  May 70
BYERS/BUYERS/BYIRS
  James L: 13 Jn 65
  John P: West Nottingham 18
  Ag 57
  Mat. P: Phila 15 Mar 64
BYNON
  David Phila 31 Ja 76
BYRD
  Thomas T. P: 16th Regt. Phila
  27 Oct 73
BYRN/BYRNE
  Ann P: New Castle 29 Ag 54
  Elizabeth P: Phila 20 Jy 69
  Garrett T: near Amwell 1 Sep
  68
  George P: Phila 12 Ja 58
  James P: Byberry 2 Ag 70;
  Dover 12 Feb 61; Kent Co 9
  Ag 59; Phila 18 Mar 62, 8
  Jy 62, 30 Ap 67
  John P: Newtown 18 Mar 62;
  Phila 21 Jy 68, 31 Ja 76
  Matthew P: Phila 3 May 70
  Redmond P: Phila-Gaz. 3 Ja 76

Richard P: Octarara 18 Feb 55
Robert P: Phila 4 Ag 63
Turence P: Kent Co 28 Oct 62
BYRNIE
  James P: Phila 19 May 63
BYRON
  William P: Phila 1 Nov 70
BYVANCK
  Evert P: Phila 12 Feb 61
BYWATER
  Margaret P: Phila 2 Ag 70
  William P: Phila 2 Sep 62

CABEEN
  Thomas P: Phila 16 Jy 72
CABELL/CABEL
  George P: Phila 27 Ja 73
  Jabez P: Reading 31 Dec 61
CACIES
  Mary P: Phila 25 Jy 65
CADDAMAN
  Warner P: Phila 3 May 70
CADDEL
  John P: Phila 24 Feb 63, 19
  May 63
CADWALLADER
  Isaac P: Phila 10 Ap 66
  Dr. Thomas P: Phila 6 Jy 58
CADY
  Abel P: Phila-Gaz 27 Oct 73
CAFFERY/CAFFREY/CAFARY
  Edward P: Phila 1 Nov 53
  Eleanor P: Phila 16 Jy 67
  George/Geo. P: Phila 24 Feb
  63 (2)
  John P: N.J. 21 Dec 58; Pa
  12 Ja 58; Phila 1 Nov 53
CAFFICY
  George P: Phila 19 May 63
CAFFIN/?/
  Joseph P: Phila 24 Feb 63
CAHILL
  Cornelius P: Phila 2 Ag 70
  Peter P: Berks Co 21 Jy 68
CAIGER
  Edmond P: Phila 28 Ap 68
CAIN/CAINE
  Benjamin P: New Castle 12 Feb
  61
  Charles P: Abington 18 Mar 62
  Daniel P: Phila 3 Ja 65
  Daniel P: Phila 2 May 65
  Hugh P: Phila 3 Ja 76
CAINS
  Francis P: Phila 26 Oct 69
CAIRD
  Archibald P: Forks of Dela-
  ware 9 Ag 59
CAIRNEY
  Ann P: Wilmington 7 Ap 57
CAIRNS/CAIRNES
  John P: Chester Co 31 Dec 61;
  Lancaster Co 24 Feb 63
William L: 29 Ja 67. P: Phila

3 May 70

CAIROS
   John   P: Chester Co 19 May 63
CALADAY & MING   P: Phila 25 Ap
   71
CALDCHREST
   Robert   P: Phila 1 Nov 70
CALDELEUGH
   Andrew   Phila 1 May 76
CALDER
   Alexander   P: Phila 20 Ap 69
CALDHOON
   James (soldier)   P: 21 Dec 58
CALDHOUND
   Audley   P: Phila 1 Nov 70
CALDWELL; see also CALWELL
   Mrs.   P: Phila 3 Ja 76
   Andrew   P: Kent Co 21 Dec 58
   Charles   P: Pa 12 Feb 61
   David   P: Pa 18 Mar 62; Phila
   4 Feb 68
   Hugh   L: near Carlisle 20 Ja
   73.   P: Lancaster Co 24 Feb
   63; Pequea 13 May 56; Pa 31
   Mar 63
   James   C: Haverford Twp 22 Ja
   67.   P: Phila 31 Jy 60 (Capt)
   John   P: Chester Co 3 Sep 61;
   East Nottingham 7 Ap 57; Pa
   28 Oct 62, 13 Ja 63; Phila
   1 Nov 70
   Jos./Joseph   C: Chester Co 18
   Jy 65; Uchland 30 Oct 66.
   L: Shearman's Valley 14 M
   72.   P: America 12 Feb 61;
   Oxford 2 Feb 64.   T: New
   Germantown 31 Ja 71
   Margaret   C: Haverford Twp
   22 Ja 67
   Martha   P: Phila 19 Ja 69
   Nevin   P: Christine Bridge 28
   Oct 62
   Peter   P: Pa 13 Oct 63
   Robert   P: Pa 2 Sep 62; Phila
   9 Ag 59, 25 Ap 71, 27 Ja 73
   Samuel   P: Pa 31 Dec 61; Phila
   12 Feb 61
   Thomas   L: Hunter's Town 2 Mar
   74; York Co 2 Mar 74.   P: Pa
   27 Jy 58, 31 Dec 61
   William, merchant   L: Brandy-
   wine Forks 20 Ja 73; York
   Co 2 Mar 74.   P: Carlisle
   3 Ja 60; York Co 12 Feb 58
CALE
   George   P: Phila 31 Mar 63,
   4 Ag 63
   Margaret   P: Lewistown 9 Ag 59
CALESTON
   John   P: Chester Co 4 Ag 63
CALHOON/CALHOUND; see also
   COLHOUN
   John   C: c/o W. Clingham, Esq.
   West Caln 28 Nov 65.   P:
   Phila 2 May 65, 10 Oct 65

CALKIN
   Reuben   P: Pennsylvania 16 Jy
   72
CALL
   Ebenezer   P: Phila 1 Nov 53
   Richard   Phila 30 Ap 77
CALLAGHAN/CALAHAN/CALAGHEN/
   CALLAGHN/CALOHAN
   Cat.   P: Phila 31 Jy 60
   Daniel   Bordentown 31 Ja 76
   Henry   P: Phila 3 Ja 76
   James   P: Phila 3 Ja 76
   Jennet   P: Chester Co 8 Jy 62
   Margaret   P: Phila 2 Ag 70
   Mary   P: Upper Makefield 3
   May 70, 1 Nov 70
   T.S.   P: Phila 2 Feb 64
   Thadee   P: Phila 3 Ja 76
   William   P: Phila 26 Jy 64, 3
   Ja 65, 25 Jy 65
CALLEN/CALLON
   Edward   P: Pa 2 Feb 64; Phila
   26 Jy 64, 4 Feb 68
CALLENDER
   Mrs.   P: Cumberland Co 13 Oct
   63
   Mr.   P: Kingston 31 Dec 61
   Francis   P: Phila 20 Oct 68
   James   P: Phila 20 Oct 68
   John   P: Phila 12 Feb 61, 31
   Dec 61
   Robert   P: Carlisle 24 Feb 63;
   Phila 2 Sep 62
   Thomas   P: 26 Oct 69; Phila
   20 Oct 68
   William   P: Phila 6 Jy 58,
   21 Jy 68
CALLOUCH
   Samuel   P: Marsh Creek 21 Jy
   68
CALLUNDEE
   William   P: Kingston 31 Dec 61
CALLY/CALLEY
   Agnes   P: Chester Co 31 Dec
   61
   Andrew   P: Pa 31 Dec 61 (2)
   Ann   P: Pequea 4 Ag 63
CALSEY
   John   P: Phila 4 Ag 63
CALTON
   Mary   P: Phila 25 Jy 65
CALVERT/CALVART
   Anthony   P: Phila 30 Ja 66
   James   P: Phila 20 Oct 68
   John   T: East Jersey 1 Sep
   68
   Capt. Thomas   P: Phila 3 Ja
   60, 28 Oct 62
   William   P: Phila 25 Jy 65,
   21 Jy 68, 19 Ja 69
CALVILL
   Ann   P: Phila 26 Jy 64
CALVIN
   Philip   P: Amwell Twp 26 Jy
   64, 31 Ja 76.   T: Amwell

1 Sep 68
CALWELL/CALLWAL; see also
   CALDWELL
   James   P: Abington 18 Mar 62;
      Haverford 8 Jy 62
   John   P: Pa 13 Oct 63
CAMBLER
   James   P: Pa 24 Feb 63
CAMBLIN
   James   P: Christine 24 Feb
      63; Pa 19 May 63
CAMBRIDGE
   Archibald   P: Pa 13 Ja 63
   Elizabeth   Phila 24 Jy 76
   William   P: Phila 28 Ap 68
CAMERON/CAMMERON
   Mr.   P: Phila 4 Ag 63
   Charles   P: Phila 25 Jy 65
   Dugald   P: Phila 2 May 65, 25
      Jy 65
   Duncan, Corporal   P: probably
      in Pittsburgh 15 Mar 64
   James   P: Pa 31 Jy 60; Phila
      16 Jy 72, 3 Ja 76
   John   P: Chester Co 31 Dec
      61; Lancaster Co 31 Dec 61;
      Pa 21 Dec 58; Phila 27 Dec
      53, 6 Jy 58, 27 Jy 58, 24
      Feb 63, 31 Mar 63, 31 Ja 76
CAMEUR
   Henry   P: Phila 9 Ag 59
CAMM/CAM
   John   P: Phila 4 Feb 68
   Thomas   T: Pennytown 17 Oct
      54
CAMMACK
   John   P: Phila 8 Jy 62
CAMPBELL/CAMMELL/CAMEL/CAMBLE/
   CAMPELL/CAMBELL/CAMPBLE
   Mr.   P: Phila 3 Ja 65, (shoe-
      maker) 2 Ag 70
   Widow   P: Phila 3 Ja 76
   Alexander   P: Bucks Co 21 Dec
      58; Foggs Manor 9 Ag 59;
      Forks of Delaware 13 Oct 63;
      Pa 21 Dec 58, 31 Dec 61, 8
      Jy 62, 28 Oct 62; Phila 6
      Jy 58, 21 Dec 58 (Capt), 3
      Sep 61, 2 Feb 64, 26 Jy 64,
      2 May 65, 27 Oct 73; soldier
      probably in Pittsburgh 15
      Mar 64 (2)
   Ann   P: West Jersey 1 Jy 56
   Anthony   P: Phila 27 Ja 73
   Arthur   P: Phila-Gaz. 27 Oct
      73
   Bernard   P: Abington 1 Feb 70
   Cha./Charles   P: Cross Roads
      12 Ja 58; Phila 23 Oct 66
   Colin/Collin   P: 21 Dec 58
      (soldier); Burlington 9 Ag
      59, 31 Dec 61
   Daniel   P: Phila 13 Oct 63,
      27 Oct 73
   David   P: New Castle 27 Dec 53,

3 Ja 60; Phila 3 Sep 61, 27
   Ja 73 (2)
Donald   P: in the army 12 Ja
   58 (Ens.), 21 Dec 58 (Sgt);
   Phila 27 Ja 73
Duncan/Dunkin   P: Phila 13 Oct
   63, 30 Ja 66
Edward   P: Phila 27 Jy 58, 21
   Dec 58, 9 Ag 59, 1 May 76
Evander   P: Phila 31 Dec 61,
   18 Mar 62
Francis   L: c/o James M'KIBBEN
   Cumberland Co 19 Dec 71
George   L: York Co 31 Ja 71.
   P: at 10 Miles Stone, Bris-
   tol Road 20 Jy 69; Phila 30
   Ja 66, 21 Jy 68, 20 Ap 69;
   York Co 18 Mar 62, 2 Sep 62
Hugh   N: New Castle Co 12 Feb
   67.   P: New Castle Co 18 Mar
   62; New London Twp 11 Sep
   55; Pa 3 Ja 60; Phila 9 Ag
   59 (2), 2 Ag 70, 27 Oct 73.
   T: 4 Nov 72
James   L: 3 Oct 65.   N: c/o
   Samuel Ruth, near New Castle
   4 Dec 66.   P: Cape Fear 12
   Ja 58; Charlestown 24 Feb
   63, 19 May 63; Foggs Manor
   9 Ag 59; Pa 12 Feb 61;
   Phila 6 Jy 58, 27 Jy 58, 3
   Ja 60, 31 Jy 60, 30 Ja 66,
   1 Feb 70, 3 Ja 76; near
   Schuylkill 2 Dec 58; Wil-
   mington 2 Feb 64.   T: 7 May
   67
John   L: York Co 19 Dec 71.
   P: Black River 21 Dec 58;
   Carlisle 2 Feb 64; Chester
   Co 12 Ja 58, 31 Jy 60;
   Cumberland Co 13 Oct 63;
   Kingsessing 26 Oct 69;
   Londonderry Twp 27 Ja 73;
   Nottingham 3 Ja 60; Phila
   31 Dec 61, 2 Feb 64, 2 May
   65, 10 Ap 66, 27 Ja 73, 30
   Oct 76, 19 Jy 80
Joseph   P: Kent Co 13 Oct 63
Josiah   P: Welch Mountains 21
   Jy 69
Margaret   N: Milford Hundred
   c/o Thomas James 4 Dec 66.
   P: Newp. 18 Ag 57; Pa 21
   Dec 58
Martin   P: Chester Co 31 Dec
   61
Mary   P: Phila 3 Ja 60; Read-
   ing-town 1 May 76
Nancy   P: Beggars Town 30 Ja
   66
Neal/Neall   P: Pa 12 Feb 61, 2
   Feb 64; Phila 26 Jy 64.   T:
   Union Furnace 31 Ja 71
Philip   P: Phila 28 Ap 68
Ro.   L: Paxton 31 Ja 71

Robert P: Caecil Co, Md. 31
Jy 60; Chester Co 21 Dec 58,
9 Jy 59; New Castle Co 27
Jy 58; Lancaster Co 28 Oct
62; Millford Hundred 31 Dec
61; Phila 31 Dec 61, 23 Oct
66 (Capt), 16 Jy 72
Thomas P: Nottingham 21 Dec
58; Phila 6 Jy 58, 27 Jy 58,
9 Ag 59
William C: c/o William Hanna
East Fallowfield 22 Ja 67.
L: Cumberland Co 2 Mar 74.
P: Baskin Ridge 27 Jy 58;
Lancaster Co 18 Mar 62; Pa
13 Ja 63, 13 Oct 63; Phila
2 May 65, 30 Ja 66, 16 Jy
67, 3 Ja 76
CAMPBIE
Alexander P: Pa 19 May 63
CAMRION
John P: Phila 3 Ja 65
CAMRON
Charles P: Phila 3 Ja 76
James P: Southampton, Bucks
Co 26 Oct 69
CANADY
Patrick P: Phila 13 Oct 63,
3 Ja 65
CANBY
Samuel T: Makefield 6 Dec 64
Theophilus P: Chester Co 13
May 56, 9 Ag 59
Thomas P: Phila 24 Feb 63
CANDEE
Joseph P: Phila 26 Oct 69
CANDELL
Thomas P: Phila 26 Jy 64,
24 Jy 76 (Capt)
CANE
Catharine P: Phila 11 Sep 55
Francis P: Phila 30 Ja 66
CANLON
Philemy P: Baltimore 31 Mar
63
CANN
John P: Phila 2 Feb 64, 26
Jy 64
CANNALT
Jonathan P: Mount Holly 16
Jy 72
CANNELL
Jenny P: Phila 10 Ap 66
CANNON/CANNAN
Mrs. P: Phila 27 Ja 73
Charles P: Phila 8 Jy 62, 15
Mar 64
James P: Phila 24 Feb 63, 2
Feb 64, 16 Jy 77, 19 Jy 80
John P: Cumberland Co 9 Ag
59
Joseph P: Phila 8 Jy 62, 5
Ag 62, 20 Jy 69
Martha P: New-Castle Co 9 Ag
59

Matthew P: New-Castle Co 3
Ja 60
Michael P: New-Castle Co 31
Dec 61
Patrick P: Phila 1 Feb 70
Robert P: York Co 3 Ja 60
Roger P: Frankfort 21 Dec 58,
9 Ag 59
William P: Phila 1 Feb 70,
27 Oct 73
CANSELL
Jacob P: Phila 9 Ag 59
CANTRIFF
John P: Lancaster Co 12 Feb
61
CANTY
Thomas P: Pa 24 Feb 63
CAPLE
John P: Phila 4 Feb 68
CAPLIN
Ded P: Germantown 21 Jy 68
Henry P: in the army 12 Ja 58
CAPP
William P: Phila 15 Mar 64
CAPPEL
Michael P: Phila 26 Jy 64
CAPPER
James P: New-Castle 2 Feb 64
CAPPICK
Mr. P: Phila 6 Jy 58
CARBEN
=Theodore P: Phila 7 Ap 59
CARD/CARDE
Eliz. P: Phila 31 Dec 61
Magness/Magnus P: Phila 13
Ja 63, 13 Oct 63
CARDIE
Jane P: Phila 9 Ag 59
CARE
Conrad P: Germantown 3 Sep 61
Daniel P: Phila 15 Mar 64
George P: Phila 12 Feb 61
CAREY/CARREY/CARRY; see also
CARY
Mrs. P: Phila 26 Jy 64
Arthur P: Phila 28 Ap 68
James P: Lancaster Co 13 Oct
63
John Bucks Co 12 Ja 58; New
Castle Co 18 Mar 62; Phila
26 Jy 64 (2), 2 Ag 70;
Plumsted 13 May 56
Matthew L: c/o John Carmi-
chael Pequea 19 Dec 71
Ralph P: Phila 3 Ja 76
William P: Phila 27 Ja 73
CARICKHER
Jacob P: Phila 31 Jy 60
CARKEY
James P: Phila 3 Ja 76
CARLEIN
Daniel P: West-New-Jersey 12
Feb 61
CARLEY
John P: Phila 10 Oct 65

CARLISLE: see also SAUNDERS &
  CARLISLE
  Col.   P: Phila 20 Jy 69
  John   P: Phila 12 Feb 61
  Lanston   P: Phila 18 Mar 62
  Nancy   P: Phila 27 Ja 73
  William   P: Christine 31 Jy
    60; Phila 4 Feb 68, 20 Oct
    68 (Col.)
CARLOW
  Joseph   P: Phila 4 Feb 68
CARMACK
  Andrew   P: Phila 1 Nov 70
CARMALT and WILSON   P: Phila 24
  Feb. 63, 19 May 63; see also
  GOUGH & CARMALT
CARMAN
  Dominick   P: Phila 26 Oct 69
  Samuel   P: Raccoon Creek 3
    Ja 60
CARMICHAEL/CARMICHEL
  Widow   P: Lancaster Co 3 Sep
    61
  Daniel   P: York Co 27 Jy 58
  Rev. J.   P: Pa 15 Mar 64
  Rev. John   C: Forks of Brandy-
    wine 18 Jy 65
  Thomas   P: Little-Britain 26
    Jy 64
  William   P: Phila 18 Mar 62
CARMICK
  George   P: Phila 26 Oct 69
  Peter   P: Phila 10 Ap 66
  Stephen   P: Phila 6 Jy 58
CARMODY
  John   P: Phila 1 Feb 70
  Michael   P: Phila 1 Feb 70
CARNAHAN/CARNAGAN/CARMIHAN/CAR-
  NAGHYN/CARNAGHAN
  John   P: Chester Co 3 Ja 60;
    Phila 4 Feb 68
  Joseph   P: Springfield, West
    New Jersey 25 Ap 71
  Sarah   P: Phila 24 Oct 54, 13
    May 56
  William   L: 29 Ja 67; c/o
    William Moore, Lancaster Co
    19 Dec 71; Londonderry Twp
    29 Jy 72.   P: 26 Oct 69
CARNAN
  John   P: Phila 2 Ag 70, 16 Jy
    77
CARNEY
  Daniel   P: Wilmington 11 Sep
    55
  David   P: Phila 2 Ag 70
  James   P: Chester Co 13 Ja 63
  John   P: Phila 4 Ag 63
  Thomas   P: Phila 12 Ja 58;
    Salem 7 Ap 57
CARNISH
  Mr.   P: Phila 2 May 65
CARNS
  Daniel   C: East Caln 30 Oct
    66

Richard   New Jersey Gaz. 1
  May 76
  Robert   P: Phila 18 Feb 55
CARON
  Capt. Daniel   P: Phila 8 Jy
    62
CARPENTER
  John   C: Haverford Twp 22 Ja
    67.   P: Chester Co 1 Jy 56,
    3 Ja 60; Gloucester Co 18
    Ag 57
  Samuel   P: Phila 31 Jy 60
  Thomas   P: Phila 12 Feb 61
  Valentine   P: Reading 3 Sep
    61
  William   P: Bucks Co 13 Oct
    63
CARR/CAR
  Widow   P: Bucks Co 25 Ap 71
  Alexander   P: Cecil Co 19 May
    63; Pa 24 Feb 63; Phila 10
    Oct 65
  Andrew   P: Lancaster Co 18
    Mar 62; Octerara 31 Dec 61
  Elizabeth   W: c/o Isaac Alt-
    wood 27 Ag 77
  George   P: Pa 15 Mar 64; Phila
    3 Ja 60 (Capt), 3 Sep 61,
    28 Oct 62
  James   P: New-Castle Co 31
    Dec 61, 18 Mar 62; Phila 21
    Jy 68 (Capt)
  John   P: Bucks Co 20 Oct 68;
    Neshaminy 2 Ag 70; Pa 13
    Ja 63; Phila Co 23 Oct 66
  Margaret   P: Phila 1 Feb 70
  Mark   P: Neshaminy 12 Ja 58
  Matthew   P: Phila 25 Jy 65
  Robert   P: Phila 6 Jy 58, 27
    Jy 58, 28 Oct 62
  Samuel   P: New Castle Co 18
    Mar 62
  Lt. Stair Campbell   P: in the
    army 12 Ja 58
  Capt. Thomas   P: Phila 4 Ag 63
CARRELL, see CARROLL
CARRICK
  Martha   P: Phila 26 Jy 64
  William   P: New Castle Co 7
    Ap 57
CARRIDINE
  Thomas   P: Phila 2 Ag 70
CARRINGTON
  Thomas   P: Abington 18 Mar 62;
    Chester Co 1 Feb 70, 2 Ag
    70
CARROLAN
  James   P: Phila 27 Ja 73
CARROLL/CARRELL/CARRILL/CARROL
  Ann   P: Phila 25 Jy 65, 28
    Ap 68
  Catherine   P: Phila 18 Mar 62
  Daniel   P: Phila 2 May 65,
    27 Ja 73
  Isabella   P: Nottingham 31 Jy

60

Jas./James L: see JONES,
  Elizabeth. P: Phila 8 Jy
  62, 15 Nov 64. T: Pitt's-
  town 4 Nov 72
Martha P: Maiden Creek 31
  Dec 61
Richard P: New Castle Co 31
  Jy 60
Robert P: Pa 4 Ag 63
Rumerly P: Phila 31 Dec 61
Timothy P: Phila 31 Dec 61,
  4 Ag 63, 30 Ja 66, 3 May 70
CARRON; see also CARON
James P: Phila 30 Ja 66
CARROW
Elizabeth P: Phila 11 Sep 55
George P: Phila 7 Ap 57
CARRUTH
Benjamin, clothier L: 2 Mar
  74
CARSELL
William P: Phila 27 Ja 73
CARSEY
James P: Phila 10 Oct 65
CARSON
Adam P: Baltimore Co 31 Dec
  61; Cumberland Co 26 Jy 64;
  Pa 3 Sep 63
Alex. P: Chester Co 12 Ja 58
Andrew P: Phila 5 Ag 62
Charles P: Duck Creek 3 Sep
  61; Lancaster 12 Feb 61;
  Paxton 24 Oct 54, 27 Jy 58;
  Phila 9 Ag 59
Cornelius P: Bucks Co 21 Dec
  58, 31 Dec 61
Frank P: Phila 3 Ja 76
Hugh P: Christine 31 Jy 60;
  Pa 13 Oct 63
Isaac C: 22 Ja 67
James L: Kennet Twp 15 Ap
  56. P: Newcastle Co 12 Ja
  58
John P: Chester Co 31 Dec 61;
  Phila 13 May 56, 31 Jy 60,
  24 Feb 63, 2 Feb 64, 26 Jy
  64, 3 Ja 65
Marcy P: Phila-Gaz. 27 Oct
  73
Martha Phila 30 Ap 77
Mary P: Pa 2 Feb 64
Richard P: Phila 3 Sep 61
Robert C: Uchland 30 Oct 66
Samuel P: Phila 6 Jy 58, 27
  Jy 58, 23 Oct 66
William P: Pa 12 Feb 61;
  Phila 28 Nov 54, 6 Jy 58,
  27 Jy 58, 20 Jy 69
CARSWALT
James P: Phila 3 Ja 65
CARSWELL
Mrs. P: Phila 31 Dec 61
James P: Phila 28 Oct 62,
  13 Oct 63, 26 Jy 64, 10 Oct

65

John P: Nottingham 5 Ag 62
Dr. Joseph P: Phila 31 Dec 61
CARTE
Michael P: Phila 1 Feb 70
CARTER/CARTHER
Alexander P: Phila 15 Mar 64
Benjamin Phila 16 Jy 77;
  Wright's Town 27 Jy 58
Edward P: Phila 5 Ag 62
James P: Phila 31 Dec 61; 18
  Mar 62, 30 Ja 66
Jane P: Phila 9 Ag 59
Johanna P: Phila 26 Oct 69
John P: New Castle Co 3 Ja
  60; Wilmington 31 Jy 60
Mary P: Phila 20 Ap 69
Robert P: Phila 15 Mar 64
Thomas P: Phila 5 Ag 56
William P: Phila 18 Mar 62,
  25 Jy 65. T: Haddonfield
  6 Dec 64
CARTHY
Charles P: Phila 26 Oct 69
CARTMILL
Thomas N: Brandywine Hundred
  29 Nov 64. P: New Castle
  Co 13 Oct 63
CARTON
Isaac P: Phila 25 Jy 65
CARTVILLE
Thomas P: Phila 7 Ap 57
CARTWELL
James P: Pa 15 Mar 64
CARTWRIGHT
Abnor P: Chester Co 8 Jy 62
Daniel P: Phila 21 Jy 68
Shackerley P: Phila 1 Nov 70
CARTY; see also CARTHY
Cornelius P: New Castle Co
  9 Ag 59
John P: Burlington 31 Jy 60
Peggy P: Phila 16 Jy 72
CARUTHERS/CARRUTHERS/CARETHERS
Alexander/Sanders Chester
  Co 12 Feb 61, 13 Oct 63
Samuel P: Forks of Delaware
  31 Jy 60; Phila 27 Jy 58,
  28 Oct 62, 13 Ja 63
William P: Cumberland Co 28
  Oct 62; Forks of Delaware
  27 Oct 73; Gloucester Co
  8 Jy 62; in Wilson's
  Settlement 19 Ja 69
CARVER
Bernard P: Phila 23 Oct 66
Jacob P: Phila 27 Jy 58
John P: Biberry 30 May 54;
  Phila 27 Jy 58
CARVIL
James P: Phila 2 Feb 64
CARWIN
Samuel P: Phila 3 Ja 76
CARY/CARYE; see also CAREY
Anthony P: Phila 9 Ag 59

John   P: Germantown 9 Ag 59;
   Phila 15 Mar 64
Mary   P: Phila Co 8 Jy 62
Samuel   P: Germantown 9 Ag 59
CASDORP/CASDORPE/CASDROP
Thomas   P: Phila 3 Ja 60, 1
   May 76, 30 Ap 77
CASENDIR
Abraham   P: Phila 12 Feb 61
CASEY/CACY
Jane   P: Phila 20 Oct 69
John   P: Phila 24 Feb 63, 26
   Jy 64
Samuel   P: Chester Co 11 Jy 54
Thomas   P: Pa 21 Dec 58
William   Phila 1 May 76
CASGIDE
Sergt. Philip   P: in the army
   21 Dec 58
CASHION
Joseph   P: Phila 27 Oct 73
CASKEY
Samuel   P: New Jersey 18 Mar
   62
CASLAND
Ann   P: Phila 20 Oct 68
CASSELAAR/CASSELER
....   P: Phila 1 Nov 53
Dougal   L: 3 Oct 65
CASSELL
John   P: Phila 28 Oct 62, 2
   Feb 64
CASSEN/CASSIN
Joseph   P: Pa 28 Oct 62
William   P: Phila 31 Jy 60
CASSIDY/CASSADY/CASSEDY/CASSE-
DAY/CASEDY/CASHEDY
Darby   P: Phila 2 May 65
Daniel   P: Phila 31 Jy 60
Hugh   P: Phila 1 Nov 70
James   P: Phila 27 Ja 73, 3
   Ja 76; Raccoon-Creek 13 Oct
   63
John   P: Phila 19 Ja 69
Patrick   P: Phila 28 Ap 68
William   P: Phila 12 Feb 61,
   3 Sep 61
CASTILINE
Mary   P: Phila 18 Ag 57
CASTLE
William   P: Phila 18 Feb 55
CASTLES
Alexander   L: 11 Ap 65
CASWELL
James   P: Phila 5 Ag 62
CATHAM
Benedictus   P: Bethlehem Twp
   3 Ja 60
CATHCART
Anne   P: Phila 20 Jy 69
John   L: c/o Mr. Strain, York
   Co 19 Dec 71
William   P: Phila 24 Feb 63,
   26 Oct 69 (Dr)
CATHE

Rosse   P: New-London 9 Ag 59
CATHER
Jasper   P: Phila 28 Ap 68
Robert   P: Phila 2 Feb 64, 26
   Jy 64, 3 Ja 65
CATHEY
Alexander   P: Phila 24 Feb 63,
   1 May 63
CATLIN
Francis   P: Phila 18 Mar 62
CATLIVE
Reese   P: Chester Co 7 Ap 57
CATON/CAYTON
Ensign Benjamin   P: in the
   army 27 Jy 58
Isaac   P: Phila 13 Oct 63, 26
   Jy 64 (2)
John   P: Kent Co 9 Ag 59, 8
   Jy 62
Robert   P: Kent Co 8 Jy 62
CATPERSON
John, Minister   L: Octarara
   2 Mar 74
CATTELL
Jonas   P: Pa 21 Dec 58
CATTERLING
Mary   P: Phila 27 Jy 58
CATTEY
Isaac   P: Phila 2 May 65
CATTON
James   P: Phila 21 Jy 68
CAUCHIN
Samuel   P: Octerara 31 Mar 63
CAUCHY
Francis   P: Fallowfield 28
   Nov 54
CAUFMAN
Jōs.   P: Phila 28 Ap 68
CAULFIELD
William   P: Phila 30 Ja 66,
   27 Oct 73 (or Pat.)
CAURCOCK
Elizabeth   P: Phila 9 Ag 59
CAVAN/CAVEN
Jane   P: Pa 24 Oct 54
Robert   P: Phila 26 Jy 64
CAVANAUGH
Bridget   P: Phila 26 Oct 69
CAWDRY
N.   P: Phila 29 Ag 54
CAWLEY
John   P: Bucks Co 7 Ap 57;
   Phila 30 Ja 66, 4 Feb 68
   (Capt)
Thomas   P: B.C. 20 Ap 69;
   Phila 25 Ap 71
CAY
Gabriel   P: Phila 12 Feb 61
CAZIE
James   P: New Jersey 3 Ja 60
CAZIER
Levi   Phila 1 May 76
Peter   T: Kingwood 17 Oct 54
CEARY
Bernard   L: Shipper's Town 14

May 72
John   P: Phila 9 Ag 59
CEILY
  Anstis/or Anstas?7   P: Phila
    25 Jy 65
CELLEY/CELLY/CELEY; see also
  KELLY
  James   P: Phila 19 Ja 69
  Joseph   P: Phila 29 Ag 54
  Roger   P: Phila 1 Feb 70
  Sarah   P: Bucks Co 13 Jan 63
CERBRIGHT
  Malen   P: Bucks Co 31 Jy 60
CERNANS
  Judah   P: Pa 18 Mar 62
CERRIGAN
  Michael   P: Pa 2 Sep 62
CERRYL
  Thomas   P: Phila 5 Jy 80-Gaz.
    19 Jy
CHABRUD
  John   P: Phila 31 Jy 60
CHADOCK
  Thomas   P: Bordentown/Burden-
    town 24 Feb 63, 19 May 63
CHADWICK
  Elizabeth   P: Phila 28 Nov 54
CHAIN
  Jo.   L: 3 Oct 65
  John   P: Phila Co 23 Oct 66
CHALDRON
  Ebenezer   P: Phila 26 Jy 53
CHALMERS
  James   P: Phila 12 Feb 61, 2
    Feb 64 (Capt), 10 Ap 66
CHALON
  Joseph   P: Phila 16 Jy 67
CAMBERLAIN/CHAMBERLIN
  Charles   P: Phila 30 Ap 67
  James   P: Lancaster Co 27 Jy
    58
  Jonas   L: Lancaster Co 15 Ap
    56.   P: Phila 13 May 56
CHAMBERS
  Alexander   P: Pa 18 Mar 62
  Col. B.   P: Conecoch. 18 Ag
    57; Cumberland Co 31 Jy 60;
    Falling-Spring 21 Dec 58
  Becke   P: Phila 16 Jy 67
  Benjamin   L: Cumberland Co 14
    May 72
  David   P: Phila 23 Oct 66
  Dorothy   P: Phila 18 Mar 62
  J.   P: Phila 19 May 63 (Capt);
    Susquehannah 2 Feb 64
  Capt. James   P: Phila 24 Feb
    63
  John   P: Kent Co 31 Jy 60, 3
    Sep 61
  Joseph   P: Kent Co 9 Ag 59;
    Salem Co 9 Ag 59; York Town
    1 Nov 53, 5 Feb 54, 4 Ap 54,
    15 Mar 64
  Robert   P: Bucks Co 10 Oct 65;
    Phila 4 Ag 63

Rowland   East Jersey 5 Ap 76-
    Gaz 1 May
  William   P: Pa 13 Oct 63
  William Hilmas   Wallpack 24
    Jy 76
CHAMP/CHAMPE
  John   P: Phila 9 Ag 59, 13
    Oct 63
CHAMPAIN
  Stephen   P: Phila 27 Ja 73
CHAMPNEYS
  Joseph   P: Pilesgrove 20 Oct
    68
CHANCELLOR
  Capt. Samuel   P: Phila 30 Ap
    67
  Dr. William   P: Phila 2 Sep
    62
CHANDLER
  George   P: Phila 4 Ag 63, 26
    Jy 64 (2), 2 May 65
  John   P: Phila 20 Jy 69
CHAPMAN
  Mr.   P: Phila 19 Jy 80
  Abraham   Wright's Town 16 Jy
    77
  Benjamin   P: Phila 10 Oct 65
  Daniel   P: Phila 11 Sep 55
  Elizabeth   P: Pa 21 Dec 58
  George   P: Marcus Hook 11 Sep
    55; Ph 1 Nov 53
  John   P: Bucks Co 7 Ap 57, 31
    Jy 60, 18 Mar 62; Cumberland
    Co 31 Jy 60, 18 Mar 62
  Mary   P: Phila 1 Nov 70
  Nathaniel   P: Phila 9 Ag 59
  Col. Russel   P: in the army
    12 Ja 58
  Samuel   Phila 30 Ap 77
  Samuel Mitchel   P: Phila 3 Ja
    65, 2 May 65
  Susanna   P: Makefield   9 Ag
    59
  Thomas   P: Phila 16 Jy 72;
    Port Penn 25 Ap 71; Wright's
    Town, Bucks Co 27 Jy 58, 4
    Feb 68
  William   P: Phila 26 Jy 64,
    2 May 65
  William Smith   P: Phila 10
    Ap 66
CHARLES
  William   P: Pa 21 Dec 58
CHARLESTOWN
  Thomas   C: Fogs Manor, see
    BEATTY, Bell
CHARLTON/CHARLETON
  Eleanor   P: Abington 13 Oct
    63
  Elizabeth   C: c/o John Jackson
    Londongrove 18 Jy 65
  Henry   P: Fogs Manor 12 Ja 58
  Richard   P: Phila 28 Oct 62
  Samuel   L: Dublin Twp 2 Mar 74
  Thomas   P: Brandywine 13 May

56; Ph 30 Ja 66

CHARTER
Isabella   P: Phila 3 Ja 76

CHASE/CHACE
John   P: Phila 16 Jy 72, 1 May
76

CHATTEN/CHATTIN
Jacob   L: near Lancaster 29
Jy 72
James   P: Phila 2 May 65, 30
Ja 66

CHATTO
William   P: Phila 16 Jy 72

CHEAS
Newby   P: Phila 11 Jy 54

CHENEY
Ann   P: Chester Co 24 Oct 54

CHERRY
James   P: Bucks Co 3 Ja 60;
Pa 21 Dec 58

CHESTER/CHESTOR
John   P: Phila 13 May 56
Samuel   P: Phila 11 Sep 55

CHESTNUT/CHESTNUTT/CHEASNUT/
CHESNUT
Alexander   P: Newcastle Co 12
Ja 58; Pa 11 Sep 55
James   P: Phila 1 Nov 70
Joseph   T: Lebanon 17 Oct 54
Robert   P: Phila 27 Ja 73
William   P: Bucks Co 31 Dec
61; Ph 28 Oct 62, 2 Feb 64,
25 Jy 65

CHEVALLIER
Mons. Henry   P: Phila 19 Jy 80

CHEVER
Ezekiel   T: Morris Town 17
Oct 54

CHEVERS
Capt. William   P: Phila-Gaz.
27 Oct 73

CHEW
David   P: Phila 10 Oct 65
Joseph   P: Phila 9 Ag 59

CHILD/CHILDS
Isaac   P: Bucks Co 21 Dec 58
Margaret   P: Phila 2 May 65

CHINA
Thomas   P: Phila 4 Feb 68

CHIPMAN
James   P: Sussex 26 Jy 53
Mary   P: America 12 Feb 61

CHISHOLM
Archibald   P: Phila 16 Jy 72

CHISLAY
Elizabeth   P: Phila 25 Ap 71

CHISNEL
Charles   P: Phila 25 Jy 65
Mary   P: Phila 26 Jy 64

CHOWNE
Samuel   P: Phila 3 Ja 65, 3
May 70

CHRESTY
Martin   P: Chester Co 24 Feb
63

CHRISTEN
Nicholas   P: Phila 15 Mar 64

CHRISTIAN
John   P: Phila 4 Ap 54
Michael   P: Phila 30 Ap 67
Thomas   P: Phila 1 Jy 56

CHRISTIE/CHRYSTIE/CHRISTY/
CRISTEY/CRISTY; see also
CHRESTY
Capt. Alexander   P: Phila 5
Ag 62
Francis   P: Phila 27 Ja 73
Hester   P: Phila 26 Oct 69
James   L: Pequea 2 Mar 74
John   P: Cheltenham, Phila
Co 28 Ap 68; Pa 31 Jy 60;
Ph 1 Feb 70
Robert   N: in Brandywine c/o
Thomas M'Cracken 4 Dec 66
Sarah   Great Valley 24 Jy 76
William   P: Phila 21 Dec 58,
27 Jy 58

CHRISTLER
Jacob   P: Phila 19 Ja 69

CHRISTOPHER/CHRISTOFOR
Mary   P: Pa 12 Feb 61; Phila
21 Dec 58

CHURCH
Ann   P: Phila 20 Ap 69
Elisha   P: Salem 1 Feb 70
Ned Huney   P: Phila 12 Feb 61
Robert   P: Phila 3 Sep 61
Capt. T.   P: Phila 5 Ag 62
Thomas   P: Phila 27 Jy 58;
Providence 26 Oct 69
William   P: Phila 1 Feb 70

CHURCHMAN
Edward   C: Thornbury 22 Ja 67.
P: 2 May 65, 21 Jy 68
Hannah   P: Pa 28 Oct 62
William   P: Phila 13 Oct 63

CHUTHAM
John   P: Phila 16 Jy 72

CILELLY
Patrick   P: Chester Co 12 Ja
58

CILLCARTH
John   P: Phila 11 Sep 55

CINNECOM
Mrs.   P: Phila 2 May 65

CIRWITHEN
Caleb   P: Lewis Town 31 Dec 61

CLACKTAGE
Patrick   P: Phila 9 Ag 59

CLAGGET/CLAGITT
Horatio   Phila 30 Oct 76
William   Phila 24 Jy 76

CLAGUE
Capt. Edward   P: Phila 11 Sep
55

CLAMINSIN
Mary   P: Phila 9 Ag 59

CLAMONE
David   P: Phila 5 Jy 80-Gaz.
19 Jy

CLAMPFFER
Elizabeth P: Phila 18 Ag 57
CLANCHY
James   P: Phila 3 May 70
CLANCY/CLANCEY
David   P: Phila 24 Feb 63
Jeremiah   P: Phila 27 Ja 73
John   P: Phila 10 Oct 65
CLANEY
Dennis   Phila 1 May 76
CLANWY
Thomas   P: Phila 27 Dec 53
CLAPHAM
George   P: Phila 1 Nov 53,
12 Ja 58
Mary   P: Bordentown 9 Ag 59,
3 Ja 60
CLARE
John   P: Phila 31 Dec 61
Polly   P: Phila 25 Ap 71
William   P: Phila 3 Ja 76
CLARENCE/CLARANCE
Rebecca   P: Phila 28 Nov 54,
2 Jy 62
Robert   P: Phila 12 Feb 61
CLARK/CLARKE
Capt.   P: Phila 9 Ag 59, 24
Feb 63
Mrs.   P: Phila 16 Jy 67
Adam   P: Pa 3 Ja 60
Alexander   P: Phila 25 Jy 65
Ambrose   P: Phila 18 Mar 62
(2)
Andrew   P: Phila 3 Ja 76
Ann   P: Phila 25 Ap 71
Catherine   P: Phila 8 Jy 62
Charles   P: Lewis Town 27 Jy
58, 21 Dec 58. T: Bucks Co
7 May 67
Cornelius   P: N. Castle Co 18
Mar 62
Daniel   P: in the army 27 Jy
58; Lancaster 31 Jy 60; Pa
21 Dec 58; Phila 3 Ja 65
David   P: America 12 Feb 61;
Frankford 2 Ag 70; New-
Castle Co 9 Ag 59
Eleanor   P: Phila 3 Ja 65
Elijah   Egg Harbour 31 Ja 76
Eliza   Little Egg Harbour 1
May 76
Elizabeth   P: Forks of Elk 31
Dec 61
Francis   P: Chester Co 13 Oct
63
Gabriel   P: Chester Co 9 Ag
59
George   P: Cumberland Co 7
Ap 57; Phila 30 Ap 67; York
Co 18 Mar 62; Yorktown 9
Ag 59
Henry   P: Phila 20 Oct 68
James   P: Baltimore Co 31 Dec
61; Lancaster 18 Ag 57; New
Castle Co 7 Ap 57; New

London 12 Ja 58; Pa 18 Mar
62; Phila 3 Ja 60, 12 Feb
61, 30 Ja 66
Jane   P: Phila 2 Feb 64
Jemima   P: Phila 31 Mar 63
John   C: 30 Jy 77 (Capt). P:
Bucks Co 23 Oct 66 (Quarter-
master), 20 Oct 68; Christ-
ine Bridge 11 Sep 55; Mount
holly 19 Jy 80; New-Castle
Co 9 Ag 59; Pa 27 Jy 58, 13
Ja 63; Phila 5 Ag 56, 6 Jy
58, 31 Dec 61, 31 Mar 63,
25 Jy 65, 30 Ap 67, 20 Oct
67, 20 Oct 68, 19 Ja 69, 20
Ap 69, 26 Oct 69, 1 Nov 70,
3 Ja 76. T: Trenton 17 Oct
54
Joseph   L: Conedogwinet 15 Ap
56. P: Pequea 9 Ag 59
Mary   P: Pa 15 Mar 64. T:
Bedminster 15 Jy 56
Michael   P: Phila 1 Feb 70
Nat.   P: Pa 24 Feb 63
Nathaniel   P: Chestnut Level
19 May 63; 31 Dec 61, 4 Ag
63, 27 Ja 73
Persillia   P: Phila 31 Dec 61
Rachel   P: Newcastle Co 12 Ja
58
Richard   P: Phila 31 Jy 60,
12 Feb 61, 25 Jy 65, 27 Ja
73, 27 Oct 73
Robert   L: c/o Thomas M'Arthur
Harris's Ferry 20 Ja 73.
P: Newcastle Co 12 Ja 58,
27 Jy 58, 21 Dec 58, 3 Sep
61; Phila 2 Feb 64, 2 Ag
70, 1 Jy 56
Sampson   P: Phila 25 Ap 71
Sarah   P: Wilmington 11 Sep 55
Stephen   P: Phila 26 Jy 64
Thomas   L: Chestnut Level 2
Mar 74. P: Phila 13 Ja 63
(Capt), 13 Oct 63, 23 Oct
66, 28 Ap 68, 1 Nov 70, 3
Ja 76; Salem Co 27 Ja 73
William   L: 29 Ja 67. P:
East Bradford 7 Ap 57, 1 Jy
56; Forks Delaware 1 Feb
70; New-Castle Co 30 May
54, 27 Jy 58; Pa 31 Jy 60;
Phila 25 Jy 65, 2 Ag 70, 16
Jy 77. T: Freehold 4 Nov 72
CLARKHOUSE
William   P: Phila 20 Jy 69
CLARKSON
John   P: Phila 10 Ap 66
Levinus   Phila 5 Jy 77-Gaz.
16 Jy
CLARY
John   P: Dover 30 May 54
CLASE
Capt.   P: Phila 7 Ap 57
Widow   P: Phila 31 Jy 60, 31

Dec 61, 8 Jy 62, 28 Oct 62
Humphry P: Phila 29 Ag 54
CLASS
  Margaret P: Phila 18 Ag 57
CLAUSON
  Daniel P: Phila 1 Nov 53
CLAVERON
  Mr. P: Phila 3 Ja 65
CLAY
  John P: Phila 28 Ap 68
  Margaret Phila 1 May 76
  Slaytor/Slater/Slator P:
    Newcastle 24 Oct 54, 11 Sep
    55, 9 Ap 57, 24 Feb 63, 19
    May 63
CLAYFIELD
  John P: Phila 3 May 70;
    Potts Town 25 Ap 71
CLAYTON/CLEAYTON
  Adam P: Chester Co 21 Dec 58,
    9 Ag 59
  Ann P: Phila 9 Ag 59
  John P: Dover 9 Ag 59; Phila
    8 Jy 62, 13 Ja 63
  Thomas C: 30 Jy 77
  William, Esq. T: Trenton 31
    Ja 71
CLEAR
  Timothy P: Phila 27 Ja 73
CLEARY
  Patrick P: Phila 4 Feb 68
CLEAVELAND/CLEAVLAND/CLAVELAND
  Aaron P: Lewes 5 Ag 56; New
    Castle Co 7 Ap 57 (Rev)
  Edward P: Phila-Gaz. 27 Oct
    73
CLEGG
  Jane Phila 5 Jy 76-Gaz. 24
    Jy
CLELAND
  James P: Phila 20 Jy 69
  Janet P: Phila 21 Dec 58
  Samuel P: Chester Co 3 Sep 61
CLEMENT/CLEMENTS/CLEMENS
  Jacob P: West New Jersey 31
    Jy 60, 12 Feb 61
  James P: New-Castle 4 Ag 63;
    Phila 4 Feb 68
  Joseph P: Haddonfield, New
    Jersey 4 Feb 68
  Samuel P: Haddonfield 1 Nov
    70; Phila 1 Nov 53
CLEMM
  Mrs. P: Phila 27 Jy 58
CLEMMONS
  James P: Pa 3 Ja 60
  Mary P: Phila 21 Dec 58
CLEMSON
  John P: Pequea 18 Ag 57
CLENDENNEN/CLENDINEN/CLINDENIN/
  CLINDENEN/CLANDINEN
  Charles P: Pa 13 Ja 63
  James P: Forks of Delaware
    3 May 70
  John P: Forks of Delaware 8

Jy 62
  Robert P: Pa 18 Mar 62
  William P: Lancaster Co 3
    Sep 61, Octorara 18 Ag 57
CLEVER/CLEIVER/CLEVERS
  Ann P: Wilmington 3 Ja 60,
    31 Jy 60
  Capt. Norman H. P: Phila 28
    Ap 68
CLIFFORD
  Benjamin P: Phila 13 Ja 63
CLIFT
  Jonathan P: Phila Co 5 Ag 56
CLIFTON
  Mrs. P: Phila 27 Jy 58
  Henry P: Phila 3 May 70
  James P: Phila 26 Jy 64, 19
    Jy 80 (Capt)
  William P: Phila 5 Ag 62; 10
    Oct 65
CLILEAND
  John P: Phila-Gaz. 27 Oct 73
CLINCH
  Robert P: Lancaster Co 9 Ag
    59
CLINDMEN
  John L: Lancaster Co 20 Ja 73
CLINE
  Jacob P: Pa 13 Ja 63
  John C: 30 Jy 77. P: Phila
    20 Oct 68
  Mary P: Phila 19 Jy 80
CLINEHOFF/CLINHOFF
  Peter P: Bohemia 31 Mar 63,
    31 Oct 63
CLINGHAM/CLINGAN
  William, Esq. C: West Caln,
    see CALHOUN, John, STEPHEN-
    SON, James, and TURNEY,
    Eleanor. P: Chester Co 27
    Jy 58 (Esq), 9 Ag 59, 31 Jy
    60, 3 Sep 61 (Esq); West-
    Caln 3 Ja 60 (Esq)
CLINTON
  Charles (surgeon in army) ' P:
    Fort Pitt 26 Jy 64; Nesha-
    miny/Shaminey 30 Ja 66 (Dr),
    10 Ap 66 (Dr); Phila Co 23
    Oct 66
  Francis P: Phila 19 Ja 69
  James P: Phila 26 Oct 69, 2
    Ag 70
  Samuel P: Phila 23 Oct 66
  William P: Chester Co 31 Dec
    61
CLITHRALL
  Hugh P: Charles Town in New
    Castle Co 7 Ap 57
CLOADE
  George P: Phila 19 Ja 69
CLOGG
  Michael P: Phila 20 Oct 68
CLOKER
  Henry P: Bucks Co 20 Oct 68
CLOSE

Neil   P: Phila-Gaz. 27 Oct 73
CLOTHIER/CLOTHER
  William/Will.   P: Phila 13 Oct
    63, 30 Ap 67, 16 Jy 67, 20
    Ap 69
CLOUGH
  Joseph   P: Phila 11 Sep 55
CLOUSTON
  Andrew   P: Phila 16 Jy 72
CLOW
  James   P: Phila 28 Ap 68, 19
    Ja 69, 3 May 70
CLOWES
  John   P: Port Lewis 10 Oct 65
CLOYD
  John   P: Pa 24 Oct 54, 24 Feb
    63, 15 Mar 64
CLULOW
  James   P: Phila 1 Nov 53, 27
    Dec 53
CLUNN
  James   T: Trenton 3 Oct 65
  Capt. John   P: Phila 2 Feb 64
CLUPTON
  John   Phila 5 Jy 76-Gaz. 24 Jy
    76
CLYMER
  George   P: Phila 2 Sep 62
  Margaret   P: Phila 28 Oct 62
COAL/COALE
  Ezekiel   T: Reading Town 7 May
    67
  Samuel S.   P: Phila 16 Jy 72
COANE
  William   P: New-Castle Co 15
    Mar 64
COATS/COATES
  James   P: James Frederick Town
    27 Jy 58
  John   P: Phila 28 Nov 54, 21
    Dec 58
  Jonathan   P: Charles-Town 5
    Ag 56, 3 Ja 60; Chester Co
    7 Ap 57, 12 Ja 58, 31 Jy 60,
    13 Ja 63.   W: Charlestown,
    Chester Co 3 Jy 76
  Lindsay   P: Phila 28 Oct 62,
    24 Jy 76
  Moses   P: Chester Co 9 Ag 59
  Samuel   P: Phila 24 Oct 54
  Thomas   P: Phila 31 Dec 61,
    26 Oct 69
COAY
  Nicholas   P: Phila 3 Ja 76
COBEEN
  William   P: Phila 12 Ja 58
COBHAM
  Robert   P: Phila 2 Sep 62, 2
    Feb 64
COBIA
  Sigmon   P: Phila 3 Ja 76
COBRIGHT
  Christopher   P: Phila 4 Feb
    68
COBURN/COBOURN

George   P: Phila 28 Nov 54
Capt. James   P: Phila 4 Ag 63
COCHRAN/COCKRAN/COCKRUM/COGHRAN/
  COUGHRAN
  Agnes   P: Phila 1 Jy 56
  Alexander   P: Md. 13 Oct 63;
    Phila 5 Ag 62
  Ann   C: at W. Rooks, near
    Charlestown, Caecil Co 28
    Nov 65
  Anthony   P: Phila 19 May 63
  Daniel   P: Leacock 13 Ja 63
  George, carpenter   P: Phila
    19 Ja 69
  James   C: West Nottingham,
    see DICKS, Alexander.   P:
    Chester Co 31 Mar 63;
    Fallowfield 2 Feb 64; Phila
    19 Jy 80
  John   L: Tom/?/s Creek, York
    Co 19 Dec 71.   P: Caecil
    Co 26 Jy 64; Fredericks Co
    5 Ag 62; Phila 31 Ja 76
  Jonathan   P: Phila 9 Ag 59
  Lawrence(soldier)   P: 21 Dec
    58
  Matthew   P: Bucks Co 8 Jy 62
  Mary   P: Kent Co 31 Dec 61
  Moses   P: Newport 12 Ja 58
  Nancy   P: Phila 26 Oct 69
  Robert   L: Shippenburgh,
    Cumberland Co 19 Dec 71.
    P: 31 Jy 60, 13 Ja 63 (Capt),
    30 Ap 67.   W: see THOMPSON,
    Margaret
  Thomas   P: Phila-Gaz. 27 Oct
    73
  William   P: Phila 27 Ja 73
COCK
  James   P: Chester Co 26 Jy 64
  John   P: Phila 3 May 70
COCKAYNE
  T.   P: Pine Grove 31 Ja 76
  Thomas   P: Pine Grove Furnace
    24 Jy 76
COCKERHAM
  Samuel   P: Phila 1 Nov 53
COCKS
  William   P: Phila 23 Oct 66,
    24 Jy 76
COCKSAN
  George   P: Chester Co 28 Nov
    54
COCKSHOT
  John, Jr.   Phila 31 Ja 76
COCY/?/
  James   P: Lancaster Co 13 Oct
    63
CODDE
  Nicholas   P: Phila 23 Oct 66
COE
  Darcus   P: Kent Co 3 Ja 60
COEL
  Mrs.   P: Phila 9 Ag 59
COFFEE/COFFIE

George   P: Phila-Gaz. 27 Oct
   73
Robert   P: Phila 20 Ap 69
COFFIN/COFFING
   Timothy   P: Phila 5 Jy 80-
      Gaz. 19 Jy
   William   P: Phila 19 Ja 69
COGHLAN/COGHLING
   Daniel   P: Phila 20 Oct 68,
      19 Ja 69, 20 Ap 69, 2 Ag
      70, 26 Oct 69
COGIN
   Peggy   P: Phila 30 Ap 67
COHEN
   Henry   P: Phila 16 Jy 67
COIN
   Benjamin   P: N.Castle Co 3
      Sep 61; Wilmington 8 Jy 62
COKER
   George   P: Phila 3 Ja 65
COKERY
   Mrs.   P: Phila 20 Ap 69
COLAN
   Richard   P: Phila 18 Mar 62
COLBERT
   William   P: Phila 9 Ag 59
COLDEN
   Mr.   P: Phila 31 Dec 61
COLDSTREAM
   Capt. William   P: Phila 16
      Jy 67
COLE; see also COAL
   Mr.   P: Phila 4 Ag 63
   Edward   P: Phila 2 Sep 62
   John   P: Phila 27 Ja 73
   William   P: Chester Co 18 Mar
      62
COLEGATE/COLGALE
   Bridget   P: Newcastle Co 12
      Ja 58
   Thomas   P: Pa 19 May 63;
      Phila 2 Sep 62, 15 Mar 64
COLEK
   Jacob   P: Lewis Town 12 Feb
      61
COLEMAN/COLMAN
   Barthol.   P: Phila 20 Jy 69
   Catherine   P: Phila 19 Jy 80
   Edmond   P: Gloucester 2 May
      65
   Jacob   P: Germantown 25 Ap 71
   Jo.   P: Phila 19 Ja 69
   John   P: Phila 10 Ap 66, 30
      Ap 77
   Nicholas   P: Pa 28 Oct 62
   Robert   P: Phila 26 Oct 69, 1
      Nov 70
   Simon   P: Phila 12 Ja 58
COLES
   William   P: Phila 6 Jy 58,
      27 Jy 58
COLESBURY
   Swen   P: Christine 31 Jy 60
COLETHATT
   Robert   P: Phila 28 Oct 62

COLGAN
   Daniel   L: Paxton 14 May 72
COLHOUN
   Andrew, Esq.   L: Carlisle 19
      Dec 71, 29 Jy 72.   P: Car-
      lisle 4 Ag 63
   David   P: Pa 2 Feb 64
   Samuel   P: Phila 13 Oct 63
COLIN
   Dr. Lewis   P: Phila 26 Oct 69
COLLERT
   Antipas   P: Phila 10 Ap 66,
      20 Jy 69
COLLETT
   Jeremiah   P: Chester Co 31
      Dec 61
COLLEY/COLEY
   John   P: Coles Town 11 Sep 55
   Samuel   P: America 12 Feb 61;
      Phila 25 Jy 65
COLLIDAY
   William   P: Germantown 3 May
      70
COLLIER
   Elizabeth   P: Phila 7 Ap 57
   Isaac   P: Darby 1 Jy 56
   Isaac, Jr.   P: Darby 13 May
      56
   Rhoadalph   P: Phila 4 Ag 68
COLLINS/COLLINGS
   Adam   P: N.J. 31 Jy 60, 12
      Feb 61; Phila 31 Jy 60
   Ann   P: Gloucester Co 31 Dec
      61
   Catharine   P: Phila 31 Jy 60,
      31 Dec 61
   Cornelius   P: Christiana 9 Ag
      59; Lancaster Co 3 Ja 60
   Daniel   P: Phila 28 Ap 68, 19
      Ja 69
   James   P: Cedar Creek 23 Oct
      66; Phila 31 Dec 61
   Jeremiah   P: Phila 3 Ja 76
   John   P: Gloucester Co 9 May
      54; Phila 9 Ag 59, 3 Ja 60,
      4 Ag 63, 19 Ja 69, 27 Ja 73,
      19 Jy 80
   Joseph   P: Sussex Co 31 Dec 61
   Mary   P: Phila 3 May 70, 30
      Oct 76
   Mat.   P: Phila 15 Mar 64
   Maurice   L: Donegall 2 Mar 74
   Ralph   P: Phila 15 Mar 64
   Sarah   P: Phila 19 Jy 80
   Stephen   P: Phila 27 Jy 58,
      19 Jy 80
COLLISON
   Richard   P: Phila 10 Ap 66
COLLY
   Edward   P: Schuylkill 10 Ap 66
   Samuel   P: Upper Dublin 12 Ja
      58
COLNS
   William   P: Christiana 7 Ap 57
COLOTY

Owen   P: Phila 13 May 56
COLSTON
  Peter   P: Phila 3 May 70
  William   P: Phila 28 Ap 68,
    21 Jy 68
COLT
  Peter   Phila 30 Oct 76
COLVIN
  Patrick   P: Phila 10 Oct 65,
    10 Ap 66
  Philip   P: Amwell 15 Jy 56;
    Phila 16 Jy 72
COLYON
  Patrick   P: Pa 11 Sep 55
COMBS, see COOMBS
COMELY
  Jacob   Smithfield 5 Oct 76-
    Gaz. 30 Oct
COMERFORD/COMOFORD
  James   P: Lancaster 3 Ja 60
  Lt. Thomas   P: In the army 12
    Ja 58
COMES, see COOMBS
COMMACK
  Jane   P: Horsham, Bucks Co 27
    Ja 73
COMMEGES/COMEGYS
  Margaret   P: Phila 3 May 70
  William   P: Chester River 31
    Dec 61
COMMIN, see CUMMINS
COMPAR
  Capt.   P: Phila 5 Jy 80-Gaz.
    19 Jy
COMPSON
  Thomas   T: Andover Furnace,
    New Jersey 1 Sep 68
COMPCTON/COMSTON
  Henry   P: Phila 13 Ja 63, 10
    Oct 65
COMPTE
  Charles   P: Phila 25 Ap 71
COMPTON
  Robert   P: Phila 20 Ap 69
  Thomas   P: Bucks Co 13 Oct 63
CONDON/CONDEN
  David   P: Phila 18 Ag 57
  James   P: Phila 3 May 70
CONDIET
  Silas   Haddonfield 5 Ap 77-
    Gaz. 30 Ap
CONELEN
  Elizabeth   P: Phila 15 Mar 64
CONGILL
  Clayton   P: Phila 9 Ag 59
CONGUERETT
  Lewis   P: Phila 4 Ag 63
CONICK
  Anthony   P: Phila 21 Jy 68
CONINGHAM, see CONYNGHAM
CONLY/CONLEY
  James   P: Phila 28 Nov 54
  John (soldier)   P: 21 Dec 58
CONN
  James   P: Phila 3 Ja 76

CONNANE
  Dominick, ship carpenter   P:
    Falls Schuylkill 19 Ja 69
CONNAUGHY
  James   P: Chester Co 1 Nov 70
CONNEL/CONNELL
  Caley   P: Phila 25 Jy 65
  Christopher   P: Phila 24 Feb
    63
  Edward   P: Phila 3 Ja 76
  Eleanor   P: Phila 10 Ap 66
  John   P: Sussex Co 13 Oct 63
  Mary   P: Phila 20 Ap 69
  Michael   P: Phila 20 Ap 69
  Morgan   P: Phila 3 Ja 76
  Patrick   P: Phila 20 Ap 69
  William   P: Phila 3 Ja 65,
    30 Ap 77; Sussex Co 13 Oct
    63
CONNEWAY
  Alley   P: Phila 25 Jy 65
CONNEYERS
  Joseph   P: Phila 21 Jy 68
CONNODGE
  Paul   P: Phila 28 Ap 68
CONNOLLY/CONNELLY/CONELY/CONNAL-
  LY/CONNOLIE
  Edward   P: Phila 1 Feb 70, 16
    Jy 72
  George   P: Phila 27 Oct 73
  John   P: Pa 21 Dec 58, 11 Sep
    55, 9 Ag 59, 10 Oct 65, 20
    Oct 68, 3 May 70, 3 Ja 76
  Mary   P: New Castle 27 Dec
    53; Phila 15 Mar 64
  Mat.   P: Lancaster Co 2 Sep 62
  Neil   P: Pa 12 Feb 61; Phila
    30 Ja 66
  Patrick   N: 29 Nov 64.   P:
    New-Castle 31 Dec 61; Wil-
    mington 13 Oct 63.   T: 7
    May 67
  Robert   Phila 5 Ap 77-Gaz. 30
    Ap
  William   P: Pa 31 Dec 61, 12
    Feb 61, 18 Mar 62
CONNOR/CONNER
  Alexander   P: Phila 1 Nov 53
  Edward   P: Bucks Co 16 Jy 67;
    Chester Co 3 Sep 61; Phila
    30 Oct 76
  Elinor   P: Phila 3 Ja 76
  Elizabeth   P: Phila 9 Ag 59
    (alias PALMER), 27 Oct 73
  James   P: Pa 4 Ag 63; Phila
    7 Ap 57, 28 Ag 57, 4 Feb 68
  Jane   P: Phila 3 Ja 76
  John   P: Pa 31 Dec 61, 25 Jy
    65, 20 Oct 68, 27 Ja 73, 27
    Oct 73, 3 Ja 76, 5 Oct 76
  Patrick   P: Phila 24 Feb 63
  Peter   P: Pa 11 Sep 55
  Terence   P: Phila 11 Sep 55
  Susannah   P: Phila 1 Feb 70
CONORD

John   P: Phila 2 Ag 70
CONQUERGOOD
   William   P: Phila 9 May 54
CONRAD/?/
   William   P: Phila 3 Ja 76
CONREA
   Gumrode   P: Phila 20 Oct 68
CONROW
   Darling   Phila 1 May 76
CONSTABLE
   Capt. Thomas   P: Phila 4 Ag
   63
CONTANCK
   Benjamin   P: Phila 3 Sep 61
CONWAY
   Daniel   P: Phila 27 Dec 53
   James   P: Phila 1 Feb 70
CONWELL/CONWILL
   Joseph   P: Lewis-Town 27 Jy
   58, 31 Jy 60
CONWIN
   Joseph   P: Phila 27 Ja 73
CONYBY
   Samuel   P: N. Castle Co 3 Sep
   61
CONYNGHAM/CONINGHAM/CUNYNGHAM;
   see also CUNNINGHAM
   Mr.   P: Phila 2 Feb 64
   Andrew   P: Phila 2 May 65
   George   P: Phila 11 Sep 55
   Grace   P: Pa 21 Dec 58
   Jo.   L: York Co 25 Dec 66
   Maganel   P: Phila 2 May 65
   Magdalen   P: Phila 3 Ja 65
   Robert   P: Phila 28 Nov 54
   William   P: Phila 3 Ja 65
COOK
   George   P: Phila 21 Dec 58
   Harman   C: c/o John Downing,
   near Brandywine Bridge 18
   Jy 65
   Henry   P: Phila 3 Ja 76
   Isaac   P: Roxborough 13 May
   56
   Jacob   P: Phila 31 Jy 60
   James   C: c/o Robert Rushton
   Oxford 22 Ja 67. L: 29 Ja
   67. P: London Derry 24 Oct
   54
   John   P: New-Castle Co 3 Ja
   60; Pa 18 Mar 62, 28 Oct
   62, 15 Mar 64
   John, Jr.   P: Chester Co 4 Ap
   54
   Mickay   P: Phila 10 Ap 66
   Nathan   P: Phila 18 Ag 57
   Nicholas   P: Pa 31 Dec 61,
   near Phila 18 Mar 62
   Robert   P: Baltimore 31 Mar
   63
   Roger   P: Yellow-Britches 24
   Feb 63, 19 May 63
   William   P: Phila 13 May 56,
   2 May 65, 30 Ja 66
COOKE

Benjamin   P: Phila 18 Mar 62
Edward   P: Phila 31 Dec 61
James   P: Chester Co 31 Dec
   61; Phila 20 Oct 68
John   P: Phila 31 Dec 61, 30
   Ap 67
Jonathan   P: Phila 2 May 65
Joseph   P: Goshen 1 Jy 56
Nathan   P: Phila 19 Jy 80
Nicholas   P: Phila 15 Mar 64
Robert   Phila 30 Oct 76
Sarah   P: Phila 15 Mar 64
COOKITT/or COOKITT?/
   George   P: Phila 3 Ja 60
COOKSON
   Thomas   P: Lancaster 24 Oct
   54
COOMBS/COMBS/COMES; see also
   GREER & COOMBS
   Capt. M.   P: Phila 2 Feb 64
   Jancelar   P: Phila 28 Oct 62
   John   L: Lancaster 29 Jy 72
   (Esq).   P: Phila 1 Feb 70
   Phineas   P: Phila 27 Ja 73
   William   P: Phila 13 Oct 63
COONON
   Timothy   P: Phila 2 Ag 70, 27
   Oct 73
COOPE
   Joseph   P: Chester Co 19 Ja
   69
   Thomas   P: Oxford Twp 27 Jy
   58
COOPER/COUPER; see also CUPER
   Archibald   L: 31 Ja 71. P:
   Lancaster Co 8 Jy 62, 13
   Oct 63; Pa 3 Ja 60, 31 Dec
   61
   Charles   P: Phila 10 Oct 65
   Christopher   P: New-Castle Co
   9 Ag 59
   Daniel   P: Gloucester Co 12
   Ja 56
   Edward   P: Hopewell 28 Nov
   54, 31 Dec 61
   Elizabeth   P: Duck Creek 9 Ag
   59
   Henry   P: Gloucester Co 30 Ja
   66; Mountholly 15 Jy 56
   Isaac   P: N.J. 18 Mar 62
   Jacob   P: Phila 9 Ag 59
   James   P: Phila 27 Dec 53, 10
   Ap 66, 30 Ap 67
   John   P: New Castle Co 7 Ap
   57; Phila 9 May 54, 28 Nov
   54
   Mary   P: Phila 21 Jy 68
   Peter   P: Phila 30 Ja 66
   Robert   P: Cumberland Co 28
   Oct 62; Hopewell 1 Nov 53;
   see also FINNEY, Robert
   Thomas   P: Mountholly 4 Ag 63
   William   P: Germantown 25 Ap
   71; Phila 25 Jy 65
COOT

Capt. Henry   P: Phila-Gaz.
  27 Oct 73
COPE
  James   P: Phila 1 Jy 56
COPELAND/COPLAND/COPLAN; see
  also COWFLAND
  George   P: Pa 3 Ja 60; Phila
    30 Ja 66
  Jonathan   P: Chester 12 Feb
    61
  William   P: Phila 4 Feb 68
COPLING
  Capt.   P: Phila 3 Sep 61
COPP
  Susannah   P: Phila 1 Nov 53,
    9 May 54, 31 Jy 60
COPPER
  Cyrus   Phila 31 Ja 76
COPPOCK
  Thomas   Phila 31 Ja 76
CORAM
  Philip and Robert   P: Phila
    27 Oct 73
CORBETT/CORBIT
  Ann   P: Phila 11 Sep 55
  Christ.   P: Phila 1 Nov 53
  Richard   P: Phila 3 Ja 76
  William   P: Bucks Co 12 Ja 58
CORD
  Thomas   P: West Nottingham 7
    Ap 57
CORDEL
  Elizabeth   P: Phila 1 Feb 70
CORDEROY
  Henry   P: Phila 13 Oct 63
CORDUS
  David   P: Phila 2 Ag 70
CORDY/CORDIE
  Cord.   P: Phila 15 Mar 64
  Jane   P: Pa 31 Jy 60
CORDOZO
  David   P: Phila 29 Ag 54
COREACE
  George   P: Phila 12 Feb 61
CORICAN
  Thomas   P: Phila 21 Jy 68
CORJEAGE
  Thomas   P: Phila 20 Ap 69
CORLEY
  Ᾱlexander   P: Phila 25 Jy 65
CORLIES
  Capt. George   P: Phila 3 Sep
    61
CORMECK
  Simon   P: Phila 20 Ap 69
CORMHELL
  William   T: c/o John Hacket,
    Esq. Trenton 3 Oct 65
CORNELIUS
  Mr.   Phila 30 Oct 76
CORNELL/CORNEL
  Aaron   P: Bucks Co 30 Ap 67
  William   P: Phila 18 Mar 62,
    2 May 65

CORNELUS
  Hannah   P: Phila 13 Oct 63
CORNER
  Thadee   L: Donegall 2 Mar 74
CORNIELLE
  Sackville   P: Phila 12 Ja 58
CORNLAY
  Henry   P: Phila 3 Ja 76
CORNMAN
  John   P: Phila 26 Jy 64
CORNS
  John   C: Chester Co 18 Jy 65
CORNWELL
  Timothy   P: Phila 6 Jy 58, 27
    Jy 58
CORPE
  John   P: Phila 18 Ag 57
CORRELL
  Daniel   P: Pa 28 Oct 62
CORREN/CORRON
  Jer./Jeremiah   P: Phila 24
    Feb 63, 19 May 63
  Neil   P: Phila 20 Oct 68
CORRY/CORY/CORREY
  Bernard   P: Phila 4 Feb 68
  Daniel   P: Phila 12 Ja 58
  David   P: New-London 31 Jy 60;
    N. Londonderry 27 Jy 58; Pa
    28 Oct 62, 13 Ja 63; Phila
    12 Ja 58
  John   P: Phila 2 May 65
  Mary   P: Phila 5 Ag 62, 24
    Feb 63
  Robert   L: Lancaster Co 20 Ja
    73.   P: East Nottingham 7
    Ap 57; Phila 13 Ja 63, 2
    Feb 64, 3 Ja 65, 2 May 65,
    25 Jy 65, 30 Ap 67, 27 Oct
    73
  Samuel   P: Phila 9 Ag 59, 19
    Jy 80 (Capt)
  Thomas   P: Chester Co 12 Ja
    58
  William   P: Phila 9 Ag 59
CORSA
  James   P: Phila 2 Ag 70
CORSIE
  Isaac   P: Phila 5 Ag 62
CORSON
  Cornelius   P: Bucks Co 3 Ja
    60
CORSSER
  John   P: Phila 12 Feb 61
CORTLANDT
  Stephen V.   P: Phila 24 Feb
    63
CORTON
  Benjamin   P: Phila 28 Nov 54
COSGROVES
  Francis   P: Pa 31 Dec 61
COSKEY
  Robert   L: Conestogoe 29 Jy
    72
COSTULY

Charles   P: Phila 28 Ap 68
COTNAM/COTTNAM
  Elizabeth   P: Salem   31 Dec
    61
  Robert   P: Phila 27 Ja 73
COTORN
  Thomas   P: Phila 10 Oct 65
COTSLER
  John   Phila 5 Jy 77-Gaz. 16
    Jy
COTTLE
  Aaron   P: Chester Co 26 Oct
    69, 2 Ag 70
COTTON/COTTEN
  Henry   P: York Co 15 Mar 64
  Capt. J.   P: Phila 27 Jy 58
  John   P: Phila 6 Jy 58 (Capt),
    1 Nov 70, 30 Ap 77
COTTRELL/COTTERIL
  Edward   P: Phila 25 Ap 71
  John   P: Chester Co 11 Sep 55
COTTRINGER
  John   P: Phila 27 Jy 58
COUCH
  William   P: Phila 13 May 56
COUFEILT
  Nicholas   P: Phila 18 Feb 55
COUGHLAN/COUGHLANE
  Cornelius   P: Phila 27 Ja 73
  Francis   P: Phila 13 May 56
  Richard   P: Phila 4 Feb 68
COUGINS
  William   P: Phila 12 Feb 61
COULSON
  Anne   P: Pa 15 Mar 64
COULSTON
  Henry   P: Phila 27 Jy 58
COULTER
  Andrew   P: Chester Co 13 Ja
    63
  James   P: Phila 20 Oct 68
  John   P: Chr/Istine/ Bridge 1
    Nov 53
  Richard   L: Cumberland Co 14
    May 72
  Thomas   P: Phila 5 Ag 62, 2
    May 65
COULTON
  Robert   P: Phila 21 Dec 58
COULTS
  James (soldier)   P: 21 Dec 58
COUNAR
  James   P: Phila 16 Jy 72
COUNCIL/COUNCILL
  Johanna   T: Arney's Town 4
    Nov 72
  Susannah   T: in Hopewell 3 Oct
    65
COURL
  Randel   P: Phila 2 Ag 70
COURSEY
  Capt. Thomas   P: Phila 28 Ap
    68
COURT
  Joseph   Phila 24 Jy 76

COURTNEY
  Francis   P: Phila 3 Ja 76
  Hercules   P: Phila 28 Oct 62,
    26 Jy 64
  James   P: Phila 4 Feb 68, 25
    Ap 71
  Mary   Phila 30 Ap 77
  Robert   P: Chester Co 18 Mar
    62
COURTS
  William   Phila 30 Oct 76
COUSBAN
  Peter   P: Phila 2 May 65
COUSINS/COUSENS/COUSIONS/CUZZ-
INS/CUZINS
  John   P: Phila 1 Nov 70, 23
    Oct 66
  William   P: Phila 11 Sep 55,
    21 Dec 58, 3 Sep 61
COUTANCHE
  Benjamin   P: Phila 31 Dec 61
COUZELL
  Sarah   T: Wells's Ferry 17 Oct
    54
COVENHOVEN
  John   P: Pilesgrove, N.J. 28
    Ap 68
COVENTON
  Mrs.   P: Phila 31 Dec 61
COW
  Thomas   P: Phila 20 Oct 68
COWAN/COWEN
  Andrew   P: Chester 28 Oct 62;
    Pa 12 Ja 58
  Joseph   P: Chester Co 13 Ja 63
  Thomas   P: Pa 18 Mar 62
COWEY
  Samuel   P: Lancaster Co 3 Ja
    60
COWIE/or COWIN?/
  George   P: Lancaster Co 15 Mar
    64
COWIS
  Robert   P: Bucks Co 15 Mar 64
COWL
  John   P: Phila 16 Jy 67
COWMAN
  Joseph   P: Phila-Gaz. 27 Oct
    73
  William   P: Phila 2 Sep 62
COWN
  James   P: New-Castle Co 31 Dec
    61
COWPER
  William, surgeon   P: German-
    town 28 Ap 68
COWPLAND
  Caleb   P: Chester Co 21 Dec
    58, 27 Jy 58
  Caleb, Jr.   P: Chester 9 May
    54
  David   P: Chester 27 Dec
    53, 4 Ap 54
  James   P: Chester Co 30 May 54
  Capt. Jonathan   P: Phila 27 Jy
    58

COX/COXE; see also COCKS
.... L: near Harris's Ferry
19 Dec 71
Benjamin P: Chester Co 9 Ag
59
Bridget P: Phila 9 Ag 59
Charles P: Phila 3 May 70,
25 Ap 71
Christopher P: Phila 10 Oct
65, 1 May 76
Daniel P: Phila 4 Feb 68
David P: Cushetunk 4 Feb 68
Elizabeth P: Phila 26 Oct 69
Gabriel P: Phila 31 Dec 61
John P: Phila 9 Ag 59, 4 Ag
63, 26 Jy 64, 3 Ja 65, 20
Jy 69, 2 Ag 70, 30 Ap 77,
19 Jy 80
Moses P: Phila 4 Feb 68
Nicholas P: Phila 26 Oct 69,
1 Nov 70
Peggy P: Phila 2 Ag 70
Richard P: Phila 27 Ja 73
Thomas P: East New Jersey 12
Feb 61
W. P: Phila 6 Jy 58
William P: Sassafras Neck 20
Oct 68
COYLE
Barbary P: Phila 26 Oct 69
James P: Pa 31 Dec 61, 8 Jy
62, 19 May 63
Pat./Patrick Batston Furnace
24 Jy 76; Phila 12 Ja 58
COYSTER
Jacob P: Phila 4 Feb 68
COYTMORE
Mr. P: Phila 23 Oct 66
CRABB
William P: Phila 12 Ja 58
CRABEN
Nancy P: Phila 3 Ja 76
CRACKNELL
John P: Phila 3 Sep 61
CRADIN
Cornelius P: Phila 28 Nov
54
CRADOCK; see also FRANCIS &
CRADOCK
Mr. P: Phila 2 Ag 70
Jane P: Phila 31 Jy 60
CRAFILS
Robert P: Phila-Gaz. 27 Oct
73
CRAFT
John P: Phila 18 Ag 57
CRAFTON
Thomas P: Lancaster Co 18 Mar
62
CRAFTS
Robert P: Phila 20 Ap 69
CRAGET
William P: Phila 25 Jy 65
CRAG/CRAGG/CRAGGE
James C: c/o J. Mathers,

Chester Co 28 Nov 65
Peter Phila 1 May 76
Capt. Robert C: 28 Nov 65
Capt. Thomas P: Phila 6 Jy 58
CRAGHTON
Robert L: Marsh Creek 14 May
72
William P: Lancaster Co 18
Ag 57
CRAIG/CRAIGE
& FALKNER P: Phila 3 Ja 65
Mr. P: Phila 18 Ag 57, 9 Ag
59
Andrew P: Phila 4 Ag 63, 2
Feb 64, 26 Jy 64, 3 Ja 65,
30 Oct 76
Eleanor P: Phila 26 Oct 69
George P: Phila 27 Ja 73
Henry, and WILLESON, Thomas
L: 11 Ap 65
James P: Phila 28 Nov 54,
9 Ag 59, 3 Ja 60, 31 Jy 60,
3 Sep 61, 2 Ag 70
John N: Dover, Kent Co 12
Feb 67. P: Cecil Co 9 Ag
59; Chester Co 31 Jy 60;
Lancaster (Co) 3 Sep 61, 4
Ag 63; Phila 6 Jy 58, 18
Mar 62, 13 Ja 63, 2 Ag 70,
3 Ja 76
Jos./Joseph P: Pa 18 Mar 62;
Phila 27 Oct 73
Margaret P: Lancaster Co 3
Sep 61
Robert P: Pa 24 Feb 63, 19
May 63, 4 Ag 63, 13 Oct 63;
Phila 31 Dec 61, 20 Ap 69,
26 Oct 69; Phila Co 16 Jy
69
Thomas P: N. London 15 Mar
64; Phila 25 Jy 65, 3 May 70
Capt. W. P: Forks of Delaware
4 Ag 63, 13 Oct 63
William P: Deep-Run 13 Oct 63,
19 Ja 69 (Schoolmaster);
Phila 28 Nov 54, 6 Jy 58, 5
Ag 62 (& Co), 3 Ja 76
CRAIGHEAD
Rev. Alexander P: Chester Co
3 Sep 61
Margaret P: Church Hill 13
Ja 63; Phila 1 Jy 56
Patrick P: Phila 5 Ag 62
CRAINS
John P: Phila 6 Sep 53
CRAMPHIN
W. P: Wilmington 5 Ag 62
CRANDLE
Levi Morris's River 30 Oct
76
CRANE/CRAIN
Eleanor P: Phila-Gaz. 27 Oct
73
Francis P: Phila 8 Jy 62
Richard P: in the army 21

Dec 58 (Sgt); Phila 21 Dec 58

CRANFORD

Samuel   P: New-Castle Co 27 Jy 58

CRANN

Hugh   P: Phila 18 Mar 62

CRASS

Margaret   P: Phila 28 Oct 62

CRASWELL

Thomas   P: Phila 31 Dec 61

CRATHORN

Jonathan   P: Phila 4 Feb 68

CRAVEN

John   P: Salem 5 Ag 62

Patrick   P: Bucks Co 16 Jy 67

Thomas   P: Bucks Co 8 Jy 62.
   T: Princeton 17 Oct 54

CRAWFORD/CRAFFORD/CRAUFORD; see also MUIR &

Mrs.   P: Phila 1 Nov 53

Mr.   P: Phila 24 Feb 63, 19 May 63

Alexander   P: Phila 5 Ag 62, 3 Ja 65, 25 Jy 65, 23 Oct 66

Andrew   P: Chester Co 9 Ag 59; Phila 2 Feb 64

Archibald/Arch   P: Bucks Co 31 Dec 61; Fishing Creek 18 Ag 57; Wilmington 5 Feb 54; York Co 3 Ja 60

Catherine   P: Chester Co 31 Mar 63

David   L: Lancaster Co 20 Ja 73.   P: Pa 4 Ag 63; Phila 13 Ja 63

Elizabeth/Eliz.   P: Phila 31 Jy 60, 19 May 63, 15 Mar 64

Felix   Phila 31 Ja 76

Hannah   P: Phila 10 Ap 66

Hugh   P: Phila 19 Ja 69

J.   P: Goshen 31 Jy 60

James   L: 13 Jn 65; York Co 2 Mar 74.   P: Bucks Co 12 Feb 61; Pa 13 Ja 63, 31 Mar 63; Phila 11 Sep 55, 3 Ja 65, 12 Feb 61, 25 Jy 65; Wilmington 15 Mar 64

John   L: near Fort Pitt 20 Ja 73.   P: Bethlehem Twp 4 Ag 63; Bucks 28 Nov 54; Kensington 4 Feb 68; Lancaster Co 15 Mar 64; Little Britain 24 Oct 54; Marcus Hook 18 Feb 55; Phila 27 Dec 53, 4 Ap 54, 4 Feb 68, 1 Feb 70; Worwood Twp 7 Ap 57

Joseph   P: Pa 13 Oct 63; Phila 27 Oct 73

Josiah   L: Earl Twp 19 Dec 71

Martha   P: Phila 25 Jy 65

Mary   P: Lancaster Co 31 Dec 61

Neil   P: Phila 27 Ja 73

Robert   N: Mill Creek Hundred 4 Dec 66.   P: Wilmington 13 Oct 63

Samuel   P: Milford Hundred 3 Ja 60

Thomas   P: Pa 3 Ja 60, 13 Oct 63

William   P: Bucks Co 26 Jy 64; Chester Co 27 Jy 58; Lancaster Co 13 Ja 63

CRAWLEY/CRAWLY

Ann   P: Phila 20 Oct 68

Michael   P: Phila 20 Oct 68

Patrick   P: Phila 28 Nov 54

CREAGE

Dennis   P: Phila 1 Feb 70

CREAN

Richard   P: near Phila 18 Mar 62

CREANOR

Patrick   P: Phila 2 May 65

CREASE

Henry   P: Phila 1 Nov 53

CREATH

William   P: New-Castle Co 9 Ag 59

CREATON

Abraham   P: Phila 4 Ap 54

CREDECK

Easter   P: Phila 23 Oct 66

CREE

Robert   L: Lancaster Co, see BOAL, Robert

CREED

Edward   P: Phila 30 Ja 66

Robert   P: Phila 30 Ja 66

CREEDON

John   P: Phila 1 Nov 53

CREELY

Mary   P: Germantown 9 Ag 59

CREGIRE

Henry   P: Phila 5 Feb 54

CREIAGE

Margaret   P: Phila-Gaz. 27 Oct 73

CREIGH

John   L: Carlisle 2 Mar 74

John   P: Pa 5 Ag 62, 13 Ja 63

CREIGHTON/CRETON

Hugh   P: Bristol 12 Ja 58; Bucks Co 12 Ja 58, 2 Feb 64; Haddonfield, N.J. 9 Ag 59, 13 Ja 63, 4 Feb 68, 26 Oct 69; Pa 3 Ja 60; Phila 25 Jy 65

Patrick   P: Deer-Creek 2 Feb 64

Robert   P: Phila 28 Oct 62

William   P: Lancaster Co 3 Sep 61

CRELEY

Patrick   P: Phila 19 Ja 69

CREMAR/CREAMER/CREMER

Dennis   P: Phila 4 Feb 68

George   P: Phila 20 Ap 69

Vertle   P: Phila 13 Oct 63
CRIBBLE
  Andreas   P: Phila 29 Ag 54
CRIDLAND
  Simmond (conductor of stores)
    P: in the army 21 Dec 58
CRIG
  Dr. Eron   P: Phila 19 Ja 69
CRIGEN
  Alexander   P: Phila 25 Ap 71
CRIGHTON
  John   P: Phila 4 Feb 68
CRIMMINE
  Dennis   P: Phila 12 Feb 61
CRIPPS
  Samuel   P: Mountholly 24 Oct
    54
CRISP
  John   P: Phila 4 Feb 68, 28
    Ap 68
CRISPIN
  Thomas   P: Phila 28 Ap 68
CRISSON
  Jeremiah   P: Phila 3 Ja 60
CRISTY, see CHRISTIE
CRITCHLOW
  James   P: Yellow-Britches 31
    Dec 61
CROAN
  James   N: York Co, Pa 29 Nov
    64
  Jon.   L: 13 Jn 65
  Nicholas   P: Phila 12 Ja 58
CROBBING
  Charles   L: York Co 20 Ja 73
CRODIE
  Easter   P: Phila 20 Jy 69
CROGAN/CROGHAN/CROHAN
  Dennis   P: Phila 30 Ap 67
  George   P: Cumberland Co
    11 Jy 54, 29 Ag 54; Lan-
    caster 19 Jy 80 (Col)
CROLTE
  James   P: Phila 7 Ap 57
CROMELY
  Alexander   P: Phila 3 Ja 65
CROMMEY
  James   P: Pilesgrove 20 Oct
    68
CRONAR
  Charles   P: Phila 25 Jy 65
CRONE
  Ann   P: Phila 2 Sep 62, 24
    Feb 63
CRONELTON
  George   P: Carlisle 2 Feb 64
CROOK/CROOKE
  Lt.(in army)   P: Fort Pitt
    26 Jy 64
  Charles W.   P: Phila 1 Nov 70
CROOKS/CROOKES
  Esther   P: Phila 27 Ja 73
  Richard   P: Greenage 15 Jy 56;
    West N.J. 7 Ap 57, 13 Oct 63
  Samuel   P: Lancaster Co 15 Mar

64 (2)
CROOKSHANKS/CRUCKSHANK/CRUCK-
  SHANKS
  Mrs.   P: near Phila 5 Ag 62
  Amelia   P: Phila 2 Feb 64
  Joseph   P: Phila 19 Jy 80
  Robert   P: Kent Co 13 Oct 63;
    Phila 31 Dec 61
CROONS
  Venlen   Phila 5 Ja 76, 31 Ja
CROSBY/CROSBEY/CROSBIE
  Ann   P: Phila 18 Ag 57
  Col. Charles   P: Chester Co
    12 Ja 58
  David   P: Pa 18 Mar 62
  Ebenezer   Phila 30 Ap 77, 16
    Jy 77 (Dr)
  John, Jr.   Ridley Creek 24 Jy
    76
  Justice   P: Chester Co 5 Ag
    56
  Thomas   P: Phila 21 Dec 58,
    27 Jy 58
  William   P: Fogs Manor 12 Ja
    58
CROSGROSE/?/
  Andrew   P: Phila 25 Jy 65
CROSHIA
  John   P: in the army 12 Ja 58
CROSLAND
  John   P: Forks of Delaware 13
    May 56; Phila 18 Ag 57
  Thomas   P: Pa 31 Dec 61
CROSS
  Frederick   P: Phila 30 Ja 66
  George   P: Phila 4 Feb 68
  Jane   P: Phila 3 Ja 76
  John   P: Lancaster 18 Ag 57,
    27 Jy 58, 31 Jy 60, 13 Oct
    63; Pa 15 Mar 64; Phila 15
    Jy 56
  Margaret   P: Phila 25 Jy 65
  Rev. Robert   P: Phila 8 Jy 62,
    2 Feb 64
  Thomas   P: Phila 2 Feb 64, 26
    Jy 64, 3 Ja 65, 23 Oct 66
  William   P: Broad-way 21 Dec
    58, 31 Dec 61; Pa 8 Jy 62
CROSSAN/CROSSEN/CROSSON/CROSEN/
  CROSAN
  Widow   P: Newcastle 28 Oct 62
  John   P: Phila 1 Feb 70;
    Whiteclay Creek 27 Dec 53
  Massey   P: Phila 3 Ja 76
  Samuel   P: Phila 9 Ag 59, 2
    Feb 64
  Stephen   P: Phila 16 Jy 72
  Thomas   P: Pa 31 Mar 63, 19
    May 63; Phila 23 Oct 66, 27
    Oct 73
CROSSY
  Neal   P: Phila 25 Jy 65
CROSTAN
  Samuel   P: Phila 26 Jy 64
CROUDAR

Harry   P: Phila 27 Ja 73
CROVASSE
  John   P: Phila 29 Ag 54
CROW/CROWE
  George   P: Wilmington 8 Jy
    62
  James   C: c/o Samuel Young
    New-Garden, Chester Co 30
    Oct 66.   P: near Mt. Holly
    1 May 76; Trenton Forge 24
    Jy 76
  Peter   P: Phila 8 Jy 62
  Robert   P: in the army 27 Jy
    58 (Lt); Lancaster Co 18
    Mar 62; Phila 24 Feb 63, 19
    May 63
  William   P: Octorara 9 Ag 59;
    Phila 11 Sep 55
CROWIN
  Thomas   P: N.J. 4 Ag 63
CROWLY
  Susannah   P: Phila 10 Oct 65
CROWTHERS
  Thomas   P: Phila 2 Feb 64
CROX
  David   P: Pa 12 Ja 58
CROXALL
  Richard   W: at the Academy,
    Wilmington 3 Jy 76
CROZIER/CROZER
  James   P: Phila 3 Sep 61
  John   P: Pennsborough 24 Feb
    63, 19 May 63; Phila 12 Ja
    58
  Margaret   P: Phila 28 Oct 62
CRULL
  Christian   P: near York Town
    24 Oct 54
CRULSTON
  Robert   P: Phila 25 Ap 71
CRUM
  William   P: Piles-grove 31
    Mar 63
CRUMBS
  Richard   P: Phila 3 May 70
CRUSE
  Nicholas   P: Germantown 9 Ag
    59
CRUSON
  Garrat   P: Baltimore 31 Mar 63
CRY
  John   P: Springfield 5 Ag 56
CUDDY
  Margaret   P: Chester Co 26
    Jy 64
CUFFENS
  Capt. N.   P: Phila 15 Mar 64
CUFFEY
  Robert   P: Lower Dublin 1 Feb
    70; Phila 28 Ap 68, 26 Oct
    69
CUGNET
  Monsieur J.P.   P: Lancaster
    Co 13 Oct 63
CULBERTSON

Esq.   C: near Forks of Brandy-
  wine, see ROSS, Robert
  John   P: Chester Co 13 Oct 63
  Joseph, student   L: Pequea 2
    Mar 74
  Mary   P: Bethlehem 31 Dec 61
  Robert   P: Pa 4 Ag 63; White-
    clay Creek 2 Feb 64
  Samuel   P: America 18 Feb 55
CULLEN/CULLIN
  Bryan   P: Whitehill 18 Mar 62
  Edward   P: Phila 19 Ja 69
  Thomas   P: Colebrookdale 26
    Jy 64; Phila 31 Dec 61, 8
    Jy 62, 5 Ag 62, 23 Oct 66
CULLY
  Samuel   P: Upper Dublin 7 Ap
    57, 31 Dec 61; Phila 25 Jy
    65
CULPIPER
  Francis   P: Phila 27 Ja 73
CULTON/CULTIN/CULTEN
  Joseph   P: Pa 24 Oct 54
  Robert   P: Phila 2 Feb 64, 26
    Jy 64
  William   P: Phila 3 Ja 76
CUMBERLIDGE
  Thomas   P: Chester Co 3 Sep
    61
CUMMINS/CUMMINGS/CUMING/CUMMIN/
  COMINGS/COMMENS/CUMMINS/
  COMMIN
  Mrs.   C: West Nottingham, see
    SCOTT, James.   P: Phila 4
    Feb 68
  Mr.   C: Nottingham, see RAN-
    DALS, Andrew.   P: Phila 23
    Oct 66
  Ballay   P: Phila 31 Dec 61
  David   P: Phila 4 Ag 63
  Elizabeth   P: Kent Co 15 Mar
    64
  George   P: Phila 25 Jy 65
  Hugh   P: Phila 27 Ja 73
  James   P: Lancaster Co 12 Ja
    58; N.J. 18 Mar 62; Pa 13
    Oct 63, 15 Mar 64; Phila 2
    Feb 64
  John   P: Chester Co 31 Dec 61;
    Chestnut Level 26 Jy 64;
    Frankford/Frankfort 31 Dec
    61, 18 Mar 62; New Castle Co
    15 Mar 64; Pa 27 Jy 58;
    Phila 5 Ag 56, 7 Ap 57, 18
    Nov 62, 13 Ja 63, 15 Mar 64.
    T: Bethlehem 17 Oct 54
  Jonathan   P: Octarara 5 Ag 62
  Margaret   P: Bucks Co 15 Mar
    64
  Mary   P: Phila 27 Ja 73
  Robert   P: East Town 20 Ap 69;
    Phila 20 Oct 68
  Samuel   P: Phila 26 Oct 69
  Susanna/Susannah   P: Falls
    Schuylkill 19 Ja 69; Frank-

ford/Frankfort 24 Feb 63,
19 May 63, 4 Ag 63; Phila 28
Oct 62, 20 Ap 69; Schuylkill
21 Jy 68
Thomas P: Phila 23 Oct 66.
T: Bethlehem 17 Oct 54
William N: 29 Nov 64. P:
Chester Co 8 Jy 62; Lan-
caster Co 15 Mar 64; North-
ampton Co 20 Ap 69; Notting-
ham 12 Ja 58, 26 Jy 64; Pa
28 Oct 62; Phila 20 Jy 69;
West Nottingham 7 Ap 57, 26
Jy 64
CUMRAINGS
John P: Phila 3 Ja 65
CUNDER
John P: Pa 18 Mar 62
CUNNIFF
Luke T: Somerset Co /?/ 7
May 67
CUNNING
John P: near Phila 3 May 70
William P: Chester Co 3 Sep
61
CUNNINGHAM/CUNINGHAM; see also
CONYNGHAM
Mrs. P: Pa 3 Sep 61
Allen C: New-Garden 22 Ja 67.
P: Pa 28 Oct 62
Andrew T: Arney's-Town 4 Nov
72
Anthony P: Phila 25 Jy 65
Archibald P: Pa 24 Feb 63,
19 May 63; Phila 3 May 70
Christopher T: near Borden-
town, see GILMORE, Samuel
Daniel P: Donegall 19 May 63
George P: Phila 9 Ag 59
Hugh P: Phila 31 Mar 63, 2
Feb 64
James P: Back Creek 3 Ja 65,
1 Nov 70; Falls Schuylkill
19 Ja 69; Lancaster Co 9 Ag
59; Phila 3 Ja 60, 31 Dec 61,
10 Ap 66
John P: Phila 13 May 56, 7 Ap
57 (Capt), 2 May 65, 21 Jy
68
Mary P: Phila 4 Feb 68
Mat. P: Pa 31 Dec 61
Patrick P: Phila 2 Feb 64
Robert P: Pa 28 Oct 62, 26
Jy 64
Samuel P: Donegall 2 Feb 64
Thomas P: Allen's Town 27 Jy
58; N.J. 18 Mar 62; Sussex
Co 2 Feb 64
Walter P: Pa 28 Oct 62
William P: Phila 27 Jy 58, 9
Ag 59, 26 Jy 64
CUOGH
Mary P: Phila 1 Jy 56
CUPPAGE
Stephen P: Phila 4 Feb 68

CUPPER
Hugh P: Gloucester Ferry 3
Ja 65
CUPER/CUPAR; see also COOPER
Alexander P: Phila 1 Nov 70
James P: Phila 19 Ja 69
CURLE
Randal P: Phila 26 Oct 69
CURLOW
Susannah P: Phila 30 Ja 66
CURLY
Capt. P: Phila 16 Jy 72
CUROTHEY
T: English-Town 31 Ja 71
CURPHY
Deborah P: Phila 8 Jy 62
CURREN
Patrick P: Phila 3 Ja 76
CURRY/CURREY/CUREY/CURRIE
Andrew P: Phila 30 Ja 66
Archibald P: Phila 7 Ap 57;
Pa 2 Feb 64; 3 Ja 66
Daniel P: Phila 27 Jy 58
David P: Phila 31 Jy 60, 30
Oct 76
James P: Bucks 1 Nov 53;
Nantmill Twp 12 Ja 58; Phila
24 Oct 54, 3 Sep 61, 2 May
65, 25 Jy 65, 27 Ja 73
John P: Bucks 1 Nov 53; Pa
13 Oct 63; Phila 2 May 65,
30 Ja 66
Mary P: Phila Co 12 Feb 61
Matthew C: Forks of Brandy-
wine 18 Jy 65 P: Phila 30
Ja 66
Peter P: Phila 20 Jy 69
Robert L: Harris's Ferry 29
Jy 72. P: Phila 2 May 65
Samuel P: New-Castle Co 13
Oct 63; Phila 2 Feb 64, 2
Ag 70, 3 Ja 76
Thomas P: York Co 31 Dec 61
Rev. William P: Great Valley
28 Oct 62; Pa 2 Jy 58
CURSON
Charles P: Duck-Creek 31 Jy
60
CURSWELL
Michael P: Phila 31 Jy 60
CURTIN
Connor P: Phila 9 Ag 59
Capt. R. P: Phila 13 Oct 63
CURTIS/CURTICE
David P: Squan-creek 31 Mar
63
George P: Little Egg-Harbour
4 Feb 68
Jonathan Kingwood, New Jersey
1 May 76
Joseph P: Pa 27 Jy 58
Thomas P: Phila 10 Oct 65
Thomas Kingwood 30 Oct 76
William P: Phila 26 Oct 69,
1 Feb 70 (Capt)

CURTIUS
Jacob F. P: Phila 4 Ap 54
CUSHIN/CUSHINE
Maurice P: Phila 2 Feb 64,
26 Jy 64, 30 Ja 66
CUSHMAN
Isaac T: Mountholly 17 Oct
54
CUSICK/CUSACK
Arthur P: Pa 15 Mar 64
Elizabeth P: Pa 3 Ja 60
Pat. P: Phila 27 Jy 58
CUSTARD
Ann N: 29 Nov 64. P:
Peckery 10 Oct 65
CUSTULO
Sarah P: Christine-Bridge
3 Ja 60
CUTHBERT
John P: Chester Co 27 Jy 58
CUTHBERTSON
Rev. P: Octorara 27 Jy 58
Rev. J. P: Octerara 26 Jy 64
John P: Chester Co 15 Mar 64;
Middle Octarara 4 Ap 54,
Phila 9 Ag 59, 19 Ja 69;
Rev John: Octorara 19 Ja 58;
Lancaster Co 12 Feb 61; Pa
3 Ja 60
Robert P: Chester Co 3 Sep
61
CUTTON
Robert P: Phila 31 Jy 60, 24
Feb 63
CUYLAR
Abraham P: Phila 31 Jy 60-

DAARN
Patrick P: Phila 3 May 70
DADE
Dr. T. P: Phila 4 Ag 63
Townshend P: Phila 13 Oct 63
DAFFT
Samuel P: Chester Co 3 Sep
61
DA FLYN
Thomas P: Pa 19 May 63
DAGWORTHY
Phebe Pen P: Phila 9 Ag 59
DAIGLE/DAIGRE
Charles (French Neutral) P:
13 May 56
John (French Neutral) P: 13
May 56
Oliver (French Neutral) P:
13 May 56
DAIL
Anthony P: Phila 28 Oct 62
DAILY/DAYLY; see also DALEY
Ann P: Phila 28 Oct 62
John P: Phila 25 Ap 71
William P: Phila 8 Jy 62
DAKES
Thomas P: Phila 3 Sep 61

DAKFORD
Aaron P: Phila 13 Oct 63
DALAMAZ
Charles P: Phila 30 Ap 67
DALE
John P: New-Castle Co 4 Ag 63
DALEY/DALY; see also DAILEY
Andrew P: Phila 18 Ag 57
Cornelius P: Phila 1 Nov 70
David P: Phila 1 Nov 53
John P: Phila 2 Ag 70, 3 Ja
76
Peter P: Phila 2 Ag 70
Thomas P: Phila 16 Jy 72
DALHOUS
George P: Phila 10 Oct 65
DALLAS/DALLASS
Duncan P: Phila 8 Jy 62
Mary P: Phila 25 Jy 65
DALLY
Michael P: Salem Co 2 Feb 64
DALS
Alexander P: Pa 12 Ja 58
DALTON; see also DAULTON
James P: Phila 16 Jy 72
Capt. John P: Phila 5 Ag 62
Margaret C: Middletown 30
Oct 66
Valentine P: Phila 26 Oct 69
William P: Phila Gaz. 27 Oct
73
DALYELL
Capt. James P: in the army
21 Dec 58
DANAGH
John P: Abington 26 Oct 69
DANCE
Joseph P: Phila Co 28 Oct 62
DANELL
James P: Phila-Gaz. 27 Oct 73
DANIEL
Catherine P: Phila 6 Sep 53
Hugh P: Phila 4 Feb 68
John P: Chester Co 9 Ag 59;
Pa 21 Dec 58
Mary P: Chester Co 13 Ja 63
Edmund P: Phila 19 May 63
DANIELSON
William P: Darby 18 Ag 57;
Phila 18 Ag 57
DANISTON
Ezekiel N: 29 Nov 64. P:
New-Castle 2 Feb 64
DANNEAD
James P: Phila-Gaz. 27 Oct
73
DANSER
George T: Allenstown 17 Oct
54, 15 Jy 56, 10 Ag 58
DARBRO
John N: Kent in Delaware 4
Dec 66
DARBY/DERBY
Abraham P: Phila 12 Ja 58
Henry P: Phila 20 Ap 69

John   P: in the army 12 Ja 58
Richard   P: Salem 9 Ag 59
Sanders   P: Lewistown 9 Ag 59,
   3 Ja 60
William   East Jersey 5 Ap 77-
   Gaz. 30 Ap
DARCY; see also DARSEY
John   P: Phila 3 Ja 76
Rachel   P: Pa 24 Feb 63
DAREACK
John   P: Pa 13 Ja 63
DAREGGER
Nathaniel   P: Phila-Gaz. 27
   Oct 73
DARKE
John   P: Phila 7 Ap 57
DARLING
Peter   P: Salem Co 4 Ag 63
DARLINGTON
Joseph   P: Chester Co 12 Feb
   61
DARMODY/DARMODE
Catharine   P: Phila 7 Ap 57
Mark   P: Phila 29 Ag 54.   T:
   Trenton 17 Oct 54
DARRAGH/DARROUGH
John   P: Phila 10 Oct 65, 20
   Oct 68
Tho./Thomas   P: Newcastle Co
   12 Ja 58 (2); Pa 15 Mar 64;
   Phila 10 Oct 65; Whitely
   Creek 1 Nov 53
William   P: Phila 21 Jy 68,
   30 Oct 76
DARROLL
Thomas   P: Bucks Co 8 Jy 62
DARROLTH
Mary   P: Bucks Co 31 Jy 60
DARSEY; see also DARCY
Capt. Elisha   P: Phila 31 Dec
   61
DARRVELL
Joseph   P: Phila 9 Ag 59
DARWAN/?/
Patrick   P: Phila 2 Feb 64
DASON
.... P: Oxford 26 Oct 69
DASSEAT
John   P: Phila 8 Jy 62
DAUGHERTY
Thomas   P: Bucks Co 18 Mar 62
DAULTON; see also DALTON
Col.   P: Phila 20 Oct 68
James   P: Phila 6 Jy 58
DAVENPORT
Isaac   P: Phila 1 Nov 53
Josiah   P: Phila 1 Nov 70
Vivian   P: Phila 13 Ja 63
DAVETEY
Alex.   P: Phila 1 Jy 56
DAVEY
Hugh   P: Phila 20 Jy 69
Robert   P: Phila 28 Oct 62
DAVID/DAVIDE
Mr./Mons.   P: Phila 19 Jy 80;

Salem 27 Jy 58
Elizabeth   P: Pa 13 Ja 63;
   Phila 30 Ap 77
Henry   P: Phila 31 Jy 60
John   P: Phila 31 Dec 61
   (Capt), 23 Oct 66, 3 Ja 76
Joseph   P: Little Duck Creek
   19 Ja 69
DAVIDS
Benjamin   P: Phila-Gaz. 27
   Oct 73
DAVIDSON; see also DAVISON
Capt.   P: Phila 31 Jy 60
Gawn   P: Phila 2 May 65
George   P: Phila 25 Jy 65
Rev. James   N: Newark 4 Dec
   66.   P: Phila 1 Nov 70
John   P: Chester Co 31 Dec 61;
   Phila 30 Ja 66, 16 Jy 67,
   28 Ap 68
Robert   L: Little Britain Twp
   19 Dec 71.   P: Phila 20 Oct
   68
Capt. Samuel   P: Phila 30 Ap
   67
Thomas   L: 25 Dec 66
Rev. W.   P: Londonderry 18
   Mar 62
William   P: Horsham 16 Jy 72;
   Phila 23 Oct 66; soldier,
   prob. in Pittsburgh 15 Mar
   64
DAVIE
Mr.   P: Phila 27 Oct 73
John   Phila 1 May 76
William   P: Phila 27 Oct 73
DAVIES/DAVVES
James   P: Phila 30 Ja 66
John   P: Chester Co 12 Feb 61
Mary   P: Phila 13 Oct 63
William   P: Phila 13 Ja 63, 2
   May 65
DAVIN
Dominick   P: Phila 1 Nov 70
DAVIS; see also WHITLOCK &
Capt.   P: Phila 4 Ag 63
Mr. (Attorney)   P: Phila 27
   Jy 58
Amos   P: Smithfield 2 May 65
Andrew   P: Nottingham 26 Jy 64
Ann/Anne   P: Phila 3 May 70.
   T: Prince-Town 6 Dec 64
Arthur   P: Phila 27 Ja 73
Benjamin   P: Plymouth 11 Sep
   55; Upper Dublin 27 Jy 58;
   West Jersey 12 Ja 58
Charles   P: Phila 3 Ja 76
Capt. Charles S.   P: Phila 27
   Ja 73
Christian   P: Phila 18 Feb 55,
   27 Ja 73
David   N: Newark 12 Feb 67
   (Rev.).   P: Oxford Twp 9 Ag
   59; Pilesgrove 21 Dec 58
Elias   C: Goshen 18 Jy 65

Elizabeth T: Trenton 1 Ag 58
Ellis P: Phila 20 Oct 68
Elnathan P: Cohansey-Gaz. 27
  Oct 73
Enoch P: Phila Co 31 Dec 61
Evan L: Carlisle 14 May 72.
  P: Bucks Co 31 Jy 60; Phila
  1 Feb 70
George P: Berks Co 7 Ap 57
  (attorney-at-law); Chester
  Co 3 Ja 60; Phila 12 Feb 61;
  Yellow Spring 18 Mar 62, 31
  Mar 63
Godfrey P: Phila 27 Ja 73
Hannah P: Phila 5 Ag 56
Henny P: Phila 24 Feb 63
Henry P: Phila 27 Ja 73
Hugh P: Pa 12 Feb 61
Isaac P: Chester Co 19 May
  63, 26 Jy 64 (Esq)
James P: Bucks Co 3 Ja 60;
  Cape May 3 Ja 76; Phila 27
  Dec 53, 29 Ag 54, 27 Jy 58
  (2), 21 Dec 58, 9 Ag 59, 20
  Oct 68
Jenkin L: Carlisle/?/ 14 May
  72
Jo. L: Carlisle/?/ 14 May 72
John P: Bucks Co 1 Jy 56, 3
  Sep 61; Montgomery Twp 5 Ag
  62; Pa 3 Ja 60, 18 Mar 62,
  13 Ja 63; Phila 24 Oct 54,
  9 Ag 59, 12 Feb 61, 15 Mar
  64, 26 Oct 69, 3 May 70, 27
  Ja 73; Radnor 1 Feb 70
Jonathan P: Reading 20 Jy 69;
  Salem Co 19 Ja 69
Joseph P: Bucks Co 9 Ag 59,
  12 Feb 61, 31 Dec 61
Lydia P: Phila 8 Jy 62
Margaret P: Phila 19 Ja 69
Mat. P: Phila 3 Sep 61
Michael P: Pa 15 Mar 64
Nathaniel P: Bucks Co 12 Ja
  58, 3 Ja 60
Owen P: Pa 12 Ja 58
Philip T: Trenton 1 Sep 68
Pressella P: Phila 24 Feb 63
Rebecca P: Darby 28 Nov 54
Richard P: Phila 3 Ja 76
Robert P: Phila 20 Ap 69
Sampson P: Conestogoe 18 Ag
  57
Samuel P: Bucks Co 1 Feb 70;
  Lewis-Town 9 Ag 59, 3 Ja 60;
  Pensalken Creek 9 Ag 59;
  Phila 1 Nov 70, 31 Mar 63
Sarah Berks Co 30 Oct 76;
  Phila 16 Feb 55
Capt. Solomon P: Phila 6 Jy
  58
Thomas P: Creesam Twp 27 Ja
  73; Phila 27 Jy 58, 3 Ja 60,
  31 Jy 60, 26 Jy 64, 30 Ja
  66, 3 May 70, 19 May 63

Truston P: Bucks Co 1 Jy 56
Walter P: Phila 31 Dec 61
William L: 29 Ja 67. P: 31
  Jy 60; Bucks Co 1 Jy 56;
  near Phila 30 Ap 67; Phila
  1 Nov 53, 1 Jy 56, 21 Dec
  58 (2), 4 Ag 63, 2 May 65,
  23 Oct 66, 28 Ap 68, 30 Ap
  77
Zacheus/Zaccheus L: Carlisle
  14 May 72. P: Radnor 1 Feb
  70
DAVISON; see also DAVIDSON
  Alexander P: Wilmington 27
    Jy 58
  Gawn P: Phila 2 May 65
  Jacob P: Phila 3 May 70
  John P: Pa 31 Jy 60, 28 Oct
    62; Phila 28 Oct 62, 26 Jy
    64
  Joseph L: Derry Twp 29 Jy 72
  Mar. L: 13 Jn 65
  Mary P: Phila 18 Mar 62
  Matthew P: New-Castle Co 12
    Feb 61; Pa 12 Feb 61
  Robert L: Carlisle 14 May 72
  William P: New Castle 1 Nov
    53; Phila 25 Jy 65
DAVITT
  Tully P: New-Castle Co 2 Feb
    64
DAVOIS
  David P: Bristol 31 Jy 60
DAWKINS
  Henry P: Phila 28 Oct 62
DAWRAH
  Mr. P: Phila 16 Jy 67
DAWS/DAWES
  Capt. Dawey P: Phila 28 Oct
    62
  John P: Phila 31 Jy 60
  Josiah P: Phila 25 Ap 71
  William P: Phila 29 Ag 54, 2
    Feb 64
DAWSE
  Abraham P: Whitpain 31 Jy 60
DAWSON
  Widow P: Phila 31 Dec 61
  Adam P: Phila 1 Nov 70
  Ann P: Phila 2 May 65
  Benjamin P: Duck Creek 11 Sep
    55
  Charles P: Phila 5 Feb 54, 4
    Ap 54
  David Phila 5 Ap 77-Gaz. 30
    Ap
  Edward T: Schoolmaster at
    Amwell 21 Ja 55
  Elias P: Phila 4 Feb 68
  Jacob C: Brandywine Ford 30
    Oct 66
  John P: Phila 28 Oct 62
  Peter P: Newcastle Co 18 Ag
    57
  Rachael P: Londonderry Twp 18

Ag 57
Richard T: Amwell Ferry 17
  Oct 54
Robert P: Phila 4 Feb 68
Samuel P: Pa 28 Oct 62
Thomas P: Phila 3 Sep 61
William Phila 30 Ap 77
William H. P: Phila 30 Ja 66
DAY
  Dr. P: Phila 27 Oct 73
  James P: Chester Co 31 Dec
    61; Phila 5 Ag 62; Upper
    Darby 11 Sep 55
  Capt. J.R. P: Phila 18 Mar
    62
  Dr. John P: Germantown 27 Jy
    58
DAYMOND
  Mr. P: Phila 19 Jy 80
DAYTON
  Joseph P: New Providence 9
    Ag 59
DEACON
  Gilbert P: Phila 2 May 65,
    30 Ja 66
  Margaret P: Phila 3 Ja 76
  Matty L: 13 Jn 65
DEAGGEOR
  John Adam P: Phila 10 Ap 66
DEAL
  Anthony P: Phila 20 Jy 69
  John P: N. Castle Co 3 Sep
    61, 8 Jy 62
  John Godfrey P: Germantown
    3 Ja 65
DEALIN
  Henry P: Phila 19 Ja 69
DEALY/DEALEY/DEALLY
  John P: Phila 28 Nov 54, 11
    Sep 55
  Patrick P: New-Ark 13 Oct 63
  William T: Newshannick 17 Oct
    54
DEAN/DEANE
  Charles P: Phila 2 Ag 70
  David P: Wilmington 12 Ja 58
  Eliz. P: Phila 18 Ag 57
  Ephraim Phila 24 Jy 76, 30
    Oct 76
  John P: Chester 13 May 56;
    Pa 18 Mar 62; Phila 18 Ag
    57, 30 Ap 77
  Joseph Phila 5 Jy 77-Gaz. 16
    Jy
  Mary P: New-Providence, Phila
    Co 28 Ap 68
  Silas P: Phila 2 Sep 62
  William P: Pa 21 Dec 58
DEANS
  Charles P: Forks of Neshami-
    ney 30 Ap 67
  Jo. L: see HARVEY, Mongo
DEARES
  Mary P: Phila 27 Jy 58
DEARFIELD

Laurence P: Phila 30 Ap 67
DEARSLY/DEARSLEY
  Richard P: Phila 8 Jy 62
  Samuel P: Phila 1 Nov 53
  Thomas P: Phila 28 Oct 62
DEAS
  Elizabeth P: Phila 3 Ja 76
DEATIN
  George P: Phila 20 Ap 69
DEAVAROUX
  Elizabeth P: Phila 11 Jy 54
DEBBEIG
  Capt. Hugh P: Phila 31 Dec
    61
DEBELLAND
  Mr. P: Phila 27 Ja 73
DE BERNIERE
  Lt. John L: Kalkaskias 20 Ja
    73
DE BOER
  Peter P: Phila 5 Ag 56
DE BOIS
  Rev. Jonathan P: Northampton
    21 Dec 58
DEBS
  John P: Amwell 15 Jy 56
DE CATOR
  Stephen P: Phila 13 May 56,
    5 Ag 56
DECOINE
  Matthew, teacher L: Lancas-
    ter 20 Ja 73
DECORNE
  Aloro P: Phila 1 Nov 70
DECORTNEY
  David P: Phila 28 Oct 62
DE COUNEY
  William P: Bucks Co 16 Jy 72
DE COURSEY/DECOURCEY
  Selham P: Phila 27 Ja 73
  William P: Bucks Co 12 Ja 58
DE CURRY/DE COUREY
  William P: Bucks Co 18 Mar
    62, 2 Feb 64
DEDEER
  John P: Germantown 13 Oct 63
DEE
  John P: Phila 30 Ja 66
DEFENDAF
  Michael P: Phila 21 Jy 68
DEFEVER
  Christian P: Bucks Co 12 Ja
    58
  John P: Fort Cumberland 7
    Ap 57
DEFLOGE
  J.A. P: Phila 26 Jy 64
DEGROFF
  John P: Poughkeepsie 15 Mar
    64
DEHAAS
  Major P: Phila 26 Oct 69
  John Philip, Esq. L: Lebanon
    19 Dec 71
DEHORSEY

Mr. P: Phila 2 May 65, 25
  Jy 65
D'KLYNE
  Barnet P: Phila 5 Jy 80-Gaz.
  19 Jy
DE LA FOREST
  Mr. P: Phila 5 Jy 80-Gaz. 19
  Jy
DE LA GARENNE
  Mons. P: Phila 24 Feb 63
DELAGE
  Mr. P: Phila 13 Ja 63
DELAHOID
  Matthew P: Phila 4 Feb 68
DE LA MAIN
  .... P: Phila 29 Ag 54
DELAMOTT
  Isaac P: Pa 3 Ja 60
DELANELLOS
  Mr. P: Phila 13 Ja 63
DELANY
  Daniel P: Phila 3 May 70
  Lloyd P: Phila 4 Feb 68
  Sharp P: Phila 26 Jy 64
DELAP/DILAP/DELLAP
  Allen P: Bucks 22 Nov 53;
    Pilesgrove 13 Oct 63
  James P: Bucks 22 Nov 53
  John P: Pa 12 Ja 58; Phila
    18 Ag 57
  Robert P: Chestnut Level 9
    Ag 59
  Samuel P: Octerara 3 Ja 60;
    Phila 3 May 70
  W. P: York Co 8 Jy 62
  William P: York Co 5 Ag 62
DE LA ROCHE
  Mons. P: Phila 5 Jy 80-Gaz.
  19 Jy
DELASON/DELASONG
  Capt. P: Phila 2 Feb 64
  Capt. John P: Phila 24 Feb
    63
DELAVIU
  Isaac Phila 5 Ja 76, 31 Ja
DELBO
  Mr. P: Phila 2 Sep 62
DELEY
  Augustus/Aug. P: Phila 2 Feb
    64, 15 Mar 64, 26 Jy 64
DE LION/DELYON
  Abr. P: Lancaster 27 Dec 53,
    11 Jy 54, 29 Ag 54
DELKER
  John P: Phila 31 Dec 61
DELL
  Mr. P: Phila 21 Dec 58
DELLET
  Hugh P: Phila 13 Oct 63
  James P: Phila-Gaz. 27 Oct
    73
DELPRATT /?/
  James P: Phila 2 Feb 64
DELSON
  James P: Phila 18 Ag 57

DE MARTIN
  Col. Phila 30 Ap 77
DEMICK
  Edward P: Phila 15 Mar 64
DEMILT
  Isaac P: Phila-Gaz. 27 Oct 73
DEMOAIN
  Mr. P: Phila 12 Feb 61
DEMON
  Joseph P: Phila 3 Ja 76
DEMPEY
  Francis,(sailor) P: Pa 21 Dec
    58
DEMPSY
  Edward P: Phila 4 Ag 63
DEMRY
  Peter P: Phila 30 Ja 66
DEMSON
  Margaret P: Jersey 1 Jy 56
DE NEILLY
  John and DURLOO, Peter P:
    Phila-Gaz. 27 Oct 73
DENISTON
  James, peruke-maker N:
    Newark 12 Feb 67
DENNEY
  John P: Cumberland Co 4 Ag 63
DENNIES
  William P: Phila 3 Sep 61
DENNING
  John P: Kent Co, Md. 7 Ap
    57
DENNIS; see also ALLEN & DENNIS
  Elizabeth P: Pa 21 Dec 58
  Henry P: Kensington 12 Ja 58,
    31 Dec 61; Phila 25 Jy 65
    (2), 10 Oct 65, 30 Ja 66, 10
    Ap 66, 26 Oct 69
  John P: Phila 19 May 63
  Littleton P: Snow Hill 31 Dec
    61
  Capt. Pat./Patrick P: Pa 24
    Feb 63; Phila 13 Oct 63
  Capt. Peter P: Pa 13 Ja 63
  Richard P: Phila 27 Dec 53;
    9 Ag 59, 19 Ja 69, 20 Ap 69.
    W: New Castle Co, see PORTER,
    Robert
  Thomas P: Phila 2 Sep 62
DENNISON/DENISON
  John P: Pa 12 Feb 61, 30 Ja
    66
DENNY
  Capt. P: Phila 27 Jy 58
  David P: Chester Co 13 May
    56, 9 Ag 59, 31 Dec 61;
    East Nantmill 7 Ap 57; Phila
    2 May 65
  Edward P: Phila 5 Feb 54, 26
    Jy 64
  Mary P: Phila 30 Ja 66
  Peter P: Phila 13 Ja 63
  William C: Uwchland Twp 22
    Ja 67. P: Pa 12 Ja 58;
    facing Reedy Island 16 Jy 72

DENORMANDY/DENORMANDIE
  A. P: Bristol 31 Dec 61
  Anthony P: Phila 21 Jy 68
  D. P: Bristol 19 May 63
  J. P: Bristol 8 Jy 62
  John P: Bristol 31 Mar 63;
    Dr. Bristol 7 Ap 57, 12
    Feb 61, 31 Mar 63, 16 Jy 77
DENSIRE /or DENFIRE?/
  Mrs. P: New-Castle Co 2 Feb
    64
DENTON/DENTEN
  Capt. P: Phila 7 Ap 57
  Mrs. P: Phila 2 May 65, 25
    Jy 65
  Henry P: Phila 2 May 65, 3
    May 70, 1 Nov 70
DE NYCE
  John P: Phila 28 Nov 54, 18
    Ag 57
DENYESEY
  Peter P: Pa 31 Dec 61
DE OLIVER
  Richard P: Phila 18 Mar 62
DE PATT
  .... P: Phila 13 May 56
DERICKSON
  Jacob P: Wilmington 26 Jy 64
DE RIPPIE
  James P: Phila 20 Ap 69
DERLINGTON
  Robert P: Phila 13 Oct 63
DERRES
  Mr. P: Phila 20 Jy 69
DERRICK/DERICK
  Christian P: Phila 25 Ap 71
  David Phila 3 Oct 76
  Thomas P: Noxontown 3 Sep 61
    (Capt); Phila 30 Oct 76
DERRY
  Jacob P: Phila 15 Mar 64
DERYMON
  Robert P: Phila 3 Sep 61
DESERCH
  Monsieur P: Phila 12 Ja 58
DESHLER
  David P: Phila 13 Ja 63
DEVEBBER
  Joseph P: Phila 3 Ja 76
DEVEERN
  Thomas P: Phila 28 Ap 68
DEVEREACK/DEVEREATH
  Mary Ann P: Phila 13 Ja 63,
    3 Ja 65
DEVERELL
  Elizabeth 1 May 76, 19 Jy 80
DEVERSON
  Capt. Wm. P: Phila 20 Jy 69
DEVESON
  George P: Phila 10 Oct 65
DEVIAS
  Mrs. P: Phila 12 Feb 61
DEVICE
  William P: Whitemarsh 23 Oct
    66

DEUICK
  Thomas P: Phila 20 Jy 69
DEVLEN
  Charles C: Marlborough 22 Ja
    67
DE VOOE
  Benjamin P: New-Castle Co 4
    Ag 63
DEVORY
  John L: c/o Michael Shriner-
    near Lancaster 19 Dec 71
DEVYER
  Richard P: Phila 28 Oct 62
DEWAR
  David P: Phila 30 May 54, 1
    Jy 56, 27 Jy 58 (Capt), 13
    Ja 63 (Capt), 23 Oct 66
DEWBYT
  Christoph. P: Germantown 6
    Sep 53
DEWEY
  John P: Phila 29 Ag 54
DEWICK
  Thomas P: Reedy Island 19
    May 63
DEWITH and Meranda P: Phila 26
  Jy 64
DEWIT/DEWITT
  Dr. P: Germantown 26 Jy 64,
    3 Ja 65
DEYN
  Daniel P: Newcastle Co 12 Ja
    58
DEYRMOND
  Tho. L: 13 Jn 65
DIAMOND/DIAMON
  Andrew P: Phila 1 Feb 70
  James P: Pa 12 Feb 61
  Mary P: N. Castle Co 15 Mar
    64
DIBBELL
  John P: Phila 25 Jy 65
DICAS
  Thomas P: Phila 30 Ap 67
DICK
  Widow P: West Nottingham 24
    Oct 54
  Archibald P: Bucks Co 26 Oct
    69; Lancaster Co 12 Feb 61
  David P: Phila 23 Oct 66
  James P: Cumberland Co 28 Oct
    62; Phila 16 Jy 67
  John P: Pa 27 Jy 58
  Mary L: 3 Oct 65. P: Cecil
    Co 13 Oct 63
  Peter P: Phila 12 Feb 61
  Dr. Samuel C: at Salem or N.
    Castle 18 Jy 65
  William L: Shippen's Town 2
    Mar 74. P: Phila 20 Jy 69
DICKE
  John P: Chester Co 12 Feb 61,
    31 Dec 61
DICKEY/DICKIE
  James P: Pa 31 Dec 61; Phila

25 Jy 65, 30 Ja 66 (2)
John P: Harris's Ferry 3 Ja
  65; Nottingham 21 Dec 58
Mary P: Phila 3 Ja 76
Peter P: Phila 3 Ja 60
Robert P: Phila 15 Mar 64
Samuel P: New-Castle Co 31
  Dec 61
DICKINSON/DICKENSON/DICKISON
Andrew L: Cumberland Co 20
  Ja 73
Cath. P: Pa 18 Mar 62
David P: Cumberland Co 27 Jy
  58
George P: Phila 8 Jy 62, 30
  Ja 66
James L: Cumberland Co 20 Ja
  73. P: York Co 31 Dec 61
John P: Pa 3 Ja 60; Phila 9
  Ag 59
Rebecca P: Phila 12 Ja 58
Richard P: Phila 12 Ja 58
Thomas P: Phila 31 Jy 60
Versell P: Sharon 8 Jy 62
William P: Phila 3 Ja 60, 10
  Ap 66, 3 May 70
DICKLEIN
Mr. P: Phila 3 Ja 76
DICKS
Alexander C: c/o James Coch-
  ran West Nottingham /?/ 22
  Ja 67
Andrew C: East Nottingham 28
  Nov 65
Jacob P: Chester Co 15 Mar 64
DICKSON; see also DIXON
Andrew P: Chester Co 26 Jy 64
Easton P: Phila 3 Ja 76
Elizabeth P: Phila 28 Oct 62,
  1 Feb 70
James P: Frederick Co 13 Oct
  63; Lancaster Co 24 Oct 54,
  13 Oct 63; Phila 2 Sep 62,
  13 Oct 63, 2 Feb 64; York Co
  12 Ja 58
John P: Pa 4 Ag 63; Phila 21
  Dec 58, 5 Ag 62, 20 Jy 69
  (Capt)
Martin P: Newcastle Co 12 Ja
  58
Thomas P: Chester Co 12 Feb
  61; Phila 4 Ap 54, 26 Oct 69
Capt. William P: Phila 4 Feb
  68
DICTION
George P: Salem Co 1 Nov 70
Joseph P: Salem Co 1 Nov 70
DIDIER
John P: Germantown 3 May 70
DIDLE
James P: Chester Co 12 Feb 61
DIGEN/DIGGEN
Edward C: 30 Jy 77. P:
  Chester Co 24 Jy 76
DIGHTON

Barney L: Lancaster Co 31
  Ja 71
Charles P: Phila 3 Ja 76
DILEPLAINE
John P: Plymouth Twp 15
  Mar 64
DILL
Mr. P: Germantown 3 May 70
James T: Amwell 17 Oct 54
Capt. John Phila 30 Oct 76
Richard P: Shamokin 7 Ap
  57
Samuel P: Phila 13 Oct 63
DILLINGHAM
Edward P: Phila 11 Sep 55,
  16 Jy 77
DILLON
James P: Phila 3 May 70
Michael P: Phila 13 Oct 63
DILLOUS
Francis P: Pa 18 Mar 62
DILWORTH
Anthony P: Lancaster Co
  13 Oct 63; Pa 21 Dec 58
James P: Birmingham,
  Chester Co 20 Jy 69;
  Chester Co 31 Jy 60
Richard P: Goshen 31 Dec
  61
DIMPSEY
James P: Phila 2 Ag 70
DIMPYS
Edward P: Pa 13 Oct 63
DINNE/DINNEE
Mons. P: Phila 19 Jy 80
John P: Phila 26 Oct 69
DINSMOR/DINSMOOR
John P: Chester Co 24 Feb
  63; Lancaster Co 13 Oct
  63
Robert P: Pa 12 Feb 61
DISHER
Capt. P: Phila 28 Ap 68
DIVEN
Hugh P: Phila 10 Ap 66
DIXON/DIXSON; see also DICK-
SON; see also FLEMING &
  DIXON
Elizabeth P: Pa 28 Oct 62;
  Phila 2 Ag 70
James P: Belfield 21 Jy 68;
  Pa 13 Oct 63
John P: Phila 5 Ag 62, 2
  Sep 62, 28 Oct 62, 30 Ap
  67, 20 Ap 69
Joseph P: New Garden 1 Nov
  53
Michael P: Phila 21 Dec 58
Richard P: Pa 2 Feb 64
Samuel C: near Chestnut
  Level 28 Nov 65. L:
  Chestnut Level 19 Dec 71
Thomas P: Pa 12 Feb 61;
  Phila 16 Jy 67
DOAG

Tho. P: Phila 3 Ja 76
DOANE
  Capt. E.   P: Phila 15 Mar 64
  Ephraim P: Phila 4 Feb 68,
    26 Oct 69, 19 Jy 80 (Capt)
DOBBIN/DOABBEN/DOBBINS
  James P: N.J. 12 Feb 61, 18
    Mar 62
  Thomas P: Phila 25 Jy 65, 19
    Ja 69
DOBBS/DOBS
  Capt. P: Phila 2 May 65
  Serjeant P: in the army 27
    Jy 58
  Richard, Esq. P: Brandywine
    26 Jy 64
  William P: Phila 3 Ja 65
DOBEL/DOBAL
  John P: Phila 1 Jy 56, 21
    Dec 58 (Capt)
DOBON
  Capt. P: Phila 26 Oct 69
DOBSON
  Joseph P: Phila 6 Sep 53, 3
    Ja 76
DOCHERTY
  Bryan P: Phila 26 Oct 69
DOCHESTER
  Capt. Ben P: Phila 1 Nov 53
DOCHETH
  John P: Phila 27 Ja 73
DOCKERY/DOCKRAY
  John P: Phila 30 May 54
  Thomas P: Pa 19 May 63, 4
    Ag 63
DODAMEED
  Ann P: L. Merion 12 Ja 58
DODD/DOD
  Jos./Joseph P: Pa 31 Dec 61;
    Phila 25 Jy 65
  Ralph P: Phila-Gaz. 27 Oct
    73
  Robert P: Phila 2 Ag 70
DODDINGTON
  Sarah P: Phila 9 May 54
DODDS/DODDES
  John P: Pa 15 Mar 64. W:
    Newark, see QUIN, John
DOFFEY
  Bridget P: Hemphill Twp 12
    Ja 58
DOGAN
  John P: Phila 30 Ja 66
DOGDEN
  Mr. P: Phila 10 Oct 65
DOHERTY/DOGHERTY
  Charles L: Peach Bottom 29
    Jy 72. P: Phila 16 Jy 72
  Daniel C: 30 Oct 66
  Henry P: Pa 12 Ja 58
  Michael C: Sadsbury 30 Oct
    66
  Richard N: near New-Castle
    4 Dec 66, 12 Feb 67
  William C: c/o John M'Gomery

West Nottingham 22 Ja 67. P:
  Pa 15 Mar 64; Sasquehannah
  24 Feb 63
DOIRON
  Paul P: Phila 2 May 65
DOLANE
  Thomas P: Pa 15 Mar 64
DOLICK
  John T: Hunterdon Co 7 May
    67
DOLLARD
  Nicholas P: Phila 11 Sep 55
DOLLES
  William P: Pa 12 Ja 58
DOLLINSON
  Joseph P: Phila 23 Oct 66
DOLUR
  Richard P: Pa 19 May 63
DOMAHON
  Richard P: Phila 3 Ja 76
DONAHOOE
  Catherine P: Phila 12 Feb 61
DONAGHY
  Huan P: Phila 1 Feb 70
DONALD/DONNALD/DONNELL/DONNAL
  Widow P: Cumberland Co 28 Oct
    62, 4 Ag 63, 13 Oct 63
  John P: Pa 12 Ja 58, 13 Ja
    63; Phila 3 Sep 61, 24 Feb
    63, 21 Jy 68, 20 Oct 68 (2),
    19 Ja 69 (2), 7 Oct 73;
    Ricklestown 1 Feb 70
  Nathaniel/Nat. P: Phila 27
    Oct 73, 30 Oct 76; Capt.
    Phila 2 Dec 58, 26 Jy 64
    (2)
  Samuel P: Wilmington 13 Oct
    63, 20 Jy 64
  Thomas L: Hopewell Twp 15 Ap
    56. P: Carlisle 3 Sep 61;
    Cumberland Co 12 Ja 58, 3
    Ja 60
  William P: Kent Co 15 Mar 64
DONALDSON/DONNALDSON; see also
  FISHER &
  & BADGER P: Phila 18 Ag 57
  Mr. P: Phila 12 Feb 61
  Dr. Alexander P: Phila 3 Ja
    65
  Arthur P: Darby 27 Jy 58, 3
    Ja 60, 31 Jy 60; Phila 2
    Feb 64
  Hugh P: Phila 2 Sep 62
  James P: Phila 28 Oct 62, 13
    Ja 63, 24 Feb 63
  John L: Cumberland Co 2 Mar
    74
  Robert P: N.J. 2 Feb 64;
    Phila 30 Ja 66
  William P: Darby 28 Nov 54,
    1 Jy 56, 2 Feb 64
DONAN
  John P: Phila 1 Nov 70
DONE
  Thomas P: Timber Creek 3 May
    70

DONNAHAN
  Catherine   P: Phila 18 Ag 57
DONNALIN
  Hans   L: Carlisle 14 May 72
DONNELLAN
  Thomas   P: Carlisle 27 Jy 58,
    13 Ja 63; Phila 21 Dec 58
DONNELY/DONNELLY/DONELY/DONNE-
    LLAY/DONNALLY
  Arthur   P: Little-Britain 26
    Jy 64
  Cornelius   P: Bedford 9 Ag 59,
    31 Dec 61
  Felix   P: Lancaster Co 15 Mar
    64
  Henry   P: York Co 28 Oct 62
  James   P: Phila 15 Mar 64,
    3 Ja 65, 3 Ja 76
  Jo.   L: 11 Ap 65
  John   P: Phila 3 Ja 76
  Michael   P: Phila 9 Ag 59
  Susanna   P: Phila 19 Ja 69
  Thomas   P: Carlisle 2 Feb 64;
    Phila 30 Ja 66
DONOUGH
  John   P: c/o Rd. Miller Abing-
    ton 2 Ag 70; Phila 10 Ap 66
DONOVAN/DONOVEN
  Francis   C: 18 Jy 65
  Jeremiah   P: Phila 12 Feb 61
  Mary   P: Phila 26 Oct 69
  Matthew   P: Phila 26 Oct 69
  Patrick   P: Phila 25 Jy 65
DOOD
  Sarah   P: Phila 20 Jy 69
DOOL
  John   P: Pa 3 Ja 60
DOOLEN
  John   L: at Martin Baar's,
    Strasburgh Twp 19 Dec 71
DOOR
  Mary   P: Phila 2 Feb 64, 26
    Jy 64
DOPERTY
  Charles   P: Phila 30 Ja 66
DORACH
  Duke   L: Lancaster Co 15 Ap
    56
DORAM
  Patrick   P: Phila 3 May 70
DORAN/DOREN/DORRON
  Andrew   P: Concord Twp 12 Ja
    58
  Dennis   P: Phila-Gaz. 27 Oct
    73
  Gayn   P: Phila 2 Ag 70
  Henry   P: Nottingham 9 Ag 59
  Peter   P: near Phila 7 Ap 57
DORMAN
  John   P: Pa 2 Sep 62
DORMONT
  John   C: at Octarara, Chester
    Co 30 Oct 66
DORNEY
  John   P: Pa 26 Jy 64

DORSEY/DORCEY
  Beates   P: Phila 27 Oct 73
  Benedict   P: Phila 12 Feb 61
  Grienbury   P: Baltimore Co 9
    Ag 59
  Patrick   T: Morris Co 1 Sep
    68
DORRELL
  John   T: near Trenton Ferry 7
    May 67
DOSCOIT
  John (Neutral)   P: Pa 27 Jy 58
DOSON
  Abraham   P: Phila 28 Oct 62
DOTSON
  Thomas   P: French Creek 1 Jy
    56
DOUBLEDAY
  Capt. J.   P: Phila 5 Ag 62
DOUBT
  Derick   P: Phila 20 Jy 69
DOUD
  John   Phila 30 Ap 77
  Michael   P: Phila 25 Jy 65
DOUDIE
  Mr.   P: York 5 Jy 80-Gaz.19
    Jy
DOUDIESKELIN
  Anna Margaret   P: Phila 10 Ap
    66
DOUDLE
  Michael   P: Sasq/uehannah/
    River 22 Nov 53
DOUDSWELL
  Thomas   P: Phila 28 Oct 62
DOUGALL/DUGGAL
  Samuel   P: N. Castle Co 13 Ja
    63
  Thomas   P: Phila 3 May 70
DOUGHERTY; see also DOHERTY
  Mr.   P: Pa 31 Jy 60
  Agnus   P: Chester Co 31 Dec 61
  Ann   Phila 30 Oct 76
  Conn.   P: Pa 21 Dec 58
  Dennis   P: Phila-Gaz. 27 Oct
    73
  Garrat   P: Fogs Manor 18 Mar
    62
  George   L: Middletown 14 May
    72.   P: Phila 3 Ja 76
  Capt. H.   P: Phila 2 Feb 64
  Henry   P: Phila 15 Mar 64
  Hugh   P: Pa 4 Ag 63 (Capt),
    27 Oct 73
  James   P: Bucks Co 2 May 65;
    N.J. 18 Mar 62; Pa 12 Feb 61,
    2 Feb 64; Phila 3 Ja 65.
    T: Hunterdon Co 10 Ag 58
  John   P: Kent Co, Md. 7 Ap 57;
    Newtown 27 Jy 58; Paxton 1
    Nov 53.   T: Hunterdon Co 10
    Ag 58
  Patrick   P: Pa 15 Mar 64;
    Phila 3 Ja 65, 30 Ap 67, 3
    Ja 76

DOUGHTY; see also DOUTY
  Mrs. P: Phila 23 Oct 66
  Edward P: Great Egg Harbour
    31 Dec 61
  Reuben T: Reading 7 May 67
DOUGLASS/DOUGLAS/DUGLESS/DUGLAS
  Adam P: Chester Co 12 Ja 58,
    9 Ag 59, 31 Dec 61; Pa 27
    Jy 58; Ukeland 18 Mar 62
  Alexander P: Phila 2 Feb 64,
    26 Jy 64
  Andrew P: Conococheague 31
    Mar 63
  Archibald P: Cumberland Co 8
    Jy 62; New-Castle Co 31 Dec
    61, 18 Mar 62
  Christian P: Phila 30 Ap 67
  Dr. Colin P: Phila 31 Dec 61
  George P: Phila 30 Oct 76.
    T: Bordentown 17 Oct 54
  Hugh P: Phila 20 Oct 68
  James P: Phila 26 Oct 69. T:
    Somerset Co 1 Sep 68
  Jane P: New-Castle Co 26 Jy
    64
  Jean N: 29 Nov 64
  John P: in the army 12 Ja 58;
    Elk River 9 Ag 59; Lancaster
    Co 18 Ag 57
  Patrick L: Carlisle /?/ 14
    May 72. P: Londonderry Twp
    27 Jy 58
  Paul Phila 31 Ja 76
  Rachel P: Phila 3 May 70
  Richard T: East Jersey 17 Oct
    54
  Robert L: Lancaster Co 15 Ap
    56
  Thomas P: Croswicks 4 Ag 63
  William L: 29 Ja 67; Leacock
    Twp 29 Jy 72. P: Gloucester
    16 Jy 72; Pa 12 Feb 61
DOULAN
  William P: Pa 31 Dec 61
DOUTY/DOUTEY; see also DOUGHTY
  Abnor/Abner P: Egg-harbour
    18 Mar 62; Gloucester Co 12
    Ja 58
DOVE
  Eleanor P: Phila 3 Ja 65
DOW/DOWE
  Ensign P: in the army 12 Ja
    58
  John N: Newport 4 Dec 66,
    cooper 12 Feb 67. P:
    Phila 10 Oct 65
  Robert P: Phila 18 Mar 62
  Capt. W. P: Phila 3 Sep 61
DOWD
  Michael P: Phila 1 Feb 70
  Terence/Terrence P: Phila
    28 Oct 62, 10 Ap 66
DOWDA
  Jupeter P: Phila 30 Ap 67
DOWDALL

Francis P: Phila 5 Feb 54,
    4 Ap 54
  Michael L: York-Town 19 Dec
    71
DOWELL
  Grace P: Phila 16 Jy 72
  Martha P: Lancaster Co 13
    Oct 63
  William P: Phila 9 Ag 59, 3
    Ja 60 (Capt), 12 Feb 61
DOWERS
  John P: Phila 3 Ja 60
  William P: Phila 4 Feb 68
DOWING
  John P: Middletown 18 Mar 62
DOWLER
  Richard C: 6 Jy 77-Gaz. 30
    Jy
DOWN
  Mary P: near Gloucester 31
    Dec 61
DOWNAM
  Joseph P: near Dover Run 7
    Ap 57
DOWNER
  Jacob L: near Lancaster 15
    Ap 56
  Jane P: Phila 13 Oct 63
  John P: Phila 9 Ag 59
DOWNEY
  Mrs. P: Pa 21 Dec 58
  Elizabeth Phila 1 May 76
  Ezekiel P: Duck Creek 18 Ag
    57
  James P: Frederick Co 31 Dec
    61; Phila 18 Mar 62, 26 Oct
    69
  John P: Pa 15 Mar 64; Phila
    4 Feb 68, 1 Feb 60
  Samuel Phila 30 Ap 77
  Susannah P: Frederick Co 31
    Dec 61; Pa 13 Oct 63
  William P: Frederick Co 31
    Dec 61
DOWNING
  Henry P: Phila 24 Feb 63
  James L: in the Valley 29 Ja
    67
  Jeffery P: Phila 3 Sep 61
  John C: near Brandywine
    Bridge, see COOK, Harman.
    P: East Caln 13 May 56
DOWNS/DOWNES
  Jonathan P: Pa 12 Ja 58, 31
    Jy 60
  Sarah P: Kent Co 2 Ag 70
DOYLE
  Barny/Bar P: Phila 11 Sep 55,
    13 May 56
  Charles P: Pa 28 Oct 62
  Edward P: Germantown 4 Feb
    68
  Fanny P: Phila 19 Jy 80
  Hannah P: Phila 26 Jy 64
  John P: Phila 30 May 54, 1

Nov 70, 3 Ja 76
Richard   P: Phila 28 Oct 62,
  15 Mar 64
Thomas   P: Pa 2 Feb 64;
  Phila 19 Jy 80
DRACE
  Morinah   P: Phila 16 Jy 72
DRAIN/DRAEN
  Hugh   P: Phila 13 May 56
  John   P: Pa 21 Dec 58
DRAKE/DREAK
  Edmond   P: N.J. 31 Mar 63
  George   P: Pa 2 Feb 64
  Jacob   P: Phila 27 Jy 58
DRAPER
  James   P: Phila 9 Ag 59, 12
  Feb 61
DRAPIER
  Rachel   P: West New Jersey
  7 Ap 57
DRASON/DRESON/DREASON
  Matthew/Mat.   P: Phila 1 Jy
  56, 21 Dec 58 (Capt), 9 Ag
  59, 3 Ja 60, 18 Mar 62
  (Capt), 10 Jy 67 (Capt), 4
  Feb 68
DREANE
  Thomas   P: Phila 19 Ja 69
DREMGOOLE
  Thomas   P: Phila 2 Feb 64
DRENNAN
  Hugh   L: c/o James Marshall
  Chestnut Level 19 Dec 71.
  P: Lancaster Co 13 Oct 63;
  Pa 13 Oct 63
DRESDALL
  William   P: Phila 16 Jy 67
DREW/DRUE
  Edward   P: Pa 4 Ag 63
  Joseph   P: Phila 3 Ja 76
  Pat.   L: Cumberland 14 May 72
DRINKER/DRINKAR; see also BELL &
  Edward   P: Phila 29 Ag 54, 6
  Jy 58
  John   P: Phila 5 Ag 62; 19 Jy
  80
DRISKEE
  Cath.   P: Phila 18 Mar 62
DRUMGOLD
  Michael   L: 13 Jn 65. N: York
  Co 29 Nov 64
DRUMMOND
  Capt.   P: New-Castle Co 8 Jy
  62
  Duncan   P: Phila 9 Ag 59;
  Whiteclay Cr 9 May 54
  William   P: Cumberland Co 23
  Oct 66
DRURY/DREWRY
  Mrs.   P: Phila 21 Dec 58
  Mr.   P: Phila 31 Jy 60
  Edward   P: Phila 1 Jy 56, 30
  Ja 66
  Sidney   P: Phila 21 Dec 58
DRYBROUGH

James   P: Phila 24 Feb 63
  Robert   P: Phila 24 Feb 63
DUANE
  James   P: Phila 25 Jy 65
DU BARREAU
  Mr.   P: Phila 1 Jy 56
DU BOIS/DUBOYS
  Abraham   P: Phila 27 Oct 73
  Jonathan   P: Bucks Co 4 Ag 63
  Lewis   P: Pilesgrove 15 Mar
  64
DUCHE
  James   P: Phila 10 Ap 66
DUCKERS
  David   P: Phila 3 Ja 76
DUCKWORTH
  Grace   P: Trenton 9 Ag 59
DUDELL
  James   P: Pa 21 Dec 58
DUDLEY
  Francis   P: N.J. 19 May 63
DUEKENNEDY
  Clarence   P: Pa 15 Mar 64
DUETRATEUR
  Monsieur   P: Phila 1 Feb 70
DUFF
  Arthur   P: Phila 16 Jy 72
  Elizabeth   P: Pa 2 Feb 64;
  Phila 19 Ja 69
  Henry   P: Phila 3 Ja 60
  James   P: Phila 2 Feb 64, 15
  Mar 64, 26 Jy 64, 27 Oct 73
  Richard   P: Phila 31 Jy 60, 12
  Feb 61
  Samuel   L: Lancaster Co 31 Ja
  71. P: Chestnut Level 28
  Oct 62
  Thomas   P: New Castle 29 Ag
  54, 31 Dec 61. W: Newport
  27 Ag 76 (Col.)
DUFFY/DUFFEY/DUFFIE
  Mr.   Phila 5 Oct 76-Gaz. 30
  Oct
  Isabella   P: Phila 30 Ja 66
  James   P: Phila 30 Ja 66, 27
  Ja 73
  John   L: Lancaster 20 Ja 73.
  P: 15 Mar 64 (2), 3 May 70,
  3 Ja 76
  Thomas John   P: Phila 30 Ap
  67
DUFFIELD
  Rev. George   P: Carlisle 26
  Jy 64; Phila 30 Oct 76
DUFTEY
  Samuel   P: 11 Sep 55
DUGAN/DOUGAN
  Michael   P: Phila 3 Ja 76
  Robert   P: Phila 31 Dec 61
  Samuel   P: Phila 26 Jy 64
  Susannah   P: Lancaster 31 Jy
  60
  Thomas   P: Roxborough 1 Jy 56
  Walter   P: Phila 1 Feb 70
DUGGABIN

Samuel N: 29 Nov 64
DUGILEAS
Mrs. P: Phila-Gaz. 27 Oct 73
DUGUID/DUGRID
John P: Pa 15 Mar 64; Phila
23 Oct 66, 16 Jy 72
Mary P: Phila 16 Jy 72
DUIEL
Denis P: Phila 31 Jy 60
DUIN
George P: Bucks Co 30 Ja 66
DUIT
Capt. P: Phila 3 May 70
DUMARE
John P: Phila 30 Ja 66
DUMMER
Elizabeth P: Pa 19 May 63
DUMVIELINES
Monsieur P: Phila 15 Mar 64
DUNAHOE/DUNNAHOE
Catharine P: Pa 3 Ja 60;
Phila 12 Ja 58
DUNALL
William C: London Britain 18
Jy 65
DUNBAR
Capt. L: 11 Ap 65
John P: Lancaster Road 7 Ap
57; Pa 13 Ja 63
Thomas P: Pa 21 Dec 58, 27
Jy 58; Phila 20 Jy 69
William T: Cranberry 17 Oct
54
DUNCAN/DUNKIN/DUNKING/DUNKEN
Capt. P: Phila 1 Feb 70
Lt. P: in the army 27 Jy 58
Alexander P: Lancaster Co 3
Sep 61, 31 Dec 61
Ann P: Phila 30 Ap 67
Benjamin P: Phila 26 Oct 69
David L: Lancaster 19 Dec 71,
merchant. P: Marcus Hook 19
Ja 69; Phila 4 Feb 68, 20
Oct 68
George P: Pa 31 Jy 60
James P: Fishing-creek 31
Dec 61; Lancaster Co 12 Ja
58, 3 Sep 61; Phila 2 Sep
62, 13 Oct 63, 3 Ja 76, 30
Ap 77
John (in army) P: Fort Pitt
26 Jy 64; Lancaster Co 1
Nov 53; Pa 3 Ja 60; Phila
6 Jy 58, 9 Ag 59, 3 Sep 61,
15 Mar 64. T: Kingston 17
Oct 54
Joseph P: Kent Co 9 Ag 59
Mary P: Phila 19 Ja 69
Nicholas P: Phila 23 Oct 66
Robert P: Pa 18 Mar 62; Phila
1 Feb 70, 3 Ja 76, 16 Jy 77
Thomas P: Phila 3 Ja 76
William P: Phila 13 Ja 63.
T: at Cranberry 21 Ja 55
DUNCK

Thomas P: Pa 27 Jy 58
DUNDASS/DUNDAS
James P: Kensington 4 Ag 63,
2 Feb 64, 26 Jy 64, 30 Ap
67, 20 Oct 68, 6 Jy 72;
Phila 21 Jy 68
Thomas P: Kensington 13 Ja
63, 24 Feb 63; Phila 2 May
65; Reading 1 Nov 70
DUNDERFIELD
William P: Phila 4 Ap 54
DUNGAN
Ganor P: Horsham 2 Feb 64
Thomas P: Phila 25 Jy 65
DUNGWORTH
Elizabeth P: Pa 28 Nov 54
DUNHAM/DONHAM
Azariah Phila 5 Ja 76-Gaz.
31 Ja
Benjamin P: Phila 31 Dec 61
Nathaniel P: Phila 31 Jy 60
DUNLAP
Allen P: Salem Co 15 Mar 64
Ann Phila 5 Oct 76-Gaz. 30
Oct
Edward P: Salem Co 15 Mar 64
Elly P: Phila 18 Mar 62
George P: Pa 31 Dec 61
Henry P: Pa 21 Dec 58; Phila
12 Ja 58
James P: Paxton 24 Feb 63;
Pa 18 Mar 62; near Phila
24 Feb 63
John L: Welsh Valley 14 May
72. P: Chester Co 24 Feb
63; Lancaster Co 2 Feb 64;
Phila 26 Jy 64, 26 Oct 69,
2 Ag 70
Samuel P: Chester Co 13 Ja
63; New-Castle Co 8 Jy 62;
Octerara 2 Sep 62
Capt. W. P: Phila 15 Mar 64
Rev. William P: Phila 4 Feb
68
DUNMAN
Jos. P: Phila 12 Ja 58
DUNN
Benjamin P: Phila 27 Oct 73
(Capt), 1 May 76
David P: Phila 2 May 65
Dennis P: Phila 3 Ja 76
Francis/Frances P: Pa 3 Ja
60, 12 Feb 61, 31 Dec 61
Capt. Henry P: Phila 23 Oct
66
James L: 3 Oct 65. P: Phila
25 Jy 65. W: Christiana
Bridge 3 Jy 76, 27 Ag 77
John L: Fort Pitt 20 Ja 73.
P: Phila 30 Ap 67, 4 Feb
68, 26 Oct 69, 3 Ja 76
Jonathan W: c/o Mr. Richard
Dowdles and James Dunn
Christiana Bridge 3 Jy 76
Jos. P: Duck Creek 18 Mar 62

Luke   P: Phila 25 Jy 65
Robert   C: West Nantmill 28
  Nov 65.   P: West Nantmill
  9 Ag 59
Thomas   P: Phila 28 Ap 68,
  26 Oct 69
DUNNER
  Elizabeth   P: Phila 30 Ap 67
DUNNING
  Thomas   P: Bucks 9 May 54
DUNPHY
  Edmond   P: Nottingham 11 Sep
  55
  Edward   T: at Robert Pearson's
  Esq. Nottingham 21 Ja 55
DUNTON
  William   Phila 30 Oct 76
DUNWODY
  William, tailor   L: 14 May 72
DUPART
  Mons.   P: Phila 2 Sep 62
DUPEE
  Susannah   P: Phila 3 Ja 60
DUPICE
  Samuel   P: Northampton Co 12
  Feb 61
DUPLESSES/DUPLESSIS
  John   P: Phila 13 May 56, 25
  Jy 65
DUPUY
  Ann   P: Phila 4 Ag 63
  Daniel   Phila 16 Jy 77
DUQUID
  John   P: Phila 1 Feb 70
DURANT
  James   Phila 5 Ja 76-Gaz. 31
  Ja
DUREL/DURELL
  Jonathan   P: Phila 5 Ag 62, 31
  Mar 63, 3 May 70
DURFEY
  Michael   P: Phila 3 May 70
DURGEN
  John /spelled Sohn in error/
  P: Phila 11 Sep 55
DURHAM
  Charles   P: Phila 25 Jy 65
  John   P: Phila 9 Ag 59, 3 Ja
  60
  Joseph   P: Phila 9 Ag 59
DURLOO, Peter, see DE NEILLY &
DURNEL
  James   P: Chester Co 18 Ag 57
DURRY
  Thomas   P: Phila 31 Dec 61
DUSDLE /?/
  William   P: Phila 31 Dec 61
DUSHANE
  Isaac   P: Newcastle Co 18 Ag
  57
DUSINBERRY
  John   T: Bethlehem 10 Ag 58
DUSSET
  Edmund   P: Phila 20 Ap 69
DUTCH

Joseph   P: Phila 26 Jy 64
DUTCH SUGAR HOUSE   P: Phila 16
  Jy 72
DUTERWHETER
  Henry   P: Germantown 19 Ja 69
DUTHILL
  Jon.   L: 13 Jn 65
DUTTON
  Isaac   P: Kensington 12 Ja 58
  Richard   C: 30 Jy 77
DUY
  Frederick   P: Germantown 12
  Feb 61
DWYER
  Cornelius   P: Phila 4 Ag 63
DYCKS
  Thomas H.   P: Phila 30 Ja 66
DYER/DYAR/DIER
  Capt. Alexander   P: Phila 16
  Jy 72, 19 Jy 80
  James   P: Kent Co 31 Dec 61
  Joseph   P: Bucks Co 19 May 63;
  Smithfield 31 Dec 61
  Mary   P: Phila 26 Jy 64
  Rebecca   P: Phila 5 Ag 56, 18
  Mar 62
  Thomas   P: Phila 8 Jy 62, 16
  Jy 67
DYMAND
  Robert   C: West Nantmill 30
  Oct 66
DYRICK
  Ralph (sailor)   P: Pa 21 Dec
  58
DYSART/DYSARD
  James   C: 30 Jy 77.   P:
  Chester Co 31 Jy 60, 30 Oct
  76, 16 Jy 77
  John   P: Chester Co 31 Jy 60
DYSTER
  James B.   P: Phila 2 Ag 70

EADISON
  Magnus   P: Phila 25 Ap 71
EADIUS
  Enoch   P: Chester Co 29 Ag 54
EADY
  John   P: Bucks Co 7 Ap 57
EAGAN
  William   T: Bordentown 4 Nov
  72
EAGER
  Mary   P: Pa 28 Oct 62
EAGLE
  Rev. John   P: Phila 23 Oct 66
EAGY
  Michael   P: Phila 9 Ag 59
EAKIN
  James   P: Nottingham 18 Ag 57
  John   P: Phila 10 Oct 65
EALY
  George   T: Wells's Ferry 17
  Oct 54
EANO
  Alexander   P: Phila 12 Feb 61

EARDLY
  Richard P: Bucks Co 31 Jy 60
EARES
  Sophia P: Phila 3 Ja 76
EARL
  John P: Pa 3 Ja 60; Phila 9
    Ag 59
  Thomas P: Burlington Co 31
    Dec 61
EARLS/EARLES
  John P: Bucks Co 12 Ja 58;
    Warminster 5 Ag 56
EARLY/EARLEY
  John P: Phila 3 Ja 76
  Stephen P: Phila 24 Feb 63
  Thomas P: Bucks Co 21 Dec 58
EARVIN
  Alexander P: Phila 2 Sep 62
EARWINE
  Jacob, merchant T: 4 Nov 72
EASHMORE
  Richard P: Phila 2 May 65
EASLEAY
  Mr. P: Phila 25 Ap 71
EASON/EASIN
  Alexander L: at the Brog
    Tavern 2 Mar 74
  Samuel P: Pa 3 Ja 60, 12 Feb
    61, 13 Oct 63; Sasquehanna
    9 Ag 59; York Co 24 Oct 54
EASTBURN
  Samuel P: Bucks Co 9 Ag 59,
    3 Sep 61
EASTINGS
  Samuel P: Phila 5 Jy 80-Gaz.
    19 Jy
EASTON
  John P: Phila 19 Ja 69
  Samuel P: Pa 15 Mar 64
EASTWICKE
  Ann P: Phila 11 Sep 55
EATON/EATTON
  Anthony P: Newcastle Co 31
    Dec 61; Pa 31 Jy 60, 12 Feb
    60
  Ezekiel P: New Castle 29 Ag
    54
  Hugh P: Phila 20 Jy 69
  Rev. Isaac P: Hopewell 21
    Dec 58
  James P: Phila 19 Ja 69
  John P: Cumberland 24 Oct
    54; N.J. 8 Jy 62 (Dr);
    Phila 27 Ja 73
  Joseph P: Whitemarsh 16 Jy 72
  Robert P: Phila 25 Jy 65
  Simon P: Phila 2 Feb 64
EATZINS
  Jon P: Phila 10 Oct 65
EAVENSON
  Richard P: Chester Co 16 Jy
    77
EBERT
  George L: 3 Oct 65
ECCLES/ECKLESS

George P: Phila 1 Jy 56
  James P: Lancaster 9 Ag 59,
    31 Dec 61; Pa 3 Ja 60
ECKERLING
  Samuel P: Germantown 20 Jy
    69
ECKOFF
  David P: Newlington 11 Sep
    55
ECKSTEIN/ECKSTEINE
  _____(joiner) P: Phila 28
    Nov 54
  Dr. Gideon L: 13 Jn 65
ECROYD
  Jos./Joseph P: Phila 18 Mar
    62, 25 Jy 65
ECTOR
  Joseph P: Pa 2 Feb 64; Phila
    3 Ja 65
EDAMS
  James P: Bucks Co 30 Ja 66
EDDY
  George, 18th Regt. P: Phila
    20 Jy 69, 2 Ag 70
  James P: Phila 28 Nov 54, 18
    Feb 55, 6 Jy 58
  Joseph P: Chester Co 31 Jy
    60; Vincent Twp 4 Ag 63
  William P: Oxford,Phila Co
    28 Ap 68
EDEN
  John, Esq. P: Phila 12 Feb 61
EDES
  Josiah P: Phila 5 Jy 80-Gaz.
    19 Jy
EDEY
  Wm. L: 13 Jn 65
EDGAR/EDGER
  Charles P: Phila 27 Jy 58,
    21 Dec 58
  Elizabeth P: Darby 18 Ag 57
  James P: Phila 27 Ja 73
  Martha P: Phila 3 Ja 76
  Mary C: Charles Town 28 Nov
    65
  William P: York Co 13 Oct 63
EDINGTON
  Mr. P: Phila 18 Mar 62
EDLESON
  James P: Phila 3 Ja 60
EDLEY
  Thomas P: Phila 27 Ja 73
EDMISTON/EDMESTON/EDMINSON
  David P: Apoquimi012y 24 Feb
    63. T: near Salem 31 Ja 71
  Robert P: Pa 4 Ag 63; Phila
    27 Ja 73
  Samuel P: Phila 27 Dec 53
  Major William P: Phila-Gaz.
    27 Oct 73
  Thomas P: Forks of Brandiwine
    9 Ag 59
  William P: Bethlehem 21 Jy
    68; Phila 3 Sep 61, 3 Ja 76
EDREY

Sally P: Phila 3 Ja 76
EDWARD/EDWARDS; see also AD-
  WARD
Capt. P: Phila 4 Ag 63
Mrs. P: Phila 20 Oct 68
Mr. P: Phila 9 Ag 59
Abraham P: Confederacy 19
  Jy 80
Arthur P: Phila 2 Feb 64
Catherine P: Phila-Gaz. 27
  Oct 73
David P: Phila 15 Mar 64,
  27 Ja 73
Edith P: Phila 19 Ja 69
Edward P: Lancaster 12 Feb
  61
Enoch P: Phila 19 Ja 69, 16
  Jy 72
Evan Phila 24 Jy 76
Henry P: /Phila?/ 2 Ag 70
John P: in the army 12 Ja
  58 (2); Lancaster Co 12 Ja
  58
Margaret P: Phila 31 Mar 63
Marshall P: Byberry 20 Jy 69
Rev. Morgan P: Phila 23 Oct
  66, 26 Oct 69
Susannah P: Bucks 9 May 54
Tab. P: Phila 8 Jy 62
Thomas P: Darby 1 Jy 56;
  Middletown, B.C. 20 Ap 69
William L: York Co 20 Ja 73.
  P: in the army 12 Ja 58;
  Phila 12 Jy 72
EESLER
Richard P: Phila 1 Feb 70
EGAN/EGON
John P: Phila 2 May 65
William P: Bordentown 2 Ag
  70
EGAR/EGGER/EGGAR
Andrew P: N. Castle Co 13
  Ja 63
Charles P: Phila 31 Jy 60
James P: Phila 9 Ag 59
Rhody P: Bound-brook 7 Ap
  57
Thomas P: Phila 31 Mar 63
EGDON
Capt. P: Phila 20 Oct 68
EGE
Michael P: Phila 3 Ja 60
EHINGUER
Daniel P: Phila 28 Ap 68
EHMANN
Geo. P: 12 miles from Phila
  5 Feb 54
EHRENZELLER
Jacob P: Phila 5 Ag 62
EIDS
Joseph P: Phila 9 Ag 59
EIGHTS
Thomas P: Phila 3 Ja 65
EILAR
Philip P: Phila 1 Nov 70

EKEN
Alexander P: Lancaster Co 2
  Feb 64
EKMAN
Andrias P: Phila 12 Feb 61
ELBERSON
Mary P: Phila 25 Jy 65
Nicholas P: Phila 24 Feb 63
William P: Phila 9 Ag 59
ELBORN
Reuben P: Duck Creek 21 Jy
  68
ELDER
Andrew P: Pa 18 Mar 62;
  Phila 27 Jy 58, 31 Jy 60
James P: Pa 18 Mar 62; Phila
  5 Ag 62, 3 Ja 65, 3 Ja 76
Rev. John P: Pa 3 Ja 60
Margaret P: Phila 12 Ja 58,
  31 Jy 60
ELDRIDGE
Ezekiel P: Cape May 11 Sep
  55
Joshua P: Phila 28 Ap 68
ELGAN
Ezra P: Phila 21 Dec 58
ELGAR/ELGER
Ervara P: Phila 8 Jy 62
Ezra P: Phila 9 Ag 59, 3 Ja
  60
ELIZABETH
Miss P: Phila 25 Ap 71
ELKIN
Isabella P: Shippack 19 May
  63
ELLET
John P: Pequea 2 Ag 70
Peter P: Phila 25 Jy 65
Thomas P: Phila 27 Ja 73
ELLICOT/ELLICOTT
Joseph P: Bucks Co 21 Dec 58,
  31 Jy 60, 4 Feb 68, 21 Jy
  68, 20 Oct 68, 26 Oct 69, 1
  Nov 70, 27 Ja 73; Solebury
  28 Nov 54
Robert L: c/o Hanse Morrison
  York Co 19 Dec 71
ELLIOT/ELLIOTT
Andrew P: Phila 6 Jy 58
Barbary P: Phila 7 Ap 57
Charles C: Oxford Twp,
  Chester Co 30 Oct 66; see
  also GRAHAM, James
Francis P: Phila 2 May 65
George P: Phila-Gaz. 27 Oct
  73
James P: Pa 2 Feb 64, 27 Oct
  73
John P: Pequea 18 Feb 55, 8
  Jy 62; Phila 6 Jy 58, 3 Ja
  60, 3 Sep 61; Whitemarsh
  18 Ag 57
Joseph P: Bucks Co 2 Ag 70,
  16 Jy 72; Pa 28 Oct 62;
  Phila 27 Oct 73

Mary   P: Phila 8 Jy 62, 3 Ja
   76
Obadiah   P: Chester Co 19 May
   63
Samuel   P: Pa 18 Mar 62
Thomas   P: Phila-Gaz. 27 Oct
   73
William   C: 30 Jy 77. P: Lan-
   caster Co 28 Nov 54; Pa 12
   Feb 61; Phila 3 May 70
ELLIS
   Alexander   P: Phila 8 Jy 62
   Amos   P: Berks Co 26 Jy 64
   Eleanor   P: Phila 12 Ja 58
   George, soldier   P: prob. in
      Pittsburgh 15 Mar 64
   James   Phila 5 Jan 76, 31 Ja
   John   P: Phila 20 Ap 69
   Joseph   P: Gloucester 2 May
      65; Haddonfield 9 Ag 59;
      N.J. 3 Ja 60 (Capt). T:
      6 Dec 64 (Capt)
   Joshua   P: Phila 25 Ap 71
   Mark   T: Allentown 15 Mar 64
   Martha   T: Trenton 17 Oct 54
   Mary   P: Phila 6 Jy 58, 27 Jy
      58, 3 Sep 61, 25 Jy 65
   Richard   P: Phila 4 Ag 63
   Robert   P: Phila 19 Ja 69
   Sarah   P: Kingsess 7 Ap 57
   Capt. Thomas   P: Phila 1 Nov
      53
   William   P: Cumberland Co 31
      Jy 60; Phila 11 Jy 54, 30
      Ja 66
ELLISON/ELLIOSON/ELISON
   Alexander   L: Blue Rocks,
      Baltimore Co 29 Jy 72
   David/Dav.   C: in Newark, N.
      Castle Co 28 Nov 65
      (weaver). L: Muddy Run 31
      Ja 71. P: Phila 26 Oct 69
   James   P: Wilmington 29 Ag 54
   John   P: Pa 5 Ag 62
   Margaret   P: Wilmington 11
      Sep 55
   Simon   Phila 31 Ja 76
   Thomas   P: Phila 12 Feb 61
   Will.   P: Phila 1 Nov 53
ELLITS
   Isabella   P: Phila 15 Mar 64
ELLSON
   William   C: Chester Co 18 Jy
      65
ELLWOOD
   William   L: Cumberland Co 2
      Mar 74
ELMER
   Dr. Jonathan   Cohansey 5 Jy
      76-Gaz. 24 Jy
ELMS/ELMES
   Elliott   P: Phila 2 Sep 62
   Stephen   P: Phila 4 Feb 68,
      19 Ja 69 (attorney)
ELMSLIE

Alexander   P: Phila 16 Jy 67
John   P: Phila 8 Jy 62
ELSCON
   David   P: Phila 3 Ja 60
ELSTRE
   Thomas   T: Trenton 6 Dec 64
ELTON
   Elizabeth   Phila 1 May 76
   John   P: Phila 19 May 63
   William   P: Phila 8 Ag 62
ELVES
   Henry   P: Phila 27 Jy 58; near
      Phila 3 Ja 60 (Capt)
ELWELL
   John   P: Pilesgrove 31 Jy 60
ELY
   George   P: Bucks Co 3 Ja 60,
      31 Dec 61, 13 Ja 63; Phila
      28 Oct 62
   Hugh   P: Bucks Co 7 Ap 57
EMBURY
   Peter   P: Phila 30 Ap 67
EMERSON/EMBERSON; see also
   AMERSON
   James   P: Phila 30 Ap 67, 16
      Jy 72
   Thomas   P: Phila 19 Jy 80
EMLEN
   Caleb   P: Phila 19 Jy 80
   Joseph   P: Phila 25 Ap 71
   Samuel   P: Phila 31 Mar 63,
      30 Oct 76
EMMIT/EMMITT/EMIT
   Abraham   N: near Newark 4 Dec
      66, 12 Feb 67; (Capt). P:
      New-London 31 Jy 60
   Ann   P: Phila 2 May 65
EMMONDS
   John   T: Hunterdon Co 17 Oct
      54
EMOCK
   John   P: Pa 27 Jy 58
EMORY
   Will. W.   P: /Phila?7 2 Ag 70
ENDERSBY/ENDERSBEY
   Thomas   P: Pa 12 Feb 61, 18
      Mar 62
ENDON
   Mr.   P: Phila 3 Ja 76
ENDT/ENT
   D.   P: Germantown 30 May 54
   Daniel   P: Germantown 11 Sep
      55, 1 Feb 70
   John Theoblt   P: Germantown
      26 Jy 53
ENGLAND
   Daniel   P: Phila 11 Sep 55
   Jane   P: Phila 20 Oct 68, 19
      Ja 69
   Samuel   C: Nottingham 28 Nov
      65. P: Chester Co 31 Dec 61
ENGLE
   Anores   P: Phila 30 Ap 67
   Elizabeth   P: Phila 23 Oct 66
   John   P: Phila 23 Oct 66

Paul   P: Germantown 21 Dec 58
ENGLEFORD
  Mrs.   P: Phila 21 Dec 58
ENGLER
  Adam   P: Phila 31 Dec 61
  Jacob   P: Bussel Town 21 Dec
    58
ENGLES/ENGLIS
  Deborah   P: Pennypack 21 Dec
    58
  Thomas   P: Phila 18 Mar 62
ENGLISH/INGLISH
  Miss   P: Phila 1 Feb 70
  Mrs.   P: Phila 29 Ag 54, 24
    Oct 54
  David   N: c/o John Thompson
    Christian Bridge 4 Dec 66.
    P: New Castle Co 12 Feb 61;
    Phila 16 Jy 72
  Francis   P: Phila 12 Ja 58
  Israel   P: Phila 21 Dec 58
  James   L: Cumberland Co 2 Mar
    77
  John (soldier)   P: 21 Dec 58
    (2); Phila 20 Jy 67
  Mary   P: Phila 5 Ag 62
  Rebecca   P: Phila 1 Jy 56
  Samuel   P: near Durham Furnace
    13 Oct 66; Pa 15 Mar 64;
    Phila 23 Oct 66
  Thomas   P: Phila 10 Oct 65
ENGRAM
  Matthew   P: Germantown 31 Jy
    60
ENNIS/ENNOS
  Ann   P: Phila 19 Ja 69, 20
    Ap 69
  Francis   P: Phila 3 May 70
  George   P: Phila 27 Oct 73
  Sarah   P: Phila 15 Mar 64
ENOCHS
  David   P: Phila 3 Ja 76
  Joseph   T: Bristol 17 Oct 54
ENSLOW
  Esther   P: Phila 20 Oct 68
ENT, see ENDT
ENTHERS
  John   P: Phila 26 Oct 69
EOLOR
  Philip   P: Phila 8 Jy 62
EPPRECH
  Saul   L: 11 Ap 65
ERCLES
  John   P: Wilmington 11 Sep 55
ERIS
  Widow   P: Phila 9 Ag 59
ERNST
  Frederick   P: Phila 31 Dec 61,
    16 Jy 67
  George   P: Yorktown 8 Jy 62
ERROMS
  Richard   P: Phila 3 Ja 76
ERSCOTT
  Capt. William   P: Phila 3 Sep
    61

ERSKIN
  Capt. Thomas   P: /Phila?/
    2 Ag 70
  William   P: Phila 2 May 65
ERVEN/ERVAN; see also EARVIN
  John   P: N.J. 19 May 63
  William   P: Phila 31 Dec 61
ERWIN/ERWING; see also EARWINE
  Anne   P: Pa 12 Ja 58
  Archibald   P: Phila 12 Ja 58
  David   P: Pa 12 Ja 58; Phila
    2 Feb 64, 27 Oct 73
  Edward   L: Antrim Twp, Cum-
    berland Co 19 Dec 71.   P:
    N.J. 18 Mar 62; West N.J. 21
    Dec 58
  Elizabeth   P: Phila 24 Feb 63
  James   P: Phila 9 Ag 59, 8 Jy
    62, 2 Ag 70, 3 Ja 76
  John   P: Bucks Co 20 Oct 68;
    Chester Co 8 Jy 62; Phila
    18 Mar 62, 10 Oct 65, 26
    Oct 69
  Jos.   P: Pa 28 Oct 62
  Matthew   P: Phila 3 Ja 76
  Robert   P: Phila 25 Jy 65
  Samuel   P: Carlisle 3 Sep 61
  Sophia   P: Donegall 2 Feb 64
  Thomas   P: Phila 26 Oct 69
ESAFT
  James   P: Salem 13 Oct 63
ESPY
  Samuel   P: Lancaster Co 13
    Oct 63
  Thomas   P: Phila 27 Ja 73
ESTAUGH
  John   P: Haddonfield 4 Ag 63
ESTILL
  John   T: Freehold 15 Jy 56
ETHERINGTON
  Capt. George   P: /Phila?/ 2
    Ag 70
  Lt. Thomas   P: Phila 30 Ap 67
ETHERY
  Jane   P: Phila-Gaz. 27 Oct 73
ETTER
  Daniel   P: Phila 5 Ag 62
ETWILL
  William   P: Phila 10 Ap 66
EUELS
  Ja.   L: Shearman,s Valley 31
    Ja 71
EUEN
  Thomas   C: West Nottingham 28
    Nov 65
EUSTACE/EUSTICE
  Charles   P: Phila 4 Ag 63, 13
    Oct 63
  Shepherd   P: Pa 12 Ja 58
  Thomas   P: Easton 1 Jy 56;
    Phila 18 Feb 55
EVANS/EVENS
  Miss   P: Phila 25 Jy 65
  Mrs.   P: Phila 4 Ag 63, 3 Ja
    65

Mr. P: Phila 13 Oct 63
Ann P: Phila 3 Ja 65, 25 Jy
  65
Caleb P: Kensington 5 Ag 62;
  Phila 24 Oct 54
Charles P: Newcastle Co 31
  Dec 61
Daniel P: Wall Kill 1 Feb 70
Edward P: Phila 24 Feb 63,
  15 Mar 64
Evan P: Phila 13 Oct 63;
  Radnor 24 Oct 54
James P: Pequea 24 Feb 63
Jane P: Phila-Gaz. 27 Oct 73
John L: Charles Town 15 Ap
  56. P: Carnarvan Twp 4 Feb
  88; Charles Town 5 Ag 56;
  Chester Co 1 Jy 56; Lan-
  caster Co 18 Mar 62; Phila
  7 Ap 57, 12 Feb 61, 25 Ap
  71 (Capt, 18th Regt)
Margaret C: London Britain
  18 Jy 65
Martin P: Duck Creek 26 Oct
  69
Mary P: Phila 11 Sep 55
Nathan C: 30 Jy 77
Owen P: Phila 27 Ja 73
Peter P: Phila Co 2 Sep 62
Robert P: Cecil Co 9 Ag 59
Rowland P: N. Providence 26
  Oct 69
Samuel P: Chester Co 27 Jy
  58, 31 Dec 61, 2 Sep 62;
  Phila 31 Jy 60, 18 Mar 62,
  3 Ja 65, 4 Feb 68
Sidney P: Phila 26 Oct 69
Susannah P: Whitemarsh 2
  Feb 64
Thomas P: Phila 18 Mar 62,
  25 Jy 65
William P: Fort Pitt 26 Jy
  64 (collar-maker in army);
  Marsh Creek 26 Oct 69;
  Phila 6 Jy 58, 27 Jy 58, 28
  Ap 68; Tredyffryn 11 Sep 55
EVART
  John P: Pa 18 Mar 62; Phila
  30 Ja 66
EVE
  Capt. P: Phila 6 Jy 58
  Benjamin P: Phila 16 Jy 67
  Oswell/Oswald P: Phila 30
  May 54, 19 Ja 69, 26 Oct 69
  Oswell, Sr. Phila 31 Ja 76
EVEN
  William T: 10 Ag 58
EVES
  John C: Kennet 22 Ja 67. P:
  Phila 28 Oct 62
EVILMAN
  William T: near Allentown 21
  Ja 55
EVING
  Walter P: Phila 25 Jy 65

EVY
  Christeen P: Mill Creek 11
  Jy 54
EWALD
  Charles P: Phila 13 Ja 63
EWART
  Frances or Elizabeth L:
  Shearman's Valley 2 Mar 74
EWEN/EWIN
  Elizabeth P: Warwick 2 Ag 70
  Samuel P: Durham Furnace 13
  Oct 63
EWING/EWINGS
  Flavell P: W. Jersey 12 Ja 58
  James Darby 1 May 76; Pa 12
  Ja 58; Phila 9 Ag 59
  John P: Phila 10 Ap 66
  Capt. Joseph P: Phila 12 Ja
  58
  Peter P: Phila 31 Jy 60
  Robert P: Pa 2 Feb 64
  Susanna P: East Nottingham
  Chester Co 25 Ap 71
  Thomas P: Cecil Co 13 Oct
  63; 13 Oct 63
  Walter P: Jersey 30 Ap 67
  William P: Cape May 13 Oct
  63; Duck Creek 12 Ja 58,
  9 Ag 59; Lancaster Co 18
  Ag 57
EYERLAND
  William P: Lancaster Co 24
  Oct 54
EYRE
  Isaac P: Phila 27 Ja 73
EYRES/EYERS; see also AYRES
  Richard P: Phila 31 Dec 61,
  18 Mar 62, 15 Mar 64

FACTER
  Nicholas T: Grigs Town 15 Jy
  56
FACY
  John P: Phila 18 Mar 62
FAESCH
  Lt. P: Phila 7 Ap 57
  Major John Rudolph P: in the
  army 12 Ja 58
FAGAN/FAGIN/FEAGAN/FEGAN; see
  also FIEGEN
  Arthur P: Phila 31 Dec 61, 8
  Jy 62, 19 Ja 69
  Barnaby/Barney P: Phila 28
  Nov 54, 30 Ap 67, 1 Nov 70
  Charles P: Chester Co 13 Ja
  63
  Henry P: Phila 9 Ag 59
  John P: Glascow Forge 2 Feb
  64; Phila 4 Feb 68, 3 Ja 76
  Pat./Patrick P: Pennypack 24
  Feb 63, 25 Jy 65, 4 Feb 68
FAHY
  Nathaniel P: Phila 20 Ap 69
  Patrick P: Phila 26 Oct 69

FAILS/?/
  John   P: Phila 13 Oct 63
FAIMS
  John   P: Phila 2 Feb 64
FAINSWORTH
  Thomas   P: Phila 4 Ag 63
FAIQUE
  John   P: N. Castle Co 12 Ja
  58
FAIRBANKS
  John   P: Phila 15 Mar 64
FAIRFAX
  Col.   P: Phila 20 Jy 69
  Hon. George, Esq.   P: Phila
  /?/ 21 Jy 68
FAIRIS
  William   C: Oxford Twp 22 Ja
  67
FAIRRY
  James   P: Phila 27 Ja 73
FAKENDOR
  John   P: Pennsylvania 16 Jy
  72
FALCON
  Peter   P: Phila 11 Sep 55
FALCONER; see also FALKNER
  Gilbert   P: Phila 1 Jy 56
  James   P: Phila 3 Ja 65, 2
  May 65
  Peter   P: Phila 5 Ag 62
  Capt. William   P: Phila 26 Jy
  64
FALDER
  Thomas   P: Phila 31 Jy 60
FALENS
  Charles   P: Chester Co 12 Feb
  61
FALKNER/FAULKNER/FALCNOR/
  FAUGHNER; see also FALCONER,
  and CRAIG & FALKNER
  Capt. (of the St. George)   P:
  Phila 7 Ap 57
  Abigail   P: Phila 1 Nov 70
  Heckless   P: Gloucester 13 Ja
  63
  John   P: 21 Dec 58 (soldier);
  Phila 20 Ap 69
  Capt. Nat.   P: Phila 24 Feb 63
  Peter   P: Phila 27 Jy 58
  Capt. W.   P: Phila 5 Ag 62
  William   P: Phila 6 Jy 58, 27
  Jy 58, 2 May 65
FALLAHE
  Patrick   P: Phila 25 Ap 71
FALLOWS
  Job   P: Spencegrove Forge 2
  Ag 70
FALLS
  Andrew   P: Cross Roads 18 Mar
  62
  James   C: Cross Roads 18 Jy
  65.   P: Pa 12 Feb 61, 2 Feb
  64
FANCOALTS
  Samuel, soldier   P: prob. in

Pittsburgh 15 Mar 64
FANN
  Rechel   L: 31 Ja 71
FANNING
  Jeffery   P: Pa 2 Feb 64
  John   Phila 30 Oct 76
  Joshua   Phila 30 Oct 76
FANNS
  Henry   Phila 5 Ap 76-Gaz. 1
  May
FARA
  Oliver   P: Chester Co 4 Ag
  63
FARD /or FORD?/
  Edward   L: Bedford Co, Vir-
  ginia 19 Dec 71
FARES
  Barakeris   P: Willis Town 12
  Feb 61
FARIES/FAIRIES
  Francis   P: Phila 1 Feb 70
  James   P: Bucks Co 24 Feb 63
  John   P: Phila 24 Feb 63, 3
  Ja 65, 19 May 63, 27 Oct
  73
FARIS/FARRIS; see also FAIRIS
  Alex   P: New Castle Co 12 Ja
  58
  James   P: New Castle Co 15
  Mar 64
  John   P: Phila 28 Oct 62
FARKER
  Ann   P: Phila 31 Dec 61
FARLEY/FARLY
  Henry   P: Phila 18 Feb 55,
  11 Sep 55
  John   L: Sadsbury Twp 29 Jy
  72
  Joseph   P: Phila 10 Ap 66
FARLO
  William   P: Kennet Twp 25 Jy
  65
FARMER/FARMAR
  Jos.   P: Phila 31 Dec 61
  Martha   P: Phila 8 Jy 62
  Mary   P: Phila 31 Jy 60
  Thomas   P: Phila 9 Ag 59, 18
  Mar 62
FARNSWORTH
  Samuel   T: Bordentown 10 Ag
  58
FARQUHAR
  Adam   P: Mount Holly 18 Feb
  55
  John, Jr.   P: Phila 23 Oct 66
FARQUHARSON
  Lewis   P: Phila-Gaz. 3 Ja 76
FARR/FAAR/FAR
  John   P: Pa 24 Feb 63; Phila
  4 Ag 63, 23 Oct 66, 31 Ja
  76
  Thomas   P: N.J. 31 Jy 60
FARRAN
  Timothy   P: Pa 24 Feb 63
FARRANT

John   C: Nantmill Twp, Chest-
er Co 28 Nov 65
FARRELL/FARREL/FERRELL/FERRALL/
FERRILL
Elizabeth   P: Chester Co 12
Feb 61
Henry   P: Marcus Hook 9 Ag
59
John   P: Phila 2 Feb 64
Dr. M.   P: Phila 15 Mar 64
Margaret   P: Frankford 20 Ap
69
Mary   P: Phila 2 Ag 70
Patrick/Pat.   P: Phila 28 Nov
54, 31 Jy 60, 5 Ag 62, 27
Ja 73 (or Andrew)
Roger   P: Phila 3 Sep 61
William   P: Phila 12 Feb 61
FARRINGTON
Mary   P: Phila 12 Ja 58
FARTA
Catherine   P: Phila 7 Ap 57
FASH
Capt.   P: Phila 2 Ag 70
FASSEP
John   P: Phila 20 Jy 69
FASSET
Philip   P: Phila 11 Sep 55
FATHAON
David   P: Phila 31 Dec 61
FAUKINGTON
Joseph   P: Great Valley 24
Oct 54
FAULKS
John   P: Chester Co 29 Ag 54
FAUNS
Capt.   Phila 5 Oct 76-Gaz.
30 Oct
FAVIERES
Capt. Samuel   P: Phila 13 Ja
63, 31 Mar 63
FAWCETT/FAWSET
Thomas   C: near Kennet Meet-
inghouse 30 Oct 66; see also
WILSON, Jane.   P: Chester
Co 15 Mar 64; Phila 27 Oct
73
FAWKES
John   P: New Town, Chester Co
1 Jy 56
FAY
Matthew   P: Phila-Gaz. 3 Ja
76
FAYER
John   P: Phila 24 Oct 54
FEACHAM
Hannah   P: Reading 24 Feb 63
FEALIS
Jn.   L: 11 Ap 65
FEAR
George   P: Pa 19 May 63
FEARIS/FEAYRES
Bernard   Phila 31 Ja 76
David   P: Wilmington 1 Jy 56
Gideon   P: Phila 27 Dec 53,

13 Oct 63
Hugh   P: Pequea 18 Feb 55
Robert   P: Phila 1 Nov 53,
27 Dec 53
Samuel   P: Pa 13 Oct 63
Tho.   P: Phila 27 Dec 53
Tim.   P: Phila 15 Mar 64
FEARLES
Bernard   Phila 5 Ap 77-Gaz.
30 Ap
FEARLY
Richard   T: Newtown 17 Oct
54
FEARS
John   L: Carlisle 29 Jy 72
FEASTER
John   P: Bucks Co 15 Mar 64
FEENAN
William   P: Phila 3 Ja 65
FEETS
Hezekiah   P: Phila 18 Mar 62,
3 Ja 65
FEGHMAN
Valentine   P: Pa 12 Feb 61
FEIREBACH
Daniel   P: Phila 25 Ap 71
FEISGER
John George   L: 13 Jn 65
FELL
James   P: Phila 27 Ja 73
(Capt), 3 Ja 76
Capt. Thomas   P: Phila 26 Jy
64, 27 Oct 73, 1 May 76
FELLEN
Mary   P: Phila 11 Sep 55
FELLERY
Stephen   P: Phila 20 Ap 69
FELLOWS
Job   P: Grove Forge-Gaz. 27
Oct 73; Pennsgrove 16 Jy
62
FELON
William   P: Phila 11 Sep 55
FELSON
Davison   C: East Fallowfield
22 Ja 67
William   P: Chester Co 15 Mar
64
FELTMAN
Nancy   P: Phila 5 Jy 80-Gaz.
19 Jy
FENDER
Dr.   P: Phila 11 Sep 55
FENNELLY
Daniel   P: Cumberland Co 2
Ag 70
FENNER
Henry   P: Phila 27 Ja 73, 30
Oct 76
FENNING/FENING
John   Phila 24 Jy 76
Joshua   P: Phila 27 Oct 73,
24 Jy 76
FENNYMORE
Joyce   P: Phila 11 Sep 55

FENTHAM
Wm. W. P: Phila 18 Mar 62,
  2 Sep 62
FENTON
Silvester N: 29 Nov 64. P:
  Phila 28 Ap 68
William P: Phila-Gaz. 3 Ja
  76
FENWICK
John P: Phila 24 Feb 63
FERER
Judey P: Phila 31 Jy 60
FERGUS/FIRGUS
& M'LEANS P: Phila 27 Ja 73
Hugh L: 11 Ap 65. P: Lan-
  caster Co 9 Ag 59, 3 Sep 61;
  Pa 31 Dec 61, 26 Jy 64, 23
  Oct 66
John P: Carlisle 8 Jy 62
FERGUSON/FORGUSON/FARGUSON/FER-
GISON
Capt. of the 70th Regt. P:
  Phila 27 Ja 73
Mrs. P: Phila 3 Sep 61
Alexander P: Jerseys 11 Sep
  55; Mount-holly 6 Sep 53
Daniel P: Phila 3 Ja 65
Elizabeth P: Phila-Gaz. 27
  Oct 73
Henry P: Bucks Co 30 Ja 66;
  Pa 15 Mar 64
Hugh P: Bucks 1 Nov 53; Pa
  12 Ja 58, 18 Mar 62
James P: Carlisle 31 Jy 60
Jean P: Phila 11 Sep 55
John P: Hudson's River 9 Ag
  59; Pa 13 Oct 63; Phila 18
  Feb 55, 9 Ag 59 (2), 2 May
  65, 26 Oct 69
Joseph Phila 5 Ja 76-Gaz. 31
  Ja
Margaret P: Bucks Co 31 Jy 60
Mary P: Bucks Co 9 Ag 59
Matthew C: 30 Jy 77. P:
  Phila 4 Feb 68; Whiteclay
  Creek 1 Feb 70
Michael P: East Jersey 9 Ag
  59; Pa 3 Ja 60
Patrick/Pat. P: Phila 11 Sep
  55, 1 Jy 56, 18 Ag 57, 27
  Jy 58, 21 Dec 58, 28 Oct 62
Richard P: Phila 9 Ag 59
Robert P: Chester Co 13 Oct
  63; Phila 18 Feb 55, 21 Dec
  58, 19 Ja 69, 26 Oct 69
Samuel P: Phila 21 Dec 58, 2
  May 65, 25 Jy 65
William P: Allentown 19 May
  63; Brandywine 11 Sep 55;
  Forks of Brandywine 8 Jy 62;
  Lancaster Co 2 Feb 63; Nant-
  mil Town 7 Ap 57
FERNAND
Manuel P: Phila 21 Jy 68
FERNLEY

George P: Bucks 11 Sep 55
FERREAR
William P: Chester Co 4 Ap
  54
FERREN
Francis P: Phila 26 Jy 64
FERRIS/FERRISS/FERICE; see
  also FEARIS
Benjamin P: Wilmington 9 Ag
  59, 15 Mar 64
David P: Wilmington 31 Jy
  60, 18 Mar 62
Gideon P: Phila 12 Ja 58
James L: Cumberland Co 2 Mar
  74
Robert P: Phila 27 Jy 58
Zech./Zacharias P: Wilming-
  ton 6 Sep 53, 18 Ag 57
FERRY
Charles P: Phila 30 Ja 66
FERSON
Jean P: Duck Creek 1 Jy 56
William P: Fellowfield 28
  Nov 54
FERVIES
David P: Pa 24 Feb 63
FETRICE
John P: Phila 31 Mar 63
William P: Phila 31 Mar 63
FETSAM
John P: Phila - Gaz. 3 Ja
  76
FEVER
Hans Martin P: Conesto 12
  Ja 58
FEW
Joseph P: Chester Co 12 Feb
  61; Forks of Brandiwine
  27 Jy 58
FIBSON
William P: Phila 30 Ja 66
FIDDIS
John T: Cohansey 15 Mar 64
Robert P: Phila 28 Oct 62
FIEGEN
Anna M. P: Lancaster Co 15
  Mar 64
FIELD
Lt. in the army P: 21 Dec
  58
James T: near Allens Town 15
  Jy 56
John P: Phila 11 Sep 55, 15
  Mar 64
Joseph P: Bucks 18 Feb 55
Robert P: Phila 27 Jy 58
FIELDING
Elizabeth P: Phila 28 Nov 54
George P: Phila 11 Sep 55,
  13 May 56, 12 Ja 58
Mary Phila 5 Jy 76-Gaz. 24
  Jy
FIFF
William, soldier P: prob. in
  Pittsburgh 15 Mar 64

FIGGIM
  Andrew   P: Phila 1 Feb 70
FILE
  John   P: Marcus Hook 9 Ag 59
FILKIN
  Cat.   P: Phila 5 Ag 62
FILLERY
  Stephen   P: Phila 1 Feb 70
FILMORE
  Jacob   P: Phila 30 Ap 67
FILSON/FILLSON
  Robert   P: Winchester 31 Dec
    61
  William   P: Chester Co 3 Sep
    61
FINCH
  Mary   P: Lancaster 9 May 54
FINLEY/FINLAY
  James   C: c/o Rev. John Col-
    bertson 22 Ja 67. P: Cecil
    Co 30 Ja 66 (Rev); Pa 24
    Feb 63
  John   C: East Nottingham,
    (Rev); see MURPHEW, Laur-
    ence. P: Cumberland Co 18
    Ag 57; Pa 27 Jy 58; Phila
    16 Jy 72
  Samuel   P: West Nottingham 9
    Ag 59
FINN
  Daniel   P: near Dover 3 Sep 61
FINNAGIN
  Patrick   P: Phila-Gaz. 27 Oct
    73
FINNEY
  Lt. Archibald   P: Whiteclay
    Creek 18 Mar 62
  Daniel   P: Dover 31 Jy 60;
    Kent Co 9 Ag 59
  David   P: Newcastle 24 Oct
    54, 1 Jy 56, 27 Jy 58. W:
    New-Castle; see JOHNSTON,
    William
  James   L: Cumberland Co 20 Ja
    73. P: Pa 28 Oct 62; Phila
    2 Dec 58
  John   P: Newcastle 18 Feb 55,
    3 Ja 60 (Dr); near Phila
    31 Jy 60
  Robert   L: c/o Rev. Robert
    Cooper Cumberland Co 29 Jy
    72. P: New Castle 29 Ag 54
FIRELING
  Philip   P: Phila 20 Oct 68
FIRST
  Ann   P: Phila 2 Sep 62, 15
    Mar 64
FISH
  Miss Keron   P: Phila 28 Ap 68
FISHER,
  DONALDSON and PRINGLE   P:
    Phila 19 Ja 69; see also
    PENROSS & FISHER
  Sgt.   P: in the army 21 Dec 58
  Adam   P: Phila 2 Sep 62

Archibald   P: Phila Gaz. 3
  Ja 76
Emanuel   P: Phila 3 Ja 60
George   P: Phila 20 Oct 68,
  1 Nov 70
Major Henry   P: Lewis Town
  19 Jy 80
James   P: Phila 20 Ap 69
John   P: Phila 27 Jy 58, 20
  Ap 69
John, Sr.   P: Phila 28 Nov
  54
Joseph   Morris's River 5 Oct
  76-Gaz. 30 Oct
Joshua   P: Phila 6 Jy 58
Justus   P: Phila 18 Mar 62
Lydia   P: Phila 5 Ag 62
Michael   P: Gloucester Co
  28 Nov 54, 16 Jy 67, 2
  Ag 70; Timber Creek 21
  Dec 58
Robert   P: Phila 29 Ag 54.
  T: Union Iron-works 6 Dec
  64
Samuel   P: Phila 2 Ag 70
FISTER
  Jaccob   P: Phila 22 Nov 53
FITCH
  Mary   P: Mountholly 19 Ja 69
FITCHAM/FITCHEM
  Elizabeth   P: Phila 9 Ag 59,
    31 Jy 60, 3 Sep 61
FITCHET
  James   P: Phila 18 Ag 57
FITIHAM
  Elizabeth   P: Baltimore 9
    Ag 59
FITTAMERRY
  John   P: Phila 5 Ag 56
FITZGERALD/FITITHGARL/FITZ-
  GARELD/FITZGERRAL
  David   P: Phila 11 Sep 55,
    2 Feb 64
  Eleanor   P: Christeen 1 Nov
    53, 1 Nov 70
  James   P: Phila 25 Jy 65, 1
    Nov 70
  John   P: Chester Co 12 Feb
    61; Phila 3 Ja 65, 30 Ap 67
  Joseph   P: Phila 31 Jy 60, 12
    Feb 61, 31 Dec 61
  Mau.   P: Phila 9 Ag 59
  Peter   P: Phila 3 Sep 61
  Rebecca   P: Kent Co 5 Ag 62;
    Phila 2 May 65
  Simon   P: Phila 1 Feb 70
  Thomas   P: Phila 9 Ag 59
  Walter   P: Phila-Gaz. 27 Oct
    73
FITZPATRICK
  Mrs.   P: Phila 3 Ja 65
  George   Phila 31 Ja 76
  Henry   P: Phila 19 Ja 69, 1
    Feb 70; Upper Maxfield 3
    May 70

James   Phila 31 Ja 76
John   31 Ja 76, 1 May 76
Michael   L: Lancaster Co 29
   Jy 72
Nancy   Phila 24 Jy 76
FITZSIMONS/FITZSIMMONS/FITZO-
MANS/FITSOMENS/FITZIMONS
Mr.   P: Christine Bridge 18
   Ag 57
Hugh   P: Phila-Gaz. 3 Ja 76
John   P: Chester Co 13 Oct 63
Judy   P: Phila 16 Jy 72
Mary   P: Wilmington 7 Ap 57
Philip   P: Phila 9 Ag 59;
   Worcester 30 Ja 66
Thomas   P: Phila 18 Mar 62
FITZWATER
Nehemiah   Phila 5 Ja 76-Gaz.
   31 Ja
FLAG
Henry C.   P: Phila 26 Jy 64
FLANIGAN/FLANAGAN/FLANNIGAN
John   P: Phila 3 Ja 60
Martha   P: Phila 15 Mar 64
Patrick   N: 29 Nov 64
FLATTELL
James   P: Phila 13 Oct 63
FLECK/FLEEK
Robert   P: Bucks Co 30 Ja 66;
   Phila 27 Ja 73
FLEMING/FLEMON/FLEMMYNG/FLIE-
MON/FLIMIN/FLEMMING
& DIXON   P: Phila 7 Ap 57
Alexander   P: Phila 1 Feb 70
Sir C.   P: Phila 2 Sep 62
Charles   P: Phila 26 Jy 64
David   C: see HAGERTY, John
Elizabeth   P: Pa 31 Jy 60
Henry   L: c/o William Kelso
   Harris's Ferry 19 Dec 71
Jacob   P: Lancaster 18 Feb 55
James   C: East Caln 18 Jy 65.
   L: 29 Ja 67; York Co 25 Dec
   66.   P: Phila 1 Nov 70
John   P: Bucks Co 31 Mar 63;
   Fogs Manor 2 Feb 63; Phila
   1 Nov 53, 30 Ap 67, 26 Oct
   69
Mary   P: Phila 12 Feb 61
Robert   P: New-Castle Co 3 Ja
   60
Samuel   T: Amwell 10 Ag 58
Thomas   L: Carlisle 31 Ja 71.
   P: Carlisle 12 Feb 61, 31
   Dec 61, 15 Mar 64; N.J. 18
   Mar 62; Phila 21 Dec 58, 3
   Ja 60, 23 Oct 66
FLENANGHAN
Onary   P: Phila 27 Ja 73
FLET
John   P: Phila 5 Ag 56
FLETCHER
James   P: Phila 27 Dec 53
John   P: Phila 30 Ap 67
Joseph   P: Phila 16 Jy 67,

   25 Ap 71
Nathan   P: Phila 27 Jy 58
Nathaniel   P: Phila 18 Mar 62
Richard   Phila 24 Jy 76
William   P: Woodberry 9 Ag 59
FLING/FLYNG
Batt   P: Phila 4 Feb 68
Edmond   P: Phila 13 Oct 63
John   P: Phila 1 Nov 53, 26
   Jy 64, 25 Jy 65
Michael   P: Phila 28 Oct 62,
   24 Jy 76
FLINT
Thomas   P: Phila 26 Jy 64
FLOOD
Mrs.   P: Phila 28 Oct 62
Patrick   P: Phila 18 Feb 55
Sophia   P: Phila 13 Ja 63
FLOUNDERS
Edward   P: Phila /?/ 21 Jy
   68
FLOWER
Capt. B.   P: Phila 19 May 63
Enoch   P: Phila-Gaz. 3 Ja 76
Henry   P: Phila 5 Ag 62
Samuel   P: Phila 6 Jy 58
Susanna   P: Phila 3 May 70
FLOWRY
Dr. P.   P: Phila 2 Feb 64
FLOYD/FLOIDE
Benjamin   P: Phila 13 May 56
Edward   P: Phila 13 Ja 63
John   P: Pa 13 Oct 63, 15 Mar
   64, 16 Jy 72
FLYNN/FLIN/FLINN/FLYN
Michael   P: Phila 1 Nov 70
Patrick/Pat/Patt   P: Phila
   1 Jy 56, 15 Mar 64, 1 Nov
   70, 3 Ja 76
Thomas   P: Phila 11 Sep 55
William   C: 30 Jy 77
FODEN
William   P: Phila 30 Ap 67
FOGGETT
Thomas   P: Phila 28 Ap 68
FOGKISON
Pat.   P: Phila 31 Jy 60
FOLCK
Adam   Phila 5 Ap 77-Gaz. 30
   Ap
FOLEY
Ann   P: Phila 3 Ja 60, 31 Jy.
   60
Patrick   P: Phila-Gaz. 3 Ja
   76
FOLICK
Barbara   P: Reading 9 Ag 59
FOLLEY
Thomas   P: Phila 10 Ap 66
FOLS
Jacob   P: Phila 2 Ag 70
FOLWELL
Goldsmith   P: Wilmington 3
   May 70
FONLOW

Edmond   P: Phila 3 Ja 60
FOOK
Paul   P: Phila 2 May 65
FORBES
Alexander   P: Phila 15 Mar 64,
   10 Ap 66
Lt. Charles   P: in the army
   12 Ja 58
Capt. George   P: Phila 4 Feb
   68
Hugh   P: Phila 6 Jy 58, 28
   Oct 62, 20 Feb 64, 23 Oct
   66
James   P: Phila 3 Ja 76
William   P: Phila 23 Oct 66
FORCITI
Jos.   P: Phila 19 Ja 69
FORD/FORDE
Col. Esq.   T: Morris Town 15
   Jy 56
Lt. Adjut.   P: Phila 16 Jy 67
Anne   P: Phila 26 Oct 69
Charles   P: Phila-Gaz. 27 Oct
   73
Francis   P: Phila 5 Ag 62
   (Esq), 1 Feb 70
Jacob, Esq.   T: Morris Town
   7 May 67
John   P: Phila 24 Feb 63
   (Capt), 25 Jy 65
Patrick   P: Phila 27 Ja 73
Richard   P: Bohemia 19 May 63
Standish   P: Phila 30 Ja 66
FORDEN
James   P: Phila 21 Dec 58
FORDHAM/FORDEM
Benjamin   P: Phila 18 Feb 55
Richard   P: N.J. 2 Feb 64
FOREE
Christian   P: Lancaster Co 18
   Mar 62
FOREMAN
Charles   L: near Fort Pitt
   20 Ja 73
FOREN
Christ.   P: Lancaster Co 15
   Mar 64
FOREST/FORREST/FORRIST
Mrs.   P: Phila 26 Oct 69
Mr.   P: Phila 27 Jy 58
Elizabeth   P: Chester Co 3
   Sep 61
George   P: Phila 16 Jy 72
James   P: Phila 4 Ag 63
Thomas   P: Phila 11 Jy 54
William   P: Chester Co 15 Mar
   64; Pa 13 Oct 63; Phila 21
   Dec 58, 28 Oct 62, 27 Ja 73
FORGGET
Susanna   P: Phila 25 Ap 71
FORLONG
Mr.   P: Phila 20 Oct 68
FORMAN
John   P: Bucks Co 26 Jy 64
Samuel   P: East Jersey 9 Ag

59, 15 Mar 64
FORRER
Christian   L: 13 Jn 65
FORRESTER/FORRISTER/FOURROUST-
ER
Arthur   1 Nov 53
Capt. Gerrald   P: Phila 19
   Jy 80
John   P: Hunterdon Co 31 Dec
   61; Phila 31 Jy 60
Margaret   P: Phila 26 Jy 64
FORRINER
Mr.   N: Warwick; see SAVIN,
   Thomas
FORSEY
Thomas   P: Phila /?/ 21 Jy
   68
FORSMAN
Robert   P: Phila 1 Feb 70
FORSTER
Andrew   T: Hopewell 10 Ag
   58
Isaac   P: Phila 2 Ag 70
John   P: Phila-Gaz. 3 Ja 76
Thomas   Phila 30 Oct 76
William   C: East Nottingham
   22 Ja 67.   P: Carlisle 24
   Feb 63; Phila 27 Oct 73
FORSYTH/FORSITH
John   P: Pa 12 Feb 61; Phila
   30 Ja 66, 3 Ja 76
Mary   L: Little Britain 20
   Ja 73
Mat.   P: Pa 18 Mar 62
Robert   P: Pa 19 May 63;
   Phila 2 Sep 62
William   P: East Nottingham
   2 Sep 62; Phila 3 Ja 76
FORTESCUE/FORTESQUE
Jane   P: Phila 29 Ag 54, 26
   Jy 64
Jean   P: Phila 9 May 54
FORTUNE
Anthony   P: Phila 4 Feb 68
FORTYE
Mrs.   P: Phila 6 Jy 58
Lt. Thomas   P: in the army 12
   Ja 58
FOSSEL
Samuel   P: Phila 15 Mar 64
FOSSETT
Robert   P: Phila 13 Ja 63
FOSTER; see also FORSTER
Alexander   P: Phila 13 May
   56, 12 Feb 61
Archibald   P: Phila 26 Jy 64
Eunis   P: Phila 3 Ja 60
Jannet   P: N. Castle Co 12 Ja
   58
Jeremiah   P: Carlisle 31 Jy
   60
John   P: Bucks Co 31 Jy 60;
   Phila 21 Dec 58
Marmaduke/Mar.   P: Phila 18
   Mar 62, 28 Oct 62

Mary   P: Phila 3 Ja 60
Nancy   Derham 24 Jy 76
Ralph   P: Phila 26 Jy 64
Richard   P: Phila 9 May 54
Samuel   P: Phila 13 May 56,
   12 Ja 58
FOTHERINHIM
   Dr. George   P: Phila 30 Ja 66
FOULISS
   Archibald   P: Phila 31 Dec 61
FOULK/FOULKE
   Adam   P: Phila 27 Ja 73
   Caleb   P: Phila 5 Ag 62
   Stephen   P: Chester Co 19 May
      63
   Robert   P: Phila 12 Ja 58
   Thomas   P: Bordentown 15 Mar
      64
   William   P: Lancaster 2 Feb 64
FOULOUGH/FOULOW
   John   Phila 30 Oct 76
   Michael   P: Phila 20 Oct 68
FOWARD
   Capt. Thomas   P: Phila 30 Ap
      67
FOWLER
   Mr.   P: Phila 1 Nov 70
   Archibald   N: 29 Nov 64
   Benjamin   T: Allen Town 17
      Oct 54
   Francis   P: Phila 4 Feb 68
   Susan   P: Phila 31 Dec 61
   Susanna/Susannah   P: Phila 31
      Mar 63, 26 Jy 64, 19 Ja 69
FOWLES
   Capt. Dennis   P: Pa 3 Ja 60
FOWLOW
   Michael   P: Phila 13 Ja 63
FOX
   Mrs.   P: Pa 12 Ja 58
   Daniel   P: Phila 3 Ja 65
   George   P: Kensington 23 Oct
      66; Phila 30 Ap 77
   Jeremiah   P: Phila-Gaz. 27
      Oct 73
   John   P: Phila 28 Oct 62, 26
      Jy 64
   Joseph   P: Phila 27 Oct 73,
      19 Jy 80
   Mary   P: Pa 3 Ja 60; Phila 9
      Ag 59
   Michael   P: Phila 2 Ag 70, 31
      Ja 76
   Thomas   P: Phila 31 Jy 60
   William   P: Chester Co 22
      Nov 53; Phila 30 May 54
FOY
   Martin   P: Phila-Gaz. 27 Oct
      73
FOX
   Matthew   P: Phila 25 Ap 71
FRAME/FRAIM
   David   P: Chester Co 13 Ja
      63; Phila 31 Dec 61
FRANCE

Job.   L: Lancaster 15 Ap 56
Joshua   P: Phila 20 Oct 68
FRANCIS
   & CRADOCK   P: Phila 15 Mar
      64
   Abraham   P: Phila 3 May 70
   James   P: Phila 31 Dec 61
   John   P: Bethlehem 26 Jy 64
   Joseph   P: Kent Co 9 Ag 59
   Reese   P: Great Valley 7 Ap
      57
   Richard   P: Phila 19 Ja 69,
      20 Jy 69
   Samuel   P: Phila 1 Feb 70
   Sarah   P: Phila 3 Ja 76
   Thomas   P: Phila 27 Jy 58
      (Capt), 2 Feb 64, 2 Ag 70
   William   P: Pa 28 Oct 62
FRANK
   George   L: 20 Ja 73
   John   P: Phila 29 Ag 54, 11
      Sep 55, 3 May 70
FRANKLIN
   Gilbert   P: Phila 31 Dec 61
   Joseph   P: Phila-Gaz. 27 Oct
      73
FRANKS
   Elizabeth   P: Phila 18 Feb 55
FRASER/FRAZER/FRASOR/FREASAR
   Mr.   P: Phila 23 Oct 66
   Alexander   P: Phila 25 Jy 65
   David   P: Marsh Creek 3 Sep
      61
   Donald, soldier   P: prob. in
      Pittsburgh 15 Mar 64
   Elizabeth   P: Phila 30 Ap
      67 (2)
   Hugh   Northumberland Co 31
      Ja 76
   Isabel   P: Phila 9 Ag 59
   Joseph   P: Phila 15 Mar 64
   Malcolm   P: Phila 30 Ap 67,
      20 Oct 68 (Lt), 19 Ja 49
   Mary   P: Phila 24 Feb 63
   Pergiter   P: Phila 6 Jy 58
   Peter   P: Phila 31 Dec 61
   William   P: Amwell, N.J. 27
      Ja 73 (Rev), 3 Ja 76 (Rev);
      N.J. 31 Jy 60 (Esq); Phila
      24 Feb 63
FRASIER/FRAZIER
   Mr.   P: Phila 26 Oct 69
   Eliz.   P: Phila 28 Ap 68
   James   P: Phila 4 Ag 63
   John   P: Phila 18 Ag 57, 12
      Ja 58, 28 Oct 62. T: East
      Jersey 17 Oct 54
   John G.   Phila 30 Oct 76
   Joseph   P: Phila 8 Jy 62
   Matthew   P: Phila 10 Ap 66
   William   P: Phila 9 Ag 59, 2
      Sep 62, 13 Oct 63. T: N.J.
      17 Oct 54
FRATY
   Jacob   P: Bucks Co 18 Mar 62

FRAYNE
  Richard   P: Phila 1 Nov 53
FREDAND
  James   P: Oxford Twp 12 Ja 58
FREDERICKS
  Rev. John Andreas   P: Phila
    12 Ja 58
FREE
  Abraham   P: Phila 29 Ag 54
FREECE
  Peter   P: Lancaster Co 9 Ag
    59
FREEHOLD
  Sarah   P: Phila 3 Sep 61
FREELAND
  Andrew   P: Cecil Co 28 Oct
    62
  James   P: Carlisle 8 Jy 62;
    Cecil Co 28 Oct 62; Pa 12
    Feb 61; Phila 26 Jy 64;
    Sheerman's Valley 18 Mar 62
FREELOW
  Michael   P: Phila-Gaz. 3 Ja
    76
FREEMAN
  Caesar   P: Phila 27 Ja 73
  Charles   Westmoreland 24 Jy
    76
  Edmond   P: Phila 8 Jy 62
  Capt. Isaac   P: Phila 24 Oct
    54
  Jonathan   P: Phila 11 Sep 55
  Robert   P: Phila 11 Sep 55,
    31 Dec 61
  William/Will.   P: Phila 7 Ap
    57, 30 Ap 67, 20 Ap 69
FREESTONE/FREESTON
  John   P: Phila 6 Sep 53, 18
    Feb 55, 1 Nov 70
FREGER
  William   P: Phila 31 Dec 61
FREKE
  John   P: Phila-Gaz. 27 Oct 73
FRELEY/FREELEY
  Christopher   P: Phila 5 Jy 76
    -Gaz. 24 Jy
  Jacob   P: Bucks Co 31 Jy 60
FRENCH
  Capt.   P: Chester Co 2 Feb 64
  George   P: Phila 10 Oct 65
  John   P: Carlisle 31 Dec 61;
    Phila 13 May, 1 Jy 56
  Robert   P: Chester Co 18 Ag
    57, 2 Feb 64
  Thomas   P: Woodberry 19 Jy 80
  William   P: Phila 25 Ap 71
FRENDEN
  Nancy   P: Phila 3 May 70
FRENE
  Patrick   P: Phila 20 Oct 68
FRENEY
  Richard   P: Pa 12 Ja 58
FRERE
  George   P: Phila-Gaz. 27 Oct
    73

FRERER
  Fisher   Phila 16 Jy 77
FRETTER
  Hendrick   P: Phila 25 Jy 65,
    10 Oct 65
FREW
  Alexander   P: Pa 13 Oct 63
FRIBEN
  Capt.   P: Phila 15 Mar 64
FRICK
  Conrad   P: Pa 12 Feb 61
  Joshua   P: Lancaster 21 Dec
    58
FRIEND
  Capt. James   P: Phila 26 Jy
    64
  John   P: Phila /?/ 21 Jy 68
FRIENDLY, see SHUENTZLYD &
FRITH
  George   P: Phila-Gaz. 3 Ja 76
FRITS
  Sebastian   P: Phila 18 Mar
    62
FRITY
  Henry   P: Phila 9 Ag 59
FRIZZELL
  John   P: Phila 28 Ap 68
FROGGETT
  Charles   Upper Preston 5 Ja
    76-Gaz. 31 Ja
FRONS
  John   P: Phila 27 Ja 73
FRUTSON
  Johan   P: Phila 5 Ag 62
FRY
  Millisent   P: Phila 7 Ap 57
FRYENMOCT
  Rev. J. Casp.   P: Claverak
    12 Ja 58
FRYER/FRYAR
  James   P: New-Castle Co 12
    Feb 61
  Thomas   P: Phila 27 Ja 73
  William   P: Pa 28 Oct 62,
    13 Ja, 24 Feb 63
FUE
  James   P: Wilmington 18 Feb
    55
FUERY
  Ann   P: N.J. 24 Oct 54
FULD
  Lt.   P: in the army 27 Jy 58
FULFORD
  Henry   P: Phila 2 Ag 70
  Capt. John   Phila 31 Ja 76
FULGHAM
  Joseph   P: Phila 12 Feb 61,
    8 Jy 62 (Capt)
FULIEN
  William   Phila 5 Jy 76-Gaz.
    24 Jy
FULLA
  James   P: Phila 13 Oct 63
FULLER
  Benjamin   P: Phila 20 Jy 69

FULLERTON
Dr. L: Leacock Twp, see
HART, James
Widow P: Phila 2 May 65
Alex./Alexander P: Chester
Co 12 Ja 58, 9 Ag 59, N.
Castle 24 Feb 63; Phila 12
Feb 61
Andrew P: Chester Co 18 Ag
57
Charles P: Pa 12 Ja 58
George P: Phila 30 Ja 66
Humphrey P: Phila 1 Feb 70
John P: Neshaminey 26 Jy 53
Richard P: Pequea 19 May 63
Samuel P: New Castle Co 12
Ja 58
William P: Pa 13 Oct 63;
Phila 24 Jy 76; Vincent 9
Ag 59
FULLMAN
Wessels P: Pa 15 Mar 64
FULTMAN
Elizabeth P: Lancaster Co
13 Oct 63
FULTON
Agnes P: Lancaster Co 13
May 56
David P: Pa 7 Ap 57
Frances P: Phila 12 Feb 61
Francis L: 3 Oct 65
George P: Phila 25 Jy 65
Henry P: Phila 20 Oct 68,
19 Ja 69, 20 Jy 69, 26 Oct
69, 1 Feb 70, 2 Ag 70
James P: Bucks Co 3 Ja 60;
Chester Co 9 Ag 59; Phila
23 Oct 66
John C: Chester Co 22 Ja 67;
Providence, see M'CULLOUGH,
James. P: Chester Co 2 Ag
70; Lancaster Co 24 Feb 63;
Little Elk 27 Jy 58; Pa 27
Jy 58, 2 Feb 64; Phila 28
Nov 54
Joseph P: Phila 1 Feb 70
Ro. L: 11 Ap 65
Samuel P: Lancaster Co 27
Dec 53; Radnor, Chester Co
25 Ap 71
William P: Phila 13 May 56,
8 Jy 62
FUNDREN
Judith P: Gloucester Co 5 Ag
56
FURMAN
& SEXSON P: Phila 10 Ap 66
Josiah P: Maidenhead 30 Ja 66
FURY
Josh. N: New-Castle 12 Feb 67
FUSSER
Adam New Jersey 5 Jy 76-Gaz.
24 Jy
FUSTELL
Solomon P: Phila 6 Jy 58

FUTTON
George P: Phila 2 May 65

GAA
Robert P: Pa 19 May 63, 4
Ag 63, 2 Feb 64
William P: Phila 26 Jy 64
GABRIEL/GABEREL
Casper P: Pa 31 Dec 61
Nicholas Eman. P: Phila 31
Dec 61
GABSON
Mary P: Phila 20 Oct 68
GADDEN
James P: Chester Co 31 Dec
61
GADDINGTON
John P: Phila 15 Mar 64
GADDIS/GADDES/GADDIES
John P: Bucks Co 15 Mar 64,
24 Jy 76
William P: Pa 3 Ja 60
GAFLEN
Alexander P: Phila-Gaz. 3
Ja 76
GAHIM
John P: Lancaster Co 12 Ja
58
GAICH
William P: Phila 2 Feb 64
GAIB /or GAIT?/
Anguiss P: Phila 13 May 56
GALBREATH/GILBREATH/GALBRATH
Catherine P: Phila 16 Jy 72
Gavin P: Chester Co 3 Sep 61
James P: Lancaster Co 28
Nov 54; Paxton T. 7 Ap 57
(esq)
John P: Phila 26 Oct 69, 3
May 70; Whiteclay Creek 12
Ja 58; York Co 13 Oct 63
Joseph/Jos. P: Phila 6 Jy 58,
27 Jy 58; 12 Ja 58
Thomas P: Pa 24 Mar 63;
Phila 2 Ag 70
GALER
Adam Phila 5 Ap 76-Gaz. 1
May
GALIAR
Mr. P: Phila 13 Ja 63
GALLAGHE
Edward P: Newcastle Co 28
Oct 62
GALLAGHAR/GALLAUGHER/GALAUGHER/
GALOUGHER/GALLAHER/GOLLACHER/
GALAHER; see also GELAGER
Abraham L: c/o Michael Gard-
ner 19 Dec 71
Fr./Francis P: Phila 19 May
63, 3 Ja 65
George L: 25 Dec 66
John L: Donnegall Settlement
19 Dec 71. P: New London
Twp 27 Dec 53

Michael   P: Phila 27 Ja 73
Peter   P: Phila 26 Oct 69
William   L: 25 Dec 66.   P:
   Pa 13 Oct 63; Phila 20 Oct
   68, 20 Jy 69, 25 Ap 71, 27
   Oct 73
Zebell   P: Doe Run 21 Dec 58
GALLIGHAWN
William   L: Anderson's Ferry
   2 Mar 74
GALLOP/GALLUP
Oliver   T: New Hanover 6 Dec
   64
William   P: Phila 16 Jy 77;
   Westmoreland 1 May 76
GALLOWAY/GALAWAY
Jane   P: Christiana Hundred
   7 Ap 57
John   L: York Co 20 Ja 73.
   P: Pa 13 Oct 63; Phila 27
   Ja 73
Joseph   L: Little Britain,
   Lancaster Co 31 Ja 71
Robert   P: Phila 2 May 65
Samuel   P: Phila 13 May 56
Sarah   P: Pa 3 Ja 60
GALLOWED
John   P: Phila 19 Jy 80
GALLSTLY
Alexander   P: Pa 12 Feb 61
GALLY
Rachel   P: Phila 27 Ja 73
GALSIN
George   P: Phila 18 Mar 62
GALT
Ro.   L: 13 Jn 65
GAMBLE/GAMBEL
George   L: Pequea 15 Ap 56
James   P: Phila 31 Dec 61
Joseph   P: Phila 2 May 65
Patrick   P: Phila 1 Feb 70
Rebecca   P: Phila 3 Ja 76
Samuel   P: Phila 24 Feb 63, 31
   Mar 63
Capt. Thomas   P: Phila-Gaz.
   27 Oct 73
William   P: Mendom Twp 12 Ja
   58
GAME
Matthew   Phila 1 May 76
GAMELING
Capt.   P: Phila 6 Jy 58
GAMWELL
Katey   P: Phila-Gaz. 27 Oct
   73
GANDUWIN
Charles   P: Phila 9 Ag 59
GANLY
Mr.   P: Phila 28 Ap 68
GANTER
Michael   P: Phila 31 Jy 60
GANTHONY
Peter   P: Phila 9 May 54
GANY
.... P: Phila 13 May 56

GARANEX
Capt. Archbold   P: Phila 7
   Ap 57
GARBETT
Henry   P: Phila 20 Oct 68
GARDINE
Charles   P: Talbot Co 8 Jy
   62
GARDINER
Alexander   P: Phila 20 Jy 69
Elizabeth   P: Phila 2 Sep 62
Francis   P: Chester Co 3 Ja
   60, 31 Mar 63
Thomas   Phila 5 Jy 77-Gaz.
   16 Jy
GARDNER
Capt.   P: Phila 31 Jy 60
Widow   P: Phila 25 Ap 71
Aleta   P: Phila-Gaz. 3 Ja 76
Andrew   P: Pa 15 Mar 64;
   Phila 3 Ja 65
David   P: Phila 21 Dec 58
Elizabeth   P: Phila 10 Ap
   66, 21 Jy 68
Henry   P: Pa 4 Ag 63
Isaac   P: Phila 31 Dec 61,
   20 Oct 68
James   P: Dover 9 Ag 59;
   Kent Co 31 Jy 60, 2 Feb 64;
   Phila 12 Ja 58, 31 Dec 61
John   P: Phila 29 Ag 54, 18
   Ag 57, 5 Ag 62, 13 Ja 63,
   4 Ag 63, 3 Ja 65, 2 May 65,
   10 Ap 66
John, Jr.   P: Phila 10 Oct 65
Martha   P: Phila 25 Jy 65
Matthew   P: Phila 30 Ja 66
Robert   P: Phila 27 Jy 58
Samuel   P: N.J. 15 Mar 64;
   Phila 18 Mar 62
Thomas   P: Phila 12 Ja 58,
   31 Dec 61, 24 Feb 63, 10
   Ap 66
Capt. W.   P: Phila 3 Sep 61
William   P: Phila 18 Feb 55,
   27 Jy 58, 1 Dec 58
GARDWEN
Charles   P: Phila 27 Jy 58
GARE
William   P: Phila 21 Jy 68
GAREY
Mary   P: Phila 9 Ag 59
GARLAND
George   P: Phila 23 Oct 66
GARLINE
Thomas   P: Phila 18 Ag 57
GARLING
Henry   P: Phila 20 Jy 69
GARMON
Samuel   P: Phila 20 Oct 68
GARNACK
James   P: Phila 20 Jy 69
GARNER
Capt.   P: Phila 10 Oct 65
Elizabeth   P: Phila 4 Feb 68

Henry P: Pa 19 May 63
Rebecca P: Phila 27 Jy 58
Robert P: Phila 18 Mar 62,
10 Ap 66
Theod. P: Phila 10 Oct 65
GARNIER
Isaac P: Phila 2 May 65, 23
Oct 66
GARRAWAY
Charles P: Phila 21 Dec 58
(Capt), 24 Feb 63
John P: Phila 27 Jy 58
Sarah P: Phila 25 Ap 71
GARRETT/GERRET/GARRET/GERRAT
Capt. Phila 30 Ap 77
Amos P: Sasquehan 27 Jy 58
Isaac Phila 1 May 76
James P: Phila 31 Dec 61
Nathaniel P: Darby 27 Jy 58
Robert N: 29 Nov 64
Thomas C: 30 Jy 77
William P: Darby 11 Sep 55,
4 Ag 63, 2 Feb 64, 21 Jy 68,
25 Ap 71; Gloucester Point
15 Mar 64
GARRETSON
John P: New-Castle 31 Jy 60
GARRIGUS
Isaac P: Phila 2 Feb 64
Mary P: Phila 18 Mar 62
GARRISON
Mr. P: Phila-Gaz. 3 Ja 76
Abraham P: Cumberland Co 27
Jy 58, 28 Oct 62
Daniel P: Phila 1 Nov 53
Johanna P: West New Jersey
5 Ag 56
John P: Newcastle Co 12 Ja
58
Nicholas P: Phila 31 Mar 63
(Capt), 3 Ja 65
Patience T: Allentown 10 Ag
58
GARRSON
John P: Newcastle 18 Ag 57
GARRY
Agnes P: Phila 30 Ja 66
GARVEY
Alexander P: Pa 27 Jy 58
GARVIN/GARVAN; see also GEARVIN
Ebenezer Phila 24 Jy 76
John L: Cumberland Co 19 Dec
71. P: Chester Co 18 Ag
57; Lancaster Co 31 Jy 60;
Phila Co 18 Mar 62
Thomas P: Lancaster Co 31 Jy
60; Sadsbury 4 Ag 63
GASCOIGN
John P: Phila 28 Oct 62
GASH
Capt. P: Phila 25 Jy 65
Capt. John P: Phila 23 Oct 66
GASKINS
Mary P: Phila 16 Jy 72
GASNE

Elizabeth P: Phila 3 Ja 60
GASPER
Anthony Phila 5 Jy 77-Gaz.
16 Jy
GASS/GAAS
John P: Pa 13 Oct 63; Phila
30 May 54
Lowick P: Phila 31 Jy 60
Sarah P: near Phila 28 Nov
54; Phila 31 Jy 60
GAST
Baarriss P: Phila 23 Oct 66
GATES
Mrs. P: Phila 27 Jy 58
Horatio P: Phila 3 Ja 65
James P: Phila 2 May 65
Sarah C: c/o D. Hollings-
worth 28 Nov 65
GATHERY
William P: Phila 27 Ja 73
GATLIVE
Rees P: Chester Co 9 Ag 59
GAUDY
George P: Phila 25 Jy 65
GAUSMAN
Benjamin Phila 30 Oct 76
GAUTIER
Peter P: Phila 21 Jy 68
GAVIN/GAVAN
Edward P: Bucks 1 Nov 53
John P: Phila 25 Ap 71
Joseph P: Phila-Gaz. 27 Oct
73
GAW
John P: Phila 22 Nov 53, 18
Mar 62
Theophilus P: Phila 13 May
56
GAY
Alexander L: Brandywine 2
Mar 74. P: Pa 12 Ja 58,
31 Jy 60; Phila 3 Ja 65, 2
May 65
John P: Phila 2 May 65
Robert P: Phila 11 Feb 70
GAYLER
George P: Phila 21 Dec 58
GAYNOR
Henry P: Phila 1 Nov 53
GEACUT
Mr. P: Phila-Gaz. 3 Ja 76
GEAR
Merion P: Phila 13 Ja 63
GEARROLL
Rito P: Phila 21 Dec 58
GEARVIN
John P: Bucks Co 9 Ag 59
GEARY/GEERY
James L: c/o Rev. Mr. Thomp-
son-Lancaster Co 13 Jn 65,
19 Dec 71. P: 3 Ja 76;
Phila 2 May 65
William P: Duck Creek 5 Ag
62
GEBBIE

William L: York Co 20 Ja 73
GEDDES/GEADIS/GEDDIS
  Alexander P: New-London 3 Ja
    60
  Ann Phila 16 Jy 77
  George P: Phila-Gaz. 3 Ja 76
  John P: Bucks Co 16 Jy 67;
    Lancaster Co 28 Oct 62
  William P: Norrington 30 Ja
    66; Phila 11 Sep 55
GEDUIS /?/
  Peggy P: Phila 19 May 63
GEEMLY
  John P: Phila 2 Feb 64
GEERS
  Ann P: Phila 15 Mar 64
GELAGER
  Henry P: Phila 4 Ag 63
GELLMORE
  James P: N. Read. F/urnace?/
    18 Ag 57
GELLY
  Robert P: Phila 10 Ap 66
GELSTON/GELLSTEN
  James P: Phila-Gaz. 3 Ja 76
  William P: Pa 12 Ja 58, 24
    Feb 63
GEMMELL/GEMMILL
  John P: Carlisle 26 Jy 64
  William P: York Co 1 Nov 53.
    T: Pa 31 Ja 71
  Zachariah P: Phila 5 Ag 62
GEMMUAL
  Ja. L: Cumberland Co 31 Ja
    71
GENINES
  Catherine P: Horsham 21 Dec
    58
GENSELL
  Matthias P: Phila 27 Jy 58,
    9 Ag 59
GEORGE
  David P: Blockley Twp 8 Jy
    62; Chester Co 18 Mar 62;
    Phila 3 Ja 76
  Jesse P: Blockley 19 May 63,
    28 Ap 68
  John P: Swedes Ford 1 Feb 70
  Mary P: Pa 12 Feb 61
  Thomas P: Pa 12 Feb 61
  William P: Bucks 28 Nov 54
GEPPS
  John P: Phila 10 Oct 65
GERDINE
  John P: Phila 6 Sep 53
GERMAINS
  Joshua Phila 1 May 76
GERMAN
  John P: Phila 28 Ap 68
GERNELL
  Christian P: Phila Co 3 Sep
    61
GERNON
  George P: Pa 31 Dec 61
  John P: Phila-Gaz. 27 Oct 73

GERRARD
  .... P: Spring Gardens 24
    Oct 54
GEST
  Richard P: Chester Co 18
    Feb 55
  William P: near Marcus Hook
    24 Oct 54
GESTᴇLOWE
  Lydia P: Phila 21 Dec 58
GETHINGS
  John P: Jerseys 11 Sep 55
GETHONG
  Isaac P: Phila 18 Mar 62
GETLIEFF
  Reese P: East Caln 21 Dec
    58
GETTER
  William P: Phila 28 Ap 68
GETTY/GETTEY
  John P: Pa 12 Feb 61; Phila
    2 Ag 70
GEUBEL
  F. P: Phila 27 Ja 73
GEVIN
  Judah P: Phila 9 Ag 59
GHIE
  John Phila 1 May 76
GHISELIN
  Caesar P: Phila 2 May 65
GIBBIS
  John P: Martick Twp 15 Mar
    64
GIBBONS/GIBBON/GIBON
  Ann P: Lancaster 18 Ag 57
  Griffith L: Carlisle 29 Jy
    72
  James Phila 31 Ja 76
  John P: East Marlborough 7
    Ap 57; Phila 26 Jy 64, 21
    Jy 68
  Jos./Joseph P: Chester Co
    3 Ja 60, 24 Feb 63
  Nicholas P: Cohansey 28 Nov
    54; Salem (Co) 7 Ap 57
    (esq), 9 Ag 59, 31 Mar 63
  Robert P: Chester Co 1 Nov
    53
  William N: near New-Castle
    4 Dec 66, 12 Feb 67. P:
    Phila 26 Jy 64
GIBBONY
  John P: Little Britain 21
    Dec 58
GIBBS
  Benjamin P: Phila 21 Dec 58,
    9 Ag 59, 3 Ja 60, 12 Feb
    61; 31 Dec 61, 20 Ap 69
  Francis Blower P: Phila 30
    Ja 66
  John P: Phila 18 Ag 57, 12
    Ja 58 (Capt)
  Martha P: Pa 9 Ag 59
  Richard P: Bucks Co 18 Ag
    57, 9 Ag 59; Pa 27 Jy 58

Solomon (sailor) P: Phila 21
  Dec 58
Thomas P: Phila 12 Feb 61
William P: Phila-Gaz. 3 Ja
  76
GIBSON
  Andrew P: Phila 1 Feb 70, 27
    Ja 73
  Daniel P: Phila 23 Oct 66
  David P: Kingsess Town 11
    Sep 55; Upper Dublin 20 Oct
    68
  Ebenezer P: Black River 16
    Jy 72
  Edward N: Head of Elk 12 Feb
    67
  George P: Lancaster Co 28 Nov
    54; Pa 28 Oct 62
  Jacob York Co 24 Jy 76
  James C: 30 Jy 77. L: Leba-
    non Twp 15 Ap 56. P: Phila
    18 Ag 57, 9 Ag 59
  Jean P: Marsh Creek 25 Jy 65
  John P: Cross Roads 3 Sep 61;
    Phila 6 Jy 58, 1 Feb 70
  Joshua Phila 30 Oct 76
  Matthew P: Phila 19 Ja 69
  Peggy P: Phila 18 Mar 62
  Richard P: Phila 18 Mar 62
  Robert P: Pa 31 Jy 60
  Samuel P: Phila 5 Ag 62
  William L: Little Britain,
    Lancaster Co 31 Ja 71. N:
    at the Head of Elk 4 Dec 66,
    12 Feb 67. P: Center House
    27 Jy 58; Little Britain 5
    Ag 62; Phila 21 Dec 58, 9 Ag
    59
GIEDEN
  William P: Bucks 1 Nov 53
GIFFEN/GIFFIN/GIFINE/GIFEN
  Andrew L: 3 Oct 65
  David P: Phila 26 Jy 64
  James P: Merion 24 Feb 63
  John P: Phila 31 Dec 61, 24
    Feb 63, 2 Feb 64, 25 Jy 65
  Robert P: Chester Co 31 Dec 61
  Stephen L: Strabane Twp, York
    Co 19 Dec 71. P: Little
    Britain 24 Oct 54
GIFFORD
  Ercher P: Germantown 9 Ag 59
  William P: Phila 1 Nov 70
GIHON
  Robert P: Concord 5 Feb 54
GILBERT/GILBARD
  Widow P: Phila 27 Jy 58
  Edward P: Phila 23 Oct 66
  Frederick P: Germantown 10
    Oct 65
  George P: Phila 27 Dec 53,
    21 Dec 58, 31 Dec 61, 10
    Oct 65
  John P: Little Britain 24
    Oct 54; Phila 10 Oct 65 (esq)

30 Ja 66, 1 Nov 70
  Joseph/Joe P: Phila 19 May
    63 (2)
GILBORNE
  George P: Phila 1 Nov 70
GILBREATH/GILBRET
  Hugh P: Chester Co 2 Feb 64
  John P: Pa 15 Mar 64
  Thomas P: Phila 28 Oct 62
GILCHRIST/GILCREAST/GILLCREAST/
  GILCRESH
  James P: Lancaster Co 31 Dec
    61, 13 Oct 63, 31 Ja 76.
    T: Trenton 31 Ja 71
  John P: Phila 29 Ag 54, 11
    Sep 55, 9 Ag 59, 7 Ap 57
    (mason) 3 Ja 60
  Robert L: Little Britain
    Twp 29 Jy 72
GILES
  Edward P: Phila 25 Ap 71
  Jacob P: Pa 21 Dec 58
  James P: Phila 20 Oct 68,
    20 Ap 69
  Nathaniel P: Lebanon 5 Ag
    56
  Roberts P: Bucks Co 1 Nov 70
GILKEY
  Walter P: Phila 2 Ag 70
GILL
  Ann P: West Jersey 9 Ag 59
  Cudjoe P: Phila 3 Ja 76
  Daniel P: Phila 10 Oct 65,
    20 Oct 68
  John P: Phila 13 Oct 63,
    26 Oct 69, 3 Ja 76
  Joseph P: Kent Island 19
    May 63
  Margaret P: Phila 27 Jy 58
  Patrick P: Wilmington 22
    Nov 53
  Richard P: Pa 21 Dec 58
  Robert P: Chestnut Level 15
    Mar 64
  Rose P: Pa 13 Oct 63
GILLAN
  Hugh P: Phila 2 May 65
GILLANDE
  John P: Pa 12 Feb 61
GILLATLY
  Rev. A. P: Octorara 3 Sep 61
GILLEAD
  Hannah P: Phila 4 Ap 54
GILLES
  Robert P: Pa 13 Oct 63
  William P: Phila 25 Ap 71
GILLESPIE/GILLASPIE/GILLASPY/
  GELESPIE/GELLASPY/GILLISPIE/
  GELESPY/GILLISPE/GILLASPY
  Rev. Mr. L: Munster, see
    M'CLAY, John
  Allen N: Newark 4 Dec 66;
    N. Castle Co 12 Feb 67.
    P: New Castle Co 2 Feb 64
  Archibald P: Pa 21 Dec 58

George   P: Pa 9 Ag 59, 3 Ja
   60 (Rev); Whit. Creek 22
   Nov 53
Henry   P: N. Castle Co 31 Dec
   61, 13 Ja 63
Col. J.   P: Lancaster Co 2
   Feb 64
James   N: 29 Nov 64 (Col).
   P: Lancaster Co 12 Feb 61
   (Col); Little Britain 24
   Oct 54, 26 Jy 64; Pa 12 Ja
   58, 18 Mar 62, 28 Oct 62,
   24 Feb 63
John   P: Little Britain 15
   Mar 64; Phila 24 Feb 63, 19
   May 63, 15 Mar 64
Jos./Joseph   P: Phila 26 Oct
   69, 1 Feb 70
Leah   P: Paxton 28 Nov 59
Rose   P: Phila 20 Oct 68
GILLIAN
John   C: Chester Co 18 Jy 65
GILLIARD
James   P: Phila 11 Sep 55
GILLIAS
James   P: Christeen 11 Jy 54
GILLIER
Hannah   P: 18 Mar 62
GILLIHAN/GILLIHEN
John   P: Lancaster Co 31 Dec
   61, 13 Ja 63
William   P: Carlisle 18 Mar 62
GILLIHEW
William   P: Carlisle 31 Dec 61
GILLILAN
Francis   P: Phila 16 Jy 72
John   P: Chester Co 27 Jy 58
GILLILAND
Dr. James   P: in the army 21
   Dec 58
William   P: Horsham 19 Ja 69;
   Phila 1 Nov 70, 27 Ja 73
GILLIN
Daniel   P: Phila 20 Ap 69
GILLIS/GILLICE
James   P: Phila 20 Jy 69
Neil   P: Phila 10 Ap 66
Robert   P: Neshaminy 2 Feb 64
GILLS
William   P: Phila 3 May 70
GILMER/GILLMER
John   P: Middle Octorara 28
   Nov 54, 3 Ja 60
GILMORE/GILMOR/GUILMORE; see
   also GELLMORE
Elizabeth   P: East Jersey 9
   Ag 59
Hugh   P: Phila 21 Dec 58
   (sailor), 5 Ag 62
James   L: Lancaster Co 29 Jy
   72. P: Haddonfield 2 Feb
   64; Pa 31 Dec 61, 13 Oct 63
John   P: Germantown-Gaz. 27
   Oct 73
Mary   L: Pequea 2 Mar 74

Robert   P: Pa 12 Feb 61;
   Somerset 2 Feb 64
Samuel   T: c/o Christopher
   Cunningham, near Borden-
   town 3 Oct 65
Thomas   P: Phila 3 May 70
GILPIN/GILPHIN
Ann   P: Chester Co 27 Jy 58
George   P: Phila 1 Nov 70
Thomas   P: Wilmington 1 Feb
   55
GINGES/GINGELS
Samuel   P: Pa 15 Mar 64;
   Phila 28 Ap 68
GINKS
Thomas   T: Bucks Co 10 Ag 58
GINNIS
James   P: Pa 31 Jy 60
GIPSON
James   N: near N. Castle 12
   Feb 67
GIRTLEY
Henry   P: Pa 13 Oct 63
GIRVAN/GIRVEN
James   P: Phila-Gaz. 3 Ja 76
Thomas   P: Middle Octorara
   18 Ag 57; Sadsbury 13 May
   56
GISCOME
William   P: Phila 21 Dec 58
GITTENS/GITTINS
John   P: Phila 29 Ag 54, 9
   Ag 59
GITURDMEN/?/
John   P: Pa 28 Oct 62
GIVEN
James   P: New-Castle Co 12
   Ja 58
John   P: New-Castle Co 12 Ja
   58
GLADEN
Joseph   P: Bucks Co 20 Oct
   68
GLADINING
David   P: Bucks Co 3 Ja 60
GLADNEY/GLADNAY
William   P: Bucks Co 2 Feb
   64, 30 Ja 66; Nesham. 18
   Ag 57
GLANVILL/GLANVILLE
Marcus   P: Reading 9 Ag 59
Maurice   P: Reeding Twp 18
   Mar 62
GLART
Capt. Patrick   P: Phila 7 Ap
   57
GLASFIELD /or GLATFIELD?/
John   P: Phila 10 Oct 65
GLASGOW/GLASCOW
Elizabeth   Phila 30 Ap 77
James   P: Fogs Manor 7 Ap 59
John   C: Nottingham 28 Nov
   65. P: Kensington 26 Oct
   69; Nottingham 12 Ja 58, 19
   May 63; Phila 18 Mar 62, 4

Ag 63

William   P: Cecil Co 9 Ag 59;
Pa 24 Feb 63; Phila 10 Oct
65; West Nottingham 24 Oct
54

GLASS
John   P: Willistown 27 Jy 58

GLASSELL
John   P: Oxford 4 Ag 63

GLASSFORD
Henry   P: Kent Co 9 Ag 59
Hugh   P: Foggs Manor 9 Ag 59;
New-Castle Co 8 Jy 62; Pa
13 Oct 63

GLAZE
Miss Sarah   Phila 30 Oct 76

GLEASON
Capt. Oliver   Phila 5 Jy 76-
Gaz. 24 Jy

GLEEN
John   P: Pa 12 Feb 61

GLENDINEN
Thomas, of the 42nd Regt.   P:
Pennsylvania 23 Oct 66

GLENN/GLEN
Governor   P: Phila 31 Jy 60
George   C: East Nottingham 30
Oct 66
James   P: New-Castle Co 21 Dec
58; Phila 25 Ap 71
John   L: Hanover Twp 29 Jy 72
Robert   P: Octorara 3 Sep 61;
Phila 18 Mar 62
William   P: Phila 18 Mar 62

GLENTWORTH
Doctor   Phila 30 Oct 76, 19
Jy 80

GLESSAN
James   L: Marsh Creek, York
Co 31 Ja 71

GLINDOR
Mich.   P: Phila 6 Sep 53

GLINN
James   P: Phila 16 Jy 72

GLISSAN
James   P: Phila 30 Ap 77, 16
Jy 77

GLOVER
Capt.   P: Phila 3 Ja 76
Ann   T: Hopewell 17 Oct 54
Capt. B es   P: Phila 4 Ag 63
Mary   P: Moreland 8 Jy 62
Richard   P: Fort Augusta 21
Dec 58, 27 Jy 58; Pa 3 Ja
60

GLYAN
Edmund   P: Phila 2 Ag 70

GMELIN
Capt.   P: Phila 18 Ag 57

GOAD
Capt. John   P: Phila 1 Nov 53

GOBBY
Peter   P: Chester Co 18 Mar
62

GOBEL

Daniel   P: Kingwood 31 Jy 60

GODDARD/GODARD
Arthur   P: Phila 20 Jy 69,
1 Feb 70
Ebenezer   P: Phila 10 Ap 66
George   P: Phila 12 Ja 58
John   P: Phila 25 Jy 65
William   P: Phila 11 Jy 54,
24 Oct 54, 20 Jy 69

GODDEN
Thomas   P: Phila 18 Feb 55

GODDINGTON
John   P: Phila 26 Jy 64

GODFREY/GODFRIE
Edmond   P: Phila 11 Sep 55
Joseph   P: Phila 15 Mar 64
William   P: Chester Co 18 Ag
57, 8 Jy 62

GODMAN
John   P: Phila 31 Dec 61

GODWIN
James   P: Phila/?/ 16 Jy 67

GOEDESCHY
John R.   P: Phila 24 Oct 54

GOETSCHY
John R.   P: Phila 18 Feb 55

GOENN
Capt.   P: Phila 25 Jy 65

GOFF
Edward   P: Phila 2 Feb 64
Eph.   P: Phila 9 Ag 59
Peter   P: Phila 27 Jy 58, 10
Oct 65, 23 Oct 66

GOFFRUM
Andr.   P: Tolpehocken 22 Nov
53

GOFORTH
William   Phila 16 Jy 77;
Reading 30 Ap 77
Zachariah   P: Kent Co 8 Jy
62

GOGGIN
George   P: Phila 1 Feb 70
John   P: Phila 25 Jy 65

GOLDEN/GOLDER
Abraham   P: New-Castle Co 9
Ag 59
William   P: New-Castle Co 9
Ag 59, 3 Sep 61; near the
Trap 2 Feb 64

GOLDING
Coals   P: North Castle 7 Ap
57

GOLDSBOROUGH
Charles   P: Phila 5 Ag 62

GOLDSWORTH
Mrs.   P: Phila 31 Dec 61

GOLDY
Joseph   P: Gloucester 31 Jy
60

GOLLEY
Susannah   P: Phila 2 May 65

GOMEZ
Mat.   P: Phila 31 Dec 61

GOMMERY

John   P: Abington 2 Ag 70
GONIGALL
  Edward   P: Phila 18 Mar 62
GONNO
  Mary   P: Duck Creek 7 Ap 57
GOOD
  Elizabeth   P: Moreland 30 Ap
  67
  Robert   P: Lancaster Co 31 Jy
  60, 3 Sep 61
GOODGION
  Lawrence   P: Pa 15 Mar 64
GOODING/GOODIN
  Jacob   P: Noxontown 27 Jy 58
  John   P: Phila-Gaz. 27 Oct 73
GOODLING
  Jacob   P: New-Castle Co 3 Ja
  60
GOODMAN
  Jean   P: Phila 29 Ag 54
  Richard   P: Phila 1 Feb 70,
  16 Jy 72
GOODSELL
  Lewis   P: Phila 10 Ap 66
GOODWIN/GOODWINS
  Charles & Co.   P: West Chester
  7 Ap 57
  George   P: Phila 8 Jy 62
  John   P: Phila 8 Jy 62, 5 Ag
  62, 2 Feb 64
  Mary   P: Phila 3 Sep 61
  Richard   P: Chester Co 13 Oct
  63
  Samuel   P: Bucks Co 18 Mar 62
  Thomas   Phila 31 Ja 76
GOOLD, see BEEKMAN &
GOORLEY
  Thomas   P: Phila 18 Mar 62
GOOS
  Charles   P: Phila 20 Jy 69
GORAN
  Andrew   P: Phila 3 Sep 61
GORDER
  George   P: Phila 20 Jy 69
GORDON/GORDIN; see also BROWN &
  Capt.   P: Phila 30 Ap 67
  Mrs.   Phila 30 Ap 77
  Alexander/Sanders   P: Pa 31
  Jy 60; Phila 16 Jy 72
  Ally   P: Phila 3 May 70
  Andrew   P: Pa 13 Oct 63, 15
  Mar 64
  Arthur   P: Cumberland Co 21
  Jy 68; Phila 2 Ag 70
  George   P: Cumberland Co 3
  Sep 61; Pa 12 Feb 61; Phila
  30 Oct 66, 1 May 76
  Isabella   P: Phila 24 Oct 54
  James   L: 29 Ja 67.   P: N.
  Castle Co 13 Ja 63; Phila
  23 Oct 66, 31 Ja 76 (Ens.,
  prisoner); York Co 12 Feb 61
  James, Jr.   P: Phila 23 Oct
  66; York Co 19 Ja 69
  Jane   P: York Co 31 Dec 61

John   P: Lancaster Co 12 Ja
  58, 3 Ja 60, 31 Jy 60;
  Phila 27 Oct 73
Lewis   P: Burdentown 9 Ag 59;
  Phila 11 Jy 54, 3 Ja 65.
  T: Bordentown 10 Ag 58
  (Esq.)
Mary   P: Phila 9 Ag 59
Patrick   P: Phila 2 May 65;
  Phila Co 19 Ja 69; Provi-
  dence 13 Oct 63
Robert   P: Phila/?/ 16 Jy 67
Thomas   L: Windsor Twp 2 Mar
  74. P: Phila 3 Ja 65, 30
  Ja 66, 1 May 76
William   L: 3 Oct 65.   P:
  Lancaster Co 8 Jy 62; Pe-
  quea 9 Ag 59, 28 Oct 62;
  Pa 12 Ja 58, 2 Feb 64
GORE
  Charles   P: Phila 3 Ja 60
GORHAM
  Stephen   Phila 5 Ja 76-Gaz.
  31 Ja
GORMAN
  Ann   P: Chester Co 11 Sep 55
GORMLY
  Samuel   P: Phila 3 Sep 61
GORRELL
  James   P: Dover 3 Ja 65
  Robert   P: Pa 31 Jy 60
GORTON
  Daniel   P: Phila 30 Ap 67,
  20 Oct 68
  Samuel   P: Phila 8 Jy 62
GORVAN
  Math.   P: Phila Co 18 Mar 62
GOSFARD
  Nathaniel   P: Phila 20 Ap 69
GOSLEY
  William   P: Kensington 19 Ja
  69, 26 Oct 69
GOSLIN/GOLLINGS/GOSLINE
  Elizabeth   P: Phila 3 Ja 65
  John   P: Phila 31 Dec 61, 4
  Feb 68
  William   P: Pa 12 Feb 61
GOSTELOU
  Jonathan   P: Phila 15 Mar 64
GOSTES
  John   T: Mountholly 17 Oct 54
GOTHER
  Edward   P: Phila 2 May 65
GOTT
  George, Schoolmaster   L:
  Lancaster Co 20 Ja 73;
  York Town 29 Jy 77
GOTTIER/GOTTEER
  Edward   P: Phila 25 Jy 65
  James   P: Phila 22 Nov 53,
  28 Nov 54, 1 Feb 70
GOUDIE/GOUDY
  James   P: Brandywine 27 Dec
  53; Chester Co 31 Dec 61;
  Shrewsbury 9 Ag 59; York

Co 3 Ja 60

GOUDRIE
James L: York Co 19 Dec 71

GOUGH
& CARMALT P: Phila 24 Feb 63
William P: Phila 5 Ag 62, 16
Jy 72

GOUL
Jacob P: Phila 30 Ap 67

GOURLEY/GOURLY
Alexander P: New-Castle Co
5 Ag 56
John P: Phila 5 Ag 62
Joseph P: Bordentown 19 May
63; Phila 3 Ja 65
Samuel P: Bucks Co 27 Jy 58

GOURREGE
Gracian P: Phila 24 Jy 76

GOUSLEY
John P: Pa 31 Dec 61

GOVER
Mary P: Sasquehanna 18 Mar
62
Philip P: Baltimore Co 31
Dec 61; Sasquehannah 24 Feb
63

GOVETT
Joseph P: Phila 13 Oct 63
W. P: Phila 31 Dec 61

GOWANS
Peter P: Phila 27 Jy 58

GOWRY
William P: Pa 26 Jy 53

GRACE
William P: Cecil Co 31 Dec
61

GRAFF
Casper P: Phila-Gaz. 27 Oct
73
Conrad P: Phila 26 Jy 64

GRAHAM/GRAHAMS/GRAEME/GRAEMS/
GREHAME
Mr. P: Phila 31 Dec 61
Adam P: Phila 19 May 63
Andrew P: Phila 23 Oct 66
Angus P: Pa 15 Mar 64
Ann P: Phila 25 Jy 65
Arthur P: Pequea 29 Ag 54;
Pa 13 Oct 65
Charles P: Marlborough 19
May 63
Elizabeth P: Newcastle Co 12
Ja 58
George P: Chester Co 2 Feb
64; Phila 28 Nov 54, 28 Ap
68
Henry Hale P: Chester Co 24
Feb 63
Hugh P: Forks of Delaware-
Gaz. 27 Oct 73
J. C: Nantmill, see KARR,
James
James C: c/o Charles Elliot
Oxford Twp 30 Oct 66. P:
Bucks Co 3 Ja 60; Chester

Co 18 Ag 57, 24 Feb 63;
Phila 24 Oct 54, 19 May
63. T: c/o Archibald
Stuart, Union Iron-works
31 Ja 71
John L: Lancaster Co 20 Ja
73. P: Pa 12 Feb 61;
Phila 1 Nov 53, 3 Sep 61,
28 Oct 62, 13 Ja 63, 16
Jy 72
Nathan P: Phila 27 Jy 58,
1 Nov 70
Nathaniel P: Phila 19 May
63, 16 Jy 77
Patrick P: Phila 24 Oct 54
Peter P: Pa 28 Oct 62
Richard P: Bucks Co 31 Dec
61
Robert L: York Co 29 Jy 72.
P: Kingsess-Gaz. 3 Ja 76;
Phila 2 Feb 64, 3 Ja 65,
20 Jy 69, 2 Ag 70, 27 Oct
73
Samuel P: New London 7 Ap
57
Sarah Phila 16 Jy 77
Capt. W. P: Phila 31 Dec 61
William L: 11 Ap 65. P:
Chester Co 2 Feb 64; Cum-
berland Co 3 Sep 61 (Capt);
Phila 28 Oct 62, 2 May 65

GRAIG
Daniel P: Phila 20 Ap 69
William P: Phila-Gaz. 3 Ja
76

GRAISBURY
Joseph P: Phila 13 Oct 63

GRAM
George P: Phila 25 Ap 71

GRAMES
Michael P: Pa 12 Feb 61

GRAMWELL
Capt. George P: Phila 2 Ag
70

GRANDINE
Samuel, Esq. T: Morris Co 7
May 67

GRANGE
Mary P: Pa 18 Mar 62

GRANGER
Mr. P: Phila 25 Ap 71
John P: Phila 16 Jy 72

GRANIER
John P: Phila 9 Ag 59

GRANNIS
Rossel P: Phila 2 May 65

GRANT; see also HARTLEY &
Adam P: Phila 21 Jy 68, 20
Jy 69
Daniel P: Phila 30 Ja 66
David P: Phila 3 May 70
Elizabeth P: Phila 30 Ja 66
James P: Phila 21 Dec 58 (soldier);
Phila 19 May 63, 4 Ag 63,
1 Feb 70 (soldier)

John   L: York Town, York Co
  19 Dec 71.   P: Phila 8 Jy
  62, 3 Ja 76
Joseph   P: 21 Dec 58 (Lt. in
  the army); Pa 5 Ag 56;
  Phila 5 Ag 62
Lewis   P: Phila 9 Ag 59, 28
  Oct 62, 30 Oct 76, 19 Jy 80
Patrick   P: Phila 4 Feb 68
Robert   P: Phila-Gaz. 3 Ja 76
Ruth   P: Pa 31 Jy 60
Thomas   P: Prince George 4 Ag
  63
William   P: East Fallowfield
  9 Ag 59; Pa 23 Oct 66 (Capt,
  42nd Rgt); Phila 23 Oct 66
GRANTLAND
  James   T: Salem Co 31 Ja 71
GRANVILL
  Maurice   P: Hunterdon Co 31
  Jy 60
GRASE
  Casper   P: Phila 3 May 70
GRASETT
  John   P: Phila 12 Feb 61
GRASLEY
  Eve   P: Phila-Gaz. 3 Ja 76
GRAVES
  Eleanor   P: Phila/?/ 16 Jy 67
  Jessey/Jesse   P: Merion 26 Jy
  64; Phila 3 Ja 65
  Richard   P: Phila 25 Jy 65
  Susanna   P: Phila 26 Oct 69
  Thomas   P: Phila 12 Feb 61, 8
  Jy 62
  William   P: Northampton Co 5
  Ag 62
GRAY/GREY
  Mrs.   P: Phila 2 Feb 64
  Adam   P: North America 1 Nov
  70
  Alexander   P: Phila 3 May 70
  Archibald   P: New-Castle Co 2
  Feb 64
  Conrad   W: Newport, see LEWS-
  TON, Matthew
  David   P: Middle Octorara 26
  Oct 69; Pa 9 Ag 59, 3 Ja 60
  Donald, soldier   P: prob. in
  Pittsburgh 15 Mar 64
  George   P: Phila 3 Ja 65, 10
  Oct 65
  Harrison, Jr.   P: Phila 23
  Oct 66
  Henry   P: Phila-Gaz. 3 Ja 76
  Hugh   P: Pa 12 Ja 58, 9 Ag 59
  Isaac   P: Phila 5 Jy 80-Gaz.
  19 Jy
  James   L: Tuscarora 20 Ja 73.
  P: Forks of Delaware 9 Ag
  59; Phila 18 Ag 57, 1 Nov
  70
  John   P: Lancaster Co 27 Jy
  58; Middle Octorara 26 Oct
  69; New-Castle Co 28 Oct 62,

  2 Feb 64; Pa 28 Oct 62;
  Phila 28 Ap 68
  Matthew   L: 11 Ap 65
  Patrick   P: Pa 31 Jy 60
  Peggy   P: Whiteclay Creek 12
  Ja 58
  Ro.   L: York Town 25 Dec 66
  Robert   P: Phila 10 Oct 65,
  30 Ja 66; York Town 2 Ag 70
  Sarah   P: Pa 12 Ja 58
  Thomas   P: Phila 21 Jy 68;
  Whiteclay Creek 12 Ja 58
  William   P: Middle Octorara
  26 Oct 69; Pa 3 Ja 60;
  Phila 25 Jy 65, 1 Feb 70,
  25 Ap 71
GRAYDEN
  Alexander   P: Bristol 31 Jy
  60
GREAM
  Samuel   P: Phila 3 Ja 65
GREAN
  Thomas   P: Phila 30 Oct 76
GREAR
  Art.   L: Pequea 14 May 72
  David   P: in the army 12 Ja
  58
  George   P: near Phila 28 Nov
  54
  James   P: Phila 27 Jy 58
GREARY
  Andrew   P: Phila 4 Ag 63
GREASBERRY
  Wm.   P: Newcastle Co 18 Ag
  57
GREATON
  Mr.   P: Phila 13 Oct 63
GREAVES
  Matthew   P: Oxford 2 Ag 70
GRECE
  Medy   P: Phila 2 Feb 64
GREEN
  Alice   P: Phila 19 Jy 80
  Ann   P: Kent Co 8 Jy 62
  Christopher   P: Dover 25 Jy
  65; Phila 2 Ag 70
  Cuff   P: Phila 3 Sep 61
  Daniel   P: Phila 31 Dec 61
  Edward   P: Phila 2 Ag 70
  Elizabeth   P: Phila-Gaz. 3
  Ja 76
  James, Jr.   P: Phila 5 Ag 62
  John   P: Phila 25 Jy 65
  Joseph   P: Cumberland Co 9
  Ag 59, 3 Ja 60; Phila 18
  Mar 62, 24 Feb 63
  Mary   P: Phila 5 Ag 56
  Matthew   P: Middle Octerara
  3 Ja 60; Phila 30 Ap 67,
  2 Ag 70
  Nathaniel   P: Phila-Gaz. 27
  Oct 73
  Neomi   P: Phila 1 Jy 56
  Nicholas   P: Phila 21 Jy 68,
  20 Oct 68

Richard P: Phila 24 Feb 63
Solomon L: Lancaster Co 20
    Ja 73
Susannah P: New-Castle Co 3
    Ja 60
Thomas P: Bucks 29 Ag 54;
    Phila 18 Mar 62, 13 Oct 63
Timothy P: Cumberland Co 9
    Ag 59, 3 Ja 60
William P: Duck Creek 18 Ag
    57; Phila 6 Jy 58, 24 Jy
    76; Wilmington 31 Jy 60, 12
    Feb 61, 24 Feb 63, 31 Mar
    63
GREENAL/GREENALL/GRENALL
Robert P: Lewis-Town/Lewes-
    Town 10 Oct 65 (Esq), 1 Nov
    70; Phila 28 Ap 68
Capt. Zibed. P: Phila 26 Jy
    64
GREENAWAY
Capt. Benjamin Phila 5 Ja 76
    Gaz. 31 Ja
GREENFIELD
James P: Pa 12 Feb 61
GREENLAN
Mary P: Phila 12 Ja 58, 4
    Feb 68
GREENLEE
William P: Forks of Delaware
    10 Oct 65
GREENLEER
John P: Pa 5 Ag 62
GREENLIES
Robert L: York Co 20 Ja 73
GREENMAN
Mrs. P: Phila 29 Ag 54, 13
    Oct 63
Rev. P: Pilesgrove 16 Jy 67
Levinia P: Phila 28 Oct 62
Mary P: Piles Grove 13 May 56
Nehemiah P: Phila 7 Ap 57
    (Rev.). T: So. Hanover 17
    Oct 54
GREENMONT
Mrs. P: Phila 6 Jy 58
GREENWAY
Robert P: Phila 2 May 65
Capt. W. P: Phila 2 Sep 62
William P: Phila 30 Ap 67
GREENWOOD
Mrs. P: Phila 20 Jy 69
Elizabeth Nova Scotia 1 May
    76
GREER/GRIER
& COOMBS, Messers Motherkill
    31 Ja 76
Andrew P: Carlisle 18 Mar 62;
    Pa 13 Ja 63
David P: Chestnut Level 30 Ja
    66
George P: Shamony 31 Jy 60
James L: Chamber's Town 20
    Ja 73. P: Chestnut Level
    30 Ja 66; Phila 1 Nov 70

John P: Bucks Co 13 Ja 63,
    24 Feb 63; Pa 28 Oct 62;
    Phila 30 Ja 66
Mary P: Phila 24 Feb 63
Thomas L: York Co 31 Ja 71
William T: Somerset Co 31
    Ja 71
GREESIE
John P: Lancaster Co 31 Jy
    60
GREESLE
Thomas P: Germantown 30 Ap
    67
GREEVE
Robert P: Phila 28 Oct 62
GREFFISS
Richard P: Phila 20 Ap 69
GREGG
Major Frederick P: in the
    army 21 Dec 58
George P: Phila 28 Ap 68
James P: Phila 20 Jy 69,
    16 Jy 77
John P: Wilmington 12 Ja 58
Samuel P: Wilmington 13 Oct
    63
Thomas P: Phila 20 Oct 68
    (Cpl), 2 Ag 70
GREGHAGAN
William P: Md. 18 Mar 62
GREGORY/GREGORIE; see also
    CREGIRE
Abraham P: Phila 2 Ag 70
David P: Cole-brook 7 Ap
    57; Phila 11 Sep 55, 31
    Dec 61, 4 Ag 63
James P: Pa 4 Ag 63, 2 Feb
    64
John P: Chester Co 2 Feb 64
Joseph, soldier in the 18th
    Regt. P: Phila 3 May 70
Mark P: Warwick Twp-Gaz. 27
    Oct 73
Martha P: Phila-Gaz. 27 Oct
    73
Thomas P: Phila 9 Ag 59, 31
    Jy 60
Walpole P: Phila 30 Ja 66
Walter P: Cumberland Co 2
    Sep 62
GREIG
David P: Phila 3 May 70, 27
    Ja 73
GRERSELY
Mr. P: Phila-Gaz. 27 Oct 73
GRESHAM
James P: Phila-Gaz. 3 Ja 76
GRESS
Gasper P: Phila 25 Ap 71
GRESWOLD
Joseph P: Phila 31 Jy 60
Thomas P: Germantown 3 Sep
    61; Phila 31 Dec 61
GREW
Thomas P: Phila 18 Mar 62

GREYER
  Andrew   P: Pa 24 Feb 63
GRIBAN
  John, 18th Regt.   P: Phila 2
    Ag 70
GRIBB
  Henry   P: Phila 25 Jy 65
GRIBBLE
  Charles   P: Phila 19 Jy 80
GRIEVE
  Matthew   P: Oxford 20 Oct 68
GRIFFIE
  Capt.   P: Phila 20 Oct 68
GRIFFIN/GRIFFING/GRIPHAN
  Edward   P: Phila 5 Ag 62
  John   P: Phila 15 Mar 64
  Capt. Moses   P: Phila 19 Jy
    80
  William   P: N. Castle Co 5 Ag
    62; Phila 28 Oct 62, 25 Jy
    65
GRIFFIS
  James   P: Phila 9 Ag 59
  William   P: Phila 15 Mar 64
GRIFFITH/GRIFFITTS/GRIFFITHS
  Ann   P: Pa 27 Jy 58
  Benjamin   P: Bucks Co 26 Jy
    64
  David   P: Frankford 3 Ja 60
  Edward   P: Phila 18 Mar 62,
    2 May 65, 25 Jy 65
  Elizabeth   P: Phila 19 Ja 69
  Giddeon   P: Phila 1 Jy 56
  John   N: 12 Feb 67.   P: Phila
    9 Ag 59, 3 Sep 61, 25 Jy 65
  Joran   P: Sussex Co-Gaz. 27
    Oct 73
  Mary   P: Pa 3 Ja 60
  Morris   P: Chester Co 18 Feb
    55, 31 Dec 61, 13 Ja 63;
    Willistown, Chester Co 9
    Ag 59, 23 Oct 66
  Richard   P: Phila 24 Oct 54
  Robert   P: Phila 10 Oct 65
  Sarah   P: Phila 31 Dec 61
  Thomas   P: Fort Ann 8 Jy 62;
    Pa 18 Mar 62; Phila 9 Ag
    59, 18 Mar 62, 5 Ag 62
  Timothy   P: New Castle Co 30
    May 54
  William   Phila 31 Ja 76
GRIGGS/GRIGE/GRIG
  David   P: Phila 1 Feb 70
  Michael   P: Chester Co 18 Ag
    57
  Rachel   P: Duck Creek 3 Sep
    61
GRIM
  Samuel   P: Phila 28 Ap 68
GRIMES/GRIMS/GRIME/GRYMES
  Mrs.   P: Phila 23 Oct 66
  Mr.   P: Phila /?/ 27 Jy 58,
    16 Jy 67
  Christiana   L: Muddy Creek
    York Co 29 Jy 72

  Daniel   P: Phila 5 Ag 62
  Nathaniel   P: Phila 11 Sep
    55
  Polly   P: Phila 26 Jy 64
  William   P: Schuylkill 24
    Feb 63
GRINDISTON
  Hugh   P: Phila 13 May 56
GRINNELL
  William   P: Phila 20 Jy 69
GRISKUM/GRISKOM
  Samuel   P: Phila 24 Oct 54
  William   P: Phila 7 Ap 57
GRISSEL/GRIZELL
  Joseph   P: Phila 12 Feb 61
  Nicholas   P: Phila 7 Ap 57
GRISSEY
  Maurice   P: Great Valley 8
    Jy 62
GROB
  Henry   P: Phila /?/ 16 Jy 67
GROGAN
  James   P: Phila 31 Dec 61
GROOM
  W.   P: Phila 31 Jy 60
GROSS
  Frederick   P: Phila 28 Ap 68
  Josiah   P: Phila 3 May 70, 2
    Ag 70, 1 Nov 70
GROTT
  James (soldier)   P: 21 Dec
    58
GROTZ
  Henry   Phila 5 Ap 76-Gaz. 1
    May
GROVE
  Capt. J.   P: Phila 13 Oct 63
  Mary   P: Germantown 20 Oct 68
  Pashley   P: Lancaster 13 May
    56
  Samuel   P: Phila 25 Jy 65
GROVER
  Dean   P: Phila 1 Nov 63
  James   P: 27 Ja 73
  Phil./Philip   C: Sasque-
    hannah Ferry 18 Jy 65, 28
    Nov 65, 30 Oct 66
GROVES
  Capt.   P: Phila 9 Ag 59
  Hugh   P: Phila 15 Mar 64
  John   P: Phila 6 Jy 58
  Peter   P: Phila 6 Jy 58
    (Capt), 9 Ag 59
  Stephen   P: Phila 19 Ja 69
  William, soldier   P: Phila 1
    Feb 70
GROWRY
  William   P: Pa 6 Sep 53
GRUBB/GRUBE
  Mr.   P: Chester 31 Jy 60
  Adam   P: New-Castle Co 5 Ag
    56
  Curtis   L: Mary-Ann Fumice,
    York Co 2 Mar 74.   P:
    Wilmington 11 Sep 55; see

also Peter

Capt. Emanuel New-Castle Co 24 Jy 76

John Adam P: Germantown 8 Jy 62

Nathaniel P: Chester Co 30 May 54, 11 Sep 55, 27 Jy 58

Peter P: Lancaster Co 24 Feb 63; Pa 26 Jy 64

Messers. Peter and Curtis L: Little Britain Lancaster Co 31 Ja 71

Rachel P: Chester Co 12 Feb 61, 3 Sep 61

Samuel P: Chester Co 11 Sep 55, 12 Feb 61

GRUMBY
Mr. P: Phila 27 Ja 73

GRUMPE
Capt. P: Phila 4 Ap 54

GRUSH
John P: Phila 26 Oct 69

GUED
Charles P: Phila 26 Oct 69

GUEHLY
John P: Bennet's Bridge 1 Feb 70

GUELING
John P: Phila /?/ 16 Jy 67

GUERIN
Mr. P: Phila 27 Oct 73, 19 Jy 80

GUEST
William P: Back Creek 12 Ja 56

GUICHARD
Joseph P: Phila 24 Oct 54

GUIG
Henry P: Phila 8 Jy 62

GUILEAND
George P: Chester Co 2 Feb 64

GUILIN /alias GUTRY/
John T: Trenton 17 Oct 54

GUIRE
Adam P: Carpenter's Island 4 Feb 68

John P: Phila 10 Ap 66

GULLAN
Alexander P: Phila 24 Feb 63

GULLE
Anthony P: Phila 26 Oct 69

GUM
Jane P: Phila 9 Ag 59

GUMNES
Enenes P: Chester Co 9 Ag 59

GUN
Moses T: Hopewell 17 Oct 54

GUNBERRY
Robert L: Carlisle 20 Ja 73

GUNDLIN
Eliz. P: Phila 16 Jy 72

GUNNING/GUNNIN
Jane P: Phila 28 Oct 62
John Berks Co 30 Oct 76

GUNNIS
Henry P: Reading Twp 31 Dec 61

GUNTER
Samuel P: Phila 10 Oct 65

GURLEY
Peter P: Phila 2 Feb 64

GURNEY
Lt. /?/ P: Phila 16 Jy 67

GUSELINE
Isaac P: Pa 27 Jy 58

GUSLY
Thomas P: Pa 13 Oct 63

GUTHRIE/GUTHRY/GUTHERY
John P: Springfield Twp 12 Ja 58

Richard P: Hopewell 9 Ag 59

Robert P: Amwell 5 Feb 54, 30 May 54; Hopewell 27 Jy 58, 3 Ja 60

William P: N. Castle Co 15 Mar 64; Whiteclay Creek 18 Mar 62

GUTRY, see GUILIN

GUTS
James P: Phila 25 Jy 65

GUTTEREZ
Jacob P: Phila 19 Ja 69

GUTTERY
Margaret P: Pa 12 Feb 61

GUVER
Adam P: Kingsess 20 Ap 69

GUY
Thomas P: Phila 8 Jy 62, 25 Jy 65

GUYER
Adam P: Kingsess 28 Ap 68

GUYNN
William L: Mary-ann Furnice York Co 2 Mar 74

GWINNETT
Bonnet P: Phila 13 Ja 63
Button P: Phila 2 Feb 64, 3 Ja 65

GWYNN/GWIN
David P: Phila 13 Oct 63
George P: Phila 31 Dec 61
Henry P: Phila 31 Dec 61

H..OCK
John P: Phila 19 Ja 69

HAAG
Godfrey P: Phila 2 Ag 70

HABERSTICK
Michael L: Lancaster Co 29 Jy 72

HACFORD
John P: Phila 4 Ag 63

HACKET/HACKETT
Mr. P: Phila 3 Sep 61
John P: Duck Creek 3 Sep 61;

Hunterdon Co 27 Jy 58; New-
castle Co 12 Ja 58; Phila
16 Jy 72. T: Trenton, see
CORMHELL, William
Robert   P: N.J. 31 Jy 60
HACKIN
John   P: Phila 26 Oct 69
HADCOCK
William   P: Phila 28 Oct 62
HADDEN/HADDIN
James   P: Phila 28 Ap 68
John   P: Phila 28 Ap 68
Mary   P: Phila 6 Jy 58
HADERETON
Mr.   P: 27 miles from Phila
1 Feb 70
HADDOCK/HADOCK
Peter   P: Phila 2 Sep 62
Walter   P: Phila 1 Nov 53, 18
Feb 55
HAEN
Christian   Phila 5 Ap 77-Gaz.
30 Ap
HAFFEY
Thomas   N: Newark /?/ 12 Feb
67
HAGAN/HAGIN/HAGGAN/HAGGEAN/
HAGGIN/HAGON
Ann   P: Phila 25 Jy 65
Arthur   P: Phila 25 Jy 65
James   P: N.J. 2 Feb 64; Nott-
ingham 15 Mar 64
John   P: Phila 13 Oct 63
Joseph   P: Chester Co 13 Oct
63
William   P: Cross Roads 7 Ap
57
HAGAR
John   Phila 24 Jy 76
HAGARTY/HEAGERTY/HEGERTY
James   N: Newark /?/ 12 Feb
67
John   C: c/o David Fleming 18
Jy 65. P: Nottingham 2 Feb
64; Pa 7 Ap 57; West Nant-
mill 9 Ag 59
HAGGETT
Edward   P: Phila 12 Ja 58
HAGLEY / or HIGLEY?/
Eliz.   P: Phila 27 Dec 53
HAGUE
Joseph   P: Phila 19 Jy 80
Nicholas   Hagarstown 24 Jy
76
HAIG
Capt. Alexander   P: Phila 20
Jy 69
Peter   P: Phila 26 Jy 53
HAIGHT
Capt.   P: Phila 31 Mar 63
Stephen   P: Bristol 15 Mar 64
HAIN
Eliz.   P: Phila 21 Dec 58
Joseph   P: Hunterdon Co 27 Jy
58

HAINES, see HAYNES
HAINLY
John   P: Chester Co 3 Sep 61
HAIR
James   P: Bethlehem 5 Ag 62
HAIRBOTTLE
Robert   P: Phila 18 Feb 55
HALDEN
Francis   P: Phila 27 Ja 73
HALE
Elizabeth   P: Phila 31 Dec
61
Walter   P: Phila 27 Ja 73
HALES
John   P: Phila 20 Ap 69
HALEY/HALY
Penelope   P: Phila 20 Ap 69
Thomas   P: Phila 2 Ag 70
HALFPENNY
Thomas   P: Germantown 26 Oct
69
HALKERSON
Robert   P: Phila 15 Mar 64
HALL
Alice   P: Phila 13 Ja 63
Andrew   P: Phila 8 Jy 62, 13
Ja 63, 20 Oct 68, 20 Jy 69
Benjamin   P: Phila 24 Feb 63
David   P: Lewis-Town 1 Jy 56
Elisha   P: Phila 25 Ap 71
Esther   P: Sussex Co 8 Jy 62
Francis   T: Prince-Town 17
Oct 54
George   P: Phila 31 Dec 61,
13 Ja 63
Hugh   L: 29 Ja 67. P: Done-
gal 7 Ap 57; Lancaster Co
12 Ja 58
Jacob   P: Phila Co 24 Feb 63
James   P: Pa 28 Oct 62;
Phila 13 Oct 63, 26 Oct 69
Jarvis   P: Phila 4 Feb 68
John   N: 12 Feb 67; in Cecil
Co, Maryland 29 Nov 64. P:
Bucks Co 18 Ag 57; Frank-
ford 20 Ap 69; Lancaster
Co 5 Feb 54; New Castle Co
7 Ap 57; Oxford Twp 4 Feb
68; Phila 7 Ap 57, 31 Dec
61, 4 Ag 63, 2 Feb 64, 10
Oct 65, 20 Ap 69, 30 Ap
69 (Capt), 16 Jy 72, 31 Ja
76
Jonathan   P: Phila 21 Jy 68
Joseph   P: Phila 3 Ja 60
Margaret   P: Phila-Gaz. 3 Ja
76
Mary   P: Phila 12 Ja 58
Moses   P: Germantown 3 Ja
60; Pa 12 Feb 61; Sussex
Co 16 Jy 72
Capt. Philip   P: Phila 31 Jy
60
Richard   P: Chester Co 1 Nov
53

Ruth T: New Jersey 10 Ag 58
Samuel P: Phila 11 Sep 55,
27 Ja 73, 3 Ja 76
Sarah P: Frankford 1 Feb 70
Solomon T: Cumberland Co 10
Ag 58
William P: Phila 9 Ag 59, 3
Ja 60, 31 Dec 61, 5 Ag 62,
2 Sep 62, 28 Ap 68
HALLAR
Jacob L: 3 Oct 65
HALLERAN
John P: Phila 20 Ap 69
HALLET/HALLOT
Joseph P: Phila 25 Jy 65
Robert Phila 30 Oct 76
HALSON
Sarah P: Phila-Gaz. 27 Oct
73
HALSTED
Matthew P: Phila 30 Ap 67
HALYBURTON
Andrew P: Phila 21 Jy 68
HAM
Mrs. N: New Castle Co, see
TURNER, Daniel
HAMBLEN
Martha P: Phila-Gaz. 27 Oct
73
HAMBRICK
Paul P: Phila 16 Jy 67
HAMBRIGHT
John P: Chester Co 5 Ag 56;
Lancaster Co 15 Mar 64
(Capt)
HAMBURG
Thomas L: White Horse 15 Ap
56
HAMERSLY
Thomas P: Pa 13 Oct 63
HAMILTON/HAMBLETON; see also
RUSSELL &
Capt. P: Phila 27 Jy 58, 21
Dec 58, 19 May 63
Lt. L: Fort Pitt 29 Jy 72
Adam P: Chester Co 9 Ag 59
Alexander L: Juniata 2 Mar
74. P: Phila 6 Jy 58, 27
Jy 58, 5 Ag 62, 28 Oct 62,
13 Ja 63, 3 Ja 65, 2 May
65, 10 Ap 66; Turner's Creek
27 Jy 58
Lt. Archibald P: in the army
21 Dec 58
Andrew P: Phila 2 Ag 70
Benjamin P: Bucks Co-Gaz. 27
Oct 73; Pa 12 Feb 61; Phila
28 Oct 62
Catherine P: Phila 13 Ja 63
Charles L: York Town 31 Ja
71
David P: Phila 12 Ja 58, 12
Feb 61; York Co 15 Mar 64
George P: Hanover Twp 2 Ag
70; Phila 15 Mar 64 (Capt)

Hans P: York Co 12 Ja 58,
13 Ja 63 (Col)
Hugh P: Phila 27 Ja 73
Rev. Jr. P: Charlestown 31
Dec 61
James P: Chester Co 7 Ap
57; Lancaster (Co.) 9 Ag
59, 3 Ja 60; Pa 4 Ag 63;
Phila 31 Mar 63, 21 Dec 58,
2 Feb 64 (Capt), 30 Ja 66,
1 Feb 70 (Esq), 27 Oct 73
Jane P: Lancaster Co 13 Oct
63; near Newcastle 28 Nov
54
Jo. L: York Town 31 Ja 71
John L: York Co 20 Ja 73.
P: Charles Town 26 Jy 64
(Rev); Chester Co 11 Sep
55; Christine 31 Jy 60;
near New-Castle 27 Jy 58;
New-Castle Co 12 Feb 61;
Phila 31 Dec 61, 18 Mar
62, 20 Jy 69, 26 Oct 69,
3 May 70, 27 Ja 73; Welch
Tract 31 Jy 60
Jonathan P: Phila 2 Feb 64
Mary P: Bucks Co 9 Ag 59,
Newtown 3 Ja 60; Phila 4
Feb 68
Nathaniel P: Phila 10 Ap 66,
23 Oct 66 (Dr)
Oliver P: Phila 28 Nov 54
Patrick P: Kent Island 19
May 63, 13 Oct 63; New-
Castle Co 12 Feb 61; Phila
28 Nov 54, 11 Sep 55, 30
Ap 77
Robert L: Cumberland Co 20
Ja 73. P: Chester Co 9
Ag 59, 28 Oct 62, 26 Jy
64; Pa 24 Feb 63; Phila
31 Dec 61 (Esq)
Ruth P: York Town 31 Jy 60
Samuel L: Cumberland Co 20
Ja 73
Thomas P: N.J. 18 Mar 62;
Patuxent River 9 Ag 59;
Pa 3 Ja 60; Somerset Co 9
Ag 59. T: 4 Nov 72
William/Wm. C: near Chester
28 Nov 65. L: Juniata 2
Mar 74. P: Baskin(g)-
ridge 12 Ja 58, 31 Dec 61,
8 Jy 62; Lancaster Co 26
Jy 64; Newcastle Co 12 Ja
58; Pa 12 Feb 61, 24 Feb
63; Phila 30 May 54, 21
Dec 58, 12 Feb 61, 3 Sep
61, 2 Ag 70
HAMISE
Catey P: Bristol 9 Ag 59
HAMLEY
Jane P: Phila 8 Jy 62
HAMLONG
Barnard P: Kent Co 8 Jy 62

HAMMELL/HAMEL/HAMIL/HAMILL
Archibald   P: Phila-Gaz. 27
 Oct 73
Daniel   P: Phila 28 Ap 68
James   P: Phila-Gaz. 3 Ja 76
John   P: Phila 3 May 70, 27
 Oct 73
Mary   P: Phila 2 Ag 70
Robert   L: Middletown, Lan-
 caster Co 19 Dec 71; Shipp-
 en's Town 2 Mar 74. P:
 Bucks Co 31 Dec 61; Phila
 20 Jy 69
Roger   P: Union Furnace 26
 Oct 69
William   L: Pequea 19 Dec 71
HAMMER
Isaac   P: Phila 29 Ag 54, 24
 Oct 54, 18 Feb 55
John   P: Germantown 29 Ag 54
HAMMERSLEY
Ralph   P: Phila 31 Dec 61
HAMMOND
James   P: N.J. 18 Mar 62
John F.   P: Phila 25 Jy 65
Leonard   P: Phila 10 Oct 65
HAMPTON
Ann   P: Phila 2 Ag 70
Elizabeth; see BELL
Mary Ann   P: Phila 2 Feb 64
HANALY
Capt. John   P: Chester Co 31
 Dec 61
HANBY/HANBEY
Elizabeth   P: Phila 27 Ja 73
Matthias   Phila 5 Ap 76-Gaz.
 1 May
HANCOCK
William, Esq.   P: Salem 8 Jy
 62
HAND
Mary   P: Cape May 27 Jy 58
Nathan   P: Cape May 21 Dec 58
Robert   P: in the army 17 Ja
 58
Samuel   P: Phila 28 Ap 68
HANDLEY
David   P: Phila 20 Jy 69
John   P: Chester Co 9 Ag 59
HANDLING
Dennis   P: Phila 29 Ag 54
HANDY
Mary   P: Phila 28 Oct 62
William   Phila 16 Jy 77
HANELMAN
Israel   P: Phila 20 Oct 68
HANERWOOD
Mrs.   P: Derby 9 May 54
HANEY
Arch.   P: St. George 18 Ag 57
Edward   Phila 5 Jy 76-Gaz.
 24 Jy
HANKNESS
William   P: Pa 13 Oct 63
HANLEY/HANLY

John   P: Chester Co 1 Nov
 53, 3 Ja 60 (Capt), 18 Mar
 62, 13 Oct 63; Phila 4 Ap
 54
Michael   P: Phila 9 Ag 59
HANLON/HANLIN/HANLEN
Mrs.   P: Phila 1 Feb 70
Mr.   P: Phila 12 Ja 58 (2)
Bryan   P: Chester Co 2 Feb
 64
Cad.   P: Phila 30 Ja 66
James   P: Phila-Gaz. 3 Ja 76
Marmaduke   P: Phila 26 Oct
 69
Patrick   P: Phila 1 Jy 56,
 19 Ja 69
HANNA/HANNAH/HANA
Abigail   P: N.J. 28 Oct 62
Francis   C: East Fallowfield,
 near Doe Run 28 Nov 65, 30
 Oct 66
James   C: Nottingham 18 Jy
 65.   L: Little Britain 2
 Mar 74.   P: Chester Co 13
 Oct 63
John   P: Norrington 26 Oct
 69; Phila 25 Jy 65
Joseph   P: Phila 10 Ap 66
Mary   P: Phila 15 Mar 64
Robert   P: near Phila 12 Ja
 58
Samuel   P: Phila 2 Feb 64, 3
 Ja 65
William   C: East Fallowfield
 see CAMPBELL, Wm.   N: 29
 Nov 64.   P: Bordentown 20
 Oct 68; Chester Co 21 Dec
 58, 9 Ag 59, 3 Ja 60; Lan-
 caster 9 Ag 59; New-Castle
 Co 28 Oct 62; Pa 28 Oct 62
HANNAS
Joseph   P: Phila 11 Sep 55
HANNEW
William   P: Newcastle 18 Ag
 57
HANNON
Catherine   P: Phila 28 Ap 68
James   C: Chester Co 18 Jy 65
HANNUM
Alice/Allice   P: Phila 20 Jy
 69, 30 Ap 77
HANRATTY/HANRATY
Patrick   P: Pa 12 Feb 61;
 Phila 10 Ap 66, 27 Oct 73
HANSDEN
Agness   P: Pa 4 Ag 63
HANSE
Lodowick   P: Phila 5 Ag 56
HANSELLMAN
Rev.   P: Phila 11 Sep 55
HANSEY
Thomas   P: Ohobo Twp 19 Ja
 69
HANSMAN
Chr.   P: Phila 15 Mar 64

HANSON
    Alexander P: Phila 2 Feb 64
    Alexander Contee P: Phila 23
      Oct 66
    Capt. H. P: Baltimore 19 May
      63
    John P: Warwick Twp 10 Oct 65
    Jonathan P: Phila 12 Feb 61,
      24 Feb 63, 1 Feb 70
    Robert P: Phila 2 Feb 64
    Samuel Phila 16 Jy 77
    Thomas Phila 16 Jy 77
HANTERAB
    Joseph P: Phila 9 Ag 59
HARBISON/HARBESON
    James P: Chester Co 18 Mar
      62
    Thomas P: Phila-Gaz. 3 Ja 76
HARBOR
    Regena P: Phila-Gaz. 27 Oct
      73
HARBORNE
    Paul P: Phila 3 Ja 65
HARDCASTLE
    Hannah P: Phila 25 Ap 71
    John P: Phila 26 Oct 69
    Capt. W. P: Phila 24 Feb 63
HARDGROVES
    Joseph P: Phila 29 Ag 54
HARDIN
    Mr. P: Phila 24 Feb 63
    Robert P: Phila 13 May 56
HARDING; see also ROBINSON &
    Mrs. P: Phila 31 Dec 61
    Aaron P: Salem Co 27 Jy 58
    Eleanor P: Christine Bridge
      31 Dec 61
    George P: Phila 2 Sep 62
    James P: Abington 18 Feb 55;
      Phila 27 Jy 58, 16 Jy 77
    Judy P: Phila 23 Oct 66
    Rachel P: Phila 16 Jy 72
    Rebecca P: Phila 9 Ag 59
    Robert P: Phila 28 Ap 68
    Samuel P: Phila 1 Nov 53
    William P: Phila 15 Mar 64,
      3 Ja 65
HARDISTY
    Joseph P: Phila 27 Ja 73
HARDS
    William P: Phila 27 Ja 73
HARDY/HARDIE
    Mrs. P: Phila 1 Feb 70, 2 Ag
      70
    Capt. Alexander P: Phila 28
      Ap 68
    Capt. James P: Phila-Gaz. 27
      Oct 73
    Thomas P: Phila 12 Ja 58, 13
      Ja 63
    William P: Phila 2 Ag 70,
      17 Jy 80 (Capt)
HARE
    Samuel P: Phila 28 Ap 68

HAREMAN
    Michael P: Lower Dublin 23
      Oct 66
HARGAN
    Daniel P: Phila 10 Oct 65
    Dennis P: Pa 28 Oct 62
HARGY
    James P: Pa 15 Mar 64
HARIGAN/HARAGAN/HARRIAGAN
    Eliz. P: Phila 15 Mar 64
    James P: Phila 29 Ag 54
    Matthew P: Phila 4 Ap 54
HARKENS
    Neal P: Pa 24 Feb 63
HARKER
    A. P: Phila 3 Ja 65
    Samuel P: Gloucester-Gaz.
      3 Ja 76; Salem Co 7 Ap 57
HARKIES
    Jeremiah P: Pa 13 Ja 63;
      Phila 28 Oct 62
HARKINSON
    John P: Mount-holly 25 Jy 65
HARKNESS
    Nat. P: York Co 2 Feb 64
    William P: Pa 28 Oct 62.
      T: Pa 31 Ja 71
HARKNIE
    William T: Barnstable /?/
      4 Nov 72
HARLAN
    George P: Pa 18 Mar 62
HARLE
    Anthony P: Phila 18 Ag 57,
      27 Ja 73
HARLEY
    Sarah N: Newark /?/ 12 Feb
      67
HARLOW
    Capt. P: Phila 31 Mar 63
HARLWOOD
    Thomas P: Phila-Gaz. 27 Oct
      73
HARMAN
    George P: Phila 15 Mar 64
HARMANSON
    John P: Phila 1 Nov 70
HARMER
    John P: Phila 9 Ag 59
HARMOND
    Capt. J. P: Phila 24 Feb 63
HARNE
    John P: Pa 3 Ja 60
HARNETT
    Cornelius, Esq. P: Phila 3
      Ja 60
    William Carpenter's Island
      16 Jy 77
HARNEY
    Alexander P: Bucks Co 7 Ap
      57
HARPER/HARPERS
    Widow P: Bucks Co 9 Ag 59
    Hannah P: Pa 13 Ja 63
    Henry P: Pa 28 Oct 62

Hugh N: 12 Feb 67
James P: Phila 24 Feb 63, 26
  Jy 64
John P: Duck Creek 27 Dec 53,
  12 Ja 58; New-Castle 18 Mar
  62; Phila 3 Ja 65, 30 Ja 66
Robert P: Phila 2 Feb 64
Samuel L: York Co 2 Mar 74.
  P: York Co 31 Dec 61, 28
  Oct 62
William P: Phila 1 Nov 70
HARRA
Robert, Esq. L: Bedford Co
  20 Ja 73
HARRINGTON
Edmond P: Phila 27 Jy 58
HARRIS
Abel P: Phila 30 Ap 67
Andrew P: Cecil Co 9 Ag 59,
  31 Jy 60
Anthony P: Phila 18 Mar 62,
  28 Oct 62
Arthur P: Phila 5 Ag 62
Charles P: Phila-Gaz. 27 Oct
  73
Edward P: Middletown Point
  15 Mar 64; Phila 16 Jy 77
Evan T: Greenwich 17 Oct 54
Francis P: Phila 20 Jy 69,
  1 Nov 70, 30 Oct 76
George P: Phila 26 Oct 69,
  1 Feb 70
Serjeant Henry P: in the army
  27 Jy 58
J. P: Phila 18 Mar 62
James P: New London 4 Ag 63;
  near Pequea 9 Ag 59; Pa 3
  Ja 60; Pittsburgh 19 May 63;
  Sasquehannah 5 Ag 62
John L: Susquehanna 20 Ja 73.
  P: Bucks Co 12 Ja 58, 12 Feb
  61, 30 Ja 66; Lancaster Co
  12 Feb 61; Newtown (Bucks
  Co) 27 Jy 58, 30 Ja 66, 1
  Feb 70; Paxton 4 Ap 54;
  Phila 1 Jy 56, 15 Mar 64,
  3 May 70 (Capt); Sasque-
  hannah 8 Jy 62; Swetara 27
  Jy 58
Jonathan P: Phila 2 Sep 62
Lancelot P: Phila 13 May 56
Margaret P: Phila 4 Feb 68
Matthew P: Phila 18 Mar 62
Robert P: Phila 28 Oct 62
Samuel L: near Harris's Ferry
  20 Ja 73
Stephen P: Phila 24 Oct 54
Thomas P: Donnegal 24 Oct 54,
  27 Jy 58; Phila 3 Ja 76
W. P: Phila 18 Mar 62
Walter/Walt. P: Phila 18 Mar
  62, 8 Jy 62
William C: 30 Jy 77. P:
  Cecil Co 9 Ag 59; Pa 28 Oct
  62; Phila 1 Nov 53, 29 Ag 54,

  18 Ag 57, 30 Ja 66, 27 Ja
  73 (2)
HARRISON
Mrs. P: Phila 28 Oct 62
Mr. P: Phila 4 Ag 63
Benjamin P: Phila 13 Oct 63
Charles P: Phila 5 Ag 62,
  27 Oct 73
Daniel P: Phila 1 Jy 56, 3
  Ja 76
Elizabeth P: Phila 25 Ap 71
Esther P: Phila 2 Ag 70
George P: Phila 27 Ja 73
Gilbert P: Phila 18 Mar 62
John P: Phila 1 Nov 53, 18
  Feb 55, 3 Ja 60, 18 Mar 62,
  19 Ja 69, 27 Ja 73, 30 Oct
  76 (Capt); White Creek 10
  Ap 66
Joseph P: Phila-Gaz. 27 Oct
  73. T: N.J. 17 Oct 54
  (Esq.)
Josiah P: Phila 19 May 63
Mary L: York Co 31 Ja 71
Mrs. Mary T: Trenton 1 Sep
  68
Richard P: Pa 27 Jy 58;
  Phila 20 Jy 69
Robert P: Phila 11 Sep 55,
  5 Ag 62
Sarah P: Phila 23 Oct 66
Thomas P: Phila 23 Oct 66
Walter P: Phila 5 Ag 62
William P: Pa 24 Oct 54;
  Phila 12 Ja 58
HARRON
Mary P: Phila 22 Nov 53
HARROT
Dr. P: Phila 19 Jy 80
HARROW
Mr. P: Phila 18 Ag 57
Isaac P: Pa 15 Mar 64
HART
Ensign Abraham P: Phila 7
  Ap 57
Charles P: Phila 2 May 65
George C: West Bradford 30
  Oct 66. P: Brandywine 5
  Ag 62; Chester Co 2 Feb
  64
Jacob L: Lancaster Co 19 Dec
  71
James L: c/o Dr. Fullerton
  Leacock Twp 19 Dec 71. P:
  Phila 15 Mar 64 (Capt)
John P: Chester Co 28 Oct
  62; Lancaster Co 26 Jy 64;
  Phila 9 Ag 59, 3 Ja 60.
  T: Hopewell 10 Ag 58;
  Hunterdon Co 10 Ag 58 (Esq.
Margaret P: Lancaster 24 Oct
  54, 18 Feb 55
Patrick P: Pa 4 Ag 63
Peter C: West Nantmell 30
  Oct 66

Seymour   Phila 5 Ap 76-Gaz.
  1 May
William   P: Deep Run 8 Jy 62
HARTFORD
  & POWELL   P: Phila 26 Oct 69
HARTLEY/HARTLY/HEARTLY
  and GRANT   P: Phila 31 Dec 61,
    18 Mar 62
  Henry   P: Phila 13 May 56, 30
    Ja 66
  James   P: Phila 8 Jy 62
  Jane   C: Brandywine Hundred
    18 Jy 65.   P: Bethel 18 Ag
    57, 27 Jy 58; Phila 25 Ap
    71; Salem 26 Oct 69
  Joshua   P: Phila-Gaz. 27 Oct
    73
  Thomas   P: Chester Co 18 Mar
    62; New-Castle Co 8 Jy 62,
    13 Oct 63; Phila 30 Ap 77
HARTMAN
  Isaac   Phila 30 Oct 76
  John   C: Pikeland 28 Nov 65
  Peter   P: Yellow Springs 30
    Ap 67
HARTUPEE
  Daniel   T: Prince Town 17 Oct
    54
HARTWICK/HARTWIG
  Rev.   P: Phila 3 Ja 65, 21 Jy
    68
HARVEY/HARVIE
  Alexander   P: Bucks Co 27 Ja
    73; Neshaminey 16 Jy 72;
    prob at Pittsburgh, drum
    major / no date /
  Andrew   P: Cecil Co 31 Dec 61
  Benjamin   P: Sasquehanna 19 Jy
    80
  Charles   P: Phila 2 Feb 64
  G.   P: Phila 12 Ja 58
  John   P: Neshaminey 27 Ja 73
  Margaret   P: Phila 1 Nov 70
  Matthias   P: Phila 30 Ja 66
  Mongo, Messrs and Jo. DEANS
    L: 29 Ja 67
  Sampson   P: Phila 31 Jy 60,
    25 Jy 65, 26 Oct 69
  Samuel   P: Phila 9 Ag 59,
    3 Ja 60
  Capt. Seth   P: Phila 5 Ag 62
  Thomas   T: Middletown Point
    15 Mar 64
  W.   P: Cecil Co 31 Jy 60
  Messieurs William or Andrew
    N: Cecil Co c/o John Picken
    4 Dec 66
  William   P: Bucks Co 25 Jy
    65; Cecil Co 31 Dec 61;
    Kennet 1 Nov 53; Pa 13 May
    56; Phila 12 Feb 61, 23 Oct
    66, 2 Ag 70
HARWOOD
  John   P: Phila 20 Jy 69
HASENCLEVER

  Peter   P: Phila 10 Oct 65
HASLET/HASLETT/HASLITT/HEAS-
  LET; see also HESLET
  Dr.   P: Phila 31 Dec 61
  John   P: Kent Co 19 Ja 69;
    Phila 31 Mar 63 (Dr)
  Joseph   P: Pa 2 Feb 64
  William   P: Chester Co 19 Jy
    80; Pa 4 Ag 63
HASMES
  Jonathan   P: Carlisle 26 Jy
    64
HASSET
  Mr. (tanner)   P: Phila 7 Ap
    57
  John   P: Phila 10 Ap 66
HASSON
  Samuel   P: Chester Co 19 May
    63
HASTINGS/HEASTING
  David   P: Octerara 2 Feb 64
  George   P: New-Castle Co 3
    Ja 60
  Henry   P: Chester Co 31 Jy
    60
  John   P: Carlisle 31 Dec 61;
    Cumberland Co 12 Ja 58;
    New-Castle Co 9 Ag 59, 3
    Ja 60
  Margaret   P: Phila 21 Dec
    58, 9 Ag 59
  Samuel   Phila 1 May 76
HATCH
  Paxton   Phila 5 Ap 76-Gaz.
    1 May
HATHORN/HATHON
  Daniel   P: Phila 24 Oct 54,
    12 Feb 61, 25 Jy 65, 23
    Oct 66
  Capt. H.   P: Phila 26 Jy 64
  Hugh   P: Phila 3 Ja 65
  John   C: East Nottingham 22
    Ja 67.   P: East Notting-
    ham 18 Ag 57, 30 Ja 66;
    New-Castle 18 Mar 62;
    Nottingham 13 Oct 63; Phila
    5 Ag 56
  Peter, Jr.   P: Concord 5 Ag
    56
  Robert   L: Cumberland Co 19
    Dec 71
HATKINSON
  John   P: Mountholly 24 Feb 63
HATRICK/HATTRICK
  Samuel   P: Phila 4 Feb 68
  Sarah   P: Phila 2 Feb 64
  William   P: Pa 13 Ja 63
HATTER
  Richard   P: Phila 31 Dec 61
HATTERSON
  Capt.   P: Phila 16 Jy 72
HATTERY
  Thomas   Phila 16 Jy 77
HATTON/HATTAN
  Charles   P: Pa 15 Mar 64

John   P: Forks of Delaware 26
  Oct 69; Middletown 20 Ap 69;
  Phila 21 Dec 58 (sailor),
  31 Dec 61 (Capt); West
  Jersey 10 Ap 66, 20 Ap 69
Thomas   P: Phila 9 Ag 59
HAUGHIAN
  Oliver   P: Bucks Co 30 Ja 66;
  Phila 28 Oct 62
HAUSVAX
  Jacob   P: Phila 25 Ap 71
HAUTZ
  John, tanner   L: Mud Creek,
  York Co 19 Dec 71
HAVEN
  Thomas   P: 11 Sep 55
HAVENOR
  Thomas   P: Phila 18 Ag 57
HAVERDSON
  Mrs.   P: Phila 31 Dec 61
HAVERS
  Edward   P: Phila 13 Oct 63
HAW
  John   P: N.J. 2 Feb 64.   T:
  Hunterdon Co 6 Dec 64
HAWEN
  Thomas   P: Phila 1 Feb 70
HAWKER
  Capt. James   P: Phila 23 Oct
  66
HAWKINS; see also HOKINS
  Mrs.   P: Pa 27 Jy 58; Phila
  6 Jy 58
  George   P: Phila 5 Ag 62, 25
  Jy 65, 30 Ja 66, 4 Feb 68,
  1 Feb 70, 1 Nov 70
  Jacobus   N: 12 Feb 67
  Jer.   P: Phila 18 Mar 62
  John   P: Phila 13 Ja 63, 3
  Ja 76
  Timothy   Phila 31 Ja 76
  Will.   P: Phila 20 Ap 69
HAWKS/HAWKES
  Samuel   P: Phila 15 Mar 64,
  30 Ap 67
HAWKSWORTH
  Enoch   L: York Co 2 Mar 74
  John   P: Phila 21 Dec 58
  William   P: Pa 11 Sep 55
HAWLEY
  Benjamin   P: Chester Co 9 Ag
  59, 2 Sep 62
HAWORTH
  John   Phila 24 Jy 76
HAXTON
  Robert   P: Phila 27 Jy 58
HAY; see also BARCLAY &
  Adam   P: Lancaster Co 24 Feb
  63
  Capt. Charles   P: Phila 2 Sep
  62
  James   P: Phila 15 Mar 64
  John   P: Phila 19 Jy 80
  Robert   L: Antrim Twp 19 Dec
  71.   P: Donegall 18 Ag 57

William   P: New-Castle (Co)
  27 Jy 58, 9 Ag 59, 3 Sep
  61, 13 Oct 63
HAYER
  John   P: Phila 21 Dec 58
HAYES/HAYS
  Charles   P: Phila 27 Ja 73
  Francis   P: Phila 26 Oct 69
  James   P: Chester Co 3 Sep
  61, 28 Oct 62; Phila 2 Ag
  70
  John   C: Oxford Twp,see
  ARNETTS, John   L: Cumber-
  land Co 2 Mar 74.   P:
  Forks of Delaware 13 Oct
  63, 3 Ja 65; Northampton
  Co 3 Sep 61; Phila 21 Dec
  58
  Malachy   P: Phila-Gaz. 27
  Oct 73
  Michael   P: Phila 2 Sep 62
  (Capt), 23 Oct 66, 16 Jy
  72, 31 Ja 76
  Nicholas   L: Bedford Co 19
  Dec 71
  Richard   P: Phila 27 Jy 58,
  2 Feb 64
  Samuel   P: Pa 12 Feb 61
  William   L: Berks Co 29 Jy
  72.   P: Hopewell-Gaz. 3 Ja
  76; Pa 1 Feb 70; Phila 1
  Feb 70; Wilmington 18 Ag
  57.   T: Barnstable 4 Nov
  72
HAYMAN
  Capt. William   P: Phila 2 Ag
  70
HAYNES/HAINES/HAINS/HANES/
  HEYNES
  Barbary   L: Lancaster 15 Ap
  56
  Charles   P: Pa 24 Feb 63;
  Phila 31 Jy 60, 27 Oct 73
  Daniel   Phila 5 Ap 76-Gaz.
  1 May
  John   P: Phila 18 Feb 55,
  25 Jy 65, 26 Oct 69
  Mat.   P: Bucks Co 12 Ja 58;
  Montgomery Twp 18 Mar 62
  Nicholas   L: 13 Jn 65
  Stephen   P: Phila 28 Nov 54
  Thomas   P: Phila 26 Oct 69
HAYWARD/HEYWARD
  Andrew   P: Phila 25 Ap 71,
  27 Oct 73
  Eliz.   P: Lancaster Co 4 Ag
  63
  George   P: Pa 12 Feb 61
  John   P: Phila 3 Sep 61
  William   Phila 24 Jy 76
HAZEL/HAZELL
  Isaac   P: Duck Creek Hundred,
  Kent Co 19 Ja 69; Phila 28
  Ap 68
HAZELHURST/HAZLEHURST

Mr. P: Phila 3 Ja 65
Isaac Phila 16 Jy 77
HAZELTON/HASELTON
& PENROSE P: Phila 3 May 70
William P: Phila 4 Ap 54,
9 May 54, 6 Jy 58, 10 Ap 66,
21 Jy 68 (Capt)
HAZELWOOD
John P: Phila 24 Oct 54
(Capt), 6 Jy 58 (Capt), 25
Jy 65
HEACOCK
Jonathan P: Chester Co 1 Nov
53, 13 May 56
HEAD
Arthur P: Phila 18 Mar 62
(2)
HEALSTON
William P: Phila-Gaz. 27 Oct
73
HEALY
Michael P: Phila 30 Ap 67
HEANDRE
James P: Phila 27 Ja 73
HEANEY/HEANY/HEENEY/HEYNEY
Henry P: Phila 1 Nov 70
Hugh P: East Fallowfield 9
Ag 59
John P: Phila 27 Ja 73
Robert P: Phila 11 Jy 54,
12 Ja 58
HEARD/HERD
John P: Phila 20 Ap 69
W. P: Phila 4 Ag 63
HEART
Catharine P: Phila 31 Jy 60
HEASLOP
George P: N. Castle Co 15 Mar
64
HEASTON
William P: Phila 21 Dec 58
HEATH
Chambers P: Phila 28 Nov 54,
9 Ag 59
HEATHER
Richard P: Chester 28 Oct
62
HEATON
John P: Phila 24 Feb 63, 24
Feb 63, 3 Ja 65
Robert P: Bucks Co 3 Ja 60
HEAVILAND
Thomas Oblong 5 Ap 77-Gaz.
30 Ap
HEBSON
Robert P: Pa 13 Oct 63
HECTH
Joshua Phila 5 Ap 77-Gaz. 30
Ap
HEDERINGTON
George P: Phila 25 Ap 71
HEDGECOCK
Thomas P: Phila 21 Jy 68
HEDGES
Abel P: Pa 12 Feb 61

HEDIAN
Myles P: Phila 20 Jy 69
HEERRETTER
Paul P: Phila 2 Ag 70
HEFFERMAN
Roger P: Phila 16 Jy 72
HEGLET
Robert P: Phila 13 Ja 63
HEINITSCH
C.H. P: Phila 16 Jy 72
HEINTZELMAN
.... P: 5 Ag 56
Jerome P: Lancaster 12 Feb
61
HEKKER
Charles L: Lancaster Co 20
Ja 73
John Charles L: Paxton /?/
14 May 72; c/o Mr. Husse-
ger, Lebanon 19 Dec 71
HELDEN
Jeremiah P: Phila 2 Ag 70
HELFER
John Christian P: Phila 28
Nov 54
HELLER
Frederick P: Phila 25 Ap 71
HELM/HELME/HELMES/HELMS
Benjamin Phila 16 Jy 77
Christopher T: Hunterdon Co
17 Oct 54
David T: Somerset Co 4 Nov
72
James P: Chester Co 31 Jy 60
Mabry P: Baltimore 31 Mar 63
Moses T: Bethlehem 17 Oct 54
HELYED
Bartholomew P: Dillworth
Town 1 Feb 70
HEMBEL
William P: Phila 23 Oct 66
HEMPHILL
David P: near Phila 28 Nov
54
James P: Edgmont 3 Ja 60;
New-Castle Co 9 Ag 59
John P: Chester Co 18 Mar
62
William L: Donegal 15 Ap 56.
P: Donegall 13 May 56; Lan-
caster Co 27 Jy 58, 3 Ja
60, 24 Feb 63, 15 Mar 64
HENCHMAN
Isaac P: Phila 3 Sep 61
HENDERSON
Mr. P: Phila 6 Jy 58
Capt. Alexander P: Phila 3
May 70
Arthur P: Phila 2 Ag 70
Daniel P: Chester Co 4 Ag 63
David P: 30 Ja 66; Notting-
ham 1 Feb 70; Phila 30
Ap 67
Eleanor P: East Jersey 21
Dec 58

George   P: Phila 2 Ag 70
Gustavus P: Phila 30 Ja 66
James   C: N. Castle Co 18 Jy
  65. N: 29 Nov 64. P: Car-
  lisle 31 Jy 60; Phila 27
  Dec 53, 26 Oct 69
Jane   P: Phila 11 Sep 55;
  Southampton, B/ucks7 C/o.7
  28 Ap 68
John   P: Lancaster Co 3 Sep
  61; Pa 30 Ap 67; Phila 13
  Ja 63, 2 Feb 64, 25 Jy 65,
  30 Ja 66, 16 Jy 67
Joseph   Phila 24 Jy 76
Margaret   P: Phila 25 Jy 65,
  4 Feb 68, 19 Jy 80
Matthew   C: Oxford 22 Ja 67
  (minister). L: 3 Oct 65.
  P: Oxford 18 Mar 62, 26 Jy
  64 (Rev.); Pa 3 Ja 60; Phila
  9 Ag 59
Resnah   P: Phila 23 Oct 66
Robert   P: Bucks Co 27 Jy 58;
  Phila 13 May 56, 27 Jy 58
  (Capt), 24 Feb 63
Rosannah   P: Phila 20 Jy 69
Samuel   T: Freehold 1 Sep 68
Thomas   P: Phila 19 May 63
William   P: Cherry Valley 2
  Feb 64; Pa 12 Feb 61; Phila
  27 Jy 58, 25 Jy 65, 16 Jy
  77. W: Christiana Bridge
  3 Jy 76
HENDRICK
  William   Upper Dublin 5 Oct
  76-Gaz. 30 Oct
HENDRICKS
  Capt. James   P: Phila 5 Ag 62
  Richard   P: Phila-Gaz. 3 Ja 76
  Tobias   P: Carlisle 3 Sep 61;
  Cumberland Co 28 Oct 62, 13
  Oct 63
HENDRICKSON
  Claus   P: Phila 1 Feb 70
  Daniel   T: Middletown 31 Ja
  71
  Hendrick   T: Middletown 17 Oct
  54
  James   P: Duck Creek 9 Ag 59,
  3 Ja 60
  Mary   P: Phila 24 Oct 54
  Robert   P: Phila 24 Oct 54,
  21 Dec 58, 5 Ag 62
HENDRY/HENDREY
  Ann   P: Phila 24 Feb 63
  James   P: Lancaster Co 13 Oct
  63; Phila 4 Feb 68
  Jo.   L: 11 Ap 65
  John   P: New Castle Co 7 Ap 57
  Samuel   N: 29 Nov 64. P: New
  Castle Co 26 Jy 64
HENDY
  John   P: Chester Co 31 Jy 60
HENEGAN
  Dr.   P: in the army 12 Ja 58

HENLY
  John   P: Phila 27 Jy 58
HENNEN
  Ja.   L: c/o Mr. Cuthbertson
  14 May 72
  James   P: Sadsbury 5 Ag 56,
  3 Ja 65
HENNERICK
  Johann   T: Prince-Town 17 Oct
  54
HENNESSY/HENESSY
  Joan   P: New London 7 Ap 57
  Capt. John   Floating Battery
  24 Jy 76; Phila 25 Jy 65
HENNEY
  John   P: Phila 2 Ag 70
HENRY; see also SIMONS &
  Capt.   P: Phila 16 Jy 72
  Dr.   Gloucester 1 May 76;
  Woodberry 24 Jy 76
  Edward   P: Phila-Gaz. 3 Ja 76
  Elizabeth   P: Lancaster Co
  21 Dec 58; Phila 16 Jy 72
  Fanny   P: Phila 10 Oct 65
  George   L: York 2 Mar 74
  Hugh   P: Chester Co 31 Dec 61
  James   L: 29 Ja 67. P: Acco-
  mack 24 Jy 76; Little Bri-
  tain 13 Ja 63, 31 Mar 63,
  19 May 63; Phila 31 Jy 60,
  25 Ap 71
  John   L: Carlisle 2 Mar 74;
  Little Britain, Lancaster
  Co 29 Jy 72. P: Kingston
  31 Dec 61; Phila 4 Feb 68,
  21 Jy 68
  Margaret   P: Hartford Twp 31
  Dec 61
  Mary   P: Phila 26 Oct 69, 27
  Ja 73
  Michael   P: Phila 27 Ja 73
  Robert   P: Abington 25 Jy
  65; Pa 12 Feb 61; Phila 13
  May 56, 10 Oct 65, 27 Oct
  73
  Samuel   P: Phila 1 Nov 70.
  T: Trenton 1 Sep 68
  Miss Sarah   Phila 30 Oct 76
  William   P: Lancaster (Co)
  21 Dec 58, 31 Jy 60, 12
  Feb 61, 3 Sep 61; Pa 12 Feb
  61; Phila 12 Ja 58, 27 Jy
  58, 1 Feb 70
HEPBURN
  Lt. John   P: Phila 1 Feb 70
  Stacy   P: Phila 25 Jy 65
HEPTENSTAL
  James, soldier   P: Phila 1
  Feb 70
HEPWORTH
  George   P: Phila 2 Ag 70, 16
  Jy 72
HERBERT/HERBURT
  Capt.   P: Phila 7 Ap 57
  Simon   P: Phila 18 Mar 62

W. P: Phila 1 Feb 70
William   P: Phila 28 Ap 68
HERCONT
William   T: Allen-town 17 Oct
54
HEREFENHEIMER
Christopher P: Phila 20 Jy 69
HERKISS
Jeremiah P: Phila 13 Oct 63
HERMOND
William   P: Phila 9 Ag 59
HERNEY
Rev. P: Phila 2 Ag 70
HERON/HERRON
Ann P: Phila 2 Feb 64
David P: Phila 2 Ag 70
David A. P: New-Castle 11
Sep 55
Isaac P: Phila 25 Jy 65, 10
Oct 65
James P: Kensington 25 Ap 71;
Phila 20 Ap 69, 2 Ag 70
Robert   Phila 5 Ja 76-Gaz. 31
Ja
Thomas P: Forks of Delaware 10
Ap 66, 20 Ap 69
HERR
John P: Lampeter Tow. 11 Sep
55
HERRENDEEN
Caleb P: Phila 20 Jy 69
HERRING
Jane Phila 1 May 76
Ensign Peter P: Phila 23 Oct
66
HERSEY
Ezekiel P: Phila 15 Mar 64
HERVEY
Thomas T: Bucks Co 6 Dec 64
HESLET/HESLETT/HESLOT
George P: New-Castle 12 Feb
61
Martha P: Phila 26 Jy 53
Mary L: 3 Oct 65
HESS
Nicholas P: Phila 31 Jy 60,
3 Sep 61
HESSILUS/HESSELUIS
Jean P: Phila 9 Ag 59
John P: Phila 28 Oct 62
HESTON
Isaac Phila 31 Ja 76
HETALEND
Roger P: Phila 11 Sep 55
HETHRINGTON
John P: Chester Co 11 Sep 55
HETT /‾or HERT?_7
Frederick P: Bethlehem 3 Sep
61
HEVIS
John P: Phila 12 Feb 61
HEWES/HEWS/HEUZE; see also
HUGHES
Mr. P: Phila 3 May 70
Charles P. P: N.J. 24 Feb 63

John P: Newtown 31 Dec 61;
Phila 27 Dec 53. T: Upper
Freehold 6 Dec 64
Josiah P: Phila 18 Feb 55,
21 Dec 58, 12 Feb 61
Patrick P: Newcastle 18 Ag
57, 12 Ja 58
Thomas P: 11 Sep 55
William T: Monmouth Co 15
Mar 64
HEWET/HUET/HUAT/HUIT
Charles P: Phila 26 Oct 69
William P: Chester Co 3 Sep
61; Cross Roads 7 Ap 57;
Oxford 26 Oct 69
HEWISON
Samuel P: Phila 3 Ja 65
HEWLIN
Andrew P: Berks Co 12 Feb
61; Phila 18 Mar 62
HEWLINGS
Ab./Abraham P: Burlington
3 Sep 61, 8 Jy 62; N.J.
24 Feb 63; Phila 27 Jy 58
HEWLIT
Adam P: N.J. 12 Feb 61
HEYATT
Mrs. P: New Garden 26 Jy
64; Phila 3 Ja 65
HEYSHAM
Capt. P: Phila 1 Feb 70
HEYSTER
Nicholas P: Phila 31 Dec 61
HIBBEARD
Ezekiah P: Phila 1 Feb 70
HIBETS
Bernard P: Lancaster Co 24
Feb 63
HICHBQRN
Benjamin P: Phila 5 Jy 80-
Gaz. 19 Jy
HICK
William P: Phila 10 Oct 65
HICKEY
John P: Phila 21 Dec 58
(sailor), 1 Feb 70
Mary P: Phila 21 Dec 58
HICKLING
Capt. John P: Phila 26 Oct
69
Sally P: Phila-Gaz. 3 Ja 76
William P: Phila 28 Oct 62,
24 Feb 63
HICKMAN
Ezekiel Westmoreland Co 1
May 76
Joseph T: Hanover 4 Nov 72
HICKS
Aug. P: Phila 24 Feb 63
Charles P: Phila 26 Jy 64
Edward P: Phila 12 Ja 58
Dr. John T: Trenton 31 Ja 71
William L: 11 Ap 65. P:
Phila 6 Jy 58
HID

John   P: N.J. 2 Feb 64
HIDELSTON/HIDELSTONE
  James   P: Chester Co 12 Feb 61,
    13 Oct 63
HIE
  Moses   P: Phila 1 Nov 70
HIELAND
  James   P: Phila 1 Nov 70
HIENSTON
  Nicholas   P: Forks of Dela-
    ware 26 Oct 69
HIGGINS/HIGGENS
  Capt.   P: Phila 28 Ap 68
  Mr.   P: Phila 20 Ap 69
  David   P: Phila 25 Ap 71
  Edmond   P: Phila 31 Jy 60
  Francis   P: Phila 3 Ja 76
  George   P: Phila 26 Jy 53
  Ichab.   P: Phila 15 Mar 64
  Isabel   P: Phila 31 Dec 61
  John   P: Phila 4 Ag 63
  Michael   P: Phila 27 Ja 73
HIGH
  John   P: Phila 30 Ja 66
HIGHLY
  Henry   P: Phila 1 Nov 53
HIGMIN
  James   P: Phila 16 Jy 72
HIGNER
  Mr.   P: Phila 4 Ag 63
HILANDS/HEYLAND
  Domnick/Dominick   P: Pa 12
    Feb 61; Phila 1 Nov 70
HILEY
  .... (sail maker)   P: Phila
    11 Sep 55
HILL
  Mrs.   P: Phila 3 May 70
  Alexander S.   P: Phila 2 Ag
    70
  Arthur   P: Phila 16 Jy 67,
    27 Oct 73
  Edward   P: Pa 2 Feb 64
  Ephraim   P: Phila Co 28 Oct
    62
  Francis   P: Phila 9 Ag 59
  George   P: New-Castle Co 31
    Jy 60
  J.   P: Phila 5 Ag 62
  Jacob   P: Phila 23 Oct 66
  James   P: Nottingham 27 Dec
    53; Phila 21 Dec 58, 8 Jy
    62.   T: near Howell's Mill
    17 Oct 54; Trenton 17 Oct
    54
  Jane   P: Pa 12 Feb 61
  Jo.   L: 11 Ap 65
  Joan   P: Pa 28 Oct 62
  John   P: Buckingham, Bucks Co
    23 Oct 66; Moreland 15 Mar
    64; Nottingham 27 Dec 53;
    Phila 4 Feb 68, 19 Ja 69
  Joseph   P: Limerick Tow. 11
    Sep 55, 13 May 56, 9 Ag 59;
    Phila 13 Oct 63, 2 Feb 64,

  1 Nov 70
  Michael   P: Northampton,
    Bucks Co 26 Oct 69
  Moses   P: Phila 1 Nov 70
  Nancy   P: Phila 21 Jy 68
  Robert   P: Phila 1 Feb 70
  Samuel   C: near Christeen
    Bridge 22 Ja 67.   P:
    Baltimore Co 31 Dec 61
  Sarah   Phila 30 Oct 76
  Sylvester   P: Phila 3 Sep 61
  Thomas   L: 3 Oct 65.   P:
    Bucks Co 10 Oct 65; Lan-
    caster Co 26 Jy 64; New-
    Castle 18 Mar 62; New
    Rochell 30 Ap 77; Phila 27
    Oct 73
  Uriah   P: Pa 12 Feb 61
  William   C: c/o Rev Blair,
    Fogs Manor 28 Nov 65.   L:
    c/o George Sanderson,
    Lancaster Co 19 Dec 71 (with
    a small box).   P: Chester
    Co 15 Mar 64; Lancaster Co
    22 Nov 53; Middletown 7 Ap
    57; Pa 15 Mar 64; Phila 16
    Jy 67, 28 Ap 68; 40 miles
    from Phila 27 Oct 73
HILLEGUS
  Susannah   P: Phila 3 Ja 63,
    26 Jy 64
HILLFORD
  Matthias   P: Kent Co 28 Oct
    62
HILLHOUSE
  James   P: Chester Co 27 Jy
    58
HILLIANDS/o̅r HILLIANGS?_/
  Polly   P̅: Newcastle I̅1 Jy 54
HILLIER
  William   P: Phila 22 Nov 53
    (Capt), 7 Ap 57
HILLINGEAN
  Thomas   P: Chester Co 3 Ja 60
HILLS
  Capt. Stephen   P: Phila 5 Jy
    80-Gaz. 19 Jy
HILLYARD
  Cornelius   P: Bucks Co 9 Ag
    59
HILTON
  Edward   P: Pa 13 Oct 63
  Lancelot   P: Phila-Gaz. 27
    Oct 73
  Simon   P: Lower Dublin 5 Ag
    62
HILTZHIMER
  Jacob   P: Phila 18 Mar 62
HINCHMAN
  James   P: Gloucester Co 21
    Jy 68
  John   P: Gloucester Co 31 Jy
    60.   T: Haddonfield 4 Nov
    72 (Esq.)
HIND

John P: Phila-Gaz. 27 Oct 73
HINDMAN/HYNDMAN
John C: 30 Jy 77
Samuel P: Pa 4 Ag 63
William P: Pa 13 Oct 63, 1
Feb 70
HINE
Edward P: Phila 28 Oct 62
Francis P: Phila 10 Ap 66
HINES
Andrew Phila 30 Ap 77
Jacob P: Phila 20 Jy 69
Matthew P: Montgomery 26 Oct
69
HINGS
Thomas P: Phila 2 Ag 70
HINKID
George P: Phila 13 Ja 63
HINKLE
Jacob P: Phila 19 Jy 80
HINKLEY
Francis P: Chester Co 7 Ap
57
Samuel P: Phila 23 Oct 66
HINSHAW/HENSHAW/HYNDSHAW
Jacob P: Monaham T. 1 Jy 56
Capt. John P: Phila 24 Oct
54
Mary P: West Jersey 3 Ja 60
Thomas P: Phila 13 May 56
HINSHELWOOD/HENSHELWOOD
Robert P: Phila 9 May 54,
23 Oct 66
HINSON
John N: near Duck Creek 29
Nov 64; see also HYNSON
HINTON
John P: Phila 2 Sep 62
HIPWELL
Jane P: Phila 20 Ap 69
HIPWORTH
George T: Trenton Forge 1
Sep 68
HITCHCOCK
Eleanor P: Phila 2 Ag 70
HITKEN
Robert, merchant L: Bedford
19 Dec 71
HIXLAND
Thomas P: Pa 28 Oct 62
HOAR
... P: Phila 11 Sep 55
William G. P: Phila 3 Ja 76
HOBBY
Winsley P: Middletown 20 Ap
69
HOBSON; see also HOPSON
John P: Lancas/ter/ 18 Feb
55; Phila 16 Jy 72
Lawrence P: Chester Co 18
Mar 62
HOCK/HOCKE
Adam P: Phila 20 Ap 69
Geo. P: Pa 11 Sep 55
John P: Phila 3 Ja 60

HOCKENHULL
John P: Phila 25 Ap 71
HOCKLEY
Richard P: Phila 20 Oct 68
HODGE; see also SCOTT &
Andrew P: Phila 19 Ja 69,
2 Ag 70
Archibald P: Chester Co 18
Mar 62; Pa 18 Mar 62
Hannah Phila 30 Oct 76
Capt. Henry P: Phila 23 Oct
66
Hugh P: Phila 9 Ag 59, 19
Ja 69, 3 May 70, 16 Jy 72
Isaac P: Pa 12 Feb 61
James L: Cumberland Co 19
Dec 71
John P: Phila 27 Dec 53
Jonathan, Esq. L: near
Carlisle 19 Dec 71
Nicholas Phila 24 Jy 76
William P: Phila-Gaz. 3 Ja
76
HODGES
Francis P: Phila-Gaz. 3 Ja
76
Joseph P: Phila 28 Oct 62,
24 Feb 63
HODGIN/HODGGIN
Isabel P: Chester Co 11 Sep
55
Robert P: Chester Co 9 Ag
59; Pa 27 Jy 58, 3 Ja 60
HODGKINSON
John P: Phila 27 Jy 58, 2
Feb 64
Peter P: Phila 21 Dec 58
HODGNETT
Jeffery P: Phila 15 Mar 64
HODGSON
Capt. Francis P: Phila 19
Jy 80
Joseph P: Phila 31 Mar 63
HODWELL
Jeffery P: Phila 2 May 65
HOE
Richard P: Phila 1 Jy 56
HOFF
Charles P: Kingwood 9 Ag 59
Rachel P: Kent Co 18 Mar 62
HOFFMAN
Jacob P: Reading 20 Jy 69,
27 Ja 73
HOGAN/HOGANS
Mr. P: Phila-Gaz. 27 Oct 73
John P: Phila 26 Oct 69, 2
Ag 70
Lawrence P: Phila-Gaz. 3 Ja
76
Mary P: Phila-Gaz. 3 Ja 76
Patrick/Pat. P: America 23
Oct 66; Phila 27 Oct 73
HOGE
William P: Bucks 11 Sep 55
HOGELAND

Catherine P: Phila 11 Sep 55
Hannah T: Peaquest 7 May 67
HOGG/HOG
  Mr. P: Phila 12 Ja 58
  Aaron P: Pequea 13 Ja 63
  Esther P: Phila 9 Ag 59
  Hester P: Phila 3 Ja 60
  Hugh P: Phila 2 Feb 64, 3 Ja
    65
  James P: Chester Co 13 Oct
    63; Phila 3 Ja 76
  John P: Lancaster Co 21 Dec
    58, Pa 12 Feb 61
  Patrick P: Chester Co 18 Mar
    62
  Richard P: Pa 27 Jy 58, 18
    Feb 55
  William/Will. P: Gloucester
    31 Dec 61, 20 Ap 69; Phila
    15 Mar 64
HOGNOR
  Frederick P: Phila 21 Dec 58
HOGSETT
  John P: Bucks Co 18 Mar 62
HOGSTER
  James P: Phila 19 Ja 69
HOGSYARD
  John P: Pa 24 Feb 63
HOISTINGS
  George P: New-Castle Co 9 Ag
    59
HOITAS/?/
  Ab. P: Pa 24 Feb 63
HOKINS
  Daniel (sailor) P: Phila 21
    Dec 58
HOLCOMB
  Sophia P: Phila 31 Jy 60
HOLDEN
  Alice P: Phila 4 Feb 68
  Jeremiah P: Phila 30 Ap 67
HOLDER
  Casper P: Salem Co 7 Ap 57
HOLDING
  James P: Phila 23 Oct 66
HOLDREN
  William T: Trenton 17 Oct 54
HOLDSTOCK
  Jos. P: Phila 25 Jy 65
HOLEURNE
  John P: Phila 31 Jy 60
HOLICH/HOLIGH
  Barberry P: Bucks Co 3 Ja
    60, 31 Jy 60
HOLL
  Gabriel P: Phila 18 Mar 62
HOLLAN
  Edward P: Phila-Gaz. 27 Oct
    73
HOLLAND
  Alice P: Gloucester Co 18 Ag
    57
  Capt. Daniel C: 30 Jy 77
  Elizabeth P: Kensington 23
    Oct 66

James P: Phila 9 Ag 59, 3
  Ja 60
John P: Phila 8 Jy 62
Nicholas P: in the army 12
  Ja 58
Richard P: Phila 4 Feb 68
Sarah P: Phila 7 Ap 57
Stephen P: Phila 31 Dec 61
Thomas P: Phila 26 Jy 53,
  27 Ja 73
HOLLANDSWORTH/HOLLENSWORTH/
  HOLENSWORTH
George P: Bucks Co 1 Feb 70
John P: Phila 11 Jy 54
Mary P: Phila 2 Ag 70
HOLLIAS
William P: Phila 18 Mar 62
HOLLIDAY/HOLIDAY/HOLADAY/HALL-
  IDAY
Alexander P: Newcastle Co
  12 Ja 58; Phila 31 Mar 63
Giles P: Berks Co 3 May 70;
  Phila 20 Jy 69
Henry P: Phila 11 Sep 55
James P: Salem 13 Oct 63
Jane P: Pequea 21 Dec 58
John P: Phila 20 Oct 68
Richard N: Newark /?/ 12
  Feb 67
Robert P: Duck Creek 4 Ag
  63
William P: Phila 26 Oct 69
HOLLINGSWORTH
Francis P: Phila 3 May 70
Jehu L: 29 Ja 67
HOLLIS
William P: Phila 12 Feb 61
HOLLOWELL
John P: Phila 15 Mar 64
Joseph P: Phila 16 Jy 67
HOLLYWOOD
Francis P: Phila 30 Ja 66
HOLM/HOLME
Charles P: Phila 29 Ag 54
John P: Pennypack 13 Oct 63
HOLMES/HOLMS
Abraham C: c/o John Mont-
  gomery at Christine Bridge
  18 Jy 65
Archibald N: Newark 12 Feb
  67
James Phila 16 Jy 77
John P: in the army 12 Ja
  58; York Co 12 Ja 58
Mary P: Baltimore 8 Jy 62
Rossey P: Phila-Gaz. 3 Ja
  76
Samuel P: Phila 12 Ja 58
Thomas P: Phila 5 Ag 62, 19
  Ja 69, 27 Ja 73
HOLMICK
Elizabeth P: Reading 31 Jy
  60
HOLMOAK
Jebediah T: Barnstable 4 Nov

72
HOLT
Ryves P: Lewis Town 18 Ag 57
HOLTON/HOULTON
Mr.   P: Phila 10 Oct 65
Azariah Phila 24 Jy 76
Benjamin P: Phila 15 Mar 64
David P: Phila 1 Feb 70, 16
Jy 72
Francis Phila 11 Sep 55 (2),
1 May 76
Jeremiah Phila 24 Jy 76
HOLTSINGER
Barrat P: Yorktown 3 Sep 61
HOLUMBY
Thomas P: Phila 13 May 56
HOME
Arthur P: Phila 31 Jy 60
HOMES
John P: Carlisle 3 Sep 61
Nathaniel P: Pa 2 Feb 64
HONEY
George P: Phila 9 Ag 59
HONKWAY
Abraham N: Newark /?/ 12 Feb
67
HONNOFLY
Isaac P: Phila 31 Dec 61
HONTNEY
Abraham N: near Dover 4 Dec
66
HOOD
Elizabeth P: Chester Co 12
Feb 61
Nathaniel P: Phila 23 Oct 66
Robert P: New-Castle Co 3 Ja
60
Capt. Seymour P: Phila 20
Oct 68
HOOFNOGLE
John P: Lancaster Co 4 Ag 63
HOOK/HOOKE
Andrew P: Phila 31 Jy 60, 3
Sep 61
John P: Phila 20 Jy 69, 26
Oct 69, 16 Jy 72
Mary P: Lewis Town 18 Ag 57;
Sussex 31 Dec 61
Samuel P: Baltimore Co 31 Dec
61. T: Trenton 1 Sep 68
William and Robert C: c/o
William Buchannan 18 Jy 65
HOOKER
John P: Phila 9 Ag 59
HOOMBREGH
Abraham P: Phila 16 Jy 72
HOOP
Thomas P: Whiteclay Creek 18
Ag 57
HOOPER
Jacob R. P: Phila 11 Sep 55
John P: Phila 28 Ap 68
Rachael P: Phila 4 Ap 54
HOOPS
Robert P: Phila 13 Oct 63

HOOTOAN
George P: Phila 3 May 70
HOPE
Martha P: Phila-Gaz. 27 Oct
73
Thomas P: Octorara 9 Ag 59,
2 Feb 64
HOPKINS
Andrew P: N.J. 24 Feb 63;
Phila 19 May 63
Archibald P: Phila 5 Ag 56
Capt. Christopher P: Phila
2 Sep 62
David P: Cumberland Co 7 Ap
57; Pa 7 Ap 57
Ebenezer P: Haddonfield 28
Nov 54, 26 Oct 69
Ephraim P: East Jersey 7 Ap
57
Gerrard P: Phila 31 Dec 61
Hannah P: Phila 30 Ja 66
Isaac P: Phila 10 Ap 66, 4
Feb 68
John P: New-Castle Co 31 Jy
60; Nutfield 13 Ja 63;
Phila 24 Jy 76
John E. P: Haddonfield 24
Feb 63, 20 Oct 68
Mary N: 12 Feb 67; New-
Castle 4 Dec 66. P: Pa 12
Feb 61; Phila 3 Ja 60, 30
Ja 66
Matthew P: Phila 5 Ag 62, 28
Oct 62, 20 Jy 69
Robert Phila 30 Ap 77
Samuel P: Lewistown 9 Ag 59;
Phila 13 Oct 63, 30 Ap 67
Sarah P: Haddonfield 9 Ag 59
Thomas P: America 23 Oct 66;
Darby Twp 27 Jy 58; Phila
30 Ap 67, 16 Jy 67
Francis P: Phila 3 May 70
Peter P: Phila 30 Ap 67
Richard P: Moore Park 21 Jy
68; Phila 4 Feb 68
HOPPER
Cosha Phila 24 Jy 76
John P: Timber Creek 9 Ag 59
Joshua P: Jersies 1 Nov 70
HOPSON
Jo. L: 25 Dec 66
John P: Lancaster 29 Ag 54
Jordan P: Amwell, N.J. 27
Oct 73, 19 Ja 76
HORDITCH
Susannah P: Phila 21 Dec 58
HORE
Elizabeth P: Spring Garden
8 Jy 62
HORMER
James C: Little Coniwago
22 Ja 67
HORN/HORNE
Rachel P: Phila 20 Jy 69
William P: Darby 2 Feb 64

HORNER
  Benjamin P: Phila 15 Mar 64
  Isaac T: near Trenton 10 Ag
    58
  James P: Forks Delaware 4 Ap
    54; Phila 3 Ja 76, 30 Oct
    76; York Co 18 Mar 62
  Joshua L: York Co 31 Ja 71
  Samuel P: Prince Town 15 Jy
    56
HORNETT
  Richard Phila 30 Ap 77
HORNING
  Vandal L: Lancaster Co 29 Jy
    72
HORROW
  David P: Phila 1 Nov 70
HORRY
  Arthur P: Phila 28 Ap 68
HORSEY
  Hannah P: Phila 26 Jy 64
HORSFORD
  John P: Pennypack 2 Ag 70
HORTON
  Edmund P: Phila 16 Jy 72
HORWELL
  Richard P: Pa 18 Mar 62
HOSE
  William P: Phila 27 Ja 73
HOSKINS
  John P: Phila 29 Ag 54
  Joseph P: Chester 29 Ag 54
HOTT
  Michael Phila 24 Jy 76
HOUGH
  Thomas Phila 31 Ja 76
HOUGHE
  Robert New Castle Co 24 Jy
    76
HOUGHTIN/HOUGHTON; see also
  STUART &
  John P: Phila-Gaz. 3 Ja 76
  Joseph P: Phila 2 Ag 70, 1
    Nov 70
HOULT
  Abel L: 3 Oct 65
HOURSTON
  James P: Phila 13 Oct 63
HOUSE
  Mrs. P: Phila 3 May 70
  Frances P: Phila 2 Ag 70
  John P: Phila 30 Ja 66
HOUSELL
  William T: Readington 17 Oct
    54
HOUSET
  John Frederick P: Chester Co
    7 Ap 57
HOUSTON
  .... P: New Castle Co 5 Ag 56
  Mr. P: Phila 20 Jy 69
  Geo. P: Phila 27 Dec 63
    (Capt), 6 Jy 58, 28 Oct 62,
    2 Feb 64, 2 Feb 64 (Capt)
  James P: Phila 13 Ja 63

HOVELMAN
  Arnold Phila 30 Ap 77
HOVENDENS
  Richard and Walter P: Phila
    25 Ap 71
  Walter P: New-Town-Gaz. 3 Ja
    76
HOW/HOWE
  Daniel P: Phila 10 Oct 65
  Capt. E. P: Phila 18 Mar 62
  Esther P: Phila 11 Sep 55
  James P: Phila 1 Nov 53
  Matthew P: Phila 3 May 70
  Thomas, on board the Lively
    P: Phila 16 Jy 72
  Will./William P: Germantown
    20 Ap 69; Phila 16 Jy 72
HOWARD
  Mr. P: Phila 5 Ag 62
  Ann P: Bucks Co 12 Feb 61
  Charles P: Phila 10 Oct 65
  Elizabeth P: Kent Co 18 Ag
    57
  George P: Phila 1 Nov 53
  Jacob P: Amity Twp 5 Ag 62
  James P: in the army 27 Jy
    58, 21 Dec 58
  John P: Phila 30 Ap 67
  Nancy T: Buck Co 10 Ag 58
  Nathaniel P: Phila 1 Nov 70
  Robert P: Phila 31 Jy 60
  Sarah P: Phila 1 Nov 70
  Thomas Gossy, merchant C: in
    Joppa 28 Nov 65
  William P: Phila 31 Dec 61
HOWELL
  Ann P: Phila 26 Jy 64
  Benjamin P: Phila 12 Ja 58
  David P: Phila 3 Sep 61
  Edward P: Welsh Tract 9 May
    54
  Israel P: Phila 15 Mar 64
  Lethea P: Phila 23 Oct 66
  Margaret P: Phila 21 Dec 58
  Mary P: Phila 2 Sep 62
  Polly P: Phila 6 Jy 58
  Reading P: Downing-Town 19
    Jn 80
  Reynold/Reynolds P: near
    Newcastle 28 Nov 54; New-
    Castle (Co) 27 Jy 58, 31
    Jy 60
  Susannah P: Gloucester 18
    Ag 57
  Thomas P: Phila 30 May 54
  William P: Cecil Co 8 Jy 62;
    Phila 9 Ag 59, 3 Ja 60
  Zepheniah P: Phila 26 Jy 64
HOWEY
  John P: Bucks Co 2 Feb 64;
    Phila 18 Mar 62, 3 Ja 65
HOY
  Richard P: Phila 19 May 63
HOYD
  John P: Phila 26 Jy 64

HUBBARD/HUBBART
  Capt. Charles Hubby P: Phila
    12 Feb 61
  Daniel P: Phila 13 Ja 63
  George P: Kent 3 Sep 61
  Peter P: Dorchester Co 4 Ag
    63; Nantioke 13 Ja 63
HUBBELL
  Abijah P: Phila 11 Sep 55
  Gershom P: Bucks Co 19 May
    63
HUBBS/HUBS
  Charles P: Germantown 3 Ja
    65, 26 Jy 64
  Capt. Henry P: Phila 16 Jy 67
  Sarah P: Phila 18 Feb 55, 19
    Jy 80
HUBERT
  Charles Phila 30 Oct 76
  Peter P: Nanticoke River 24
    Feb 63
HUBNER
  George P: Phila 27 Ja 73
HUCKLEY
  Col. C: 30 Jy 77
HUDHAM
  Richard P: Phila 24 Oct 54
HUDNUT
  John T: Amwell 4 Nov 72
HUDSON/HUTDSON; see also HUTSON
  John P: Phila 9 Ag 59, 3 Ja
    60
  Joseph P: Chester Co 3 Ja
    60; Phila 12 Ja 58
  Josiah P: Mount-Joy Forge 1
    Nov 70
  William P: N.J. 2 Feb 64
HUEST
  Thomas P: Little Elk 3 Sep
    61
HUEY/HUIE
  James P: Phila 2 Feb 64
  Jerrard L: Bedford Co 20 Ja
    73
  Mary P: Phila 5 Feb 54, 11
    Sep 55
  Samuel P: Hunterdon Co 9 Ag
    59, 3 Ja 60; Phila 27 Dec
    53 (Capt)
HUFF
  Elizabeth P: Haddonfield 26
    Jy 64
  Richard, Jr. L: Conococheague
    Creek 19 Dec 71
HUGAN/HUGANS
  Jacob P: York Co 7 Ap 57, 18
    Ag 57
  William P: Freehold 24 Oct
    54
HUGAR/HUGER
  Benjamin Phila 16 Jy 77
  Daniel P: Phila 26 Jy 64, 3
    Ja 65
HUGARTY
  John P: Phila 27 Ja 73

HUGEY
  Robert T: Oxford Furnace 17
    Oct 54
HUGGENS/HUGGINS
  Matthew P: Rays-Town 8 Jy
    62
  Thomas P: Phila 27 Ja 73
HUGH
  Griffitt P: Phila 19 May 63
HUGHES/HUES/HUGHS; see also
    HEWES
  Rev. Dr. P: Phila 4 Feb 68
  Barney/Barnabas P: Lancas-
    ter Co 12 Feb 61, 3 Sep 61
  Bernard P: Pa 2 Feb 64
  Catherine P: Pa 27 Jy 58
  Charles P: 21 Dec 58, sol-
    dier; Bucks Co 31 Dec 61;
    Phila 31 Jy 60 (Capt), 3
    Ja 76. W: merchant in
    Wilmington on Delaware 3
    Jy 76
  Daniel Phila 5 Jy 77-Gaz.
    16 Jy
  Dennis P: Phila 27 Ja 73
  Elisha P: Chester Co 1 Nov
    53, 31 Dec 61
  Francis P: Phila 3 Sep 61
  George P: Phila 30 Ap 67
  Henry P: Phila 27 Ja 73
  Isabel P: Phila 4 Ag 63
  James P: Lancaster Co 12
    Feb 61; Phila 30 Ja 66, 26
    Oct 69
  John L: Little Britain,
    Lancaster Co 29 Jy 72. P:
    Chester Co 8 Jy 62; Phila
    19 Ja 69, 2 Ag 70, 3 Ja 76
  Jonathan P: New-Town-Gaz.
    3 Ja 76
  Joseph P: Phila 21 Jy 68
  Martin P: Phila 31 Mar 63
  Mary P: Phila 27 Ja 73. T:
    Prince-Town 17 Oct 54
  Nicholas P: Bucks Co 4 Feb
    68
  Robert L: Carnarvon 2 Mar
    74
  Susanna P: Phila 27 Ja 73
  Thomas P: Phila 18 Mar 62
  Thomas P: Phila 27 Ja 73
  Uriah, Sen. Buckingham 31
    Ja 76
  William P: Phila-Gaz. 3 Ja
    76
HUGHSON
  John P: Bucks 9 May 54
HUGS
  James P: Phila 11 Sep 55
HUKILL
  Mary P: New-Castle Co 9 Ag
    59
HULBERT/HULBERD
  P. P: Phila 11 Sep 55
  William T: 21 Ja 55

HULD
  Joseph P: Phila 1 Jy 56
HULL
  Mr. P: Phila 13 Oct 63
  Anthony P: Phila 18 Feb 55,
    28 Oct 62, 2 Feb 64, 26 Jy
    64, 3 Ja 65
  Daniel P: Reading 8 Jy 62
  Isaac P: Sussex 24 Feb 63
  Jonathan P: Phila 2 Feb 64
  Stille P: Phila 27 Ja 73
HULLES/HULLIS
  Abraham P: Neshaminy 28 Oct
    62; Upper Dublin 27 Ja 73
HULME
  Robert P: Phila 3 Ja 65
HULSE
  R. P: Phila 27 Ja 73
HULSKEMP
  Garret P: Phila 27 Ja 73
HUME
  James P: Phila 21 Jy 68
  Sarah P: Phila 17 Jy 80
HUMES/HUMS
  Ann P: Phila 7 Ap 57
  Samuel P: Phila 24 Oct 54
  John P: New-Castle Co 21 Jy
    60
HUMPHRY/HUMPHRYS/HUMPHREYS/HOM-
FRAY/HUMPHREY
  Mr. P: North East 9 Ag 59
  Alexander N: near Dover 4
    Dec 66
  David L: Cumberland Co 20 Ja
    73. P: East Nottingham 24
    Oct 54; Upper Octarara 23
    Oct 66
  Hannah P: Phila 26 Jy 53
  James P: Chester Co 13 Oct
    63; Phila 9 Ag 59
  John P: Lancaster Co 13 Oct
    63
  Joshua Phila 30 Ap 77
  Samuel P: Cumberland Co 13
    Oct 63. T: 7 May 67
  Thomas T: Kingwood 1 Sep 68
  William P: New Castle 11 Jy
    54; Phila 6 Jy 58, 27 Jy 58
HUNKARD
  Jo L: 29 Ja 67
HUNLY
  Sergt. John P: in the army
    21 Dec 58
HUNN
  John P: Dover, Kent Co 11
    Feb 70, 3 May 70
  Jonathan Phila 30 Oct 76
HUNSLEY/HUNSLAY
  Robert P: Moyamensing 15 Mar
    64; Phila 3 Ja 65, 2 Ag 70
HUNT
  Andrew P: Phila 2 Feb 64
  Edward P: Phila 1 Nov 53
  Isaac P: Phila 2 Ag 70
  Capt. J. P: Phila 15 Mar 64

  John P: Phila 9 Ag 59, 8 Jy
    62, 1 May 76
  Jonathan T: Hopewell 6 Dec
    64
  Joseph P: Chester Co 9 Ag
    59, 12 Feb 61
  Robert P: Cole's Town, N.
    Jersey 4 Feb 68
  Roger P: Great Valley 5 Feb
    54; Phila 9 Ag 59
  Thomas Germantown 31 Ja 76
  William P: Kent 31 Dec 61
HUNTER
  Alex./Alexander P: Forks
    Delaware 6 Sep 53, 4 Ap
    54; Phila 1 Nov 53
  David P: Pa 28 Oct 62, 13
    Oct 63; Phila 18 Mar 62 (2)
  George P: Pa 28 Oct 62, 13
    Ja 63; Phila 18 Mar 62, 27
    Ja 73, 19 Jy 80 (Capt)
  Hannah P: Phila-Gaz. 27 Oct
    73
  James P: Chester Co 7 Ap
    57, 9 Ag 59, 3 Ja 60, 28
    Oct 62, 2 Feb 64; Marple
    Twp 7 Ap 57; Phila 8 Ag
    62, 13 Ja 63, 25 Jy 65, 1
    Nov 70; Radnor 30 Ap 77
  John L: Leacock 2 Mar 74.
    P: Delaware Forks 12 Feb
    61, 31 Mar 63, 3 Ja 65; Pa
    12 Feb 61, 13 Ja 63, 13 Oct
    63; Phila 13 Oct 63, 15 Mar
    64, 28 Ap 68
  Joseph/Jos. P: Pa 12 Feb 61;
    Phila 12 Ja 58
  Margaret P: Phila 26 Oct 69
  Capt. Peter P: Phila 26 Oct
    69
  Richard P: Phila 27 Jy 58,
    21 Dec 58 (sailor)
  Robert P: Cumberland Co 28
    Oct 62; Nottingham 27 Dec
    53; Phila 27 Oct 73
  Samuel P: Phila 10 Oct 65
  Thomas P: Phila 12 Ja 58.
    T: Lebanon 31 Ja 71
  William L: 29 Ja 67; Martick
    Furnice 2 Mar 74; Octarara
    2 Mar 74. P: Lancaster Co
    8 Jy 62; Pa 13 Ja 63; Phila
    2 Feb 64, 10 Oct 65, 30 Ja
    66
HURRAN
  George P: Phila 3 Ja 65
HURRY
  Arthur P: Phila 18 Feb 55,
    7 Ap 57 (cooper), 9 Ag 59,
    26 Oct 67
HURST
  Charles, Esq. T: 4 Nov 72
  Elizabeth P: Pa 21 Dec 58
  Timothy P: Phila 13 Oct 63
  William P: Phila 1 Feb 70

HURSTON
 George P: Phila 2 Feb 64
HUSCHIRON
 Elizabeth L: Octorara 15 Ap
  56
HUSSEGER
 Mr. L: Lebanon, see HEKKER,
  John Charles
HUSSEY
 Jacob P: Phila 28 Nov 54, 18
  Feb 55
 James P: Phila 18 Mar 62, 25
  Jy 65
 Nathaniel P: Phila 13 May 56
 William P: Phila 28 Oct 62,
  25 Jy 65, 16 Jy 67, 28 Ap 68
HUSTON
 Mr. P: Phila 25 Jy 65
 Agnas/Agnes L: Cumberland Co
  25 Dec 66. P: Cumberland
  Co 13 Oct 63
 Ann P: Pa 2 Feb 64
 George P: Phila 20 Ap 69
 James N: Brandywine 27 Jy 58,
  2 Feb 64; New Castle Co 7 Ap
  57; Phila 9 Ag 59, 18 Mar 62,
  4 Ag 63, 2 Feb 64, 21 Jy 68,
  2 Ag 70, 3 Ja 76
 John L: York 2 Mar 74 (Dr).
  P: near Pequea 9 Ag 59; Pe-
  quea 3 Ja 60
 Jos./Joseph C: c/o Rev.
  Allison 18 Jy 65. P: Lan-
  caster Co 18 Mar 62; Pa 3 Ja
  60, 4 Ag 63
 Nathaniel P: Phila-Gaz. 3 Ja
  76
 Robert P: Lancaster Co 3 Sep
  61; N. Castle Co 3 Sep 61
 William P: Pa 18 Mar 62;
  Phila 21 Jy 68
HUTCHINS/HUTCHINGS/HUTCHENS
 Benjamin P: Phila 26 Jy 64
  (Dr), 3 Ja 65 (2)
 James Phila 16 Jy 77
 John P: Phila 29 Ag 54, 25
  Jy 65
 Jos. P: Phila 31 Dec 61
 Rigdon P: Kent Island 31 Dec
  61
 Stephen P: Phila 9 Ag 59
 Capt. Thomas P: Phila 21 Dec
  58, 18 Mar 62, 26 Oct 69
 Capt. Z. P: Phila 5 Ag 62
 Zachariah/Zach. P: Pa 2 Feb
  64; Phila 8 Jy 62
HUTCHINSON/HUTCHESON/HUTCHISON/
 HECHISON/HUCHESON
 Sergt. Charles P: in the army
  21 Dec 58
 Christian P: Phila 19 Ja 69
 Eliz. P: Octerara 11 Sep 55
 James C: New London Cross
  Roads 30 Oct 66; see also
  ORR, John. L: York Co 20 Ja

73. P: Bucks Co 3 Ja 60;
  Chester Co 31 Jy 60, 18 Mar
  62; Pa 18 Mar 62, 24 Feb
  63, 18 Ag 57, 30 Ja 66, 16
  Jy 67
 Jane P: Bucks Co 26 Oct 69
 John C: London Grove Chester
  Co 30 Oct 66. P: Pa 26 Jy
  64; Phila 30 May 54; sol-
  dier, prob. in Pittsburgh
  15 Mar 64 (2)
 Robert P: Newtown 8 Jy 62
 Miss Sally Phila 30 Oct 76
 Thomas P: Pa 12 Feb 61. T:
  Greenwich 17 Oct 54
 William P: Chester Co 31 Jy
  60; Phila 27 Oct 73. T:
  Middlesex Co 10 Ag 58
HUTHESON
 Agness P: Brandywine 13 Oct
  63
HUTHINGS
 Daniel P: Phila 21 Dec 58
HUTSICAN
 David P: Donegal 7 Ap 57
HUTSON
 Samuel P: Phila 30 Ja 66
HUTTON
 Capt. J. P: Phila 18 Mar 62,
  2 Feb 64
 James P: New Castle Co 12
  Feb 61
 John P: Chester Co 7 Ap 57;
  Pa 31 Jy 60; Phila 21 Dec
  58 (sailor)
 William P: Phila 5 Ag 62
HUWELL
 Thomas P: Phila 3 Ja 65
HUY/HWEY
 John L: Pequea 15 Ap 56. P:
  Phila 5 Ag 56
HUXLAND
 James P: Pa 15 Mar 64; Phila
  2 Feb 64
 Thomas P: Phila 18 Mar 62
HYDE
 Mary P: Phila 3 May 70
 William P: Phila 15 Mar 64
HYLANDS
 Hercules P: West Fallowfield
  7 Ap 57
HYLIE
 Samuel P: Cumberland Co 4
  Ag 63
HYLON
 James P: Phila 1 Nov 70
HYMAN
 Jane P: Phila-Gaz. 3 Ja 76
 Peter P: Phila 9 Ag 59
HYNMAN
 Archibald P: Pa 12 Feb 61;
  Phila 18 Mar 62
HYNSON; see also HINSON
 F. P: Phila 24 Feb 63
 Francinah P: Phila 9 Ag 59,

3 Ja 60
Francis P: Phila 28 Oct 62
J.C. P: Pa 31 Jy 60
HYTCH
  Capt. R./Ro P: Phila 5 Ag 62

IBBIT
  - Serjeant P: New Castle 7
  Ap 57
IBESON
  William P: Phila 23 Oct 66
IGNEW
  John P: Phila 12 Feb 61
ILLIGENES
  Christian P: Phila 16 Jy 67
IMLAY/IMLEY
  John P: Burlington 27 Jy 58
  William P: Phila 3 Ja 65. T:
  Bordentown 7 May 67
IMSLEY
  Charles P: Phila 1 Feb 70
INGELS
  Hannah P: Germantown 19 Ja
  69
INGERSOL
  Capt. Jonathan Phila 5 Ja 76-
  Gaz. 31 Ja
INGHAM
  Thomas P: Phila 3 Ja 60
INGLE
  Stuffle P: Phila 25 Ap 71
INGLIS
  Rev. P: Phila 2 May 65
  Mary P: Phila 2 May 65
INGLISH, see ENGLISH
INGRAM/INGRAHAM
  George P: Phila 18 Mar 62,
  5 Ag 62
  James P: Phila 16 Jy 67
  John P: Phila 24 Oct 54, 27
  Jy 58, 21 Dec 58, 9 Ag 59,
  28 Oct 62, 24 Feb 63, 31 Mar
  63
  Margaret P: Phila 11 Jy 54
  Thomas P: Phila 1 Nov 70
INKISTER
  Thomas P: Phila 21 Jy 68
INNES/INNIS
  Brice L: 14 May 72. P:
  Hanover Twp 24 Oct 54;
  Lancaster Co 12 Feb 61
  Frances P: Phila 9 Ag 59
  Col. James Phila 30 Ap 77
INSKEEP
  Abraham P: Jersey 28 Ap 68
  Benjamin P: Gloucester Co 25
  Ap 71
INTHILL
  Dr. T: Morris Town 31 Ja 71
IRELAND
  Mr. P: Phila 27 Jy 58, 26
  Oct 69
  Edward P: Phila 15 Mar 64
  Henry P: West Jersey 31 Jy

60; Phila 2 May 65
  James P: Lancaster Co 3 Sep
  61
  Jo. L: Chestnut-Level 31 Ja
  71
  Capt. John P: Phila 13 Ja 63
  Thomas P: Phila 21 Dec 58,
  9 Ag 59, 25 Jy 65
IRINTON
  Samuel P: Pa 13 Oct 63
IRONS
  Thomas P: Pa 3 Ja 60
IRVIN; see also ERVIN
  Archibald P: Phila 27 Dec 53
  Gerrard Phila 24 Jy 76
  John P: Horsham Twp 13 Ja
  63; Phila 25 Jy 65
  Samuel T: Durham Furnace 7
  May 67
IRWIN; see also ERWIN
  Anna P: Phila 3 Ja 65
  Elizabeth P: Pa 3 Ja 60;
  Phila 9 Ag 59
  Erter P: Bucks Co-Gaz. 3 Ja
  76
  George L: York-Town 31 Ja
  71, 2 Ja 73
  Gerad L: near Carlisle 19
  Dec 71
  James P: Bucks Co 13 Ja 63,
  31 Mar 60; Pequea 13 Ja 63,
  4 Ag 63; Phila 19 Ja 69
  John P: Bucks Co 3 Ja 60;
  Harris's Ferry 30 Ja 66;
  Horsham 24 Feb 63, 19 Ja 69,
  20 Ap 69, 26 Oct 69; Pa 31
  Dec 61; Phila 15 Mar 64, 2
  May 65; Warrington Twp 28
  Ap 68
  Samuel P: Carlisle 3 Sep
  61; Pa 31 Dec 61
  Thomas P: Phila 12 Feb 61
  William P: Bucks Co 1 Feb 70
ISAAC
  Mr. P: Phila 4 Feb 68
  George P: Phila 1 Nov 70
  Jonathan P: Andover Furnace
  26 Jy 64. T: Andover
  Furnace 6 Dec 64
ISAAKS
  Asher P: Newtown 13 Oct 63
ISBESTER/ISBUSTER
  George P: Germantown 11 Sep
  55; Phila 27 Dec 53, 5 Ag
  62
ISER
  Frederick P: Lancaster 26 Jy
  64
ISERY
  Mary P: Phila-Gaz. 27 Oct 73
ISLES
  Rev. Samuel P: Bethlehem 18
  Mar 62
ISLOP/ISLUP
  Mr. P: Phila 2 May 65,25 Jy

65
ISRAEL
Israel P: Phila 3 Ja 65
Mary P: Phila 18 Ag 57
IVINS
Isaac P: Phila 27 Ja 73
IVORY
Thomas P: Phila 10 Ap 66, 30
Ap 67
IZARD/ISARD
Ralph P: Phila 25 Jy 65, 10
Ap 66

JACK
John P: Chester Co 2 Feb 64
Thomas C: 30 Jy 77
JACKLYN
Edmund P: Phila 27 Jy 58
JACKSON/JACSON; see also WILLS
& JACKSON
Mrs. P: Phila 12 Ja 58, 21
Dec 58, 9 Ag 59
Mr. P: Phila 26 Oct 69
Agnus P: Phila 5 Ag 62
Ann P: Nottingham 31 Jy 60;
Phila 21 Dec 58
Benjamin P: Phila 24 Oct 54
David C: N. London 18 Jy 65.
P: New-London 2 Feb 64;
Phila 2 May 65
Elizabeth P: Kent Co 28 Oct
62
George P: Phila 7 Ap 57
(Capt), 8 Jy 62, 28 Oct 62,
25 Ap 71
Hugh P: Phila 19 May 63
James P: Phila 31 Jy 60, 19
Ja 69, 27 Ja 73. T: Borden-
town 7 May 67
John N: Cumberland Co 12 Feb
67. P: Bibary Twp 7 Ap 57;
Pa 18 Mar 62; Phila 21 Dec
58, 8 Jy 62, 2 Sep 62, 30 Ap
67, 3 May 70, 27 Ja 73
Jos. P: East Jersey 2 Feb 64;
Gloucester Co 23 Oct 66; Pa
2 Sep 62; Phila 2 Sep 62, 1
Feb 70
Josiah P: Phila 24 Oct 54
Mary P: Abington 15 Mar 64;
Monmouth Co 13 Ja 63
Capt. Nathaniel P: Phila 2
Ag 70
Richard P: Phila 15 Mar 64
Robert P: Lancaster Co 3 Ja
60 (Dr); Phila 27 Dec 53,
30 May 54, 6 Jy 58, 31 Dec
61 (Dr)
Samuel C: c/o Benjamin M'Coul
18 Jy 65
Thomas P: Phila 21 Dec 58,
28 Oct 62, 16 Jy 67, 28 Ap
68, 26 Oct 69
William P: Phila 28 Oct 62;

16 Jy 77
Wolsly P: Phila 20 Jy 69
JACOBS
and JOHNSTON P: Phila 30 Ap
67
Mr. P: Germantown 12 Ja 58
Bar. P: Lancaster 28 Oct 62
Benjamin P: Pa 20 Ap 69;
Phila 23 Oct 66
Christopher P: Germantown
27 Jy 58, 21 Jy 68
Israel P: Reading 9 Ag 59
Jacob P: Wilmington 31 Jy 60
James P: Phila 31 Dec 61
Job P: Wilmington 9 Ag 59
Joseph P: Phila 5 Feb 54, 6
Jy 58. T: Trenton 17 Oct
54
JACOBY/JACOBEY
Christopher P: Bakers-Town
31 Jy 60; Germantown 24 Oct
54, 4 Feb 68
JACQUET/JAQUET
Joseph P: Newcastle Co 31
Dec 61, 5 Ag 62; Noxontown
15 Mar 64
Capt. Pet. P: Christine
Ferry 31 Jy 60, 3 Sep 61;
New-Castle Co 8 Jy 62
Thomas P: Christine Ferry 1
Jy 56, 27 Jy 58, 21 Dec 58,
9 Ag 59, 3 Ja 60; N. Castle
Co 9 Ag 59
JACQUIRE
Daniel P: in the army 27 Jy
58
JAFFRAY
Henry P: Kent Co 1 Nov 53
JAGO
Edward P: Phila 11 Sep 55
JAKOAKS
Mary P: Phila 2 Ag 70
JAMES
and WRIGHT P: Phila 30 Ap
67, 16 Jy 67
Mr. C: c/o James Loghary
Oxford Twp 18 Jy 65. P: 1
Nov 70
Andrew P: Phila 9 Ag 59;
Wilmington 18 Feb 55
Daniel P: Phila 3 May 70, 2
Ag 70, 1 Nov 70
Edward P: Phila 3 Sep 61
Elizabeth P: Phila 13 May 56
Ezekiel C: 30 Jy 77
Hugh P: in the army 27 Jy
58; Phila 9 Ag 59
Iseac P: Phila 28 Oct 62
James P: Phila 23 Oct 66.
T: Piles-Grove 31 Ja 71
John L: Lancaster Co 29 Jy
72. P: Brandywine 2 Feb
64; Phila 20 Oct 68 (Capt)
Joseph P: Chester Co 12 Ja
58; Willis-Town 3 Ja 60;

Wilmington 9 Ag 59
Margaret   Phila 16 Jy 77
Mary   P: Chester Co 31 Jy 60;
   Pa 12 Ja 58; Phila 27 Jy 58
Nicholas   P: Phila 26 Oct 69
Thomas   N: 29 Nov 64 (Esq).
   P: Christine Bridge 26 Jy
   64; Phila 18 Feb 55, 21 Dec
   58
William   L: 11 Ap 65. P:
   Phila 28 Oct 62, 3 Ja 65,
   30 Ap 67
William H.   P: Phila 16 Jy 72
JAMESON/JAMISON; see also
   JEMISON
   B.   P: Phila 3 Ja 65
   Benjamin/Begn   P: Pa 9 Ag 59,
   3 Ja 60
   David   P: Phila 13 Ja 63
   Edward   L: 3 Oct 65
   Ezekiel   P: Pa 18 Mar 62
   Henry   P: Pa 12 Feb 61
   John   L: 14 May 72; Shippens-
   burgh 2 Mar 74. P: Phila 15
   Mar 64
   Martha   P: Md. 7 Ap 57
   Mary   P: Buckingham 16 Jy 72
   Robert   P: Bucks 11 Sep 55
   Thomas   P: Phila 4 Feb 68
JAMPSON
   Moses   P: Cumberland Co 9 Ag
   59, 3 Ja 60
JANES
   Anna   P: Pa 12 Feb 61; Phila
   9 Ag 59
JANN
   Mary   Phila 31 Ja 76
   Capt. Thomas   Phila 31 Ja 76
JANSEN
   Barbary   P: Chester Co 7 Ap 57
JANSION
   Nathaniel   P: Phila 6 Jy 58
JANUARY
   Joseph   P: Phila 8 Jy 62
   Peter   P: Lancaster Co 13 May
   56; Phila 5 Ag 62
   Sarah   P: Phila 31 Dec 61
JAPPRA
   Thomas   P: Pa 18 Mar 62
JAQUES/JEQUEYS
   Jeane   P: Phila 16 Jy 67
   Nathan   Phila 24 Jy 76
   Dr. Richard   T: Middletown 31
   Ja 71
JAQUET
   Joseph   N: 29 Nov 64
JARMAN
   John   P: Phila 28 Ap 68
   Lewis   P: Chester Co 31 Mar
   63
   William   T: Bordentown 17 Oct
   54
JARNIE
   John   P: Phila 30 Ja 66
JARRARD

Mary   P: Phila 7 Ap 57
JARVIS
   Leonard   P: Phila 4 Ag 63
JASEPH
   William   P: Bucks 11 Sep 55
JAYSSER
   Frederick   P: Lancaster 27
   Jy 58
JEAN
   Matthew   P: Phila 24 Oct 54,
   11 Sep 55, 7 Ap 57, 3 Sep
   61
JEAY
   John   P: Phila 31 Jy 60
JEFFERTS
   George W.   Phila 5 Jy 76-
   Gaz. 24 Jy
JEFFERY/JEFFREYS/JAFERIES
   Amos   P: Brandywine 18 Ag 57
   Margaret   P: Phila 31 Mar 63
   Michael   P: Phila 9 May 54,
   30 May 54
   Samuel   P: Phila 17 Jy 80
   William   P: Wilmington 4 Ap
   54, 9 May 54, 11 Sep 55, 1
   Jy 56
JEKYLL/JEAKLE
   John   P: Phila 3 Ja 65, 2 May
   65, 25 Jy 65
JEMISON/JEAMISON; see also
   JAMESON
   Alexander   P: Phila-Gaz. 3
   Ja 76
   David   P: Phila 27 Jy 58, 25
   Jy 65, 20 Oct 68
   Hark.   P: Phila 15 Mar 64
   John   P: Bucks Co 3 Ja 60;
   Phila 3 May 70
   Robert   P: Fogs Manor 3 Ja
   60
JENKERSON
   John   P: Phila 21 Jy 68
JENKINS
   Aaron   P: Phila 7 Ap 57
   Ann Elizabeth   P: Phila 3
   Sep 61
   Charles   P: Phila 30 May 54,
   12 Feb 61, 5 Ag 62
   Lt. Edward   P: in the army 27
   Jy 58
   James   P: Phila-Gaz. 27 Oct
   73
   Jane   P: Chester Co 13 May 56
   John   P: Phila 21 Dec 58, 28
   Oct 62, 4 Ag 63
   Nathaniel   P: New Garden 3 Sep
   61
   Richard   P: Chester 27 Jy 58
   Robert   P: Phila 21 Dec 58
   Samuel   P: Phila 18 Mar 62
   Timothy   P: Kent Co 9 Ag 59
   W.   P: Conestogoe 15 Mar 64
   William   P: Phila 5 Ag 62,
   28 Oct 62
JENKS

Thomas P: Bucks Co 27 Jy 58
JENNEY/JENNY
Rev. Dr. Phila 24 Jy 76
Abel P: Phila 21 Jy 68
Edward P: Phila 31 Mar 63
Thomas P: Bucks Co 10 Oct 65
JENNINGS
Henry P: Phila 26 Jy 64, 2
Ag 70
James T: Allen-Town 4 Nov 72
John P: Easton 3 Sep 61; Phila
3 Ja 65
Redmond P: Phila 2 May 65
Thomas P: Phila Co 31 Jy 60,
3 Sep 61, 18 Mar 62
JENSION
Nathaniel P: Phila 27 Jy 58
JEPSON
William P: Pa 13 Oct 63
JERGAN
Elizabeth P: Phila 24 Oct 54
JERMAN
John P: Phila 31 Dec 61; Rad-
nor 6 Sep 53, 9 May 54
JEROM
David P: in Lord Fred. Caven-
dish's Regt. 19 Ja 69;
Phila 20 Oct 68 (34th Regt)
JERSON
James P: Allentown-Gaz. 27
Oct 73
JERVIES
David P: Phila 15 Mar 64
JERVIS; see also JARVIS
Elizabeth P: Pa 13 Ja 63
Esther P: Lancaster Co 8 Jy
62
John P: Phila 19 Jy 80
Thomas P: Phila 31 Jy 60
JESERT
Joseph T: Somerset Co 10 Ag
58
JESSEN/JESSENN
D. Christopher P: Pa 12 Feb
61
Gotthard P: Goshen 11 Sep 55;
Phila 28 Nov 54
JESSOP/JESSEP
John P: Phila 11 Jy 54, 9 Ag
59, 3 Ja 60
William P: Bucks Co 18 Mar
62
JEWER
John P: Phila 31 Mar 63
JEWSON
Thomas P: Phila 4 Ag 63
JIHMA
John Phila 16 Jy 77
JOAB
Tho. P: Chestnut-level 12 Ja
58
JOB
Jeremiah P: Leacock Twp 8 Jy
62
John P: Pa 12 Feb 61

JOBBIN
Richard P: New Castle 1 Jy
56
JOBS
Deborah P: Phila 20 Oct 68
JOCELYN
Thomas P: Phila 9 Ag 59
JOHANNA
Mr. P: Phila-Gaz. 3 Ja 76
JOHN
Mat. P: Phila 26 Jy 64
Robert P: Phila-Gaz. 27 Oct
73
Samuel P: Chester Co 3 Sep
61
William P: Chester Co 28 Ap
68
JOHNS
Matthew P: Phila 28 Oct 62
Richard P: Phila 21 Dec 58;
near Woodbury 19 Ja 69;
Woodberry 20 Ap 69
Samuel P: Phila-Gaz. 27 Oct
73
William P: Pa 21 Dec 58
JOHNSON
Mrs. P: Kensington 12 Ja 58
Alexander C: at the Cross
Road, New London Twp,
Chester Co 28 Nov 65 (Esq).
P: New-London 4 Ag 63
Ann P: Phila 1 Jy 56
Benja. P: Bucks Co 12 Ja 58
Catherine P: Phila 13 Oct 63
Charles P: Phila 1 Nov 53
Colin P: Phila 31 Jy 60, 2
Sep 62
David P: Pa 13 Oct 63;
Phila 28 Ap 68
Edward P: Donnegal 24 Oct
54
Francis P: Phila 30 Ap 77
(Col.). W: near Christia-
na 27 Ag 77 (Esq.)
George P: Bucks Co 4 Ag 63;
Phila 15 Mar 64
Holland P: Phila-Gaz. 3 Ja
76
James P: Bucks Co 12 Ja 58;
Phila 12 Ja 58, 25 Ap 71
Job P: Frankford 20 Oct 68
John L: c/o Alexander John-
son Lancaster Co 29 Jy 72.
N: Brandywine 4 Dec 66.
P: Allenstown 30 Ja 66;
Bucks Co 10 Oct 65; Chester
Co 12 Ja 58, 13 Oct 63, 2
Feb 64; Edgmont 5 Feb 54;
Germantown 24 Oct 54, 1
May 76; Pa 21 Dec 58, 19
May 63; near Phila 24 Oct
54; Phila 4 Feb 68, 28 Ap
68, 16 Jy 72, 30 Oct 76;
Timber Creek 20 Jy 69
Joseph P: Phila 1 Nov 53, 28

Ap 68. T: Amwell 10 Ag 58
(Capt)
Leonard P: Phila 15 Mar 64
Lownam P: Lancaster 19 Jy 80
Mary P: N.J. 13 Ja 63; Phila
13 May 56, 21 Dec 58
Moses T: Morris-town 17 Oct
54
Nicholas P: Bristol 3 Sep 61
Prezeley N. England Town 30
Oct 76
Richard L: c/o Thomas Clark
Lancaster 19 Dec 71
Robert P: Bucks Co 26 Jy 64;
Hunterdon Co 9 Ag 59; Phila
31 Dec 61, 10 Oct 65, 10 Ap
66, 23 Oct 66
Samuel P: Hunterdon Co 9 Ag
59; N.J. 4 Ag 63
Thomas (gunner) P: in the
army 21 Dec 58; Marcus-hook
18 Mar 62, 8 Jy 62; Phila
7 Ap 57, 2 Feb 64, 15 Mar
64, 26 Jy 64, 25 Jy 65
William P: Phila 3 Ja 65, 10
Oct 65, 30 Ja 66, 23 Oct 66,
20 Oct 68, 3 May 70, 27 Oct
73; carpenter, near Schuyl-
kill 16 Jy 72 ("Much time
hath been spent, and strict
Enquiry made, to forward this
letter, but to no Purpose.")
JOHNSTON/JOHNSTONE; see also
JACOBS &
Capt. P: Phila 2 Ag 70
Mrs. P: Phila 26 Oct 69
Adam W: c/o Mrs. Ann Mont-
gomery /Wilmington/ 3 Jy 76
Alexander L: Shippensburgh
2 Mar 74. P: Chester Co 3
Sep 61; New London Twp 27
Jy 58
Andrew P: Phila 25 Jy 65
Ann P: Phila 2 Ag 70, 1 Nov
70
Benjamin P: Pa 26 Jy 64
Charles P: Pequea 18 Mar 62;
Phila 5 Feb 54
Collin P: Phila 31 Dec 61
David P: Cumberland Co 28
Oct 62; Pa 28 Oct 62
Elizabeth P: Phila 1 Nov 53
George P: Bucks Co 18 Ag 57;
Falls Twp 9 Ag 59
Isabella P: Phila 1 Feb 70
James P: Bucks Co 3 Ja 60;
Christine Bridge 31 Dec 61;
Somerset Co 3 Sep 61. T:
Maidenhead 4 Nov 72
John L: Leacock 15 Ap 56. P:
Bucks Co 3 Ja 60; Carlisle
9 Ag 59; Forks of Brandiwine
25 Ap 71; Germantown 28 Nov
54; Nottingham 18 Mar 62, 13
Ja 63; Octararo 7 Ap 57; Pa

28 Nov 54, 13 Ja 63; Phila
31 Dec 61, 8 Jy 62, 27 Oct
73, 3 Ja 76; Timber Creek
3 May 70
Joseph P: Phila 18 Mar 62,
8 Jy 62
Mary P: Kent Co 18 Ag 57;
near The Gap 3 Sep 61;
Pequea 30 Oct 76
Nathan P: Cumberland Co 28
Oct 62
Nathaniel P: N.J. 18 Ag 57
Obadiah P: Darby 31 Jy 60
Paul P: Phila 1 Nov 70, 25
Ap 71, 1 May 76
Richard P: Phila-Gaz. 3 Ja
76
Robert P: Bucks Co-Gaz. 27
Oct 73; Chester Co 27 Dec
53, 30 May 54; Pa 2 Feb 64;
Phila 15 Mar 64, 16 Jy 77
Samuel P: Haverford 7 Ap 57,
18 Ag 57; Phila, Capt 19 Ja
69
Thomas P: Chester Co 11 Sep
55
Thomas G. P: Phila 25 Ap 71
William P: Phila 31 Dec 61,
13 Ja 63, 30 Ja 66, 30 Ap
67, 30 Ap 77 (Capt). W:
in Milltown, c/o David
Finney, Esq. in New Castle
3 Jy 76
JOHONNOT
Col. Gabriel Phila 5 Ap 77-
Gaz. 30 Ap
JOLLEY/JOLLY
Charles P: Phila 2 Feb 64,
3 Ja 65
James P: Bucks Co 21 Dec 58;
New Conaity Twp 23 Oct 66;
Pa 28 Oct 62
JOLLIFFE
William P: Jersey 13 May 56
JONES
....., counsellor P: in Red-
hill 19 Ja 69
Capt. P: Phila 5 Ag 62
Mrs. P: Phila 21 Dec 58, 3
Ja 76
Rev. P: Phila 3 May 70
Widow P: Phila 3 Ja 65
Abraham P: Phila 25 Ap 71
Amos C: Chester Co 18 Jy 65.
P: 25 Jy 65; Wilmington 18
Feb 55
Ann Great Valley 30 Oct 76;
Phila 3 Ja 65
Benjamin P: Phila 2 Sep 62.
T: Kingwood 4 Nov 72
Cadwallader C: Uwchland, see
SPEARY, James
Catherine P: West Nottingham
26 Jy 64
Charles P: Kensington 2 Feb

64; Kingston 13 Oct 63;
Phila 28 Oct 62
Daniel   P: Phila 1 Nov 70
David   P: Carnarvan, Bucks Co
26 Oct 69; Middletown 31 Mar
63; Phila 21 Jy 68, 3 Ja 66
Doughty   P: Phila 28 Oct 62
Capt. E.   P: Phila 31 Jy 60
Edward   L: Lancaster Co 15 Ap
56. P: Phila 21 Dec 58, 26
Jy 64, 3 May 70, 1 Nov 70,
27 Ja 73; Vineyard 23 Oct 66
Elizabeth   L: at Jas. Carroll's
13 Jn 65. N: 29 Nov 64. P:
Phila 12 Ja 58, 27 Ja 73,
27 Oct 73, 30 Ap 77
Capt. Ephraim   P: Phila 28 Oct
62
Evan   P: Northampton 13 May
56; Phila 1 Jy 56
Griffith   P: Pa 12 Feb 61, 19
Jy 80
Hannah   P: Pa 19 May 63
Henry   P: Phila 25 Jy 65, 1
Feb 70 (Capt)
Hugh   P: Merion   25 Ap 71
Humphrey   P: Phila 2 Ag 70
Isaac   P: Phila 11 Sep 55, 5
Ag 62
Isabella   P: Kent Co 12 Ja 58;
Phila 10 Ap 66
J.   P: Phila 31 Jy 60, 18 Feb
55 (Rev.)
James   P: Blockley 11 Jy 54;
Chester Co 31 Dec 61; Pe-
quea 18 Mar 62
Jane   P: Phila 18 Ag 57
Jesse   P: Phila 26 Jy 53
John   C: 30 Jy 77. P: Apoqui-
nimy 27 Jy 58; Bucks Co 8 Jy
62; Chester Co 22 Nov 53, 11
Jy 54; East Bradford 18 Feb
55; Germantown 30 Ap 67;
Newtown 27 Jy 58; Penkader
Hundred 27 Oct 73; Phila 26
Jy 53, 18 Ag 57, 21 Dec 58,
3 Ja 60, 19 May 63, 4 Feb
68, 21 Jy 68, 27 Ja 73; Welch
Tract 15 Mar 64. T: Chester-
field 7 May 67
Joseph   P: Pa 19 May 63; Phila
28 Nov 54, 4 Feb 68
Joshua   P: Phila 18 Mar 62
Justice   P: Germantown 13 Ja
63
Katherine   P: Phila 29 Ag 54
Latimor   P: Phila 21 Dec 58
Mary   P: Phila 1 Jy 56, 12 Ja
58, 27 Jy 58, 21 Dec 58, 31
Jy 60, 28 Oct 62; Strasburg
21 Dec 58
N.   P: Kingsess 2 Sep 62; Lower
Ferry 28 Oct 62
Nancy   P: Gloucester 9 Ag 59;
Phila 25 Ap 71

Nathaniel   P: Bucks Co 13 Ja
63
Neil   P: Lower Ferry 31 Mar
63
Nicholas   P: Phila 16 Jy 67
Peregrine   P: Phila 25 Jy 65
Polly   P: Marcus Hook 26 Jy
64
Richard   P: Talbot Co 31 Dec
61
Robert   P: Abington 19 Ja 69;
Chester Co 12 Feb 61
Samuel   P: Phila 30 May 54,
9 Ag 59, 27 Oct 73
Sarah   P: Phila 9 Ag 59, 3
Ja 60, 31 Dec 61, 2 Feb 64
Stephen   P: Phila 26 Oct 69.
T: Maidenhead 17 Oct 54
Thomas   P: Berks Co 31 Jy 60;
Bucks Co 21 Dec 58; Phila
11 Sep 55, 31 Dec 61, 27
Oct 73; Salem 12 Ja 58
William   P: Carpenter's Is-
land 5 Ag 62; Phila 7 Ap
57, 31 Dec 61, 2 Feb 64, 30
Ja 66, 30 Ap 67, 16 Jy 72,
27 Ja 73, 27 Oct 73, 3 Ja 76;
Reading Furnace 27 Jy 58
JONNESTON/JONNERTON
Dr.   P: Phila 13 Ja 63, 24
Feb 63
JORDAN
James   P: Phila 16 Jy 72
John   P: Limerick Twp 8 Jy
62; Pa 28 Oct 62, 13 Ja 63,
24 Feb 63
Mary   T: Allen-Town /?/ 4
Nov 72
Michael   Phila 5 Ap 76-Gaz.
1 May
Tho.   P: Chester Co 27 Dec 53
JORONEY
William   P: Phila 24 Oct 54
JOSEPHSON
Myer/Mayer   L: Reading 29 Jy
72. P: Phila 3 Sep 61, 3
Ja 65
JOSIAH
Emanuel   P: Phila 6 Jy 58, 27
Jy 58
JOSSELIN
Amaziah   Phila 5 Ap 77-Gaz.
30 Ap
JOUCE
Isaac, 18th Regt.   P: Phila
Gaz. 27 Oct 73
JOWSAN
Mr.   P: Phila 16 Jy 72
JOY
Capt.   P: Phila 25 Jy 65
Mr.   P: Phila 30 Ja 66
Capt. Daniel   P: Phila 26 Jy
64, 16 Jy 67, 25 Ap 71
JOYCE
David   P: Phila-Gaz. 3 Ja 76

JUDAH
  Abraham P: Phila 26 Jy 64;
    Wilmington 27 Jy 58, 21 Dec
    58
JUDGE
  Barbary L: near Lancaster
    15 Ap 56
  Katherine P: Pequea 18 Mar
    62
JUDKIN
  George P: Phila 31 Jy 60
JUDWIN
  Capt. Thomas Smith P: Phila
    1 Feb 70
JURDEN
  James P: Phila 1 Nov 70
JURRYMAY
  Hans P: Phila 1 Nov 53
JUSTICE/JUSTUS
  Alexander P: Phila 1 Nov 70
  George P: Phila 25 Jy 65
  John L: Ballenfels 2 Mar 74
    (Dr). P: Phila 1 Feb 70
  Peter P: Nottingham 12 Ja 58

KABETER
  Mr. P: Pa 3 Ja 60
KABLER
  Mr. P: Phila 9 Ag 59
KACHAN
  John C: Reading Furnace 18
    Jy 65
  William P: Phila 30 Ja 66
KAIGHN/KAIGHEN
  Charles P: Pa 13 Ja 63
  John P: Phila 10 Ap 66
KALDRIDGE
  William P: Phila 25 Jy 65
KALLIE
  James P: Phila 27 Jy 58
KALS/KALES
  Rev. John W. P: Germantown
    5 Ag 62; Phila 13 Oct 63
KAMMIN
  Alexander P: Bucks 28 Nov 54
KAN
  Charles P: Phila 27 Ja 73
KANE
  Catherine P: Phila 18 Ag 57
  Francis, Schoolmaster L:
    Carnarven Church 19 Dec 71
  Jo. L: York 14 May 72
  Robert P: Phila 3 Ja 65
  William P: Phila 19 Ja 69
KANGHIE
  Samuel P: Octorara 28 Nov 54
KAPPELL
  Michael P: Phila 4 Ag 63
KARCHER
  Lewis Phila 1 May 76
KARNAN
  Hugh P: Chester Co 8 Jy 62
KARR
  Capt. Abraham P: Phila 6 Jy

58
  Capt. Alexander P: Phila 27
    Jy 58
  George P: Phila 19 Ja 69
  Henry P: Phila-Gaz. 27 Oct
    73
  Capt. J. P: Phila 21 Jy 60
  James C: c/o J. Graham at
    Nantmill, Chester Co 28
    Nov 65. P: Donegal 12 Ja
    58; Lancaster Co 13 Oct
    63, 26 Jy 64
  Joseph P: Phila 10 Oct 65
  Mark P: Bucks Co 12 Ja 58
  Samuel P: N. Castle Co 31
    Dec 61
  Thomas P: Phila 26 Jy 53
  William P: Duck-creek 12 Ja
    58; Nesham 7 Ap 57; Phila
    27 Oct 73
KARSWIL
  Mark P: Phila 5 Jy 80-Gaz.
    19 Jy
KASS
  William T: Amwell 15 Mar 64,
    6 Dec 64, 1 Sep 68
KAST
  Jerg. P: Germantown 18 Feb
    55
  Martin P: Reading 15 Mar 64
KASTER
  William P: Phila 10 Ap 66
KATTER
  Alexander P: Phila 9 Ag 59
KAUFF
  Andreas P: Lancaster Co 3
    Ja 60
KAUFFMAN
  Andreas P: Lancaster 9 Ag
    59
KAVANAGH
  Garret P: Lancaster Co 12 Ja
    58
KAY
  John P: Phila 15 Mar 64, 3
    Ja 65
  Philip L: York Co 14 May 72
  William P: Phila 15 Mar 64,
    3 Ja 65
KEAGY
  John P: Blue Rock 28 Oct 62
KEAIS
  Capt. William P: Phila 19 Ja
    69, 3 May 70
KEALE
  Capt. Robert P: Phila 4 Feb
    68
KEAN
  John L: York-Town 20 Ja 73,
    2 Mar 74
  Lawrence P: Phila 30 Ap 67
  William C: near Doe Run 22
    Ja 67
KEARNEY/KEARNY
  Edward P: Phila 16 Jy 67

Capt. Michael P: Phila 16 Jy
  67
Patrick P: Phila 1 Feb 70
Philip P: Phila 2 May 65, 25
  Jy 65, 30 Ja 66, 21 Jy 68
Thomas P: Salem Co 26 Jy 64
KEARNS
  James, soldier P: Phila 1 Feb
  70
KEARSLEY
  Jonathan P: Lancaster Co 1
  Nov 53, 11 Jy 54
KEARY/KEAREY
  John P: Welsh Tract 2 Feb 64
  Patrick P: Phila 1 Nov 53
KEASBEY
  Sarah P: Salem 19 Jy 80
KEAT
  Mr. P: Phila 21 Dec 58
KEATEN
  George P: Phila 18 Feb 55
KEATES
  Thomas P: Phila 16 Jy 67
KEATON
  George P: Phila 21 Dec 58
  James P: Phila 25 Jy 65
KEDDICE
  John P: Phila 27 Jy 58
KEDEY
  John P: Phila 18 Mar 62
KEEDY
  William, soldier P: Phila 20
  Oct 68
KEEF
  Dennis T: New Jersey 17 Oct
  54
KEEFFE
  Mary P: Phila 1 Nov 70
KEELY
  Thomas P: Baltimore Co 9 Ag
  59
KEEMER
  George P: Germantown 27 Jy
  58
KEEN
  Daniel P: Phila 1 Feb 70
  James L. P: Phila 2 Ag 70
  Matthew P: Pa 18 Mar 62;
    Phila 13 Ja 63
  Peter P: Phila 4 Ag 63
  Reynold P: Phila 27 Jy 58
KEENS
  George P: York Town 18 Mar
  62
KEEPERS
  William P: Chester Co 27 Jy
  58
KEEPING
  Agnes P: near Phila 7 Ap 57
KEERAN
  John P: Phila 2 May 65
  Patrick P: Apoquimenick 1 Feb
  70
KEES
  Robert P: Phila 25 Jy 65

KEESBY
  Phoebe Salem 24 Jy 76
KEHR
  Abraham P: Phila 1 Feb 70
KEIF
  Patrick P: Phila 16 Jy 72
KEIGHLEY
  Mrs. P: Phila 31 Dec 61
KEILY
  John P: Phila-Gaz. 3 Ja 76
KEIMEN
  Robert T: Somerset 15 Jy 56
  Thomas P: Somerset 15 Jy 56
KEIMER
  Dr. Thomas P: Phila 19 Ja 69
KEIRL
  John P: Phila 21 Dec 58
KEISE
  Thomas P: Phila 24 Feb 63
KEITH
  Alexander P: Phila 25 Jy 65
  George P: Bucks Co 9 Ag 59,
    12 Feb 61
  William P: Bucks Co 2 Feb
    64; Phila 20 Ap 69 (Capt)
KEITNOR
  Paulus P: Phila 4 Ap 54
KELEZ
  Thomas P: Brandywine 4 Ag 63
KELL
  James C: c/o Jos. Pennock,
    Chester Co 18 Jy 65. P: Pa
    15 Mar 64
  John P: West Marlborough 7
    Ap 57
KELLAM
  William N: 29 Nov 64
KELLER/KELLAR/KELLOR
  George P: Phila 13 Oct 63,
    3 Ja 65
  John P: Lancaster Co 15 Mar
    64
  Michael L: 13 Jn 65
KELLET
  Capt. Roger P: Lancaster Co.
    31 Jy 60
KELLOCK
  John P: Pa 13 Ja 63
KELLOP
  Philip P: Phila 16 Jy 67
KELLUM
  Richard P: Phila 13 Oct 63
KELLY/KELLEY/KELLIE; see also
  CELLEY
  Mr. P: Phila 26 Jy 64
  Ann P: Phila 2 Ag 70
  Charles P: Phila 25 Jy 65
  Daniel P: Phila 30 Ap 67
  Erasmus P: Bucks Co 2 Ag 70
  George P: Buckingham 16 Jy
    72
  Hugh P: Chester Co 15 Mar
    64
  Isaac P: Pa 12 Feb 61
  James P: Phila 9 Ag 59, 31

Dec 61, 29 Feb 63, 30 Ja 66,
1 Nov 70, 27 Oct 73; White-
clay Creek 18 Ag 57
John P: Cumberland Co 8 Jy
62; Pa 13 Ja 63; Phila 21
Dec 58, 3 Ja 60, 1 Nov 70,
3 Ja 76
Marcus P: Phila 27 Jy 58
Margaret P: Phila 28 Ap 68
Mary P: Cumberland 9 Ag 59,
3 Ja 60; Whiteclay Creek 2
Feb 64
Matt. L: Octerara 14 May 72
Maurice P: Phila-Gaz. 3 Ja
76
Patrick P: Phila 28 Nov 54,
16 Jy 72
Peter P: Chester Co 31 Dec 61
Richard P: Pa 11 Sep 55
Robert P: Anderson's Ferry
24 Feb 63
Terence P: Chester Co 3 Sep
61
Tho./Thomas P: Chester Co 12
Ja 58, 27 Jy 58, 9 Ag 59,
28 Oct 62; Newcastle Co 18
Mar 62; Pa 11 Sep 55, 12 Feb
61; West-Caln 21 Dec 58
Tobias N: 12 Feb 67
Waldren P: Phila 2 Feb 64
William P: Nottingham 9 Ag
59; Phila 24 Feb 63, 27 Oct
73
KELLS
George P: Phila 28 Nov 54
KELSEY/KELSY/KELSE/KELSAY/KELSY
Mr. P: New-Castle Co 9 Ag 59
John P: Phila 9 Ag 59, 16 Jy
67
Rev. R. P: N.J. 15 Mar 64
Rev. Robert P: Cumberland Co
13 Oct 63
Sam. P: Phila 28 Ap 68
KELSO/KILSOE
Catherine P: Phila 2 May 65
George P: Bucks Co 13 Ja 63,
30 Ja 66; Phila 16 Jy 72
James P: Phila 21 Jy 68, 1
Feb 70
John P: Darby 4 Ag 63; Pa
12 Feb 61; Phila 30 Ja 66
Jr. Phila 30 Ap 77
William L: Harris's Ferry,
see FLEMING, Henry; Lan-
caster Co 29 Jy 72. P:
Paxton 7 Ap 57; Phila 27
Jy 58 (sailor), 15 Mar 64.
William, Jr. P: Paxton 19 Jy
80
KELSOR
Rev. P: Pilesgrove 11 Sep 55
KEMBLE
Conrad P: Phila 21 Dec 58
KEMENS
Alexander P: Phila 23 Oct 66

KEMERLE
Jacob P: Phila 19 Ja 69
KENAMAN
Susannah P: Phila 12 Feb 61
KENCHER
Jacob P: Phila 31 Jy 60
KENDALL/KENDAL
Benjamin P: Phila 6 Jy 58
Henry P: Phila 1 Nov 70
KENDRY
William L: Little Britain 20
Ja 73
KENERLY
Randel P: East Nottingham
28 Nov 54
KENILLY
Duncan T: at William Boyd's
near Trenton 3 Oct 65
KENION
David P: Pa 15 Mar 64
KENKEAD
Anne P: Phila 12 Feb 61
John P: Chester Co 31 Jy 60
Joseph (soldier) P: 21 Dec
58
KENMAN
Sam. P: Upper Dublin 12 Ja
58
KENNAGHAN
John P: Strabane Twp 13 Ja
63
KENNAN
Henry P: Newcastle 24 Oct
54; Phila 26 Jy 64
Hugh P: Chester Co 8 Jy 62
KENNED
Richard P: Chester Co 12 Feb
61
KENNEDY/KENNADY/KENEDY
Capt. P: Phila 8 Jy 62
Mr. P: Phila 20 Oct 68
Ann P: Chester Co 24 Feb 63
David P: Chester Co 21 Dec
58, 9 Ag 59; Phila 30 Ja
66; Whangsworth 1 Nov 53
Dennis P: Phila 29 Ag 54,
11 Sep 55
Mrs. Elizabeth Phila 30 Oct
76
Francis P: Chester Co 3 Ja
60
George P: Pa 28 Oct 62;
Phila 2 May 65
James L: 29 Ja 67. P:
Chester Co 9 Ag 59, 5 Ag
62, 24 Feb 63, 4 Ag 63, 13
Oct 63, 15 Mar 64; Pa 3
Ja 60; Phila 20 Jy 69
John C: London Britain 22
Ja 67. L: York Co 2 Mar
74. P: America 9 Ag 59;
Bucks Co 20 Oct 68; Chester
31 Dec 61, 18 Mar 62;
Leacock Twp 31 Dec 61; Pa
3 Ja 60; Phila 12 Feb 61,

18 Feb 55 (2), 5 Ag 62 (Capt),
13 Ja 63, 24 Feb 63, 3 Ja 76
Joseph   P: Phila-Gaz. 3 Ja 76
Katherine   P: Phila 18 Mar 62
Mary   P: Montgomery Twp 18
Mar 62; Phila 25 Jy 65, 27
Ja 73
Murdoch   P: Phila 2 Feb 64
Patrick   P: Phila 3 Sep 61,
2 Ag 70 (18th Regt)
Prudence   Chester Co 1 May 76
Richard   P: Chester Co 3 Ja 60
Robert   P: Pa 20 Oct 68; Phila
(Co) 5 Ag 62, 13 Ja 63, 3
Ja 65, 16 Jy 67, 26 Oct 69
Dr. S.   P: Lancaster Co 15
Mar 64
Samuel   P: Chester Co 9 Ag
59; Phila 10 Ap 66; Dr.,
Chester Co 21 Dec 58, 3 Ja
60, 3 Sep 61
Thomas   P: Monmouth Co., N.J.
20 Oct 68; Pa 13 Ja 63;
Phila 27 Oct 73, 3 Ja 76
William   L: Cumberland Co 29
Jy 72; Carlisle 20 Ja 73.
P: Baltimore Co 9 Ag 59;
Nottingham 18 Mar 62; Pa 24
Feb 63; Phila 4 Feb 68, 21
Jy 68
KENNELY
Johannah   P: Phila 1 Nov 70
KENNOCHAN
Hugh   P: Pa 2 Feb 64
KENNON/KENON
John   P: Harris's Ferry 27 Jy
58; Phila 23 Oct 66
Robert   P: Pa 12 Feb 61
Rowan   P: Lancaster Co 12 Ja
58
KENNY/KENNEY
John   P: Phila 31 Jy 60, 3 May
70
Jos.   P: Phila 3 Sep 61
Nancy   P: Chester Co 31 Dec 61
KENSEY
Frasher   P: Phila 23 Oct 66
KENT
John   P: Phila 19 Ja 69
KENTON
Richard   P: Phila 31 Dec 61
KENYON
Enoch   P: Phila 4 Feb 68
KERBER
Valentine   P: Phila 1 Nov 70
KERBRIGHTS
Messieurs   P: Phila 30 Ap 67
KERBY
Thomas   P: Phila 18 Ag 57
KERCHER
Lud. Henry   P: Phila 24 Feb
63
KERCK
John   P: New-Castle Co 27 Jy
58

KERLIN
John   P: Chester Co 18 Mar
62
Capt. William   P: Phila 30
Ap 67
KERLY
Sally   P: Phila 19 Ja 69
KERMOND
William   P: Phila 3 Ja 60
KERNAGHEN
John   P: Strabane Twp 3 Sep
61
KERNS
Mary   P: Bucks Co 2 Feb 64,
3 Ja 65
KERR/KER
Mrs.   P: Phila 27 Jy 58
Adam   P: Pa 13 Oct 63;
Phila 31 Dec 61, 30 Ja 66
Arthur   P: Pa 13 Oct 63
Edward   P: Phila 9 May 54,
1 Jy 56, 5 Ag 56
Elizabeth   P: Phila 11 Sep
55, 18 Mar 62
George   P: Pa 13 Oct 63;
Phila 3 Ja 65, 2 Ag 70
James   C: c/o John Graham
Nantmell, Chester Co 30
Oct 66, 22 Ja 67.   P:
Forks of Delaware 30 Ja
66; Phila 30 Ja 66
John   P: America 9 Ag 59;
Bucks Co 20 Oct 68; Marsh
Creek 7 Ap 57; Phila 2 May
65, 3 Ja 76; York Town 18
Mar 62
Joseph   P: Chester Co 2 Sep
62
Mark   P: Bucks Co 13 Ja 63
Martha   P: Octerara 13 Oct
63
Peter   P: Phila 2 Ag 70
Robert   C: in Upper Octo-
raro 22 Ja 67.   P: Chester
Co 27 Jy 58, 12 Feb 61;
Pa 3 Sep 61; Phila 12 Feb
61
Samuel   N: 29 Nov 64.   P:
Pa 8 Jy 62, 2 Feb 64;
Phila 16 Jy 77
Thomas   P: near Phila 21 Jy
68
Walter   P: Phila 25 Jy 65
William   P: Bucks Co 4 Feb
68; Pa 13 Ja 63, 13 Oct
63; Phila 28 Oct 62, 10
Ap 66
KERRON
Hugo   P: Phila 3 Ja 65
KETCHUM/KECHAM
Daniel   P: Phila 9 Ag 59;
West Jersey 30 Oct 76
Capt. Stephen   P: Phila 3
Sep 61
KETTEMAN

Andreas   L: 13 Jn 65
KEW
  Elizabeth   P: Phila 22 Nov 53
KEYS
  John   P: Nesham/Iney7 7 Ap 57
  Robert   P: Nesham/iney7 7 Ap
    57
KIAH
  George   Spring Mill 1 May 76
KIDD/KID/KYD
  Alexander   P: Lampiter Twp 3
    Sep 61; Lancaster Co 4 Ag
    63
  Andrew   P: Cecil Co 9 Ag 59
  Capt. George   P: Phila 28 Oct
    62
  Hugh   P: Pa 28 Oct 62
  John   P: Phila 1 Feb 70, 2 Ag
    70
  Samuel   P: New-Castle 2 Feb 64
  Capt. William   P: Phila 21 Jy
    68
KIDDE
  Peter   P: Phila 3 Ja 65
KIDDEY/KIDDY
  John   P: Phila 5 Ag 56, 31 Dec
    61
KIDNEY
  John   P: Phila 28 Oct 62, 13
    Oct 63
KIDWALLD
  John   P: Phila 21 Jy 68
KIGHTLEY
  James   P: Chester Co 7 Ap 57;
    Kennet 13 May 56
KILBURNE/KILLABORN
  Patrick   P: Pa 31 Dec 61
  Thomas   T: Maidenhead 15 Jy 56
KILDEN
  John   P: Phila 23 Oct 66
KILGOUR/KILLGORE
  William   P: Pa 31 Dec 61, 23
    Oct 66
KILKENNY/KILKINNY
  Mary   P: America 9 Ag 59, 31
    Jy 60
KILL
  Martin   P: Gloucester 24 Feb 63
  Thomas   P: Pa 24 Feb 63
KILLCRIST
  John   P: Paxton Twp 8 Jy 62
KILLEN/KILLON/KILLIN/KILLENS
  Hannah   P: Wilmington 21 Dec
    58
  William   P: Dover 26 Oct 69
    (Esq); Kent Co 8 Jy 62, 2
    Feb 64
KILLOCK
  John   P: Chester Co 13 Oct 63
KILMICHAEL
  Thomas   P: Susquehannah 8 Jy
    62
KILPATRICK/KILLPATRICK
  Elizabeth   P: Pa 18 Mar 62
  Hugh   C: Chester Co, see

  NESBITT, John.   P: Nott-
    ingham 26 Jy 64
  Jane   P: Phila 5 Ag 62
  Patrick   P: America 9 Ag 59;
    New-Castle Co 21 Dec 58;
    Pa 3 Ja 60
  Richard   P: Cumberland Co 31
    Dec 61
  Samuel   P: Charlestown, Cecil
    Co 23 Oct 66
  William   P: Phila 20 Oct 68
KIMREY
  John   P: Phila 2 Feb 64
KIMSEY
  Sarah   P: Gloucester 31 Jy
    60
KINDER
  Samuel   Phila 30 Ap 77
KINDEY
  John   P: Phila 2 May 65
KINDLY
  William   P: Phila 16 Jy 72
KINEMIN
  John   P: Talbot Co 9 Ag 59
KING
  Abraham   P: Lancaster Co 27
    Jy 58, 21 Dec 58
  Anna Maria   P: Lancaster Co
    27 Jy 58, 9 Ag 59
  Benjamin   P: Phila 18 Feb 55
  Isaac   P: Joneykake Landing
    3 Sep 61
  James   L: Chestnut Level 20
    Ja 73; Bucks Co 4 Feb 68;
    Phila, soldier 20 Oct 68
  Joel, stay-maker   L: Lancas-
    ter Co 19 Dec 71
  John   C: Whiteland Twp 22 Ja
    67.   P: Bridgwater 1 Nov
    70; Phila 31 Dec 61, 18 Mar
    62, 2 May 65, 26 Oct 69.
    T: Somerset Co 1 Sep 68
  Nehemiah   P: Phila-Gaz. 3 Ja
    76
  Patrick   P: Lancaster Co 21
    Dec 58
  Patty   P: Lancaster Co 3 Ja 6(
  Richard   P: Phila 5 Ag 62
  Robert   P: Little Britain 24
    Oct 54; Phila 20 Oct 68
  Thomas   L: c/o James Wilson
    Carlisle 20 Ja 73.   P:
    Lancaster Co 13 Oct 63;
    Lower Dublin 5 Ag 56;
    Phila 8 Jy 62, 27 Ja 73, 3
    Ja 76
  Tristram   Phila 30 Ap 77
  William   P: Chester Co 3 Sep
    61; Phila 19 Jy 80
KINGSBURY
  Margaret   L: Paxton 2 Mar 74
KINGSLAND
  Isaac   P: Phila 4 Ap 54
KINKEAD
  George   P: Cumberland Co 2

Feb 64; Lancaster Co 18 Mar
62
James P: Phila 30 Ja 66
John P: Pa 13 Oct 63
KINLEY
Robert P: Cumberland Co 2
Feb 64
KINLOCK
Samuel P: Northampton Co 16
Jy 67
KINNAN/KINAN/KINNON
Roan P: Phila 3 Ja 60
Robert P: Phila 4 Feb 68
William P: East New Jersey 12
Feb 61; Phila 25 Jy 65
KINNEER
Joseph L: Lancaster Co 29 Jy
72
KINSEY
Abraham P: Phila 2 Ag 70, 30
Ap 77
James P: Phila 2 Sep 62 (Esq),
20 Oct 68, 16 Jy 72
KINSLEY
Zeph. P: Phila-Gaz. 3 Ja 76
KIOGH
James P: Phila 24 Feb 63
KIRD
John P: Cumberland Co 2 Feb
64
KIRK; see also M'CREARY, Widow
Adam P: Pa 12 Feb 61
Alexander P: Phila 30 Ap 67
Francis P: Deep-Run, Bucks Co
23 Oct 66
James P: Phila-Gaz. 3 Ja 76
John P: Chester Co 27 Jy 58;
Mill Creek 1 Feb 70; Pequea
18 Mar 62, 2 Sep 62
Roger P: Nottingham 27 Jy 58;
West Nottingham 12 Ja 58
Thomas P: Cumberland Co 4 Ag
63
William P: Nottingham 12 Ja
58; Phila 3 Ja 76
KIRKBRIDE
Mahlon P: Bucks Co 9 Ag 59.
T: Pa 15 Jy 56
KIRKBY/KIRKEBY
Robert P: Phila 11 Sep 55
William P: Pa 13 Ja 63
KIRKER
James P: Phila 2 Ag 70
KIRKPATRICK
Gavin P: Phila 24 Feb 63
Hugh P: West Nottingham 12
Ja 58
Isaac P: Pa 3 Sep 61
James P: Rocky-hill 2 Feb 64
William P: Pa 7 Ap 57. T:
10 Ag 58; Trenton 1 Sep 68
KIRNAN
Hugh P: Schuylkill 18 Ag 57
KIRSTED
Benjamin P: Phila 2 Feb 64

KITCHEN
Samuel T: Amwell-Mills 4 Nov
72
KITE
Charles Abington 5 Ja 76-
Gaz. 31 Ja
KITHTE
William or Cornelius P: Phila
21 Jy 68
KITTEN
John P: Chester Co 8 Jy 62
KIZEY
James P: Phila 2 Ag 70
KLEINHOOFF
Peter P: Bohemia 5 Ag 62
KLIMER
Henrick P: Phila 19 Ja 69
KLOMBAK
Philip P: Phila 21 Dec 58
KLUGH
Charles L: Lancaster 19 Dec
71
KLUMBERG
Mr. P: Phila 25 Jy 65
KLUTZ
Hon. Justice P: Phila 10 Oct
65
KNADY/KNEDY
George P: Phila 15 Mar 64
Murden P: Phila 26 Jy 64
KNAPP
Thomas P: on board the Vi-
per sloop of war - Phila
20 Jy 69
William P: Phila 25 Jy 65
KNARESBOROUGH/KNAVESBRAUGIT
John P: Bohemia 8 Jy 62, 5
Ag 62
Wm. P: Phila 6 Sep 53
KNAUT
Philip P: Phila 18 Mar 62
KNEAL
John P: Lewis-Town 1 Nov 53
KNIGHT
Charles P: Phila-Gaz. 3 Ja
76
Isaac P: Phila 26 Oct 69
Jannet P: Pa 3 Ja 60
Nicholas P: Lancaster Co 27
Jy 58
Peter P: Phila 6 Jy 58, 2 Ag
70, 24 Jy 76
Phiby P: Phila 7 Ap 57
Thomas P: Biberry 29 Ag 54
KNILE
George P: Phila 16 Jy 72
KNIPE
Jonathan T: 10 Ag 58
KNOCK
Thomas N: 29 Nov 64
KNOT
Mary P: Phila 5 Ag 62
KNOWLES
Edward P: Phila 3 Ja 65
John P: Chester Co 9 Ag 59;

New-Castle Co 21 Dec 58;
Phila 30 Ja 66, 10 Ap 66
KNOX/KNOCKS
Alexander P: Phila 19 Ja 69
Andrew P: Pa 12 Feb 61;
Whitpain Twp 27 Oct 73
David P: Bucks Co 13 Ja 63;
Norrington, Phila Co 25 Jy
65, 28 Ap 68; Pa 15 Mar 64
James P: Peach-Bots 9 May 54
John C: Chester 30 Oct 66.
P: Darby 30 Ja 66; Pa 12 Feb
61; Phila 28 Ap 68
Joseph P: Phila 23 Oct 66
Mary P: Phila 24 Oct 54
Oliver P: Phila 13 Oct 63
Patrick P: near Swatara 24
Oct 54
Robert P: Phila 3 Sep 61, 16
Jy 77
Thomas P: Mill Creek 9 Ag 59;
Pa 3 Sep 61
William P: Phila-Gaz. 3 Ja
76; Welsh Tract 7 Ap 57
KOBB
Philip P: Phila 11 Sep 55
KOCK
Johannes P: Germantown 26 Oct
69
KOERNER
Jean Christian P: Phila 1 Nov
53
KOLLER
Rodolph P: Phila 18 Mar 62
KOLLERIS
Anna Maria P: Phila 5 Ag 56
KOLLOCK/KOLLICK
Cornelius P: Phila 27 Jy 58
Jacob P: Lewistown/Lewes
(Town) 9 Ag 59, 31 Jy 60,
2 Ag 70, 1 Nov 70; Pa 12
Feb 61
KOPPLE
Michael P: Phila 5 Ag 62
KOST
John P: Lancaster Co 31 Jy
60
KOSTER
William P: Phila 9 Ag 59
KOWASAFER
Richard T: Amwell 7 May 67
KOWN
George P: Phila 24 Feb 63
KRAUSKOP
John P: Pa 26 Jy 64
KRIDER
Mr. P: Phila 27 Ja 73
KRIPNER
Poulus/Paulus P: Pa 26 Jy
64; Phila 13 May 56, 3 Ja
65, 10 Ap 66
KRUYTER
Martin P: Phila 1 Nov 70
KUENTZLY
Conrad P: Cumberland Co 3 Ja

60
KUFF
Arthur P: Pa 31 Dec 61
KUHN/KUHNS
Dr. Adam Simon P: Lancaster
12 Feb 61
Michael P: Phila 4 ₮g 63
KUL
Richard P: Phila 8 Jy 62
KULLEY/KULLY
Elisabeth P: Carlisle 31 Dec
61
Mary P: Cumberland Co 31 Jy
60
KUNTZ
Rev. Mr. Phila 30 Ap 77
KURTZ
Ernst P: Phila 6 Jy 58
Peter P: Phila 1 Nov 70
KUTNELL
Joseph P: West Jersey 1 Feb
70
KUYPER
Dirk P: Phila 19 Ja 69

LA_DAN
S̄arah P: Phila 3 Ja 65
LA BORDE
Mons. P: Phila 19 Jy 80
LACEY/LEACY/LACY/LACE
.... P: Phila 13 May 56
Edward P: Cumberland Co 1
Nov 53
Elizabeth P: Phila 31 Jy 60
John Bucks Co 24 Jy 76;
Phila 13 Ja 63
Mary P: Phila 27 Jy 58
Thomas P: Phila 9 Ag 59
LACKEY
James P: Phila 27 Ja 73
Tho. P: Whiteclay Creek 12
Ja 58
LACKLAN
John P: Chester Co 31 Dec
61
LACKUY
James P: Salem 26 Oct 69
LADD
John P: Gloucester Co 31 Dec
61 (Esq), 1 Nov 70
Thomas T: Bordins-town 17
Oct 54; Burlington 17 Oct
54
LADWICK
Ladiway P: Phila-Gaz. 3 Ja
76
LAFERTY
James P: New London 3 Sep
61; Phila 27 Ja 73
LAGHLIN
John P: Chester Co 3 Ja 60
LAHUE
Mary Darby 5 Oct 76-Gaz. 30
Oct

LAID
Ⅰ James   P: Pa 12 Ja 58
LAIDLER
Ⅰ Mr.   P: Phila 28 Ap 68
LAIGHT
Ⅰ Edward   P: Phila 3 Ja 65
LAING
Ⅰ Benjamin   P: Phila 10 Ap 66
Ⅰ Samuel   P: Phila 1 Jy 56
LAIRD
Ⅰ Alexander   P: Phila 31 Jy 60
Ⅰ Archibald   P: Forks of Dela-
   ware 9 Ag 59, 3 Ja 60, 31
   Jy 60
Ⅰ David   P: Pa 3 Ja 60
Ⅰ James   P: Chester Co 26 Jy
   64; Octorara 18 Ag 57
Ⅰ John   P: Lancaster Co 3 Sep
   61; near Marcus Hook 9 Ag
   59
Ⅰ William   P: Freehold 3 Sep
   61
LAKE and VANCOURT
Ⅰ Messieurs   T: Bronly 15 Mar
   64, 6 Dec 64
Ⅰ David   P: Pa 31 Dec 61
Ⅰ Francis   P: Phila 20 Ap 69
Ⅰ Mary   P: Great Egg-Harbour
   21 Dec 58; West Jersey 3
   Ja 60
Ⅰ Thomas   P: Phila 7 Ap 57,
   9 Ag 59, 26 Jy 64, 19 Ja
   69, 1 May 76
Ⅰ William   P: Phila 1 Nov 53
LAKER
Ⅰ Thomas   P: Phila 3 Ja 65
LALER
Ⅰ Cornelius   P: Pa 13 Ja 63
LALLEY/LALLY
Ⅰ Francis   P: Norrington 31
   Dec 61; Phila 3 Sep 61;
   Providence 26 Oct 69
LAMAR
Ⅰ Marien   P: Phila 4 Ag 63,
   25 Jy 65
Ⅰ William   Carlisle Co 16 Jy
   77
LAMB/LAMBE
Ⅰ Capt. G.   P: Phila 15 Mar 64
Ⅰ James   P: Pa 24 Oct 54; Phila
   11 Sep 55
Ⅰ John   P: Phila 3 Sep 61, 31
   Dec 61
Ⅰ Joseph   P: Phila 15 Mar 64, 3
   Ja 76
Ⅰ Moses   P: Chester Co 15 Mar 64
Ⅰ William   P: Phila 27 Ja 73
LAMBERT
Ⅰ Mr.   P: Phila 2 Feb 64
Ⅰ Mary   P: Phila 25 Jy 65
Ⅰ Matthew   P: Chester Co 1 Nov
   53, 28 Nov 54
Ⅰ Thomas   P: Pa 3 Ja 60; Phila
   9 Ag 59
LAMBURN

Ⅰ Robert   P: Chester Co 15 Mar
   64
LAME
Ⅰ Isabel   P: Phila 21 Dec 58
LAMEY
Ⅰ James   L: 29 Ja 67
LAMLUR
Ⅰ Solomon   P: Phila 21 Dec 58
LAMON
Ⅰ John   Phila 30 Ap 77
Ⅰ Robert   P: Wilmington 4 Ap 54
LAMONT/LAMOUNT/LAMANT
Ⅰ John   P: Phila 18 Ag 57, 15
   Mar 64
Ⅰ Joseph   P: Phila 1 Feb 70
LAMPKIN/LAMKIN
Ⅰ John   P: Phila 9 Ag 59, 3 Ja
   60, 31 Jy 60, 31 Dec 61
LAMSA
Ⅰ James   P: Pequea 5 Ag 56
LAMSON
Ⅰ Nathaniel   P: Phila 9 Ag 59
LANAGAN/LANAGIN
Ⅰ Mary   C: at the Dial, in
   Charlestown, Maryland 30
   Oct 66
Ⅰ Patrick   P: Phila 30 Ap 67
LANCASTER
Ⅰ John   P: Phila 4 Feb 68
Ⅰ Joseph   P: Phila 3 Ja 65
LANCKS
Ⅰ John   P: Phila 28 Ap 68
LAND
Ⅰ Mr.   Phila 1 May 76
Ⅰ Ann   P: New Castle Co 31 Dec
   61
Ⅰ William   P: New-Castle 21 Dec
   58
LANDER
Ⅰ Henry   P: Huntington Co 8 Jy
   62
LANDERHUSEN
Ⅰ Peter   P: Phila 22 Nov 53
LANDIS
Ⅰ Henry   T: Amwell 1 Sep 68
LANDRY
Ⅰ Mrs.   P: Phila 19 Jy 80
Ⅰ Pire/Peter   P: Pa 12 Feb 61;
   Phila 31 Dec 61
LANE
Ⅰ Balshazar   L: Lancaster 20
   Ja 73
Ⅰ Edward   P: Phila 12 Ja 58
Ⅰ Elizabeth   P: North River 9
   Ag 59
Ⅰ Richard   P: Pa 24 Oct 54
LANG
Ⅰ James   P: Phila 15 Mar 64
Ⅰ Margaret   P: Phila-Gaz. 27
   Oct 73
LANGAN
Ⅰ Jere.   P: Phila 26 Oct 69
LANGDON
Ⅰ Henry   P: Phila 24 Feb 63
Ⅰ John   P: Phila 27 Jy 58

LANGE
William   P: Phila 26 Oct 69
LANGEN
John   P: Phila 30 Ja 66
Thomas   P: Phila 10 Ap 66
LANGFORD
Francis   P: Phila 27 Ja 73
LANGLEY
Anna Rebecca   Phila 31 Ja 76
James   P: Pa 27 Jy 58
John   P: Phila 13 Oct 63
LANGSTROTH
Thomas   P: Phila 1 Nov 70
LANGWELL
William   P: Pa 12 Feb 61
LANNING/LANING
John   L: 14 May 72.   P:
   Greenwich, N.J. 27 Oct 73
Richard   T: Amwell 1 Sep 68
LANNOX
Henry   P: Phila 30 Ja 66
LANTHIE
John   P: Phila 31 Dec 61
LAPELLS
Ralph   T: 4 Nov 72
LARD
John   P: Phila 26 Oct 69
LARDNER
B.   P: Duck Creek 31 Dec 61
Benjamin   N: 29 Nov 64.   P:
   Cross Roads 4 Ag 63; Duck
   Creek 31 Jy 60, 2 Sep 62,
   13 Oct 63, 15 Mar 64; Pa 12
   Feb 61; Wilmington 1 Nov 53
John   P: Chester 5 Ag 62
LARGE/LARG
Mr.   P: Phila 2 Feb 64
Ebenezer   Buckingham 31 Ja 76
LARGELOM
Nicholas   P: Pa 31 Mar 63
LARIMORE/LARAMOR/LAREMAR/LAW-
   REMORE
Mrs.   P: Kensington 26 Oct 69
Hugh   P: New-Castle Co 13 Ja
   63
Samuel   P: Kingston 31 Jy 60
Thomas   P: Phila 7 Ap 57
LARKHILL
Andrew   Phila 30 Ap 77
LARKIN
John   Phila 16 Jy 77
LARMORE
Jo.   L: Chestnut-Level 31 Ja
   71
LARNER
John   P: Chester 12 Feb 61;
   Phila 1 Nov 53
LA ROYERIE
Col.   P: Phila 19 Jy 80
LARY
Mary   P: Phila 28 Oct 62
LASCELLS/LASCELL
Geo.   P: Phila 31 Dec 61
Matthew   P: Phila 26 Jy 64
LASHER

John   P: Pa 28 Oct 62
LASHLY
Edmund   P: Phila 27 Jy 58
LASLIE/LASSLY
James   P: Phila 28 Oct 62
William   P: Whitemarsh 3 Ja
   65
LASON (or LAFON?)
Robert   P: Phila-Gaz. 3 Ja 76
LATHAM/LATHIM
James   P: Christine Br. 27 Jy
   58; Phila 31 Ja 76
LATHORP/LATROUP
Francis   P: Phila 28 Oct 62
Q.   P: Phila 2 Feb 64
LATTA
Robert   P: Phila-Gaz. 3 Ja 76
William   P: Pa 15 Mar 64
LATTIMORE/LATIMORE/LATTIMER/
   LETTIMORE/LEATTMORE
Arthur   P: Forks of Delaware
   18 Mar 62
James   N: 29 Nov 64.   P: New-
   Castle Co 13 Ja 63; Newport
   9 Ag 59
John   P: Phila 28 Oct 62, 27
   Ja 73
Mary   P: Phila 16 Jy 72
Mat.   P: Lancaster Co 4 Ag 63
Robert   P: Phila 21 Jy 68
LATTIN
Edward   P: America 9 Ag 59;
   Pa 3 Ja 60
LAUDERDALE/LAUTHERDAIL
Eleanor   P: Phila 13 Oct 63
Capt. Thomas   P: Phila 30
   May 54
LAUGHBRIDGE
John   P: East Nottingham 31
   Dec 61
LAUGHLIN/LAUCHLIN
M.   P: Lancaster Co 18 Mar
   64; Phila 31 Mar 63
James   P: Phila-Gaz. 3 Ja 76
John   P: America 9 Ag 59;
   Chester Co 31 Dec 61; Lan-
   caster Co 13 Oct 63
Joseph   P: Lower-Dublin 3 Ja
   60
Patrick   P: Phila 27 Ja 73
Robert   L: Fort Ligonier 19
   Dec 71
LAUTHIE
John   P: Phila 4 Ag 63, 2 May
   65
LAVENS
William   near the Head of Elk
   /?/ N: 12 Feb 67.   P: Phila
   25 Ap 71
LAVERS
Richard   P: Phila 31 Jy 60
LAVERTY
Catherine   P: Phila 3 Sep 61
Henry   P: Phila 18 Mar 62
LAVERY

Isabel N: 29 Nov 64. P: New Castle Co 26 Jy 64

LAW
Jacob P: Phila 15 Mar 64
Mat. P: Pa 13 Oct 63, 2 Feb 64
Robert P: Nottingham 18 Mar 62
Thomas C: West Caln 28 Nov 65 (shoemaker). P: Chester Co 12 Feb 61
Upton P: Phila 1 Nov 70

LAWED
Samuel P: Duck Creek 7 Ap 57

LAWLOR/LAWLER
Lawrence Phila 30 Ap 77
Martin P: Phila-Gaz. 27 Oct 73

LAWRENCE/LAURANCE
Mrs. P: Phila 12 Feb 61
Adam P: Lancaster Co 3 Sep 61
Anthony P: Phila 30 May 54
Charles P: Phila 26 Jy 64
Dan./Daniel P: Cape May 18 Feb 55 (Rev.); Carlisle 1 Nov 53; Phila 25 Jy 65
Elisha T: West Jersey 18 Mar 64
Elisha, Jr. T: West Jersey 6 Dec 64
Jacob P: Salem 3 Sep 61
James P: Bucks Co 21 Dec 58
Joseph P: Phila 25 Ap 71
Mary P: Phila 10 Ap 66
Robert P: Phila 30 May 54
Thomas P: Phila 3 Ja 65
William P: N.J. 18 Mar 62

LAWRENSON
Peter P: Phila-Gaz. 3 Ja 76

LAWRIE
Mr. T: Allen-town 17 Oct 54

LAWS
Robert P: Phila 10 Oct 65

LAWSON
Anthony P: Phila 27 Ja 73
George N: Head of Elk 4 Dec 66, 12 Feb 67. P: Cecil Co 5 Ag 62
James P: Pa 13 Ja 63
Peter P: Phila 25 Jy 65

LAWTON
John P: Phila 18 Mar 62
Robert P: Phila 2 Feb 64

LAY
Mary P: Phila-Gaz. 3 Ja 76

LAYDEN
Elizabeth P: Phila 25 Ap 71

LAYER
Elizabeth P: Phila 27 Ja 73

LAYMAN
Michael P: Phila 5 Ag 62

LAYSHARE
Henry P: Phila 2 May 65

LEA

James P: Wilmington 30 May 54, 18 Feb 55
John P: Wilmington 18 Feb 55

LEACH/LEECH
Alexander P: Pa 18 Mar 62
Benjamin P: Pa 3 Ja 60; Phila 9 Ag 59
Fra., Esq. L: Pequea 31 Ja 71
Francis L: Lancaster Co, see MOORE, William. P: Lancaster Co 12 Feb 61; Leacock 7 Ap 57
James L: at the Gap 2 Mar 74
John P: Christine Bridge 23 Oct 66
Joseph P: Frankford 30 May 54; Phila 6 Jy 58, 27 Jy 58 (Esq)
Thomas P: Phila 3 Ja 60

LEACOCK
Joseph P: Phila 11 Sep 55

LEADBETTER/LEDBETTER
Geo. P: Phila 1 Nov 53, 31 Dec 61
James P: Phila 28 Ap 68

LEADLIE
John P: Salem 4 Feb 68
William P: Phila 15 Mar 64

LEALAND
Thomas P: Phila 27 Ja 73

LEAMING
Aaron P: Cape-May 31 Dec 61

LEAMY
Mat./Matthias/Matthew P: Chester Co 24 Feb 63; Whiteland 13 May 56, 8 Jy 62

LEARD
William P: Bucks Co 27 Jy 58; N.J. 13 Ja 63

LEARNE
John P: Chester 27 Jy 58

LEARNED
Robert P: Phila 4 Feb 68, 25 Ap 71

LEARY/LEARRY
Cornelius P: Newport 3 Ja 60
Dennis T: Trenton 17 Oct 54

LEASING
Mr. L: York-Town, see STEPHENS, Mary

LEATH/LEATHS
John P: Phila 2 Sep 62
Capt. T. P: Phila 2 Feb 64
Thomas P: Phila 3 Ja 65

LEAVE
William P: Phila 3 May 70, 16 Jy 72

LE BLANC
Charles (French Neutral) 13 May 56
Mons. Rene P: Phila 1 Jy 56

LEBLAND
Mrs. P: Phila 21 Jy 68

LEBLANE

Daniel   P: Phila 23 Oct 66
LECHLER
  George   Phila 30 Ap 77
LECIE
  Catherine   L: Dorchester Co
    15 Ap 56
LECK
  Henry   P: Phila 5 Ag 62
LECKEY/LECKY/LEECKEY/LECCY/
  LECKE
  George   P: New London 1 Nov
    53; York Co 12 Ja 58, 26 Jy
    64
  James   P: Phila 7 Ap 57
  John   P: Phila 8 Jy 62
  Thomas   P: Phila 25 Jy 65
LE COEG
  Capt. Peter   P: Phila 20 Oct
    68
LECONT/LE CONTE
  John Etton   T: Monmouth Co 31
    Ja 71, 4 Nov 72
  Peter   T: Monmouth Co /?/ 4
    Nov 72
  Dr. Peter   T: East New Jersey
    1 Sep 68
LEDBY
  Henry   P: Phila 8 Jy 62
LEDDELL
  George   P: Phila 20 Jy 69
LEDLIE; see also LEADLIE
  Andrew   P: Easton 2 Ag 70
  Joshua   P: Eastown 27 Ja 73
LEE
  Capt.   P: Phila 19 Jy 80
  Abraham   P: Phila 4 Ag 63
  Ann   P: Phila 31 Jy 60, 15
    Mar 64
  Eleanor   P: Kent Co 12 Feb 61
  Gasham   P: Amwell 1 Feb 70
  George   P: Phila 16 Jy 72
  James   P: Phila 3 Ja 65;
    Wilmington 2 Feb 64
  John   L: Lancaster Co 15 Ap
    56. P: Phila 28 Nov 54, 12
    Feb 61, 13 Ja 63, 1 Nov 70,
    27 Oct 73; Wicacoa 5 Feb 54
  Mrs. Mary   T: c/o Capt. Ander-
    son near Trenton 1 Sep 68
  Michael   P: Cumberland Co-Gaz.
    27 Oct 73
  Mordecai   Bucks Co 24 Jy 76
  Richard   P: Phila 23 Oct 66
  Robert   P: Phila-Gaz. 3 Ja 76
  Thomas   Phila 1 May 76, 19 Jy
    80 (Capt)
  William   L: Guilford Twp, Cum-
    berland Co 19 Dec 71. P:
    America 9 Ag 59; Tinicum 28
    Ap 68
LEECH, see LEACH
LEEDS
  Jonathan   Phila 31 Ja 76
LEES
  Abraham   P: Phila 1 Jy 56

James   P: Phila 27 Jy 58, 12
  Feb 61, 2 Feb 64
John   P: Phila 28 Oct 62
LEESHOLTZ
  David   P: Phila 9 May 54
LEFEVER
  Samuel   L: Pequea 31 Ja 71;
    Strasburg Twp, see BUGLESS,
    Mary
LEG
  John   P: Chester Co 15 Mar 64
LE GAY
  Samuel   P: Phila 25 Jy 65
LE GRON
  Da.   L: 29 Ja 67
LEHMAN
  Christian   P: Germantown 26
    Oct 69
LEIGH
  Benjamin   P: Phila 27 Ja 73
  Michael   T: Salem Co 15 Jy 56
  Sherwood   P: Carlisle 9 Ag
    59, 3 Ja 60
LEIN
  Ann   P: Phila 31 Jy 60
  Charles   P: Chester Co 18 Feb
    55
LEITH
  Edward   P: Phila 2 May 65
LEIVING
  Sarah   P: Pa 4 Ag 63
LELLY
  Thomas   P: America 9 Ag 59
LEMAN/LEMON/LEMEN
  Henry   P: Phila 15 Mar 64,
    10 Oct 65
  Jo.   L: 11 Ap 65
LENARET
  William   P: Phila 9 Ag 59
LENDEN
  William   P: Phila 16 Jy 67
LENEY
  John   P: Paxton 2 Feb 64
  Samuel   P: Paxton 2 Feb 64
LENHEAR
  Philip   P: Lancaster 30 May
    54
LENNON
  Thomas   P: Phila 1 Feb 70
LENOX/LENNOX
  John   P: Phila 19 Ja 69, 26
    Oct 69
  Margaret   P: Pa 12 Feb 61
  Thomas   L: Cumberland Co 31
    Ja 71. P: Phila 15 Mar 64
LENVEL
  Edward   C: near Marcus Hook
    28 Nov 65
LEO
  Mary   P: Phila 31 Mar 63
LEONARD/LENARD/LENNARD; see
  also LEYNARD
  James   P: Kingston 4 Ag 63.
    T: Kingston 17 Oct 54
  John   P: Phila 2 May 65

Michael   P: Phila 26 Oct 69
Thomas, Esq.   T: Prince Town
  15 Jy 56
LEPPANTON
  Joshua   P: Phila 3 May 70
LEROWAN
  Thomas   P: Lancaster Co 3 Sep
  61
LE ROY
  Monsieur A.   P: Pa 13 Oct 63
LESHER
  John   P: Pa 18 Mar 62
  William Germantown 1 May 76,
  24 Jy 76
LESLIE/LESLEY/LESLE
  Capt.   P: Phila-Gaz. 27 Oct 73
  Andrew   P: Bucks Co 2 May 65;
  Phila 16 Jy 67
  Charles   P: Phila-Gaz. 3 Ja 76
  Dr. Charles Shaw   T: Prince-
  town 17 Oct 54
  Elizabeth   P: Phila 2 Sep 62
  George   C: c/o Robert Griffin
  N. London 18 Jy 65.   P: Phila
  20 Ap 69, 3 Ja 76
  John (sergeant in army)   P:
  Fort Pitt 26 Jy 64
  Joseph   P: Leacock 13 May 56;
  Pa 27 Jy 58, 21 Dec 58;
  Phila 6 Jy 58
  Peter   P: Phila 16 Jy 67, 20
  Oct 68
  Robert   P: Phila 1 Feb 70
  Samuel   P: Chester Co 2 Ag 70
  Thomas   P: Phila 4 Feb 68
  William   P: Phila 15 Mar 64,
  10 Oct 65
LESLIR
  William   P: Phila 26 Jy 64
LESTER
  Adam   P: Phila 18 Feb 55
  Capt. Eliphalet   P: Phila-
  Gaz. 27 Oct 73
  Elizabeth   P: Phila 12 Ja 58
  James   P: Pa 3 Ja 60
  John   P: Pa 3 Ja 60; Phila 1
  Nov 53, 18 Feb 55, 9 Ag 59
  Michael   P: Phila 3 Sep 61
  Thomas   P: Phila 19 Jy 80
  William   P: N.J. 13 Ja 63;
  Pa 8 Jy 62
LETSON
  Joseph   P: Phila 9 Ag 59
LETTO
  Michael   P: Phila 9 Ag 59,
  3 Ja 60
LETUE /?/
  Jacob   P: Phila 28 Oct 62
LEUTON
  Sarah   P: Phila 3 Ja 65
LEVAN
  Dr.   L: 13 Jn 65
LEVERING
  Abraham   P: Pa 12 Feb 61
  Nathan   P: Roxborough 19 Jy 80

Thomas   P: Phila 5 Ag 62
LEVERS
  Robert   P: Phila 3 Ja 65 (2),
  30 Ja 66
LEVESTON
  Samuel   P: Mountholly 20 Oct
  68
LEVINE
  John   P: Phila 21 Jy 68
LEVRISTON
  Robert   P: Phila 28 Oct 62
LEVY/LEVI/LEAVY
  Abraham   P: Buckingham 31 Ja
  76
  Himan   P: Phila 16 Jy 72
  I.,Jr.   P: Phila 2 Sep 62
  Isaac   P: Phila 26 Jy 64, 1
  Feb 70
  Jacob   P: Phila 20 Oct 68
  Levi Samuel   P: Phila 20 Ap
  69
  Martha   P: Chester Co 28 Nov
  54
  Myer   P: Kingston 31 Jy 60;
  Salem 12 Ja 58
  Sampson/Samson   P: Phila 12
  Feb 61.   W: New-Castle 27
  Ag 77
  Thomas   P: Phila 23 Oct 66
LEWELLEN
  Thomas   P: Phila 26 Oct 69
LEWIN
  Eleanor   P: Phila 31 Mar 63
LEWIS/LEWES
  Rev. Mr.   Phila 1 May 76
  Anna   P: Carlisle 26 Jy 64
  David   P: Pa 11 Jy 54, 24
  Oct 54
  Elisha   P: Baltimore 31 Dec
  61, 31 Mar 63; Phila 27 Jy
  58, 3 Ja 60
  Ellis   P: Phila 6 Jy 58
  Francis   P: Phila-Gaz. 3 Ja 76
  George   P: Phila 18 Ag 57, 1
  Feb 70
  Hannah   P: Phila 31 Dec 61
  Harvey   P: Chester Co 3 Sep
  61
  Jacob   P: Phila 10 Ap 66
  John   P: Radnor 1 Jy 56
  Jonathan   P: Phila 27 Dec 53
  Margaret   P: Chester Co 28 Nov
  54
  Mary   P: Phila 3 Sep 61
  Michael   P: Phila 3 May 70
  Nathaniel   P: Phila 1 Nov 70
  Robert   P: Phila 3 Ja 60;
  Wilmington 22 Nov 53, 24 Oct
  54, 18 Feb 55, 1 Jy 56, 18
  Ag 57
  Sarah   P: Phila 1 Nov 53
  Thomas   P: Phila 18 Ag 57, 16
  Jy 67
  Ursula (wife of Thomas)   P:
  Phila 16 Jy 67

Walter   P: Phila 13 Oct 63
William   P: Newtown 13 May
   56; Phila 1 Feb 70 (sol-
   dier), 25 Ap 71
LEWSTON
Matthew or GRAY, Conrad   W:
   Newport /Wilmington P.O./
   3 Jy 76
LEWTON
Sarah   P: Phila 2 May 65
LEYBOURN
Robert   P: Phila 18 Feb 55
LEYNARD
George, Sr.   P: Great Valley
   3 Ja 60; Lancaster Co 9 Ag
   59
LIANS
Betty   P: New-Castle 9 Ag
   59, 3 Ja 60
LICKY
Margaret   P: Derry Twp 28
   Oct 62
LIDDON
Samuel   P: Gloucester Co 9
   Ag 59; Raccoon Creek 31 Dec
   61
LIDENEUS
John Abraham   P: Phila 1 Jy
   56
LIEUT
Rev. Mr.   Buckingham 31 Ja
   76
LIGGET/LIGGIT
John   P: Octerara 13 Ja 63;
   Oxford 2 Feb 64
LIGHT
John   P: Octerara 13 Oct 63
LIGHTBODY
Michael   P: Pa 31 Jy 60;
   Wilmington 13 Oct 63
LIGHTBOURN/LIGHTBURN
Capt. James   P: Phila 4 Ag
   63
Capt. Samuel   P: Phila 21 Dec
   58, 28 Oct 62
Capt. W.   P: Phila 31 Dec 61
LIGHTFOOT
Susanna   P: Phila 1 Nov 70
Thomas   P: Phila 6 Jy 58, 30
   Ap 67, 16 Jy 67, 28 Ap 68,
   1 Feb 70
William   P: Phila 6 Jy 58,
   30 Ap 67, 28 Ap 68, 1 Feb 70
LIKEN
John   P: Oxford Twp 31 Jy 60
Thomas   P: Oxford Twp 31 Jy 60
LILE
Alexander   P: Phila 30 Ja 66
John   P: Ballemone 9 Ag 59
LILLEY
John   P: in the army 12 Ja 58;
   Phila 30 Ap 67
Robert   P: Phila Co 26 Oct 69
LIMASNY
James   P: Phila 20 Ap 69

LINCHEAN
John   P: Phila 31 Jy 60
LINCHOAS
Thomas   P: Phila 2 Ag 70
LINCOLN
Thomas   P: Bucks Co 3 Ja 60,
   3 Sep 61; Reading 2 Feb 64
LINDALL/LINDALE/LINDAL/LYNDALL
John   P: Oxford 2 Feb 64, 15
   Mar 64; Phila 28 Nov 54, 5
   Ag 62, 2 May 65; at Tacony
   in Oxford Twp 19 Ja 69
LINDEN
Sarah   P: Phila 18 Ag 57
LINDER
John Jacob   P: Phila 27 Jy 58
LINDERMAN
Martin   P: Phila 3 Sep 61
LINDLEY/LINDELE
George   P: Pa 12 Feb 61;
   Phila 13 Ja 63
John   P: Tacony 3 May 70
Jonathan   P: London-Grove 3
   Sep 61
Susannah/Susanna   P: Phila 11
   Sep 55, 21 Jy 68
LINDO
Abraham   P: Phila 21 Jy 68
Dinnah   P: Phila 21 Dec 58
LINDSEY/LINDSAY/LINSEY
Mrs.   P: Phila 20 Oct 68
Charles   P: Phila 27 Ja 73
David   P: Phila 21 Jy 68
Elizabeth   P: Phila 4 Ag 63,
   2 Feb 64
Ja., coppersmith   L: 25 Dec
   66
James   P: Phila 13 May 56, 21
   Dec 58
Robert   P: Pa 3 Ja 60
Walter   P: Lancaster Co 5 Feb
   54; Phila 27 Dec 53
William   P: Bucks Co 27 Jy
   58; Little Britain, Lan-
   caster Co 1 Jy 56; Phila 2
   May 65
LINE
Thomas   P: Chester Co 9 May 54
LINGARD
Mary   P: Phila 5 Ag 56
LINGEY
Robert   P: Phila-Gaz. 27 Oct
   73
LINLEY
Jenneah   T: Morris Co 17 Oct
   54
LINN; see also LYNN
Alexander   P: Somerset Co 13
   Ja 63
James   P: Chester Co 15 Mar
   64; Phila 10 Ap 66
Joseph   P: Phila 27 Ja 73
Robert   P: York Co 31 Dec 61
William   L: Shippensburg 31
   Ja 71

LINNEN
John   P: Phila 7 Ap 57
LINNEY
John   P: Phila 25 Ap 71
LINTON
John   P: Phila-Gaz. 27 Oct
73, 16 Jy 77
William   P: Bucks Co-Gaz. 27
Oct 73
LION/LIONS, see LYON/LYONS
LIPPINCOTT/LIPINCUT
Deborah   P: Gloucester Co 15
Mar 64; West Jersey 24 Feb
63
Hezekiah   P: Phila 9 May 54
Samuel   P: Springfield-Gaz.
27 Oct 73
LISCHY
Rev. Jacob   L: 13 Jn 65
LISENBY
Henry   P: New-Castle Co 8
Jy 62
LISLE/LISLIE
Alexander   P: Plymouth, Phila
Co 4 Feb 68
Henry   P: Phila 5 Ag 62, 21
Dec 58
John   P: Phila 12 Feb 61
(Capt), 18 Mar 62, 5 Ag
62, 13 Oct 63
LISTER
Ann   P: Burlington 8 Jy 62
Gilbert   P: Phila 2 May 65
James   P: Phila 9 Ag 59
John   P: near Phila 2 Feb 64;
Phila 18 Ag 57, 3 Ja 65
William   P: Burlington 5 Ag
62; West Jersey 24 Feb 63
LISTON
Capt. John   P: Phila 5 Ag 62
LITHGO/LITHGOW
Daniel   P: Phila 16 Jy 67;
Salem 3 May 70
Hannah   P: Phila 15 Mar 64
LITHROP
Edward   P: Pa 2 Feb 64
LITTEL/LITTELL; see also LYTTEL
Mary   P: Phila 28 Oct 62
Michael   P: Phila 28 Oct 62
Robert   P: Christeen Bridge 18
Ag 57
LITTLE
Adam   P: Phila 15 Mar 64
Arch./Archibald   P: Wilming-
ton 12 Ja 58, 9 Ag 59
Benjamin   P: Phila 10 Oct 65
James   P: Phila 27 Ja 73
John   P: Phila 3 Ja 65, 25 Ap
71, 27 Ja 73
Joseph   P: Hunterdon Co 2 Ag
70
Michael   P: Phila 25 Jy 65, 10
Ap 66
Nancy   P: Phila 5 Ag 56
Richard   P: Phila 8 Jy 62

Robert   P: Lancaster Co 31
Dec 61, 18 Mar 62; Phila
27 Oct 73
Rose   P: Forks Brandywine 22
Nov 53
Simon   P: Phila 23 Oct 66
Thomas   P: Phila-Gaz. 3 Ja 76
William   C: c/o A.M'Gomery
Christeen Bridge 28 Nov 65.
P: Phila 3 May 70
LITTLEFIELD
Jer.   P: Phila 18 Mar 62
LITTLER
Joshua   P: Wilmington 21 Dec
58
Thomas   P: New Castle Co 7
Ap 57; Wilmington 18 Ag 57
LITTLEWOOD
Benjamin   Pitt's-town 30 Ap
77
Joshua   P: Phila 16 Jy 67
LIVAS
Rev. Arnold   P: St. Mary's
Co 19 May 63
LIVERDAY
Katherine   P: Phila 18 Mar
62
LIVESEY
Thomas   P: Lancaster Co 3 Sep
61
LIVINGSTON/LEVINGSTON
& TEMPLETON   P: Phila 5 Ag 62
Mrs.   Phila 16 Jy 77
Alexander   Phila 1 May 76
Mita   P: Phila-Gaz. 27 Oct 73
Robert   P: Frankford 13 Ja 63
Sarah   C: near the Rev. Mr.
Boyd's, Octarara, Chester
Co 18 Jy 65.   P: Pecquea
9 May 54; Pa 2 Feb 64
LIVISTON
John   P: Pa 12 Feb 61
LLEWELLIN
David   P: Haverford 13 May 56
LLOYD/LOYD; see also POUSSETT
& LOYD
Widow   P: Limerick Twp 3 Sep
61
Henry   P: Phila 28 Ap 68, 21
Jy 68
Isaac   P: Pennypack 13 Ja 63
Lewis   P: Abington 1 Nov 53,
16 Jy 67, 26 Oct 69, 2 Ag
70
Mary   P: Pa 27 Jy 58
Nicholas   P: Phila 5 Ag 62
Thomas   P: Phila 27 Jy 58
(Dr).   T: Burlington 17 Oct
54
William   P: Phila 25 Jy 65
LOAGE
John   P: Phila-Gaz. 3 Ja 76
LOAKEY
John   P: Phila 25 Jy 65
LOARDAN

LOARDAN
Charles P: Phila 18 Mar 62
LOB
Lorens P: Phila-Gaz. 27 Oct
73
LOBDELL
Isaac P: Phila 1 Jy 56, 26
Jy 64
LOCHRIDGE
John C: near the meeting-
house, East Nottingham 28
Nov 65
LOCK
Rev. P: Lewis-Town 18 Feb 55
Englebert P: Phila 31 Jy 60
Richard P: Phila 4 Feb 68
LOCKAN
Patrick P: Phila 28 Ap 68
LOCKER
Mary P: Newcastle 12 Ja 58
LOCKERMAN
Susannah P: Dover 9 Ag 59
LOCKHART/LOCKART/LOCKERT/LOCK-
ARD/LOKART
Mrs. T: Freehold 7 May 67
Aaron P: Abington 1 Jy 56
Alexander P: Chester Co 3 Sep
61; Pa 18 Mar 62
Elizabeth P: Phila 18 Mar 62
John P: Pa 18 Mar 62; Phila
23 Oct 66
Mary P: Phila 22 Nov 53
Robert P: Phila 15 Mar 64,
28 Ap 68
LOCKERY
James P: Chester Co 4 Ag 63
LOCKTON/LOCKTOWN
John P: Pa 24 Oct 54
Martha P: Wilmington 31 Jy 60
LOCKWOOD
Capt. Jos. P: Phila 3 Sep 61
LOCREY
Mrs. P: Phila 21 Dec 58
LOCUS
Joseph P: White Marsh 19 Jy
80
Tacey P: White Marsh 19 Jy
= 80
LODER
Elizabeth P: Salem 3 Ja 60
LOEDEY
Daniel P: Chester Co 12 Ja 58
LOESER
Jacob P: Lancaster 4 Ap 54
LOGAN/LOGEN/LOGENS/LOGGAN
Alexander P: Bucks Co 24
Feb 63; Phila 30 Ja 66
Daniel P: Abington 25 Ap 71
David L: Lancaster Co 29 Jy
72. P: Abington 21 Dec 58;
Brandywine 26 Jy 64; East
Jersey 12 Ja 58; Morris Co
28 Oct 62; New-Castle 13
May 56
George P: Phila 10 Oct 65.

T: Trenton 17 Oct 54
James P: Northampton 5 Jy
80-Gaz. 19 Jy
John L: Lancaster Co 29 Jy
72. P: Phila 21 Dec 58,
20 Ap 69, 31 Ja 76, 30 Oct
76. T: Baskin(g)-Ridge 15
Mar 64, 6 Dec 64; Bucks Co
15 Mar 64
Margaret P: Bucks Co 12 Feb
61
Samuel L: Shippensburg 31
Ja 71
Thomas C: 30 Jy 77. P:
Baskingridge 13 Oct 63;
Conywago 5 Feb 54; Pa 18
Mar 62
LOGG
Thomas P: Kingsess 21 Jy 68
LOGHARY
James C: Oxford Twp, see
JAMES, Mr.
LOGMAN/?/
Thomas P: at Kingsess 19 Ja
69
LOGUE
David C: Brandywine 18 Jy 65
LOLLNER
.... P: Phila 1 Jy 56
LONDON
Mr. P: Phila 26 Oct 69
LONG/LONGE
Mr. P: Phila 9 Ag 59, 3 Ja
60
Alexander P: Chester Co 7
Ap 57
Ann; see PAMER
James P: Cumberland Co 12
Ja 58; Phila 28 Oct 62
John L: Earl Twp 15 Ap 56.
P: Lancaster Co 7 Ap 57,
7 Ag 59, 3 Ja 60; Phila 3
May 70, 19 Jy 71
Matthew P: Phila 25 Ap 71
Patrick P: Phila 8 Jy 62
Peter P: Pa 24 Oct 54;
Capt., Phila 19 Ja 69
Richard P: Phila-Gaz. 27 Oct
73
Risking L: 11 Ap 65
Robert P: Lancaster Co 4 Ag
63
Thomas P: Bucks Co 20 Oct
68; at Durham Furnace 19
Ja 69; Pa 13 Oct 63; Phila
26 Oct 69 (soldier), 1 Nov
70
William P: Phila 28 Ap 68,
27 Oct 73
LONGBOTTOM
John P: Phila 25 Jy 65
LONGMEAD
Richard P: Phila 18 Ag 57
LONGSTREET
Daniel P: Phila 27 Ja 73

LONGWILL
  James P: Pa 12 Feb 61; Phila
    31 Dec 61
LOOCK
  John P: Phila 16 Jy 67
LORAIN
  Barnabas P: Phila 10 Ap 66
LORD
  Abraham P: Phila 20 Oct 68
  Elizabeth P: Phila Co 31 Dec
    61
  John P: Pa 5 Ag 56
LORDSMAN
  Robert P: Bucks Co 2 Ag 70
LORIMER/LOREMAR/LOREMER/LOR-
  MOR
  Capt. P: Phila 16 Jy 72
  James P: Kingston 24 Feb 63;
    Lancaster Co 13 Ja 63
  Jos. P: Kensington 2 Feb 64
  Samuel P: Phila 12 Feb 61, 1
    Nov 53
  Thomas P: Bucks Co 3 Ja 60
LORGE
  Elizabeth P: Buckingham 5
    Ag 56
LORIN
  Lisagreth P: Phila 27 Dec
    53
LORRAIN
  John Phila 5 Ja 76-Gaz. 31
    Ja
LOSCH/LOSH
  George P: Germantown 12 Ja
    58, 18 Mar 62; Phila 27 Jy
    58
  Robert P: Pa 12 Feb 61
LOSCHNER
  John P: Phila 3 Ja 65
LOSEN
  James P: Phila 18 Mar 62
LOSK
  Elizabeth P: Lancaster Co
    3 Sep 61
LOTT
  John P: Phila 4 Feb 68
LOTTE
  William P: Phila 2 Ag 70
LOUDON/LOUDOUN; see also LOW-
  DEN
  James P: Cumberland 15 Mar
    64
  Susannah P: Phila 18 Ag 57
  Thomas P: Phila 2 May 65,
    27 Oct 73
LOUGH
  John P: Bucks Co 2 Ag 70
LOUGHEAD
  Robert P: New-London 21 Dec
    58
LOUGHREY
  James P: Nocomixon Twp 28
    Ap 68
LOUGHRIGH
  John P: Pa 24 Feb 63

LOUGHUDGE
  John P: Pa 13 Oct 63
LOUTNEAN
  Robert P: Phila 28 Nov 54
LOUTTIT
  George P: Phila 20 Jy 69 (2)
  Mary P: Phila 30 Ap 67, 1
    May 76
LOVE
  Alexander P: York Co 13 Oct
    63
  Daniel P: Phila 22 Nov 53
  Henry P: Cheltenham-Gaz. 3
    Ja 76
  James P: Chester Co 9 May
    54, 11 Sep 55; Lancaster
    Co 24 Feb 63
  Matthew P: Phila 27 Ja 73
  Robert, see William &
  Samuel A. Phila 30 Ap 77
  Dr. Thomas W: Wilmington 3
    Jy 76
  William P: Chester Co 18
    Mar 62; Pa 18 Mar 62;
    Phila 18 Ag 57, 16 Jy 67;
    & Robert, Pa 16 Jy 72
LOVEDAY
  Mary P: Phila 13 May 56
LOVEGROVE
  Robert P: Phila 20 Jy 69
LOVELL
  Charles P: Londonderry 18 Mar
    62
  Michael P: Phila 6 Jy 58
  William N: near the Head of
    Elk /?/ 12 Feb 67
LOVELY
  William Phila 5 Jy 76-Gaz.
    24 Jy
LOVERBE
  Ann P: Phila 26 Oct 69
LOW
  Charles P: Phila 10 Ap 66
  Elizabeth P: Phila-Gaz. 3
    Ja 76
  Jennet/Jannet P: Chester Co
    4 Ap 54, 3 Ja 60
  Margaret P: Phila 1 Jy 56
  Thomas L: Chester Co 29 Jy
    72. P: Phila 4 Ag 63
  Thomas Brown P: Phila 10 Ap
    66
  William P: Chester Co 1 Nov
    53
LOWBER
  Jonathan Kent on Delaware
    16 Jy 77
LOWDON; see also LOUDON
  Mat. P: Mount Nebo 12 Ja 58
  Samuel P: West Jersey 8 Jy
    62
  Thomas P: Phila 18 Mar 62
LOWE
  Capt. John Hawkins Phila 30
    Oct 76

LOWHER
  Miriam   P: Pa 8 Jy 62
  Peter   P: Kent Co 9 Ag 59
LOWLAND
  ....   L: near Harris's Ferry
    29 Jy 72
LOWNDES/LOWNDS
  Christopher   P: Md. 21 Dec
    58; Phila 3 Ja 65
  Charles   P: Phila 18 Ag 57
  John   P: Phila 21 Dec 58, 9
    Ag 59, 13 Ja 63
LOWNSBERRY
  Samuel   T: Bordentown 15 Jy
    56
LOWRY/LOWRIE/LOWREY/LOWRAY
  Alexander   P: Anderson's
    Ferry 18 Mar 62; Lancaster
    Co 3 Sep 61
  Andrew   P: Phila 9 Ag 59 (2),
    3 Ja 60, 31 Jy 60, 3 Sep 61
    (2), 15 Mar 64
  David   P: Phila 23 Oct 66
  George   P: Pa 4 Ag 63
  James   P: Hospital 26 Oct
    69; Phila 27 Ja 73
  John   C: in Bourdeaux Tract,
    Virginia 28 Nov 65.   P:
    Sussex Co, West Jersey 20 Jy
    69.   T: 4 Nov 72
  Robert   P: Phila 2 May 65
  Stephen   P: Phila 1 Feb 70, 3
    Ja 76
  William   P: Pa 2 Feb 64
LOYHED
  Jchn   P: Chester Co 2 Sep 62
LUCAS/LEUCAS
  Capt.   P: Phila 27 Jy 58
  George   L: York Co 2 Mar 74
  James   C: 30 Jy 77 (Capt).   P:
    Phila 30 Ja 66
  Robert   P: Bucks Co-Gaz. 27
    Oct 73; Phila 20 Oct 68
  Roger   P: Phila 27 Jy 58
  Thomas   P: Near Phila 18 Mar
    62; Phila 3 Ja 65, 10 Oct
    65, 3 May 70
LUCK
  Sylvester   N: 29 Nov 64.   P:
    Phila 5 Ag 56
LUCKET
  Col. William   Phila 30 Ap 77
LUCKEY/LUCKIE
  Hugh   P: Chester Co 31 Dec 61
  Samuel   P: Phila 27 Ja 73
LUCKS
  William   P: Phila 20 Ap 69
LUDERT
  W.L.   Phila 31 Ja 76
LUDLOM
  Jeremiah   P: Cape May 1 Nov
    70
LUDLOW
  George D.   P: Phila 31 Dec 61
LUFF

  Dr. Nathaniel   Phila 24 Jy 76
LUGHTON
  James   P: Newcastle 12 Ja 58
LUKENS/LUKINS
  Jesse   P: Phila 1 Feb 70, 2
    Ag 70, 25 Ap 71; Roxbury
    3 Sep 61
  William   P: Phila 1 Nov 70
LUKERANIER
  William   P: Phila 9 Ag 59
LUMSDEN/LUMSDAIN
  Rob.   P: Phila 31 Jy 60, 20
    Ap 69, 3 Ja 76
LUNDEY
  Thomas   P: Phila 1 Nov 70
LUNGLEY
  Thomas   P: Bucks Co 18 Ag 57;
    Phila 18 Feb 55
LUNN
  Thomas   P: Queen Ann's Co 3
    Sep 61
LUNT
  Benjamin, Jr.   P: Phila 30
    Ja 66
LUNTZ
  Julian   P: Phila 1 Nov 70
LUPTON
  Thomas   P: Phila 24 Feb 63
  William   P: Phila 2 Ag 70
LURTING
  Robert   P: Phila-Gaz. 27 Oct
    73
LUSH
  Andrew   P: Phila 11 Sep 55
LUSHER
  Benjamin   P: Phila 31 Jy 60
  Capt. G.   P: Phila 18 Mar 62,
    5 Ag 62
  Jacob   P: Frankford-Gaz. 27
    Oct 73
  James   P: Germantown-Gaz. 27
    Oct 73
LUSK
  Robert   P: Chester Co 31 Jy
    60; Pa 12 Feb 61, 31 Dec
    61; Phila 3 Sep 61
  Thomas   P: Pa 31 Jy 60;
    Phila 26 Oct 69
LUTTON
  Robert   P: Pa 13 Oct 63
LUXTON
  Alexander   P: Phila 30 Ja 66
LYBURT
  Peter   P: Germantown 30 Ja 66
LYDDALL
  William   P: Pa 13 Oct 63;
    Phila 3 Ja 65
LYFAGHT
  Nicholas   P: N.J. 18 Ag 57
LYLE/LYLLE/LYELL
  Alexander   P: Plymouth 9 Ag
    59
  Eleanor   P: Middletown 13 Ja
    63
  Hugh   P: New London 7 Ap 57

John   P: Chester Co 9 Ag 59;
  N.J. 13 Ja 63; Phila 10 Ap
  66, 4 Feb 68
Robert   P: Pa 12 Feb 61
LYNAH
  Eleanor   P: Phila 2 Sep 62
LYNCH/LINCH
  Charles   P: Phila 3 Sep 61
  David   L: Conegocheague 20
    Ja 73
  Dennis   L: c/o ...Liggly,
    merchant-Phila 19 Dec 71.
    P: near Phila 28 Oct 62
  Elizabeth   P: Phila 4 Ag 63
  James   P: Newcastle Co 18
    Ag 57; Pa 8 Jy 62
  John   P: Phila 28 Ap 68
  Philip   L: 11 Ap 65. P:
    Yellow Springs 1 Feb 70
  Robert   P: Lancaster Co 15
    Mar 64
  Thomas   P: Phila 28 Oct 62
LYND
  Archibald   P: Salem 9 Ag 59
  Robert   P: Homminy 28 Nov 54
LYNDALL, see LINDALL
LYNDON
  John   P: Phila 20 Oct 68
LYNMIRE
  Sally   P: Phila 13 May 56
LYNES
  Eleanor   P: Phila 30 Ja 66
LYNN; see also LINN
  Charles   P: Phila 2 Sep 62
    (Capt), 25 Jy 65
LYNNENTON
  John   P: Great Valley 3 May
    70
LYNNOX
  John   P: Phila 25 Jy 65
LYNOTT
  Thomas   P: Phila 3 Ja 65
LYNOUGH (alias SUMMERS)
  Mary   P: Phila 19 Ja 69
LYON/LION/LIONS/LYONS
  Benjamin   P: Phila 27 Jy 58
  Capt. Charles   Mount Holly 24
    Jy 76; Phila 21 Dec 58, 13
    Ja 63
  Gloud   P: Wilmington 26 Jy 64
  James   P: Carlisle 2 Feb 64;
    Cumberland Co 2 Sep 62; Pa
    12 Ja 58; Phila 25 Jy 65
  John   P: Cape-Fear 21 Dec 58
  Patrick   P: Phila 20 Oct 68,
    19 Ja 69, 20 Jy 69
  Thomas   P: Chester Co 11 Sep
    55
  William   P: Cumberland Co 3
    Sep 61
LYS
  Henry   L: Lancaster Co 15 Ap 56
LYSAGHT
  Nicholas   P: N.J. 31 Jy 60

LYTHCOH
  Sarah   P: Phila 25 Ap 71
LYTTEL; see also LITTELL
  John   P: Bucks Co 27 Jy 58
LYTTELTON/LYTTLETON
  Rev. Mr.   P: Phila 19 Ja 69
  Thomas   P: Phila 8 Jy 62

M'ABRAHAM
  Bryan   L: 20 Ja 73
M'ADAM/M'ADAMS/M'CADAM
  John   P: Pa 15 Mar 64
  Robert   P: Pa 12 Feb 61;
    Phila 21 Dec 58
  Tim   P: Phila-Gaz. 3 Ja 76
  William   P: Phila-Gaz. 27
    Oct 73
M'AFEE/M'AFFEE
  George   P: Phila 26 Oct 69
  John   P: Pa 12 Feb 61
  Joseph   P: Pa 13 Oct 63, 2
    Feb 64
M'ALAW
  Charles   P: near Phila 24 Feb
    63
M'ALEXANDER
  Hector   P: Pa 2 Feb 64
  William   P: Phila 2 Ag 70
M'ALLAIR
  Dennis   P: Mountholly 2 Feb
    64
M'ALLEN; see also M'CALLAN
  William   P: Pa 12 Feb 61
M'ALLICE
  Manus   P: Pa 12 Ja 58
M'ALLISTER/M'ALLASTER/M'ALIST-
  ER/M'CALLASTER/M'CALLISTER/
  M'COLISTER
  Mr.   P: Phila 2 May 65
  Alexander   P: Phila Co 28 Oct
    62
  Archibald   L: 27 Ja 67. P:
    Great Valley 13 Ja 63; N.J.
    24 Feb 63; Pa 13 Oct 63;
    Salem Co 7 Ap 57, 26 Jy 64
  Charles   P: Lancaster Co 27
    Dec 53; Phila 18 Mar 62, 13
    Ja 63, 24 Feb 63, 2 Feb 64
  Daniel   P: Pa 12 Ja 58;
    Phila 11 Sep 55
  George   P: Pa 13 Oct 63
  Hugh   P: Phila 30 Ap 67
  James   P: Phila 18 Ag 57, 10
    Ap 66
  John   L: Lancaster Co 15 Ap
    56. P: Lancaster Co 24
    Oct 54; Morris Co 3 Sep 61;
    Pa 3 Ag 58, 13 Oct 63;
    West Fallowfield 26 Jy 53
  John, Jr.   P: Lancaster Co 29
    Ag 54
  Mary   Phila 30 Ap 77
  Michael   P: Phila 1 Nov 70
  Randel/Randle   P: Pa 18 Mar

62, 2 Feb 64; Phila 28 Oct
62
Richard L: York Co 2 Mar 74
(Esq). P: Pa 31 Dec 61
William P: Forks of Delaware
25 Ap 71; Newcastle Co 18
Mar 62; Pittsburgh 2 Sep 62
M'ALPIN/MACKALPIN/M'ALPINE
Lt. P: in the army 12 Ja 58
Mrs. P: Phila 19 Jy 80
Robert P: Phila 16 Jy 72
M'ALWEE
Unity P: Pa 13 Oct 63
M'ALY
George P: Phila 3 Ag 58
M'ANLIN
Henry L: 11 Ap 65
M'ANULLY
Ann P: Phila 27 Ja 73
M'ARDLE
Lawrence P: Phila 20 Oct 68
M'ARTHUR
John P: Pa 4 Ag 63; Phila 3
Ja 65, 23 Oct 66 (of the
42nd Regt)
Thomas L: Harris's Ferry, see
CLARK, Robert
M'ATEE
Cormick P: Schuylkill 4 Ag 63
MACAULAY/M'AULAY/M'AULLY/
M'AULEY/M'CAULY/M'ALLEY/M'-
CAWLY
Widow Phila-Gaz. 27 Oct 73
Aulav/Ally/Alla P: Phila 24
Oct 54, 28 Oct 62, 26 Jy
64, 23 Oct 66
George P: Pa 13 Ja 63; 12
Feb 61
Capt. James Phila 31 Ja 76
John P: Phila 31 Jy 60
Rose P: Pa 3 Ja 60
M'BETH/M'BEATH/M'BATH/MACKBETH
Alexander N: White-clay Creek
12 Feb 67
Andrew P: New-Castle Co 9 Ag
59; New-London 13 Ja 63
James P: Phila 10 Oct 65, 1
Nov 70
John P: Phila 18 Feb 55, 28
Ap 68
M'BRATNOW
Alexander P: Phila 28 Oct 62
M'BRIAR/M'BRAYER
David P: Conegogee 24 Oct 54;
Pa 13 Oct 63
M'BRIDE/M'BRYDE
Agnus/Agness P: Phila 3 Ag
58, 31 Jy 60
Alexander/Alex. L: 3 Oct 65.
P: Bucks Co 21 Dec 58; Pa
12 Ja 58, 24 Feb 63; Phila
13 Ja 63, 26 Jy 64, 3 Ja 65
Daniel P: Pa 12 Feb 61
David L: Lancaster Co 20 Ja
73. P: Pa 28 Oct 62

Hannah L: near Boyd's Meet-
ing-house 15 Ap 56
Hugh P: Phila 25 Jy 65, 10
Oct 65
Isaiah P: Chester Co 3 Sep
61
James L: Chestnut Level 2
Mar 74. P: Baskinridge 8
Jy 62; East New Jersey 12
Feb 61; Phila 26 Oct 69, 27
Oct 73
John P: Phila 29 Ag 54
Josiah P: Octerara 3 Ja 60
Mary T: N.J. 15 Jy 56
Samuel P: Pa 31 Mar 63;
Pequea 13 Ja 63
M'BRIDEN
John P: Phila 26 Jy 53
M'BURNIE
John P: Phila-Gaz. 3 Ja 76
M'CABE
John P: Phila 27 Ja 73
M'CACHAN
Dennis P: Phila 3 Sep 61
M'CAFFERTY
Arthur P: near New-Castle
31 Jy 60
M'CAGE
George P: Kensington 1 Feb
70
M'CAGHY
Samuel P: Phila 3 May 70
M'CAIG
James P: Phila 26 Oct 69
M'CAINE
Thomas P: Phila-Gaz. 27 Oct
73
M'CALCHEN
Mr. P: Phila 3 Ja 60
M'CALL/M'COLL
& TODD, Messieurs, students
L: Pequea 2 Mar 74
Mr. P: Duck-creek 12 Ja 58
Andrew P: Pa 13 Oct 63
Archibald P: Phila 19 Jy 80
James P: Pa 4 Ag 63, 13 Oct
63; Phila 10 Ap 66. T:
Springfield, Monmouth Co 1
Sep 68
John P: Phila 28 Nov 54;
York-Town 30 Ap 77
Judith P: Phila 3 May 70
M'CALLA/M'CALA;see also McCULLOCH
Alexander L: Lancaster Co
15 Ap 56
John P: in the army 12 Ja
58
Joseph P: Phila 19 Ja 69
Wm. L: Lancaster Co 31 Ja 71
M'CALLAN; see also M'ALLEN
James P: Phila 16 Jy 67
M'CALLEY
Edward P: Phila 1 Feb 70
M'CALLISTER, see M'ALLISTER
M'CALLOM/M'CALLUM/M'CALUM;

see also M'COLLOM
Archibald P: Phila 25 Ap 71
David P: Salem 20 Oct 68
Duncan, soldier P: prob. in Pittsburgh 15 Mar 64
John (soldier) P: 21 Dec 58
M'CALMAN
John P: Phila 2 Feb 64
M'CALMOUNT/M'CALMONT/M'CALMOND
John P: Phila 30 Ap 67, 2 Ag 70, 27 Oct 73
Robert P: Phila 19 Ja 69, 1 Feb 70
Samuel P: Lancaster Co 31 Dec 61
M'CAMCOCK
William P: Phila 9 Ag 59
M'CAME
Archibald P: Phila 26 Jy 64
M'CAMISAH
William P: Phila 13 Oct 63
M'CAMISH
Mary P: Phila 13 Oct 63, 25 Ap 71
Milliam /sic!/ P: Phila 31 Dec 61
M'CAMONT/M'CAMOUNT
Alex./Alexander P: Bucks Co 12 Ja 58, 27 Ja 73
M'CAMON/M'CAMMON
John P: Phila 1 Nov 70, 28 Ap 68
M'CAMOND
Mary P: Lancaster Co 9 Ag 59
M'CANCE
David P: Conewaga 3 Ag 58
M'CANDER
Charles P: Pa 4 Ag 63
M'CANDLISH
George P: Phila-Gaz. 3 Ja 76
William P: Phila-Gaz. 3 Ja 76
M'CANDREMAN
John P: Phila 9 Ag 59
M'CANE
David P: Brandywine 13 Ja 63
Mary P: Pa 13 Oct 63
M'CANN/M'CAN
Catherine P: Phila 27 Ja 73
Daniel P: Phila 7 Ap 57
Henry P: Somerset 21 Dec 58
Hugh P: Phila 27 Ja 73; West Jersey 12 Ja 58. T: Princetown 17 Oct 54
John P: Bohemia 2 Feb 64
Marcy P: Phila 30 Ja 66
M'CANTS
James L: Chestnut Level 19 Dec 71
M'CAPEN
James P: Phila 27 Ja 73
M'CARDY/M'CARDEY
Archibald P: Phila 19 Ja 69
Hugh P: Pa 2 Feb 64
M'CARGER
Robert P: Phila-Gaz. 27 Oct 73

M'CARMICK, see M'CORMICK
M'CARNETY
Wm. P: Cumberland Co 12 Ja 58
M'CARRELL/M'CARRILL/M'CARROLL/M'CARROL
James L: Strabane Twp, York Co 19 Dec 71. P: Phila 24 Feb 63 (Mathmaker)
John P: York Co 2 Feb 64
John, Jr. P: Octorara 24 Oct 54
William P: Pa 31 Jy 60; Phila 5 Ag 62
M'CARTER
Daniel P: Phila 30 Ja 66
John P: East Jersey 15 Mar 64. W: Christiana Hundred 3 Jy 76 (schoolmaster)
M'CARTEY/M'CARTY/M'CARTHY
Abigail Timber Creek 5 Jy 76-Gaz. 24 Jy
Cornelius P: N.Castle Co 13 Ja 63
Capt. Daniel P: Phila 4 Ag 63
Jeremiah P: Phila 4 Feb 68, 19 Ja 69
John P: Christine Bridge 18 Mar 62; Pa 19 May 63, 4 Ag 63, 4 Feb 64; Phila 21 Jy 68, 19 Jy 80
Capt. Just./Justin P: Phila 18 Mar 62, 28 Jy 64
Margaret P: George-Town 3 Sep 61
Owen P: Greenwich-Gaz. 3 Ja 76
Thomas P: Phila 13 Oct 63, 3 Ja 65
M'CARTNEY
Benjamin P: Brandywine 30 Ja 66
Calix P: Phila 19 Jy 80
James P: Phila 3 Ja 65
John P: Pennypack Mill 20 Oct 68
Joseph P: Phila 25 Jy 65
Robert, miller W: Brandywine 3 Jy 76
William P: Phila 3 Ja 76
M'CASCORA
Michael P: New-Castle 28 Oct 62
M'CASHLAND
James P: Cumberland Co 2 Feb 64
M'CAUGHRY
Thomas T: Mimebrook /?/ 4 Nov 72
M'CAUS
Alexander P: Abington 20 Jy 69
M'CAUSLAND/M'CAUSLIN
Isabel P: Whiteclay Creek

7 Ap 57
James L: c/o John Montgo-
mery-Christiana Bridge 19
Dec 71
John L: Lancaster Co 2 Mar
74
William P: Lancaster Co 12
Feb 61
Thomas L: Leacock Twp 20
Ja 73
William L: Leacock Twp 15
Ap 56

M'CAVLEP
Alexander L: York Co 25
Dec 66

M'CAY
Alexander P: Lampeter 5 Ag
56; Phila 3 Ja 76
George P: Phila 29 Ag 54
John P: Lancaster Co 3 Sep
61; Phila 13 Ja 63
Margaret P: Pa 3 Ja 60
Neal L: Lancaster Co 31 Ja
71
William P: Phila 13 Ja 63

M'CELUGAN
John P: Cumberland Co 24
Feb 63

M'CEMMON
John P: Phila 16 Jy 72

M'CHANCE
George L: Strabane Twp,
York Co 19 Dec 71

M'CHERON
Charles P: Pa 2 Sep 62

M'CHESNEYM
T: c/o Rev. William Tennent
/?/31 Ja 71

M'CHESTER
Daniel P: Phila 27 Ja 73

M'CHICTOCK
Samuel P: Brandywine 2
Feb 64

M'CIME
James P: East-New-Jersey
12 Feb 61

M'CITIRAGE
John P: Phila 20 Oct 68

M'CLANACHEN/M'CLANAGAN/M'CLA-
NEGAN/M'CLANAHON/M'CLANACHAN
M'CLANEGHAN; see also
M'CLENAHAN
Mr. P: Bucks Co 2 May 65
Alex. P: Newcastle 24 Oct 54
James P: Pa 26 Jy 64
John P: Chester Co 31 Dec 61;
Pa 18 Mar 62, 19 May 63, 4
Ag 63, 2 Feb 64

M'CLANG
Matth. P: Lancaster Co 28 Oct
62

M'CLARY/M'CLAREY
John P: Phila 13 May 56, 1
Jy 56

M'CLATTEN

Barbara P: N.J. 28 Oct 62

M'CLAY/M'CLEA/M'CLEAY; see
also M'LEA
John L: New-Munster, Mil-
ford Hundred, near the Rev.
Mr. Gillespie's Meeting-
house 19 Dec 71. N: 29
Nov 64. P: Cumberland Co
18 Mar 62; near New-Castle
31 Jy 60; N. Castle Co 31
Dec 61; Pa 12 Feb 61
Robert P: Phila-Gaz. 3 Ja 76
Samuel Buffaloe Valley 24
Jy 76
William P: near Christeen 8
Jy 62; Phila 18 Mar 62, 4
Ag 63

M'CLEAN/M'CLAIN/M'CLANE/M'-
CLEANE/M'CLEEN; see also
M'LANE/M'LEAN
Alexander P: Phila 27 Ja 73
Allen P: Pa 31 Dec 61, 13
Oct 63
Archibald P: Phila 25 Jy 65;
Upper Dublin 28 Ap 68
Bridget P: Pa 3 Ag 58
Daniel P: Fort Cumberland
21 Dec 58; Pa 13 Oct 63
David P: Bucks Co 20 Oct 68;
Delaware 15 Mar 64; Forks
of Delaware 31 Dec 61, 28
Oct 62; Phila 10 Oct 65,
30 Ja 66, 1 May 76
Hugh P: Phila 26 Jy 64, 30
Ja 66
James P: Pa 26 Jy 64; Phila
16 Jy 77
John P: Phila 3 Ja 65 (2)
Robert P: Phila 31 Dec 61
Thomas P: Conewaga 24 Oct 54
William P: Pa 13 Ja 63 (2);
near Phila 19 May 63; Upper
Dublin 13 Ja 63. T: Hunter-
don Co 31 Ja 71

M'CLEARY
Thomas P: Marsh Creek 13 Oct
63

M'CLELLAND/M'CLELLEN/M'CLELIN/
M'CLELLAN/M'CLELAN/M'CLELAND/
M'CLILAND
Arch./Archibald P: Phila 28
Ap 68, 27 Ja 73
Alexander P: Lancaster Co 12
Feb 61
Daniel P: Lancaster Co 18
Mar 62
George P: Phila 31 Mar 63
James P: Chestnut-Level 3
Ja 60; Pa 31 Dec 61
John L: Back Leacock 15 Ap
56. P: Cumberland Co 26
Jy 64; Pa 13 Oct 63; Phila
5 Ag 56
Jos. P: Phila 3 Sep 61, 31
Dec 61

William L: York Town 29 Jy 72.
  P: Phila 1 Nov 70. T: Mine-
  brook 4 Nov 72
M'CLEMOND
  Benjamin P: Pa 13 Oct 63
M'CLENACH
  Blair P: Phila 25 Jy 65
M'CLENAHAN/M'CLENEHAN/MACCLEN-
  ACHAN/MACLANACHAN; see also
  M'CLANACHEN
  Mr. P: Phila 2 Ag 70
  Blair P: Phila 12 Feb 61
  John P: Pa 18 Mar 62. W:
    Fogs Manor 3 Jy 76
M'CLENAN
  John P: Conecochegue 31 Mar
    63
M'CLEVER
  Jane P: Hanover, Lancaster
    Co 1 Jy 56
M'CLIFTON
  James P: Phila 3 Ja 65
M'CLINTOCK/M'CLINTOGH
  John C: Londonderry 30 Oct
    66
  Matthew P: Phila 30 Ja 66
M'CLINTON
  Mary P: Phila-Gaz. 3 Ja 76
M'CLISH
  Catherine P: Phila 27 Ja 73
  John P: Yellow Springs 20 Jy
    69
M'CLISTER
  Malcom L: Lancaster Co 31 Ja
    71
M'CLORG
  Alexander P: Phila-Gaz. 27
    Oct 73
M'CLOSKEY/M'CLOSKY
  Christian P: Phila 25 Jy 65
  Henry P: Phila 20 Ap 69
  James P: Pequea 26 Jy 64
  Thomas L: 29 Ja 67
M'CLUGHAN/M'CLAUGHAN/M'CLUAN
  Anthony P: Phila 13 May 56
  Gilbert P: Phila 13 Ja 63
  John P: near New Castle 18
    Feb 55; New-Castle 27 Dec
    53, 11 Jy 54, 3 Ja 60, 31
    Jy 60; Phila 23 May 56
M'CLUNG
  Matt. L: 3 Oct 65. P: Lan-
    caster Co 24 Feb 63
M'CLURE/M'CLEUR/M'CLUR/M'CLUER
  Alexander L: Lancaster Co 29
    Jy 72
  Fra. L: in Paxton 31 Ja 71
  James P: Pa 3 Ag 58; Phila
    4 Feb 68
  John P: Lancaster Co 3 Ag
    58; Pa 28 Oct 62; Phila 15
    Mar 64 (Capt), 20 Ap 69
  Mat. P: Lancaster Co 4 Ag 63
  Richard P: Phila 30 Ja 66
  Robert P: East Nantmill 21

Dec 58
  Samuel P: Phila 4 Feb 68
  William C: Cross Roads 18 Jy
    65. L: Hanover Twp 19 Dec
    71
M'CLURG
  Thomas P: Phila 28 Oct 62
M'CLUSKY
  James L: Pennsylvania 29 Jy
    72
M'CLUZE
  John P: Baltimore Co 19 May
    63
M'COGHAN
  John P: Phila 19 Ja 69
M'COHNICK
  Mr. P: Phila 27 Ja 73
M'COLEMAN
  N. P: Pa 31 Jy 60
  Nicholas P: Pa 13 Ja 63
M'COLLEY
  John P: Phila 28 Ap 68
M'COLLIN
  Allen P: Phila 27 Ja 73
M'COLLOCK, see M'CULLOUGH
M'COLLOM/M'CULLOM; see also
  M'CALLOM
  Allen P: Phila 23 Oct 66,
    30 Oct 76
  Andrew P: Salem-Gaz. 27 Oct
    73
M'COMB/M'COMBE/M'COOMBS
  Archi/Archibald P: Phila 12
    Feb 61, 26 Jy 64
  Charles P: Phila 10 Oct 65
  Eleazer P: Phila 28 Oct 62
  George L: 14 May 72
  John P: Phila 27 Ja 73, 3
    Ja 76
M'COMGALL
  William P: Phila 31 Dec 61
M'CONAUGHEY/M'CONAGHY/M'CONO-
  UGHY/M'CONNACHIE
  James P: New-Castle Co 21
    Dec 58
  John P: Lancaster Co 12 Ja
    58; Newcastle Co 18 Mar 62
  William P: Phila 25 Jy 65
M'CONEGILL; see also M'GONI-
  GEL
  Peter P: Phila 13 Ja 63
M'CONN/MACCON
  Finlaw P: Goshen 9 Ag 59
  William L: 11 Ap 65
M'CONNACHAN
  Samuel P: Phila 28 Oct 62
M'CONNALY
  Daniel P: Phila 4 Feb 68
M'CONNELL/M'CONNEL/M'CONNOLL
  Ann P: Christine Bridge 3
    Sep 61
  James P: Pa 31 Dec 61
  Lettice P: Phila 31 Dec 61
  Martha P: Pa 3 Ag 58
  Mary Ann P: Phila 31 Dec 61

Neal   P: Phila 9 Ag 59
Thomas   P: Somerset Co 31 Jy
   60
William   P: New-Castle Co 13
   Oct 63; Pa 31 Dec 61; Phila
   10 Oct 65, 20 Oct 68
M'COOK
John   N: c/o John Steward
   New-Castle 4 Dec 66. P: Pa
   24 Feb 63, 19 May 63; Phila
   3 Ja 65, 2 May 65
M'COOL
Samuel   C: 18 Jy 65
M'COOR
John   N: Kent Co 12 Feb 67
M'CORCAIN
William   P: Pa 12 Feb 61
M'CORD
John   P: Pa 12 Feb 61
Robert   P: Darby 3 Ja 65
Thomas   L: Paxton 19 Dec 71,
   2 Mar 74. P: Paxton 9 Ag 59
William   L: 20 Ja 73. P: Pa
   12 Feb 61
M'CORDY/M'CORDIE
Eleanor   P: Chestnut Level 12
   Ja 58
Robert   P: Phila 3 Ja 60
M'CORGAN
Hugh   P: Patowm/ack/ R/iver/
   12 Ja 58
M'CORKLE/M'CORKAL/M'CORKILL/
   M'CORKEL/M'CORKIL/
Archibald   P: Phila 18 Mar 62
Darius   P: Pa 12 Ja 58
James   P: Pa 4 Ag 63
John   P: New-Providence 3 Ag
   58; Pa 2 Feb 64 (2); White-
   land 18 Mar 62
Samuel   P: Phila 18 Mar 62
M'CORMICK/M'CARMICK
Widow   P: Sweetara Creek 31
   Jy 60
Alexander   P: Pa 4 Ag 63, 13
   Oct 63, 26 Jy 64; Phila 3
   Ja 65
Benjamin   P: Pa 28 Oct 62
Daniel   P: Lancaster Co 24 Feb
   63
Dennis   P: Phila 11 Sep 55,
   3 Ja 76, 31 Ja 76
Isabel   P: Chester Co 21 Dec 58
James   P: Fallo. 18 Ag 57;
   Lancaster Road 12 Ja 58;
   Phila 9 Ag 59; West Bradford
   7 Ap 57
Jeremiah   P: Phila 1 Nov 70.
   T: Monmouth Co 21 Ja 55
John   L: 13 Jn 65. P: Phila
   11 Sep 55, 3 Ja 60, 30 Ja 66,
   20 Oct 68
Joseph   P: New-Castle Co 9 Ag
   59; Pa 9 Ag 59, 18 Mar 62
Samuel   P: Phila 15 Mar 64
William   P: Phila 3 Sep 61, 28

Oct 62
M'CORMIE
Charles   P: Phila 1 Feb 70
M'CORNE
James   P: Phila 3 Ja 65
M'CORTY
Patrick   P: Christeen 13 Ja
   63
M'COSKY
James   P: Fogg's Manor 8 Jy
   62
MAC COURT
Anthony   P: Phila 1 Feb 70
M'COWEY
Francis   P: Chester Town 2
   Feb 64
M'COY/M'KOY
Alexander   P: Lancaster Co
   18 Ag 57
Anges, soldier   P: prob. in
   Pittsburgh 15 Mar 64
Daniel   P: Phila 13 Oct 63,
   20 Ap 69
Gane   P: Pa 26 Jy 64
John   P: Pa 24 Feb 63
Mary   P: Lancaster 12 Feb 61
William   P: Chester Co 8 Jy
   62
M'CRAB
John   P: Pa 15 Mar 64
M'CRACKEN/M'CRAKEN/M'CRACAN/
   M'CRAKIN
Anthony   P: Lancaster Co 3
   Sep 61
Archibald   P: Pa 18 Mar 62
David   P: Caecil Co 4 Ag 63;
   Phila 5 Ag 62
James   L: 11 Ap 65, 13 Jn 65,
   3 Oct 65. P: Brandywine
   31 Dec 61; Pa 31 Jy 60,
   18 Mar 62; Phila 24 Oct 54,
   3 Ag 58, 13 Ja 63, 26 Jy
   64, 26 Oct 69
John   P: Pa 8 Jy 62; Phila
   16 Jy 72
Jos.   P: Chester Co 31 Dec 61
Thomas   N: Brandywine, see
   CHRISTIE, Robert. P:
   Brandywine 15 Mar 64;
   Forks of Delaware 7 Ap 57
William   P: Phila 13 Oct 63,
   26 Jy 64, 3 Ja 65
M'CRAKER
Thomas   P: Brandywine 28 Nov
   54
M'CRANCH
Joseph   P: Pa 18 Mar 62
M'CREA/M'CRAE
Alexander   P: Phila-Gaz. 3 Ja
   76
Hugh   P: nigh Elk 7 Ap 57;
   Elk 2 Feb 64
James   P: Lancaster Co 13 Oct
   63
Robert   P: Pa 28 Oct 62; Phila

30 Ja 66
William P: Elk River 3 Sep
61; Phila 10 Ap 66;
Whiteclay Creek 9 Ag 59
M'CREAGHT
Anthony P: Swatara 24 Oct
54
M'CREARY/M'CRERY/M'CREREY/
M'CREERY/M'CRIREY
Mr. P: Phila 7 Ap 57
Widow P: Bucks 28 Nov 54
(alias KIRK), 12 Ja 58
James L: York Co 29 Jy 72.
P: Phila 1 Nov 70; 16 Jy
72
Jo. L: 11 Ap 65
John L: 29 Ja 67. P:
Lancaster Co 24 Oct 54
Robert P: Yorks Co 18 Mar 62
M'CREE
Hugh N: 29 Nov 64
M'CREIGHT
Anthony L: Lancaster Co 2 Mar
74
M'CREW
John P: Phila 4 Feb 68
M'CROCHAN
Wm. P: Bucks Co 18 Ag 57
M'CRONEY
Jane P: Upper Dublin 3 Ag 58
M'CROREY
Jane P: Upper Dublin 3 Ag 58
Samuel or James P: Upper Dub-
lin 25 Ap 71
William P: Augusta Co 13 Oct
63
M'CROSSEN
James P: Phila 27 Ja 73
M'CROY
John P: Pa 4 Ag 63
M'CUISHANE
John P: Phila 27 Ja 73
M'CULHEIN
Alexander P: Phila 16 Jy 72
M'CULLAN
Alexander P: Phila 11 Sep 55
M'CULLOUGH/M'CULLOCK/M;COLLAUGH/
M'CULOUGH/M'COLLOCH/M'COLLOGH/
M'COLLOCK/MECOLLOK/M'CULLA;
see also M'CALLA
Alexander L: Hanover Twp 15
Ap 56. P: New-Castle Co 4
Ag 63; Sussex Co 7 Ap 57
Andrew P: Phila 4 Feb 68
Anthony P: Phila 5 Ag 56;
Queen's Town 13 Ja 63
Barbary/Barbara P: Pa 21 Dec
58; Phila 9 Ag 59, 3 Sep 61
Barnaby P: Cumberland Co 24
Feb 63
Barney P: Pa 13 Ja 63
David P: Phila 28 Ap 68, 1
Feb 70, 3 May 70
Elizabeth P: Phila 16 Jy 67,
20 Jy 69

Geo. P: Nottingham 3 Sep 61
James C: c/o John Fulton,
Providence 22 Ja 67. L:
Carlisle 19 Dec 71. P: Pa
28 Oct 62, 13 Oct 63;
Phila 2 May 65, 19 Ja 69,
16 Jy 77; Reading 5 Ag 56
Jannet P: Phila 3 Sep 61
John C: East Bradford 22 Ja
67. P: Bucks Co 30 Oct
76; Fort Cumberland 12 Ja
58; Hopewell 31 Ja 76;
Phila 18 Mar 62
Mary P: Phila 21 Dec 58, 8
Jy 62
Patrick P: Bucks Co 27 Ja 73
Robert P: Pa 28 Oct 62
Samuel P: Marsh Creek 31 Dec
61; Phila 16 Jy 72
Timothy P: Broughton 9 Ag 59
William L: Hanover Twp 20 Ja
73. P: Phila 28 Nov 54,
30 Ja 66, 1 Feb 70, 25 Ap 71
M'CUNE/M'CUNN/M'CUN/M'CUEN;
see also M'EUIN/M'KEWIN
James P: New Castle Co 19
May 63
Thomas L: York Co 2 Mar 74.
P: Bucks Co 26 Jy 64;
Cumberland Co 3 Sep 61; Pa
3 Ja 60; Phila 3 Ja 65;
York Co 31 Dec 61
M'CURDY
Angus P: Phila-Gaz. 27 Oct 73
Archibald/Arch. P: Abington
5 Ag 56; Phila 28 Ap 68
Edward P: Newcastle Co 7 Ap
57, 4 Ag 63
Ellis P: Lancaster Co 21 Dec
58
Hugh P: Pa 28 Oct 62
John P: Londonderry 12 Ja 58,
3 Ag 58; Phila 30 Ja 66
Robert P: Springfield 5 Ag
56, 12 Ja 58; Upper Dublin
Twp 9 Ag 59
M'CURRY
Jonathan P: Phila 3 Sep 61
Loughlin P: Pa 13 Ja 63
M'CURTEN
Mr. P: Pa 12 Ja 58
M'CUSICK
James P: Chester Co 31 Dec 61
M'CUTCHEON/M'CUCHON/M'CUTCHEN/
M'CUTCHIN/M'CUTCHON
Hugh P: Fishkill 11 Sep 55
James P: Phila 13 Oct 63, 3
Ja 65
Samuel P: Cumberland Co 26 Jy
64; Pa 28 Oct 62; Phila 23
Oct 66 (Capt)
Susannah P: Pa 26 Jy 64,
York Town 26 Jy 64
M'DAIRET
Alexander P: Phila 24 Feb 63

M'DANIEL
    Catharine P: Phila-Gaz. 3
        Ja 76
    Daniel P: Phila 4 Ag 63
    Hugh P: Phila 5 Ag 62
    James P: Phila 23 Oct 66
        (Capt); St. George's Hun-
        dred 21 Dec 58
    John P: Phila 21 Dec 58, 25
        Ap 71
    Mary P: Phila 10 Oct 65
    Michael P: New Jersey 1 Feb
        70
    William P: Bucks Co 9 Ag 59
    Zachariah T: Hunterdon Co
        10 Ag 58
M'DAVID
    Patrick P: Newtown 5 Ag 62
M'DAVIL
    Daniel P: Bucks Co 28 Oct
        62
M'DEAD
    William P: Pa 15 Mar 64
M'DERMED
    Archibald P: Phila 31 Jy 60
    John P: Phila 31 Jy 60
M'DERMOT/M'DORMOT
    Michael P: Germantown 3 May
        70
    William P: Phila-Gaz. 27 Oct
        73
M'DEVIT/M'DEVITT/M'DEVID/
    M'DIVIL
    Daniel P: Bucks Co 24 Feb 63
    Edward L: 25 Dec 66
    John L: Cumberland Co 19 Dec
        71
    Patrick/Pat. P: Phila 2 Feb
        64, 15 Mar 64
M'DILL
    Jacob L: Pequea 15 Ap 56
    James L: Pequea 19 Dec 71
M'DOAL
    Sarah P: Phila 24 Oct 54
M'DON
    John P: Phila 2 Ag 70
M'DONALD/M'DONNALD
    Mr. P: Phila 28 Oct 62
    Alexander P: Kent Co 2 Ag
        70; Pa 4 Ag 63; Phila 5 Ag
        56, 30 Ap 67
    Ann/Anne P: Phila 8 Jy 62, 23
        Oct 66
    Charles P: Phila 26 Jy 64,
        3 Ja 65
    Cornelius P: Nottingham 31
        Jy 60
    Donald Phila 24 Jy 76
    James P: Abington 27 Dec 53;
        Lancaster Co 27 Dec 53, 31
        Jy 60; Phila 12 Ja 58, 4 Ag
        63; soldier, prob. in Pitts-
        burgh 15 Mar 64
    John P: Fort Pitt 26 Jy 64
        (soldier); Pa 18 Mar 62;

Phila 28 Nov 54, 3 Ag 58
    Lewis, Esq. T: Bedford 15
        Jy 56
    Mary Phila 5 Jy 77-Gaz. 16
        Jy
    Michael T: Allentown 10 Ag
        58
    Norman (sergeant in army)
        P: Fort Pitt 26 Jy 64
    Rowland P: Cumberland Co 18
        Mar 62
    William P: Phila 11 Jy 54,
        10 Oct 65
M'DONALL/M'DONNELL/M'DONNALL
    Dr. L: Cumberland Co 19 Dec
        71
    Alexander P: Phila-Gaz. 3 Ja
        76
    Angus (soldier) P: Fort Pitt
        26 Jy 64
    Archibald P: Phila 30 Ja 66
    George P: Phila 15 Mar 64
    Henry P: Pa 12 Feb 61
    James P: Chestnut Level 12
        Ja 58
    Mary P: Kent Co 28 Oct 62;
        Lancaster Co 4 Ag 63
    Michael P: Phila-Gaz. 3 Ja
        76
    Randall L: Carlisle 29 Jy
        72
M'DONOUGH/M'DONOGH
    Bryan P: Phila 18 Ag 57
    James P: Ready Island 4 Ag
        63
    Norah P: Phila 8 Jy 62
M'DOUGALL/M'DOUGEL/M'DUGALD/
    M'DOUGALD
    Mr. P: Phila 25 Jy 65
    Allen P: Pa 13 Ja 63
    Duncan P: Phila 3 Ja 65
    Capt. Henry P: Phila 1 Nov
        53
    John P: Pa 12 Feb 61; Phila
        3 May 70
    John Douglass Phila 5 Ap 76-
        Gaz. 1 May
M'DOWELL/M'DOWEL/M'DOWAL/M'-
    DOUAL/M'DOOL
    Alexander P: Chester Co 3 Ja
        60; Lancaster Co 18 Mar
        62; Pa 9 Ag 59; Phila 24
        Oct 54, 5 Ag 56, 19 Jy 80
        (Rev.)
    Andrew P: Chester Co 5 Ag
        62; near Christeen 8 Jy 62;
        Pa 13 Oct 63
    Edward P: Phila 4 Feb 68
    Ephraim P: East Jersey 8 Jy
        62
    George P: Phila 26 Jy 64
    James P: Donegall 19 May 63;
        Lancaster Co 24 Feb 63, 2
        Feb 64; Pa 13 Oct 63; Phila
        2 May 65

Jane P: Cross Roads 31 Jy 60
John N: in Cecil Co 29 Nov
   64. P: Lancaster Co 12 Feb
   61; Phila 3 Sep 61, 28 Oct
   62, 26 Jy 64, 25 Jy 65. T:
   Lomington 4 Nov 72
Matthew C: Chester Co 28 Nov
   65. P: East Fallowfield 8
   Jy 62
William P: Cross Roads 21 Dec
   58; Pa 12 Feb 61, 2 Sep 62;
   Phila 27 Ja 73
M'DUFF
   Alexander L: Paxton 2 Mar 74
   John P: Phila 19 Ja 69
   Lawrence P: Phila 23 Oct 66
   Richard P: Phila 3 Ag 58
M'DUFFEY/M'DUFFEE/M'DOFFE
   Daniel P: Great Valley 18 Mar
      62; Pa 9 Ag 59; Phila 12 Feb
      61
   Robert P: Pa 12 Feb 61
M'DUNER
   James P: Trap-Town 4 Ag 63
M'EACHREN/M'EACHEN/M'EACHM/
   M'EACHARN
   James P: Brandywine 31 Dec
      61; Forks of Brandywine 3
      May 70; Pa 12 Feb 61
   Laughlin, soldier P: prob.
      in Pittsburgh 15 Mar 64
M'EADAM
   Henry P: Phila 30 Ja 66
MACEL
   Mary P: Phila 26 Jy 64
M'ELHAGY
   James P: Mountholly 2 Feb
      64
M'ELHATTEN
   John P: Phila 3 May 70
M'ELHENNEY
   William P: Darby 25 Ap 71
M'ELMOY
   Patrick L: Chestnut Level
      31 Ja 71
M'ELROY/MICKELROY
   Archibald P: Phila 2 Feb 64,
      27 Oct 73
   Thomas or James L: Cumber-
      land Co 2 Mar 74
M'ELTHINNEY
   Andrew P: Kent Co 3 Ja 60
M'ELWAIN
   Robert P: Whiteclay Creek
      7 Ap 57
M'ELWEE
   Frank P: Pa 28 Oct 62
M'ENROE
   John C: c/o John Hays, Oxford
      Twp 30 Oct 66
M'ENTAGGART
   Michael P: Phila 16 Jy 67
M'EUIN; see also M'CUNE
   John P: Alloway's Creek

16 Jy 67
M'EULISPY
   John P: N.Castle Co 13 Ja 63
M'EVAN
   James P: Phila-Gaz. 3 Ja 76
M'EVERS
   Charles P: Phila 31 Dec 61
M'EVITY
   Thomas P: in the army 12 Ja
      58
M'FADDEN/M'FADEN/M'FADON
   Margaret P: Phila-Gaz. 27
      Oct 73
   Sa. L: 14 May 72
   William P: Phila 27 Ja 73,
      30 Ap 77
M'FALL; see also PATT & M'FALL
   Hugh P: Bucks Co 26 Oct 69
   Patrick P: Phila 30 May 54,
      2 Feb 64, 30 Ja 66
M'FARAN/MACFAREN
   George P: Bucks Co 9 Ag 59
   William P: Mount-bethel 27
      Oct 73
M'FARLAND/M'FARLIN/M'FARLING/
   M'FARLAN/M'FARLON
   Alex. P: Phila 9 Ag 59
   Andrew L: Fort Pitt 19 Dec
      71
   Arthur P: Yellow-Spring 3
      Sep 61
   Benjamin P: Bethlehem 12 Ja
      58
   Catharine P: Phila-Gaz. 3
      Ja 76
   Charles P: Pa 4 Ag 63
   Daniel P: Mount-holly 1 Nov
      70; Phila 26 Jy 64
   Edward P: Pa 4 Ag 63; Pe-
      quea 3 Sep 61
   Francis P: Phila 30 Ap 67
   George P: Phila 21 Jy 68
   James P: Bucks Co 1 Jy 56;
      Carlisle 31 Jy 60, 4 Ag
      63; Chester Co 12 Feb 61;
      Forks Bridge 9 May 54
   John P: America 1 Nov 53;
      Chester Co 4 Ag 63; Phila
      20 Ap 69
   Neil P: Phila 28 Nov 54
   Nelly P: Phila 12 Feb 61
   Patrick P: Phila 25 Jy 65
   Walter,grenadier P: prob. at
      Pittsburgh 15 Mar 64
   William P: Kennet Twp 26 Jy
      64
M'FAUL/M'FAULE/M'FOWELL
   Dennis P: Christine Bridge
      21 Dec 58
   Neale P: Phila 12 Feb 61
   Pat. P: Pa 15 Mar 64
M'FEALL
   Henry P: Pa 12 Ja 58
M'FEE

Daniel   C: c/o William Fee-
  Chester 22 Ja 67
M'FEELY
  Daniel   P: Phila-Gaz. 27 Oct
  73
  Edward   L: Pequea 31 Ja 71
M'FERREN/M'FERRON/M'FERAN
  George   P: Bucks Co 24 Feb
  63; Pa 26 Jy 64; Phila 3
  Ja 65
  Samuel   Phila 16 Jy 77
M'FERRER
  John   P: Bucks Co 18 Mar 62
M'FETRICK/M'FATRICK
  Archibald   P: Phila 30 Ap 67
  John   P: Phila 19 Jy 80
MACKFIELD
  John   P: Phila 10 Oct 65
M'FIER/M'FIRE
  James   P: Phila 1 Nov 70
  Samuel   P: Phila 27 Ja 73
M'FORREN
  John   P: Pa 3 Ja 60
  Matthew   P: Pa 3 Ja 60
M'FUN
  Thomas   P: Bucks Co 2 Feb 64
M'GAA
  John   P: Phila 27 Ja 73, 27
  Oct 73
  William   P: Pa 3 Ja 60
M'GAGEWH
  W.   P: Phila 31 Dec 61
M'GAILLARD
  Robert   T: Lomington /?/4
  Nov 72
M'GALL
  George   P: Phila 28 Oct 62
M'GALLART
  John   P: Bucks Co 18 Mar 62;
  East Jersey 3 Sep 61
M'GALTIER
  John   P: N.J. 24 Feb 63
M'GAMON
  Michael   P: Phila 25 Ap 71
M'GANNON/M'GANNOU
  Michael   Darby 23 Oct 66;
  Phila 30 Ap 67
M'GARGOL
  Mr. Garret Roger   P: Phila 20
  Oct 68
M'GARNER
  David   P: Phila-Gaz. 27 Oct
  73
M'GARRICK
  James   P: Phila 3 Ja 65
M'GARRY
  John   N: 29 Nov 64
M'GASOCK
  Benjamin   P: York Co 3 Sep
  61
M'GAVOCK
  James   P: Bucks Co 13 Ja 63
  Patrick   P: Phila 19 Ja 69
M'GAW; see also MAGAW
  Ro.   L: York Co 31 Ja 71

M'GEACH
  Agnes   P: Pa 18 Mar 62
  Ann   P: Newcastle Co 18 Ag
  57
  Eliz./Elizab.   P: Newcastle
  Co 18 Ag 57, 12 Ja 58
M'GEE; see also MAGEE
  Henry   P: Phila 26 Oct 69
  James   P: Phila 10 Oct 65
  John   P: Lancaster 19 Jy 80
  (Col.); Phila 28 Ap 68
  Samuel   P: N.Castle Co 26
  Jy 64
  Thomas   P: Phila 26 Jy 64 (2)
M'GEGHAGAN
  William   P: New Castle Co 15
  Mar 64
M'GENLY
  James   P: Phila 20 Oct 68
M'GHARRAHER
  James   P: Pa 13 Oct 63
M'GILL/MAGILL
  Alice   P: Phila 18 Ag 57
  Catharine   P: Phila-Gaz. 3 Ja
  76
  Elizabeth/Betsy   P: Phila 3
  Ja 60, 13 Oct 63, 3 Ja 65
  Hugh   P: Phila 10 Oct 65
  Ja.   L: near Fort Loudon 25
  Dec 66
  James   P: Pa 31 Dec 61; Phila
  3 Ja 65
  Neil   P: Phila 30 Ja 66
  Patrick   N: merchant, Elk-
  ridge, Md. 12 Feb 67.   P:
  Phila 30 Ap 67, 26 Oct 69,
  1 Nov 70
  Robert or Henry   P: Phila 19
  Ja 69
  William   P: Phila 31 Mar 63,
  19 May 63
M'GILLIERE
  John   P: Phila-Gaz. 27 Oct
  73
M'GILTON
  John   P: Phila 28 Oct 62
M'GINLY
  James   P: Phila 20 Ap 69
M'GINNES/M'GENNIS/M'GENIS/
  M'GENNESS/MACKANESS/MAGENNIS/
  MAGINNIS/MAGINESE; see also
  M'HANGIS
  Catherine   P: Phila 16 Jy 72
  Edward   P: Phila-Gaz. 3 Ja 76
  James   P: Pa 31 Jy 60; Phila
  20 Oct 68
  John   L: 19 Dec 71 (school-
  master).   P: Phila 3 Ja 76
  Samuel   P: 21 Dec 58 (soldier);
  Pa 26 Jy 64
  Thomas   Phila 1 May 76
  Timothy   P: Phila 23 Oct 66
M'GLASHAN
  Leonard, sergeant   P: prob.
  at Pittsburgh 15 Mar 64;

Fort Pitt 26 Jy 64
M'GLATHERY/M'GLATHRY
  Henry P: Norrington-Gaz. 3
    Ja 76
  John P: Bucks Co 15 Mar 64
  Matthew P: Phila 31 Dec 61
  Thomas P: Phila 3 Ja 76
M'GLAUGHLIN/M'GLAUGHLEN/M'GLACK-
LIN; see also M'LAUGHLIN
  Hugh T: Bordentown 17 Oct 54
  John P: Phila 30 Ja 66
  Neal P: N.J. 24 Feb 63
  Patrick P: Chester Co 2 Feb
    64
  Philip P: Phila 26 Oct 69
M'GOM
  Humphrey P: Pa 3 Ja 60
M'GOMERY/M'GOMRIE
  Mr. C: Christeen Bridge, see
    STORY, William
  John C: West Nottingham, see
    DOHERTY, William
  Wm. P: Little Br. 12 Ja 58
M'GONIGEL; see also M'CONEGILL
  Robert P: Muspilion 1 Nov
    70
M'GOROWN
  Daniel P: Phila 10 Oct 65
M'GOUGE
  James P: Pa 19 May 63, 4 Ag
    63
M'GOUSH
  John P: Phila 21 Jy 68
M'GOWAN/M'GOWEN/M'GOWN; see also
M'COGHAN,MAGOWN,M'KOUN
  John L: Pequea 29 Jy 72. P:
    Phila 1 Nov 70
  Patrick P: Octerara 3 Ja 60
M'GRADEN
  John P: Phila 31 Dec 61
M'GRADY/M'GREADY/M'GREDDY/M'-
GREDY/M'GRADAY
  Dennis P: Phila 8 Jy 62
  James P: Chester Co 31 Jy 60
  John P: Chester Co 28 Oct 62;
    Phila 16 Jy 72
  Samuel P: Neshaminey 2 Feb 64
M'GRANAGHAN
  Patrick P: Phila 27 Ja 73
M'GRAW/M'GRAH/M'GRAGH/M'GRAUGH/
M'CRAW/MAGRAH
  Ann P: Bucks Co 21 Dec 58
  Arnold P: Phila 2 May 65
  Mary P: Pa 12 Feb 61
  Martin P: Salem 8 Jy 62
  Michael P: Phila 31 Dec 61,
    20 Ap 69, 20 Jy 69
  Morris T: Hunterdon Co 6 Dec
    64
  Perkins P: Phila 9 Ag 59
  William Phila 16 Jy 77
M'GREAL
  Owen P: Chester Co 12 Feb 61
M'GREGOR/M'GRAGGER/M'GRAIGER/
M'GRIGER

Mr. P: Phila 2 May 65
  Esther P: in the army, prob.
    at Pittsburgh 15 Mar 64
  John P: Pa 7 Ap 57; Phila
    21 Dec 58, 9 Ag 59
  Rachel P: Phila 3 Ja 60
M'GREW
  Alexander P: Leacock 3 Ag 58
  John P: Leacock 3 Ag 58
M'GROARRY
  Pat. P: Phila 30 Ja 66
M'GROUGAR
  James P: Pa 4 Feb 64; Phila
    21 Dec 58
M'GUCHAN
  Patrick P: Phila 30 Ja 66
M'GUE
  David P: Phila 25 Jy 65
M'GUFFOY
  Jane P: Pa 3 Ja 60
M'GUIRE/MAGUIRE; see also MA-
QUIRE
  Mrs. P: Lancaster Co 4 Ag 63
  John P: Phila 28 Ap 68
  Patrick C: 18 Jy 65. P:
    N. Castle Co 13 Ja 63; Pa
    26 Jy 64; Phila 24 Feb 63
  Thomas P: Chester Co 2 Sep
    62
  William P: Chester Co 24 Feb
    63; Phila 8 Jy 62
M'GUMORE
  William P: New London 31 Mar
    63
M'GURDY
  Hugh P: Phila 3 Ja 65
M'GUSSOCK
  Joseph T: Allen's Town 1 Sep
    68
M'HAFFY/M'HAFEY
  Moses P: Pa 9 Ag 59
  Thomas N: Christeen Bridge
    4 Dec 66
M'HANGIS
  John P: Phila-Gaz. 3 Ja 76
M'HARGY
  Archibald P: Chester Co 24
    Feb 63
M'HENRY
  Daniel P: Pa 13 Oct 63
  Rev. H. P: Phila Co 31 Dec
    61
  James P: Phila 13 Ja 63
  John (soldier) P: Fort Pitt
    26 Jy 64
  Dr. Matthew P: Phila 19 Ja
    69
M'HERGAN
  James P: Bucks Co 27 Ja 73
M'HONNEY
  William L: Caecil Co, near
    Christiana-Bridge, Maryland
    19 Dec 71
M'HUGH/MACHEW
  .... P: Phila 3 Ag 58

James   P: Phila 2 Ag 70
M'ILDUFF
    John   P: Phila 18 Mar 62
M'ILHENEY/M'ILHENNEY
    Ezekiel   P: Lancaster Co 3
    Sep 61
    William   Phila 30 Ap 77
M'ILLHAGNEY
    Hugh   P: Phila 26 Oct 69
M'ILLURAY
    James   P: Phila 28 Ap 68
M'ILRATH
    Thomas   P: N.J. 2 Feb 64
M'ILVAINE/M'ILVANE
    Capt.   P: Phila 31 Mar 63,
    2 May 65
    Archibald   P: Phila 9 Ag 59
    David   P: Phila 2 May 65
    Forgeson   P: Phila 18 Mar
    62
    Gilbert   P: Norrington 26
    Jy 64; Phila Co 28 Oct
    62
    John   P: Lancaster Co 4 Ag
    63; Ridley Twp 1 May 76
    William   P: Bristol 2 Feb
    64; Fair View 10 Oct 65,
    10 Ap 66; Pa 4 Ag 63; Phila
    13 Oct 63, 2 Feb 64, 15 Mar
    64, 26 Jy 64, 2 May 65, 25
    Jy 65
M'ILVIDY
    Daniel   P: Chester Co 13 Oct
    63
M'ILLVRAY
    Arch./Archibald   P: Pa 12 Ja
    58; Phila 26 Jy 64
    Kitty   P: Phila-Gaz. 3 Ja 76
M'INELY
    Arthur   P: Phila 4 Ag 63
M'INTIRE/M'ANTIER/MACKINTIRE/
M'ENTIRE/M'INTYRE
    Alex   P: Christine 4 Ap 54
    Andrew   L: Lancaster 2 Mar 74
    Dugal   C: 18 Jy 65
    Henry   P: Bucks Co 28 Oct 62
    James   P: 21 Dec 58 (soldier);
    Pa 28 Oct 62
    Jane   P: Phila 27 Ja 73
    John   P: Bucks Co 12 Feb 61;
    Phila 30 Ja 66
    Malcom   P: in the army 12 Ja
    58
    Michael   P: Phila 29 Ag 54,
    15 Mar 64
    Neil   P: Phila 2 May 65, 25
    Jy 65
    Peter   P: Phila 10 Oct 65
    Samuel   N: New-Castle 4 Dec 66;
    White-clay Creek /?/ 12 Feb
    67
    William   P: Bucks Co 3 Sep 61,
    27 Ja 73
M'INTOSH/M'ENTASH
    John   P: Phila 11 Sep 55

Peter   P: Phila 1 Nov 70
M'ISAAC
    Daniel   P: Phila 28 Ap 68,
    19 Ja 69
M'IVITY
    Cromwell   P: Brandiwine 18
    Mar 62
M'JANNET
    Thomas   P: Phila 12 Feb 61
M'JEFFERY
    Dennis   P: Phila 27 Dec 73
MACK
    Archi.   P: Pa 12 Feb 61
    George   P: Phila 13 Oct 63
    Jacob   P: Phila 11 Sep 55
    William   P: Phila 1 Feb 70
M'KACHAN
    James   P: Pa 4 Ag 63
M'KADDAN
    Henry   P: Phila 19 May 63
M'KAGHANIS
    Dennis   P: Phila 27 Ja 73
M'KAN/M'KANN
    Mary   P: Phila 30 Ja 66
    Nancy   P: Phila 9 Ag 59
    Timothy   P: Phila-Gaz. 3 Ja
    76
M'KANE
    Margaret   P: Phila 15 Mar 64
M'KARDY
    Samuel   T: 7 May 67
M'KASSON
    Mary   P: Salem 8 Jy 62
M'KAUCHEN
    Wm.   P: Phila 25 Jy 65
MACKAY/MACKEY/MACKY/M'KAY/
M/KEY/MACKIE/MAKEY
    Aeneas   L: Fort Pitt 20 Ja 73
    Alexander   P: Pa 3 Ja 60;
    Phila 25 Jy 65, 23 Oct 66,
    26 Oct 69, 19 Jy 80 (Capt);
    West Nottingham 7 Ap 57
    Andrew   P: Pa 18 Mar 62
    Angus   P: Pa 12 Feb 61
    Christian   L: 13 Jn 65
    Daniel   P: Phila-Gaz. 27 Oct
    73
    David   P: Pa 13 Ja 63; Phila
    3 Sep 61
    Ealce   P: East-Town 3 Ag 58
    James   P: Chester Co 31 Dec
    61; Elk River 21 Dec 58;
    Phila 23 Oct 66; Salisbury
    1 Feb 70
    John   P: Elk River 13 May 56;
    Pa 26 Jy 64; Phila 18 Ag 57,
    3 May 70, 27 Oct 73
    Neal   L: 29 Ja 67
    Robert   P: Chester Co 3 Sep
    61 (Capt); Lancaster Co 7
    Ap 57; Little Elk 1 Feb
    70; New London Town 21 Dec
    58
    Roger   P: Phila 16 Jy 72
    Capt. Solomon   P: Phila 11 Sep

55
Wallock P: Phila 19 May 63
William L: c/o Samuel Lefevre
   Lancaster Co 19 Dec 71. P:
   Phila 9 Ag 59, 24 Feb 63
M'KEAGHNY
Hugh P: Phila 20 Jy 69
M'KEAMAN
Daniel P: Octorara 7 Ap 57;
   York-Town 1 Nov 53
M'KEAN/M'KEANE
Lt. T: 10 Ag 58
Andrew P: Phila 26 Oct 69
James P: Pa 12 Feb 61
Thomas P: Chester Co 9 Ag 59,
   8 Jy 62; Lancaster Road 7
   Ap 57. W: Wilmington 27 Ag
   77 (Esq)
William P: Donegall 18 Mar 62
M'KEASEN
Patrick P: Phila 28 Ap 68
M'KEE/MACKEE
Alexander/Alex. P: Chester Co
   27 Dec 53, 12 Feb 61, 13 Oct
   63; Fort Pitt, in army 26 Jy
   64; Pa 13 Oct 63; Phila 24
   Oct 54
Andrew N: Brandywine Hundred,
   c/o Mr. Steward, New Castle
   4 Dec 66
David L: Northumberlan Co 20
   Ja 73. T: near Trenton 7
   May 67
Jane P: Chester Co 31 Jy 60;
   Pa 3 Ag 58
John P: Cumberland Co 13 Ja
   63, 24 Feb 63; near New-
   Castle 31 Jy 60; Phila 28 Ap
   68, 27 Ja 73
Margaret P: Pa 12 Ja 58
Mary P: Phila 26 Jy 64
Robert P: B.C. 20 Ap 69; Lon-
   don Derry 24 Oct 54, 12 Ja
   58
Rodde P: Phila 8 Jy 62
William L: in Shearman's
   Valley 14 May 72. P: Chest-
   er Co 26 Oct 69; N. Castle
   Co 13 Ja 63
M'KEEHAN
George P: Pa 12 Feb 61
M'KEIGAN
John P: Bethlehem 12 Ja 58
M'KEEN
James P: Pa 24 Feb 63
Thomas, Esq. P: Phila 31 Mar
   63
M'KELEY
James P: Forks of Brandywine
   3 May 70
MACKELL/M'KELL
Mr. P: Phila 9 Ag 59
Adam P: Phila 18 Feb 55
M'KELVEY
Atness P: Bucks Co 9 Ag 59

Owen P: Phila 1 Feb 70
M'KEMAN
Daniel P: Marshcreek 13 Ja
   63
Neal P: Peach-bottom 13
   Ja 63
M'KEMMY
George P: Cumberland Co
   28 Oct 62
M'KEMOR
Neil L: 13 Jn 65
M'KENNAN/M'KENIN
Rev. P: Whiteclay Creek
   2 Ag 58
John P: Pa 31 Dec 61
M'KENNERA
Rev. T: Trenton 17 Oct 54
M'KENNEY/M'KENNY
Andrew P: Pa 26 Jy 64
Janet P: Baskin-Ridge 21
   Dec 58
Mat. P: Pa 2 Feb 64
Robert P: Marsh Creek 18
   Mar 62
William P: Phila-Gaz. 3 Ja
   76
M'KENRIE
Elizabeth P: Pa 12 Feb 61
M'KENZIE/M'KENSEY/MACKENZIE/
   M'KINSEY/M'KINZIE
Capt. A. P: Pa 3 Ag 58
Alex./Alexander P: Phila
   28 Ap 68, 2 Ag 70
Ann P: Phila 3 Ag 58
Daniel L: Lancaster Co 29
   Jy 72
John P: Phila 3 Ag 58;
   soldier, prob. in Pitts-
   burgh 15 Mar 64 (2)
Capt. K. P: Phila 18 Feb
   55
Capt. Kenneth P: Phila 3
   Ja 60
M'KEON
Gilbert P: Chester Co 19
   May 63
M'KEOVIN
Thomas P: Pa 3 Ja 60
M'KER
John (soldier) P: Fort
   Pitt 26 Jy 64
MACKERATH
Michael P: Pa 4 Ag 63
M'KERTTIN
Alexander P: Phila 13 Oct
   63
M'KETRICK
Mary P: Phila 28 Ap 68
M'KEWERS
Felix P: Phila 1 Feb 70
M'KEWIN
Isaac P: Pa 12 Ja 58
M'KIBBEN
James L: Cumberland Co,
   see CAMPBELL, Francis

M'KICHAM/M'KICHAN
 George   P: Chester Co 9 Ag
  59.   T: Lomington 4 Nov
  72
M'KILLUP/M'KILLEP/M'KELLOP/
 M"KILLOP
 Archibald   P: near New Castle
  3 Ja 60
 Gilbert   P: Phila 28 Ap 68
 Henry   P: Pa 13 Ja 63
 Hugh   P: Phila 4 Feb 68
 James   P: Hunterdon 28 Oct
  62
 Randel   P: Phila 3 Sep 61,
  25 Ap 71
M'KIM/M'KIMM
 Sarah   New Jersey 31 Ja 76
 Thomas   P: Wilmington 12 Ja
  58
 William   P: Pa 2 Feb 64
M'KINBY
 John   P: Phila 27 Ja 73
MACKINGTON
 Philip   P: Phila 27 Ja 73
M'KINLA
 Mr.   P: Phila 1 Nov 70
M'KINLEY/M'KINLAY/M'KINLY;
  see also M'GINLEY
 Dr.   P: New Castle Co 9 Ag
  59
 Daniel   P: Phila-Gaz. 3 Ja
  76
 Hugh   P: Phila-Gaz. 3 Ja 76
 John   P: Pa 13 Ja 63, 13 Oct
  63; Pa 26 Jy 64 (Dr), 30
  Oct 76; Wilmington 12 Ja
  58 & 26 Jy 64 (Dr), 21 Dec
  58 (Esq), 2 Feb 64
 Robert   P: Pa 31 Dec 61
 William   P: Phila 26 Jy 64,
  3 Ja 65
M'KINNIE/M'KINNY
 Ewill   P: Phila 13 Oct 63
 John   P: Phila 25 Jy 65,
  28 Ap 68, 3 Ja 76
 Kattirn   P: Phila 9 Ag 59
 Matthew   Phila 24 Jy 76
M'KINNON
 Daniel   P: Charles Co 31 Jy
  60
M'KINSLEY
 Dr. William   T: 7 May 67
M'KINSTRY
 John   P: Phila 31 Dec 61
M'KIRGAN
 Daniel   P: N. Castle Co 31
  Dec 61; Pa 12 Feb 61;
  Upper Dublin 31 Dec 61 (2)
M'KISSACK
 John, schoolmaster   L: York
  Co 19 Dec 71
M'KITRICH/MICKTRICK/MAC-
 ITRICK
 John   P: Northampton 13 May
  56, 18 Ag 57; Pa 13 Ja 63

M'KNIGHT
 Elizabeth   P: Phila 8 Jy 62
 George   P: Pa 19 May 63;
  Phila 7 Ap 57, 13 Oct 63,
  26 Jy 64, 3 Ja 65, 16 Jy
  67
 John   P: Phila 1 Nov 53
 Mary   P: Lancaster Co 9 Ag
  59; Rapho Twp 21 Dec 58
 Michael   P: N. Castle Co 31
  Dec 61
M'KNIVE
 Mr.   Phila 5 Jy 76-Gaz. 24 Jy
M'KNOWN
 John   P: Lancaster Co 24 Feb
  63
M'KNOWNS
 Robert   P: Phila-Gaz. 3 Ja 76
MACKON
 Mr.   P: Phila 3 Ag 58
M'KONKY
 Andrew   P: Chester Co 28 Oct
  62
M'KONNE
 James   P: Freehold 9 Ag 59
M"KOSKY
 John   P: New-Castle 3 Ja 60
M'KOUN/M'COWN/M'KOWIN/MIKOWAN;
  see also M'GOWAN
 James   L: 13 Jn 65.   P:
  Chester Co 3 Sep 61; Octo-
  rara 18 Ag 57.   T: Pea-
  pack 17 Oct 54
 Richard   P: Pa 2 Feb 64
 Samuel   P: Charles Town 12
  Ja 58
M'KLUSKEY
 Patrick   C: New London 30 Oct
  66
M'KUIM
 Robert   P: Phila 18 Ag 57
M'LANE; see also M'CLEAN, M'LEAN
 Alexander   P: Bucks Co 16 Jy
  67
 Daniel   P: Allens-Town 3 Ag
  58
 John   P: Phila 27 Ja 73
M'LAREN
 Robert   P: Phila 25 Ap 71
M'LAUGHLEY
 James or Daniel   L: at the
  Head of Opekin, Frederick
  Co., Virginia 25 Dec 66
M'LAUGHLIN; see also M'GLAUGH-
 LIN
 Alexander   P: Phila 3 May 70
 Edward   C: West Fallowfield
  30 Oct 66
 Charles   P: Phila 30 Ja 66
 Cornelius   P: Pa 2 Feb 64
 David   P: Phila 21 Dec 58
 Edward   P: Phila 19 May 63
 James   P: Bucks Co 3 Ag 58;
  Pa 26 Jy 64; Phila 3 Ja 65,
  3 May 70

Neal   P: Pa 31 Dec 61
Nicholas   P: Phila 20 Ap 69
M'LEA
  John   P: New-Castle Co 9 Ag
  59
M'LEAMIN
  Hugh   P: Phila 20 Oct 68
M'LEAN; see also M'CLEAN,M'-
  LANE
  Alex.   P: Phila 20 Jy 69
  Andrew   L: c/o Robert Thomp-
  son Lancaster Co 19 Dec 71
  Betsey   P: Phila 5 Jy 80-
  Gaz. 19 Jy
  Hugh   P: Phila 3 Ja 65
  Capt. Robert   P: Phila 28 Ap
  68 (& Capt)
M'LEARY
  George   T: Maidenhead 1 Sep
  68
M'LELAND
  Thomas   P: Lancaster Co 31
  Dec 61
M'LELLON
  Widow   P: Cumberland Co 2
  Feb 64
MACKLEMAR
  Nathaniel   P: Phila 24 Oct
  54
M'LEOD/M'LOUD/M'LOAD
  Capt.   P: in the army 3 Ag 58,
  21 Dec 58
  Colin   P: Phila-Gaz. 3 Ja 76
  Isabel   P: Pa 3 Ja 60
  Norman, Corporal   P: prob.
  at Pittsburgh 15 Mar 64
  William   P: Pa 2 Feb 64
M'LEROY
  William   P: Phila 2 Ag 70
M'LETTRING
  Capt. John   P: Phila 3 Ag 58
M'LEUIR
  David   P: Phila 2 May 65
MACLEWE
  Latice   P: Cecil Co 31 Dec 61
M'LIESH/M'CLIESCH
  John   P: Pa 19 May 63; Yellow
  Springs 1 Nov 70
M'LINAN
  Daniel   P: Phila 18 Mar 62
M'LONE
  John   P: Phila-Gaz. 27 Oct 73
M'LOUEN
  Robert   P: New-Castle 21 Dec
  58
M'LOWRY
  William   P: Phila 3 Ja 65
M'LYLE
  Alexander   P: Phila Co 3 Sep
  61
M'MACKEN
  James   P: Phila 26 Jy 64, 3
  Ja 65
M'MAHON/M'MAGHAN/M'MAHAN/M'-

MAHEN
  Constantine   P: Phila 5 Ag
  62, 28 Oct 62
  Daniel   P: Pa 28 Oct 62
  Hannah   P: Pa 13 Oct 63;
  Phila 10 Oct 65
  James   P: Phila 25 Jy 65
  John   L: Paxton 19 Dec 71
  Timothy   P: Phila 26 Jy 64
M'MALAN
  Margaret   P: Phila 8 Jy 62
M'MANN/M'MAN
  James   C: Orange Co., North
  Carolina 30 Oct 66
  Susanna   P: Phila 18 Mar 62
M'MANUN
  Cane   P: Phila 31 Jy 60
M'MANUS
  Daniel   P: Phila 1 Jy 56
  Patrick   P: Phila 1 Jy 56
M'MARTIN/M'MARTINE
  Robert   P: Phila 26 Jy 64,
  3 Ja 65
M'MASTER/M'MASTERS
  Gilbert   P: Conestogoe 9 Ag
  59
  Ja.   L: 14 May 72; Lancaster
  Co 19 Dec 71
  James   P: Upper Maxfield 23
  Oct 66
  Jane   P: Phila 12 Ja 58
  Robert   P: Nottingham 9 Ag
  59, 3 Ja 60
  William   P: Nottingham 3 Ja
  60; Phila 24 Oct 54, 3 Ja
  65
M'MATHE
  Daniel   C: Youghlan 22 Ja 67
M'MATHEL
  Andrew   P: Pa 1 Jy 56
M'MAYBER
  James   L: 11 Ap 65
M'MAVER
  Alexander   P: Phila 27 Ja 73
M'MECHAN/M'MEAKEN/M'MEKEN/M'-
  MEAKING
  Andrew   P: Blue Mountains 31
  Dec 61; Phila 28 Nov 54
  James   P: near Newcastle 24
  Oct 54, 21 Dec 58 (Esq);
  Phila 28 Ap 68
M'MEEN
  William   P: Sasquehannah 12
  Ja 58
MACKMELLON
  Robert   P: Phila 19 Ja 69
M'MENOMY
  John   P: Phila 21 Dec 58
M'MICHAEL
  Alexander   P: Phila 27 Oct 73,
  3 Ja 76
  Archibald   P: Pa 3 Ja 60
  John   P: Pa 19 May 63, 4 Ag
  63; Phila 27 Ja 73
  Robert   P: Pa 18 Mar 62

M'MICKEN/M'MICHEN
  Andrew P: near Phila 2 Feb
    64; Phila 26 Jy 64
  James P: Pa 19 May 63, 4
    Ag 63, 2 Feb 64
  William P: Carlisle 28 Oct
    62; near Christeen; Chris-
    teen 5 Ag 62 (Dr)
M'MICKONING
  Andrew P: Phila 3 Sep 61
M'MILLAN
  Duncan P: Phila 24 Feb 63,
    25 Jy 65
  E. P: Phila 13 Oct 63
  Iver P: Pa 13 Oct 63
  James P: Fogs Manor 12 Ja
    58, 3 Ja 60; New-Castle Co
    3 Sep 61
  John P: York Co 18 Mar 62
  William P: Little Britain
    21 Dec 58
M'MILLEANS
  John P: Phila 31 Jy 60
M'MIN/M'MINN
  Casber P: Pa 13 Oct 63
  Esther P: Pa 18 Mar 62
  John P: Ashton Twp 7 Ap
    57; Chester Co 18 Mar 62
  Robert P: Chester Co 28
    Nov 54, 12 Ja 58, 9 Ag 59;
    Marlborough 13 Ja 63; Pa
    3 Ja 60, 12 Feb 61
M'MITCHELL
  James C: c/o John M'MICKEL
    Providence 22 Ja 67
  John P: Pa 2 Feb 64
M'MOHAN
  Timothy P: Phila 3 Ja 65
M'MOKEN
  Andrew P: East New Jersey
    12 Feb 61
M'MONAGLE/M'MONIGILL/M'MUNA-
GLE
  James L: Cumberland Co 19
    Dec 71
  William P: 21 Dec 58 (sol-
    dier); Pequea 2 Feb 64
M'MORDY
  Rev. R. P: Marsh Creek 2
    Feb 64
M'MORLAN
  John P: New-Castle Co 9
    Ag 59
M'MULLAN/M'MULLEN/M'MULLON
  Mr. N: White-clay Creek /?/
    12 Feb 67
  Alcom P: Phila-Gaz. 3 Ja 76
  Charles P: Rock Creek 12 Ja
    58; York 24 Oct 54
  Christian P: Phila 27 Ja 73
  David P: Phila 13 Ja 63
  Dennis P: Phila 5 Feb 54
  Eph. P: Pa 2 Feb 64
  Hugh P: York Co 13 Oct 63
  James C: 30 Jy 77. L: Lower

    Ferry 2 Mar 74. P: Bucks
    Co-Gaz. 27 Oct 73; Duck-
    Creek 31 Dec 61, 18 Mar
    62; Phila 25 Ap 71 (sol-
    dier); Sasquehanna 30 Ap
    77
  John P: Chester Co 28 Oct
    62; near Derby 24 Oct 54;
    Pa 13 Ja 63
  Margaret P: Phila 26 Jy 64
  Neal P: Pa 13 Ja 63
  Oliver P: Phila 24 Feb 63
  Patrick P: Phila-Gaz. 3
    Ja 76
  Robert P: Darby 7 Ap 57,
    12 Ja 58, 31 Jy 60
  Thomas P: Hanover Twp 24
    Oct 54
  W. P: Little Britain 31
    Dec 61
  William P: Fogs Manor 3
    Ja 60; Pa 24 Feb 63;
    Phila 31 Mar 63
M'MULLAR
  Ja. L: York Co 31 Ja 71
M'MUN
  John P: New-Castle Co 9
    Ag 59
  Robert N: 29 Nov 64
M'MURPHY
  James P: Huntington 3 Sep
    61; York Co 13 Oct 63
M'MURTRIE
  William Phila 5 Oct 76-
    Gaz. 30 Oct
M'MYNE
  Dr. P: in the army 12 Ja
    58
M'NABB/M'NAB
  Agnes P: Chester Co 18 Ag
    57
  Ann P: Chester Co 31 Jy 60
  Archibald P: Phila 7 Ap 57
  John P: West Caln 7 Ap 57,
    12 Ja 58
  Richard P: Phila 16 Jy 72
M'NAIL
  Alexander P: New-Castle
    Co 9 Ag 59
  Capt. John P: Fort Cum-
    berland 8 Jy 62
M'NAIR
  Archibald P: Pa 31 Dec
    61; York Co 12 Ja 58, 31
    Jy 60
  Robert P: Bucks Co 18 Mar
    62
MACNALLY
  ... P: Phila 5 Ag 56
M'NAMARA/M'NEMARA
  Capt. Mich. P: Phila 22
    Nov 53
  George 30 Oct 76, 30 Ap
    77
  Ketty P: Pa 3 Ja 60

M'NAMEE
   Ann   P: Northampton Co 26
      Oct 69
M'NAPPER
   James   L: Little-Britain,
      Lancaster Co 19 Dec 71
M'NAREY/M'NARY
   Francis   P: Phila 13 May 56
   Richard   P: Phila 1 Nov 70
M'NARGHTAN
   Malcom   P: Pa 12 Feb 61
M'NAUGHT
   James   C: c/o William Max-
      well Nottingham 22 Ja
      67.   L: York Co 14 May 72.
      P: Cumberland Co 1 Nov 53;
      Pa 2 Feb 64
M'NEAL/M'NEIL/M'NIELL/M'NEALE/
   M'NIEL; see also M'NAIL
   and TALBERT   P: Phila-Gaz.
      27 Oct 73
   Dr.   P: Newcastle Co 18 Ag
      57
   Anthony   P: Abington-Gaz.
      27 Oct 73
   Archibald   P: Cumberland Co
      26 Jy 64; Phila 31 Jy 60
   Daniel   P: Phila 31 Dec 61
   Elizabeth   P: Phila 3 Ja 65.
      T: Trenton Ferry 17 Oct 54
   Hackler   C: near Doe Run 30
      Oct 66
   Hecter   P: Pa 26 Jy 64; Phila
      1 Feb 70
   Henry   P: Phila 26 Jy 64, 10
      Oct 65, 30 Ja 66
   James   P: Bristol 9 Ag 59;
      Pa 12 Ja 58; Phila 24 Oct
      54, 26 Jy 64, 3 Ja 65, 2 May
      65, 27 Oct 73
   John   P: Pa 26 Jy 64; Phila
      3 Ja 65, 20 Oct 68
   Malcom   P: Phila 1 Feb 70
   Neil   P: New-Castle 5 Ag 56
   Rachel   P: Pa 18 Mar 62
   Richard   P: Phila 3 Ja 60,
      18 Mar 62, 8 Jy 62
   Samuel   P: Chester Co 3 Ja 60;
      Londonderry Twp, Pa 31 Dec 61
M'NEAR
   John, tailor   L: 14 May 72
   Margaret   P: Cumberland Co 18
      Mar 62
M'NEELY/M'NEILLY/M'NELLEY
   Alexander   P: Phila 19 Ja 69
   David   P: Chester Co 24 Feb 63
   Robert   P: Bucks Co 31 Dec 61;
      Phila 30 Ja 66
M'NEWCH
   Patrick   P: Phila 28 Ap 68
M'NISH
   Samuel   P: Pa 13 Ja 63
MACNOICEL
   William   P: Kensington 2 Ag 70

M'NUTT
   John   L: Cornwall 19 Dec 71.
      P: Pa 8 Jy 62; Phila 30
      Ja 66
   Joseph   P: Lancaster Co 12
      Ja 58
   Thomas   P: Phila 30 Ja 66
M'PEAKE
   John   P: near Flushing 9 Ag
      59
M'PHALL
   Dennis   P: Pa 12 Feb 61
M'PHEE
   John   P: Phila 16 Jy 67
M'PHERSON/M'FERSON/M'FARSON/
   M'PHEARSON
   Capt.   P: Phila 25 Jy 65
   Alexander, soldier   P: prob.
      in Pittsburgh 15 Mar 64;
      in Upper Octorara 30 Oct
      66
   Arthur, of the 42d Regt.   P:
      Phila 23 Oct 66
   Daniel, Sergt.   P: in the
      army 21 Dec 58; Phila 5 Ag
      56; Phila or New-Castle
      7 Ap 57
   Donald   P: Phila 30 Ja 66
   Frederick   L: Lancaster Co
      29 Jy 72
   John   P: Chester Co 31 Jy
      60; Phila 12 Feb 61, 25 Jy
      65; William & Mary Parish
      18 Mar 62 (Rev.)
   Margaret, in the army   P: prob.
      at Pittsburgh 15 Mar 64
   Richard   P: Chester Co 13
      Oct 63
   Robert   L: York Co 19 Dec 71
      & 2 Mar 74 (Esq.).   P:
      Chester Co 1 Nov 53; near
      Phila 4 Ag 63; near Wil-
      mington 11 Sep 55
   William   L: Cumberland Co
      14 May 72.   P: Phila 3 Ja
      65
M'PHILLEMY/M'PHELIMAN/M'PHILL-
   IMY
   Hugh   P: Phila 26 Oct 69, 2
      Ag 70, 3 Ja 76
MACPLACK
   Richard   P: Gloucester Co 11
      Sep 55
MACPRIDE
   James   P: Pa 18 Mar 62
M'QUATTERS
   Betty   Cross-Roads 1 May 76
M'QUAID/M'QUEAD/M'QUID
   Arthur   P: Earl Town 12 Ja 58
   Henry   P: Chester Co 18 Mar
      62; Phila 25 Jy 65, 26 Oct
      69
M'QEAN
   Patrick   P: Chester Co 13 Oct
      63

M'QUILKIN
  Neal   P: Newcastle Co 12 Ja
    58
M'QUOWN/M'QUON
  James   P: Pa 20 Oct 68
  Rebecca   P: Phila 26 Oct 69
M'ROY
  John   P: Pa 19 May 63
  Mary   P: Salem 2 Sep 62
M'ROYALL
  Charles   P: Brandywine 15
    Mar 64
M'SEIMMEN /or M'SESMMEN?7
  Thomas   P: near N. Castle 18
    Feb 55
M'SHANE
  Francis   T: Union Iron-Works
    6 Dec 64
M'SHANNON
  Charles   P: Phila-Gaz. 3 Ja
    76
M'SHERRY
  Barnabas   L: York Co 29 Jy
    72
  Patrick   P: Conewaga 1 Feb 70;
    Lancaster Co 12 Feb 61, 24
    Feb 63; Phila 30 Ja 66, 27
    Oct 73
M'SLOAN
  Felix   P: Phila-Gaz. 3 Ja 76
M'SPARRAN/M'SPARRON
  Archibald   P: Phila-Gaz. 3 Ja
    76
  James   P: Forks of Delaware
    3 Ag 58; Pa 12 Feb 61
M'STRAVOGE
  Henry   P: Phila 25 Ap 71
M'SWEEN
  Hugh, soldier   P: prob. in
    Pittsburgh 15 Mar 64
M'TAGGART/M'TAGERT
  Archibald   P: Phila 3 Ja 65,
    1 May 76
M'TEAR
  Ro.   L: 3 Oct 65
M'TYRE
  Henry   P: New-Castle Co 9 Ag
    59
M'VAUGH
  Nancy   P: Pa 26 Jy 64; Phila
    3 Ja 65
  William   P: Phila 1 Feb 70
M'VAUGHTAN
  Donald   P: Phila 24 Oct 69
M'VEIGH
  Mat.   P: Phila 3 Ag 58
M'VICAR/M'VICKER/M'VICEAR
  Archibald   P: Phila 2 Feb 64
  Duncan   P: Phila 26 Jy 64
  John   P: Pa 26 Jy 64
M'VINSEE
  Mary   P: Phila 31 Dec 61
M'WHINEY
  John   P: Phila-Gaz. 3 Ja 76
M'WHISTER

  David   P: Pa 13 Ja 63
M'WHORTER
  Hugh   N: New Castle c/o
    Robert Morrison 4 Dec 66,
    12 Feb 67
  John   P: Bucks Co 2 Feb 64;
    Phila 3 Ja 65
M'WHORTON
  John   P: Pa 26 Jy 64
M'WILLIAM/M'WILLIAMS
  Abraham   L: Lancaster Co 2
    Mar 74
  David   P: Pa 24 Feb 63
  Hugh   L: Paxton 31 Ja 71
  James   P: York Co 2 Feb 64
  John   P: Phila 10 Ap 66
  Mary   P: East Nottingham 8
    Jy 62
  Patrick   P: Phila-Gaz. 3 Ja
    76
  Richard   P: Newcastle Co 18
    Ag 57, 21 Dec 58, 9 Ag 59,
    31 Jy 60, 24 Feb 63, 4 Ag
    63, 26 Jy 64
  William (soldier)   P: 21 Dec
    58; Md. 18 Mar 62
M'YAY
  William   P: Pa 19 May 63
MADDEN/MADDIN/MADING
  Elizabeth/Betsy   P: Phila 1
    Jy 56, 7 Ap 57
  James   P: Pa 31 Dec 61
  Michael   P: Phila 2 Ag 70
MADDORS
  John   P: Chester Co 9 Ag 59
MADDOX
  Alexander   P: Phila 9 Ag 59
MADEWELL
  John   P: Trenton 9 Ag 59
MAFFIS /or MAFFIE?7
  William   P: Phila 25 Jy 65
MAGA
  Margaret   P: Phila 12 Ja 58
MAGAVOCK
  James   P: Fishing Creek 18
    Ag 57
MAGAVRIK
  Jane   P: Pa 3 Ja 60
MAGAW; see also M'GAW
  David   P: Pa 28 Oct 62
  Elizabeth   P: Phila 28 Oct 62
MAGEE
  Mr.   P: Phila 28 Oct 62
  Alexander   L: c/o Mrs. Hop-
    kins near Peaquea 19 Dec
    71
  Daniel   P: Phila 25 Ap 71
  John   L: Carlisle, see BASH-
    FORD, William, Cumberland
    Co, see MORRISON, Jane.   P:
    Phila 4 Ag 63, 27 Ja 73
  Capt. Nathaniel   P: Phila 7
    Ap 57
  Patt.   L: c/o Geo. Stakes
    Little York 19 Dec 71

Thomas   P: Phila 21 Dec 58,
  20 Ap 69
William   P: N.J. 4 Ag 63
MAGG
  Jacob   P: Phila 28 Nov 54
MAGHAN
  /Illeg.7....h P: Pa 24 Feb
  63
MAGHLIN
  William   P: Octerara 4 Ag
  63
MAGILARD
  -   T: Monmouth Co 3 Oct 65
MAGILL, see M'GILL
MAGILT
  Charles   P: Conegocheague
  3 Ja 60
MAGNET
  John   P: Phila 10 Ap 66
MAGNIET
  Daniel   P: Phila 16 Jy 67
MAGOR
  Alexander   P: Phila Co 12
  Ja 58
MAGORMAN
  David   P: Newcastle Co 7
  Ap 57
MAGOWN; see also M'GOWAN
  Mighail   L: 11 Ap 65
MAGREY
  William   P: Phila 20 Ap 69
MAGUFUG
  Joseph   P: N. Castle 2 Feb
  64
MAHAFFY
  Samuel   P: Phila 21 Jy 68
MAHANY
  Jeremiah   P: Phila 25 Ap 71
  Timothy   P: Pa 31 Dec 61
MAHER
  Matthew   P: Phila 2 Sep 62
MAHON
  John   P: Phila 23 Oct 66
MAHONEY/MAHONY
  Elizabeth   P: Phila 18 Mar
  62
  Francis   P: Phila 8 Jy 62,
  25 Ap 71
  James   P: Phila 21 Jy 68
  Timothy   Phila 31 Ja 76
  William   P: Phila 20 Ap 69
MAIN
  William   P: Fogs Manor 1 Nov
  53
MAINGESNEER
  John   P: Phila 3 Ag 58
MAINT
  James   P: Phila 3 Ja 65
MAIR
  Henry   P: Pa 3 Ja 60
  Walter   L: York Co 29 Jy 72.
  P: Providence 1 Jy 56
MAIRNS
  John   P: N.J. 15 Mar 64
MAISE

John   P: Phila 1 Feb 70
  Samuel   P: Lancaster 18 Ag 57
MAISLIN
  Samuel   P: Phila-Gaz. 3 Ja 76
MAITLAND
  Capt. Richard   P: Phila 31 Jy
  60
MAIZE AND MILLER
  P: Phila-Gaz. 3 Ja 76
MAJOR
  Alexander   P: Phila (Co) 18
  Mar 62, 2 May 65, 16 Jy 72,
  North Wales 3 Ja 65, 1 Feb
  70
  James   P: Phila 31 Dec 61;
  Tarten Twp 8 Jy 62; Trenton
  Twp 31 Dec 61
MALCOLM/MALCOM
  Rev. A.   P: Queen Ann's Co
  3 Sep 61
  Alexander   P: East New Jer-
  sey 12 Feb 61 (Rev.);
  Phila 30 Ja 66, 10 Ap 66
  Donald   P: Phila 20 Oct 68,
  20 Ap 69
  John   P: Phila 1 Feb 70, 27
  Ja 73; near Christiana 27
  Ag 77 (Esq.)
  Robert   P: Phila 3 Ja 65,
  23 Oct 66
MALIN
  Gidian/Gideon   P: Upper
  Providence 5 Ag 56, 12
  Ja 58
MALKATTON
  Alexander   P: Pa 2 Feb 64
MALLEY
  John   P: Chester Co 18 Ag 57
MALLISON
  Thomas Obee   P: Phila-Gaz.
  3 Ja 76
MALLORIE
  Walter   P: Durham 25 Ap 71
MALLOT
  John   P: Phila 18 Mar 62
MALOBY
  Thomas   P: Phila 24 Feb 63
MALONE/MALOONE
  James   P: Phila 18 Mar 62,
  5 Ag 62
  Patrick   P: Phila 30 May 54
MALONY
  Robert   P: Newcastle Co 18
  Mar 62
MALOW
  Patrick   P: Chester Co 13 Oct
  63
MALPASS
  Thomas, soldier 18th Regt.
  P: Phila 1 Nov 70
MALYBAY
  Thomas   P: Phila 9 Ag 59
MANCHESTER
  John   P: Phila 25 Jy 65
MANDERSON

Adam   P: Phila-Gaz. 3 Ja 76
MANDESLEY
   Ann   P: Phila 4 Ag 63
MANFORD
   James   P: Pa 12 Ja 58
MANICH
   Daniel   L: Leacock Twp 19
      Dec 71
MANIE
   James   P: Phila 5 Ag 56
MANIX
   James   P: Pa 13 Oct 63
MANLOVE
   George   P: Kent Co 4 Ag
      63
MANN/MAN
   Adam   P: New-Castle Co
      9 Ag 59; Whiteclay
      Creek 3 Ja 60
   Fergus/Fourgass   P: North-
      ampton Co 27 Oct 73;
      Phila 27 Ja 73
   George   Phila 31 Ja 76
   Henry   P: Phila 3 Ja 60
   Margaret   P: Lon. Gr. 24
      Oct 54
   Susanna   P: Phila 25 Ap 71;
      Wilmington 8 Jy 62
   William/Wm.   P: Lon. Gr. 24
      Oct 54.   W: c/o James
      Glenn, merchant, Christ-
      iana Bridge 3 Jy 76
MANNIN
   Edmund   P: Phila /?/ 19 Ja
      69
MANNING/MANING
   Daniel   P: Phila 2 Feb 64
   John   P: Phila 18 Mar 62
   William   P: Phila 30 Ja 66
MANOE
   William   P: Phila 1 Nov 70
MANSFIELD
   David   P: Phila 19 Jy 80
   William   P: Pa 3 Ag 58
MANSIR
   John   P: Charles-Town 12 Ja
      58
MANSON
   James   P: Phila 1 Nov 70
   Nathaniel, sergeant   P: prob.
      at Pittsburgh 15 Mar 64
MANY
   Francis   P: Phila 9 Ag 59
MANYATTY
   Mrs.   P: Phila 10 Ap 66
MANZANO
   Toref   Phila 16 Jy 77
MAQUIRE
   Edmund   P: Pa 31 Jy 60
MALRACH
   Solomon   P: Phila 25 Jy 65
MARBURG
   Johan Casper   P: Phila 5 Ag
      56
MARBURGER

Caspar   P: Phila 3 Ag 58
MARBURRY
   Dr.   P: Phila 5 Jy 80-Gaz.
      19 Jy
MARCHAL
   John   P: Brandywine 4 Ag 63
   Robert   P: Phila 3 Ja 65
MARCILLOT
   Peter   P: Coopers-Town 5 Ag
      56
MARCKT
   Goodfrey   P: Phila-Gaz. 27
      Oct 73
MARDIN
   Mary   P: Phila 1 Nov 53
MARE
   Mar.   L: 3 Oct 65
MARGERUM/MARJORUM
   Edward   P: Pa 3 Ag 58
   Henry   P: 8 Jy 62; Wakefield
      9 Ag 59, 3 Ja 60
MARGREEN
   John   P: Phila 18 Mar 62
MARHAR
   Mr.   P: Phila 26 Jy 64
MARIS
   Ann   P: Springfield 30 Ja 66
MARKS
   Elizabeth   P: Phila 2 Ag 70
   James   P: Hunterdon Co 20 Ap
      69
   John   P: Phila 31 Jy 60
   Joseph   P: Phila 1 Feb 70
   Michael   P: 11 Sep 55
MARL
   John   P: Phila 5 Ag 62
   Thomas   P: Phila-Gaz. 3 Ja 76
MARLEY
   John   P: Phila 2 Feb 64
MARNY
   William   P: Phila-Gaz. 3 Ja
      76
MARO
   Robert   P: Lancaster Co 18 Mar
      62
MARR
   Andrew   P: Pa 3 Ja 60
MARRIN/MARIN/MARREN
   David   P: Phila 28 Nov 54
   John   P: Pa 18 Mar 62
   William   N: 29 Nov 64
MARRIOT/MARRIOTT
   Henry, corporal   P: Phila 23
      Oct 66
   Thomas   P: Pa 12 Feb 61;
      Phila 3 Ja 60
MARRITT
   Ephraim   T: Kingston 17 Oct
      54
MARSDEN
   Humphrey   P: Phila 21 Dec 58
   Capt. William   P: Phila 6 Jy
      58
MARSH
   Mr.   P: Pa 13 Oct 63

Ann   P: Phila 2 Ag 70
J.   P: Chester Co 31 Jy 60
Capt. James   P: Phila 28 Ap
  68
John   P: Chester Co 9 Ag 59
Joseph   P: Phila 27 Ja 73
Waltson   P: 9 May 54
MARSHALL
  ....   P: West Nottingham 13
  May 56
Mrs.   P: Phila 20 Jy 69
Widow   P: Nottingham 3 Ja 60
Benjamin   P: Phila 21 Dec 58,
  30 Oct 76
Christopher   P: Phila 3 Ag 58
David   P: Duck Creek 1 Jy 56
Eliz.   P: Phila 16 Jy 72
Geo.   P: Lancaster Co 31 Dec
  61
Gilbert   P: Albermarle Co
  23 Oct 66
James   L: see DRENNAN, Hugh,
  25 Dec 66. N: White-clay
  Creek 2 Feb 67.   P: Bradford
  Twp 3 Sep 61; Lancaster Co
  31 Dec 61
John   P: Lancaster Co 18 Mar
  62; Marcus-Hook 3 Sep 61,
  2 Feb 64; Phila 18 Mar 62,
  27 Ja 73, 30 Ap 77
Jos.   P: Phila 3 Ja 60
Margaret   P: Phila 3 May 70
Moses   P: Phila-Gaz. 27 Oct 73
Rachel   P: Chester Co 9 Ag 59
Thomas   P: Phila 22 Nov 53,
  30 May 54, 30 Ap 77 (Dr.)
Walter   Phila 1 May 76
Capt. W.   P: Phila 4 Ag 63
William   P: Chester Co 4 Ag 63,
  15 Mar 64; Pa 12 Feb 61;
  Phila 12 Ja 58, 3 Ag 58, 13
  Ja 63 & 26 Jy 64 (Capt)
MARSTON
  John Susanna   P: at Phila 16
  Jy 77
MARTELL
  Thomas   P: Phila 30 May 54
MARTHER
  John   P: Pa 2 Feb 64
MARTIN
  and SMYLEY, Messers Snow
  Hill 30 Oct 76
  Mr.   P: Phila 25 Jy 65
  Rev.   P: Newtown 3 Ag 58
  Agnes   N: 29 Nov 64
  Andrew   P: Phila 31 Mar 63
  Ann/Anne   P: Chestnut Level
  3 Ag 58; Pa 18 Ag 57
  Dr. C.F.   P: Phila 24 Feb
  63
  David   T: Trenton 17 Oct 54
  (Esq.).   P: Phila 7 Ap 57
  Elizabeth   P: Phila 28 Oct
  62
  Esther   P: Cooper's Creek 11

Sep 55
George   P: Chester Co 18 Mar
  62, 2 Sep 62; Duck Creek 29
  Ag 54; Pa 3 Ag 58; West
  Bradford 8 Jy 62, 4 Ag 63
Hugh   P: Phila 18 Mar 62
Isaac   P: Phila 9 Ag 59, 26
  Jy 64 (Capt)
Jacob   L: Pequea 19 Dec 71
James   P: Chester Co 18 Mar
  62; Pa 3 Sep 61, 25 Jy 65,
  16 Jy 67, 16 Jy 72 (on
  board ship Lively). T:
  Hunterdon Co 17 Oct 54
John   P: Chester Co 3 Sep
  61; Mantua Creek 27 Ja 73;
  New Castle Co 15 Mar 64;
  Pa 13 Ja 63; Phila 3 Ja
  60, 18 Mar 62 (Capt), 25
  Jy 65, 30 Ja 66, 25 Ap 71,
  27 Oct 73, 24 Jy 76, 30 Oct
  76, 19 Jy 80
Jos.   P: Pa 3 Ja 60; Phila 31
  Mar 63, 2 Feb 64, 1 Nov 70
Josiah/Josias   P: Sussex on
  Delaware 24 Oct 54, 28 Ap
  68
Laughlin   P: Phila 27 Ja 73
Capt. Lynn   P: Phila 16 Jy
  72
Mary   P: Phila 4 Feb 68
Nicholas   P: Phila 10 Ap 66
Patrick   P: Duck Creek 9 Ag
  59, 3 Ja 60
Paul   P: Bucks Co 21 Dec 58,
  26 Oct 69; Phila 10 Oct 65
Peter   C: 30 Jy 77
Roger   P: Chester Co 12 Ja
  58; Pa 3 Ag 58, 2 Feb 64,
  26 Jy 64; Phila 21 Dec 58,
  9 Ag 59
Samuel   L: Paxton Twp 15 Ap
  56.   P: Cumberland Co 13 Ja
  63; Neilson's Ferry 31 Dec
  61; Phila 12 Ja 58, 5 Ag
  62, 13 Oct 63, 3 Ja 65,
  25 Jy 65, 20 Oct 68, 3 Ja
  70
Thomas   L: Leacock Town 15
  Ap 56.   P: Bucks Co 3 May
  70; Nottingham 2 Feb 64;
  Phila 13 Oct 63, 3 Ja 65,
  25 Jy 65
William   L: 11 Ap 65.   P:
  Bucks Co 7 Ap 57, 3 Ja 60;
  N.J. 13 Ja 63; Pa 2 Feb 64
  (2); Phila 30 May 54, 12
  Feb 61, 31 Dec 61, 30 Ja
  66, 28 Ap 68, 1 Feb 70
MARTLEW
  Peter   P: Phila 21 Jy 68
MARTON
  Mary   P: Phila-Gaz. 27 Oct 73
  William   P: Phila 4 Feb 68
MARVIN

William   P: Phila 30 Ja 66
MASDEN/MASDON
  Mary   P: Phila 12 Ja 58
  Wm.   P: Manor of Mor/land/
    12 Ja 58; Phila 20 Jy 69
MASE
  Jo.   L: 14 May 72
MASH
  Henry   T: Allentown 10 Ag
    58
MASON
  and DIXON   P: Phila 23 Oct
    66
  Sergt.   P: Fort Pitt 26 Jy
    64
  Abraham   P: Phila 6 Jy 58;
    3 Ag 58
  Charles   P: Phila 26 Jy 64
  Deborah   P: Phila 10 Oct 65
  George   W: near Wilmington
    27 May 77
  James   P: Phila 31 Dec 61
  John   P: Phila 27 Ja 73
  Jonathan   P: Pa 31 Mar 63
  Joseph   Phila 16 Jy 77
  Robert   P: Phila 1 Nov 53
  Russell   P: Pa 13 Oct 63
  Stephen   P: Phila 30 Ap 67,
    16 Jy 67
  Thomas   C: Darby 18 Jy 65.
    P: Pa 12 Feb 61, 31 Dec 61;
    Phila 18 Mar 62, 5 Ag 62,
    10 Ap 66
  William   P: East Marlborough
    24 Oct 54
MASSET
  Robert   Phila 30 Ap 77
MASSEY
  George   P: Phila 24 Feb 63
MASSMORE
  John   P: Phila 31 Dec 61
MASTERCHEEK
  Frederick   P: Phila 11 Jy
    54
MASTERS
  Agness   P: N.J. 13 Ja 63;
    Phila 26 Jy 64
  John   P: Phila 13 Oct 63
  Joseph   Phila 31 Ja 76
MASTERSON
  Robert   P: Phila 12 Feb 61
MASTIN/MASTON
  Mrs.   P: Bucks Co 2 Ag 70
  James   P: Phila 16 Jy 72
MATCHET
  Richard   T: Freehold 17 Oct
    54
MATER
  Hugh   Phila 5 Jy 77-Gaz. 16
    Jy
MATHALIN
  Capt. J.   P: Phila 5 Ag 62
MATHAS
  Neil   P: Phila 25 Jy 65
MATHER/MATHERS

Bartholomew   P: Phila 28 Ap
  68
Edward   P: Lancaster Co 23
  Oct 66
James   P: Chester 24 Oct 54,
  13 May 56, 7 Ap 57, 21
  Dec 58, 3 Ja 60, 18 Mar 62;
  Phila 21 Dec 58
John   P: Bucks Co 23 Oct 66;
  Carlisle 19 May 63 (Esq);
  Chester (Co) 30 May 54, 11
  Jy 54, 24 Oct 54, 12 Ja 58;
  Green-Law, N. Britain 30
  Oct 76; Pa 3 Ag 58; Pecks-
  land 28 Oct 62
Thomas   P: Bucks Co 23 Oct 66
MATHIAS/MATTHIAS
  David   P: Chester Co 28 Nov
    54
  John   P: Phila 30 Ja 66
  John Fuller   C: East Caln 18
    Jy 65
MATLACK
  Timothy   P: Phila 2 Sep 62
MATLER
  John   P: Phila 3 Ja 65
MATSON
  Jane   P: Phila 20 Ap 69
MATTHEWS/MATTHEW/MATHEWS
  Alexander   P: Pa 12 Feb 61
  Calcut   P: Phila 25 Ap 71
  Catharine   P: Lancaster Co
    1 Nov 53
  Ebenezer   P: Phila 2 Ag 70
  Elizabeth   P: Pa 31 Dec 61
  George   P: Phila 27 Ja 73
  Isaac   N: Kent Co 4 Dec 66,
    12 Feb 67.   P: Pa 2 Feb 64
  James   P: Phila 10 Ap 66
  John   P: Chester Co 13 Ja
    63; New-Castle Co 13 Oct
    63; N.J. 24 Feb 63; Pa 8
    Jy 62; Phila 26 Jy 64, 31
    Ja 76
  Mussend.   L: York Co 2 Mar 74
  Nathaniel   P: 9 May 54
  Samuel   P: Phila-Gaz. 3 Ja 76
  William   P: Phila 16 Jy 67
MATTHIE
  John   P: Pa 13 Oct 63
MATTISON
  Thomas   Olee 31 Ja 76
MAUGHAN/MAUGHIN
  Katherine   P: Phila 18 Mar 62
  Thomas   P: Newcastle Co 2 Sep
    62
  William   P: Phila 26 Jy 64
MAUGRIDGE
  William   P: Berks 29 Ag 54
MAURAKEN
  James   P: Phila 3 Ja 65
MAURICE
  Mrs.   P: Phila 2 May 65
  Theodore   P: Kent Co 3 Ag 58
MAUS

And.   P: Pa 31 Dec 61

MAW

Abey, Esq., 32d. Regt.,   P:
  Phila 25 Ap 71
Ensign Crank   P: Phila 3 Sep
  61
Edmund   P: Phila 5 Jy 80-
  Gaz. 19 Jy

MAXFIELD

Elizabeth   Phila 5 Ap 77-
  Gaz. 30 Ap
Henry   P: Phila 25 Ap 71
James   P: Phila 18 Feb 55
John   P: Phila 26 Oct 69

MAXTON

George   P: Ch. Co. 20 Jy 69;
  Yellow Springs 26 Oct 69

MAXWELL

Capt.   P: Phila 27 Ja 73
Alexander   P: Ebbet's-Town-
  Gaz. 27 Oct 73
David   P: Monmouth, N. Jersey
  20 Oct 68
George   P: Phila 2 Feb 64
James   L: Chestnut Level 20
  Ja 73.   P: New Land 18 Ag
  57; Pa 12 Feb 61, 26 Jy
  64; West Nottingham 18 Ag
  57
Jennet   P: Phila 10 Ap 66
John   P: Pa 21 Dec 58, 12 Feb
  61, 18 Mar 62; Phila 9 May
  54, 18 Feb 55, 16 Jy 72.
  T: Hunterdon Co 10 Ag 58
Jos.   L: York Co 31 Ja 71
Robert   N: c/o Rev. John
  Rogers St. George's 4 Dec
  66; Kent Co 12 Feb 67.   P:
  Phila 18 Mar 62
Solomon   W: Christiana 27 Ag
  77
William   C: Nottingham, see
  M'NAUGHT, James.   P: N.J.
  3 Ja 60; Nottingham 12 Ja
  58; Pa 31 Dec 61; Phila 21
  Dec 58 (Capt), 18 Mar 62

MAY

Mr.   P: Phila 26 Jy 64
Elizabeth   P: Schuylkill 31 Dec
  61
Richard   P: Phila 16 Jy 72
Robert   L: Hanover Twp 15 Ap
  56.   P: Fogs Manor 13 Oct
  63
Thomas   P: Phila-Gaz. 3 Ja 76

MAYBURY/MAYBURRY/MAYBERY/MAY-
  BERRY

Francis   P: Northeast 8 Jy 62
James   P: Phila 12 Feb 61
Richard   P: Newtown, Bucks Co
  25 Ap 71
Thomas   P: Phila 16 Jy 67, 30
  Ap 77

MAYDUEL

John   P: Phila 18 Feb 55

MAYDWELL

John   P: Phila 31 Jy 60

MAYES

John   P: Phila 25 Ap 71

MAYGOR

Richard   P: Cranberry 11 Sep
  55

MAYHEW

John   P: Pilesgrove 20 Jy
  69; West Jersey 24 Jy 76

MAYNADIER

Dr. Henry   Phila 5 Jy 77-Gaz.
  16 Jy
William   P: Phila 28 Ap 68

MAYNE

Joseph   P: Phila 28 Nov 54

MAYOR

James   P: Pa 3 Ag 58

MAYRATY

Hannah   P: Phila 5 Ag 62

MAYS

Charles   P: Phila 26 Oct 69
William   P: Phila 11 Sep 55

MAZINE

William   P: Phila 28 Ap 68

MEAD/MEADE

Garret   P: Phila 9 Ag 59
John   P: Phila 21 Dec 58
Patrick   P: Phila 19 Ja 69
Samuel   T: Prince Town 15 Jy
  56

MEADLEY

Jane   L: 13 Jn 65

MEADOWS

Edward   P: Phila-Gaz. 27 Oct
  73

MEAKER

Matthew   P: Phila 31 Mar 63

MEAL

Benjamin   P: Phila 16 Jy 72
Frederick   Germantown 1 May
  76

MEALLY

Elizabeth   P: Phila 27 Ja 73

MEANS

Hugh   P: New Castle Co 19 May
  63; Pa 18 Mar 62; Phila 30
  Ap 77; Wilmington 5 Ag 62
Isaac   P: Phila-Gaz. 27 Oct
  73
Jacob   L: Strabane, York Co
  19 Dec 71
Samuel   P: Phila 4 Ap 54, 30
  May 54, 11 Jy 54; Williston
  19 May 63

MEARE

William   P: Phila 3 Ag 58

MEARIS

Samuel   P: Wilmington 7 Ap 57

MEARNS

John   P: Phila 3 Sep 61

MEASE

& MILLER   P: Phila 2 May 65
Mr.   P: Phila 18 Mar 62
James   P: Phila 18 Mar 62, 26

Oct 69
Samuel P: Phila 26 Jy 64, 3
    Ja 65
William P: Pa 13 Oct 63
MEASON
Catharine P: Pa 9 Ag 59
MEATHERS
Edward L: Lancaster Co 20
    Ja 73
John P: Pa 13 Ja 63
MEAUS
Ja. L: York Co 31 Ja 71
MECOCHLAN
James P: Phila 7 Ap 57
ME COLLOK, see M'CULLOUGH
MECOM
Benjamin P: Phila 19 Ja
    69, 20 Jy 69
MECOMBS
Mary P: Phila 1 Feb 70
MEE
John P: Phila Co 18 Mar 62
Thomas P: Frankford 24 Feb
    63; Pa 4 Ag 63
MEEK
Robert P: Cecil Co 13 Oct
    63
MEGAS
Robert P: Baltimore Co 13
    Oct 63
MEGAWAN
Robert P: Phila-Gaz. 3 Ja
    76
MEGILL
John and Rowland P: Phila
    21 Jy 68
MEGOSOY
Jos. P: Phila 25 Ap 71
MEGREALE/MEGREATE
Owen P: Pa 28 Oct 62, 2
    Feb 64
MEHARIE
John P: Phila 20 Oct 68
MEIN
Andrew P: Phila 2 Ag 70
MEINZIES
James P: Phila 3 Ja 60
Thomas P: Phila 27 Ja 73
MEIR
Dr. Adolf P: Phila 19 Ja
    69
MEKERY
Daniel P: Pa 2 Feb 64
MELCHELL
John P: Phila 8 Jy 62
MELCHER
Leonard P: Phila 4 Ag 63
MELDRUM
John P: Phila 26 Oct 69
MELEBUN
James (soldier) P: Fort
    Pitt 26 Jy 64
MELLEY
John P: Chester Co 9 May 54
MELLIAND

Class. P: Phila 15 Mar 64
MELLON/MELLEN
Joshua P: Willistown 24 Jy
    76
Phelise Phila 1 May 76
Ross P: Burlington 28 Oct 62
MELLOWS
Philip P: Phila 9 Ag 59
MELOY
Hugh P: Pa 18 Mar 62
Manus P: Pa 18 Mar 62
MELVIN
Abraham C: Chester, near the
    Meeting-house 18 Jy 65
MEMAGHEN
James P: Pa 26 Jy 64
MENAL
James P: Phila 27 Ja 73
MENARY
Edward P: Bucks Co 20 Oct 68
MENDENHALL
Benjamin P: Chester Co 31 Jy
    60
MENEALY
Hugh P: Phila 26 Oct 69
MENESIE
Alexander P: Phila 1 Feb 70
MENSCH
John Nicholas P: Phila 22
    Nov 53
MEQUAID
Henry P: Chester Co 12 Feb
    61
MERANDA, see DEWITH &
MERCA
Mr. P: Phila 28 Oct 66
MERCER
Edward P: Frederick Co 15
    Mar 64
George P: Phila 10 Oct 65
Capt. Henry P: Phila 4 Ag
    63
Hugh P: Fort Morris 3 Ag 58
Ja. L: 14 May 72
James P: Pa 26 Jy 64
John P: Phila 28 Oct 62
Nicholas P: Frederick Co 15
    Mar 64
MERCHANT
John P: Bulkley 6 Jy 58;
    Phila 21 Dec 58, 19 Jy 80
Portague P: Phila 25 Ap 71
Thomas P: Phila 21 Jy 68
MEREDAY
Widow of William P: Phila
    25 Ap 71
MEREDITH/MERRIDITH
Charles P: Phila 2 Sep 62
Elizabeth P: Phila 25 Ap 71
Francis P: Kent Co 12 Ja 58
Hugh P: Phila 26 Jy 53
Jonathan P: Bucks Co 26 Oct
    69, 3 May 70; Phila 27 Ja
    73
Reese/Rice P: Chester Co 19

May 63; Phila 27 Ja 73
Thomas P: Bucks Co 26 Oct
69
William P: Bucks Co 26 Oct
69
MERGAN
Godfrey P: Chester Co 9 Ag
59
MERICA
Peter P: Phila 18 Mar 62
MERICK
Lewis P: Phila 9 Ag 59
MERION
Ezekiel P: Phila 24 Jy 76
MERONEY
Thomas P: Lancaster 19 Jy
80
MERRIOTT/MERRIOT
Sarah P: Bristol 31 Dec 61,
2 Sep 62
MERROW
John P: Phila 5 Jy 80-Gaz.
19 Jy
MERRY
Ann P: Phila 20 Oct 68
John T: Morris Co 15 Jy 56
MERRYWEATHER
Issac P: Phila 5 Ag 56
MERSHON
Aaron P: Phila 26 Oct 69
MERTON
Jane P: Pa 18 Mar 62
MESSERSMITH
Matthias Phila 24 Jy 76
METCALF/METCALFE
Richard P: Lewis-Town 31
Jy 60; Pa 9 Ag 59, 12 Feb
61
Rob., Esq. P: Lewes 12 Ja
58
MEW
William P: Marsh Creek-Gaz.
27 Oct 73
MEWHINEY
Ro. L: 3 Oct 65
MEYER
Capt. P: in the army 12 Ja 58
George E. P: York-Town 24
Feb 63
MEYLER
Stephen P: Phila 1 Feb 70
MICHAEL
David P: Moreland Twp 9 Ag
59
MICHELL
James P: Pa 3 Ja 60
Richard P: Phila 19 Ja 69
MICKELBOURK
Ludowick P: Phila 3 Ja 60
MICKER
Barbary P: Willistown 3 Ag 58
MIDDLETON/MIDLETON
Widow P: Phila 9 Ag 59
Alexander Phila 30 Ap 77
Edward P: Phila 7 Ap 57

George P: N. Jersey 4 Feb 68
Jo. L: Martick Twp 31 Ja 71
John P: Donegal 12 Ja 58,
3 Ag 58; Haddonfield 27 Ja
73, 27 Oct 73; Phila 2 Sep
62
Capt. Powell P: Phila 16 Jy
67
Rachel P: Phila 9 Ag 59
Robert P: Wilmington 28 Oct
62
William P: Octora 12 Ja 58
(2)
MIDGLEY
Robert P: Phila 1 Feb 70
MIDWINTER
Sarah P: Phila 13 May 56
MIER
Mr. Phila 30 Ap 77
MIFFLIN
John, Jr. P: Phila 3 Ag 58
Jonathan Phila 16 Jy 77
Samuel P: Jerseys 12 Ja 58
MIHER
Edward P: Phila 31 Jy 60
MILETON
Richard P: Chester Co 7 Ap
57
MIKELL
Thomas P: Phila 25 Jy 65
MILBOURN
Henry P: Phila 24 Oct 54
William P: Phila 18 Feb 55
MILES
Israel P: Merion 16 Jy 72
James P: Phila 3 May 70
Samuel P: Phila 8 Jy 62
MILIKEN
James P: Phila-Gaz. 27 Oct
73
MILLARD
Benjamin P: Pa 5 Ag 56
John P: Phila 28 Oct 68
MILLEMAN
Ann P: Chester 13 May 56
MILLEN
Edward P: Phila 21 Dec 58
MILLER/MILLAR/MILLOR; see also
MEASE & MILLER
Mr. P: Pa 13 Oct 63; Phila
3 Ag 58, 31 Dec 61
Alexander/Alex. C: Newport
18 Jy 65. L: Pequea 31 Ja
71. P: Bucks Co 15 Mar 64;
Pequea 1 Feb 70; Phila 21
Jy 68, 27 Oct 73
Andrew C: London Briton 28
Nov 65. P: Leacock 2 Feb
64; Phila 25 Ap 71
Bridget P: Phila 19 May 63
Campbell P: Newcastle Co 12
Ja 58
Catherine P: Phila 16 Jy 67
Charles P: Phila 16 Jy 72
Christian L: Lampeter Twp 15

Ap 56
David   P: Pa 31 Jy 60
Eleanor   P: Phila 20 Oct 68
Eleazer   P: Phila 8 Jy 62
Elizabeth   P: Phila 6 Jy 58,
  9 Ag 59
Francis Jacob   L: 13 Jn 65.
  N: 29 Nov 64
George   C: Upper Providence,
  Chester Co 18 Jy 65.   P:
  Germantown 19 Ja 69; Phila
  18 Mar 62, 5 Ag 62, 16 Jy
  72, 19 Jy 80; Upper Provi-
  dence 5 Ag 56, 7 Ap 57
George Adam   L: 31 Ja 71
Hannah   P: Phila 3 Sep 61
Henry   P: Germantown 19 Ja
  69; Phila 24 Feb 63, 25 Ap
  71, 27 Oct 73, 3 Ja 76
Hugh   C: Fogs Manor, see SMYTH,
  John.   P: Chester Co 9 Ag
  59, 13 Oct 63; Londonderry
  12 Ja 58
Jacob   P: Phila 4 Feb 68
James   L: near Caldwell's 15
  Ap 56; Colerain Twp 20 Ja
  73; Pequea 19 Dec 71.   P:
  Chester Co 28 Nov 54; Cobb's
  creek 8 Jy 62; Lancaster Co
  12 Feb 61; New-Garden 9 Ag
  59, 2 Feb 64; Pequea 9 Ag 59,
  13 Ja 63, 2 Feb 64; Phila 11
  Sep 55, 1 Jy 56, 31 Dec 61,
  8 Jy 62, 13 Ja 63 (Capt), 27
  Ja 73; West Jersey 21 Jy 68
Jane   P: Phila 16 Jy 72
Jean   P: Phila 19 Ja 69
John   P: Church-Hill 13 Ja 63;
  Dover 5 Ag 56; Dover Town 21
  Dec 58 (Rev.); Germantown 19
  Ja 69; Kingwood 9 Ag 59 Lan-
  caster Co 21 Dec 58; New-
  Castle Co 3 Ag 58; N.J. 18
  Mar 62; Pa 27 Dec 53, 18 Ag
  57, 21 Dec 58, 31 Dec 61, 26
  Jy 64 (Capt), 1 Nov 70; Read-
  ing 31 Jy 60, West Caln 7
  Ap 57
John Peter   P: Pa 7 Ap 57
Joseph   L: 29 Ja 67.   P:
  Phila 2 May 65 (2), 25 Jy
  65, 2 Ag 70
Judah   P: Phila 9 Ag 59
Lawrence   P: Phila 28 Nov 54
Capt. Magnus   P: Phila 5 Ag 62
Margaret   P: Phila 23 Oct 66
Mary   P: Pa 3 Ja 60; Phila 30
  Oct 76
Michael   P: Phila 30 Ap 67
Patrick   P: Phila 11 Sep 55
Peter   P: Phila 6 Jy 58, 3
  Ja 65, 30 Oct 76, 30 Ap 77
Rd.   Abington; see DONOUGH,
  John
Richard   P: Pa 13 Ja 63, 2 Feb

64; Phila 7 Ap 57, 7 Ap
  57 (or East Jersey), 12
  Ja 58, 9 Ag 59 (3), 31
  Jy 60, 12 Feb 61, 3 Sep
  61, 31 Dec 61, 31 Mar 63,
  26 Jy 64
Robert   P: Carlisle 13 Oct
  63; Chester Co 3 Sep 61;
  Phila 2 Ag 70, 1 Nov 70,
  27 Ja 73; see also MONT-
  GOMERY, John
Severn   P: Phila 7 Ap 57
Thomas   P: Bucks Co 19 Ja
  69; Chester Co 18 Mar 62;
  N.J. 31 Jy 60; Oxford,
  West Jersey 4 Feb 68
Warrick   P: Chester Co 2 Feb
  64
William   C: Veson Forge 18
  Jy 65.   L: 3 Oct 65.   P:
  19 Ja 69 soldier in the
  Royal Irish Regt.; Beth-
  lehem Twp 21 Dec 58;
  Phila 10 Ap 66, 20 Jy 69,
  19 Jy 80
MILLIGAN/MILLEGAN
James   P: Pa 18 Mar 62;
  Phila 27 Oct 73
John   P: Chester Co 13 Oct
  63; Yellow Breeches 31 Ja
  76
MILLIKEN
Brice   P: Phila 1 Nov 70
James   T: 4 Nov 72
John Cumberland Co 31 Dec
  61, 18 Mar 62
MILLIN
Capt. Sampson   P: Phila 6
  Jy 58
MILLINBOURGER
Peter   P: Phila-Gaz. 3 Ja
  76
MILLS
Alexander   P: Phila 2 Feb
  64, 10 Oct 65, 16 Jy 67
  (Capt), 1 Feb 70, 16 Jy
  72 (Capt)
Francis   P: Phila 31 Jy 60
James   L: York Co 29 Jy 72
John   P: Chester Co 26 Oct
  69; East Nottingham 13 Ja
  63; Pa 12 Feb 61, 31 Dec
  61, 18 Mar 62, 28 Oct 62;
  Phila 13 Oct 63, 3 Ja 65,
  23 Oct 66
Jonathan   P: New-Castle Co
  9 Ag 59
Matthew   T: Sussex Co 31
  Ja 71
Richard   P: Phila 19 Jy 80
Robert   P: Nottingham 12 Ja
  58
William   P: Phila 13 Oct
  63.   T: Arney's-Town 4
  Nov 72

MILNE/MILN/MILLNE
  Dr.   P: in the army 12 Ja
    58
  Alexander   P: Phila 3 May 70
  Edmund   P: Phila 12 Feb 61,
    23 Oct 66, 20 Ap 69, 2 Ag
    70
  George   P: Phila 16 Jy 67
  James   P: Phila 5 Ag 55, 31
    Dec 61, 25 Jy 65
MILNER/MILNOR/MILLNER
  Bridget   P: Phila 21 Dec 58
  Isaac   P: Phila 5 Feb 54, 31
    Jy 60
  John   P: Pa 21 Dec 58; Phila
    11 Sep 55, 31 Jy 60, 10 Oct
    65 (Rev)
  Joseph   P: Bucks Co 23 Oct 66.
    T: near Trenton Ferry 7 May
    67
  William   P: Phila 12 Ja 58
MILTON
  Ann   Phila 30 Ap 77
MILWARD
  James   P: Phila 30 Ja 66
  Samuel   P: Phila-Gaz. 3 Ja 76
MIMNAGH
  Neal   P: Phila-Gaz. 3 Ja 76
MINAUGHT
  Widow   P: Phila 13 Oct 63
MINEALL
  David   P: Pa 18 Mar 62
MINEN
  Mr.   P: Phila 20 Oct 68
MING; see also CALADAY &
  Mr.   P: Germantown 10 Oct 65
  Melchior   P: Germantown 2 May
    65
MINNION
  Margaret   P: Phila 16 Jy 67
MINOR/MINORS
  Nathan   P: Pa 9 Ag 59
  William   P: Phila 19 May 63
MINOW
  John   P: Pa 3 Ag 58
MINSHALL/MINSHAL
  Griffith   P: Wilmington 5 Feb
    54, 9 May 54, 11 Sep 55, 13
    May 56, 7 Ap 57
  Moses   P: Wilmington 30 May 54
  William   P: Phila-Gaz. 27 Oct
    73
MINTHORN
  Capt. W.   P: Phila 31 Dec 61
MIRES
  George   P: Phila 31 Mar 63
MIRICK
  George   P: Falls of Delaware
    16 Jy 72
MISKIMINE
  John   P: Pa 28 Oct 62
MISSET
  Garret   P: Phila 20 Jy 69
•MISSICO
  Ephraim   P: Somerset Co 18 Ag

    57
MITCHELL/MITCHALL
  Mrs.   P: Phila 28 Oct 62
  Mr.   P: Bucks Co 3 Ja 65;
    Phila 30 Ja 66
  Abraham   P: Phila 21 Jy 68
  Alex./Alexander   P: Notting-
    ham 4 Ap 54; Phila 18 Ag
    57, 25 Jy 65
  Andrew   P: Chester Co 12 Feb
    61, 31 Dec 61
  Da.   L: 13 Jn 65; or Jo. 25
    Dec 66
  David   L: Cumberland Co 20
    Ja 73.   P: Bucks Co 18 Mar
    62; Cumberland Co 15 Mar
    64; Hopewell 28 Oct 62
  Edward   P: Charlestown 24 Feb
    63
  Elizabeth   P: Conewa. 18 Ag
    57; Pa 31 Dec 61
  Esther   P: Lancaster Co 9 Ag
    59
  Isaac   P: Phila 30 Ja 66
  James   L: York Co 29 Jy 72.
    P: Newcastle Co 18 Ag 57
    (Capt); Phila 1 Nov 53, 3
    Ag 58 (Capt), 5 Ag 62, 3
    Ja 65
  Jane   P: Phila 3 Ag 58, 21
    Dec 58
  Jo.   L: 11 Ap 65; see also
    Da.
  John   P: Bucks 30 Ja 66;
    Lancaster Co 31 Dec 61;
    Phila 5 Ag 62, 28 Oct 62,
    13 Oct 63 (Capt), 3 Ja 65,
    25 Jy 65, 30 Ja 66, 4 Feb
    68, 19 Ja 69, 1 Feb 70
    (soldier), 3 Ja 76, 1 May
    76
  Joseph   C: 30 Jy 77.   P:
    Blockley 28 Ap 68, 20 Jy
    69; Newcastle Co 18 Mar 62;
    N.J. 18 Mar 62
  Nancy   P: Phila 3 May 70
  Randle/Randel   P: Phila 18 Ag
    57, 6 Jy 58, 3 Ag 58, 21
    Dec 58
  Richard   P: Phila 26 Jy 64
  Ro.   L: 25 Dec 66
  Robert   L: Shippensburgh 2
    Mar 74.   P: Pa 4 Ag 63;
    Phila 1 Nov 70, 3 Ja 76
  Samuel   P: Bucks Co 13 Oct
    63; Chester Co 13 Oct 63;
    Pa 18 Mar 62; Phila 13 Ja
    63; Whitemarsh 13 Ja 63.
    T: Cumberland 7 May 67
  Thomas   P: Bucks 22 Nov 53,
    30 May 54, 9 Ag 59, 2 Feb
    64, 16 Jy 67, 16 Jy 72;
    New-Castle Co 4 Ag 63; New-
    town 8 Jy 62, 5 Ag 62;
    Phila 24 Oct 54, 11 Sep 55,

19 May 63, 2 Feb 64, 26 Jy
64, 3 Ja 65 (2), 3 Ja 66;
Capt., Phila 18 Ag 57, 2
Sep 62, 28 Oct 62 (2), 4
Ag 63
William C: see MOORE,
Frostram. L: Shippens-
burg 31 Ja 71. P: Pa 26
Jy 64; Phila 13 Oct 63
(Capt), 2 Feb 64
MITCHELTREE
James P: Bucks 22 Nov 53
MIXCAU
George P: Lancaster Co 9 Ag
59
MOAKS
James P: Peqeca 27 Ja 73
MOAT
David P: Phila 20 Ap 69
MODE
Eleonar P: Phila 23 Oct 66
MOEAR/?/
Monsieur P: Phila 24 Feb 63
MOFFIT/MOFIT
David P: Phila 27 Dec 53
John P: Chester Co 3 Sep 61
William P: Phila 13 May 56
MOGAW
David P: Cumberland Co 3 Sep
61
MOIES
George P: Phila 31 Mar 63
MOLAND
_____ P: Phila 28 Nov 54
Dr. T: Bucks Co 31 Ja 71
Elizabeth P: Phila 28 Oct 62
Thomas P: Phila 23 Oct 66
William P: Phila 2 Ag 70
MOLDER/MOULDER/MOLEDER/MOLDOAR
Joseph P: Phila 21 Dec 58
Mary P: Phila 30 May 54,
3 Ja 60
Robert P: Marcus Hook 28 Nov
54, 7 Ap 57 (Capt), 12 Ja
58 (Capt), 9 Ag 59, 12 Feb
61, 2 Sep 62; Phila 12 Ja 58
Thomas P: Marcus-Hook 4 Ag 63
William P: Phila 2 May 65
MOLLEY/MOLEY
Alexander P: Phila 27 Ja 73
Patrick P: Phila 12 Ja 58
William P: Baltimore 31 Mar
63
MOLLISON/MOLISON
Mr. P: Phila 20 Ap 69
Charles P: Phila 19 Ja 69
MOLLOY
John P: Phila 3 Ja 65
MOLONNY
Catherine P: Phila 1 Nov 70
MOLSBY
John P: Wilmington 5 Ag 56
MOLYNEAUX
Frederick P: Phila 20 Jy 69
Rev. Robert P: Phila 19 Jy 80

MONCRIEFFE
Capt. Richard P: Pa 3 Ag 58
MONIES
Margaret L: Lancaster Co 20
Ja 73
MONDOCHOG
Isaac P: Phila 18 Ag 57
MONEY
Michael P: Phila 10 Oct 65
William P: Phila 24 Feb 63
MONFORT
Monsieur Phila 16 Jy 77
MONIER
John P: Phila 26 Jy 64
MONIGUELL
William P: Phila 3 Sep 61
MONK/MONKE
Charles P: Phila 3 Ag 58,
13 Ja 63 (Capt)
MONKHOUSE
Jonathan P: Pa 8 Jy 62
MONOTTO
Daniel P: Phila-Gaz. 27 Oct
73
MONRO/MONROW/MUNRO/MONROE/MUNROW
Ann P: Phila 30 May 54
Sergt. Daniel P: in the army
21 Dec 58
Donald P: Phila 23 Oct 66
George P: New-Castle 5 Feb
54, 11 Jy 54, 11 Sep 55, 3
Ag 55, 9 Ag 59, 2 Feb 64
Rev. H. P: Phila 31 Dec 61
Jane P: Phila 10 Oct 65
John L: 29 Ja 67. P: Phila
30 Ap 67, 27 Oct 73
MONTGOMERY/MOUNTGUMBRY
Dr. P: Phila 19 Jy 80
Mr. P: Lancaster 26 Jy 64
Alexander P: Christine-
Bridge 21 Dec 58, 3 Ja 60,
3 Sep 61; New-Castle Co 3
Ag 58, 13 Oct 63; Pa 12 Ja
58; Phila 3 Ag 58, 9 Ag 59,
31 Dec 61, 28 Oct 62, 2 Feb
64
Ann W: see JOHNSTON, Adam
Charles L: Rappo 31 Ja 71
Hugh Phila 16 Jy 77; York
Co 8 Jy 62
James P: Pa 12 Ja 58
Jo., carpenter L: Pequea 31
Ja 71
John L: 29 Ja 67; Esq.,
Carlisle 20 Ja 73; or
Robert MILLER, Carlisle 2
Mar 74. P: Carlisle 31 Jy
60, 2 Sep 62, 23 Oct 66;
Lancaster Co 24 Feb 63;
Makefield 3 Ja 60; New-
Castle Co 4 Ag 63 (2), 13
Oct 63, 26 Jy 64; Phila 18
Mar 62, 1 Feb 70, 27 Ja 73,
30 Oct 76
Jonathan P: Phila 16 Jy 72

Katherine   P: Bound Brook 18
  Mar 62
L.   P: Phila 30 Ja 66
Ro.   L: 25 Dec 66
Robert   P: Chester 19 Jy
  80; Lancaster Co 13 Ja
  63; Paxton 2 Sep 62, 13
  Oct 63; Pa 18 Mar 62;
  Phila 28 Nov 54; Phila Co
  28 Oct 62
Samuel   P: Pa 13 Oct 63;
  Phila 12 Feb 61, 31 Dec 61
Tho./Thomas   P: Christine
  Bridge 27 Dec 53, 4 Ap
  54, 11 Jy 54, 28 Nov 54, 11
  Sep 55, 7 Ap 57, 18 Ag
  57, 12 Ja 58, 6 Jy 58, 21
  Dec 58; New-Castle 3 Ja 60;
  Phila 10 Ap 66
William   L: Lancaster 2 Mar
  74; Little Britain 20 Ja
  73.   P: Phila 20 Oct 68
MONTIHOUSE
  Jonathan   P: Pa 18 Mar 62
MONTSEIR
  Jonathan   P: Phila 23 Oct 66
MOODY
  Alexander   P: Whiteclay Creek
    13 Oct 63
  James   P: New Yaar 21 Dec 58;
    Pa 9 Ag 59
  John   P: Phila 27 Dec 53
  Robert   P: Phila 2 Ag 70
  Thomas   P: Pa 31 Dec 61
MOON
  Ch.   P: Phila 15 Mar 64
  Francis   P: Phila 25 Jy 65
  Jacob   T: Prince-town 17 Oct
    54
  James   P: B(ucks) Co. 20 Ap
    69, 20 Jy 69; Phila 27 Ja
    73
  Nicholas   P: Brandywine 18
    Ag 57
  Robert   P: Phila 3 Ja 65
  Samuel   P: Phila-Gaz. 27 Oct
    73
MOONEY
  Kitty   P: Phila 2 May 65
  Owen   P: Germantown 20 Jy 69
MOORE/MOOR
  Capt.   P: Phila 24 Feb 63,
    25 Jy 65
  Widow   L: Pequea 15 Ap 56
  Alexander   N: near New-Castle
    c/o Margaret Olden 4 Dec
    66, 12 Feb 67.   P: near
    New-Castle 3 Ja 60; N.
    Castle Co 31 Dec 61; N.J.
    13 Oct 63.   T: Bordentown
    Dr 15 Jy 56; 10 Ag 58
  Allen   P: Phila 31 Mar 63
  Andrew   P: Lancaster Co 3 Ja
    60; Pa 8 Jy 62, 24 Feb 63,
    19 May 63

Ann   P: Phila 12 Feb 61
Arthur (soldier)   P: 21 Dec
  58
Augustine   P: Salem 12 Feb 61
Charles   P: Chester Co 1 Nov
  53, 18 Feb 55; Marple Twp
  29 Ag 54; Pa 26 Jy 64
David   L: Lancaster Co 2 Mar
  74.   P: Pa 18 Mar 62; Phila
  2 May 65; West Nottingham
  3 Ja 65
Edward   Phila 5 Ja 76-Gaz.
  31 Ja
Elizabeth   P: Pa 3 Ag 58;
  Phila 24 Oct 54, 21 Dec
  58, 27 Oct 73
Francis   P: Phila 3 Ja 60
  (Capt), 27 Ja 73, 3 Ja 76
Frank   T: Stoney-brook 17 Oct
  54
Frostram, and MITCHELL,
  William   C: c/o James
  Watson Forks of Brandywine
  18 Jy 65
George, carpenter   L: West
  Florida 20 Ja 73; White-
  clifts, on the Mississippi
  19 Dec 71.   P: Chester Co
  31 Jy 60; Phila 12 Ja 58,
  3 May 70
Henry   C: Marcus Hook 18 Jy
  65.   L: Pequea 31 Ja 71
  (schoolmaster).   P: East
  Jersey 8 Jy 62 (Esq);
  Middlesex 9 Ag 59
Howard   L: Paxton 2 Mar 74
Hugh   L: Lancaster Co 19 Dec
  71
Jacob   P: Phila 16 Jy 67
James   L: Pequea, Leacock Twp
  19 Dec 71; near Carlisle,
  see RICHEY, Adam.   P:
  Brandywine 24 Feb 63;
  Chester Co 12 Ja 58; Cross
  Roads 2 Feb 64; Fogs Manor
  13 Oct 63; London Twp 26
  Oct 69; Newcastle Co 18 Mar
  62; Pa 31 Dec 61, 2 Feb 64
  (2), 15 Mar 64; Capt., Phila
  3 Ag 58, 21 Dec 58; Phila
  30 Ja 66 (2), 3 Ja 76;
  Whitemarsh 1 Nov 53.   T:
  @ Trenton 21 Ja 55
James, Jr.   L: Forks of
  Brandywine 19 Dec 71
Jane   P: New-Castle Co 9 Ag
  59
Jo.   L: Cumberland Co 14 May
  72
John   C: N. London 18 Jy 65,
  cooper, at the Cross Roads
  30 Oct 66.   L: Cumberland
  Co 19 Dec 71.   P: Chester
  Co 13 Ja 63; Cumberland Co
  2 Feb 64; Hampsted 3 Ja 65;

Moreland 18 Mar 62; N.J.
31 Jy 60; New London 26
Jy 64; Pa 2 Sep 62, 13
Ja 63; Phila 30 May 54
(2) 28 Nov 54, 7 Ap 57,
24 Feb 63, 26 Jy 64, 3 Ja
65, 4 Feb 68, 28 Ap 68, 21
Jy 68, 24 Jy 76; Provi-
dence 24 Feb 63. T: at Mr.
Henry's 7 May 67; Trenton
1 Sep 68
Jonathan P: Phila 3 Sep 61
Joseph C: New-London 22 Ja
67. P: New London Twp 28
Nov 54
Lucretia P: N.J. 31 Jy 60
Martha P: Phila 27 Ja 73
Mary P: Mountholly 31 Dec
61; Phila 25 Jy 65, 1 Feb
70, 1 Nov 70
Michael P: Phila 24 Oct 54
Mordecai P: Bucks Co 9 Ag 59;
Newtown 21 Dec 58, 3 Ja 60
Nathaniel T: Hopewell 1 Sep
68
Nicholas P: New-Castle Co 9
Ag 59
Philip P: Phila 25 Ap 71
Rachel P: Delaware 26 Jy 64;
Phila 23 Oct 66
Richard P: Phila 23 Oct 66,
30 Ap 67
Robert N: in Christeen 4 Dec
66; Christeen Bridge 12 Feb
67. P: New-Castle Co 3 Sep
61, 8 Jy 62, 24 Feb 63; Pa
3 Ja 60; Phila 26 Jy 64, 30
Ja 66
Sampson C: East Nottingham,
Chester Co 30 Oct 68. P:
Pa 18 Mar 62
Samuel P: Pa 31 Jy 60; Phila
12 Feb 61, 13 Sep 61, 2 May
65, 2 Ag 70, 16 Jy 72; Polt's
Valley 13 Ja 63; West New Jer-
sey 18 Ag 57
Sarah P: Phila 9 Ag 59, 3 Ja 76
Stephen P: Phila 12 Feb 61
Susannah P: Phila 28 Oct 62
Tho., fuller L: near Carlisle
31 Ja 71
Thomas P: Chester Co 3 Ja 60;
Kent Co 31 Dec 61; Marcus-
Hook 5 Ag 62; Phila 1 Nov 53,
12 Ja 58, 31 Jy 60; 2 Sep 62,
10 Ap 66, 4 Feb 68, 20 Jy 69,
27 Oct 73 (Capt). T: 3 Oct
65
Thomas William P: Phila 3 May 70
Walter P: Moreland 1 Jy 56
William L: c/o William Pollock
Carlisle 19 Dec 71; c/o Francis
Leech, Lancaster Co 19 Dec 71.
P: Baltimore 31 Mar 63; Chest-
er Co 18 Mar 62; Lancaster Co

12 Ja 58, 8 Jy 62; Mill-
Creek 3 Ag 58, 21 Dec 58;
Phila 3 Ja 60 (Capt), 2 Feb
64, 10 Oct 65, 16 Jy 67,
20 Oct 68, 25 Ap 71, 3 Ja
76; Tuskeny Creek 3 Ja 60
MOOREHEAD/MOORHEAD/MOREHEAD
Joseph L: Shippensburg 29
Jy 72, 20 Ja 73. P:
Brandywine 7 Ap 57
Samuel P: Cumberland Co 24
Feb 63
William P: Phila 18 Mar 62
MOORES
George C: Phila, or TREANOR,
John, Chester 30 Jy 77
MORAN
James P: Pa 2 Feb 64
MORDAGH
Andrew P: Salem 23 Oct 66
Robert P: Pa 13 Ja 63
MORDICA
Elizabeth P: Phila 5 Ag 62
MORDON
Mattolleno P: Phila 9 Ag 59
MORDOUGH
Mat. P: Tyrone Twp 8 Jy 62
MORELAND/MORLAND
William P: N. Castle Co 24
Feb 63; Lancaster Co 13 Oct
63; Pa 18 Mar 62
MORGAMRE
John C: Christine Bridge 18
Jy 65
MORGAN/MORGAIN/MORGON/MORGANS
General P: North America 25
Ap 71
Widow T: Hopewell 17 Oct 54
Benjamin P: Phila 2 Sep 62
Cattern P: Phila 9 Ag 59
Charles P: Phila 9 Ag 59, 10
Oct 65
Daniel P: Phila 27 Ja 73
Rev. Mr. Enoch P: Welsh
Tract 25 Ap 71
George P: Phila 3 Ja 65
Jacob P: Phila 9 Ag 59, 31 Jy
60, 3 Ja 65
John P: Phila 31 Dec 61
Mary C: London Britain 18 Jy
65. P: Chester Co 26 Jy 64
Michael L: York Co 20 Ja
73. P: Phila 27 Ja 73;
Yellow Breeches 1 May 76
Morgan P: Phila 9 May 54, 11
Sep 55
Owen P: Phila 25 Jy 65
Phael P: Phila 12 Feb 61
Reese P: Lancaster Co 13 Ja
63
Samuel P: Pilesgrove 19 Ja
69
Tabitha P: Manti Creek 7 Ap
57
Thomas C: 30 Jy 77 (2)

Tobias   P: Gloucester Co 31
  Jy 60
William   P: Phila 28 Oct 62,
  26 Jy 64, 1 Nov 70
MORGUE
  Henry   P: Phila 17 Jy 80
MORIARTY/MORARTY
  James   P: Phila 15 Mar 64,
    26 Jy 64
  Sylvester   P: Phila 1 Jy 56
MORON
  Francis, hatter   P: Phila 19
    Ja 69
MORONEY
  William   P: Phila 11 Sep 55
MORRAY/MORREY
  Charles   T: Prince-town 17
    Oct 54
  Nathaniel   T: Trenton 17 Oct
    54
MORRELL/MORRIL
  Hugh   P: Phila 2 Feb 64
  John   P: Phila-Gaz. 3 Ja 76
  Nathaniel   P: Phila 11 Sep
    55
  Sarah   P: Great Valley 13 May
    56
MORRIN/MORREN
  Joseph   P: Pa 12 Feb 61
  Sarah   P: Phila 3 Sep 61, 19
    May 63
MORRIS
  Deborah   P: Phila 9 Ag 59
  Elizabeth   P: Phila 3 Ag 58,
    27 Ja 73
  Hugh   P: Phila 27 Ja 73, 27
    Oct 73, 3 Ja 76
  Jacob   P: East Jersey 31 Dec
    61
  James   P: Bucks Co 31 Jy 60;
    Phila 2 Ag 70
  John   L: York Co 29 Jy 72.
    P: Bethlehem 19 May 63; Pa
    3 Ja 60, 13 Oct 63; Phila
    9 Ag 59, 4 Feb 68, 28 Ap
    68; Reading 19 Jy 80
  Jonathan   C: East Marlborough
    28 Nov 65
  Joseph   P: Paxton 20 Jy 69;
    Phila 2 May 65
  Luke   P: Phila 29 Ag 54, 13
    May 56
  Mary   P: Phila 12 Ja 58, 8
    Jy 62
  Rachel   P: Phila 8 Jy 62
  Richard   P: Phila 9 Ag 59,
    25 Jy 65
  Robert   Haddonfield 30 Ap 77;
    Phila 6 Jy 58, 4 Ag 63, 30
    Ja 66
  Capt. Samuel   P: Phila 19 Jy
    80
  Susannah   P: Phila 30 Ja 66
  Thomas   P: Bucks 24 Oct 54;
    Chester Co 2 Feb 64; Pa 2

  Feb 64; Phila 3 Ja 65 (Esq),
    30 Ja 66, 10 Ap 66
  William   N: 29 Nov 64. P:
    Phila 12 Ja 58 (Capt),
    1 Feb 70, 30 Ap 77; Wil-
    mington 30 May 54
  William, Jr.   P: Wilmington
    9 Ag 59
MORRISON/MORISON
  Mr.   P: Phila 8 Jy 62, 28 Oct
    62
  Widow   L: Cumberland Co 29 Jy
    72
  Alexander   P: Chester Co 13 Ja
    63; New-London 26 Jy 64
  Angus   P: Phila 12 Feb 61
  Andrew   L: Conecochig 15 Ap
    56. P: Cumberland Co 13
    Oct 63
  Benjamin   P: Pa 13 Ja 63;
    Phila 31 Jy 60
  Daniel   P: Carlisle 4 Ag 63
  David   P: Chester Co 18 Ag
    57, 31 Dec 61, 2 Feb 64
  Edward   P: Pa 3 Ag 58
  Elizabeth   P: Phila 1 Feb 70
  Ephraim   C: New London 28
    Nov 65
  Rev. Evander   P: Pa 11 Sep
    55
  Francis   P: Phila 26 Jy 64
  Gabriel   P: Bucks Co 2 Feb
    64; Lancaster Co 24 Feb 63;
    Phila 3 Ja 65
  Gaunt   P: Pa 28 Oct 62
  George   P: Phila 1 Jy 56, 26
    Jy 64 (Capt), 19 Jy 80
  Hance   P: Carlisle 4 Ag 63;
    Cumberland Co 26 Jy 64
  James   C: Chestnut Level 18
    Jy 65. P: Chester Co 9
    Ag 59; Fogs Manor 3 Ag 58;
    Pa 12 Feb 61, 4 Ag 63; Sus-
    quehannah 31 Dec 61
  Jane   L: c/o John Magee-
    Cumberland Co 29 Jy 72
  Jennet   L: Cumberland Co 20
    Ja 73
  John   P: Phila 25 Ap 71, 27
    Ja 73; York Co 31 Dec 61
  Margaret   T: Quaker-Town 31
    Ja 71
  Neil   P: Chester Co 13 Ja 63
  Robert   C: c/o Rev. John
    Beard 18 Jy 65. P: New-
    Castle 28 Oct 62
  Samuel   P: Bucks Co 3 May 70
  Thomas   P: Phila 9 Ag 59
  William   N: 29 Nov 64. P:
    Chester Co 31 Jy 60; Peach
    Bottom 31 Dec 61; Pa 12 Feb
    61; Phila 21 Dec 58, 3 May
    70, 27 Ja 73; Susquehannah
    28 Oct 62, 2 Feb 64
MORROW/MORROWS

Arthur P: Phila 25 Jy 65
Charles P: Chester Co 13 Oct
  63; York-Town 1 Nov 53
Francis P: Phila-Gaz. 27
  Oct 73
George P: Newcastle 24 Oct
  54
James P: Newcastle 24 Oct
  54; Pa 3 Ja 60, 13 Oct 63;
  Phila 25 Jy 65, 10 Oct 65
John P: Jersey 26 Oct 69
Joseph P: Phila 13 Ja 63,
  24 Feb 63. T: Prince-
  town 17 Oct 54, 15 Jy 56
Luke P: Phila 26 Jy 64
Samuel P: Chester Co 28 Oct
  62; Pa 2 Sep 62
William P: Phila 25 Jy 65
MORSE/MORS
  John P: Phila 21 Jy 68, 30
    Ap 77
MOSCHELL/MOSCHEL/MUSCHELL
  Frederick P: Phila 31 Jy 60
  George P: Phila 24 Oct 54,
    18 Feb 55
  Geo. Frederick P: Phila 11
    Jy 54
MORTON/MORETON
  Capt. P: Phila 2 Feb 64
  Andrew P: Phila 30 May 54,
    9 Ag 59
  David P: East Jersey 8 Jy
    62
  Capt. Edmond/Edmund P: Phila
    30 Ap 67, 28 Ap 68
  Edward L: 25 Dec 66, 29 Ja
    77. P: Phila 8 Jy 62 (Capt)
  George P: Phila 12 Feb 61
  Jacob P: near Christeen 8 Jy
    62
  James L: 29 Ja 67. P:
    Chester Co 5 Ag 56; Phila
    18 Mar 62, 26 Jy 64, 2 May
    65, 4 Feb 68
  John P: Pa 18 Mar 62; Phila
    12 Feb 61, 28 Oct 62, 1 Feb
    70, 31 Ja 76
  Magnus P: Pa 26 Jy 64
  R. P: Phila 26 Oct 69
  Robert P: Pa 18 Mar 62
  Samuel C: 30 Jy 77. P:
    Amer 5 Ag 56; Phila 1 Feb
    70
  Thomas P: Phila 8 Jy 62,
    (Capt), 13 Ja 63 (Capt),
    1 May 76
  William P: Pa 2 Sep 62; Phila
    7 Nov 53 (Capt), 18 Ag 57
  William Henry P: Phila 21 Dec
    58
MORVIS
  Margaret P: Chester Co 12 Ja
    58
MOSER
  Jacob C: 30 Jy 77

MOSES
  .... P: Phila 11 Sep 55
  Benjamin P: Phila 1 Jy 56
  David P: Phila 1 Nov 53
  George P: Christian Sound
    3 Ja 66
  Mortica P: Phila 29 Ag 54
  Rachel P: Phila 1 Nov 70
  Thomas P: Phila Co 19 Ja 69
MOSS
  John P: Phila 2 Ag 70
  Joseph C: near Miller's
    Mill, London Grove 30 Oct
    66
  Michael P: Phila 28 Ap 68
MOSSMAN
  Archibald P: Phila 3 Sep 61,
    3 Ja 65
MOTLEY/MOTTLEY/MOTTELY
  John P: Phila 5 Jy 80-Gaz.
    19 Jy
  Pat./Patrick P: Phila 26 Jy
    64, 3 Ja 65
  William P: Phila 26 Oct 69,
    1 Nov 70, 27 Ja 73
MOTS
  John P: Phila 19 Ja 69
MOUATT
  James P: Oxford 5 Jy 80-Gaz.
    19 Jy
MOULDER, see MOLDER
MOULSDALE
  Robert P: Phila 20 Jy 69
MOUNT
  Alexander N: 29 Nov 64
  James P: Pa 12 Feb 61, 26
    Jy 64
  Matthias T: Middletown 15
    Jy 56
MOUNTEER
  Susanna Phila 30 Oct 76
MOUSE
  Frederick P: Phila 26 Jy 64
MOUSON
  Robert P: New-Castle Co 3 Ag
    58, 21 Dec 58
MOUTTON
  Capt. Edward P: Phila 23 Oct
    66
MOWLAN
  Thomas, soldier P: Phila 1
    Feb 70
MOYCE/MOYES
  John P: Phila 5 Ag 62
  Richard P: Phila 10 Ap 66
MOYLE
  Mary P: Phila 13 Oct 63
MOYNAHAN
  Andrew P: Phila-Gaz. 3 Ja 76
MUBBIT
  Joseph P: Phila 10 Ap 66
MUCKELWAIN
  William P: Phila 3 Ja 65
MUCKLE
  Archibald P: Pa 21 Dec 58

Capt. Samuel P: in the army
21 Dec 58
MUCKLEDATH
John N: 29 Nov 64
MUFFAN
Thomas P: Phila 3 Sep 61
MUHLENBERG
Rev. H. P: Germantown 31
Jy 60
Hen. P: Providence Twp 1
Nov 53
MUIR/MUER
& CRAWFORD P: Phila 8 Jy 62,
5 Ag 62, 19 May 63
Alexander P: Pa 9 Ag 59,
3 Ja 60
James P: Pa 5 Ag 62
Thomas P: Phila 28 Oct 62
MUIRHEAD/MUREHEAD
James C: East Nottingham
18 Jy 65. P: Chester Co 13
Ja 63
MULAND
John P: Pequea 3 Sep 61
MULDRAGH
Hugh P: Newcastle Co 7 Ap 57
MULFORD
Thomas P: Phila 24 Feb 63
(Capt), 27 Ja 73
MULHERAN
James P: Milltown 9 Ag 59;
Pa 8 Jy 62
MULHOLLAND/MULHOLLAN/MOLHOLLAND/
MULHOLAN/MULLHOLLEN
Arthur P: Jersey 26 Oct 69
Barnard P: Pa 28 Oct 62
Daniel P: Phila 2 Ag 70
James P: Phila 3 Ag 58, 18
Mar 62
John P: Pa 12 Feb 61
MULL
Martin Phila 24 Jy 76
MULLALLY
William P: Phila 12 Feb 61
MULLCADY
Robert P: Phila 1 Nov 53
MULLEN/MOLON/MULLON/MOLLON/
MULLAN
Alexandon London Britain,
Chester Co 23 Oct 66
Charles P: Phila-Gaz. 27
Oct 73
George P: Phila 26 Jy 64
James P: Phila 28 Ap 68
Jane P: Hanover Twp 18 Mar
62
John P: Phila 10 Ap 66
Jos./Joseph P: Phila 2 Feb
64, 10 Ap 66
Mary P: Willis Town 12 Ja
58
Robert Phila 16 Jy 77
Thomas P: Phila 6 Jy 58,
3 Ag 58, 21 Dec 58, 3 Ja
60, 13 Ja 63, 4 Feb 68, 28

Ap 68, 3 Ja 76
William P: Pa 13 Oct 63
MULLER
John Peter P: Pa 22 Nov 53
MULLHOLD
Barnard P: Phila 13 Ja 63
MULLIGAN/MULLIGHAN/MOLLIGAN/
MULLICAN
George P: Octerara 15 Mar
64
Isaac P: Pa 26 Jy 64 (2)
John P: Bucks Co 15 Mar 64,
26 Jy 64; Pa 18 Mar 62, 2
Feb 64, 15 Mar 64
Joseph L: Middle Octorara 15
Ap 56
Richard P: Lancaster Co 12
Ja 58
MULLINAY
Richard P: Phila 5 Feb 54
MULLINS/MULLENS
Mr. P: Phila 12 Feb 61
James P: Phila 30 Ap 67
MULLYDOU
Mary P: Phila 9 Ag 59
MULOCK
James P: Haddonfield 2 Sep
62
MULONE
James P: Phila 3 May 70
MULVENNAN
Charles P: Pa 3 Ja 60
MULWEE
William P: Pa 13 Ja 63
MUNN/MUN
John P: New-Castle Co 9 Ag
59
Neil P: in the army 12 Ja 58
Pollard P: Phila 12 Ja 58
William P: Phila 3 Ag 58
MUNDLE
James P: Phila 27 Ja 73
MUNRO/MUNROW, see MONRO
MURATT
Gasper P: Phila 21 Jy 68
MURCHEE
Daniel P: Pa 26 Jy 64
MURCHLAND
John C: East Nottingham 22
Ja 67
MURDEY
Isabella P: Phila 10 Ap 66
MURDOCK/MURDOCH/MURDAGH/MURDAH
Andrew P: Phila 10 Oct 65,
30 Ja 66; Salem 12 Feb 61
Ann Phila 1 May 76, 30 Oct
76
Ebenezer P: Kensington 1 Feb
70
George P: Phila 26 Jy 64
James L: surgeon's mate to
the Royal Highland Regt. 25
Dec 66. P: Wilmington 2 Sep
62
Jo. L: Carlisle 31 Ja 71

Patrick P: Phila-Gaz. 3 Ja 76
William P: Salem 3 Ag 58
MURGATROYD
  John P: Phila 27 Ja 73
  Thomas P: Phila 25 Jy 65
MURIATE
  Hugh P: Phila 2 May 65
MURLAND
  John P: Pequea 18 Mar 62,
    13 Ja 63
MURPHEW
  Laurence C: c/o Rev. John
    Finley East Nottingham /?/
    22 Ja 67
MURPHY/MURPHEY/MORPHEY
  Mr. Phila 31 Ja 76
  Andrew P: Phila 6 Sep 53
  Ann P: Phila 30 Ja 66
  Archibald P: New-Castle Co
    3 Sep 61
  Daniel Phila 5 Ja 76-Gaz.
    31 Ja
  Edward P: Mount-Holly-Gaz.
    3 Ja 76; Phila 19 Ja 69
  Gilbert P: Phila 25 Ap 71
  James P: Oxford 28 Nov 54;
    Pa 3 Ag 58; Phila 10 Ap 66
  John N: near Red Lion 12 Feb
    67. P: Bucks Co 13 Oct 63,
    10 Oct 65; Gloucester Co 26
    Jy 64; Haddonfield 26 Oct
    69; N. Castle Co 26 Jy 64;
    Pa 3 Ja 60; Phila 31 Mar 63,
    28 Ap 68, 1 Nov 70, 27 Oct
    73, 16 Jy 77
  Luke P: Phila 31 Jy 60
  Mary P: Phila 24 Oct 54
  Maurice P: Phila 3 Ja 65, 23
    Oct 66, 4 Feb 68
  Michael P: Phila 20 Oct 68
  Neel P: Pa 24 Feb 63
  Nicholas P: Phila 29 Ag 54
  Philip P: Pa 3 Ag 58
  Samuel P: Phila-Gaz. 3 Ja 76
  Dr. Thady P: Phila 12 Ja 58
  Thomas P: Phila 31 Dec 61, 28
    Oct 62, 27 Ja 73, 27 Oct 73
  William P: New-Castle 1 Jy 56;
    Phila 30 Jy 60
MURPRATT
  Thomas P: Kent Co 9 Ag 59
MURRA
  Alexander L: Shearman's Valley
    14 May 72
MURRAY/MURREY/MURRY/MURRIE
  ... P: New Castle 27 Dec 53
  Capt. P: Phila 18 Mar 62
  Mrs. P: Phila 21 Dec 58
  Mr. P: Phila 19 May 63, 25
    Jy 65
  Rev. (Mr.) Reading P: 21 Jy
    68, 19 Ja 69, 1 Feb 70
  Widow P: Phila 3 Ja 65
  Rev. Alexander P: Pa 19 May
    63; Reading 27 Ja 73

Anne P: Lancaster Co 3 Ag 58
Anthony P: Berks Co 30 Ap 67
Capt. Duncan P: Phila 8 Jy
  62
Francis P: Gloucester 31 Dec
  61; Phila 19 Jy 80
Henry P: Phila 31 Dec 61
James P: Bucks Co 30 Ap 67;
  Lancaster Co 9 Ag 59; Phila
  18 Feb 55, 3 Ag 58, 12 Feb
  61
John L: 29 Ja 67. P: Pa 13
  Oct 63; Phila 11 Sep 55, 8
  Jy 62, 23 Oct 66, 3 Ja 76;
  Capt., Phila 24 Oct 54, 28
  Nov 54, 3 Sep 61, 31 Dec 61,
  28 Oct 62, 13 Ja 63, 19 May
  63, 26 Jy 64, 19 Ja 69
John Harding P: Phila 2 May
  65
Lindly P: Phila 5 Ag 62
Mary T: Somerset Co 31 Ja 71
Neill Westmoreland 1 May 76
Thomas P: Nottingham 3 Ja 60
William L: 29 Ja 67 (Capt).
  P:21 Dec 58 (soldier); Bucks
  Co 3 Jy 60, 24 Feb 63, 19
  May 63; Lancaster Co 18 Ag
  57; Neshaminy 3 Ja 60; Pa
  26 Jy 64; Phila 1 Nov 53,
  31 Mar 63
MURRIAL
  Hugh P: Phila 3 Ja 65
MURPIN
  William P: Phila 29 Ag 54
MUSEMICK
  William P: Phila 3 Ja 65
MUSGERN
  Robert P: Phila 9 Ag 59
MUSGROVE
  Mrs. T: near Prince-Town 10
    Ag 58
  William P: Phila 27 Dec 53
MUSKEY
  Daniel P: Cumberland Co 3
    Ag 58
MUSTARD
  William C: sadler at London-
    grove 28 Nov 65
MUTHERAN
  Mary P: Phila 1 Nov 70
MYER
  Ad. L: 11 Ap 65
  Susanna L: near York Town 29
    ' Jy 72
MYERS
  Ann/Anne P: Phila 13 Ja 63,
    31 Mar 63
  Joseph P: Phila 31 Jy 60, 12
    Feb 61
MYNCE
  William P: Phila 30 Ap 67
MYNGASNER
  John P: Phila 1 Jy 56

NABLE
  Lydia T: Maidenhead 6 Dec 64
NAILE
  Robert P: Phila 21 Jy 68
NANNA
  Abraham P: Phila 31 Dec 61
NANNER
  Dianah P: Lewis Town 18 Ag
  57
NANTICOOK
  William (Chief of the Kanea-
  way Nation)-Phila 24 Jy 76
NAP
  Mr. P: Phila 15 Mar 64
NAPIER
  James P: New Castle 27 Dec
  53
NARES
  Ephraim Cumberland Co 30 Oct
  76
NARRY
  John P: Phila 31 Dec 61
NAYLOR/NAILOR/NEALOR
  Francis P: 21 Dec 58 (sol-
  dier); Sasquehannah 12 Ja
  58
  John P: Sasquehannah 12 Ja
  58
  Ralph P: Pa 19 May 63, 4 Ag
  63
  Thomas P: Phila-Gaz. 3 Ja 76
NAPLETON, see WORKMAN &
NASH
  Edward P: Phila 26 Jy 64
  Patrick P: Phila 12 Ja 58
NA/?/ZUM
  Thomas P: Phila 10 Oct 65
NEADHAM
  John P: Phila 4 Ag 63
NEAL/NEILL/NEIL/NEALE/NIEL; see
  also NAIL
  Mr. P: Phila-Gaz. 27 Oct 73
  Andrew P: N. Castle 18 Mar 62
  Ann P: Pa 31 Dec 61
  Arthur P: Phila 30 Ja 66
  Geo. P: Lancaster Co 12 Ja 58
  Henry P: Phila 28 Oct 62
  Rev. Hugh P: Dover 21 Dec 58
  James L: Lancaster Co 20 Ja
  73. P: Phila 1 Jy 56, 13 Ja
  63
  John P: Chester Co 24 Feb 63;
  N. Castle 18 Mar 62; Pa 3
  Ja 60, 13 Ja 63
  Mary P: Wapping Twp 31 Jy 60
  Neal P: Lancaster Co 3 Sep 61
  Patrick P: Pa 3 Ja 60. T:
  Trenton 4 Nov 72
  Philip P: Phila 13 Ja 63, 24
  Feb 63
  Sarah P: Phila 3 Ja 76, 24 Jy
  76
  Thomas L: Lancaster Co 29 Jy
  72
  William P: N. Castle Co 2 Feb

64; Shippeys Town 4 Ag 63
NEALEN
  James T: Reckless-Town 4
  Nov 72
NEALSON; see also NEILSON
  Robert P: Nottingham 21 Dec
  58, 9 Ag 59
NEAR
  Edward L: at Smith's Forge
  14 May 72
NEARY
  Peter Phila 31 Ja 76
NEBLET
  Henry P: Phila-Gaz. 27 Oct
  73
NEELY
  John P: Wilmington 24 Feb 63
NEEPER
  Joseph P: Pa 13 Ja 63
NEES
  Jane P: Phila 28 Oct 62
NEGLEY/NEGLIE
  Jacob P: Germantown 10 Ap
  66, 23 Oct 66
NEIDE
  Jacob P: Phila-Gaz. 3 Ja 76
NEIDHAM
  Elizabeth P: Phila 25 Jy 65
NEILSON
  Alexander P: Phila 15 Mar 64
  James L: 29 Ja 67. P: N.J.
  13 Ja 63; Pa 15 Mar 64
  Samuel P: Phila 5 Ag 56
  William P: Phila 30 Ja 66,
  3 Ja 76
NEIMAN
  Emanuel P: Pennsylvania 20
  Oct 68
  Zacharias P: Phila 12 Feb 61
NEISSER
  Augustine P: Phila 3 Ag 58
NELL
  Martin P: Pa 12 Feb 61
NELMES/NELMIS/NELRES
  Capt. Thomas P: Phila 18 Mar
  62, 2 Feb 64, 31 Jy 60
NELMS
  Benjamin P: Phila 13 Oct 63
NELSON/NELLSON
  Capt. P: Pa 21 Dec 58
  Mr. P: Phila 28 Oct 62
  Alexander P: Phila 28 Ap 68
  Ant. P: Phila 15 Mar 64
  Duncan P: Pa 3 Ja 60; Phila
  9 Ag 59
  Eleanor P: Potts-Grove 25
  Ap 71
  Elizabeth P: Chester Co 1 Jy
  56
  Rev. G. P: Phila 2 Sep 62
  George P: Phila 19 Ja 69
  Hugh P: Phila 16 Jy 67, 20
  Ap 69, 3 Ja 76
  James P: Abington 1 Nov 70;
  Donegall 2 Feb 64; Lan-

caster Co 3 Ag 58, 4 Ag 63;
Manor of Moreland 30 Ja 66
(2), 28 Oct 69; Phila 3 Sep
61, 27 Ja 73
John   P: Bucks Co 13 Oct 63;
Phila 18 Feb 55, 3 Sep 61,
3 Ja 76
Jonathan   P: Delaware 28 Oct
62; Mount Bethel 27 Ja 73;
Pa 13 Oct 63; Phila 3 Ja 65
Mary   P: Phila 9 May 54, 9 Ag
59, 5 Ag 62
Samuel   P: Phila 9 Ag 59, 3
Ja 60, 8 Jy 62, 13 Ja 63,
10 Oct 65, 10 Ap 66 (Capt).
T: Kingston 17 Oct 54
W.   P: Pa 31 Dec 61
William   P: Bucks Co 26 Oct
69; Phila 15 Mar 64; York-
Town 9 Ag 59
NEMAN
George   P: Phila 4 Feb 68
NEPEN
John   P: Phila 3 Ja 65
NEPHEW
James   T: Somerset Co 31 Ja
71
NERGHT
Petrus   P: Phila 5 Ag 56
NERSELY
John   P: Lancaster 19 Jy
80
NESBITT/NISBETT/NISBITT
Albert   P: Phila 4 Ag 63
Catern   P: Donegall 3 Ja 60
David   C: near the Brick
meeting 28 Nov 65.   P:
Bucks Co 31 Dec 61, 25 Ap
71; Wright's Town 18 Mar 62
James   P: Phila 3 Ag 58, 25
Jy 65
John   C: c/o Hugh Kilpatrick
Chester Co 28 Nov 65.   P:
Carlisle 13 Oct 63; Cum-
berland Co 7 Ap 57; Onion's
Ironworks 9 Ag 59
Joseph   P: Nottingham 13 Oct
63
Katherine   P: Donegall 9 Ag
59
Kirlar   P: Phila 9 Ag 59
Tho.   P: Back Creek 12 Ja 58
William   P: New Castle Co 15
Mar 64
NESMITH
John   P: Phila 20 Ap 69
Robert   P: Phila 20 Ap 69
NETT
Joseph   P: Phila 2 Feb 64
NEVILL/NEVELL
Esther   P: Phila 3 Ja 65, 30
Ap 67
James   L: Cumberland Co 14 May
72
Thomas   P: Phila 15 Mar 64,

16 Jy 67
NEVIN
Moses   P: Phila 2 Sep 62
NEVITT
Thomas   P: Pa 5 Ag 56
NEWBOLD
Capt. John   P: Lewes Town 18
Feb 55
NEWBOROUGH
Joshua   P: Wilmington 18 Ag
57
NEWBURN
Thomas   Phila 31 Ja 76
NEWCOMB/NEWSCOMB
Silas/Sylas   P: Cumberland
Co 28 Oct 62; West-Jersey
31 Dec 61
NEWELL/NEWEL
Dr.   P: Allenstown 30 Ja 66
Elizabeth   P: Phila 23 Oct 66,
16 Jy 67
Hugh   P: Phila 28 Nov 54, 4
Feb 68, 26 Oct 69
James   P: Allenstown 2 Ag 70;
Phila 20 Oct 68.   T: near
Allen's Town 15 Jy 56
Robert   P: Phila 28 Nov 54
NEWFORME
Capt. Thomas   P: Phila 12 Feb
61
NEWLAN/NEWLAND/NEWLEN
Ensign Edmund   P: in the army
21 Dec 58
John   P: Phila 9 Ag 59
William   P: Phila 20 Ap 69
NEWMAN
George   P: Phila 13 Oct 63
John   P: Phila 9 Ag 59
Paine   Phila 24 Jy 76
Samuel   P: Phila 18 Mar 62
William   P: Phila 27 Ja 73
NEWMARCH
Henry   P: Phila 9 Ag 59, 3
Ja 60
NEWMARSH
Joseph   P: New-Castle 3 Ja 60
NEWPHY
John   P: Phila 15 Mar 64
NEWPORT
Richard   P: Kensington 1 Nov
70; Phila 10 Ap 66
Stephen   P: Phila 21 Jy 68,
20 Oct 68
NEWSTON
John   P: Phila 2 Ag 70
NEWTON/NEWTOWN
Ambrose   P: Phila 21 Dec 58
Christopher   P: Phila 30 May
54
Dounham   P: Phila 31 Dec 61,
3 Ja 65
Elizabeth   P: N.J. 3 May 70;
Pa 3 Ja 60
Isaac   P: Cape May 18 Mar 62
Jean   P: Phila 11 Sep 55

Pat.   P: Pa 15 Mar 64
Robert   P: Pa 31 Dec 61
Thomas   P: Phila-Gaz. 27 Oct
  73
William   P: Bucks Co-Gaz. 27
  Oct 73
NEWVILLE
Edward   P: Phila 3 Ja 60
NIBBS
Septimus   Phila 31 Ja 76
NIBLOCK/NIBLOG
William   C: 28 Nov 65. P:
  Phila 30 Ja 66
NICALL
Ellenor Ellizt   P: Phila 9
  Ag 59
NICE
George   P: near Phila 25 Ap
  71
John   P: Germantown Road 28
  Ap 68
NICHELL
Maurice   P: Phila 3 Ja 60
NICHOLAS/NICHOLIS
Richard   P: Phila Co 18 Ag
  57
William   P: Jerseys 9 Ag 59;
  Pa 3 Ja 60; Phila 28 Oct
  62
NICHOLLS/NICHOLL/NICHOLS/NICOLS/
  NICKOLS/NICKOLLS/NICOLLS
Charles   P: Phila 1 Nov 53
Edward   P: Pa 28 Oct 62, 13 Ja
  63; Phila 4 Ag 63
George   L: York Co 14 May 72
James   P: Charles-town 12 Ja 58
John   L: Lancaster Co 20 Ja
  73, 2 Mar 74. T: Phila 3
  Sep 61 (Capt)
Mary   P: Center 12 Ja 58
Philip   P: Phila-Gaz. 3 Ja 76
William   P: N.J. 3 May 70;
  Phila 25 Jy 65
NICHOLSON/NICKELSON/NICOLSON/
  NICKLESON
Mrs.   P: Phila 12 Ja 58
Ann   P: Phila 10 Ap 66
Archibald/Arch   P: Pa 31 Dec
  61; Phila 18 Mar 62, 2 May
  65, 28 Ap 68
Cornelius   P: Phila 18 Feb 55
Edward   P: Phila 15 Mar 64
George   P: Pa 12 Feb 61; Phila
  9 Ag 59, 18 Mar 62, 10 Oct
  65
James   C: 30 Jy 77
John   P: Blockley 9 May 54;
  Phila 30 Ap 67
Margaret   P: Phila 25 Jy 65
Mary   P: Phila 27 Ja 73
Richard   L: Carlisle 2 Mar 74
Richen   P: Pa 13 Oct 63
Robert   P: New Jersey 3 May 70;
  Phila 18 Mar 62
Sarah   P: Blockley 30 Ja 66;

Phila 2 Ag 70
Thomas   P: Phila 27 Ja 73
William   P: New Jersey 3 May
  70; Phila 3 Ag 58, 18 Mar
  62
NICK
Mary   P: Phila 9 Ag 59
NICKELLS/NICKELL
James   P: Pa 31 Jy 60; Phila
  3 Ja 65
John   P: Great Valley 31 Jy
  60
NICKINSON
John   P: Blockley 11 Sep 55,
  9 Ag 59
Sarah   P: Phila 18 Mar 62
NICOLA
Lewis   P: Allen-town-Gaz. 27
  Oct 73; Phila 30 Ap 67
  (Major)
NIGHEL
Edmond   P: Phila 16 Jy 67
NIGHT
Charles   Phila 1 May 76
NIHILL/NIHELL
Edmund   P: Phila 21 Dec 58,
  13 Ja 63, 20 Ap 69; &
  Morris, Phila 12 Feb 61;
  Laurence &, Phila 12 Feb 61
Edward   P: Phila 28 Nov 54
Maurice   P: Phila 31 Jy 60,
  19 May 63
NIKIRRIS
William   P: Phila 30 Ja 66
NILL
Samuel   P: Lancaster Co 9 Ag
  59; Pa 3 Ja 60
NILSON
Hugh   P: Phila 13 Ja 63
James   P: Phila 12 Feb 61
Jonathan   P: Forks of Dela-
  ware 3 Ja 60
NIMMAN/NIMMON
George   P: Abington 2 Feb 64;
  Pa 15 Mar 64
NINIAN
David   P: Pa 31 Dec 61
NIPE
Mr.   P: Nottingham 3 Sep 61
NIVIN/NEVEN
John   P: Bucks Co 30 Ja 66;
  Chester Co 11 Sep 55; Pa
  31 Dec 61; Phila 18 Mar 62,
  28 Ap 68
NIXON
Andrew   P: Phila-Gaz. 3 Ja 76
John   P: Phila 3 Ag 58
Joseph   P: Pa 19 May 63
Pat./Patt   P: E. New Jersey
  12 Ja 58; N.J. 3 May 70
Sidney   P: Bethlehem 30 Ja 66
Stephen   L: Lancaster Co 2
  Mar 74; Pequea 31 Ja 71
Thomas   P: Pa 31 Dec 61; Phila
  24 Feb 63, 15 Mar 64

NOAR
  Michael   P: West New Jersey 18
    Ag 57
NOBILEAU
  Charles   P: Phila 20 Jy 69
NOBLE
  George   P: Phila 2 Ag 70
  James   C: East Nottingham,
    Chester Co 30 Oct 66
  Joseph   P: Phila 21 Jy 68
  Lydia   T: Maidenhead 15 Mar
    64
  Margaret   P: Phila 25 Ap 71,
    27 Ja 73
NOBLIT/NOBLETT/NOBLET
  Richard   P: Chester Co 24 Oct
    54, 9 Ag 59
  William   P: Chester Co 5 Feb
    54, 31 Jy 60
NOCHER/NOCKER
  John   P: Phila 12 Feb 61, 3
    Ja 65
NOCO
  Henry   P: Phila 16 Jy 67
NOLAN/NOALAN
  John   P: Phila 3 Ja 76
  Nicholas   P: Phila 27 Oct 73
NOON
  Thomas   P: Lancaster 18 Ag 57
NORBURY
  Joseph   P: Cape-May 21 Dec 58
NORCALL
  James   P: Whitemarsh 18 Mar 62
NORD
  Capt. Edward   P: Phila 28 Oct
    62
NORE
  Mr.   P: Phila 25 Ap 71
NORGROVE
  Nathaniel   Phila 1 May 76
NORIE/NORREY
  Peter   P: Phila 26 Oct 69, 3
    Ja 76
  Robert   P: Phila 3 Ja 76
NORRINGTON
  Thomas   P: Phila 2 Sep 62
NORRIS
  Mrs.   P: Phila 5 Ag 62
  Mr.   P: Bristol 19 May 63
  Garret   P: Phila 3 Sep 61, 4
    Ag 63
  George   T: Prince-town 17
    Oct 54
  Henry   L: Dill's Town 2 Mar
    74
  James   P: Phila-Gaz. 3 Ja 76,
    1 May 76
  Robert   P: Phila 1 Feb 70
  Thomas   P: Bristol 4 Ag 63,
    13 Oct 63, 2 Feb 64, 15 Mar
    64; Phila 13 Ja 63, 27 Ja 73.
    T: Prince-town 17 Oct 54
NORTH
  Capt.   P: Phila 7 Ap 57
  Elizabeth   C: 6 Jy 77-Gaz. 30

  Jy
  Hen. James   P: Pa 12 Feb 61
  John   P: Phila 12 Ja 58
  Rev. Mr. Joseph   P: Phila 27
    Ja 73
  Roger   P: Phila 1 Feb 70;
    Providence (Twp) 1 Nov 53,
    2 Feb 64
  William   P: Phila-Gaz. 3 Ja
    76
NORTHEY
  Ebenezer   P: Pa 9 May 54
NORTON
  Dr.   T: Trenton 4 Nov 72
NORWOOD
  Benjamin   P: Phila 12 Ja 58
  John   P: Phila 3 Ja 65
NOTT
  John   P: Phila 3 Ja 60
NOWLAND
  Peter   Phila 31 Ja 76, 30 Oct
    76
NOWLS
  Rachel   P: Phila 21 Jy 68
NOYES
  Thomas   P: Phila 26 Oct 69
NUGENT/NEWGENT
  Lawrence   P: Phila 13 Ja 63
  Patrick   L: Juniata 20 Ja 73.
    P: Head of Bohe 7 Ap 57
NULLS
  Mr.   P: Phila-Gaz. 3 Ja 76
NUNER
  Daniel   P: Lewis Town 1 Feb
    70
NUNESS
  Anthony   N: in Cecil Co 29
    Nov 64
NUNEY
  Daniel   P: Pa 31 Jy 60
NUNN
  William   P: Phila 30 Ja 66
NUNNS/NUNS
  Joseph   P: Phila 3 Ja 65
  Capt. Thomas   P: Phila 27
    Ja 73
NUNRY
  Diana   P: Lewes-Town 3 Ag 58
NUSUM/NUZUM
  Andrew   P: Fort Bedford-Gaz.
    27 Oct 73
  Thomas   P: Phila 23 Oct 66,
    16 Jy 67 (Capt); Providence
    27 Oct 73
NUTT
  John   P: Middle Octorara 9 Ag
    59
NUTTER
  Simon   P: Phila-Gaz. 3 Ja 76
NUTTLE
  Samuel   P: Phila 13 Ja 63

OAKFORD
  Aaron   P: Phila 15 Mar 64

Isaac P: Glass-house 26 Oct
  69
OAKMAN/OACKMAN
  Henry P: Phila 25 Ap 71,
    31 Ja 76
  Isaac P: one of the print-
    ing offices, Phila-Gaz.
    27 Oct 73
OAKLEY
  John P: Bethlehem-Gaz. 27
    Oct 73
OARMS
  Dr. Samuel P: Phila 3 Ag 58
O'ARROM
  James P: Phila 25 Jy 65
OBERLING
  John Francis P: Bethlehem
    30 Ap 67
O'BRIAN/O'BRIEN/O'BRYAN
  Christopher P: Pa 18 Ag 57;
    13 Oct 63
  Edward P: Phila 19 Ja 69
  Joel P: Chester Co 26 Oct 69
  John P: Phila 1 May 76
  Margaret P: Bucks Co 3 Ag 58;
    Pa 31 Dec 61; Phila 24 Feb
    63
  Mary T: Bordentown 15 Jy 56;
    Trenton 6 Dec 64, 3 Oct 65
  Mortogh/Morthough P: Phila
    2 Ag 70, 27 Oct 73
  Rosanna P: Phila 1 Feb 70
  Timothy P: Phila 26 Oct 69
  Will./William P: officer of
    the customs at Lewes Town
    2 Ag 70; Phila 24 Oct 69
O'BRIANT
  Daniel P: Phila 2 May 65
  John P: Phila 20 Ap 69
O'CAIN/O'CANE
  Pady P: Phila 1 Nov 70
  Thomas P: 15 Miles from Lan-
    caster 28 Ap 68
O'CALLANS
  Dennis P: Phila 1 Feb 70
OCKMEY
  James P: Phila 25 Ap 71
O'CONAN
  Patrick P: Phila 16 Jy 72
O'CONEL
  Isabel L: 13 Jn 65
O'CONNER/O'CONNOR
  Dennis P: Phila Co 12 Ja 58
  Johannah T: at Benjamin
    Stout's-Hunterdon Co 31 Ja
    71
  Michael P: near Phila 24 Oct
    54
O'CORRIREN
  Philip P: Darby 27 Ja 73
OCQUENEUR
  Anne P: Phila 16 Jy 72
O'DAINE
  John P: Phila 25 Jy 65
O'DANIEL

Hugh P: Phila-Gaz. 27 Oct 73
O'DEA
  John P: Phila 20 Ap 69, 20
    Jy 69
ODEAR
  Neil P: Pa 13 Oct 63
ODENELY
  Cornelius P: Bradford 4 Ag
    63
ODENHAMER
  John P: Phila 24 Oct 54
ODIER
  William P: Newcastle Co 12
    Ja 58
ODLING
  Robert P: Phila 30 Ja 66,
    23 Oct 66
O'DONNELL/O'DONELL
  Charles P: Phila 28 Nov 54
  Hugh P: Phila 20 Jy 69
O'DONOLY/O'DONALLY
  Arthur P: New Castle 28 Oct
    62
  James P: Lancaster Co 12
    Feb 61
O'DORAN
  Patrick P: Pa 2 Feb 64;
    Phila 3 Ja 65
O'DORNAN
  Murtegh L: c/o William
    Armer-Cumberland Co 2 Mar
    74
ODOUR
  Mary P: Phila 15 Mar 64
ODREAN
  Hugh P: Phila 13 May 56
OFALLEN
  Barnet L: Lebanon Twp 15 Ap
    56
O'FARRILL
  Dennis P: Phila 12 Feb 61
O'FEE
  Molly P: Phila 26 Jy 64
OFFENBEHEN
  Henry P: Phila 3 May 70
OFFERALL
  Lewis P: Phila 20 Jy 69
OGBORNE
  William P: Phila 31 Jy 60
OGDEN
  Abraham P: Phila 6 Jy 58
  Amos, Esq. P: Phila 19 Ja 69
  David P: Phila 27 Ja 73
  John T: Roxbury 17 Oct 54
  Joseph P: Phila 4 Ag 63. T:
    Roxbury 17 Oct 54
  Margaret P: Reading Town 16
    Jy 67
  Nathan P: Reading Town 16 Jy
    67. T: Reading Town 1 Sep
    68
  Stephen P: Chester Co 31 Dec
    61
OGHSTON
  Andrew P: Pa 31 Dec 61

OGILBY
    Patrick P: Phila 4 Ap 54
OGILLIN
    William P: Pa 13 Oct 63
OGIN
    Peter P: Phila 13 May 56
OGLE
    Benjamin P: Phila-Gaz. 3 Ja
        76
    Thomas P: New-Castle Co 21
        Dec 58, 8 Jy 62; Phila 4
        Feb 68 (Dr)
OGLEBY/OGLEBEE/OGELBY
    James (soldier) P: 21 Dec
        58
    John P: Phila 2 Feb 64
    Mary P: Pa 31 Jy 60
O'HAMSEY
    Bryan P: Pa 2 Sep 62
OHANLON
    Patrick P: Burlington 8 Jy
        62
O'HARLAN
    Charles P: Phila Nov 53
OHARA/O'HARRA/O'HARROW
    Barney P: Salem 24 Feb 63
    Bryan/Brian P: N.J. 18 Mar
        62; Phila 6 Jy 58, 4 Ag
        63, 1 Feb 70, 1 Nov 70;
        Salem Co 9 Ag 59; West Jer-
        sey 31 Dec 61
    Dennis P: Phila 18 Mar 62, 8
        Jy 62, 10 Oct 65
    Elizabeth P: Phila 12 Feb 61
    Capt. Henry P: Phila 19 Jy 80
    Michael P: Phila 1 Nov 53
OHARN
    Henry P: Phila 13 Oct 63
O'HAUGHIAN
    Oliver P: Phila 27 Ja 73
O'HURRY
    Sampson P: Phila 28 Ap 68
O'KELLY
    Richard P: Phila-Gaz. 27 Oct
        73
    Mr. P: Bethlehem 26 Oct 69
OKILL
    George P: Phila 3 Ag 58, 21
        Dec 58
OLD
    James L: Lancaster Co, see
        PRICE, Peter
OLDEN
    Margaret N: near New-Castle,
        see MOORE, Alexander
OLDENBRUCK
    Daniel P: Phila 3 May 70
OLDES
    Ann P: Phila-Gaz. 3 Ja 76
OLDFIELD
    Ann P: Phila 22 Nov 53
    William P: Phila 31 Jy 60
OLDHAM
    George L: 18th Regt. Fort
        Pitt 19 Dec 71

OLDRIDGE
    Abiah P: Phila 5 Ag 62
OLEVERTY
    Dennis P: Phila 28 Oct 62
OLIPHANT
    Samuel P: Phila-Gaz. 3 Ja 76
    William P: Phila 26 Jy 64,
        27 Oct 73
OLIVER
    Andrew P: Phila 27 Ja 73
    Ann P: Phila 18 Mar 62
    Elizabeth T: Pa 17 Oct 54
    John P: Bordentown 31 Dec
        61; Phila 8 Jy 62 (Capt),
        8 Jy 62, 15 Mar 64, 3 Ja 65,
        30 Ja 66, 3 May 70
    Joseph P: Point-no-Point 15
        Mar 64
    Samuel P: Goshen 30 Ja 66
    Tho./Thomas P: Phila 27 Dec
        53, 24 Oct 54, 28 Nov 54,
        27 Ja 73
    William P: Marsh Creek 9 Ag
        59; Phila 31 Ja 76
OLTON
    Ralph P: Phila 28 Oct 62
OMONEY
    Catherine P: Phila 13 Ja 63
O'MOREY
    Henry P: Phila 23 Oct 66
O'MULLAN
    Thomas P: Phila 30 Ja 66
O'NEILL/O'NEAL/O'NEILE/O'NAILE
    Arthur P: Phila 23 Oct 66,
        27 Ja 73
    Arthur J. P: Phila-Gaz. 3 Ja
        76
    Constantine P: Bethlehem 19
        May 63
    Daniel P: Phila 26 Jy 64
    Edward P: Phila 16 Jy 72
    Felix P: Phila 24 Oct 54
    Francis P: Oxford 13 Oct 63
    Henry P: near Newcastle 24
        Oct 54; Phila 19 Ja 69, 1
        Nov 70
    James P: New Castle Co 15
        Mar 64; Phila 25 Jy 65, 28
        Ap 68
    Owen P: Phila 1 Jy 56
    Patrick P: Phila 11 Sep 55,
        1 Nov 70
    Peter P: Phila 8 Jy 62
    Robert P: Phila 28 Nov 54
    Tarrance P: Phila 3 Ja 65
ONIX
    John P: Phila 25 Ap 71
OPDYKE
    Joseph T: Amwell 17 Oct 54
ORD
    John P: Phila 19 Jy 80
O'RILEY
    James P: Phila-Gaz. 3 Ja 76
ORME
    Sarah P: Phila 2 Ag 70

ORMES
  Mr.   P: Phila 27 Ja 73
ORMSBY
  George   P: Pa 13 Oct 63
  John   P: Bedford 21 Jy 68;
    Phila 6 Jy 58, 3 Ag 58
ORMSLEY
  Mr.   P: Phila 2 May 65
ORNDT
  Major Jacob   P: Fort Allen
    21 Dec 58
ORNER
  Hermanus   P: Whitemarsh 13
    May 56, 5 Ag 56
  Thomas   P: White-marsh 9 Ag
    59
O'ROARK
  Alexander   P: Phila 9 Ag 59
ORR/OAR
  Daniel   P: Phila 3 Ja 65
  George   P: Phila 30 May 54
  James   P: Phila 30 Ja 66;
    Shearman's Val. 13 Ja 63
  John   C: c/o James Hutche-
    son, New London 30 Oct 66.
    P: Bedford 15 Mar 64; Cum-
    berland Co 2 Feb 64; Pa 24
    Feb 63; Phila 3 Ja 76
  Robert   P: Phila 20 Jy 69, 27
    Ja 73
  Thomas   P: Phila 9 Ag 59
  William   C: Kennet Twp,
    Chester Co 28 Nov 65. L:
    Pennsborough Town 15 Ap
    56. P: Christine Bridge 18
    Feb 55; Sasquehanna 3 Ag 58;
    near Schuylkill 30 Ap 67
ORRAM
  James   P: Chester Co 2 Feb 64
ORRAN
  Thomas   N: 29 Nov 64
ORRE
  John   L: Paxton 2 Mar 74
ORSMORE
  John   P: Phila 2 May 65
OSBORN/OSBOURN/OSBORNE/OSBONE
  Catherine   P: Phila 31 Dec 61
  Eleanor   P: Phila 30 Ja 66
  Elizabeth   P: Worcester 5 Ag
    56
  James   P: Phila 31 Dec 61
  Peter   P: Phila-Gaz. 27 Oct
    73 (Capt); Wilmington 12
    Feb 61, 31 Dec 61
  Robert   P: Phila 12 Feb 61,
    2 Ag 70
OSELAND
  Mr.   P: Phila 31 Jy 60
OSHER
  Walter   P: Phila 6 Sep 53
O'SKELLY
  Robert   P: Phila 27 Ja 73
OSSITAR
  James   P: Chester Co 21 Dec 58
OSTLER

William   P: Phila 15 Mar 64
O'SULLIVAN
  Mortough   P: Cape-Fear 1 Nov
    70
OSWALD
  John   P: Phila 16 Jy 67
OTENHAMMER
  John   P: Phila 13 May 56
OTIS/OTEIS
  Richard   P: Phila 3 Ja 65,
    30 Ap 67, 16 Jy 67, 21 Jy
    68
OTLEY
  Ann   C: Goshen 30 Oct 66
  Mary   P: Chester Co 12 Feb 61
O'TOLE
  Darby   P: Phila 25 Jy 65
OTORA
  Manus   P: Phila 26 Jy 53
OTTERBEIN/OTTERBERN
  Mr.   P: Phila 26 Oct 69
  Rev.   P: Lancaster 22 Nov 53
OTTO
  Bodo   P: Phila 1 Jy 56
  Col. Bodo, Jr.   P: Gloucester
    19 Jy 80
OTTONE
  Manus   P: Phila 6 Sep 53
OTWAY
  Robert   P: Phila-Gaz. 27 Oct
    73
OUGHELTREE/OUGHITREE
  James   C: East Nottingham
    Chester Co 30 Oct 66
  Matthew   P: Phila 30 Ja 66
OUGHTERSON
  Andrew   P: Phila-Gaz. 27 Oct
    73
OULSTONE
  William   P: Phila 31 Jy 60
OUTERBRIDGE
  Rumse   P: Phila 16 Jy 72
  Stephen   P: Phila 1 Nov 70
OVELTON
  Edward   P: Phila 18 Mar 62
OWEN/OWENS/OWINGS
  Ann   Phila 30 Ap 77
  Benjamin   P: Bucks 1 Nov 53
  Edward   L: at the Pot-ash
    Manufactory 2 Mar 74;
    merchant, Juniata, Cumber-
    land Co 29 Jy 72. P:
    Juniata 27 Oct 73; Phila 1
    Nov 70, 16 Jy 72
  Hugh   P: New-Castle 28 Oct 62
  James   P: Pa 2 Feb 64
  James Alexander   T: 4 Nov 72
  John   Germantown 24 Jy 76;
    Phila 7 Ap 57; Shippens-
    burg 21 Dec 58
  Owen   P: Phila 10 Ap 66
  Robert   P: N. Castle Co 2
    Feb 64; Pa 31 Dec 61, 18 Mar
    62
  Samuel   P: Phila 20 Oct 68

Sarah P: Phila 9 Ag 59, 19
   Ja 69
OWNER
Robert P: Pa 15 Mar 64
OXLEY
Edward P: Phila 23 Oct 66,
   20 Ap 69
OXSTON
Thomas P: Phila 23 Oct 66

P--LE
John P: Phila 2 Ag 70
PACEY
Mark Hugh P: Phila 24 Oct 54
PACKER
Daniel P: Phila 2 May 65
PACKET
Samuel P: Phila-Gaz. 3 Ja
   76
PADRICK
John P: Marcus-Hook 5 Ag
   56, 31 Jy 60; Pa 12 Feb 61
PAGAN
Andrew P: Pa 12 Feb 61
Giles P: near Phila 18 Ag 57
PAGE
Ann P: Phila 21 Dec 58
Joseph P: Chester Co 5 Feb 54
William P: Pa 4 Ag 63
PAINE/PAIN/PAYN/PAYNE
James P: Phila 11 Sep 55, 12
   Feb 61
Mary P: Phila 26 Jy 64
Capt. S./Stephen P: Phila 3 Ag
   58, 21 Dec 58, 18 Mar 62
Tho./Thomas P: Phila 27 Dec 53,
   3 Ja 76
William P: in the army 12 Ja
   58
PAINES
Adam P: Phila 9 May 54
D--con P: Phila 9 May 54
PAINTER
John P: Chester Co 7 Ap 57
Philip Darby Twp 30 Oct 76
PAINTY
John P: Germantown 13 Ja 63
PAIR
William P: Phila 3 Ag 58
PAISLEY
John P: Lancaster Co 18 Ag 57
PAKER
Catherine Phila 1 May 76
PALL
Andrew P: Pequea 2 Feb 64
PALLER
Elizabeth P: Phila 1 Feb 70
PALMER
Alice P: Chester Co 3 Sep 61,
   31 Dec 61
Elizabeth; see CONNOR
H. P: Phila 16 Jy 72
John P: New-Castle 15 Mar 64;
   Phila 22 Nov 53, 29 Ag 54,

11 Sep 55, 16 Jy 77
Jonathan P: Pa 3 Ag 58
Joseph P. P: Germantown 19
   Jy 80; Pa 31 Mar 63; Phila
   19 May 63
Richard P: Phila 4 Feb 68
Thomas C: Charlestown,
   Maryland 18 Jy 65
William P: Coles-Town 18
   Feb 55
PAMER (alias LONG)
Ann P: Phila-Gaz. 3 Ja 76
PAMMER
Mr. P: Phila 28 Ap 68
PAMPER
Widow P: Bethlehem Co 31 Dec
   61
PANCOAST
Edward T: Bordentown 10 Ag
   58
PAPON
Lt. Stephen P: in the army
   12 Ja 58
PAPPS
William, bombardier P: prob.
   at Pittsburgh 15 Mar 64;
   Fort Pitt 26 Jy 64
PARCOCK
John P: Phila 3 Ag 58
PARE
Ralph P: Phila 27 Ja 73
PARHAM
Samuel P: Phila 24 Feb 63
PARIL
Joseph P: Phila 24 Feb 63
PARIS/PARISE/PARISS
Peter P: Phila 3 Ag 58, 21
   Dec 58, 31 Jy 60, 10 Oct
   65, 3 May 70, 25 Ap 71,
   19 Jy 80
PARISH
Edward P: Phila 21 Dec 58
Peter Phila 24 Jy 76
PARK
John L: Middle Octarara 2
   Mar 74. P: N.J. 13 Oct 63
Thomas P: Bucks Co 10 Oct 65
PARKER
Miss P: Chester Co 9 Ag 59
David P: Lancaster Co 18 Mar
   62
Edward C: East Nottingham,
   Chester Co 30 Oct 66; near
   the Brick Meeting-house 22
   Ja 67. P: Pa 18 Mar 62
Elisabeth P: Pa 31 Dec 61
Hannah P: Phila 20 Oct 68
Henry P: Phila 1 Jy 56
Hugh P: Phila 5 Ag 56
James P: New Providence 5
   Ag 56, 21 Dec 58, 9 Ag 59;
   Phila 4 Feb 68, 28 Ap 68.
   T: 4 Nov 72
John P: Phila 1 Nov 70, 2 Ja
   73

Jonathan P: Phila 20 Oct 68.
  T: Trenton 17 Oct 54
Martin P: Phila 20 Ap 69
Matthew P: Phila 25 Jy 65
Nicholas P: Sturbridge 1
  Jy 56
Capt. Reuben P: Phila 7 Ap
  57
Richard P: Limerick 13 May
  56; Phila 6 Jy 58, 3 Ag 58,
  19 Ja 69
Robert P: Montgomery Twp
  9 Ag 59; Pa 12 Feb 61, 31
  Dec 61, 18 Mar 62, 26
  Jy 64
Thomas P: Dover 3 Ag 58
Timothy P: Phila 26 Oct 69
William P: Cumberland Co 31
  Jy 60; Gilbert's Manor 7 Ap
  57; Phila 3 Ja 65
PARKIN
  John P: Octerara 15 Mar 64
  Richard P: Phila 1 Nov 70,
  27 Oct 73
PARKINSON
  Barnard P: Phila 13 Oct 63
  James P: Phila 27 Dec 53, 9
  May 54
  Thomas P: Phila 18 Feb 55
PARKLE
  Thomas P: Phila 31 Dec 61
PARKS
  Mrs. P: Chester Co 3 Ja 60
  Charles P: Phila 13 Ja 63
  George P: Chester Co 3 Sep 61
  James P: Phila 31 Dec 61
  John P: Pa 31 Dec 61
  Jonah P: Bethlehem Co 31 Dec
  61
  Ruben P: Phila 12 Feb 61
  Thomas P: Dover 8 Jy 62;
  Kent Co 2 Feb 64
PARKSON
  Mary P: Phila-Gaz. 3 Ja 76
PARLIN
  Rev. O. P: Phila 6 Jy 58;
  Wicacoa 1 Jy 56
PARON /or possibly PATON?/
  Robert P: Phila 11 Sep 55
PARR/PAR
  Caleb P: Phila 9 Ag 59
  Peter P: Phila 6 Jy 58
  William P: near Phila 18 Ag
  57
PARRISEEN
  Mr. P.O. P: Phila 1 Jy 56
PARROCK
  John P: Phila 21 Dec 58
PARROT/PARROTT
  Abner Phila 1 May 76
  George P: Salem 1 Feb 70
  John P: Talbot 19 Jy 80
PARRY
  Lewis P: Phila 12 Ja 58
  Peter P: Phila 18 Ag 57

PARS
  Peter P: Phila 3 Ag 58
PARSELL
  James P: Montgomery Twp 13
  Ja 63
PARSONS/PARSON
  Widow P: Phila 20 Jy 69
  Elizabeth Phila 1 May 76
  Richard P: Phila 2 May 65,
  25 Jy 65; Rights-Town 31
  Jy 60
  Weldon P: Phila 26 Oct 69,
  1 Nov 70
PART/?/
  Elihu T: Kingwood 10 Ag 58
PARTINSON
  Pat. P: N.J. 13 Oct 63
PARTON
  Elizabeth P: Phila 20 Jy 69
PARTRAY
  Ch. P: Phila 15 Mar 64
PARTRIDGE
  James P: Phila 28 Oct 62
  Capt. Sohn /for John?/ P:
  Phila 3 Ag 58
PARVIN/PARVAN
  Jer. P: Piles-grove 18 Ag
  57
  Mary P: Phila 4 Ag 63
  Matthew P: Cohansie 20 Oct
  68; Cumberland Co 12 Feb 61
  Pearson P: Phila 13 Oct 63
  Silas P: Phila 13 Oct 63
  Thomas P: Phila 24 Feb 63
PASCHALL/PASCHAL/PATCHALL
  Dr. P: Salem 3 Ag 58
  Hugh P: Pa 2 Feb 64
  James P: Phila 6 Jy 58, 3 Ag
  58
  Jonathan P: Phila 10 Ap 66
  Stephen P: Phila 3 Ag 58,
  26 Jy 64, 3 Ja 65
  Thomas P: Phila 6 Jy 58, 2
  Sep 62, 13 Ja 63, 24 Feb 63
PASSMAN/PASMAN
  John P: Bucks Co 31 Jy 60;
  Pa 31 Dec 61
PATERSON, see PATTERSON
PATIENCE
  James P: Phila 21 Jy 68
PATON
  Robert P: Pa 3 Ag 58
PATOUN
  John P: Phila 2 Feb 64, 1 Nov
  70
PATRICK
  Mr. P: Marsh-Creek 31 Dec 61
  James T: Baskinridge 3 Oct
  65
  John P: Bucks Co 4 Feb 68
  Thomas P: Gloucester Co 31
  Jy 60
PATSUL
  Hugh P: Phila 3 Ja 65
PATT

and M'FALL   P: N. Castle Co
  9 Ag 59
PATTEN
  Hugh   P: Phila 31 Dec 61
  Joseph   L: Lancaster Co 29 Jy
  72
  Mary   P: Phila 28 Nov 54
PATTERSON/PATERSON
  Mrs.   P: Phila 9 Ag 59, 3
  Ja 60
  Anthony   P: Bucks Co 7 Ap 57
  Andrew   P: Little Edgmont 10
  Oct 65; Pa 2 Feb 64; Phila
  3 Ja 65
  Arthur   P: Octerara 2 Feb 64
  Benjamin   P: Phila 15 Mar 64
  Catharine   P: Phila-Gaz. 3 Ja
  76
  Charity   P: in the Manor 21
  Dec 58
  Hardon R.   P: Phila 4 Feb 68
  Hugh   N: c/o Mrs. Spencer-New-
  Castle 4 Dec 66; near N.
  Castle 12 Feb 67
  James   L: Fogg's Manor 20 Ja
  73; Lancaster Co 31 Ja 71.
  P: Bucks Co 26 Jy 64;
  Manor of Moreland 13 Ja 63,
  3 Ja 76; Pa 12 Ja 58; Phila
  30 Ja 66
  John   P: Baskinridge 18 Ag 57;
  Chester Co 31 Dec 61; Cumber-
  land Co 13 Oct 63; Phila 2 May
  65, 25 Jy 65, 4 Feb 68, 27
  Ja 73, 3 Ja 76; Reading 15
  Mar 64
  Margaret   P: Phila-Gaz. 3 Ja
  76
  Mary   L: Pequea 2 Mar 74
  (widow).   P: Phila 25 Jy 65
  Moles   P: Phila 28 Ap 68
  Moreland   P: 19 May 63
  Nathaniel   P: Bucks Co 31 Jy 60,
  10 Oct 65
  Nicholas   P: Chester Co 12 Feb
  61
  Peter   P: Londonderry Twp 13
  Ja 63
  Richard   P: Pa 24 Feb 63; Phila
  19 May 63
  Robert   P: New-Castle Co 3 Sep
  61, 18 Mar 62; Pa 3 Ja 60;
  Phila 30 May 54, 3 Ag 58, 21
  Dec 58, 9 Ag 59, 3 Sep 61, 15
  Mar 64, 30 Ja 66, 3 Ja 76;
  Pilesgrove 3 Ag 58, 21 Dec 58,
  9 Ag 59, 13 Ja 63, 2 Feb 64;
  Salem Co 28 Oct 62
  Samuel   N: 29 Nov 64.   P: Cum-
  berland Co 13 Ja 63; Phila 18
  Mar 62, 8 Jy 62
  Samuel, Jr.   W: and Col. Christ-
  iana Bridge 3 Jy 76
  Thomas   P: Bucks Co 21 Dec 58;
  Phila 3 Ag 58, 21 Dec 58, 3
  Ja

  65, 23 Oct 66, 30 Ap 67
  William   C: Chester 22 Ja 67.
  N: 29 Nov 64.   P: Carlisle
  31 Dec 61; Christine Bridge
  1 Jy 56, 3 Ja 60; Cumber-
  land Co 3 Sep 61; N.
  Castle Co 9 Ag 59; Pa 2
  Feb 64; Phila 9 Ag 59, 30
  Ja 66, 20 Jy 69
PATTISON/PATYSON
  Charles   P: Carlisle 9 Ag 59;
  Cumberland Co 3 Ja 60
  John   P: Duck-creek 12 Ja 58;
  Phila 13 Oct 63
  Joseph   P: Phila 30 May 54
  Robert   P: Duck Creek 26 Jy
  64
PATTON
  Andrew   P: Phila 2 Sep 62, 27
  Oct 73
  George   P: Phila 21 Jy 68
  James   P: N.J. 13 Oct 63
  Jean   P: Phila 13 Ja 63
  Capt. Jo.   L: Lancaster Co 31
  Ja 71
  John   P: Nottingham 18 Ag 57
  Robert   P: Phila 5 Ag 56, 3
  Ag 58
  William   P: Octorara 3 Ag 58;
  Pa 8 Jy 62; Phila 26 Oct 69
PAUL
  Andrew   P: Falling Spring 18
  Mar 62
  John   P: Phila 3 Sep 61, 27
  Ja 73
  William   P: Phila 18 Mar 62
PAVCOCK
  John   P: Phila 6 Jy 58
PAXON
  Samuel   Ruddy Creek 16 Jy 77
PAXTON/PACKSTON
  Alexander   P: Lancaster Co 15
  Mar 64
  Andrew   P: Octorara 28 Oct
  62; Pa 12 Feb 61, 13 Oct 63
  Edward   P: Phila 28 Oct 62
  Jane   P: Phila 3 Ag 58
  Samuel   P: York Co 26 Jy 64
PAYLER
  Capt. Geo.   P: Phila 4 Ag 63
PAYNE; see PAINE; also YARREL
  & PAYNE
PEACH
  Jacob   P: Phila 13 May 56
PEACOCK
  Mr.   P: Stoney Batter 27 Ja
  73
  Clement   P: Phila 5 Ag 62
  Ja.   L: Donnegall 14 May 72
  James   P: Christine Bridge 12
  Ja 58; Little Britain 8
  Jy 62; Phila, soldier in the
  34th Regt 19 Ja 69
  Michael   P: Phila 20 Jy 69
PEAKEN

William P: Phila 2 Ag 70
PEAL/PEALE; see also PEEL
Nathaniel C: c/o S.
Boyers-near the Blue Ball
Chester Co 28 Nov 65
Robert P: Pa 31 Jy 60
PEARCE/PEARSE; see also PIERCE
Andrew P: Phila 1 Nov 53
Edward P: Chester Co 3 Ag 58
Henry P: Phila 20 Jy 69
John P: Pa 2 Feb 64; Phila
13 Ja 63, 4 Ag 63 (2), 26
Oct 69, 1 May 76
Mary P: Phila-Gaz. 3 Ja 76
Rebecca P: Bucks Co 21 Jy
68; Phila 10 Ap 66, 20 Ap
69, 2 Ag 70
Robert Phila 1 May 76
Timothy P: Phila 31 Dec 61,
15 Mar 64
PEARCH
Thomas P: Phila-Gaz. 3 Ja 76
PEAREY
James P: Phila 30 Ap 67
PEARIS
Richard P: Phila 9 Ag 59;
Capt., Phila 3 Ja 60, 18
Mar 62
PEARNE
Richard P: Phila 28 Oct 62
William P: Phila 18 Ag 57
PEARSALL/PEARSOLL
John P: Phila 20 Ap 69
Jos./Joseph P: Phila 12 Ja 58,
31 Jy 60
Thomas P: Phila 23 Oct 66
PEARSLEE
Thomas P: Phila 21 Jy 68
PEARSON; see also PIERSON
Anthony P: Phila 19 May 63
Christopher P: Phila 2 Ag
70, 25 Ap 71
Francis C: Middletown 22 Ja
67. P: Chester Co 20 Ap 69
Frederick P: in the army 12
Ja 58
James P: Phila 4 Ag 63, 30
Ja 66, 16 Jy 72
John P: Phila 11 Sep 55, 3
Ag 58, 24 Feb 63, 3 Ja 65,
19 Jy 80
Joseph P: Burlington 9 Ag 59;
Chester Co 23 Oct 66; West
New Jersey 21 Dec 58
Nancy P: Phila 3 Ja 65
Samuel P: Phila 26 Jy 53;
Richland 1 Nov 53
William P: Kensington 4 Ag
63; Phila 3 Ja 60. T:
Trenton 31 Ja 71
PEARST
Jacob P: Phila 29 Ag 54
PEARY
George P: Phila 7 Ap 57
PEASENCE

Samuel P: Phila 3 Ja 65
PEASLEY
William P: Phila 2 May 65
PECHEM
Mr. P: Phila-Gaz. 3 Ja 76
PECK
Abby L: Cumberland Co 2 Mar
74
Joseph L: Cumberland Co 2
Mar 74. P: Cumberland,
West Jersey 3 Ja 76; West
Jersey 31 Ja 70
Patrick P: Sadsbury 5 Ag 56
William Aug. P: Phila 18
Mar 62
PECKAN
Samuel, weaver C: in Fogs
Manor 30 Oct 66
PECKING
Robert P: Phila 26 Oct 69
PECKWORTH
John P: Phila 20 Jy 69
PEDDAL
Joseph Phila 5 Ja 76-Gaz.
31 Ja
PEDDIE
Alexander P: Pa 21 Dec 58
PEDLEY
Jeremiah Phila 5 Jy 76-Gaz.
24 Jy
PEDRICK
John P: Marcus Hook 4 Ap 54
PEE
George P: Pennsylvania 16 Jy
72
PEEK
Nathaniel, the 3rd P: Green-
wich 2 Ag 70
PEEL
Ann P: Phila 7 Ap 57
Sarah P: Phila 16 Jy 67
William P: Phila-Gaz. 27 Oct
73
PEERS
Thomas (soldier) P: 21 Dec
58
PEET
Thomas P: near Phila 18 Ag
57
PEFFER
Mr. P: Phila 18 Mar 62
PEGG
Henry P: Pa 12 Feb 61
PEGNOM
Robert P: Bucks Co 26 Oct 69
PEIRCE, see PIERCE
PEIRCY
Susannah P: Pa 31 Mar 63
PEIRSON, SEE PIERSON
PEIRYORD
Samuel P: Phila 29 Ag 54
PELL
Thomas P: Potomack 8 Jy 62
PELLER
James P: Phila 18 Mar 62

PELLES
  Isaac P: Phila 27 Ja 73
PELLSON
  Henry P: Phila 27 Ja 73
PELTON
  Benjamin P: Hopewell 31 Dec
    61. T: Hopewell 17 Oct 54
PELTS
  John P: Phila 23 Oct 66
PEMBERTON
  Israel P: Phila 2 Ag 70
  John P: Phila 3 Ja 65
  Mary P: Germantown 31 Jy
    60
PENCER
  Margaret P: Phila 3 Ja 60
PENDERGAST
  Martin P: Phila 20 Oct 68
  Thomas P: Phila 16 Jy 72
PENDLEBOROUGH
  James P: Phila 1 Feb 70
PENEWILL
  John P: Phila 27 Ja 73
PENFORD
  Mary P: Pa 12 Feb 61
PENIER/PENEIR
  Margaret P: Phila 9 Ag 59
  Peter P: North Wales 31 Dec
    61
PENN
  Richard P: Phila 1 Nov 70
  Thomas P: Phila 1 Nov 70
PENNELL
  John P: Phila 28 Nov 54,
    30 Ap 67
  Joseph P: Phila 25 Jy 65 (2),
    10 Oct 65, 30 Ja 66, 10 Ap
    66, 19 Jy 80
  Joshua P: Chester Co 31 Dec
    61
  William P: Phila 24 Feb 63
PENNINGTON/PENINGTON
  Ebenezer P: Phila 3 Ja 65
  Edward P: Phila 6 Jy 58
  Miles P: Phila 30 Ap 67
  Thomas P: Mooreland 5 Ag 62,
    28 Oct 62
PENNIS
  Lewis P: Pa 31 Jy 60
PENNISTON
  Jeremiah P: Phila 26 Jy 64
PENNOCK
  Joseph P: Marlborough 18
    Mar 62; Pa 21 Dec 58; Phila
    24 Feb 63
PENNY/PENNEY
  Archibald P: Phila-Gaz. 27 Oct
    73
  James L: Colrain Twp 15 Ap 56
  Robert John /?/ Phila 27 Oct
    73
  Thomas P: Cumberland Co 13 Oct
    63; Lancaster Co 18 Ag 57
  William P: Lancaster Co 3 Sep
    61

PENNYCOOK
  James and David P: Phila 21
    Jy 68
PENROSE; see also HAZELTON &
  Joseph P: Tinicum Island 16
    Jy 72
  Thomas P: Phila 6 Jy 58
PENROSS
  and FISHER, Messers P: Phila
    19 Ja 69
PENSONBY
  John P: Phila 18 Ag 57
PENTHENY
  Augustine P: Phila 4 Ap 54
  Peter P: Phila 24 Feb 63
PERAN
  Giles P: Goshen 9 Ag 59
PERCE
  Alexander C: 30 Jy 77
PERDRIAN/PERDRIAU
  Stephen P: Phila 5 Feb 54,
    31 Dec 61, 13 Ja 63
PEREI
  Martin P: Phila 26 Oct 69
PERES
  Samuel P: Phila 28 Nov 54
PERKINS
  Christopher P: Phila 9 Ag 59
  Henry P: Pa 3 Ja 60
  James P: Phila 5 Ag 62, 31
    Mar 63
PERKINSON
  Charles P: Phila-Gaz. 27 Oct
    73
  John P: Phila 27 Ja 73
  Thomas P: Evesham, W. Jersey
    4 Feb 68
PERRINE
  Peter T: 4 Nov 72
PERRY
  Alexander P: Phila 5 Ag 56
  Ann P: Phila 9 Ag 59
  George P: Phila-Gaz. 3 Ja 76
  John C: Whiteland Twp 30 Oct
    66. P: Phila 28 Oct 62
  William P: Christine Bridge
    28 Nov 54
PERSIVAL
  Capt. John P: Phila 3 May 70
PERSOY
  Anna Silia P: Phila 3 Sep 61
PESCOD
  John P: Phila-Gaz. 27 Oct 73
PETERS/PETER
  Mr. P: Phila 3 Ja 76
  George P: Phila-Gaz. 27 Oct
    73
  John P: Phila 3 Ag 58, 21
    Dec 58, 12 Feb 61
  Mannas P: Phila 3 Ag 58
  Valentine, Esq. P: Phila 23
    Oct 66
  William P: Phila 3 Ag 58
PETERSON
  Widow L: Little Britain Twp

19 Dec 71

Henry P: Pequea 30 Oct 76;
Phila 30 Ap 77

James P: Bucks Co 3 Ag 58

Capt. Jos. P: Phila 2 Feb
64

Margaret P: N.J. 24 Feb 63

Nathaniel P: Bucks Co 13 Oct
63

Thomas P: Phila 9 Ag 59

PETILL

Martha P: Phila 18 Feb 55

PETRY

Jacob P: Phila 27 Ja 73

PETTEBONE

Charles P: Phila 4 Feb 68

PETTENBY

Rev. Mr. P: Lancaster Co 24
Feb 63

PETTICREW/PETTYCREW/PETTECREW/
PETTICRUE

David L: Hanover Twp 19 Dec
71, 29 Jy 72. P: Fogs Manor
31 Jy 60; Phila 10 Oct 65

James P: Lancaster Co 24 Oct
54

Margaret P: Phila 12 Ja 58

William P: Christine 28 Oct
62

PETTIT

Charles P: Phila 10 Oct 65

Nathaniel P: Phila 18 Mar 62

PETTY

Arthur P: Phila 2 Feb 64

John P: Phila 31 Dec 61, 5
Ag 62, 24 Feb 63

Mat. P: Phila 15 Mar 64

PHARIS

David P: Wilmington 3 Sep 61

PHELPS

Col. Alexander P: Phila 16
Jy 67

Jonathan P: Phila 25 Jy 65

William P: Phila 3 Ja 65

PHENEMON

Isaac P: Penn's-Neck 31 Ja
76

PHENISE

Cornelius P: Phila 1 May 76

PHENIX; see also PHOENIX

Effie P: Phila 4 Feb 68

Fel. P: Phila 24 Feb 63

Fortune P: Phila 26 Jy 64

PHIFER

Michael P: Phila 28 Oct 62

PHILAN

Thomas P: Chester Co 3 Sep
61

PHILE

Frederick P: Phila 23 Oct 66

PHILIPPE

M. P: Phila 28 Ap 68

PHILIPS/PHILLIPS

Mr. T: Maidenhead 17 Oct 54

Andrew, soldier P: prob. in

Pittsburgh 15 Mar 64

Catharine/Catherine P: 25 Jy
65; Phila 21 Dec 58, 3 Sep
61, 31 Mar 63

Christian P: Phila 16 Jy 67

Col. Frederick P: Phila 1 Feb
70

Henry P: Phila-Gaz. 3 Ja 76

Capt. J. P: Phila 31 Jy 60

James P: Phila 30 May 54

John P: Newcastle 24 Oct 54;
Phila 24 Oct 54, 12 Ja 58,
3 Ag 58, 4 Ag 63, 16 Jy 67;
Capt., Phila 6 Jy 58, 5 Ag
62

John Randle P: Phila 9 Ag 59

Jonas P: Phila 13 Ja 63

Jonathan P: Phila 18 Mar 62,
21 Jy 68

Capt. Joseph T: N.J. 17 Oct
54

Leonard P: Phila 3 Sep 61,
31 Dec 61

Mark P: Phila 25 Jy 65

Mary P: Phila 25 Jy 65

Philip T: Maidenhead 17 Oct
54

Robert L: Lancaster Co 29 Jy
72

Samuel P: Bucks Co 26 Oct 69

Simeon T: Penington 7 May 67

Thomas P: Phila 1 Jy 56, 13
Ja 63

William P: New Castle Co 31
Jy 60

PHILIPSON

Hannah P: Phila 23 Oct 66

William P: Phila 18 Feb 55,
18 Mar 62, 3 Ja 65

PHILLIZYEES

John P: Lancaster Co 12 Feb
61

PHILPOT/PHILPOTT/FILLPOT

Mrs. T: Trenton 6 Dec 64

Widow P: Bucks Co 10 Oct 65

Erick P: Salem (Co) 15 Mar
64, 26 Jy 64

George P: Pa 24 Feb 63

Gregory P: Phila 13 Ja 63,
2 Feb 64, 15 Mar 64

John P: Salem 18 Mar 62

PHIPPS

Nathan P: Chester Co 22 Nov
53

Thomas P: Phila 31 Jy 60

PHOENIX

Mrs. P: Phila 28 Oct 62

Telamon P: Phila 28 Oct 62;
Capt. Telemon-Phila 1 Feb 70

PIATT; see also PYATT

Jacob P: Lancaster Co 12 Feb
61

PICKEN/PICKAN/PICKENS

John N: Cecil Co, see HARVEY,
William. P: Phila 21 Dec

58, 31 Dec 61
Jonathan P: Pa 31 Mar 63;
  Phila 28 Oct 62
Robert P: West New Jersey 21
  Dec 58
Samuel P: Chester Co 31 Dec
  61; Pa 18 Mar 62
PICKERING/PICKERIN
George and James P: Phila
  25 Ap 71
James P: Phila 15 Mar 64
Thomas P: Phila 20 Jy 69
PICKERTON
George P: Phila 12 Ja 58
PICKESS
George P: Germantown 19 Ja
  69
PICKET
John P: Woodbury 16 Jy 67
PICKING
Robert P: Pa 26 Jy 64; Phila
  3 Ja 65
PICKLE
John P: Phila 11 Jy 54
PICKLES
Joseph P: Phila 23 Oct 66
PICKLESS
Letitia P: Wilmington 1 Jy
  56
PICKMAN
Sally P: Phila 20 Ap 69
PIDDLE
Jos. P: Pa 15 Mar 64
PIDGEON
Charles P: Chester Co 4 Ag
  63
PIERCE/PEIRCE; see also PEARCE
Mr. P: Phila 30 Ja 66
Edward P: Phila 3 Ag 58
John P: Thornbury Twp 1 Jy
  56
Jonas P: Phila 3 Sep 61
Joseph P: Brandywine 8 Jy
  62
Lewis P: Phila 16 Jy 72
Paul P: Chester Co 8 Jy 62;
  Cumberland Co 24 Feb 63
Thomas P: Phila 18 Mar 62,
  2 May 65
Capt. Timothy P: Phila 19
  Jy 80
PIERRE
Monsieur Phila 1 May 76
PIERSON/PEIRSON; see also PEAR-
  SON
Christopher P: Phila 16 Jy 72
Joseph P: West New Jersey 5
  Ag 56
Wyllys Red Stone 15 Jy 77
PIETY
Austin P: Fort Chartres 25
  Ap 71
PIGNAL
Hugh P: up Delaware River 25
  Ap 71

PIGOTT
Thomas P: Phila 31 Ja 76
PILE
Hannah P: Phila 30 Ap 77
Mary P: Maidenhead 1 Jy 56
Pet./Peter P: Germantown 15
  Mar 64, 3 Ja 65
PILES
Samuel Phila 16 Jy 77
PILL
Peter P: Phila 2 Ag 70
PILYON
James P: Duck-creek 12 Ja
  58
PIM/PIMM
Rich. P: Great Valley 9 Ag
  59
Thomas L: the Valley 15 Ap
  56. P: Caln 5 Ag 56
PINCHON
William P: Phila 18 Jy 80
PINDAR
John P: Phila 25 Jy 65
PINE
Lawrence P: Phila 28 Oct 62
Lazarus P: Gloucester 3 Ag
  58
PINES
John P: Phila 11 Sep 55
PINKERTON/PENKERTON
David P: Pa 21 Dec 58
Henry P: Phila 3 Ja 60, 28
  Oct 62
William T: c/o Dolly Clark
  31 Ja 71
PINKS
Samuel P: Phila-Gaz. 27 Oct
  73
PINNY
William P: Chester Co 3 Ag
  58
PINTER
Lewis Phila 16 Jy 77
PINYARD
Rachel P: Phila 24 Oct 54
PIPER
James P: Cumberland Co 18
  Ag 57; Shippenstown 2 Feb
  64; Col., Phila 24 Jy 76
John P: Phila 28 Ap 68
Mary P: Pa 3 Ag 58
PIRRIE
Mary P: Pa 13 Oct 63
PITMAN
John P: Phila-Gaz. 3 Ja 76,
  24 Jy 76
PITNES
Henry P: Phila 16 Jy 67
PITT
Benjamin P: Phila 13 Oct 63
John P: Phila 27 Ja 73
William P: Phila 18 Mar 62,
  3 Ja 76
PITTS
Bradley Phila 16 Jy 77

PLACE
  Charles Frederick P: Phila
    19 Ja 69
  Capt. W. P: Phila 13 Ja 63,
    24 Feb 63
PLAISEWAY
  Robert P: Phila 27 Ja 73
PLANT
  Mary P: Phila 3 May 70
PLASKETT
  Capt. John P: Phila 30 Ap
    67
PLATT
  Charles P: Phila 27 Ja 73
  Samuel P: New-Castle Co 9
    Ag 59, 3 Ja 60
PLAYTER
  Mr. P: Phila 1 Nov 70
PLEASANTS
  Samuel P: Phila 27 Ja 73
PLEMIN
  Thomas P: Phila 12 Feb 61
PLIM
  George P: Phila 24 Oct 54
PLUARD
  John P: Pa 13 Oct 63
PLUMSTED
  Thomas P: Phila 25 Ap 71
PLUNKET
  William L: 14 May 72 (Capt).
    P: Lancaster 19 Jy 80
POAK/POAKE/POKE
  Charles P: Phila 31 Mar 63,
    10 Oct 65
  Robert P: Phila 2 May 65
POCOCK
  Nicholas P: Phila 4 Ag 63
POE
  John P: Octorara 21 Dec 58
POET
  Mrs. P: Phila 31 Jy 60
  John P: Phila 11 Sep 55
  Juliana P: Phila 21 Dec 58
POFF
  Nancy P: Phila-Gaz. 3 Ja 76
POGUE/POAG/POGU
  John L: Carlisle 19 Dec 71.
    P: Salem Co 4 Ag 63
  William P: Merion 20 Jy 69
POLAND
  Joseph Phila 24 Jy 76
POLICK
  Thomas P: Phila-Gaz. 3 Ja
    76
POLKE
  Joseph P: Pa 7 Ap 57
  William P: Phila 4 Ag 63
POLLARD
  Jacob P: Phila 15 Mar 64
  Capt. Job P: Phila 31 Jy 60
  William P: Phila 1 Jy 56, 9
    Ag 59
POLLINS
  Rachel P: Pa 31 Dec 61
POLLOCK

Cutlin P: Phila 3 Sep 61
James L: Carlisle 29 Jy 72,
  20 Ja 73
Jo. L: in Carlisle 14 May 72
John L: Carlisle 2 Mar 74.
  P: Carlisle 13 Ja 63; Phila
  9 Ag 59
Oliver P: Phila-Gaz. 27 Oct
  73
Thomas P: Phila 2 Sep 62
William L: Carlisle, see
  MOORE, William
POLSON
  Francis P: Baltimore Co 31
    Dec 61
POLTON
  Ann P: Phila 23 Oct 66
POMPIN
  Joan P: Phila 25 Jy 65
PONDER
  John P: Sussex Co 3 Ag 58
PONTLONEY
  Margarette P: Phila 9 Ag 59
POOCK
  Elizabeth P: Phila 18 Mar 62
POOL/POOLE
  Mrs. P: Phila 3 Ag 58, 21
    Dec 58
  Mr. P: Phila 3 Ja 76
  David P: Pa 18 Mar 62; Phila
    3 Ja 65
  Joseph P: Bucks Co 18 Ag 57
  Richard P: Little Darby 19
    Ja 69. W: Wilmington 27
    Ag 77
  William P: Wilmington 1 Jy
    56
POOLEY
  Hester P: Cumberland Co 18
    Ag 57
  William P: Wilmington 26 Jy
    64
POOLS
  Henry P: Phila 3 May 70
POOR
  John P: Chester Co 31 Dec 61
  Thomas P: Phila-Gaz. 3 Ja 76
POPE
  & THOMAS Duck-Creek 24 Jy 76
  John P: Phila 30 Ap 67
POPHAM
  James P: Phila 3 Ja 65, 10
    Ap 66
POPKINS
  Mary P: Reading 3 Ja 60
POPPLEWELL
  Richard P: Bethlehem 30 Ap
    67
PORDEY
  Archibald P: York Co 3 Ag 58
POREE
  Peter P: Phila 2 Feb 64
PORTER
  Andrew C: Chester Co., see
    THOMPSON, Alexander. P:

Nottingham 3 Ag 58; Phila
28 Ap 68
Catherine   P: Chester Co 12
Feb 61
Elisabeth   P: Pa 31 Dec 61
James   L: 13 Jn 65.   P:
Phila 31 Jy 60, 16 Jy 67,
3 Ja 76
Jane   L: c/o Mr. Cuthbertson
14 May 72.   P: Phila 2 May
65
John   P: Phila 24 Feb 63;
West Jersey 18 Ag 57, 12
Ja 58
Jonathan   P: Pa 12 Feb 61
Richard   P: Phila 26 Oct 69
Robert   W: New Castle Co c/o
Mr. Richard Dennis, ship-
carpenter 3 Jy 76.   P:
Phila 9 Ag 59, 3 Ja 60, 28
Oct 62, 15 Mar 64
Samuel   P: Marsh Creek 27 Ja
73
William   L: 29 Ja 67; Leacock
Twp 30 Ja 73.   P: Frankford
20 Ap 69; Lancaster Co 12
Feb 61; Leacock (Twp) 13 May
56, 13 Oct 63; near Newcastle
24 Oct 54; Phila 7 Ap 57, 18
Ag 57
PORTH
John   P: Phila 28 Ap 68
PORTIS
George   P: Phila 5 Ag 56
James   P: Phila 5 Ag 56
PORVELL
Mary   P: Phila 4 Ag 63
POST
Peter   T: 1 Sep 68
Samuel   P: New Castle Co 9
Ag 59, 3 Ja 60
POTTER
Col. David   P: Cohansey 30 Ap
77
Edward   P: Goshen 9 Ag 59;
Pa 3 Ja 60; Phila 5 Feb 54,
5 Ag 56
Eleanor   P: Phila 23 Oct 66
James   P: Phila 1 Feb 70, 27
Oct 73
John   P: Chester Co 3 Ja 60;
Phila 13 Ja 63
Martha   P: Conecocheague 15
Mar 64
Mary   P: Chester Co 12 Feb 61
Matt./Matthew   P: Phila 13 Ja
63, 31 Mar 63
Seagoe   P: Phila 31 Ja 76
POTTMAN
William   P: Phila 10 Oct 65
POTTS
Alexander   P: Phila 23 Oct 66
David   P: Phila 20 Oct 68,
26 Oct 69, 3 May 70
John   P: Cumberland Co 31 Jy

60; Pottsgrove 31 Ja 76
Jonathan   P: Phila 30 Ap 77
(Dr).   T: Kingston 17 Oct
54
Jos./Joseph   P: Phila 3 May
70
Thomas   P: Cross-roads 13 Ja
63; Manatawny 7 Ap 57;
Pa 18 Mar 62; Phila 3 May
70; Capt., Phila 4 Feb 68
William   P: Pa 24 Feb 63
(Capt); Phila 2 May 65, 10
Oct 65
POULSON
Patt.   P: Phila 18 Ag 57
POULTNEY/POULTNAY
Thomas   P: Lancaster (Co) 24
Feb 63, 19 May 63, 13 Oct
63; Phila 30 Ja 66, 25 Ap
71
POUND
Elijah   T: Piscatawa 17 Oct
54
William   P: Phila 4 Feb 68
POUNDER
Andrew   P: Phila 15 Mar 64
POUSETT
and LOYD   P: Phila 2 Feb 64
POVLIN
Mr.   P: Phila 28 Ap 68
POWDEN
Samuel   P: Phila 18 Mar 62
POWELL; see also HARTFORD &
POWELL
Edward   P: Phila 2 Ag 70
Elisha   P: Deer Creek 19 May
63
James   P: Phila 27 Ja 73
John   T: Kingwood 10 Ag 58
Joseph   P: Sadsbury 30 May
54, 11 Sep 55, 9 Ag 59
Mary   P: Phila 3 Ag 58
Nicholas   P: Phila 1 Nov 53
Richard   P: Timber Creek 24
Jy 76
Samuel   P: Phila 29 Ag 54
Stephen (soldier)   P: 21 Dec
58
Thomas   P: Phila 13 Ja 63,
31 Mar 63 (Capt)
Trueman/Truman   P: Kinderhook
9 Ag 59; Pa 21 Dec 58
William   P: Phila 24 Oct 54
POWER/POWERS
Mrs.   P: Phila 2 May 65
Alexander   P: Phila 10 Oct 65
Bridget   P: Phila-Gaz. 3 Ja 76
Edward   P: Phila 23 Oct 66
Eleanor   P: Phila 13 Oct 63,
3 Ja 65
Jane   P: Nottingham 27 Dec 53
Jeffery/Gaffery   P: Phila 31
Mar 63, 30 Ap 67, 19 Ja 69,
27 Ja 73 (Capt)
John   P: Phila 8 Jy 62, 23

Oct 66, 21 Jy 68
Joseph   P: Phila 27 Ja 73
Mary   P: Phila 18 Feb 55
Patrick   C: near Oxford
   Meeting-house 22 Ja 67.
   P: Phila 5 Ag 62
Richard   P: Phila 31 Dec 61
   (Capt), 27 Ja 73
Robert   P: Phila 31 Jy 60
   (Capt), 31 Mar 63, 30 Ja
   66
Thomas   L: Paxton 19 Dec
   71.   P: Phila 12 Feb 61
POWERT
Charles   P: Phila 6 Sep 53
POWIL
John   P: Lancaster 26 Jy 64
PRALL
John   T: near Corryell's
   Ferry 6 Dec 64
PRATT
Alexander, soldier   P: Phila
   26 Oct 69
John, Jr.   T: Amwell 15 Mar
   64
Shubael   Phila 30 Oct 76
   (Dr), 16 Jy 77
Thomas   P: Land Office, Phila
   21 Jy 68
PRAUL
John, Jr.   P: Bucks Co 25 Ap
   71
PRECKETT
Ang. /or Ane?/ P: Kent Co 7
   Ap 57
PREMIER
Adam   P: Phila 30 Oct 76
PRENNES
Thomas   P: New Jersey 3 May
   70
PRENTICE/PRINTIS
Dr.   P: Lancaster 9 Ag 59, 3
   Ja 60
John   P: Phila 3 Ja 65, 2 May
   65, 30 Ap 67
PRESCOTT
John   P: Pa 12 Feb 61
PRESLY
John   P: Phila 3 Ag 58
PRESTON
Ann   P: Cumberland Co 8 Jy 62
James   P: Chester Co 3 Ag 58
John   P: Bucks Co 4 Ag 63, 20
   Ap 69; Phila 3 Ja 60, 27 Ja
   73
Jonathan   P: Upper Dublin 11 Jy
   54
Nathaniel   P: Phila 20 Oct 68,
   1 Feb 70
Samuel   P: Phila 3 May 70
Thomas   P: Bucks Co 16 Jy 67;
   Phila 6 Jy 58, 12 Feb 61
William   P: Phila 2 Ag 70
PRICE
tanner,...   P: Phila 29 Ag 54

Mrs.   P: Phila 19 Ja 69
Anna/Anne/Ann   P: Phila 9 Ag
   59, 3 Ja 60, 18 Mar 62;
   Roxbury 3 Ag 58
Catherine   P: Phila-Gaz. 27
   Oct 73
David   T: Hopewell 15 Mar 64,
   6 Dec 64
Eb.   P: Phila 13 Ja 63
Edward   P: Merion Twp 27 Ja
   73
Elizabeth   P: Phila 7 Ap 57,
   2 Sep 62, 25 Jy 65, 10 Oct
   65
Esther   P: Phila 18 Mar 62
George D. (soldier)   P: Fort
   Pitt 26 Jy 64
Isaac   P: Phila 11 Sep 55
James   P: Phila 19 Ja 69
Jasper   P: Phila 29 Ag 54
Jesse   P: Phila 9 Ag 59, 3
   Ja 60, 18 Mar 62
John   P: Phila 3 May 70
Joseph   P: Phila 3 Ja 60
Mary   T: Burlington Co 17 Oct
   54
Peter   L: at James Old's,Lan-
   caster Co 19 Dec 71, 29 Jy
   72
Philip   P: Kingsess 13 Oct
   63.   T: Morris Twp 7 May
   67
Reese   P: Chester Co 3 Sep 61
Richard   P: Phila 19 May 63,
   25 Jy 65, 21 Jy 68, 19 Jy
   80
Robert   P: Haddonfield 3 Ag
   58.   T: Sussex Co 7 May 67
Sophia   P: Phila 3 Sep 61, 18
   Mar 62
Thomas   T: Maidenhead 17 Oct
   54; Crosswicks 17 Oct 54
W.   P: Phila 31 Dec 61
William   P: Phila 11 Sep 55,
   13 May 56, 21 Dec 58, 9 Ag
   59, 31 Dec 61, 18 Mar 62,
   5 Ag 62, 1 Feb 70 (Capt)
PRICHARD
Rowland   P: Phila 2 Sep 62
Thomas   P: Phila 2 Sep 62
PRIESTLY
John   P: Phila 24 Feb 63
PRINCE
Elizabeth   P: Phila 2 May 65
PRINGLE; see also FISHER &
PRINGLE
Hugh   P: Phila 2 Ag 70
James   P: Phila 2 May 65
John   P: Phila 13 Ja 63, 25
   Jy 65, 21 Jy 68
PRIOR
Mr.   P: Phila 28 Ap 68
Andrew   P: Chester Co 12 Feb
   61
Elizabeth   P: Phila 20 Ap 69

John   P: Phila-Gaz. 3 Ja 76
Thomas   T: Yeardly's Ferry
   10 Ag 58
PRITCHARD
William   P: Phila 30 Ap 77
PRITCHETT
William   P: Phila 11 Sep 55
PRIZLEY
John   P: Phila 11 Sep 55
PROBY/PROBYE
Jacob   P: Phila 2 Feb 64
John   P: Phila 16 Jy 72
Mary   L: 13 Jn 65. P: Phila
   31 Ja 76
PROCTO
John   Phila 24 Jy 76
PROCTOR
Benjamin   P: Phila 4 Feb 68
Thomas   P: Phila 23 Oct 66
PROSSER
John   P: Phila 1 Nov 53
PROUD
Robert   P: Phila 24 Feb 63
PROUDFOOT
Rev.   P: Pequea 2 Feb 64
Dav.   L: 31 Ja 71
Rev. James   P: Pequea 18 Mar
   62, 24 Feb 63, 4 Ag 63, 26
   Jy 64
John   P: Phila 25 Jy 65
Ro.   L: 31 Ja 71
PROVOST
Hon. Bartisan   P: Phila 2 Ag
   70
PUFF
Peter   P: Phila 18 Mar 62
PUGH
James   P: Phila 30 Ja 66
Jonathan   P: Lancaster Road
   13 Ja 63
William   T: Union Iron-Works
   7 May 67
PUHEN
Loftues   P: Phila 15 Mar 64
PULLEN/PULLIN
Loftus/Loftis   P: Chester Co
   28 Nov 54; Phila 21 Dec 58
Samuel   P: Kensington 4 Ap 54
PUMROY
George   P: Shippensburg 18 Mar
   62
PUNCH
James   P: Chester Co 31 Dec 61;
   Pa 18 Mar 62
Nicholas   P: Pa 31 Dec 61; Phila
   16 Jy 72
PUNSMANTLE
Clara Marie   P: Phila 3 Ag 58
PURCELL
Capt. Michael   P: Phila 5 Ag 62
PURD
Robert   Phila 24 Jy 76
PURDON
Fergus/Farges   P: Phila 13 Ja
   63, 27 Ja 73

PURDY/PURDEY/PURDAY
James   P: Near Phila 20 Oct
   68
John   P: Phila 29 Ag 54. T:
   near Allen's Town 1 Sep 68
Thomas   P: Pa 2 Feb 64; Phila
   30 Ap 77
PURFIELD
Lawrence   P: Phila 10 Ap 66
PURISS
Thomas   P: Phila 1 Jy 56
PURNER
Henry   P: Phila 13 Oct 63,
   3 Ja 65
PURSELL/PURSSELL
Jane   P: Newcastle Co 7 Ap
   57
John   P: Phila 12 Feb 61, 3
   Sep 61
William   P: Phila 28 Ap 68
PURTLE
James   P: Chester Co 3 Sep 61
PURVIANCE
James   P: Phila 19 Ja 69
Samuel   P: Phila 13 May 56
William   P: Phila 26 Oct 69
PURVIS
William   P: Phila 2 Ag 70
PYATT; see also PIATT
Alexander   P: Phila 3 Ja 65
James   P: East New Jersey 21
   Dec 58
PYNES
John   P: Phila 28 Nov 54, 3
   Ag 58
PYRES
John   P: Phila 13 May 56

QUA
Alexander   T: Monmouth Co 1
   Sep 68
QUAINTANCE
William/Will.   P: Chester Co
   12 Feb 61; East Bradford 24
   Oct 54; Pa 31 Dec 61
QUALE
Mr.   P: Phila 9 Ag 59
QUALL
Jane   P: Little Britain 18
   Mar 62
QUAZY
Peter   P: Phila 10 Oct 65
QUAN
Thomas   P: New Castle Co 30
   May 54
QUANTON/QUANTIN
Mary   P: Warwick, Bucks Co 26
   Oct 69
Samuel   P: Bucks Co 30 Ja 66
QUEE
Rachel   P: Horsham 4 Ag 63
QUERY
John   L: Lancaster Co 15 Ap
   56

QUICK
John   P: Phila 4 Ap 54
QUIG
James   P: Phila 13 May 56
QUIGLEY/QUIGLY
John   N: 29 Nov 64.   P:
Cumberland Co 13 Oct 63
QUILHOT
Dr.   P: Phila 13 Oct 63
QUILY
Daniel   P: Phila 18 Mar 62
QUIM
Charles   P: 13 May 56
John, tailor   T: 7 May 67
QUINLAN
Ralph   P: Phila 5 Ag 56
QUINN/QUIN
Barnabas   L: 25 Dec 66
Charles   P: 3 Ag 58, 9 Ag
59, 31 Dec 61
Hugh   P: Phila 26 Oct 69
James   P: Phila 25 Jy 65
John   P: Phila 31 Jy 60.
W: c/o Mr. John Dodd's
Newark
Theodosia   P: Phila 27 Ja
73
QUIRKS
John   P: Phila 27 Ja 73

RABOTT
Rev. Jacob   P: Phila 19 Jy
80
RACOP
Christian   P: Phila 2 May
65
RADCLIFF/RATCLIFFE
Henry   P: Pa 3 Ja 60; Phila
21 Dec 58, 4 Ag 63
John   P: Phila 24 Feb 63
Thomas   P: Pa 3 Ja 60
RADDEN
William   P: Phila 27 Ja 73
RAFF
John   P: Kensignton 4 Ag 63
RAFFERTY
John   P: Pa 13 Ja 63
RAGON
William   P: Cooper's Creek 9
Ag 59
RAHN
Casper   P: Phila 24 Jy 76
RAIN
Samuel   P: Marcus Hook 9 Ag
59
RAINEY/RAINY
Mrs.   P: Cape-May 2 Feb 64
David   P: Lancaster Co 3 Ja 60
James   P: Cape-May 31 Dec 61,
18 Mar 62
RAINS
John   P: Phila-Gaz. 3 Ja 76
RAIT
Robert   P: Phila 9 Ag 59

RAKESTRAW
Hannah   P: Phila 9 Ag 59
William   P: Phila 9 Ag 59
RAKLIN
Mary   P: Phila 30 Ap 67
RALLON
George   P: Phila 30 Oct 76
RALSTON/RALSTAN
Andrew   P: Cumberland Co 2
Feb 64
David   L: Middletown Twp,
Cumberland Co 19 Dec 71
Gavin/GAUN   P: Baltimore Co
3 Ja 60; Pa 12 Feb 61
John   P: Baltimore Co 3 Ja
60, 31 Dec 61; Pa 12 Feb
61; Pine Grove Iron Works
27 Ja 73
RAMAGE/RAMADGE
Archibald   P: Pa 13 Ja 63
James   P: Phila 26 Oct 69, 3
Ja 76
Thomas   L: Paxton 19 Dec 71.
P: Pa 13 Oct 63
RAMBO
John   P: Phila 24 Feb 63
RAMBRIDGE
Peter   P: Chester Co 12 Feb
61
RAMSAY/RAMSEY; see also WILTON
& RAMSAY
Mrs.   P: Cape-May 15 Mar 64
Ann   L: Donegall 15 Ap 56
Benjamin   Phila 5 Ap 76-Gaz.
1 May
Ja.   L: in Drummore 14 May
72
James   P: Great Valley 18 Mar
62
John   P: N. Castle Co 15 Mar
64; Pa 15 Mar 64; Phila 4
Ag 63, 3 Ja 76
Joseph   P: Phila-Gaz. 27 Oct
73
Margaret   P: Pa 4 Ag 63
Rebecca   P: Lancaster Co 12
Ja 58
Robert   P: Chester Co 4 Ag
63; Lancaster 2 Feb 64, 15
Mar 64; Octerara 2 Feb 64;
Pa 18 Mar 62, 19 May 63
Sa.   L: 14 May 72
William   L: Marsh Creek 2 Ma
74.   P: Bucks Co 30 Ja 66;
Chester Co 2 Feb 64; N.
Castle Co 13 Oct 63; Lan-
caster Co 31 Dec 61, 2 Feb
64, 15 Mar 64; Phila 20 Ap
69
RAMSHAW
Benjamin   P: Phila 25 Jy 65,
10 Ap 66
RANDAL/RANDELL/RANDEL/RANDOL
Mr.   L: 29 Ja 67
Dr. Ananias   P: Alloways

Creek 1 Feb 70
Ed. F. P: near Chester 5 Ag
   62
John P: Phila 31 Jy 60
William C: c/o George Ash-
   bridge Willistown 22 Ja 67
RANDALS
Andrew C: c/o Mr. Cummins-
   near Nottingham Meeting-
   house 28 Nov 65
RANDOLPH
Benjamin P: Phila 5 Ag 62,
   30 Oct 76
John P: Phila 25 Jy 65
RANKIN/RANKEN/RANKINS/RANKON/
   RENKEN
Capt. P: Phila-Gaz. 27 Oct
   73
Mr. P: Phila 20 Ap 69
David P: Phila 19 Ja 69
Elizabeth P: Phila 11 Sep 55
Hugh P: Pa 2 Feb 64
James L: Lancaster 20 Ja 73.
   P: Forks of Delaware 21 Dec
   58, 1 Nov 70, 27 Oct 73;
   Northampton Co 31 Dec 61,
   13 Oct 63; near Nutfield 24
   Oct 54; Pa 2 Feb 64
John L: Pequea Creek 15 Ap
   56; cooper 2 Mar 74. P:
   New-Castle Co 3 Ag 58, 21 Dec
   58, 9 Ag 59, 31 Jy 60; Pequea
   27 Dec 53; Phila 4 Ag 63, 4
   Feb 68, 1 May 76; Red-Lion 3
   Sep 61
Joseph P: Milford 13 Oct 63;
   Phila 27 Oct 73
Capt. Moses P: Phila 19 May
   63, 3 May 70
Richard P: Phila 30 Ja 66
Samuel L: Lancaster Co 20 Ja
   73. P: Lancaster Co 31 Jy 60
Thomas P: Pa 24 Feb 63
William P: Lancaster Co 31 Jy
   60; Phila 2 Ag 70
RANLISS
William P: Phila 25 Jy 65
RANSOM
George P: Phila 28 Ap 68
RAPALJE
Garret P: Phila 25 Ap 71
RAPER
Robert, Esq. P: Phila 23 Oct
   66
RAPP
Rev. Phil. Henry P: Germantown
   12 Feb 61, 3 Sep 61
RARITON
Henry P: Marcus-Hook 9 Ag 59
RATAN
Joseph P: Sussex Co 2 Feb 64
RATCHFORD
Hugh L: Pequea 19 Dec 71
RATHMILL
John P: Bucks Co 10 Oct 65

RATTRAY
Andrew P: Phila 31 Dec 61
RAVENCROFT
Richard P: Phila-Gaz. 3 Ja 76
RAWLE
Rebecca P: Phila 5 Ag 62
RAWLING/RAWLINGS
Thomas P: Phila 30 Ap 67, 28
   Ap 68, 19 Ja 69
RAWN
Charles P: Chester Co 24 Feb
   63
RAY
Alexander P: Phila 21 Dec
   58 (2)
Lt. J. P: in the army 3 Ag
   58
Jane P: Pa 21 Dec 58
Peter P: Phila-Gaz. 27 Oct
   73
Robert P: Newcastle 11 Jy 54
William Phila 30 Ap 77
RAYLY
William P: White Horse, Lan-
   caster Road 9 Ag 59
RAYSE
John P: Phila 3 Ja 65
RAYWORTH
William P: Phila 9 Ag 59
RAZER/RAZOR
Baltzo P: Phila 3 May 70
Peter P: Pa 12 Feb 61
REA/REAH; see also REAY, RHEA
Alexander P: Kingwood 13 Oct
   63
Edward N: 29 Nov 64
Elizabeth P: Phila 20 Oct 68
Ja. L: 14 May 72
James, of the 42d Regt. P:
   Phila 23 Oct 66
Jos. P: Pa 15 Mar 64
Patrick P: New-Castle 3 Sep
   61
Rebecca P: New-Castle Co 4
   Ag 63
Robert P: Christine Bridge
   9 Ag 59
William P: Christine Bridge
   9 Ag 59
REACE
David P: Pa 31 Mar 63
READ
Mrs. P: Chester Co 28 Oct 62
... Mr. P: Christine 31 Mar
   63
Andrew, Esq. P: Phila 23
   Oct 66
Ann P: Phila 3 Ja 65
Charles P: Phila 13 Ja 63
   (Esq.), 2 May 65
Charles, Jr. P: Phila 10
   Oct 65
George P: Lancaster Co 28
   Oct 62
Jacob P: Phila 15 Mar 64, 26

Jy 64
James/Jas. L: 20 Ja 73
   (collier). P: Artena-
   raroo 2 May 65; Lancaster
   15 Mar 64; New London 18
   Ag 57 (Esq.); Octerara 31
   Dec 61; Pa 12 Feb 61;
   Phila 21 Dec 58, 31 Dec 61,
   31 Mar 63, 25 Jy 65, 19
   Ja 69; Reading 2 May 65
John P: Christine 21 Dec 58;
   Cumberland Co 3 Sep 61; Pa
   31 Mar 63, 2 Feb 61; Phila
   18 Mar 62, 24 Feb 63, 20
   Jy 69, 1 Nov 70
Mary T: Freehold 4 Nov 72
Ned P: Phila 19 Ja 69
Richard P: Phila-Gaz. 27
   Oct 73
Robert P: Pa 18 Mar 62, 28
   Oct 62; Phila 15 Mar 64, 26
   Jy 64
Samuel P: Pa 28 Oct 62
Thomas P: Pa 18 Mar 62; Phila
   24 Feb 63, 27 Oct 73
William C: New Town, Chester
   Co 18 Jy 65. P: Lancaster
   Co 3 Ag 58, 2 Sep 62, 13 Ja
   63 (Esq.); Pa 13 Ja 63;
   Phila 28 Oct 62; York Co 13
   Oct 63
READING/REDING
Rev. P: Phila 3 May 70
Elizabeth P: Phila-Gaz. 3 Ja
   76
John, Esq. T: Amwell 17 Oct
   54
Miss Margaret Phila 30 Oct 76
Rev. Philip P: Apoquinimy
   3 Ag 58
Robert P: Phila-Gaz. 27 Oct 73
REAGAN
Lawrence P: Phila 15 Mar 64
REALLY
Cornelius P: Phila 3 Ja 65
REANY/RENEY
Alexander, cooper L: 2 Mar 74
James N: 29 Nov 64. P: Pa 2
   Feb 64; Phila 11 Jy 54
REARDON
John P: Phila 24 Oct 54
REARLIN/REARLINE
Joseph P: Chester Co 31 Jy
   60; Concord 12 Ja 58
REARY
Ann P: Phila 25 Ap 71
REASE
Rev. Edward P: Phila 2 Ag 70
REASON/REAZON
George P: Phila 11 Sep 55
Jer. P: Phila 2 Feb 64
REAUGH
John P: Phila 27 Ja 73
REAY
George P: N. Providence 26

Oct 69
RECH
Joseph P: Pa 24 Feb 63
RED
Philip P: Phila 19 Ja 69
REDDICK/REDICK
Sarah P: Cumberland Co 12
   Ja 58
William L: 3 Oct 65
REDGRAVE/RIDGRAVE
Ann P: New-Castle Co 21 Dec
   58, 9 Ag 59, 3 Ja 60
RED HEAD
Robert Phila 30 Oct 76
REDIN
John P: Phila 9 Ag 59
REDMAN
Patrick P: Phila 20 Ap 69
REDMOND
John P: Chester Co 13 Oct 63
Patrick P: Phila 23 Oct 66
REDSTREAK
John P: Salem 30 Ap 67
REE
John P: Little-Britain 13 Oct
   63
REECE/REESE/REES
David P: Radnor 7 Ap 57
Given/Givin P: Lower Merion
   9 Ag 59, 3 Ja 60
John P: Bucks Co 9 Ag 59;
   Phila 21 Dec 58
Joseph P: Bucks Co 3 Ja 60
Margaret P: Phila 3 Ja 65
Robert P: Kingwood 9 Ag 59
Thomas P: Chester Co 28 Nov
   54; Phila 16 Jy 67
Valentine P: Phila 27 Ja 73
William P: Phila 1 Nov 70
REED
Capt. P: Phila 16 Jy 67
Mrs. P: Phila 1 Feb 70
Mr. & storekeeper C: at
   Christeen Bridge 28 Nov 65
Rev. P: New-Castle Co 30 May
   54
Adam P: Lancaster 9 Ag 59
Andrew P: N.J. 3 Ja 60; Pa
   9 Ag 59; Phila 28 Nov 54, 28
   Ap 68. T: East Jersey 3 Oct
   65; Freehold 15 Mar 64, 6
   Dec 64
Charles P: Phila 25 Jy 65
David P: Phila 3 Ja 65
George P: 21 Dec 58 (soldier);
   New-Garden 11 Sep 55
Henry L: Cumberland Co 29 Jy
   72
James P: Phila 3 Ag 58, 3 Ja
   76, 30 Ap 77
John C: c/o J. Reed, Reed's
   Mill, New London, Cross
   Roads 28 Nov 65. L: Cum-
   berland Co 29 Jy 72; Han-
   over Twp 15 Ap 56; Lancaster

Co 19 Dec 71. P: near
Phila Co 3 Ja 60; Phila
3 Ja 65, 3 Ja 76. T:
Maidenhead 10 Ag 58
John, Jr. P: Cumberland
Co 7 Ap 57
Joseph Phila 16 Jy 77
Jos., Jr. P: Phila 30 Ja 66
Margaret P: York Co 3 Ja 60
Mary P: York Co 9 Ag 59
Philip P: Pa 3 Ja 60
Robert L: c/o John Wilkins,
Carlisle 29 Jy 72. P:
Somerset Co 13 Oct 63
Samuel P: Phila 18 Ag 57,
12 Ja 58. T: Monmouth Co 3
Oct 65
Timothy P: Forks Delaware 1
Nov 70
William L: York Co 19 Dec
71. P: Bucks Co 21 Jy 68;
Chester Co 28 Oct 62, 2
Feb 64; Chestnut Level 12
Ja 58; Cumberland Co., N.J.
29 Ag 54, 18 Feb 55; Lan-
caster Co 27 Dec 53, 31 Jy
60; Little Britain Twp 12
Ja 58; Phila 5 Ag 56, 28 Ap
68, 27 Ja 73; York Co 3 Ja
60
REEDE
Robert, shoemaker C: 22 Ja
67
REELY
William P: Sweetarra Creek 26
Oct 69
REEVES
Benjamin P: Phila 11 Jy 54,
24 Oct 54
Elijah, soldier P: Phila 1
Feb 70
Elizabeth P: Kensington 2 Feb
64
Francis P: Phila-Gaz. 3 Ja
76
John P: West Nottingham 24 Oct
54
Mary Phila 1 May 76
REID
David P: Pa 13 Oct 63; Phila
20 Ap 69, 1 Nov 70; prob. in
Pittsburgh, Sgt. 15 Mar 64
James P: Phila 30 Ja 66
John P: Phila 30 Ja 66, writing
master 4 Feb 68
Robert P: Phila 25 Jy 65
William P: 12 Feb 61; York
Co 3 Sep 61
REIGER
Jacob P: Phila-Gaz. 27 Oct 73
REILY/REILLY/REILEY
Ann P: Pa 31 Dec 61; Salem Co
30 Oct 76
Benjamin P: Sussex on Delaware
26 Oct 69

Charles P: Phila 3 Ja 65
Edward P: Germantown 3 Ag
58, 21 Dec 58; Phila 21
Dec 58 (Capt.), 9 Ag 59
Farrel P: Phila 18 Feb 55
John P: Phila 23 Oct 66
Luke P: Phila-Gaz. 27 Oct
73
Mary P: Chester Co 3 Ja 60,
31 Jy 60
Polly P: Lancaster 12 Feb
61
Robert P: Pa 31 Dec 61
William P: Chester Co 4 Ag
63; Whieteland Twp 12 Ja
58
REINHART
Jacob P: Phila 19 Jy 80
REINHERD-GLASS
George P: Phila 31 Jy 60
REINHOLT
Monsieur P: Pa 7 Ap 57
REISNER
Joseph P: Phila 31 Dec 61
REKEY
James P: Phila 28 Oct 62
RELF/RELFE
Capt. Jas. P: Lancaster 15
Mar 64
John P: Phila 3 May 70
Capt. Joseph P: Little
Britain 13 Oct 63
REMSON
John P: Phila 3 Ja 65
RENARD
John P: Phila 27 Ja 73
RENEAR
James P: N.J. 15 Mar 64
RENFEW
William P: Phila-Gaz. 3 Ja
76
RENFREW
John P: Phila-Gaz. 3 Ja 76
Robert P: Pa 5 Ag 62
RENICK
Henry P: Lancaster Co 22
Nov 53
RENIFFE
Charles P: Phila 24 Oct 54
RENNARD
Dr. P: Great Egg-Harbour
16 Jy 77
RENNILS
James P: Phila 24 Feb 63
RENNOLDSON
Charles P: Phila-Gaz. 27
Oct 73
RENOT
Charles P: Phila 1 Jy 56
RENOUF
Charles P: Phila 11 Sep 55,
7 Ap 57
RENSHAW
Richard P: Gloucester Point
28 Ap 68, 21 Jy 68

Thomas   P: Phila 31 Jy 60,
   31 Dec 61
RENSON
   John   P: Phila 3 Ja 60
RENTCH
   Andrew   L: 29 Ja 67
RENTFORD
   Henry   P: Pa 15 Mar 64
RESIDE/RESID
   James   P: Phila 5 Ag 56
   John   P: 12 Feb 61; London-
      derry 31 Dec 61; New Lon-
      doner 18 Ag 57; Pa 9 Ag
      59
RETTOW
   John   P: Ashton Twp 13 Ja
      63
REVELL/REUIL
   Mary   P: Phila 11 Sep 55, 6
      Jy 58
REVERLDS
   James   Phila 1 May 76
REWMAN
   John   P: Phila 3 Ja 60
REYN
   Mr.   P: Pa 18 Ag 57
REYNARD
   Simon   P: Richland /or Phila?7
      1 Nov 53
REYNIE
   Mrs.   P: Phila 24 Feb 63
REYNOLDS/REYNALDS/RENOLDS/
   RANNALDS; see also RENNILS/
   REYNELLS
   Alexander   P: Dover, Kent Co
      20 Jy 69
   Anthony   P: Pennsylvania 20 Oct
      68
   Catherine   P: Kent Co 9 Ag 59,
      3 Ja 60
   David   P: Germantown 12 Ja 58;
      Phila 6 Jy 58, 31 Dec 61
   Edward   P: Phila 3 Sep 61,
      3 Ja 76
   Jackson   P: Phila 27 Ja 73
   James   P: Phila 30 May 54, 3
      Ag 58, 21 Dec 58, 24 Feb 63.
      T: Mountholly 15 Mar 64
   John   P: Cranberry 1 Feb 70;
      Phila 26 Oct 69
   Joseph   P: Pa 4 Ag 63; Phila
      21 Dec 58, 9 Ag 59
   Michael   Phila 24 Jy 76
   Pat.   P: Mount-holly 8 Jy 62
   Robert   P: Kent Co 12 Ja 58
   Samuel   P: Marcus-Hook 3 Sep
      61, 31 Dec 61
   Sarah   P: Phila 21 Dec 58, 30
      Ap 77
   William   P: Lancaster Co 5 Feb
      54, 4 Ap 54
RHEA; see also REA
   David   P: Pikeland 24 Feb 63
   William   T: 10 Ag 58; Trenton
      15 Jy 56

RHODES
   Joseph   P: New-Castle Co 31
      Jy 60
   Reuben   P: Phila 2 Feb 64
   Capt. William   P: Kent Co
      8 Jy 62
RIB
   Mary   P: Phila 9 Ag 59, 3
      Sep 61
RIBIERE
   Mons.   P: Phila 19 Jy 80
RIBOLT
   Jacob   P: Germantown 2 May
      65
RICE (or PRICE)
   tanner...   Phila 29 Ag 54
   Mrs.   P: Phila 16 Jy 67
   Caleb   P: Phila 20 Ap 69
   David   P: Phila 8 Jy 62
   Capt. E.   P: N. Castle Co
      2 Feb 64
   Henry   P: Phila-Gaz. 3 Ja
      76
   Isabel   P: Cranberry 9 Ag
      59
   James   P: 24 Oct 54
   John   P: Phila 2 Ag 70
   Patrick   P: Phila 4 Feb 68
RICH
   Betsy   P: Phila 20 Jy 69
RICHAN
   George   P: Phila 5 Ag 56
RICHARD
   Monsieur, Baron de Reichel
      P: Phila 19 Jy 80
   Stephen   P: Phila 24 Feb 63
   William   P: Pa 13 Oct 63
RICHARDS
   Burnet/Barnet   P: Bristol
      9 Ag 59; Pa 12 Feb 61;
      Phila 2 May 65
   Charles   P: East New Jersey
      13 Oct 63
   David   P: Phila 31 Dec 61,
      30 Ap 67
   Elizabeth   P: Allen-Town/
      Allens Yown 3 Ag 58, 21
      Dec 58; Phila 16 Jy 77
   Henry   P: Phila 2 Feb 64,
      15 Mar 64 (2), 3 Ja 65, 20
      Ap 69
   James   P: Phila 31 Jy 60
   John   P: Phila 18 Mar 62,
      31 Mar 63, 27 Oct 73:
      Capt. -Phila 31 Jy 60
   Joseph   P: Phila 19 Ja 69
   Richard   P: Chester Co 9 Ag
      59
   Thomas   P: Phila 3 Ag 58,
      21 Dec 58, 9 Ag 59, 3 Ja
      60
RICHARDSON
   ... (timber merchant)   P:
      Pa 11 Sep 55
   Alexander   P: Pa 15 Mar 64;

Phila 26 Jy 64

Daniel P: Abington 26 Oct
  69. T: Trenton 4 Nov 72

Eliz. P: Richland /or
  Phila?7 1 Nov 53

Isaac P: Bucks Co 31 Dec 61;
  Lancaster Co 3 Sep 61; Pequea 12 Ja 58

James N: c/o Joseph Barton
  Mill Creek Hundred 4 Dec 66.
  P: Phila 10 Ap 66

John P: in the army 12 Ja 58;
  Phila 8 Jy 62

Jos. P: N. Prov. Town 6 Sep
  53, 15 Mar 64 (Capt); Providence, Phila Co 2 Jy 69

Richard P: Chester Co 3 Ja 60;
  Phila 31 Dec 61; Wilmington
  30 May 54

Samuel P: Lancaster Co 24 Feb
  63; Phila 28 Oct 62

Thomas P: Phila 3 Ja 65

William L: c/o William Bell-
  Lancaster 20 Ja 73, 2 Mar
  74. P: Phila 24 Oct 54, 11
  Sep 55, 4 Ag 63

RICHART
  Thomas P: Chester Co 18 Ag 57

RICHE
  John P: Phila 11 Sep 55
  Mary P: Phila 24 Oct 54
  Robert P: Forks Delaware 4 Ap
  54
  Thomas Bucks Co 30 Ap 77; Phila
  12 Feb 61

RICHESON
  Mary P: West Jersey 7 Ap 57
  Pleasant P: Phila 2 Feb 64
  William (soldier) P: 21 Dec
  58

RICHEY
  Adam C: c/o James Moore-near
  Carlisle 29 Jy 72

RICHMOND/RICHMONT
  Dr. P: in the army 21 Dec 58
  George P: Phila 30 Ap 67
  Jacob P: Pilesgrove 31 Dec 61
  John L: 13 Jn 65
  Joseph P: Phila 21 Jy 68; Salis-
  bury 3 Ag 58
  Mary P: in the army-prob. in
  Pittsburgh 15 Mar 64
  Nemo P: Phila 21 Dec 58
  Neomey P: Phila 21 Dec 58
  Robert P: Phila 2 Ag 70

RICKETS
  Elizabeth P: Phila 3 Ja 65

RICKLESS
  Joseph P: West Jersey 13 Ja 63

RID
  Thomas P: Phila 3 Ja 65

RIDDLE/RIDDEL/RIDDALL/RIDDELL/
  RIDDAL/RIDEL
  James P: Phila 27 Dec 53, 3 Ja
  65, 27 Oct 73

John P: Forks of Delaware
  9 Ag 59, 31 Dec 61; Phila
  7 Ap 57, 16 Jy 67; Capt.
  Phila 6 Jy 58, 3 Ag 58,
  4 Ag 63

Joseph P: Phila 16 Jy 67

Samuel P: New-Castle Co
  9 Ag 59

Thomas P: Pa 13 Oct 63;
  Phila 3 Ja 65

William P: Jerseys 9 Ag
  59; N.J. 3 Ja 60; Pa 2
  Feb 64

RIDDICK
  William P: Phila 19 Ja 69

RIDE
  Henry P: Phila 3 Ja 65

RIDER
  Eleanor T: Bordentown 17
  Oct 54
  James P: Phila 15 Mar 64

RIDGE
  Lt. William P: in the army
  12 Ja 58

RIDGLEY
  Charles P: Dover 31 Dec 61

RIDGWAY
  Margaret P: Phila 21 Dec 58

RIDLEY
  Thomas P: Phila 2 May 65

RIDOCK
  Robert P: Phila 27 Ja 73

RIE
  Owen P: Springfield 2 Feb
  64

RIGBE
  Henry P: Phila 28 Nov 54

RIGDEN
  William P: Phila 24 Feb 63

RIGGS
  Edward T: Hanover 17 Oct
  54
  George P: Cumberland 28
  Nov 54

RIGH
  William P: Phila 9 May 54,
  27 Oct 73

RINGHOUS
  Michael L: 3 Oct 65

RILEY
  Catharine P: Phila-Gaz. 3
  Ja 76
  Charles P: Phila 11 Sep 55
  Daniel P: Newtown 13 May
  56
  Edward P: Phila 21 Dec 58
  Timothy P: Egg Harbour 1
  May 76
  William P: Chester Co 1 Nov
  53

RINCKER
  Henry P: Easton 1 Jy 56

RIND
  Edward P: Phila 25 Jy 65

RINDLESS

Alexander   P: Phila 11 Sep 55
RING
   Richard   P: Phila 28 Oct 62
RINN
   John   P: Chester Co 19 Jy 80
RINNELLS
   James   P: Phila 10 Oct 65
RIORDON
   Michael   P: Phila 27 Ja 73
RIPETH
   William   P: Lancaster 15 Mar
   64
RIPPY
   Hugh   P: Chestnut Level 3 Sep
   61
RISK
   Charles   P: Chester Co 18 Mar
   62
   William   P: Cumberland Co 28
   Oct 62
RISSEL
   Thomas   P: Phila 11 Sep 55
RISSETT
   Christian   P: Phila 19 Jy 80
   Paul   P: Phila 24 Oct 54
RISTINE
   David   P: Germantown 20 Ap 69
   John   P: Germantown 19 Ja 69
RITCHIE
   James   T: Kingwood 4 Dec 64
   Capt. John   P: Phila 3 May 70
   Robert   P: Phila-Gaz. 3 Ja 76
RITEW
   Matthew   L: Berks Co 25 Dec 66
RITTEN/RITTON
   John   P: Chester Co 8 Jy 62;
   Pa 4 Ag 63, 15 Mar 64; 2 Sep
   62, 13 Oct 63, 15 Mar 64
RIVERS/RIVER
   Joseph   P: Phila 16 Jy 72
   Walter   P: Phila 21 Dec 58
   William   P: Phila 3 Ag 58, 9
   Ag 59
ROACH/ROAGH
   James   P: Phila-Gaz. 27 Oct 73
   John   P: Phila-Gaz. 3 Ja 76 (2)
   Thomas   P: Phila 15 Mar 64
   William   P: Egg-harbour 2 Ag 70;
   Phila 5 Ag 62, 4 Feb 68,
   27 Oct 73
ROADS
   James   P: Phila-Gaz. 27 Oct 73
   Joseph   P: Phila 1 Feb 70
ROAN
   Dr.   P: Phila 26 Jy 64
   Andrew   L: Derry Twp 2 Mar 74
   James   P: Phila 18 Mar 62
   John, minister   L: 2 Mar 74
ROARK
   Alexander   P: Pa 21 Dec 58
ROBB/ROB
   Mary   P: Phila 21 Dec 58
   Richard   P: Germantown 28 Nov
   54; Phila 3 Ja 76
   William   P: Octerara 13 Ja 63

ROBBARDS
   John   P: Pa 13 Oct 63
ROBBINS; see also ROBINS
   Mary   P: Phila-Gaz. 27 Oct
   73
   Thomas   P: Phila 15 Mar 64
   William   P: Phila 3 Ja 65
ROBERTS
   Mr.   P: Phila 2 May 65
   Albert   P: Phila 3 Ja 65
   Ben./Benjamin   L: 13 Jn 65.
   P: Phila 16 Jy 67
   Blanch   P: Phila 4 Ag 63
   Bradford   P: Phila 10 Ap 66
   David   P: Chester Co 28 Oct
   62
   Henry   P: B. Co. 20 Ap 69
   Isaac   P: Phila 11 Sep 55
   Dr. J.   P: Kent Island 31
   Dec 61
   Jacob   P: Phila-Gaz. 3 Ja
   76
   Capt. James   P: Phila 8 Jy
   62
   John   N: 29 Nov 64.   P:
   Cumberland Co 7 Ap 57;
   Salem 7 Ap 57
   Margaret   P: Phila 3 Ja 60
   Mary   P: Chester Co 12 Feb
   61, 18 Mar 62; Cumberland
   Co 7 Ap 57; Goshen 21 Dec
   58, 31 Dec 61
   Nancy   P: Phila 16 Jy 72
   Patrick   P: Phila 2 May 65
   Philip   P: Pa 3 Ja 60
   Richard   P: Phila 26 Jy 64,
   1 Feb 70
   Robert   P: Phila 2 Ag 70,
   27 Oct 73
   William   P: Chester Co 9 Ag
   59; Phila 16 Jy 72; Salem
   7 Ap 57
ROBERTSON
   Mrs.   P: Phila 27 Ja 73, 27
   Oct 73
   Widow   P: Phila 3 Sep 61
   Alexander   P: Phila 23 Oct
   66
   David   P: Phila 2 Ag 70
   Donald   P: Phila 3 Ja 65
   Easter   P: Phila Co 3 Ja 60
   George   P: Phila 1 Jy 56, 21
   Dec 58 (soldier)
   Henry   P: Phila 28 Ap 68
   Hugh   P: Pa 21 Dec 58
   James   P: Pa 3 Ja 60; Phila
   25 Jy 65, 19 Jy 80 (Capt)
   John   P: New Providence 16
   Jy 67; Pa 31 Jy 60;
   Phila 24 Feb 63 (Capt), 3
   Ja 65, 2 May 65, 23 Oct
   66, 3 Ja 76
   Michael   Phila 30 Oct 76
   Robert   P: Phila 3 Ja 76
   Thomas   P: Phila 11 Sep 55

William P: Fogs Manor 3 Ag
  58, 9 Ag 59; Phila 29 Ag
  54, 3 Ja 65, 2 May 68, 2
  Ag 70
ROBESON
  James P: Phila 4 Feb 68
  Jonathan P: Phila 2 May 65
  Mary P: Phila 16 Jy 67
  Peter P: Whitemarsh 24 Oct
    54, 28 Nov 54
  Robert P: Phila 6 Sep 53
  William P: Pa 24 Feb 63
ROBINETT/ROBINET
  Eliz. P: Pa 4 Ag 63
  Joseph P: Chester Co 11 Sep
    55; Marcus-hook 8 Jy 62
  Samuel P: Phila 19 Ja 69
ROBINS; see also ROBBINS
  James P: Phila-Gaz. 3 Ja 76
  John P: Phila 21 Jy 68.
    T: Allentown 3 Oct 65
  Sarah P: West Jersey 7 Ap
    57
ROBINSON/ROBENSON; see also
  THOMPSON & ROBINSON
  ... P: Phila 13 May 56
  & HARDING P: Phila 21 Dec 58
  Capt. P: Phila 24 Feb 63
  Abraham, Esq. P: Phila 1 Nov
    70
  Alexander P: Phila 31 Dec 61
  Andrew L: Little Britain 20
    Ja 73. P: Phila 3 Ja 76
  Budd P: Phila 3 Ag 58, 21
    Dec 58
  Daniel P: Phila 18 Mar 62,
    15 Mar 64, 3 Ja 65
  Esther P: Pa 9 Ag 59
  George P: in the army 12 Ja
    58; N. Castle Co 31 Dec 61
  Capt. H. P: Phila 15 Mar 64
  Henry P: Phila 12 Ja 58,
    10 Ap 66, 27 Ja 73 (Capt)
  Humphry P: Phila 6 Jy 58
  Isaiah Phila 30 Ap 77
  James L: Chestnut Level,
    Chester Co 19 Dec 71. P:
    Bohemia 31 Dec 61; Christeen
    Bridge 18 Ag 57; Cohansey 2
    Feb 64; Lancaster Co 18 Mar
    62; Little Britain 1 Nov 53;
    Phila 2 Feb 64, 2 Feb 64, 20
    Ap 69, 1 Nov 70
  John L: Little Britain 2 Mar
    74. N: 29 Nov 64. P: 3 Ag
    58, in the army; 21 Dec 58
    (soldier); Cumberland Co 13
    Oct 63; Hopewell 15 Mar 64;
    Muddy Creek 18 Ag 57, 12 Ja
    58; Phila 4 Ap 54, 4 Feb 68,
    21 Jy 68, 20 Jy 69, 27 Ja 73,
    3 Ja 76; Shrewsbury 9 Ag 59
  Jonathan P: Phila 3 Ja 65
  Joseph T: Trenton 17 Oct 54
  Magdalen P: Phila 3 Ag 58

Morris P: Oxford Furnace 21
  Dec 58
Paul P: Phila 28 Nov 54
Philip P: Lancaster Co 12
  Feb 61
Capt. Richard P: Phila 28
  Oct 62
Robert P: Phila 16 Jy 72
Saunders P: Gloucester,
  W. Jersey 4 Feb 68
Thomas/Tom P: Chester Co
  13 Ja 63; Naaman's Creek
  7 Ap 57; N.J. 3 Ja 60, 31
  Jy 60; Phila 8 Jy 62, 24
  Feb 63, 2 Feb 64, 20 Oct
  68
Vasti Phila 24 Jy 76
William L: 3 Oct 65. P:
  Cape-May 6 Sep 53;
  Cumberland Co 18 Mar 62;
  Fogs Manor 12 Ja 58, 3 Ja
  60; Londonderry Twp 7 Ap
  57; New Castle Co 9 Ag 59;
  Phila 29 Ag 54, 28 Ap 68
  (34th Regt), 27 Oct 73,
  3 Ja 76, 31 Ja 76, 19 Jy
  76 (& son), 30 Oct 76
ROBISON
  Andrew P: Phila 27 Ja 73
  Catherine Phila 5 Ap 77-
    Gaz. 30 Ap
  George P: Brandywine 24
    Feb 63
  Hugh Phila 1 May 76
  James P: Phila 26 Jy 64
  John P: Phila 30 Ap 67
  Sally P: Phila 31 Dec 61
  William P: Phila 4 Ag 63
    63
ROBOTEAU
  Charles P: Providence 31
    Dec 61
ROBOTHOM
  John P: Phila-Gaz. 27 Oct
    73
ROBSON
  Saul P: Phila 25 Ap 71
ROCHE
  Mary L: at William Ross's,
    tavern keeper,Lancaster
    19 Dec 71
ROCHSBERRY
  Maily P: Phila-Gaz. 3 Ja
    76
ROCK/ROK
  Francis P: Charlestown 13
    Oct 63
  George P: Phila 9 Ag 59
  James P: Phila 23 Oct 66
  John P: Wilmington 3 Sep
    61
  Joseph P: Phila 31 Jy 60
  Capt. Moses P: Phila 5 Ag
    62
  Samuel P: Phila 13 Oct 63

ROCKAFIELD
  John   L: Lampeter Twp 19
    Dec 71
ROCKETT
  John   P: Phila 12 Feb 61
RODDEN
  Patrick   P: Phila 12 Feb 61
RODDY
  Andrew   P: Pa 24 Feb 63
  Henry   P: Phila 27 Ja 73
RODGERS; see ROGERS
RODMAN
  Joseph   P: Egg-harbour 8 Jy
    62
  Seamon   P: Burlington 18
    Mar 62
  Thomas   P: Pa 15 Mar 64
  William   P: Bensalem 26 Oct
    69; Phila 27 Oct 73
RODMENT
  William   P: Pa 9 Ag 59
RODS
  Isabel   P: Lancaster 9 Ag 59
ROE
  George   P: Phila 24 Feb 63
  James   N: 29 Nov 64
  Samuel   P: Phila 20 Oct 68
ROFFE
  John   P: Phila 3 Ja 65
ROGERS/RODGERS/ROGER
  Mr.   P: Phila 25 Ap 71
  Alexander   P: Chester Co 9
    Ag 59
  Andrew   L: 20 Ja 73; York Co
    2 Mar 74
  Ann   P: Phila 19 Jy 80
  Benjamin   P: Phila 31 Dec 61
  Charles   P: Phila 5 Ag 62
  David   P: Chester Co 12 Ja
    58, 4 Ag 63; Pa 31 Dec 61
  Edward   P: Chester Co 11 Sep
    55
  Francis   P: Neshaminy 12 Ja
    58
  George   P: Phila 2 May 65
  Isaac   P: AllenTown 13 Ja 63.
    T: Allentown 10 Ag 58
  Jacob   P: Phila 31 Dec 61
  James   P: Pa 26 Jy 64; Phila
    15 Mar 64, 26 Oct 69
  John   P: Chester Co 8 Jy 62,
    28 Oct 62; New Castle Co 3
    Ag 58, 21 Dec 58, 9 Ag 59,
    3 Ja 60; Pa 12 Feb 61; Phila
    27 Oct 73; St. George's Hun-
    dred 3 Sep 61
  John, Jr.   T: near Trenton 21
    Ja 55
  Margery   P: New Jersey 12 Ja
    58
  Matthew   P: Winchester 12 Ja
    58
  Michael   P: Phila 3 Sep 61
  Nurse   P: Phila 30 Ja 66
  Rebecca   P: Reading 21 Dec 58

Richard   P: Phila 3 Ja 60
Robert   P: Pa 12 Feb 61, 31
  Dec 61, 30 Ja 66
Samuel   P: Phila 27 Ja 73.
  T: Bordentown 3 Oct 65
Mrs. Sarah   T: Reckless
  Town 1 Sep 68
Thomas   P: Pa 31 Mar 63, 10
  Ap 66, 4 Feb 68
William   P: Md. 24 Feb 63;
  Pa 15 Mar 64; Phila 31
  Dec 61, 5 Ag 62, 30 Ja 66
ROGERSON
  John   P: Phila 3 May 70
  William   P: Phila 21 Jy 68
ROHDENBUELER
  Salo   P: Phila 16 Jy 67
ROHLEIG
  John Henry/Johan Henrick
    P: Pa 3 Ag 58; Phila 9
    Ag 59
ROLARS
  John   P: Phila 15 Mar 64
ROLINSON
  Daniel   P: Philà 19 May 63
ROLLO
  Mrs./Madam   P: Phila 19 Ja
    69, 1 Feb 70, 25 Ap 71
ROLSTON/ROULSTON
  Samuel   P: Whiteclay Creek
    3 Ag 58
  William   P: Phila 1 Feb 70,
    3 May 70
ROMALHO
  Emanuel   P: Phila 26 Oct 69
RONALDS
  Jas.   P: Phila 15 Mar 64
RONELS/RONOLS
  Agnes   P: Forks of Delaware
    13 May 56
  George   P: Phila 30 Ap 67
RONEY
  James   P: Phila-Gaz. 3 Ja
    76
ROOK/ROOKE
  Bartholomew   P: Phila 21 Jy
    68
  James   P: Phila 19 Ja 69
  William   C: c/o Mr. Curry-
    at N.E. Maryland 30 Oct
    66; at Elisha Hughes's
    East Nottingham 22 Ja 67
  William   P: Phila 16 Jy 72
ROOKER
  Abraham   P: Wilmington 29
    Ag 54
ROONY
  Barny   P: Phila-Gaz. 3 Ja
    76
ROOPE
  John   P: Richland /or
    Phila?7 1 Nov 53
ROOPER
  John   P: Great Swamp 9 Ag
    59

ROOS
   Robert   T: or Jeremiah Thatcher
   Kingwood 7 May 67
ROOSEL
   Thomas   P: Phila 30 Ja 66
ROOSEVELT
   Isaac   P: Phila 12 Feb 61
ROSALL
   Rebecca   P: Salem 8 Jy 62
ROSBOROUGH/ROSBROGH
   Alexander   C: East Nottingham
   22 Ja 67
   John   P: Earl Town 12 Ja 58
ROSBOTTOM
   Benjamin   P: Phila 8 Jy 62
   James   P: Phila-Gaz. 3 Ja 76
ROSE
   Capt.   P: Phila 15 Mar 64
   Alexander   Phila 30 Ap 77
   Ann   P: Phila 30 Ap 67, 16 Jy
   72
   Bethia   P: Phila 31 Jy 60
   David   Phila 1 May 76
   James   P: Phila 2 Feb 64,
   15 Mar 64, 24 Jy 76, 30
   Ap 77
   Samuel   P: Phila 16 Jy 72
   Thomas   P: Germantown 1 Jy 56,
   3 Ja 76; Phila 11 Sep 55
   William   P: Phila 2 Feb 64
ROSS
   Capt.   P: Phila 4 Ag 63
   Alexander   P: Mount-holly 27
   Dec 53, 7 Ap 57; Dr.,
   Mountholly 28 Ap 68, 20 Oct
   68, 1 Feb 70; Capt., Phila
   27 Oct 73.   T: Mt. Holly 1
   Sep 68 & 31 Ja 71 (Dr)
   Capt. Charles   P: Phila 12 Ja
   58
   David   L: Octarara 19 Dec 71.
   P: Phila 30 Ap 77
   Ezekiel   P: Phila 6 Jy 58
   Frances   P: Phila-Gaz. 27 Oct
   73
   Geo./George   P: Lancaster 9 Ag
   59; Cpl., Lancaster Co 19 Jy
   80; Capt., Phila 18 Mar 62,
   24 Feb 63, 31 Mar 63, 19 May
   63
   Hugh   L: Stephenson's Ferry 2
   Mar 74
   Ja.   L: York Co 31 Ja 71
   Jacob   P: New-Castle 11 Sep
   55, 1 Jy 56
   James   P: near Newcastle 24
   Oct 54; Phila 18 Mar 62,
   2 Ag 70, 3 Ja 76; Capt.,
   Phila 6 Jy 58, 13 Ja 63, 2
   Ag 70; York Co 18 Ag 57, 2
   Ag 70
   Jane   P: Phila 13 Ja 63
   John   L: York Co 2 Mar 74.   P:
   New London 5 Ag 56; Phila 6
   Jy 58, 3 Ag 58, 31 Dec 61, 25

Jy 65, 10 Oct 65 (2), 10
   Ap 66, 23 Oct 66 (2), 20
   Jy 69, 1 Feb 70, 16 Jy 77.
   T: Ringwood Furnace 4 Nov
   72
   Peter   P: Phila 10 Oct 65,
   23 Oct 66
   Robert   C: 18 Jy 65;
   commissary in N. York,
   c/o J. Culbertson, Esq.
   near the Forks of Brandy-
   wine 28 Nov 65.   P: N.J.
   24 Feb 63; Pa 31 Dec 61;
   Col., Phila 13 Ja 63
   Thomas   P: Phila 2 Ag 70;
   Capt., Phila 18 Ag 57
   William, weaver   C: London-
   grove 22 Ja 67.   L: York
   Co 2 Mar 74.   P: Brandy-
   wine 15 Mar 64; Fogs
   Manor 21 Dec 58; Nesha-
   miny 26 Oct 69; Pa 2
   Feb 64; Phila 7 Ap 57, 3
   Ja 65, 30 Ja 66, 23 Oct
   66, 16 Jy 67
ROSSITER/ROSITER
   Daniel F.   P: Phila 1 Nov
   70
   Richard   P: Phila 2 May 65
ROTHENBUHLER
   Mr.   P: Phila 13 Ja 63
ROTHWELL
   Henry   P: Phila 2 May 65
ROUCE
   Mr.   P: Phila 4 Ag 63
   John   P: Phila 5 Ag 62
ROUCH
   Henry   P: Phila 27 Ja 73
ROUND
   James   P: Worcester 24 Feb
   63
ROUNSAVELL/ROUNSIFER
   Richard   P: West Jersey 5 Ag
   62.   T: Hunterdon Co 7 May
   67
ROUSKOFF
   John P.   P: Phila 2 Ag 70
ROW
   Joseph   P: Phila 23 Oct 66
   Samuel, miller   C: Charles-
   town, Maryland 18 Jy 65
ROWAN/ROWEN
   Rev.   P: Lancaster 9 Ag 59
   Andrew   P: Phila-Gaz. 3 Ja
   76
   Geo./George   P: Phila 18
   Mar 62, 24 Feb 63, 31 Mar
   63, 4 Ag 63
   Henry   P: Pequea 13 Ja 63
   James   P: Marcus Hook 18
   Mar 62; Phila 20 Oct 68
   John, Rev.   P: Lancaster
   Co 3 Ja 60; Phila 4 Feb
   68; Dr., Phila 6 Jy 58,
   3 Ag 58

Margaret P: Phila 26 Oct 69;
  Williams-Town 3 Ag 58, 21
  Dec 58
Michael C: c/o Rev. J.
  Blair, Fogs Manor 28 Nov
  65
Matthew P: Williams-Town
  21 Dec 58
ROWE
  Stephen P: Salem Co 18 Mar
  62
ROWER
  Robert P: Phila 8 Jy 62
ROWES
  John P: Phila 28 Oct 62
ROWLAND
  Charles P: Phila 2 Feb 64
  John P: Chester Co 24 Feb
  63
  Peggy P: Phila 20 Oct 68
  Robert, Esq. P: Pa 13 Ja 63
  Samuel P: 12 Feb 61
  Thomas P: Chester Co 1 Jy
  56; 8 Jy 62; Great Valley
  7 Ap 57
  William P: Pa 21 Dec 58
ROWLS /or ROWIS?/
  Reason P: 28 Nov 54
ROWNEY
  Alexander P: Phila 20 Oct
  68
ROXBOROUGH/ROXBROUGH/ROXBURGH
  Adam P: Phila 2 Sep 62, 28
  Oct 62, 24 Feb 63
  John P: Phila 5 Ag 62
ROY
  Abraham P: Lancaster 31 Dec
  61
ROYAL
  Sarah P: Cumberland Co 8 Jy
  62
ROYLE
  James, soldier P: Phila 1
  Feb 70
  William P: Phila 26 Jy 64
ROYLEY
  William P: Phila 9 Ag 59
ROYSTRUP
  Rev. Otto P: Pa 3 Ja 60
ROZEL
  Charles P: Phila-Gaz. 27 Oct
  73
RUBY/RUBIE
  Henry L: Reading Forge 15 Ap
  56
  Hugh P: Perkiomen 3 Sep 61
RUCHEL
  John P: Jersey 13 May 56
RUDDERFORD
  Alex. P: Phila 4 Ag 63
RUDENIN
  Jacob P: Phila 11 Sep 55
RUDOLPH/RUDULPH
  John Phila 30 Oct 76
  Tobias P: Phila 9 Ag 59

RUECASTLE/RUCCASTLE/RACCASTLE/
  RERECASTLE/REVECASTOL
  Robert P: Phila 30 Ap 67,
  28 Ap 68, 21 Jy 68, 20 Oct
  68, 19 Ja 69, 20 Ap 69
RUFF
  Jacob P: Shippack 8 Jy 62
RULE
  John P: Grigs-Town 18 Mar
  62
  William P: Pa 3 Ag 58
RULIDGE
  John P: Phila 16 Jy 72
RUMFORD
  John P: Wilmington 5 Ag 56
  Jonathan P: Phila 25 Jy 65;
  Plymouth 1 Nov 53, 13 May
  56, 5 Ag 56
RUMLEY
  William P: Phila 30 Oct 76
RUMSEY; see also WILTON &
  RUMSEY
  Benjamin C: Charles-Town,
  Maryland 30 Oct 66. P:
  Phila 5 Feb 54, 28 Nov 54
RUNDALL/RUNDEL
  Jacob T: Princetown 17 Oct
  54
  John P: Phila-Gaz. 3 Ja 76
RUNNELS
  James P: Phila 31 Mar 63
RUPP
  John Phila 1 May 76
RUSH
  Jacob P: Phila 9 Ag 59, 19
  Jy 80
  John P: Phila 21 Dec 58
  Patrick Phila 1 May 76
  William P: Phila 3 Ag 58, 3
  Ja 76
RUSHTON
  Robert C: Oxford, see COOK,
  James
RUSK
  David P: Baltimore 31 Mar
  63
RUSLY
  Isaac P: Pa 12 Feb 61
RUSSELL/RUSSALL/RUSELL/ROUSSELL
  & Co. P: Phila 16 Jy 72
  & HAMILTON P: Phila 28 Ap 68
  Abraham P: Phila 5 Ag 62, 15
  Mar 64, 26 Jy 64
  Alexander P: Chester Co 3
  Sep 61; Lancaster Co 12 Feb
  61, 3 Sep 61; Phila 3 May
  70, 2 Ag 70
  Charles P: 12 Feb 61
  Christopher, Esq. C: N.
  Castle 18 Jy 65
  Edward P: Chester Co 31 Jy
  60; Phila 19 Ja 69, 20 Ap
  69
  George P: Phila 30 Ja 66, 16
  Jy 67, 26 Oct 69

Hugh P: Fogs Manor 13 May 56
James L: York Co 19 Dec 71.
  P: Chester bounty /sic!/ 31
  Dec 61; Gloucester 19 Jy
  80; Pa 18 Mar 62; Phila 3
  Ja 60, 3 Ja 65, 1 Nov 70;
  Wilmington 9 Ag 59
John P: Bucks Co 15 Mar 64,
  10 Oct 65, 30 Ja 66; Chester
  Co 22 Nov 53; Marlborough 28
  Oct 62; Pa 13 Oct 63; Phila
  25 Jy 65, 20 Jy 69, 1 Feb 70.
  T: Somerset Co 15 Jy 56
Joseph/Jos. P: Chester 5 Ag
  56, 12 Feb 61, 3 Sep 61;
  Phila 5 Ag 62
Mat./Matthew P: Newark 15 Mar
  64; Pa 28 Oct 62, 4 Ag 63
Nathaniel P: Phila 8 Jy 62
Nicholas P: Phila-Gaz. 27 Oct
  73
Robert P: Pa 9 Ag 59; Phila
  1 Feb 70; York Co 3 Ja 60
Thomas C: c/o Rev. John Beard,
  Nottingham 22 Ja 67. P:
  Coambs-creek 12 Ja 58; Pa
  28 Oct 62; Phila 3 Ag 58,
  21 Dec 58, 27 Ja 73
William P: Chester Co 8 Jy
  62; New-Castle Co 9 Ag 59;
  Phila 30 Ja 66, 20 Oct 68,
  20 Ap 69, 3 May 70; York Co
  24 Oct 54
RUSSELSON
  Joseph P: Pa 4 Ag 63
RUSTON/RUSTIN
  Job P: Fogs Manor 11 Jy 54;
  Phila 28 Ap 68
  Samuel P: N. Castle Co 28 Oct
  62
RUTH
  Rosannah P: Leacock Twp 31
  Dec 61
  Samuel N: near Newcastle, see
  CAMPBELL, James
RUTHERFORD
  John T: Trenton 15 Jy 56, 15
  Mar 64
  Joseph P: Nottingham 3 Ag 58
  Robert T: Phila; see TAYLOR,
  Crad
  Thomas L: Lancaster Co 29 Jy
  72; Paxton 14 May 72. P:
  Phila 28 Nov 54
  William P: Pa 21 Dec 58
RUTHVEN/RUTHREN
  John P: Pa 13 Oct 63; Phila
  3 Ja 65
RUTLAND
  Elizabeth P: Phila 23 Oct 66
  Thomas, Jr. W: Newark /Del./
  School 3 Jy 76
RUTLIDGE
  Elizabeth P: Yellow Breeches
  28 Oct 62

RUTTER
  Widow P: Phila 3 Ag 58
  John P: Phila 6 Jy 58, 21
  Dec 58
  Moses C: at the Head of
  Elk River, Maryland 30
  Oct 66
  Samuel P: Concord 5 Ag 56
RUXBY
  John P: Phila 6 Jy 58, 21
  Dec 58
RUZBY
  Isaac P: near Phila 31 Dec
  61
RYAL
  Mary T: Trenton 17 Oct 54
RYAN/RYON/RIAN
  Bryan P: Phila 21 Jy 68
  Cornelius P: Phila 25 Jy
  65
  Daniel P: Newtown 27 Dec
  53; 25 miles from Phila
  11 Sep 55
  Elizabeth P: Phila 18 Mar
  62, 2 Ag 70
  John P: Phila 1 Feb 70,
  25 Ap 71
  Mary P: Richland /or
  Phila?/ 1 Nov 53
  Patrick C: Marcus-Hook 18
  Jy 65. P: Phila 13 May
  56
  Philip P: Phila 1 Feb 70,
  3 Ja 76
  Polly P: Phila-Gaz. 27 Oct
  73
  Rachel P: Phila 3 Ag 58,
  21 Dec 58
  Peter T: Trenton 1 Sep 68
  Richard P: Phila 24 Oct 54
  Thomas P: Black Horse,
  Lancaster Co 1 Feb 70;
  Phila 31 Jy 60, 20 Oct 68
RYCANT
  Capt. Paul P: in the army
  21 Dec 58
RYERSON
  Martin, Esq. T: Amwell 3
  Oct 65
RYLE
  John P: Phila-Gaz. 3 Ja 76
RYN
  Matt. L: in Middletown 14
  May 72

SACKET
  Jos. P: Bucks Co 18 Ag 57
SADLER
  Isaac P: Huntingdon 30 Ja
  66; York Co 2 Feb 64. T:
  c/o Rev. Mr. Thompson,
  Pa 3 Oct 65
SAFTON
  James P: Phila 27 Ja 73

SAGE
  Alexander   P: Phila 11 Jy 54
  Comfort   T: Middletown 6 Dec
    64
  John   P: Phila 30 May 54
  Joshua   P: West-Jersey 12 Feb
    61
  Nathan   Phila 30 Ap 77
SAGRODS
  Patrick   P: Phila-Gaz. 3 Ja
    76
SAINT
  John   P: Phila 18 Mar 62
ST. MAURICE
  James   P: Phila 11 Sep 55
SALE
  David   P: Phila 21 Jy 68
SALERFIELD
  Thomas   P: Phila 31 Dec 61
SALISBURY
  Ann   P: Phila 8 Jy 62
  William   P: Kent Co 13 Oct
    63; Pa 3 Ag 58, 21 Dec 58
SALKELD
  Isaac   P: Phila 4 Ag 63, 13
    Oct 63
SALLOWS
  Jacob   P: Phila 1 Nov 53
SALSER
  Thomas   P: Phila 26 Jy 64
SALTER/SALTAR
  Capt.   P: Phila 9 May 54
  John   P: Phila 13 Ja 63
  Thomas   P: Phila 26 Jy 64
SALTERBACKEN
  John   P: Phila 6 Jy 58
SALTMOUTH
  Mary   P: Phila 2 Ag 70
SALTONSTALL
  Winthrop   P: Phila 13 Ja 63
SALTUS
  Norwood   P: Phila 6 Jy 58
SAMELS
  Jehu   L: 13 Jn 65
SAMMON/SAMIN
  Robert   P: Phila 16 Jy 72,
    27 Ja 73
SAMPLE
  James   P: Bucks Co 8 Jy 62;
    Lancaster Co 8 Ag 57
  John   P: Bucks Co 31 Dec 61;
    Chester Co 13 Oct 63
SAMPSON/SAMSON
  James   P: Phila 31 Mar 63,
    19 Ja 69
  John   P: Phila 13 Oct 63
  Elizabeth   P: Phila 20 Jy 69
SAMUEL
  Richard   P: Phila 3 Ja 65
  Robert   P: Phila 3 Ja 76
  Rosser   P: Phila 10 Oct 65
SANDERLIN
  John   P: Salem 7 Ap 57
SANDERS
  George; see also SAUNDERS   P:

Phila 21 Dec 58
  James   P: Pa 4 Ag 63; Phila
    13 Oct 63
  John   P: 12 Feb 61
  Katherine   P: Phila 3 Ag 58
  Robert   P: Phila 15 Mar 64
  William   P: Phila 3 Ja 76
SANDERSON
  George   L: Lancaster Co;
    see HILL, William.   P:
    Phila 19 Ja 69 (Esq)
  Henry/Hendrey   P: Milton 23
    Oct 66; N. Castle Co 2
    Feb 64; Phila 3 Ja 65;
    Welsh Tract 13 Sep 63
  Richard   P: Chester Co 9
    May 54, 18 Mar 62, 8 Jy
    62
SANDHAM
  Matthias   P: in the army
    3 Ag 58
SANDMAN
  Matthias   P: Phila 2 Ag 70
SANDOS
  John   P: Phila 31 Dec 61
SANDRY
  Hanebel   P: Pa 18 Mar 62
SANDS
  John   P: Pa 18 Mar 62
  Michael   T: Trenton 1 Sep
    68
  Prince   P: Phila 2 Sep 62,
    13 Ja 63
SANDY
  Anne   P: Bucks Co 30 Ap 67
  Sares   P: Phila 23 Oct 66
SANNON
  Samuel, student   L: Pequea
    2 Mar 74
SANSOM
  and SWETT   P: Phila 2 Sep
    62, 24 Feb 63
SARGANT
  Eliz.   P: Mackfield 24 Feb
    63
SARJAN
  Samuel   P: Carlisle 19 Jy
    80
SASCOMB
  John   P: Phila 3 May 70
SATTERTHWAITE/SATTERTHWAIT
  James   P: Phila 7 Ap 57,
    3 Ja 60, 2 Sep 62, 31
    Mar 63
  Wm.   P: Lower Makefield 12
    Ja 58
SAUER/SOUR/SOWER
  Christopher   P: Germantown
    29 Ag 54, 11 Sep 55, 13
    May 56, 1 Jy 56, 7 Ap 57,
    30 Ap 67, 28 Ap 68, 21
    Jy 68, 20 Ap 69, 3 May
    70, 3 Ja 76, 30 Ap 77,
    16 Jy 77
SAUL

Joseph P: Phila 13 Oct 63
SAUNDERS; see also SANDERS
and CARLISLE P: Phila 3
  May 70
Alexander P: Phila 2 Ag 70
Christopher P: Phila 21 Dec
  58
Francis/Fr. P: Gloucester
  15 Mar 64; West Jersey 13
  Ja 63
Hannah P: Nesham 12 Ja 58
Henry P: Phila 4 Feb 68
James P: Phila 4 Ag 63, 30
  Ap 67
John P: Phila-Gaz. 27 Oct
  73
Dr. Joseph 24 Jy 76
Parnell P: Phila 3 Ja 76
Thomas P: Phila 1 Nov 70
SAUNDERSON ; see also SANDERSON
Joseph P: Phila 30 Ap 67
Richard C: Chester Co 18
  Jy 65
SAVAGE/SAVADGE/SAVIDGE
Darby P: Phila 15 Mar 64,
  21 Jy 68, 2 Ag 70
Eliz. P: Phila 5 Ag 56
Gerral P: Phila-Gaz. 3 Ja
  76
Habiah P: Phila 26 Jy 64
Henry P: Pa 12 Ja 58; Phila
  5 Ag 56
Jeremiah P: Phila 18 Mar
  62, 27 Ja 73
Patrick P: Pa 13 Ja 63
Robert P: East Jersey 7 Ap
  57; Middletown 21 Dec 58;
  Phila 23 Oct 66
Thomas P: Phila 26 Oct 69
William P: Phila 3 Ja 76,
  31 Ja 76
SAVEY /or SAVOY?/
Peter Phila 30 Ap 77
SAVIN
Thomas N: 12 Feb 67; c/o
  Mr. Forrimer Warwick 4 Dec
  66
William P: Phila 20 Jy 69
SAVORY
Jos. P: Phila 31 Dec 61
SAWDERBURN
Frederick P: Phila 3 May 70
SAWEL
Joseph P: Phila 3 Ja 65
SAWELDER
Jos./Joseph P: Phila 26
  Jy 64 (2)
SAWLER
Mr. P: Phila 10 Oct 65
SAWYER/SAWER
Elizabeth P: Phila 25 Ap 71,
  19 Jy 80
Capt. Thomas P: Phila 31 Dec
  61
SAXTON/SAXTYN

Frederick Prince-Town 5
  Ap 77-Gaz. 30 Ap
James P: Yellow Springs
  19 Ja 69
SAYRE/SAYER/SAYERS
Ananias P: Phila 1 Feb 70
Ann P: Phila-Gaz. 3 Ja 76
Hugh L: Carlisle 2 Mar 74
Stephen P: Phila 30 Ap 67
SAYS
Malachi L: 14 May 72
SAYWORD
Capt. Jeremiah P: Pa 12
  Feb 61
SCALE
John P: Queen Ann's Co.
  28 Oct 62
SCALES
Thomas P: Phila 20 Ap 69
William P: Phila 20 Jy 69
SCALLAN
James P: Chester Co 12 Ja
  58
SCANDELON
Co. P: Phila 31 Jy 60
SCANLON/SCANLAN/SCANLEN
Dr. L. P: Phila 2 Feb 64
Luke P: Phila 24 Feb 63
Mary P: Phila 19 Ja 69, 20
  Ap 69
Nancy P: Pa 31 Jy 60
SCANNEL/SCANNELL
Johanna P: Phila 11 Sep 55
John L: Lancaster Co 19 Dec
  71
SCANT
John P: Phila 9 Ag 59
SCARON
Mr. P: Phila 12 Feb 61
SCATES
Lucy P: Germantown /error
  for Phila?/ 13 May 56
SCHAFFER
Adam P: Phila 3 Ag 58
SCHENCK
Maria P: Phila 19 Jy 80
SCHERALL
Ann P: Phila 3 Ag 58
SCHETTWELL
Abraham P: West Jersey 12
  Ja 58
SCHLATTER
Michael P: Phila 1 Jy 56
SCHLEWEIS
Gotlieb P: Phila 12 Ja 58
SCHLEYDHORN
Elizabeth P: Phila 1 Feb
  70
SCHLOSSER
George P: Phila 2 Sep 62,
  28 Oct 62
Jacob Phila 30 Ap 77
SCHMIDT
Simon P: Bucks Co 28 Ap 68
SCHNEBERGER, see SHUENTZLYD &

SCHOFIELD
Rachel P: Bucks Co 18 Ag
57, 12 Ja 58
SCHORELL
J. P: Phila-Gaz. 3 Ja 76
SCHOTLER
Corbit P: East Jersey 24
Jy 76
SCHOUHOTZAR
Henry P: Phila 1 Nov 70
SCHRIBER
Jonathan P: Phila 2 Ag 70
SCHRINER
Jacob P: Phila 19 Jy 80
SCHRIVER
George P: Germantown 28 Ap
68
SCHROCK
John P: Phila Co 5 Ag 56
Simon P: Phila 31 Jy 60
SCHUTZ
Conrad P: Phila 3 Ja 65,
25 Ap 71
SCHUYLER
Casparus T: Trenton 17 Oct
54
SCHWARTZ
Andrew P: Phila 3 Ja 65
SCHWERDSFEGER
Rev. J.S. P: York Co 31
Dec 61
SCHWERNER
Lawrence P: Germantown 11
Sep 55
SCHWIND
Dr. John Phila 24 Jy 76
SCHWOERER
Melchior P: Phila-Gaz. 27
Oct 73
SCOLEY
David P: Phila 30 Ja 66
SCOONE
Peter P: Phila 10 Oct 65
SCORS
James P: Bucks Co 13 Oct 63
SCOTCH
William (sailor) P: Phila
3 Ag 58
SCOTHORN
Lewis P: Merion Twp 18 Ag
57
SCOTLAND
John P: Phila 1 Feb 70
SCOTT/SCOT
& HODGE P: Phila 2 Sep 62
Lt. of his Majesty's schooner
HALIFAX P: Phila 1 Nov 70
Alexander P: Lancaster Co 9
Ag 59; Pa 4 Ag 63
Ann P: N. Castle Co 3 Sep 61
Archibald P: Pa 18 Mar 62
Charles Phila 30 Ap 77
Elisabeth/Elizabeth P: Phila
31 Dec 61, 27 Oct 73
Francis L: Lancaster Co 19 Dec

71. P: Lewes 22 Nov 53;
Phila 1 Nov 53, 3 Sep 61
Hugh P: Phila 15 Mar 64
Ja. L: Cumberland Co 14 May
72
James C: at Mrs. Cummings, in
West Nottingham 22 Ja 67.
P: at the Capes 30 Ja 66;
Chester Co 18 Mar 62, 24
Feb 63, 31 Mar 63, 2 Feb
64; Donegall 21 Dec 58;
Nottingham 13 Oct 63;
Octorara 21 Dec 58; Pa 3
Ag 58, 12 Feb 61, 2 Feb 64;
Capt., Phila 31 Mar 63
John P: Brandywine 26 Oct
69, Bucks Co 30 Ja 66;
Chester 24 Feb 63, 31 Mar
63; Forks of Delaware 31
Dec 61; Germantown 13 May
56; Phila 9 Ag 59, 3 Ja 60,
16 Jy 67, 3 May 70, 3 Ja 76;
Sheerman's Valley 5 Ag 59,
3 Ja 60; Capt., Phila 20
Jy 69, 1 Feb 70, 24 Jy 76
Joseph P: Lancaster Co 4 Ag
63
Josiah P: Lancaster 2 Feb 64
Margaret P: Phila 27 Ja 73
Capt. N. P: Phila 18 Mar 62
Patrick L: 29 Ja 67
Richard P: Phila 31 Dec 61
Robert P: Bucks Co 9 Ag 59,
31 Jy 60, 3 Sep 61; New
Castle Co 29 Ag 54, 31 Jy
60; Phila 24 Feb 63, 4 Ag
63, 2 Feb 64, 3 Ja 65, 26
Oct 69, 27 Oct 73, 3 Ja 76,
16 Jy 77
Samuel L: Leacock 11 Ap 65.
P: Donegal 7 Ap 57; near
Lancaster 21 Dec 58; Lan-
caster 26 Jy 64; Lancaster
Co 12 Feb 61, 31 Dec 61, 2
Feb 64; Pa 28 Oct 62
Thomas P: Phila 28 Nov 54
William P: Bucks Co 4 Feb
68; Lancaster Co 4 Ag 63;
Neshaminy 26 Oct 69; Pa 4
Ag 63; Phila 1 Jy 56, 3 Ja
65, 20 Ap 69, 1 Feb 70, 27
Oct 73, 24 Jy 76
SCOVEL
J. P: Phila 13 Oct 63
SCUDDER
Thomas P: Salem 1 Nov 70
SCUGGALL
Allen P: Wilmington 3 Ja 60
John P: Wilmington 9 Ag 59
SCULL
Hezekiah P: Cape-May 8 Jy
62
Capt. Peter Phila 1 May 76
Richard P: York Co 19 May
63

SCULLY/SCULEY
  Christopher P: Pa 12 Feb 61
  Thomas P: Phila 20 Oct 68
SEABURY
  Rev. Samuel P: Phila 19 Ja
  69
SEAGROVE
  John P: Phila 19 Jy 80
SEALY
  Samuel P: near Schuylkill 24
  Oct 54
SEAMAN/SEMAN
  Geo. P: Phila 18 Mar 62
  John P: Phila 25 Ap 71
SEANT
  John P: Phila 21 Dec 58
SEARISBROOK
  James P: Phila 31 Jy 60
SEARLES/SEARLS/SURLS/SERLS
  Mrs. P: Phila 3 Ja 60
  Elizabeth P: Phila 26 Jy 64
  Mary P: Pa 18 Mar 62
  William P: Phila 31 Dec 61
SEARS/SEARES
  Antonia P: Phila 19 Ja 69
  Isaac P: Phila 25 Ap 71
  Capt. Joseph P: Phila 31 Dec
  61, 19 May 63
  Molly P: Phila 30 Ap 67
  Sandy P: Phila 28 Ap 68
SEARSON/SERSON
  John P: Phila 10 Ap 66,
  19 Ja 69
SEAVER
  Elizabeth P: Phila 9 Ag 59
SEAWRIGHT
  Gilbert L: 14 May 72
  William L: Leacock 15 Ap
  56
SEAYER
  John P: Phila-Gaz. 27 Oct
  73
SEDDIS
  Henry P: West New Jersey 24
  Jy 76
SEDGWICK
  Mary P: 11 Sep 55
SEED
  Francis N: 29 Nov 64
SEELEY; see also CEILY
  Jonas, Esq. L: 14 May 72
SEGGERSON
  John P: Phila 5 Ag 62
SEIDEL
  Nicholas Worcester Twp 5 Ap
  76-Gaz. 1 May
SEILLE
  Nathaniel P: Bethlehem 1 Nov
  70
SEIMENTON
  John P: Pa 12 Feb 61
SEIPPEL
  Jean P: Germantown 13 May 56
SEITZ
  Lewis P: Phila 26 Jy 64

SELEDOR
  William P: Nottingham 31
  Mar 63
SELFLECE /?/
  Nathan P: Phila 31 Mar 63
SELLAR
  Capt. James P: Phila 23 Oc·
  66
SELLERS
  John P: Darby 25 Ap 71
SELLIVANT
  David P: Duck Creek 15 Mar
  64
SELLON (or SILLON)
  Samuel P: Pa 18 Mar 62
SELLY
  William P: Phila 16 Jy 72
SEMANS
  William P: Schuylkill 10
  Ap 66
SEMPLE
  David L: Shippensburgh 2
  Mar 74. P: Phila 30 Ja
  66
  James P: Bucks Co 12 Ja 58;
  Phila 11 Sep 55
  John P: Pensborough 24 Oct
  54; Phila 28 Ap 68
  Nathaniel P: Nassau Hall 1
  May 76. T: Lebanon 17 Oct
  54
  William P: Chester Co 9 Ag
  59; Phila 30 Ap 77
SENGEL
  Benjamin P: Phila 28 Ap 68
SENNELL
  John P: Newcastle Co 12
  Ja 58
SENTANCE
  Matthew P: Phila 12 Ja 58
SERDES
  Johan Hd. P: Phila 9 Ag 59
SERLO
  Catherine P: N. Castle Co
  31 Dec 61
SERVICE
  John Phila 31 Ja 76
SEURD
  Ephraim T: Morris-town 17
  Oct 54
SEVERNE/SEVERNS
  Luke P: Bucks Co 18 Mar 62
  Theophilus T: Trenton 15
  Mar 64, 6 Dec 64
SEWARD
  James P: Phila 28 Nov 54
SEWELL
  Thomas, 18th Regt. P:
  Phila-Gaz. 27 Oct 73
  William P: Phila 19 Jy 80
SEWRIGHT
  George P: Pa 13 Oct 63
SEXSON, see FURMAN &
SEXTON
  Isaac T: Amwell 7 May 67

SEYDICH
  Monsieur   P: Phila 19 Ja 69
SEYMOUR
  John   P: Phila 19 Ja 69
  Capt. Thomas   P: Phila 13 Ja
    63
SEYVERDIZ
  Charles   P: Phila 1 Jy 56
SHACKLETON/SHAKLETON
  Richard   P: Oxford 1 Nov
    53; Oxford Furnace 12 Ja
    58; Phila 27 Ja 73
SHADD
  John   P: Phila 30 Ap 67
SHADDOCK
  John   P: 12 Feb 61
SHADES
  Ann   P: Phila 1 Nov 53
SHADRACK
  Rev. Daniel   P: Phila 19 Jy
    80
SHADWICK
  Jonathan   P: Phila 27 Ja 73
SHADY
  Matthias   P: Phila 31 Mar 63
SHAEL
  James   P: Phila 10 Oct 65
SHAFFER
  David   P: Phila 12 Ja 58, 21
    Dec 58
  Michael   P: N.J. 4 Ag 63
SHAFTOUR
  Ludwick   P: Phila 20 Oct 68
SHAKES
  James   P: Pa 31 Jy 60
SHAKESPEAR
  David   Phila 31 Ja 76
  Samuel   P: Phila 2 Ag 70
  Susanna   P: Phila 2 Ag 70
SHALE/SHALES/SHALLES
  Edward   P: Phila 18 Mar 62
  James   P: Phila 5 Ag 62
  Valentine   P: Phila 3 Ag 58,
    21 Dec 58, 31 Dec 61
SHALER
  Abraham   P: Berkiomen 13 May
    56
  Sibel   Egg-Harbour 30 Oct 76
SHALCROSS/SHALLCROSS
  Leonard   P: Pa 3 May 70;
    Phila 16 Jy 72
SHAMNON
  Standhope Mason   N: 29 Nov
    64
SHANBERGER
  Jo.   L: York Co 14 May 72
SHAND
  George   P: Phila 19 Ja 69
  Margaret   P: Phila 21 Jy 68
SHANNON/SHANON/SHANNAN
  Mrs.   P: Phila 8 Jy 62
  Andrew   P: Phila 3 Ag 58
  David   P: Bucks Co 4 Feb 68,
    27 Ja 73
  Elizabeth   L: 13 Jn 65.   P:

Phila 20 Jy 69
  James   L: Cumberland Co 19
    Dec 71.   P: Phila 27 Oct
    73
  John   N: Apoquinimy Hundred
    12 Feb 67.   P: Coecil Co
    4 Ag 63; Cross Roads 7 Ap
    57; Phila 9 May 54; 18
    miles from Phila 26 Oct
    69
  Michael   P: Phila 3 Sep 61
  Richard   N: 29 Nov 64.   P:
    Pa 3 Sep 61; Phila 18 Mar
    62, 19 May 63
  Robert   C: 30 Jy 77.   P:
    Germantown 13 May 56; Pa
    12 Ja 58
  Samuel   P: Bucks Co 18 Mar
    62, 13 Oct 63; Neshaminey
    19 Ja 69; Pa 4 Ag 63;
    Phila 27 Oct 73
  Thomas   P: Md. 24 Feb 63
SHARK
  Jos./Joseph   P: Berks Co 31
    Mar 63; Bucks Co 24 Feb
    63
SHARMONT
  John   P: Phila 28 Oct 62
SHARON
  James   L: Carlisle 19 Dec 71
SHARP/SHARPE
  Messieurs & Co   P: Phila 30
    Ap 67, 28 Ap 68, 21 Jy
    68, 20 Oct 68
  Alexander   P: Chester Co
    12 Ja 58
  Andrew   P: Pa 15 Mar 64
  Christine   P: Phila 20 Jy
    69
  Elizabeth   T: Somerset-
    Court-House 4 Nov 72
  James   P: Chester Co 31 Dec
    61
  Joseph   P: Phila 13 Oct 63,
    3 Ja 65
  Mary   P: Phila 3 May 70
  Samuel   P: Pa 26 Jy 64;
    Phila 16 Jy 67, 27 Ja 73,
    27 Oct 73
  William   C: Chester Co 18
    Jy 65.   P: Chester Co 13
    Oct 63; Tredyffrin 5 Ag
    56
SHARPLESS
  Edmund, soldier   P: Phila
    1 Feb 70
  Nathan   L: Chester Co 15
    Ap 56
  Samuel   P: Chester Co 4 Ap
    54
SHARPNECK
  Henry   P: Germantown 26 Jy
    64
SHAW
  Alexander   P: Phila 18 Mar
    62

Ant. P: Phila 31 Dec 61
Catherine P: Bucks Co 9 Ag
  59
Daniel P: Hanover Twp 2 Sep
  62
Dennis P: Phila 21 Dec 58,
  3 Ja 60
James L: York 14 May 72.
  P: New-Castle Co 9 Ag 59,
  3 Sep 61, 31 Dec 61, 18
  Mar 62; Lancaster Co 31 Dec
  61; Phila 9 Ag 59, 20 Jy
  69, 30 Oct 76
Dr. James P: New-Castle Co 3
  Ja 60; Phila 12 Feb 61
John P: Bucks Co-Gaz. 27
  Oct 73; Charles-Town 21 Dec
  58; Phila 28 Oct 62, 20
  Jy 69
Mary P: Phila 16 Jy 72
Michael P: Lower Dublin 10
  Oct 65
Moses P: Wilmington 13 Sep
  63
Nathan P: Cumberland Co 4
  Ag 63
Richard P: Morris's River 29
  Ag 54
Robert P: Phila 7 Ap 57.
  T: Somerset Co 4 Nov 72
S. P: Phila 2 Sep 62
Samuel L: Hanover Twp 15 Ap
  56. P: Bucks 28 Nov 54;
  Chester Co 18 Mar 62; Lan-
  caster Co 13 Oct 63; North-
  ampton 18 Mar 62; Phila 5
  Ag 62
Thomas P: Phila 8 Jy 62
William P: N.J. 2 Feb 64;
  Phila 10 Oct 65, 2 Ag 70
SHAWAR
Andrew P: Phila 20 Jy 69
SHEA
Martin P: Phila 3 Ja 65, 1
  Nov 70
SHEARMAN/SHEERMAN
Agness P: Kennet Twp 4 Ag
  63; N. Castle Co 3 Sep 61
John P: Phila 23 Oct 66,
  3 Ja 76
SHED
George P: Phila 6 Jy 58
SHEE
Edward L: c/o Robert M'-
  Pherson "ork Co 29 Jy 72
Joseph P: Phila 1 Nov 70
Michael P: Phila 3 May 70
SHEEBY
John P: Phila 12 Feb 61
SHEED
Peter P: Phila 27 Ja 73
SHEEHAN/SHEEHON/SHEAHANE
Daniel P: Phila 27 Ja 73
David P: Phila 4 Ag 63
Eleanor P: Phila 28 Ap 68

John P: Phila 11 Sep 55
SHEELS/SHEALS/SHEELES
Allen P: Phila 13 Ja 63
Patrick P: Pa 13 Oct 63;
  Phila 3 Ja 65
William P: Burlington 31
  Dec 61
SHEERE
Capt. W. P: Phila 2 Sep 62
SHEES
Michael P: Phila 20 Oct 68
SHEETS/SHEETZ
Henry P: near Phila 26 Oct
  69; Phila 28 Ap 68
SHEIL /?/
James P: Montgomery 27 Oct
  73; Phila 30 Ja 66
Joseph P: Phila 28 Oct 62
SHELDON
Joseph P: Chester Co 13 May
  56
Richard P: Phila-Gaz. 3 Ja
  76
SHELLENBERGER
Simon P: Phila 18 Mar 62
SHELLEY/SHELLY
Abraham P: Phila 7 Ap 57
John P: Pa 3 Sep 61
William C: 30 Jy 77
SHELMAN
Thomas P: Frankford 26 Oct
  69
SHELMER
David L: at Lauchlin M'-
  Cartney's Lancaster 29
  Jy 72
SHENEN
William P: Pa 2 Feb 64
SHEPHERD/SHEEPARD/SHEPPARD/
  SHEPHARD
Mr. P: Phila 27 Ja 73
Ezekiel P: Phila 4 Ap 54
George P: Phila 19 Ja 69
Giles P: Phila 16 Jy 67
James P: Phila 30 Ja 66
Jane Phila 16 Jy 77
John P: Phila 31 Jy 60,
  3 Ja 65; Shrewsbury 12
  Ja 58. T: Shrewsbury 10
  Ag 58
Jos. P: Phila 15 Mar 64
Josiah P: Phila 18 Mar 62,
  3 Ja 65, 10 Oct 65
Michael P: Phila 20 Jy 69
Nathaniel P: Phila 19 Ja 69
Robert P: Phila 28 Ap 68
Samuel P: Phila 19 Ja 69,
  3 Ja 76
William P: Pa 7 Ap 57
SHEPPART
Mary P: Lancaster Co 12 Ja
  58
SHERER/SHEARER
Hugh C: c/o Rev. John
  Beard Chester Co 18 Jy 65

J. L: Lancaster Co 20 Ja 73
SHERIDAN
  George   P: Juniata 18 Mar 62
SHERIFF/SHERIF
  Cornelius_ N: Apoquinimy Hun-
    dred /?/ 12 Feb 67. P: Pa
    15 Mar 64
  William   P: Pa 3 Ja 60; Phila
    9 Ag 59
SHERLOCK/SHURLOCK
  Easter P: Phila 20 Jy 69
  Simon   P: Phila 19 May 63
SHERMAN; see also SHEARMAN
  Josiah T: Trenton 17 Oct 54
  William P: Phila 3 May 70
SHERTALL
  Richard   P: Phila 23 Oct 66
SHERWOOD
  Robert   T: Burlington Co 1 Sep
    68
SHETON
  Richard   P: Phila 5 Ag 56
SHEVE
  George   P: Phila 27 Ja 73
SHEVERS
  Samuel   P: Racoon Island 18
    Ag 57
SHEWALL /?/
  Thomas   P: Phila 25 Jy 65
SHEWARD
  Caleb   P: Lancaster Co 3 Ja
    60, 31 Dec 61; Phila 1 Jy
    56, 28 Ap 68
  Elizabeth   P: Phila 25 Ap 71
SHEWCROFT
  Lt. John   P: Phila 20 Ag 70
SHEWEL
  Thomas   P: Plumstead, Bucks
    Co 26 Oct 69
SHICKLETON
  William   P: Phila 18 Mar 62
SHIDMORE
  Mary   P: Oxford Twp 31 Jy 60
SHIELDS/SHEALDS/SHEELDS/SHEILDS/
    SHIELD
  Capt.   P: Pa 15 Mar 64
  Mr.   P: Phila 26 Oct 69
  Daniel   P: Mount-holly 1 Nov
    70
  David   P: Pa 9 Ag 59, 31 Jy
    60
  Edmond   P: Phila 23 Oct 66
  Edward   P: Phila 27 Ja 73
  Eliz.   P: Germantown / error
    for Phila?/ 13 May 56
  John   P: Kent Co 8 Jy 62;
    Phila 9 Ag 59, 3 Ja 60, 19
    Ja 67
  Martha   P: Chester Co 13 Oct
    63, 2 Feb 64; Cross Roads 26
    Jy 64
  Thomas   P: Phila 19 Jy 80
  William   P: Bucks Co 10 Oct 65
SHIEFFIN
  Jacob   P: Phila 31 Dec 61

SHIEHY
  John   P: Phila 12 Feb 61
SHIFFLIN
  Jacob   P: Phila 9 Ag 59
SHILLING/SHILLIN/SHILLEN
  Philip   P: Phila 19 Jy 80;
    Spring Garden 24 Feb 63
  William   P: Kent Co 8 Jy 62
SHINDER
  George   P: Phila 3 Ag 58
SHINE
  John   P: Phila 28 Oct 62,
    25 Jy 65
  William   P: Phila 13 Ja 63
SHINGLETON
  Capt. John   P: in the army
    3 Ag 58
SHIPLEY
  William   P: Pa 12 Feb 61;
    Phila 19 Ja 69, 3 May
    70; Wilmington 3 Ag 58
SHIPPEN/SHIPPIN
  Mr.   P: Lancaster Co 9 Ag
    59; Phila 25 Jy 65
  Edward   P: Phila 3 Ag 58
    (Esq) 30 Oct 76
  Joseph   P: Germantown 26
    Oct 69; Phila 1 Jy 56, 9
    Ag 59, 3 Ja 60
  Mary   P: Germantown 24 Feb
    63
  William   Phila 30 Oct 76
SHIPPY
  Edward   P: Phila 31 Mar 63
SHIRLAND
  Daniel   P: Phila 5 Ag 62
SHIRLEW/SHERLEW
  Robert   P: Bucks Co 21 Dec
    58, 9 Ag 59
SHIRLEY/SHIRLY
  Catherine   P: N. Castle Co
    31 Dec 61
  Ferrers   P: Phila 15 Mar 64
  Lydia   P: Phila 3 Ja 65
SHIVERS
  Samuel   P: Gloucester Co
    20 Ap 69
SHOE
  Catharine   P: Newtown 31 Jy
    60
SHOEMAKER/SHUMAKER
  Benjamin   P: Phila Co 16
    Jy 67
  David   P: Phila 13 Ja 63
  Daniel   P: Phila 9 Ag 59
  Frederick   L: 13 Jn 65
  John   P: Cheltenham 16 Jy
    72; Conestogoe 31 Jy 60;
    Phila 27 Ja 73
  Joseph   P: Chestnut Hill,
    near Germantown 4 Feb
    68; Germantown 27 Oct 73;
    Phila 19 Jy 80
  Thomas   P: Phila 28 Oct 62
SHORBACK

Peter   P: Phila 25 Ap 71
SHORE
  Michael   P: Phila 24 Oct 54
SHORRY
  Thomas   P: Phila 28 Ap 68
SHORT/SHOURT
  John   P: Phila 2 Ag 70, 27
    Ja 73
  Oliver   P: Phila 6 Sep 53
  Robert   P: Phila 16 Jy 72
SHORTAL/SHORTALL
  Richard   P: Phila 19 Ja 69
  Thomas   P: Phila 2 Ag 70
SHOTWELL
  Nicholas   P: Phila 1 Nov 53
SHOWCROSS
  Lt.   P: Phila 20 Jy 69
SHOWECKER/SHOWAGER/SHOWEKER
  Martin   P: Germantown 2 Ag
    70, 25 Ap 71, 6 Jy 72
SHRUMPHIN
  Maria   P: Phila 5 Ag 56
SHUENTZLY
  SCHNEBERGER and FRIENDLY- P:
    Cumberland 9 Ag 59
SHULTS
  John   P: Phila 16 Jy 67
SHUN
  Thomas   P: Phila 7 Ap 57
SHURLY
  Mr.   P: Phila 3 Ja 65
SHUTE
  James   P: Phila 21 Dec 58
  John   P: Bridge-Town 12 Ja
    58
  Joseph   P: Phila 29 Ag 54, 7
    Ap 57
  Mary   P: Phila 12 Ja 58
  Rebeccah   P: Phila 1 Nov 53
  Susannah   P: Oxford Twp 21
    Dec 58, 9 Ag 59
  William   P: Phila 11 Sep 55;
    Salem 24 Feb 63
SHUTER
  Charles   P: Phila 3 Ja 65
SHUTLOCK
  Alexander   P: Phila 9 Ag 59
SHUTS /?/
  Benjamin   P: Phila 25 Jy 65
SICAN
  Samuel   P: Phila 30 Ja 66
SICHELS
  George David   P: Phila 9
    Ag 59
SICKLES
  John   T: Princetown 7 May 67
SICKER
  John, 18th Regt.   P: Phila 2
    Ag 70
SICKLEY
  John   P: Chester Co 15 Mar
    64
SIDDAL
  Mary   P: Phila 21 Dec 58
SIDDON

John   P: Phila 11 Sep 55
SIDING
  Mary   P: N.J. 12 Ja 58
SIDWELL
  John   C: Nottingham,
    Chester Co 30 Oct 66
SIFFANY
  Stephen   P: America 7 Ap
    57
SILBEY
  Henry   P: Phila 2 May 65,
    25 Jy 65
SILCOCK
  Henry   P: East Jersey 12 Ja
    58; N.J. 28 Oct 62
SILDEN
  Richard   P: Phila 31 Dec 61
SILK
  Michael (soldier)   P: Fort
    Pitt 26 Jy 64
SILKS
  Henry   P: Phila-Gaz. 3 Ja
    76
SILLIMAN/SILLYMAN
  Alexander   P: Phila 27 Ja
    73
  Thomas   P: Phila 3 Ja 65
SILVER
  Aaron   P: Pilesgrove 15 Mar
    64
  Archibald   P: Salem Co 12
    Ja 58
  Francis   P: Cumberland Co
    12 Ja 58
  Sarah   P: Bristol 3 Sep 61
SILVERWOOD
  Joseph   P: Phila 2 May 65,
    25 Jy 65
SILVESTER
  Zebulon _Phila 1 May 76
SIMENSON /‾or SIMENTON?/‾
  John   P: Great Valley 31
    Dec 61
SIMERALL
  Andrew   P: Fogs Manor 28
    Oct 62
SIMESON
  Robert   P: Lancaster Co 3
    Sep 61
SIMM
  John   P: Phila 27 Ja 73
SIMMONS
  Elizabeth   L: 3 Oct 65
  Capt. Jeremiah   P: Phila 19
    Jy 80
  Thomas   Phila 31 Ja 76
SIMMONTON
  Robert   P: Pa 3 Sep 61
SIMONS/SYMMONS/SIMANS
  and HENRY   P: Lancaster 13
    Ja 63, 19 May 63
  Mr.   P: Phila 9 Ag 59
  Elizabeth   P: Phila 24 Oct
    54
  Jacob   L: 11 Ap 65

James P: Phila 13 Ja 63
John P: B.C. 20 Ap 69; Pa
  13 Oct 63; Spring Garden
  24 Feb 63, 13 Oct 63
Joseph P: Lancaster 3 Ja
  60, 9 Ag 59, 12 Feb 61
Joseph P: Lancaster 13 Oct
  63; Phila 30 Ja 66
SIMONTON/SIMENTON
John P: Christine 31 Mar 63;
  New-Castle 31 Mar 63; Pa
  21 Dec 58; Wilmington 9 Ag
  59
SIMPSON/SIMSON
Mrs. P: Phila 1 Nov 53, 30
  Ja 66
Arthur P: Lancaster Co 28
  Oct 62
George P: Phila 5 Ag 62
Henry P: Oxford Twp 30 Ap
  67
James P: Fogs Manor 31 Dec
  61; N.J. 18 Mar 62; Phila
  18 Feb 55
John L: Upper Paxton 2 Mar
  74. N: 29 Nov 64. P:
  Chester Co 12 Ja 58; Phila
  28 Nov 54, 26 Oct 69. T:
  Trenton 15 Jy 56 (Capt.,
  Gen. Lascalle's Regt.)
Joseph P: Christ. Hundred 11
  Sep 55; Phila 19 Ja 69, 3
  May 70; Wilmington 28 Oct
  62
Margaret P: Chester Co 3
  Sep 61; Lancaster 21 Dec
  58; Newcastle Co 12 Ja 58
Peter P: Phila 5 Ag 62
Samuel P: Abington 1 Nov 70,
  3 Ja 76; Bucks Co 9 Ag 59,
  31 Jy 60; Phila 21 Dec 58,
  25 Jy 65
Thomas P: Pextang 13 May 56
William P: Germantown 13
  May 56; Lancaster Co 7 Ap
  57; Pa 12 Ja 58; Phila 7 Ap
  57 (Sgt)
SIMRAONS
John P: Phila 10 Ap 66
SIMS
Mr. P: Phila 25 Ap 71
James P: Phila 25 Jy 65
Joseph P: Phila 6 Jy 58
Ralph P: Pa 4 Ag 63
Thomas P: Phila 3 Ag 58, 21
  Dec 58
William P: Phila 18 Feb 55,
  11 Sep 55, 31 Jy 60
SIMUND
Henry P: Phila 4 Feb 68
SINCLAIR/SINKLER/SINCLARE/SIN-
  CLEAR
Capt. P: Phila 31 Mar 63
Alexander, sergeant P: prob.
  in Pittsburgh 15 Mar 64

Lt. Arthur L: Ligonier 20
  Ja 73
Christian P: Phila 19 Ja
  69
Donald P: Phila 31 Mar 63
Ebah P: York Co 4 Ag 63
Elisha P: Chestnut Level
  12 Ja 58
Eliz. L: 14 May 72
George P: Phila 12 Ja 58
John P: Bucks Co 10 Oct
  65; Capt. in the army 21
  Dec 58
Joseph P: Quaker Town 26
  Oct 69. T: Quaker Town
  1 Sep 68
Magnus/Magnous P: Phila
  4 Ag 63, 26 Jy 64
Peter P: Phila 20 Ap 69
SINGER
Paul P: Phila 28 Ap 68
SINGERSON
Lewis P: Phila-Gaz. 3 Ja
  76
SINGIFER
Ludwick P: Phila 19 May
  63
SINGLETON
Benjamin P: Phila 8 Jy 62
John P: New London Twp 11
  Sep 55
Neally P: Phila 20 Jy 69
William P: Phila 15 Mar
  64
SINKS
Mary P: Brussel Twp 11 Sep
  55
SINNEX
Henry P: Phila 2 Ag 70
James P: New-Castle Co
  8 Jy 62
SINNIKSON
Andrew P: Penns Neck 26
  Jy 64
SINNOT/SINNOTT/SINNET
Christopher P: Phila 30
  May 54
H. P: Pa 31 Dec 61
Richard P: Phila 31 Jy 60,
  3 Sep 61
SINTON
Benjamin P: Phila 28 Ap 68
SIPEL
Conrad P: Pa 11 Sep 55
SITGREAVES
Thomas P: Chester Co 9 May
  54
William P: Phila 3 Ag 58
SIVEL
Patty P: Phila 31 Dec 61
SKAFAS
Lucy P: Bethaven 31 Jy 60
SKEELS
William P: Burlington 31
  Dec 61

SKELMAN
  Thomas   P: Frankford 2 Ag
    70
SKELTON
  Samuel (schoolmaster)   P:
    Phila 24 Oct 54
SKENDELEEN
  Cornelius   P: Pa 12 Feb 61
SKETCHLEY
  John   P: Chester Co 1 Nov
    53
  Mary   P: Springfield 13 May
    56, 31 Dec 61
SKILLEN
  William   L: Lancaster Co 19
    Dec 71
SKILLING/SKILLIN
  Samuel   Phila 30 Ap 77, 16
    Jy 77
  William   P: Pa 13 Ja 63;
    Phila 27 Oct 73
SKILLMAN
  Jacob   P: N.J. 24 Feb 63
  Robert   P: Kings-Town 21 Dec
    58
SKINNER/SKYNNER
  Cornelius   T: Germantown
    31 Ja 71
  David   P: York Co 3 Ag 58
  Elizabeth   P: Phila 20 Oct
    68
  Lt. Henry   P: in the army 21
    Dec 58
  John   P: Nottingham 31 Dec
    61
  Richard   P: Phila 19 Jy 80
  Samuel   P: Phila 31 Dec 61,
    13 Oct 63
  Sarah   P: Pa 3 Ag 58; Phila
    21 Dec 58
  Thomas   P: Phila 20 Jy 69
  Ensign W.A.   P: in the army 3
    Ag 58
SLACK
  John   P: Phila 28 Ap 68
  Sarah   P: Phila 20 Oct 68
SLADE
  Mr.   P: Phila-Gaz. 3 Ja 76
SLATER/SLEATER/SLATTER/SLAYTER
  Rev. Dr.   P: Phila 31 Dec 61
  Alexander   P: Phila 9 May 54
  John   P: Phila 19 Ja 69
  Jonathan   P: Phila 8 Jy 62
  Michael   P: Phila 12 Feb 61
  Robert   P: Lancaster Co 24 Feb
    63; Pa 3 Sep 61; Phila 31
    Jy 60
  W.   P: Phila 8 Jy 62
  William   P: Nottingham 24
    Feb 63
SLAYGELT
  Christopher   L: near York town
    19 Dec 71
SLEEPER
  John   P: Phila 28 Oct 62

SLEETH
  Abraham   P: Phila 31 Dec 61
SLEMENS/SLEMMONS
  Thomas   P: Pequea 21 Dec 58
  William   L: Pequea 2 Mar 74
SLEUCH
  Patrick   P: Phila 11 Sep 55
SLEYGEL
  Christopher   P: York Co 3
    Ja 60
SLIFER /or SLISER?/
  Mrs.   P: Phila-Gaz. 27 Oct
    73
SLIGHT
  Henry   P: Bucks Co 31 Jy 60
SLOAN/SLONE
  James   P: N.J. 13 Oct 63;
    Paxton 18 Mar 62
  John   P: Neshaminy 8 Jy 62
  Robert   P: Chester Co 3
    Sep 61; N. London 15 Mar
    64
  William   L: Paxton Twp 20
    Ja 73. P: Pa 13 Oct 63
SLOO
  Capt. Nathaniel   P: Phila
    28 Oct 62
SLOOAM
  Robert   P: Phila 20 Ap 69
SLOSS
  Duncan   P: Pa 31 Dec 61
  Robert   P: Phila 11 Sep 55
SLOVEN
  Samuel   P: Pa 3 Sep 61, 31
    Dec 61
SLOVERSWILER
  Mr.   P: Phila 20 Jy 69
SLOW
  Mat.   P: Lancaster 3 Ja 60
SLUNKELY
  Peggy   Phila 31 Ja 76
SLUTH
  John   P: Phila 28 Oct 62
SMALL
  Drum-Major   P: Phila 16 Jy
    67
  Alexander   P: Phila 12 Ja
    58
  Edward   P: Phila 23 Oct 66
    (& Capt.)
  George   P: Pa 3 Ag 58
  Henry   C: Chester Co 18 Jy
    65, New London 28 Nov 65.
    P: New-London 10 Oct 65
  James   P: Phila 2 Feb 64,
    15 Mar 64 (2), 20 Jy 69
  William   P: Pa 9 Ag 59
SMALLTHS
  Michael   P: Phila 3 Ja 60
SMART
  Anne   P: East New Jersey 18
    Ag 57
  John   P: N.J. 2 Feb 64; Pa
    4 Ag 63
  Rev. John   P: Chester Co 2

Sep 62; Pa 18 Mar 62

SMEDLY

Hannah C: Chester Co 22 Ja
67

SMELT

Capt. Thomas (of Gen. Lasce-
lles's Regt.) - /Trenton?/
15 Jy 56

SMILEY/SMYLEY/SMYLIE/SMILIE/
SMYLLY

Messers MARTIN & Snow Hill
30 Oct 76

James P: Phila 3 Ja 60, 26
Jy 64

Jane P: Phila 26 Jy 64

Jo. L: 3 Oct 65

John P: Pa 13 Ja 63

Robert P: N. Castle 11 Sep
55, 13 May 56

William L: 29 Ja 67. P:
York Co 3 Sep 61

SMITH

and STERRITT P: Phila 24
Feb 63

Capt. P: Phila 6 Jy 58,
3 Ag 58

Mrs. P: Phila 31 Jy 60

Mr. P: Phila 3 Ja 65

Abigail P: Gloucester 28
Oct 62

Adam P: Germantown 13 May
56; near Phila 13 Ja 63.
T: Trenton 10 Ag 58

Mrs. Agnes C: 30 Jy 77.
P: Phila 15 Mar 64

Alexander P: 21 Dec 58
(soldier), 10 Ap 66;
Manor of Moreland 27 Oct
73; Phila 10 Oct 65

Andrew P: Mill-Creek 12 Ja
58; Sgt., prob. in Pitts-
burgh 15 Mar 64

Ann P: Phila 20 Ap 69

Anthony P: Phila 30 May 54

Armstrong P: Phila 28 Oct
62

Arthur Phila 30 Ap 77

Capt. C. P: Phila 15 Mar 64

Caspar/GASPER/GASPAR/CASPER
P: near Gloucester 21 Dec
58; Gloucester (Co) 9 Ag
59, 3 Ja 60, 5 Ag 62, 15
Mar 64; N.J. 4 Ag 63

Catherine P: Phila 19 Ja 69

Charles P: Phila 9 Ag 59,
3 Ja 60, 15 Mar 64

Capt. D. P: Phila 18 Mar 62

Daniel P: Chester Co 2 Feb
64; Pa 12 Feb 61

David P: Nottingham 13 Ja
63

Dougald T: Somerset Court-
house 4 Nov 72

Ebenezer Aug. Phila 1 May 76

Edward P: Bucks Co 12 Ja 58;

Phila 25 Jy 65

Elizabeth P: Phila 11 Sep
55, 3 Ja 76

Ellis P: Pennsylvania 20
Ap 69

Ephraim P: Phila 2 Feb 64

Esther P: Phila 27 Ja 73

Ezekiel P: Pa 3 Ag 58.
T: Allentown 15 Mar 64

Francis P: Pa 3 Ag 58;
Phila 28 Ap 68, 19 Ja 69

Frederick P: Wilmington
9 Ag 59

George P: Phila 3 Ag 58,
31 Mar 63, 27 Oct 73

Gilbert P: Little Britain
Twp 12 Ja 58; Phila 6 Jy
58. T: Bordentown 10
Ag 58

Grace P: Phila 18 Ag 57

Hannah P: Phila 9 Ag 59,
3 Ja 60

Henry P: Pa 31 Mar 63;
near Phila 24 Feb 63

Capt. Henry Secheverall
P: Phila 25 Ap 71

Hester P: Newcastle Co
18 Ag 57

Hezekiah T: Hopewell 10
Ag 58

Hugh P: Bucks Co 2 Feb 64,
15 Mar 64, 10 Oct 65; Pa
4 Ag 63; Phila 18 Mar 62,
3 Ja 65

Humphrey P: Phila 21 Dec
58

Isaac P: Phila 10 Oct 65.
T: Trenton 31 Ja 71

James P: Antedotum Creek
9 Ag 59; Christine Bridge
28 Oct 62; Germantown 31
Mar 63; Lancaster Co 8
Jy 62 (Esq.), 4 Ag 63;
New Groves 31 Dec 61;
Phila 1 Nov 53, 6 Jy 58,
3 Ag 58, 13 Oct 63, 26 Jy
64, 25 Jy 65, 20 Jy 69,
3 May 70, 27 Oct 73; York
Co 5 Ag 62. T: Somerset
Court-house 4 Nov 72

Janet L: Conestoge 15 Ap
56

Jehlel P: Phila 11 Sep 55

Jeremiah P: Phila 18 Feb
55, 3 Ag 58, 9 Ag 59, 28
Oct 62, 25 Jy 65

John L: Pequea 19 Dec 71.
P: 12 Feb 61; Chester Co
5 Ag 56, 12 Feb 61, 3 Sep
61, 15 Mar 64; Donegall
9 Ag 59, 18 Mar 62;
Kingsess 26 Jy 64; Lan-
caster Co 3 Sep 61; Nott-
ingham 31 Jy 60; Pa 13 Ja
63, 2 Feb 64; Phila 9 May

54, 7 Ap 57 (of the Royal
Americans), 7 Ap 57, 6 Jy
58 (Capt), 3 Ag 58 (Capt),
3 Ja 65, 2 May 65, 3 Ja 65
(Lt), 30 Ja 66, 30 Ap 67,
28 Ap 68, 21 Jy 68, 20
Jy 69 (2), 26 Oct 69, 3
May 70, 27 Ja 73, 31 Ja
76, 1 May 76; Sgt., prob.
in Pittsburgh 15 Mar 64;
Rodney's Mill 9 Ag 59;
Thunder Hill 8 Jy 62. T:
Hopewell 17 Oct 54 (2,
Capt)
John, Jr. T: Maidenhead 10
Ag 58
Capt. Johnson P: Phila 24
Jy 76, 30 Oct 76
Jonathan P: Phila 9 Ag 59
Joseph P: Bucks Co 12 Ja
58; New London 13 Ja 63;
Phila 5 Ag 56, 4 Feb 68,
1 May 76, 30 Oct 76. T:
Wright's Town, Bucks Co 6
Dec 64
Josiah P: Phila 30 Ap 77
Lydia P: Pa 3 Ag 58
Margaret P: Lewistown 31
Dec 61; Pa 21 Dec 58;
Phila 27 Ja 73
Mary L: Mill Creek 15 Ap
56. P: Kent Co 7 Ap 57;
Lancaster Co 24 Oct 54; Pa
12 Feb 61; Phila 26 Jy 53,
31 Jy 60, 8 Jy 62, 25 Jy
65, 16 Jy 72
Mildred P: New-Providence
27 Ja 73
Pat./Patrick P: Lancaster
(Co) 31 Jy 60, 31 Dec 61,
2 Feb 64
Peggy P: Phila 2 May 65
Peter P: Carlisle 19 May
63, 4 Ag 63, 2 Feb 64;
Lancaster Co 9 Ag 59;
Pennypack 1 May 76; Phila
30 Ja 66
Philip P: Phila 26 Oct 69
Richard P: Phila 9 May 54,
1 Jy 56, 18 Ag 57, 6 Jy
58, 3 May 70, 30 Ap 77;
Salem Co 15 Mar 64
Robert L: Marsh-creek, York
Co 19 Dec 71. P: Bucks
Co 2 Feb 64; Chester Co
27 Dec 53, 12 Ja 58, 12
Feb 61, 18 Mar 62, 13 Oct
63; 15 Mar 64; near Chester
4 Ag 63; Fog's Manor 13
Oct 63; Horsham 18 Ag 57,
31 Dec 61; Octorara 31 Dec
61; Phila 6 Sep 53 (Capt),
11 Sep 55, 6 Jy 58, 3 Ag
58 (Capt), 3 Ag 58, 21 Dec
58, 31 Dec 61, 18 Mar 62,13

Ja 63,24 Feb 63 (Capt),
13 Oct 63, 2 Feb 64 (2),
26 Jy 64, 3 Ja 65, 1 Nov
70, 30 Oct 76, 19 Jy 86.
P: Phila Co 12 Ja 58;
Uwchland 19 Jy 80; York
Co 24 Feb 63, 4 Ag 63.
T: Prince Town 15 Jy 56
Rosanna P: Phila 1 Feb 70
Sampson P: Chestnut Level
27 Dec 53, 12 Ja 58 (Rev);
Lancaster Co 3 Sep 61, 31
Dec 61 (Rev), 13 Oct 63
(Rev)
Samuel P: Chester 13 May
56; Phila 31 Dec 61, 3
Ja 76, 1 May 76
Sarah P: Bucks Co 18 Mar
62; New-Castle 13 Ja 63
Susannah P: Chester Co 13
Oct 63
Thomas P: Bucks Co 3 Ja
60; Lancaster Co 3 Ja 60;
Pequea 9 Ag 59; Pa 13 Ja
63; Phila 24 Oct 54, 31
Dec 61, 25 Jy 65, 2 Ag
70, 1 May 76
Timothy, Esq. P: Bucks Co
3 Ja 60
Valentine P: Phila 9 Ag 59
Capt. W. P: Wilmington 2
Feb 64
Warner P: Phila 11 Sep 55
William L: York Town 29
Jy 72 (tailor). P:
Chester Co 21 Dec 58;
Christine Bridge 3 Ag 58;
Duck Creek 24 Feb 63; Md.
19 May 63; Northampton
Co 31 Jy 60; Pa 12 Ja 58,
3 Ag 58; Phila 28 Nov 54,
3 Ag 58, 6 Jy 58, 13 Ja
63, 24 Feb 63, 13 Oct 63,
3 Ja 65, 4 Feb 68, 28 Ap
68, 25 Ap 71, 27 Oct 73
(2), 31 Ja 76 (Dr), 19 Jy
80 (Rev); Wilmington 4 Ag
63 (Capt)
William, Jr. P: Phila 10
Oct 65
SMITHERS/SMITHER
John P: Dover 30 Ja 66;
Kent Co 3 Ja 60, 31 Jy 60
SMETHURST
Gamalid P: Phila 3 Ja 60,
31 Jy 60
SMOCK
and Co., Messieurs T:
Middletown Point 15 Mar
64, 6 Dec 64
SMOUT
Elizabeth P: Lancaster 29
Ag 54
Jacob P: Phila 9 Ag 59
John Phila 30 Ap 77

Mary   P: Phila 21 Jy 68
SMYLEY; see MARTIN & SMYLEY;
   also SMILEY
SMYTH/SMYT
   Adam   P: Blockley 9 Ag 59
   Capt. Alexander Lawson   Phila
      30 Oct 76
   Charles   P: Phila 2 Ag 70
   Ezekiel   T: Allentown 3 Oct
      65
   Frederick, Esq.   P: Phila 3
      Ja 65
   Hugh   P: Phila 20 Jy 69
   James   P: Darby 19 May 63;
      Phila 2 Feb 64, 30 Oct 76
   John   C: at Hugh Miller's
      in Fogs Manor 22 Ja 67.   P:
      Fort Pitt 2 Jy 64, sergeant
      in army 26 Jy 64; German-
      town 13 May 56; Phila 3 Ja
      65 (Esq)
   Jonathan   Morris's River 30
      Oct 76
   Thomas   P: Bucks Co 9 Ag 59
SNAIL
   Philip   P: Gloucester Co 12
      Feb 61
SNAVELY
   Caspar   Lebanon 1 May 76
SNEAD
   Edward   P: Phila 24 Oct 54
      (Capt), 3 Ja 60 (Capt), 24
      Feb 63
SNELL
   William   P: Pa 24 Feb 63
SNIDER/SNEIDER
   Christian   P: Phila 28 Nov
      54
   Jacob   Phila 30 Ap 77
   John   P: Phila 16 Jy 72
SNIDMAN
   Bastian   P: York Co 8 Jy 62
SNODGRASS
   John   L: 14 May 72
SNOOK
   William   P: Phila 11 Sep 55
SNOW
   Silas   Duck Creek 16 Jy 77
   Lt. William, of the 55th
      Regt.   P: Phila 3 May 70
SNOWDON/SNOWDEN
   Widow   P: Phila 31 Mar 63
   Isaac   P: Phila 3 Ag 58, 4
      Ag 63, 30 Oct 76, 30 Ap 77
   Jedediah   P: Phila 9 Ag 59
   John   Phila 1 May 76
   Leonard   P: Burlington 3 May
      70, 26 Oct 69; Phila 1 Nov
      70, 25 Ap 71
   Michael   P: Phila 27 Ja 73
   Ruth   P: Phila 9 Ag 59,
      27 Ja 73
SNYDER; see also SNIDER
   Mr.   P: Phila 26 Oct 69
   Christian   P: Phila 11 Sep 55

Henry   T: Kingwood 6 Dec 64
SOABUST
   John   P: Phila 31 Jy 60
SOBER
   Elizabeth   P: Phila 9 Ag
      59
SOLE
   Alexander   P: Haverford 1
      Feb 70
SOLOMAN/SOLOMON
   Mr.   P: Phila 3 Ja 65
   John   P: Phila 23 Oct 66
SOMERVILL
   Joseph   P: Phila 27 Ja 73
SORDS
   John   P: Lancaster Co 7 Ap
      57
SORTER
   James   P: Phila 2 Feb 64
SOTHERN
   Christopher   P: Phila-Gaz.
      3 Ja 76
SOUMAIN/SOUMAINE/SOUMANE
   Mr.   P: Phila 23 Oct 66
   Samuel   P: Phila 5 Ag 56,
      9 Ag 59, 3 Ja 65, 25 Jy
      65, 30 Ja 66, 30 Ap 67,
      16 Jy 67
SOUR, see SAUER
SOUTER
   Peter   P: Phila 3 Ag 58, 9
      Ag 59
SOUTH
   Daniel   T: Kingston 10 Ag
      58
SOWER, see SAUER
SOWERWOLD
   Michael   Phila 30 Ap 77
SOWIN
   William   P: Phila 20 Ap 69
SPACHMAN/SPAKMAN
   Mary   P: Phila 1 Jy 56
   Thomas   P: Phila 1 Jy 56
SPAIN
   Edward   P: Phila 6 Jy 58,
      3 Ag 58
SPALON
   Richard   P: Phila-Gaz. 27
      Oct 73
SPANGENBERG/SPANGENBERY
   John   T: Newtown, Sussex
      Co 1 Sep 68, 31 Ja 71
   Johniust   P: the Jerseys
      12 Feb 61
   Rev. Jos.   P: Phila 5 Ag 62
SPANGLER
   Catharine   P: Phila-Gaz. 3
      Ja 76
SPANTON
   Elizabeth   P: Phila 25 Ap
      71
SPARK/SPARKS/SPARKES
   Mr.   P: Phila 25 Ap 71
   James   P: Phila 16 Jy 67
   John   P: Phila 16 Jy 67;

Salem Co 12 Ja 58
Robert P: Phila 3 Ag 58, 21
  Dec 58
Walter P: Pa 19 May 63
William P: Phila 3 Ja 65
SPARROTT
Edmund P: Phila 4 Ag 63
SPARROW
Thomas P: Phila 11 Sep 55,
  26 Oct 69
SPARRY
James P: Phila 3 Ja 60
SPAVOLD
James P: Phila 9 Ag 59
SPEAKMAN
T. Phila 24 Jy 76
SPEAR/SPEARS/SPEER
David P: Bucks Co 28 Oct
  62, 30 Ap 67
James P: New-Castle Co 9
  Ag 59, 31 Jy 60
John P: N. Castle Co 31
  Dec 61
Joseph P: Carlisle 15 Mar
  64; Phila 27 Ja 73
Robert P: Lancaster Co 31
  Dec 61; New-Castle Co 31
  Jy 60
William P: Lancaster Co 27
  Dec 53
SPEARY
James C: at Cadwallader
  Jones's, Uwchland 22 Ja 67
SPEISE
John Jacob P: Phila 18 Ag
  57
SPENCE
Mr. P: Phila 21 Dec 58
Edward P: Phila 8 Jy 62
Henry P: Carlisle 3 Sep 61
James, Esq. P: Pa 31 Jy 60,
  18 Mar 62
John P: Phila 26 Oct 69
John R. P: Phila 21 Jy 68
Peter P: Phila 5 Ag 62
  (Capt), 23 Oct 66, 28 Ap
  68, 19 Ja 69
Capt. Thomas P: Phila 3 Ag
  58
William P: Phila 27 Dec 53
SPENCER/SPENSOR
Mrs. N: New-Castle, see
  PATTERSON, Hugh. P: Phila
  20 Oct 68
Douglass Phila 1 May 76
Rev. Elihu P: Pa 4 Feb 68
Jo. L: 11 Ap 65
John P: Phila 26 Oct 69
Joseph P: Phila 27 Ja 73,
  30 Ap 77, 19 Jy 80
Capt. Peter P: Phila 13 Oct
  63
Capt. Samuel P: Phila 19 Jy 80
William P: Newcastle Co 18
  Ag 57, 9 Ag 59, 28 Oct 62,

4 Ag 63; Pa 3 Ja 60;
  Phila 2 Oct 62, 28 Ap 68
SPENSERD
William P: Pa 26 Jy 64
SPICER
Jacob P: Cape-May 9 May
  54, 6 Jy 58, 12 Feb 61
  (Esq), 3 Sep 61 (Esq),
  28 Oct 62; N.J. 7 Ap 57
  (Esq)
James P: Cape May 9 Ag 59
SPIDIE/SPIDY
William P: Phila 31 Dec
  61, 13 Oct 63
SPIER
John P: Pa 31 Dec 61
SPIKES
Jacob P: Phila 29 Ag 54
Susannah P: Phila 21 Dec
  58
SPIKFADEN
Benedick P: Lancaster 26
  Jy 64
SPINAS
Richard P: Phila 24 Oct 54
Sarah P: Phila 24 Oct 54
SPINKS
James P: Phila 18 Feb 55
SPOFFORD
John P: Phila 5 Feb 54
SPOONER
William P: Phila 3 Ja 65
SPOULL
Andrew P: Durham 1 Feb 70
SPOUTSMAN
Mrs. P: Lancaster Co 31
  Dec 61
SPRAGUE
John P: Phila 25 Ap 71
SPRAIGHT
James P: Phila 15 Mar 64
SPRATLY
Walter Phila 30 Ap 77
SPRATT/SPRAT
David P: Phila 3 Sep 61
John L: 13 Jn 65. P:
  N. Castle Co 3 Sep 61;
  Phila 3 May 70
SPRET
Jo. L: 11 Ap 65
SPRING
Capt. Benjamin P: Phila
  26 Jy 64
John P: Phila 26 Oct 69
SPRINGER
Benjamin P: Burlington Co
  19 May 63
John P: Freehold 9 Ag 59
SPROAT
James P: Phila 19 Jy 80
SPROGEL
Lodwig P: Phila 2 Ag 70
SPROTT
William P: Nottingham 28
  Oct 62

SPROUL/SPROULL
  Andrew P: Durham 26 Oct 69,
    1 Nov 70; Sussex Co 27 Ja
    73
  John P: N. Castle 24 Feb 63
  Thomas P: New-Castle 1 Jy
    56
  William P: Chester Co 24 Feb
    63; Pa 31 Mar 63
SQUARE
  Michael P: Northampton 30
    May 54
SQUIRE/SQUIRES
  John N: 12 Feb 67
  Thomas P: Phila 20 Jy 69,
    2 Ag 70
SRAPNELL
  John P: Phila 10 Oct 65
SROCK
  John P: Providence Twp 1 Nov
    53
STABLER
  Edward P: Phila 11 Sep 55
STACKHOUSE
  Michael P: Phila 3 Ja 65
  William P: Bucks Co 3 Ag
    58
STACY
  John Phila 1 May 76
  Richard N: near Weatherspoon's
    c/o Mrs. Smith New Castle Co
    4 Dec 66; near Witherspoons
    12 Feb 67
STADLER
  Jacob P: Phila 9 Ag 59
  Robert Phila 24 Jy 76
STAFBACK
  Michael P: Phila 3 Ja 65
STAFFORD
  Elizabeth P: Conegogee 28 Nov
    54
  George P: Lower Dublin 10 Oct
    65; Phila 15 Mar 64
  James P: Conegogee 28 Nov 54
  W. P: N. Castle Co 31 Dec 61
  William P: Newcastle Twp 12
    Ja 58
STAGG
  John P: Phila 5 Ag 56
STAHLER
  Edward P: Phila 18 Feb 55
STAINMAIT
  Daniel P: Phila 6 Jy 58
STAKES
  Dr. B. P: Phila 31 Mar 63
STALFORD
  Samuel P: New Providence 9
    Ag 69
  Thomas P: Great Swamp 26 Oct
    69
STALL
  Christian P: Heidelberg 11
    Sep 55
  Gasper/Casper P: Phila 23 Oct
    66, 27 Oct 73

STAMPER
  John P: Phila 12 Feb 61
  William P: Phila-Gaz. 3 Ja
    76
STANALAND
  John P: Phila 1 Jy 56
STANBURY
  Jonathan P: Germantown 2
    Ag 70
STANCLIFF/STANCLIFFE
  John P: Phila 19 Ja 69, 2
    Ag 70
STANDIN
  Henderson W:/Wilmington/
    3 Jy 76
STANDLEY/STANDLY
  David P: Phila 11 Sep 55
  James P: Phila 8 Jy 62
  Margaret P: Germantown 31
    Jy 60
  Marshal P: Phila 25 Jy 65
  Peter P: Easton 16 Jy 77
STANFORD
  Robert L: Lancaster Co 20
    Ja 73
STANLAND
  John P: Roxborough 16 Jy
    72
STANLEY/STANLY
  and Co P: Phila 24 Feb 63
  John L: Cumberland Co 20
    Ja 73. P: 11 Sep 55, 7
    Ap 57
  Joseph P: Phila 11 Sep 55
  Mary P: Germantown 3 Ja 60
  William P: Phila 24 Feb 63
STANNEX
  James P: N. Castle Co 3
    Sep 61
STANTON
  Capt. P: Phila 6 Jy 58
  Capt. Giles P: Phila 27
    Ja 73
STAPLER
  and SMITH P: Phila 24 Feb
    63
  John P: Wilmington 9 May
    54, 31 Dec 61
STAPLETON
  Thomas P: Phila 30 Ap 67
STARBUCK
  Joseph P: Pa 3 Sep 61
  Samuel P: Phila 3 Ja 65
STARK
  Nancy P: Phila 31 Dec 61
STARLING
  James P: Bucks Co 21 Dec
    58
STARMAN
  Jacob P: Phila 18 Ag 57
STARR
  Jeremiah P: Phila 31 Dec 61
  John P: New-Garden 8 Jy 62
  Moses P: Whiteland Twp 12
    Ja 58

STARRET/STARRAT
  John   P: Pa 3 Ag 58; Phila
    24 Oct 54
  Robert   P: Phila 26 Oct 69
STATES
  John   P: Phila 19 Ja 69
STARTIN
  Charles   Phila 30 Ap 77
STEANS
  Thomas   P: Phila 19 Jy 80
STEATTON
  Hill   P: Lewis Town 9 Ag 59
STEDMAN
  Alexander   P: Phila 4 Feb
    68
  John   P: Phila 28 Ap 68
  Richard   P: Phila 26 Jy 64
STEEL/STEIL
  Miss   P: Pa 2 Feb 64
  Alexander   Phila 30 Ap 77,
    19 Jy 80
  Col. Archibald   P: Phila 5
    Jy 80-Gaz. 19 Jy
  Brice   T: Trenton 1 Sep 68
  Henry   P: Phila 2 Sep 62,
    26 Jy 64, 21 Jy 68
  James   P: Phila 5 Ag 62, 2
    Sep 62, 15 Mar 64
  John   L: Paxton Twp 20 Ja
    73.   P: Carlisle 12 Feb
    61 (Rev); New London 3 Ag
    58 (Rev); Pa 9 Ag 59, 2
    Feb 64; Phila 2 Ag 70, 1
    Nov 70.   T: Somerset Co 4
    Nov 72.
  Margaret   P: Phila 31 Mar 63
  Peggy   P: Phila 31 Dec 61
  Robert   P: Chestnut Level 12
    Ja 58; Cross Roads 7 Ap 57
  Thomas   P: Pa 12 Ja 58;
    Phila 2 Feb 64, 20 Jy 69,
    16 Jy 72
  William   P: Germantown 24 Feb
    63; Pa 9 Ag 59, 3 Ja 60,
    31 Jy 60; Phila 28 Ap 68
STEEN
  Mary   P: Octorara 3 Ag 58
  Robert   P: Pa 13 Oct 63;
    Radnor 12 Ja 58
  Thomas   P: Phila 18 Ag 57
STEENIN
  Mary   P: Middle Octorara 18
    Ag 57
STEENSON
  John   P: Phila 3 Ja 65
STEER
  Joseph   P: Lancaster Co 13
    Oct 63
  William   P: Phila 3 Ja 76
STEINER
  Conrad   P: Germantown 11 Sep
    55; Phila 5 Ag 62 (Rev)
STEINMEYER
  Ferdinand   P: Phila 2 Ag 70
STEINSON

John   P: Phila 26 Jy 64
STELWAGEN
  George   P: Phila 28 Oct 62
STENBECK
  William   P: Phila 31 Mar 63
STENCH
  John   P: Phila 1 Jy 56
STENNER
  Charles   P: Phila 21 Dec 58
STENSON
  John   P: Phila 13 Oct 63
STENTON
  John   P: Pa 21 Dec 58
STEORT
  Mary   P: Phila 2 May 65
STEPHENS/STEPHEN; see also
  STEVENS
  Mrs.   P: Pa 7 Ap 57
  Alexander   P: Phila 27 Ja
    73
  Capt. Andrew   P: Paxton 19
    Ja 69
  Col. Edward   Phila 24 Jy
    76
  Elizabeth   P: Phila 21 Jy
    68
  Francis, Esq.   P: in the
    army 3 Ag 58
  J.   P: Phila 2 Sep 62
  John   P: Phila 25 Jy 65,
    30 Ja 66; Wilmington 5
    Ag 56
  Mary   L: c/o M. Leasing
    York-Town 20 Ja 73
  Richard   P: Pa 12 Feb 61
  Robert   P: Chester Co 12
    Ja 58; Lancaster Co 3 Ja
    60, 3 Sep 61
  Thomas   P: Phila or Md.   7
    Ap 57 (Esq); Phila 27 Oct
    73
  Walter   P: Phila-Gaz. 27
    Oct 73
STEPHENSON; see also STEVEN-
  SON
  George   P: Phila 24 Oct 54
  Grisel   P: Chester Co 1 Nov
    53, 27 Dec 53
  Hugh   P: Pa 15 Mar 64
  James   C: c/o W. Chinghan
    Esq.-West Caln 28 Nov 65
  John   P: Donegall 12 Ja 58
  Robert   P: Phila 27 Oct 73
  William   P: Pa 2 Feb 64
STERLING/STIRLING
  Rev. A.   P: Chester Co 15
    Mar 64
  Alexander   P: Pa 18 Mar 62;
    Phila 15 Ag 62
  Rev. Andrew   P: Octorara 18
    Mar 62
  Archibald   C: East Caln 28
    Nov 65
  Isabella   P: Pa 18 Mar 62
  James   Burlington 30 Ap 77

John   C: near Little Conewago
22 Ja 67.   P: Pa 18 Mar
62, 28 Oct 62; Phila 3 Ja 65
Jos.   P: Chester Co 15 Mar 64
Martha   P: Phila 30 Ja 66
Matthew   P: Phila 28 Oct 62
Lt. Robert   P: in the army 21
Dec 58; N. Providence 20
Oct 68
STERNLE
John Fred.   P: 13 miles from
Phila 11 Sep 55
STERRITT; see SMITH &
STEVENS; see also STEPHENS
Mr.   P: Phila 27 Ja 73
Benjamin   P: Maidenhead 5 Ag
62.   T: Maidenhead 3 Oct
65, 31 Ja 71
Elizabeth   P: Phila 22 Nov 53,
21 Dec 58, 23 Oct 66, 30 Ap
67, 16 Jy 67, 4 Feb 68, 20
Oct 68
George   P: Phila-Gaz. 3 Ja 76
John   P: Phila 24 Oct 54, 21
Dec 58, 25 Jy 65, 30 Ja 66
Philip   P: Phila 3 Ja 76
Richard   P: Bethlehem 15 Dec
61; Phila 23 Oct 66, 30 Ap
67, 16 Jy 67, 20 Oct 68
Sarah   T: near Trenton 31 Ja
71
William   P: Phila 3 Ja 76,
16 Jy 77
STEVENSON; see also STEPHENSON
Adam   P: Phila-Gaz. 3 Ja 76
Daniel   T: Middletown 7 May
67
David   P: Cumberland Co 2
Feb 64
Edward   T: Middletown 15 Mar
64, 6 Dec 64
George   L: Carlisle 29 Jy 72
& 20 Ja 73 (Esq).   P:
York Town 9 Ag 59
James   P: Cecil Co 13 Ja 63;
Phila 30 Ja 66, 28 Ap 68
Jennet   P: Kent Co 7 Ap 57
John   P: Chester Co 27 Dec 53;
New Castle 5 Feb 54; Phila
23 Oct 66, 28 Ap 68.   T:
Middle T/own/, Capt 15 Jy
56
Jos.   P: in the army 12 Ja
58
Richard   L: Stiegle's town,
near Lancaster 19 Dec 71
Robert   L: Carlisle 29 Jy 72.
P: Phila 10 Oct 65, 23 Oct
66; York Co 3 Ja 60; York
Town 7 Ap 57
Samuel   P: Pa 13 Ja 63, 13 Oct
63, 3 Sep 61, 18 Mar 62 (2);
Phila 8 Jy 62, 26 Jy 64, 3
Ja 65
William, Esq.   C: Chester Town

Maryland 18 Jy 65;
Merchant, Charlestown
Maryland 28 Nov 65
STEWAR
John   P: Chester Co 21 Dec
58
STEWARD/STEUARD
Adam   Phila 5 Jy 77-Gaz.
16 Jy
Agnus   P: Phila 13 Ja 63
Capt. Alexander   P: 12 Feb
61
David   P: Phila 30 Ap 67
Elizabeth   P: Phila 30 Ap
67
Henry   P: Phila 23 Oct 66
James   P: Pa 9 Ag 59; Phila
25 Jy 65
John   N: Brinigar Twp 4
Dec 66
Michael   P: Phila 30 May 54
Dr. Patrick   P: Noxonton 7
Ap 57
Summerset   P: Phila 25 Jy
65
STEWART/STEUART; see also
STUART
Dr.   P: in the army 3 Ag 58
Mr.   P: Pennsylvania 4 Feb
68
Agnes   P: Phila 27 Ja 73
Alexander   P: Pa 13 Oct
63; Phila 8 Jy 62;
soldier, prob. in Pitts-
burgh 15 Mar 64
Andrew   P: Phila 4 Feb 68
Ann   P: Newport 7 Ap 57
Archibald   P: Pa 13 Oct 63,
15 Mar 64; Phila 9 Ag 59,
13 Ja 63; Union Iron-Works
28 Oct 62, 15 Mar 64.   T:
see WRIGHT, Thomas
Lt. C.   P: Phila 2 Feb 64
Caleb   P: Phila 28 Oct 62
Charles   P: Delaware 5 Ag
62; Kingwood, N. Jersey
28 Ap 68; Phickenin 27
Ja 73; Phila 28 Nov 54,
25 Jy 65, 2 Ag 70
Daniel (agent)   P: in the
army 21 Dec 58; Phila 27
Ja 73
David   P: Chester Co 31 Dec
61
Donald (soldier)   P: Fort
Pitt 26 Jy 64
Elizabeth   P: Phila 18 Mar
62, 24 Feb 63
Francis   P: Frankford 24 Feb
63; Pa 31 Mar 63; Phila
10 Oct 65
George   P: Chester Co 2 Feb
64; Pequea 8 Jy 62; Phila
19 Jy 80 (Capt)
Hugh   P: Radnor 19 May 63

Isabel P: Phila 2 Sep 62
James P: Bucks Co 27 Ja
  73; N. Castle Co 31 Dec
  61; Pa 12 Feb 61, 28
  Oct 62, 2 Feb 64; Phila
  31 Jy 60, 8 Ag 62, 28
  Oct 62, 26 Jy 64, 3 Ja 65,
  23 Oct 66, 4 Feb 68, 31
  Ja 76
Jane P: Phila 31 Mar 63
Janet P: Chester Co 28 Oct
  62
Jennet P: Pa 24 Feb 63
Jenny P: Phila 26 Oct 69
John L: Cumberland Co 20 Ja
  73. N: near N. Castle 12
  Feb 67. P: Brandywine 31
  Dec 61; Chester Co 12 Ja
  58; Marsh Creek 15 Mar 64;
  Morris Co 5 Ag 56; Newcastle
  Co 7 Ap 57; Pa 31 Jy 60, 13
  Ja 63, 19 May 63, 26 Jy 64,
  25 Jy 65, 10 Ap 66, 20 Oct
  68, 27 Oct 73; near Wilming-
  ton 11 Sep 55. T: Middle-
  town 31 Ja 77
Joseph, sergeant 18th Regt.
  P: Phila 1 Nov 70
Margaret P: Phila 10 Oct 65
Mary P: Chester Co 27 Dec 53
Nancy P: Phila 24 Feb 63
Neil P: Phila 25 Jy 65, 23
  Oct 66
Peter P: Phila-Gaz. 27 Oct
  73, 1 May 76
Robert P: Bucks Co 21 Dec 58;
  Neshaminy 10 Ap 66; Pa 12
  Ja 58, 5 Ag 62, 15 Mar 64;
  Phila 9 Ag 59, 3 Ja 60, 8 Jy
  62, 19 May 63 (Col.), 4 Ag
  63, 27 Ja 73; York Co 23 Oct
  66
Samuel P: Brandywine 18 Mar 62
Thomas P: Phila 1 Nov 70
Walter P: Chester Co 3 Sep 61;
  Phila 3 Ja 76
William L: York Co 2 Mar 74.
  P: America 7 Ap 57 (Lt.);
  Chester Co 27 Dec 53; Pa 3
  Ag 58, 13 Oct 63 (3); Sussex
  Co 28 Oct 62. T: N. Jersey
  31 Ja 71
STICKNEY
  William Phila 30 Ap 77
STILES/STYLES
  Benjamin P: Phila 3 Ja 65
  Daniel P: Phila-Gaz. 3 Ja 76,
    31 Ja 76, 24 Jy 76
  Edw. P: Phila 8 Jy 62
  Henry P: Phila 25 Ap 71
  Richard P: Phila 2 Sep 62
  Robert P: Germantown /error
    for Phila?/ 13 May 56
STILL
  Benjamin P: Elizabeth Town 30

  Ap 77
STILLWAGGON/STILWAGGON
  John P: Phila 3 Ag 58, 3
    Sep 61, 31 Mar 63
  Samuel P: Phila 31 Mar 63
STILLWELL/STILWELL
  John P: Phila 3 Ag 58
  Nicholas P: Upper End of
    Cape May 21 Jy 68
STILLY
  Peter P: Phila 19 May 63
STILTS
  Adam P: Roxborough 16 Jy
    72
STINGIS
  Joseph P: Phila 30 Ap 77
STINSON
  James P: Phila 1 Jy 56
  John P: Phila 3 Ja 65, 20
    Jy 69
  Michael P: Pa 12 Feb 61
  William P: Phila 18 Mar 62
STINYARD
  Joseph P: Phila 30 Ap 67
STIRLING, see STERLING
STITSON
  Theophilus P: Phila 23 Oct
    66
STITT
  James L: 20 Ja 73
STOCKHOUSE
  Michael P: Bristol 2 Feb
    64
STOCKTON/STUCKTON
  Betsey P: Phila-Gaz. 27
    Oct 73
  Thomas P: York Co 31 Dec
    61
STOCKWELL
  John P: Phila 20 Jy 69,
    26 Oct 69
STOCO
  Mr. P: Phila 31 Dec 61
STODDARD
  Benjamin P: Phila 12 Feb
    61, 3 Sep 61
STODDERT
  Henry P: New-Castle 18
    Feb 55
STODGRASS
  William L: 11 Ap 65
STODMON
  John P: Phila 12 Feb 61,
    5 Ag 62
STOI
  Rev. P: Phila 30 Ap 67
STOKALD
  Conyers P: Phila 3 May 70
STOKER
  James P: Phila 2 Ag 70
STOKES
  George P: Phila 13 Oct 63
  James P: Phila 21 Jy 68
STOKLY
  Cornelius P: Angola Twp 19

Ja 69

STOLE
William P: Phila 11 Sep 55

STOLESBURY/STOLSBOROUGH
John P: Phila 19 Ja 69, 1
  Feb 70

STOMMER
Leattice /?/ P: Phila 5 Ag
  56

STONE
John P: Phila 10 Oct 65
Sophia P: Phila 3 May 70
Walter P: Phila 16 Jy 72
William P: Phila 16 Jy 67

STONEMAN
Tobias L: 3 Oct 65

STONLEY
John P: Phila 18 Mar 62

STOOBER
Widow P: Phila 3 Ja 60

STOOK
Robert P: Phila 11 Sep 55

STOOPS
John P: Phila 29 Ag 54
Mary P: Pa 18 Mar 62

STOR_SE
Abraham P: New-Castle Co 8
  Jy 62

STORE
James P: Phila 18 MAr 62

STOREY/STORY
John P: Phila 16 Jy 72
Lydia T: Allentown 10 Ag 58
Mary P: Phila 5 Ag 62
Peter P: Duck Creek 13 Ja
  63; Kent Co 13 Ja 63 (Dr)
Robert P: Newcastle Co 18 Ag
  57, 21 Dec 58
Simon P: Phila 11 Sep 55
William C: c/o Mr. M'Gomery-
  Christeen Bridge 28 Nov 65
Zebediah P: Phila 10 Oct 65;
  Capt., Phila 4 Ag 63, 2 Feb
  64

STOUCK
Adam P: Phila 4 Ap 54

STOUT
Benjamin T: Hunterdon Co, see
  O'CONNER, Johannah
Catharine P: N.J. 18 Mar 62
David P: Lancaster Co 4 Ag 63
Hannah P: Middletown 21 Dec 58
John P: Phila 3 Ag 58 (sailor),
  19 Jn 80 (Capt)
Col. Joseph T: Hopewell 1 Sep
  68
Margaret P: Phila 25 Ap 71
Philip P: Jersey 16 Jy 72
Rachel T: Hunterdon Co 10 Ag
  58
Samuel, Esq. T: Hopewell 17
  Oct 54

STOY
Mary Eliz. P: Phila 24 Feb 63
Peter P: Phila 26 Jy 64

Rev. W. (Dutch) P: Phila
  3 Ag 58

STRADLING
John C: 30 Jy 77

STRAFFORD
James P: Welch-Tract 31 Jy
  60

STRAIN
Mr. York Co, see CATHCART,
  John

STRANGE
John P: Wilmington 9 Ag
  59, 31 Jy 60 (Capt)

STRATTON/STRATTAN
David P: West New Jersey 1
  Jy 56
Fithian Deerfield 31 Ja 76
Capt. John P: Phila 31 Jy
  60

STRAWBERRY
Robert P: Bucks Co 3 Ja 60

STRAWBRIDGE
Robert P: Little Pipe
  Creek 1 Nov 70

STREAN
William P: Pa 13 Oct 63

STREET
Francis P: Phila 20 Oct 68,
  20 Jy 69
Mary P: Phila 27 Ja 73
Samuel P: Phila 16 Jy 67

STREIGHT
Godgrey P: Bucks Co 19
  Ja 69

STREMBECK
William P: Phila 29 Ag 54

STREPER
William P: Whitemarsh 18
  Mar 62

STRETCH
Daniel P: Cumberland Co
  26 Jy 64

STRETCHER
Edw. Phila 31 Ja 76

STRICKER
Martin P: Germantown 13
  May 56

STRICKLAND
Mr. P: Biberry 19 Jy 80

STRICKLER
Peter P: Phila 20 Ap 69

STRIKE
Edward P: Lower Dublin 9
  Ag 59

STRINGER
Thomas P: Phila 5 Ag 62
William P: Octorara 12 Ja
  58; Upper Octarara 29 Ag
  54

STRODE
John C: East Bradford 22
  Ja 67
Richard P: Chester Co 27
  Ja 73

STRUMBECK/STRUMBOK

William Phila 3 Ja 60,
   10 Ap 66, 30 Ap 67
STRONFELS
   George P: Phila-Gaz. 27
      Oct 73
STRONG
   Matthew Phila 31 Ja 76
   Peter P: Phila 16 Jy 72
STROUD; see also STRODE
   Isaac P: Phila 2 Feb 64
STROWGER
   William P: Phila 19 Ja 69
STRUTHERS
   William, soldier P: prob.
      in Pittsburgh 15 Mar 64
STUART; see also STEWART
   and HOUGHTON P: Phila 25
      Ap 71
   Alexander P: Phila 31 Jy
      60, 1 Feb 70, 3 May 70
   Archibald P: Union Iron-
      Works 25 Ap 71. T: Union
      Iron-Works, see GRAHAMS,
      James
   Christopher P: Phila 27 Oct
      73
   David Phila 30 Ap 77
   George P: Phila 20 Jy 69
   Hugh P: Phila 2 Ag 70
   Jean Phila 1 May 76
   Jenny P: Phila 10 Oct 65
   John P: Brandywine 18 Ag
      57; near Newcastle 7 Ap 57
   Robert P: Phila 20 Ap 69.
      T: Basking-ridge 17 Oct
      54
   Rosanna P: Phila 1 Feb 70
   Ruth P: Phila 1 Nov 70
   Susannah L: Cork Co 25 Dec
      66
   Wm. P: Brandywine Forks 20
      Ap 69; Phila 25 Jy 65, 3
      Ja 76
STUBER
   Mrs. P: Phila 5 Ag 62
   Dr. Frederick P: Phila 6
      Jy 58
STUCKLEY
   John P: N. Hanover 30
      May 54
STUMP
   John P: Springfield 11 Sep
      55
STURGEON/STOURGEN
   Mr. P: Chester Co 3 Sep 61
   Hannah P: Phila 18 Mar 62
   Jeremiah P: Chester Co 28
      Oct 62
   John P: Lancaster Co 7 Ap
      57; Phila 1 Nov 70
STURGES/STURGIS
   John P: Chester Co 24 Feb 63,
      31 Mar 63; Pa 28 Oct 62,
      13 Ja 63
STWALT

Charles P: Phila 6 Jy 58,
   3 Ag 58
STYCER
   Thomas C: at Elisha Hughes's
      22 Ja 67
STYMETS
   Daniel P: Phila 6 Jy 58
SUBERING
   William P: Sussex 28 Ap 68
SUBERRY
   Elizabeth P: Phila 12 Feb
      61
SUDLOW
   Richard Phila 31 Ja 76
SULLIVAN/SULLEVAN/SULEVANE/
   SULLIVANE/SULLAVANT
   Capt. P: Phila 3 Ja 60,
      10 Oct 65
   Andrew P: Phila 3 Ja 65;
      soldier, Fort Pitt 26 Jy
      64
   Cornelius P: Lancaster 13
      Oct 63; Phila 18 Feb 55,
      11 Sep 55
   Darby P: New-Castle Co 3
      Ag 58
   David N: Kent Co 29 Nov
      64. P: Duck Creek 24
      Feb 63; Kent Co 13 Oct
      63
   Dennis P: Phila 20 Jy 69
   James P: Phila 31 Mar 63
   Jeremiah P: Christeen 26
      Jy 64
   John P: Allens-Town 3 Ag
      58; Phila 13 Ja 63, 27
      Ja 73
   Mary P: Pa 12 Ja 58; Phila
      18 Ag 57
   Oyne P: the Jerseys 12
      Feb 61
   Patrick P: Phila 20 Jy 69
   Silvester/Sylvester P:
      Middletown 16 Jy 67, 19
      Ja 69
   Thomas P: Northampton Co
      2 Ag 70
SUMMERS
   Benjamin P: Phila 12 Ja 58
   George P: Phila 18 Mar 62
   James L: Pequea 19 Dec 71
   Mary, see LYNOUGH
SUMMERSET
   John P: Phila 18 Ag 57
SUMRALE
   Alexander P: Octarara 5 Ag
      56
SUNDERLIN
   Peter P: the Jerseys 12 Ja
      58
SUNTER
   Michael P: Germantown
      /error for Phila?/
      13 May 56
SUPPLE

Jonas   P: Norrington 1 Feb 70
SURDELONG
  Constantine   P: Phila 20 Jy 69
SUTHARD
  Thomas   P: Phila-Gaz. 27 Oct
    73
SUTHERLAND
  Alexander   P: Phila 2 Sep 62
  Christian   P: Phila 4 Feb 68
  David   P: Phila 28 Nov 54
  John   L: York Co 2 Mar 74
SUTOR
  William   P: Phila 18 Mar 62
SUTTER
  Ann   P: Phila 20 Ap 69
  John   P: Chester Co 2 Sep 62
  Mary   P: Phila 31 Jy 60
  Peter   P: Phila 19 Jy 80
SUTTERLAND
  Donald   P: Phila-Gaz. 3 Ja
    76
SUTTON
  Mr.   P: Phila 30 Ja 66
  Bartholomew   P: Phila 16 Jy 72
  James   P: Phila 2 Feb 64
  John   P: Chester Co 11 Sep 55;
    Darby 18 Feb 55; Frankford
    7 Ap 57
  Mary   P: Phila 8 Jy 62
  Rachel   P: Phila 3 Ag 58, 26
    Oct 69
  Richard   P: Phila-Gaz. 27 Oct
    73
  William   P: Newport 9 Ag 59
  Capt. Woolman   Phila 31 Ja 76
SWAIN/SWAINE
  Capt. Г: Phila 18 Mar 62
  Mrs. Margaret   Phila 30 Oct 76
  Francis   Phila 31 Ja 76
  John   P: Phila 24 Feb 63
SWAING
  John   P: Phila 23 Oct 66
SWALLOW
  James   P: Germantown-Gaz. 3
    Ja 76
SWAN/SWANN
  Alexander   P: Chester Co 13
    May 56; Sweetara 4 Ag 63
  Hugh   L: Lancaster Co 15 Ap
    56. P: Huston's Ferry 28
    Oct 62; Lancaster Co 13 Ja
    63; Sasquehannah 4 Ag 63
  Lt. Rowd   P: Phila 20 Jy 69
  Thomas   P: Pa 12 Feb 61, 3
    Sep 61, 31 Dec 61
SUANSON
  Joshua   P: Phila 9 Ag 59
SWANSTON
  William   P: Phila 3 May 70
SWANZEY
  John   L: Cumberland Co 29 Jy
    72
SWARTS
  Kitty   P: Lancaster 31 Dec 61
SWAYEZE

Matthias   T: Bethlehem 6
  Dec 64
SWEARINGEN
  Samuel   P: Carlisle 9 Ag
    59, 3 Ja 60
SWEENEY/SWEANY/SWENY/SWINY
  Archibald   L: Derry Twp
    19 Dec 71. P: Derry Twp
    3 Ja 65
  Barnaby   P: Pa 3 Ag 58
  Edward   P: Phila 20 Oct 68
  Isaac   P: Chester Co 18 Ag
    57
  Margaret   P: Phila 26 Jy
    53
  Nancy   P: Pa 26 Jy 64
  Walter   P: Phila 2 May 65
SWEET
  John   P: Phila 1 Feb 70
  Jos.   P: Oley 31 Dec 61
SWEETING
  William   P: Phila 12 Feb 61
SWEILER
  Jacob L.   P: Phila 19 Jy 80
SWETT/SWEAT; see also SANSOM
    & SWETT
  Benjamin   P: Phila 30 Ap 67
  Thomas   P: Phila 2 May 65,
    25 Jy 65
SWIFT
  Godwin   P: Phila 25 Jy 65
  John   P: Phila 1 Jy 56, 5
    Ag 56
  Joseph   P: Phila 1 Jy 56,
    5 Ag 56
  Joseph, Jr.   Phila 30 Ap 77
SWIM
  Rebecca   P: Kings-Town 21
    Dec 58
SWINSEN
  John   P: Phila 24 Feb 63
SWITMAN
  ...   P: Phila 28 Nov 54
SWORD
  John   P: Lancaster Co 3 Ja
    60
SYCINGER
  Godfrey   L: Dunkertown 19
    Dec 71
SYDE
  John   P: Phila 5 Ag 56
SYDER
  George   P: Germantown 19 Ja
    69
SYGET
  George   P: Forks of Brandi-
    wine 21 Dec 58
SYKES/SIKES
  George   Phila 31 Ja 76
  William   P: Phila 1 Feb 70
SYMENTON
  John   P: Great Valley 3
    May 70
SYME
  Alexander   P: Phila 16 Jy 67

SYMER
Andrew P: Phila 7 Ap 57
SYMES/SIMES
Dr. Phila 5 Oct 76-Gaz.
30 Oct
Sarah P: Lewis-Town 13
May 56
SYMMER
Andrew P: Phila 10 Oct
65, 30 Ja 66
SYMONDS
Capt. Edward P: Phila 13
Ja 63
SYNDALL
John P: Pa 26 Jy 64
SYNG
Abigail P: Phila 6 Jy
58
Philip P: Phila 6 Jy 58,
3 May 70
Susannah P: Pa 31 Dec 61

TABB
Edmond P: Phila 31 Dec 61
TAGGARD
Mr. P: Phila 16 Jy 72
TAGGART/TAGART
Jacob C: at John Baldwin's
Kennet 22 Ja 67. P:
Salem 20 Oct 68
James P: Pa 18 Mar 62; Pe-
quea 8 Jy 62
Jo. L: 14 May 72
John P: Pa 13 Ja 63
Joshua P: Pilesgrove 19 Ja
69
Nelly P: Phila 25 Jy 65
TAIL
David L: Cumberland Co 20
Ja 73
TALBOT/TALBOTT
Capt. P: Phila-Gaz. 27 Oct
73
Benjamin Berks Co 30 Oct 76
Williamson Phila 30 Ap 77
TALEM
John P: Phila 21 Dec 58
TALLS
Andrew P: Pa 13 Ja 63
TALLY
Michael P: Phila 5 Ag 62
TAMSON
Joseph P: Phila 3 Ja 65
TANE
John P: Phila 18 Mar 62,
8 Jy 62
TANKIN
John P: Phila 31 Dec 61
TANNER/TANNOR
Mrs. Ann Phila 30 Oct 76
Benjamin P: Hopewell 18
Ag 57, 26 Oct 69
James P: Phila 20 Jy 69
Capt. John P: Phila 19 Jy

80
Joseph P: Chestnut Hill
21 Jy 68
Michael P: in Negalister,
40 English miles from
Lancaster, Pa. 2 Ag 70
Nancy Phila 31 Ja 76
William Phila 1 May 76,
19 Jy 80
TANNINGER
Jacob P: Germantown 31 Jy
60
TARBERT
Robert P: Christine Bridge
12 Ja 58
TARRANT
Capt. M. P: New-Castle Co
31 Mar 63
TARTENSON
Bellerue P: Phila 30 Ap 77
TARVEY
Sophia P: Phila 1 Nov 70
TATE/TAIT
Andrew P: Phila 18 Mar 62,
8 Jy 62
Anthony P: Bucks Co 7 Ap
57, 13 Oct 63, 2 Feb 64;
Phila 10 Oct 65
George P: Phila 7 Ap 57
John P: Phila 28 Ap 68;
St. George's 26 Oct 69
Samuel C: Oxford Twp 22
Ja 67. L: Cumberland
Co 20 Ja 73. P: Chester
Co 3 Ag 58; Phila 3 Ja 76
William P: Gloucester Point
26 Oct 69; Phila 23 Oct
66
TATEM/TATEN
William P: Gloucester 25
Ap 71; Phila 4 Ag 63
TAUNTON
John P: Phila-Gaz. 3 Ja 76
TAYLOR
Adam P: N. Castle Co 31 Dec
61
Capt. Alexander P: Phila
4 Ag 63
Benjamin P: Chester Co 31
Jy 60; Kennet Twp 5 Ag 56
Catherine N: Head of In-
dian River 12 Feb 67.
P: Phila 27 Ja 73
Charles P: Phila 26 Jy 64
Christopher P: Phila 2
May 65, 25 Jy 65
Claudius/Glaud P: Phila
10 Oct 65, 20 Oct 68
Trad T: c/o Robert Ruther-
ford Phila 3 Oct 65
Cusery P: N.J. 3 Ag 58
Daniel P: Northern Libert-
ies 3 May 70; Phila 5 Ag
56
David P: Phila 10 Ap 66

Edward   P: Phila 1 Nov 53
Eleanor   P: Pa 31 Dec 61
George   L: 2 Mar 74 (shoe-
    maker).   P: Bucks Co 31
    Dec 61; Cape May, 16 Jy
    77; Phila 21 Dec 58, 19
    May 63, 20 Oct 68.   T:
    Derham Iron-Works 10 Ag
    58
Gilliam   Phila 30 Oct 76
Greenwood   P: Phila 3 Ja
    76
Henry   P: Phila 27 Ja 73
Isaac   P: Burden's Tract 4
    Ag 63; Phila 10 Oct 65
James   N: 29 Nov 64.   P:
    Bucks Co 1 Nov 70; North-
    ern Liberties 26 Oct 69;
    Pa 2 Feb 64; Phila 18 Ag
    57, 13 Ja 63, 20 Jy 69
Capt. James   P: Northern
    Liberties 3 May 70; Phila
    24 Oct 54, 28 Oct 62,
    4 Ag 63, 16 Jy 67, 2 Ag
    70, 27 Oct 73, 1 May 76,
    24 Jy 76; York Town 12
    Feb 61
John   P: Middle Octorara
    21 Dec 58; Pa 2 Feb 64;
    Phila 3 Ja 60, 13 Ja 63,
    19 May 63, 25 Jy 65, 20
    Oct 68, 20 Ap 69.   T:
    Bordentown 7 May 67;
    Trenton 10 Ag 58
Joseph   P: Phila 19 Jy 80
Josiah   P: Phila 18 Mar 62,
    8 Jy 62
Judith   P: Phila 16 Jy 72
Mary   L: Leacock Meeting
    19 Dec 71.   P: Newtown,
    Bucks Co 23 Oct 66
Matthew   N: near N. Castle
    12 Feb 67.   P: Phila 27
    Oct 73
Medad   P: Phila 29 Ag 54
Nicholas   P: Phila 26
    Jy 64
Peter   P: Chester Co 12 Feb
    61, 18 Mar 62, 8 Jy 62;
    Phila 2 May 65, 25 Jy 65
Phiby   P: Chester Co 21 Dec
    58
Richard   P: Phila 28 Oct 62,
    26 Oct 69, 24 Jy 76
Robert   P: Bucks Co 25 Ap
    71; Cumberland Co 2 Feb 64;
    Pa 13 Oct 63, 15 Mar 64;
    Phila 13 Oct 63, 28 Ap 68;
    Yellow Breeches 3 Ag 58
Thomas   P: 12 Feb 61; Free-
    hold 31 Mar 63; Meadstone/
    Medstone 1 Nov 53, 11 Sep
    55; St. George's 12 Ja 58
Thompson   P: Phila 27 Ja 73
William   P: Phila 8 Jy 62,

19 May 63, 13 Oct 63
TAYS
William   P: Phila 27 Ja 73
TEADARO
Christian   P: Phila 20 Jy
    69
TEAMASON
Martha   P: Phila 3 Ja 65,
    2 May 65, 25 Jy 65
TEASSE
Michael   P: Sasquehanna 3
    Ag 58
TEAT/TEATE
Anthony   P: Middletown 31
    Jy 60; Newtown 31 Dec 61
Samuel   P: Marsh Creek 30
    Ja 66; Pa 3 Sep 61
TEE
Richard   P: Phila 25 Jy 65,
    23 Oct 66
TEESON
Daniel   P: Phila 1 Feb 70
TELFORD
David   P: Phila-Gaz. 3 Ja
    76
TELLES
John   P: Phila 23 Oct 66,
    20 Jy 69
TELLEUR
Capt. W.   P: Phila 26 Jy
    64
TEMPLE
Thomas   P: Phila 10 Ap 66
William   P: Phila 28 Ap
    68, 27 Ja 73
TEMPLEMAN
John   P: Phila 5 Jy 80-
    Gaz. 19 Jy
TEMPLER
Mrs.   P: Phila 26 Oct 69
TEMPLETON; see also LIVING-
    STON &
James   P: Pa 19 May 63
John   P: Great Valley,
    Chester Co 3 May 70;
    Whiteland 18 Mar 62
Samuel   P: Phila-Gaz. 27
    Oct 73
TEN EYCK
Andrew   P: Phila 19 Jy 80
Thomas   P: Phila 30 Ap 77
TENNENT/TENNANT/TENANT
Rev. C.   P: Whiteclay-
    creek 12 Ja 58
Rev. G.   P: Phila 5 Ag 62,
    13 Ja 63
James   P: Phila 16 Jy 72
Richard   P: Phila 3 Ja 65
William   P: Phila 18 Mar
    62, 8 Jy 62, Rev.
    William   P: Monmouth Co
    18 Ag 57.   T: 7 May 67
TENNISON/TENISON
John   P: Phila 3 Ja 65, 25
    Jy 65

TERANCE
  William   P: Cross Roads 2
    Feb 64
TERRELL/TERRIL
  John   P: Phila 2 Feb 64
  Mary   Deerfield, Cumberland
    Co 30 Oct 76
TERRY
  James   P: Phila 1 Feb 70
  Capt. John   P: Phila-Gaz.
    27 Oct 73
TERVET
  Thomas   P: Phila 30 Ja 66
TESHLER
  Anthony   P: Phila 11 Sep 55
TESLEN
  Godhard   P: Phila 12 Ja 58
TEST
  Edward   P: N.J. 31 Jy 60;
    Salem 18 Ag 57, 8 Jy 62
TETFORD
  Walter   P: Phila 30 Ap 67
TETIGSOM
  Godfried   P: Phila 7 Ap 57
THACKER
  Catharine   P: Phila 23 Oct 66
THAMPERNOE
  Peter   P: Phila 24 Feb 63
THARP
  William   P: Pa 28 Oct 62
THATCHER
  Jeremiah /see ROOS, Robert/
    T: Kingwood 7 May 67
  Richard   P: Kennet 7 Ap 57
  Samuel   P: Phila 4 Feb 68
THAXTER
  Samuel   P: Phila 4 Ag 63, 2
    Feb 64, 15 Mar 64
THEDE
  Capt. Jacob   P: Phila 19 Ja 69
THELWELL
  John   C: Londonderry, Chester
    Co 30 Oct 66
THENE
  Elizabeth   P: Phila 3 Ag 58
THICKPENNY
  James   P: Phila 18 Feb 55,
    11 Sep 55
THISTLE
  Thomas   P: Phila 16 Jy 67
THOMA
  Madam   P: Phila 19 Jy 80
THOMAS; see also POPE & THOMAS
  Alexander   P: Phila 12 Ja 58
  Arthur   P: Phila 23 Oct 66
  Azariah   P: Great Valley 11 Sep
    55
  Benjamin   P: Phila 3 Ja 65
  David   P: Bucks Co 18 Mar 62,
    26 Oct 69; Pa 13 Ja 63;
    Phila 8 Jy 62
  Edward   P: Phila 1 Jy 56, 3
    Ag 58, 3 Ja 60, 23 Oct 66
  Eleanor   P: Abington 30 Ja 66
  Henry   T: Trenton 10 Ag 58

  Isaac   C: at Willis Town,
    Chester Co 18 Jy 65
  John   P: near Phila 28 Nov
    54; Phila 25 Jy 65, 4
    Feb 68
  Jonathan   P: Phila 16 Jy 67
  Joseph   P: Phila 24 Feb 63;
    York-Town 12 Feb 61
  Capt. Lewis   P: New-Castle
    Co 21 Dec 58
  Margaret   P: Phila 21 Dec
    58
  Nathan   P: Newcastle Co 7
    Ap 57
  Oliver   P: Phila 31 Dec 61,
    5 Ag 62
  Peter   P: Lancaster Co 22
    Nov 53, 4 Ap 54
  Philip   P: French Creek 2
    Feb 64
  Richard   P: Phila 12 Ja 58
  Samuel   P: Phila 3 Ag 58,
    5 Ag 62, 30 Ja 66, 20
    Ap 69
  Sarah   P: Phila 10 Ap 66
  Thomas   P: Guinnedth Twp
    27 Ja 73; Phila 11 Sep 55
  William   P: Chester Co 28
    Nov 54. T: near Bound
    Brook 6 Dec 64
  William, Jr.   P: Oxford 19
    May 63
THOMASIN
  Samuel   P: Phila 1 Jy 56
THOMPSON
  and BONNELL   P: Phila 24
    Feb 63, 19 May 63
  and ROBINSON   P: Phila 3 Ag
    58
  Dr.   P: Phila 1 Feb 70
  Mrs.   P: Phila 4 Ag 63
  Abraham   P: Pa 3 Sep 61
  Alexander   C: blacksmith,
    c/o Andrew Porter,
    Chester Co 28 Nov 65. P:
    Londonderry Twp 28 Oct
    62; Lower County 18 Ag
    57; Phila 26 Oct 69, 16
    Jy 72, 31 Ja 76
  Andrew   P: 12 Feb 61
  Ann   P: Phila 25 Jy 65
  Ant.   P: Holly Hill 2 Feb
    64
  Archibald   P: Phila 25 Ap
    71
  Barshaba   Phila 31 Ja 76
  Catherine   P: Phila 12 Ja
    58
  Charles   P: Phila 19 Jy 80
  David   P: New-Castle Co 31
    Jy 60, 24 Feb 63; Pa 3
    Sep 61, 13 Oct 63; Phila
    3 Ag 58, 28 Oct 62
  Edward   P: Phila-Gaz. 27 Oct
    73

Eleanor P: Elk 3 Ja 60
Elizabeth P: Phila 31 Jy 60, 24 Feb 63
Frances P: Salem Co 25 Ap 71
Capt. G. P: Phila 24 Feb 63
George P: Pa 26 Jy 64; Phila 16 Jy 67; Wilmington 31 Dec 61
Grace P: Jersey 7 Ap 57
Hugh L: Cumberland Co 19 Dec 71; Phila Co 29 Jy 72. P: Christine Bridge 12 Ja 58; Kent 15 Mar 64; Phila 18 Mar 62, 4 Ag 63
James P: Bucks Co 10 Oct 65; Chester Co 18 Ag 57; Oxford 3 Ja 60; Pa 31 Dec 61; near Phila 18 Mar 62, 8 Jy 62; Phila 31 Dec 61, 2 Sep 62, 13 Oct 63, 23 Oct 66 (2), 27 Ja 73; Upper Marlborough, Phila Co 4 Feb 68; West Caln 31 Dec 61
Jane P: Phila 19 May 63
Jem P: Phila 3 Ja 65
Jo. L: 3 Oct 65
John L: Cumberland Co 14 May 72; Lancaster Co 29 Jy 72; schoolmaster 19 Dec 71, 2 Mar 74. N: Christeen Bridge, see ENGLISH, David. P: Bucks Co 8 Jy 62, 26 Oct 69, 16 Jy 72, 24 Jy 76; Chester Co 4 Ag 63; Lancaster Co 15 Mar 64; Little Britain 28 Oct 62; Montgomery Twp 28 Ap 68; New Castle Co 21 Dec 58, 31 Jy 60; N. Jersey 20 Ap 69; Northeast 12 Ja 58; Pa 31 Dec 61, 2 Feb 64, 15 Mar 64; near Phila 4 Feb 68; Phila 18 Feb 55, 5 Ag 56, 6 Jy 58, 3 Ag 58, 18 Mar 62, 8 Jy 62 (2), 23 Oct 66, 19 Ja 69, 27 Oct 73; Shippensburg 12 Ja 58
Jonah P: Phila 1 May 76
Joseph P: Bucks Co 28 Oct 62; Cumberland Co 13 Ja 63, 13 Oct 63; Phila 1 Jy 56, 24 Feb 63
Margaret W: c/o Robert Coughran 3 Jy 76
Martha P: Pa 13 Oct 63; Phila 21 Dec 58
Molly P: Phila 20 Oct 68
Moses P: Antrim 26 Oct 69; York Co 3 Ag 58
Peter P: Phila 28 Oct 62, 24 Feb 63, 2 Ag 70
Reuben P: Phila 15 Mar 64

Robert P: Chester Co 21 Dec 58; Lancaster 13 Ja 63; Northern Liberties 3 May 70; Pa 3 Sep 61; Phila 30 Ap 67, 1 Feb 70 (soldier), 25 Ap 71, 30 Oct 76; Whiteclay Creek 18 Ag 57, 12 Ja 58
Rev. S. P: Conewa. 12 Ja 58
Samuel L: Cumberland Co 29 Jy 72; Little Britain 19 Dec 71. P: Phila 28 Ap 68
Rev. Samuel L: Strabane Twp York Co 19 Dec 71. P: Carlisle 28 Oct 62; York Co 4 Ag 63
Susannah P: Phila 13 Oct 63
Thomas P: near Phila 31 Dec 61; Phila 4 Ag 63, 30 Ap 77, 16 Jy 77; Salem Co, West New Jersey 23 Oct 66
William L: Carlisle 20 Ja 73. P: Bucks 27 Dec 53, 3 Ja 60; Chester Co 1 Nov 53; Phila 24 Oct 54, 1 Nov 70; York-Town 12 Feb 61. T: Maidstone 15 Jy 56
Rev. William P: Carlisle 8 Jy 62, 28 Oct 62, 24 Feb 63; Phila 5 Ag 62
THOMSON/TOMSON
Abraham P: Whiteland 5 Ag 56
Alexander P: Phila 20 Jy 69, 3 Ja 76
Andrew P: Phila 7 Ap 57
Catharine P: Phila 21 Dec 58
Lt. Charles P: Phila 30 Ap 67
David P: Phila 5 Feb 54, 29 Ag 54, 28 Nov 54, 27 Ja 73
James P: Phila 25 Jy 65
John P: Bucks Co 18 Mar 62; Phila 7 Ap 57, 30 Ap 67, 1 Nov 70, 3 Ja 76
Joseph P: Phila 28 Nov 54
Mary P: Phila Co 4 Ap 54
Nelly P: Phila 23 Oct 66
Rebecca P: Phila 27 Ja 73
Richard P: Phila 18 Ag 57
Robert P: Nottingham 25 Jy 65
Thomas P: Chester 11 Sep 55
William P: Phila 27 Ja 73, 27 Oct 73
THOMSTON/THONSON
Alexander P: Phila 18 Mar

62, 8 Jy 62
THOPE
John   P: Phila 1 Nov 70
THORN/THORNE
Jane   P: Baltimore 31 Dec
61, 19 May 63
John   L: Lebanon 20 Ja 73.
P: Christine Bridge 12
Ja 58
Sydenham-Kent Co 1 May 76
THORNBER
John   Phila 5 Ja 76-Gaz.
31 Ja
THORNBRUGH
Daniel   L: York Co 29 Jy
72
THORNBURGH
Mr.   P: Pa 15 Mar 64
THORNBURY/THORNBROUGH
Margaret   P: Phila 18 Mar
62, 13 Ja 63, 24 Feb 63,
4 Ag 63
Tho.   P: Lancaster 12 Ja
58
THORNHILL
John   P: Phila 30 Ja 66
THORNTON
Ann   P: Phila 18 Mar 62,
13 Ja 63
James   P: Germantown /error
for Phila?7 13 May 56
John   P: Phila 18 Mar 62,
8 Jy 62, 20 Jy 69; York
Co 31 Dec 61
Capt. Joshua   P: Phila 4 Ag
63
Solomon   P: Phila 3 Sep 61
THROP/THROPP
John   P: Burlington Co 26
Oct 69; Phila 20 Jy 69
THUMB
George   P: Phila 30 Ap 77
THURSTON
Capt. Levit   P: Phila 11 Sep
55
TIDMARSH
Giles   P: Phila 5 Ag 62
TILBURY
Thomas   P: Phila 3 Ag 58
TILGHMAN
Edward, Jr.   Phila 30 Oct 76
TILLINGHAST
Nicholas   P: Phila 6 Jy 58,
3 Ag 58
TILLIT/TILLET
Capt. Thomas   P: Phila 3 Ag
58, 4 Ag 63
TILLOTSON
Dr. Thomas   P: Phila 31 Ja 76
William   L: 3 Oct 65
TILTON
William   P: Phila-Gaz. 27 Oct
73
TIMOTHY
John   P: Phila 27 Ja 73

TINGES
Henry   P: Phila 30 Oct 76
TINKER
John   P: Germantown 2 Feb
64
TINKLER
John   P: Phila 16 Jy 67
TINLEY
....   P: Phila 5 Ag 56
TIOLI
Mr.   P: Phila 28 Ap 68
TISDALE
Joseph   P: Phila 11 Sep 55
TITCOMB
Jos.   P: Phila 5 Ag 62;
Capt., Phila 24 Jy 76,
30 Oct 76
TITUS
Francis   P: Pa 26 Jy 64.
T: Pa 3 Oct 65
Jacob   P: Cold-Spring 15
Mar 64
Philip   P: Pa 15 Mar 64
Richard   P: Phila 13 Ja 63
TOAM
Mary   P: Chestnut Level 15
Mar 64
TOBY
Nathaniel   T: E. N. Jersey
31 Ja 71
TODD/TOD
____   L: student, Pequea
see M'CALL
Andrew   P: Great Valley 26
Jy 64.   T: Morris-Town 4
Nov 72
Ann   Phila 30 Oct 76
David   P: Phila 2 May 65,
27 Oct 73; Providence
2 Ag 70, 3 Ja 76
James   P: Phila 31 Dec 61;
Providence Twp 1 Nov 70
Mary   P: Phila 27 Ja 73
Capt. Nath.   P: Phila 3 Sep
61
Robert   P: N. Providence
18 Mar 62, 28 Ap 68
TODERINGHAM
Francis   P: Phila 27 Ja 73
TOFFIELD
Catherine   P: Phila-Gaz.
27 Oct 73
TOGGETT
Ann   P: Phila 21 Dec 58
TOLBERT
John   P: Phila 19 Jy 80;
Sussex Co 31 Dec 61
Mary   P: Phila 31 Mar 63
Samuel   Phila 30 Ap 77
TOLE
Darby   P: Phila 25 Jy 65
TOLLIS
Samuel   P: Phila 20 Ap 69
TOLMIE
Alexander   P: Phila-Gaz. 3

Ja 76

TOMB/TOM
  Hugh   P: Phila 2 Feb 64;
    Dr., Phila 24 Feb 63, 13
    Oct 63, 15 Mar 64, 10 Ap
    66, 27 Oct 73
  Samuel   P: Sussex Co 2 Feb
    64
TOMINES/TOMINS
  Patrick   P: Phila 5 Ag 62,
    15 Mar 64
TOMLINSON
  John   P: Phila 2 May 65,
    25 Jy 65 (2), 30 Oct 76
  Richard   P: Phila 12 Ja 58
    (Capt), 27 Ja 73
  Robert   P: Phila 18 May 57
TOMLISTON/TOMLISTONE
  James   P: Phila 26 Jy 64,
    3 Ja 65
TIMPKINS/THOMKINS/TOMKINS
  Charles   P: Phila 8 Jy 62,
    5 Ag 62
  Robert   P: Bucks 28 Nov 54
  Thomas   P: Phila 3 Ja 65
TONAMORE
  Mary   P: Kensington 4 Feb
    68
TOOD
  John   P: Christine 13 Ja 63
TOOLE
  Bartholomew   P: Phila 11 Sep
    55, 26 Oct 69
TOOLS
  Samuel   P: Phila 28 Ap 68
TOOP
  Joseph   P: Phila 25 Ap 71
TORANCE
  Hugh   P: Cumberland Co 12
    Ja 58
TORBERT
  James   T: Bucks Co 7 May 67
  Samuel   P: 12 Feb 61
TORBUT
  Robert   P: Chester Co 12 Ja
    58
TORHERT
  Samuel, tanner   P: Bucks Co
    19 Ja 69
TORKER
  John   P: Phila 3 Ja 65
TORRANT
  John   P: Phila 3 Sep 61
TORREY
  Capt. Benjamin   P: Phila 8
    Jy 62
TORRONS
  Robert   P: Phila 20 Jy 69
TOWNART
  Jacob   P: near Lancaster 12
    Feb 61
TOWNSEND/TOWNSHEND
  Charles   P: Phila 18 Ag 57,
    4 Feb 68
  Isaac   P: Phila 25 Jy 65

Rev. Jacob   P: Phila 18
    Mar 62, 8 Jy 62, 15 Mar
    64, 3 Ja 65, 16 Jy 67
  James   P: Phila 3 Ag 58
  Joseph   P: Bucks Co 25 Ap
    71
  Thomas   P: Phila 23 Oct 66
TOYE
  Patrick   P: Phila 3 Ja 65
TRAIL/TRAILLE
  Dr.   P: in the army 12 Ja
    58
  Robert   P: Phila 15 Mar 64;
    Northampton 1 Feb 70
TRAINER/TRAINOR
  James   P: Pa 31 Dec 61
  Philip   P: Phila 3 Ja 65
TRALY
  Samuel   P: Phila 16 Jy 72
TRANBERG
  Andrew   P: Wilmington 24
    Oct 54, 1 Jy 56
  Catharine   P: Wilmington
    18 Feb 55
TRAP
  John   P: Kingsess 21 Dec 58
TRAPNELL
  John   P: Kingsess 24 Feb 63
TRAPNUT
  John   P: near Phila 31 Dec
    61
TRAVERS
  Patt   P: Phila 1 Feb 70
TRAXEL
  Monsieur   P: Conogigie 28
    Oct 62
TREADWELL
  David   P: Phila 3 Ja 65
  Sarah   P: Phila 25 Jy 65
  William E.   P: Phila 3 Ag 58
TREANOR
  John   C: Chester-or MOORES,
    George, Phila 30 Jy 77
TREAT
  Richard   P: Abingdon 24
    Oct 54, 1 May 76; Rev.
    5 Oct 76
TREBY
  John   P: Phila 3 Ja 65
TREDWAY
  David   P: Phila-Gaz. 27 Oct
    73
TREE
  Capt. Lambert   P: Phila 2
    Feb 64
TREICHEL
  =Lewis   P: Phila 25 Jy 65
TREISLER
  Peter   P: Phila 1 May 76
TREMPER
  William   P: Phila 10 Oct 65,
    21 Jy 68
TRENCH
  George   P: Salem 30 Ja 66
TRENCHARD

George, Esq. T: West Jersey
    6 Dec 64
TRENT
    Rev. Jos. P: Phila 24 Feb
        63
    Sarah P: Carlisle 2 Feb 64
    Capt. W. P: Carlisle 4 Ag
        63
    William P: Lancaster 12 Feb
        61; Phila 3 Ja 65
TREVOR
    John P: Whiteclay Creek 19
        Ja 69
TRIBIT
    George P: Pa 18 Mar 62
    Govy P: Phila 8 Jy 62
TRICHARD
    Peter P: Phila 4 Feb 68
TRICKER
    Christopher P: Phila 13 Oct
        63
TRICKETT
    William P: Phila 19 Jy 80
TRICKEY
    Charles P: Phila 2 Feb 64
TRIM
    Christopher P: Phila 27 Ja
        73
    Moses P: Delaware 4 Ag 63
TRIMBLE/TRIMBELL
    John P: Cumberland Co 31
        Dec 61
    Joseph P: Phila 6 Jy 58, 13
        Ja 63
    Robert P: Phila 1 Nov 70
    William P: Phila 13 Ja 63
TRINNEL/TRINNELL
    Alexander P: Cumberland Co
        28 Oct 62
    William P: Cumberland Co
        3 Sep 61
TRINNEY
    John P: Phila 21 Dec 58
TRIPPETT
    John P: Phila 8 Jy 62
TRISBACH
    Simeon P: North Co 12 Ja 58
TROTT/TROOT/TROTH
    Mr. P: Chester Co 9 May 54
    Ann P: Chester Co 1 Nov 53,
        28 Nov 54, 18 Feb 55
    Capt. John P: Phila 31 Jy 60
    William P: Phila-Gaz. 27 Oct
        73
TROTTER
    James P: Phila 25 Jy 65
    John P: West Jersey 12
        Feb 61
TROUCHARD
    George T: West Jersey 15 Mar
        64
TROUGHLAND
    Thomas C: Marlborough Twp 30
        Oct 66
TROUTEN/TROUGHTON

James P: Phila 1 Feb 70
    Thomas P: Chester Co 15
        Mar 64
TROY
    Matthew P: West Jersey 12
        Feb 61
    Michael P: Phila 10 Ap 66
    Peggy P: Phila 30 Ja 66
TRUELOVE
    Samuel P: Phila 25 Ap 71
TRUETT/TRUITT
    Jos. P: Phila 25 Jy 65
    Solomon P: Phila 20 Jy 69
TRUMBLE
    Francis P: Phila 2 Sep 62
    Sarah P: Phila 24 Feb 63
TRUMMOLD
    John P: near Phila 28 Oct
        62
TRUNY
    Capt. John P: Phila 1 Nov
        53
TRUSS
    Andrew P: Phila 21 Dec 58
TRUSTLOVE
    Samuel P: Phila 26 Oct 69
TRYALL
    George Phila 30 Oct 76
TUBRID
    James P: Phila-Gaz. 3 Ja
        76
TUCKER
    Benjamin P: Phila 1 Feb 70
    George Phila 5 Ap 77-Gaz.
        30 Ap
    Henry P: Phila 2 Feb 64,
        15 Mar 64
    John P: Phila 13 Oct 63;
        Upper Merion 1 Feb 70
    Jonathan P: Upper Merion
        24 Jy 76
    Joseph P: Tredyffrin 11
        Sep 55, 1 Jy 56; Abington
        5 Ag 56, 7 Ap 57; Great
        Valley 31 Dec 61
    Nicholas P: Bucks Co 7 Ap
        57
    Robert P: Pa 31 Dec 61
    Ruth P: Phila 27 Ja 73
    Samuel P: Phila 3 Ag 58;
        N.J. 13 Ja 63
    Stephen P: Phila 27 Ja 73
    Thomas P: Chester Co 24 Jy
        76
TUCKEY
    William P: Cape-Fear 3 Ag
        58
TUDOR
    Edward P: Phila 27 Ja 73
TUFF
    Mr. Bruff P: Salem 30 Oct
        76
TUFTS
    Simon P: Phila 18 Feb 55
TULLINGER

Casper N: 29 Nov 64. P:
  New Castle Co 31 Mar 63
TILLOW
  Charles P: Phila 10 Ap 66
TULLY/TULEY
  Abraham P: Phila 2 Ag 70
  Charles P: Phila-Gaz. 27
    Oct 73
TULLIKEN
  Major P: in the army 21
    Dec 58
TUNNICLIFF/TUNICLIFFE
  Mr. P: Phila 1 Nov 70
  John P: Phila 3 Ja 65
TUNNYMORE
  Richard P: Phila-Gaz. 27
    Oct 73
TURBERT/TURBETT
  James P: Phila 3 Ag 58,
    18 Mar 62
TUREY
  Michael P: Pa 4 Ag 63
TURK/TURKE
  Andrew P: Charles-Town 21
    Dec 58
  James P: Pa 3 Sep 61
TURLEY
  Joseph P: Phila 3 Ja 65
TURNER
  Miss P: Phila-Gaz. 3 Ja 76
  Barchebe P: Phila 20 Jy 69
  Daniel N: c/o Mrs. Ham-
    New Castle Co 4 Dec 66. P:
    Christeen 2 Feb 64
  Edward P: Phila 1 Feb 70
  George P: Phila 31 Jy 60,
    8 Jy 62
  James P: Lancaster Co 22
    Nov 53
  John P: Phila 4 Ag 63, 2 Feb
    64, 10 Oct 65, 10 Ap 66
  Joseph P: Phila-Gaz. 3 Ja 76
  Lt. Sam. P: Phila 20 Ap 69
  Peter W: New Castle Co 3
    Jy 76
  Susannah P: Pa 13 Ja 63,
    24 Feb 63
TURNEY
  Eleanor L: near William
    Clingan's, Esq. 31 Ja 71.
    P: Little Brandywine 1 Nov
    70; Chester Co 28 Ap 71
TURNLEY
  Joseph P: 12 Feb 61
TURNOVES
  James P: York-Town 12 Feb 61
TURPIN
  William P: Phila 19 Jy 80
TURVERT
  Martin L: L# Jn 65
TUTTLE/TUTTELL
  Capt. Jehiel P: Phila 11 Sep
    55
  Samuel T: Morris-Town 4 Nov 72
TWADDEL/TWADDELL

James P: Phila 1 Nov 53
William P: Phila-Gaz. 27
  Oct 73
TWADDEY
  Alexander P: Phila 1 Feb
    70
TWEED
  James (sailor) P: Phila 3
    Ag 58
  Robt. P: Lancaster Co 27
    Dec 53
TWEEDY
  William P: Phila 3 Ag 58
TWENTYMAN
  Joseph P: Phila 27 Ja 73
TWIGS
  John P: New-Castle Co 3
    Ag 58
TWINEM
  James P: York Co 13 Oct 63
TWINING
  Stephen P: Bucks Co 31 Jy
    60; Springfield 18 Mar 62
TYBOUT/TYBOUTT/TYBOUTE
  Andrew P: Phila 24 Feb 63,
    23 Oct 66
  James P: Phila 13 Oct 63
  Joseph P: Phila 24 Feb 63
TYERAL
  Capt. Thomas P: Phila 29
    Ag 54
TYLER
  Daniel P: Phila 13 Oct 63,
    3 Ja 65
  Robert P: Andover Creek
    13 Oct 63
TYNG
  John A. P: Phila 15 Mar
    64
TYRRIL/TYRRELL/TYRELL
  John P: Pa 13 Ja 63
  Thomas P: Germantown 13
    May 56; Phila 5 Ag 56
TYRER
  Thomas P: Phila-Gaz. 3 Ja
    76, 31 Ja 76
TYSON
  Enos Upper Dublin 5 Ja
    76-Gaz. 31 Ja

UGEE
  John P: Phila-Gaz. 27 Oct
    73
ULLERICK
  Philip P: Phila 8 Jy 62
ULLY
  Lewis P: Phila 27 Ja 73
UMPTON
  Edward P: Phila 24 Oct 54
UNDERHILL
  John P: West Bradford 31
    Dec 61
  Jos. P: Dover 26 Jy 64
UNDERWOOD

Samuel P: York-Town 31 Jy
  60
Thomas P: Phila 19 Ja 69
UPTON
  Giles P: Phila 6 Jy 58
URWIN
  James P: Phila 27 Ja 73,
    27 Oct 73
USHER
  .... , merchant L: York Town
    19 Dec 71
  John P: Phila 19 Ja 69
UTNEY
  Mr. P: Phila 2 May 65
UTSMAN
  Mary P: Lancaster 12 Feb 61

VAGNAL
  Mrs. T. P: Phila 15 Mar 64
VAIN
  Mary P: Phila 21 Dec 58
VALATON
  Mr. P: Phila 13 Oct 63
VALENTINE/VALINTINE
  Ann P: Phila 28 Nov 54,
    31 Jy 60
  Henry P: Phila 27 Ja 73
VALLACOT
  Mary P: Phila 11 Sep 55
VALLANCE
  Nicholas P: Phila-Gaz. 3 Ja
    76
  Robert Phila 16 Jy 77
VALLEAU
  John P: Phila 5 Ag 56, 10
    Oct 65
  Peter P: Marcus-hook 10 Oct
    65
VAN AKEN/VANAIKE
  Roelof T: near Prince Town
    15 Jy 56
  William P: Germantown 5 Ag
    56, 19 May 63, 13 Oct 63
VAN BEARETH
  William P: Phila 3 May 70
VANBEBBER
  Isaac C: Charles-Town,
    Maryland 30 Oct 66
  Jacob, Esq. P: Newcastle Co
    12 Ja 58
VANBRISKER
  Ann P: Phila 12 Ja 58
VANBURKELOW
  Jacob P: Phila 8 Jy 62
VANBUSKIRK/VAN BUSKARK
  Hannah T: Shaminy 15 Jy 56
  Jacob P: near Phila 3 Ag 58
VANCE/VAUNCE
  Esther P: near Phila 13 Oct
    63
  James P: Naghan 3 Ja 60;
    Phila 3 Ja 76
  John P: New-Castle Co 3 Ja
    60, 31 Jy 60

Joseph C: West Nottingham
  22 Ja 67
William P: Phila 27 Ja 73
VANCORT/VAN COURT, see LAKE
  Moses P: Moreland 20 Jy
    69
V.CORTLANDT
  Stephen Phila 24 Feb 63
VAN DAM
  Anthony Shrewsbury 5 Ap
    77-Gaz. 30 Ap
VANDEGRAFT
  John P: Neshaminy 1 Jy 56
VANDERBELT
  John P: Phila 15 Mar 64
VAN DEREN
  John P: (Falls of) Schuyl-
    kill 28 Ap 68, 3 May 70
VANDERGRIETH
  Elias P: Phila 2 Ag 70
VANDERGRIFT/VANDERGRIFFT
  John P: Phila 28 Ap 68
  Nicholas P: Pennypack 16
    Jy 72
VANDERHERST
  Arnoldus P: Phila 19 Ja 69
VANDERLIP
  Dolly P: Phila 31 Jy 60
VANDER VELDEN
  Isaac P: 12 Feb 61
VAN DERVER
  Jacob P: Currier's Ferry
    19 Ja 69
VANDUCHREN
  John P: Phila 20 Ap 69
VANDYKE/VANDYCK
  Lydia T: 10 Ag 58
  William P: Phila 31 Dec 61
VAN EMBERG
  Mr. P: Bordentown 25 Ap 71
VANGENY
  Airy T: Trenton Goal 17
    Oct 54
VANGEZELL
  John P: New-Castle 3 Ja
    60, 31 Jy 60, 12 Feb 61,
    3 Sep 61, 2 Feb 64, 15
    Mar 64
VANHAUZER
  Felty L: 19 Dec 71
VAN HORN/VANHORNE
  David P: Phila 31 Dec 61
  James T: Rocky-Hill 17 Oct
    54
  Jane P: Bucks Co 3 Sep 61
  Rev. William P: Phila 19 Jy
    80
VAN HUBEN
  Hans P: Lancaster 7 Ap 57
VANKIRK
  William P: Freehold 31 Jy
    60
VANLAASHERT
  Christian P: Germantown 30
    Ap 67

VANLEER/VANLIER
  Dr. Branson   C: Chester Co
    18 Jy 65
  John George   P: Germantown
    11 Jy 54, 24 Oct 54
VAN LUVENER/V. LUVENAH
  Zacharias/Zachary P: New
    Castle 31 Jy 60, 2 Feb 64
VANNEMAN
  Andrew   P: near Wilmington 24
    Oct 54
VANOST
  Isaac   P: Phila 28 Nov 54
VANOSTEN
  John   P: Phila 2 May 65
VANSANT/VANSAND
  Hannah   Bucks Co 30 Ap 77,
    16 Jy 77
  Jacob   P: Smithfield 15 Mar
    64
  Joshua   P: Kent Co 31 Dec 61
  Judith   P: Bristol 7 Ap 57
  Margaret   P: Smithfield 26
    Jy 53
  Stoffs   P: Bucks 24 Oct 54
VANSCIVER
  Jacob   P: Phila 2 May 65
VANSEIUA
  Jacob   P: Germantown /?/ 30
    Ap 67
VANSICKLE
  James   Reading-Town 30 Oct 76
  John   T: Readington 17 Oct 54
VAN SPRAUN
  G.   P: Phila 18 Mar 62
VANTENKYES
  Samuel   P: Phila 24 Jy 76
VANUAGLAM
  Benjamin   P: Phila 3 Ja 65, 2
    May 65
VAN VLEET
  Derrick   T: Readington 17 Oct
    54
VAN WIESSENFELS
  Lt.   P: Phila 7 Ap 57
VAN WYCH
  Theodorus   P: Phila 8 Jy 62
VAREE
  James   P: Phila 31 Jy 60
VAUGH
  Benjamin   P: Frankford 26 Jy
    64
VAUGHAN/VAUN
  Edward   P: Phila 29 Ag 54,
    21 Dec 58, 31 Jy 60
  John   P: Chester Co 28 Nov 54;
    Phila 28 Oct 62
  Sergt. Thomas   P: in the army
    21 Dec 58
  William   P: Phila 2 May 65
VAUSE
  William   T: Crosswicks 17 Oct
    54
VAWIN
  James   P: Phila 28 Ap 68

VEAL
  John   P: Mount Pleasant 12
    Ja 58
VEASY/VESEY
  John   P: Chester Co 18 Ag
    57
  Joseph   Slvop Providence
    30 Oct 76; Phila 30 Ap
    77
VEERE
  James   P: Phila 3 Ja 60
VEINTER
  Margaret   P: Phila 30 Ap 77
VELLIGOT
  Samuel   P: Phila 6 Jy 58
VELURE
  Jacob   P: Phila 21 Dec 58
VENABLES
  Richard   P: Phila 10 Ap 66
VENDER VAUSSEN
  Ensign, of the 17th Regt.
    P: Germantown /?/ 30 Ap
    67
VEREIN
  Thomas   P: Phila 23 Oct 66
VERNON
  Agnus   P: 13 Ja 63
  Benjamin   P: Lancaster Co
    31 Mar 63
  Martha   P: Leacock 12 Ja 58
  Samuel   P: Montgomery Twp
    8 Jy 62; Plymouth, Phila
    Co 4 Feb 68
VERNOR
  Samuel   P: Phila 28 Nov 54
VERT
  John   P: Phila 1 Feb 70
VICARY
  John   P: Phila 1 Nov 53
VICKERS
  Peter   T: Bucks Co 7 May 67
VICTOR
  Mr.   Phila 30 Ap 77
VINCENT/VINSONT
  John   P: Phila-Gaz. 3 Ja 76
  Joseph   P: (French Neutral)
    13 May 56
  Nancy   P: Phila 27 Ja 73
  Thomas   P: Chester Co 1 Nov
    53
VINEY
  Henry   P: Newport 11 Sep 55
VINING/VINNING
  Henry   P: Phila 20 Ap 69
  Capt. Wm.   P: Phila 18 Ag
    57
VINSON
  John   P: Gloucester Co 1
    Nov 53
VINTER
  Ensign   P: in the army 12
    Ja 58; Lt. in the army 12
    Ja 58
VIRGAN
  John   P: Kent Co 31 Jy 60

VIRGINT
  Thomas   P: Phila 13 Oct 63
VOGHT
  Dr. C.   P: Lancaster 31 Jy 60
VOLLAR
  John   P: Phila 18 Feb 55
VON BEVERD
  Wilhelm   P: Phila 20 Oct 68
VOORHEES
  Court   T: 4 Nov 72
VUTLOR
  John   P: Sussex Co 28 Oct 62

WACHTEL
  George   P: Lancaster 12 Feb
  61
WADDEL/WADDLE/WADDELL
  Widow   P: Phila 3 May 70
  David   P: Pa 13 Oct 63
  Henry   P: Phila 3 Ag 58
  James   P: Pa 3 Ja 60
WADDINGHAM
  Samuel   P: Pa 31 Jy 60
WADE/WAID
  Andrew   P: Phila 30 Ap 67
  Capt. John   P: Marcus Hook 18
  Ag 57
  John   P: Marcus-Hook 15 Mar
  64
  Martha   P: Phila 28 Oct 62
WAGLOM
  John   P: Phila 3 Ja 65
WAGNER
  Clarida   P: Phila 3 Ag 58
WAGONER/WAGENER/WAGGONER/WAAGE-
  NAAR
  Gerss /?/ P: Phila 5 Ag 56
  Henry   P: New Jersey 27 Ja 73
  John   P: Chester Co 31 Jy 60
  Peter   Phila 1 May 76
WAGSTAFFE
  James   P: Phila 3 Ag 58
WAGWORTH
  William   P: New London 28 Oct
  62
WAIKINSHAW /¯could it be WALKIN-
  SHAW?7
  John¯   P: Pa 12 Feb 61
WAINES
  Isaac   T: Squire's Point 1
  Sep 68
WAINRIGHT
  Sarah   P: Phila 2 Ag 70
WAKE
  Capt. John   P: Phila 20 Oct 68
  Joseph   P: Phila 21 Jy 68
  William   P: Charlestown 2 Feb
  64
WAKEFIELD
  J.   P: Phila 2 Sep 62
WAKELY
  George   P: Phila 12 Ja 58, 24
  Feb 63, 2 May 65; Wilmington
  3 Ag 58

  John   P: Phila 28 Oct 62
  Mary   P: Phila 2 May 65
WAKER
  Robert   P: Chester Co 31
  Jy 60
WALBERTON
  Charles   P: Pa 19 May 63,
  13 Oct 63
WALCH
  Dr. James   P: Phila 12 Feb
  61
WALCOTT
  Lucy   P: Phila 13 Oct 63
WALDEN
  James   P: Phila-Gaz. 3 Ja
  76
WALDRICK
  Mary   P: Phila 28 Nov 54
WALDRON
  Daniel   T: Readington 17
  Oct 54
  Edward   P: Darby 1 Nov 53
WALES
  William   P: Albermarle Co
  23 Oct 66
WALIES
  John, Esq.   P: Phila 3 Ja
  60
WALK
  Capt. John   P: Phila 19 Jy
  80
  William   P: New-Castle Co
  3 Sep 61
WALKER
  Mr.   P: Phila 26 Oct 69
  Andrew   P: M'Dowell's Mill
  18 Mar 62
  Arthur   L: Lancaster Co 2
  Mar 74
  Charles   Phila 30 Ap 77
  David   P: Phila 3 Ja 60
  George   P: Phila 20 Ap 69
  Henry   P: Chester Co 31 Jy
  60
  James   P: New-Castle Co 31
  Jy 60; Phila 21 Dec 58,
  13 Ja 63
  John   P: Pa 2 Feb 64; Phila
  18 Mar 62, 23 Oct 66, 20
  Oct 68, 1 Feb 70, 16 Jy
  72, 30 Oct 76
  Jos.   P: Octorara 31 Dec 61
  Justus   P: Phila 31 Ja 76
  Margaret   P: Bucks Co 30
  Ap 67; Lancaster Co 29
  Jy 72; Phila 16 Jy 72
  Marian   P: Phila 11 Jy 54
  Mary   P: Cumberland Co 21
  Dec 58, 3 Ja 60; Phila 30
  Ja 66
  Michael   P: Phila 5 Ag 62
  Moses   P: Bucks Co 7 Ap 57
  Patrick   P: Pa 15 Mar 64
  Peggy   P: Phila 27 Ja 73
  Peter   P: Phila 31 Dec 61

Ralph   P: Wilmington 22 Nov
   53
Capt. Ralph P: Pa 12 Feb
   61; Phila 3 Ag 58; Wilming-
   ton 3 Ag 58, 3 Ja 60, 31
   Jy 60, 2 Sep 62, 13 Ja 63
Richard   P: Phila 4 Feb 68
Robert   P: Carlisle 3 Sep 61;
   Chester Co 12 Feb 61;
   Cumberland Co 15 Mar 64;
   New London 26 Jy 64; Phila
   20 Ap 69
Capt. S. P: Wilmington 8 Jy
   62
Sarah   P: Phila 18 Feb 55,
   21 Dec 58
Simon   Phila 30 Ap 77
Thomas   P: Phila 29 Ag 54,
   21 Dec 58; N.J. 24 Feb 63;
   Phila 1 Feb 70; West Brad-
   ford 8 Jy 62
W.   P: Lancaster Co 8 Jy 62
William   L: Lancaster Co 2 Mar
   74. P: Chestnut Level 24
   Oct 54; Del. 4 Ag 63; Dover
   3 Sep 61; East-Fallonfield
   13 Oct 63; Fishing Creek 31
   Dec 61; Kent Co 12 Ja 58;
   Pa 21 Dec 58; Phila 7 Ap 57
WALKINSON
   Widow   P: New-Castle Co 31 Jy
   60
   John   P: 12 Feb 61; New-
   Castle Co 31 Jy 60
WALL
   Capt.   P: Phila 19 May 63, 4
   Feb 68, 2 Ag 70
   Casper, skinner   P: Phila 31
   Ja 76
   Capt. Gurney   P: Phila 26 Oct
   69
   John   P: Goshen 1 Jy 56; Phila
   30 Ap 77; West Caln 3 Ja 60
   Nicholas   P: Phila 20 Ap 69
WALLACE/WALLES/WALLIS/WOLLIS/
   WALLAS
   Mr.   P: at Mr. Thompson's
   Phila 19 Ja 69
   Mrs.   P: Phila 31 Dec 61
   Alexander   P: Phila 3 Ja 65
   Andrew   P: Horsham 12 Ja 58
   Arthur   P: Wilmington 31 Dec 61
   Benjamin   L: 11 Ap 65
   Eleanor   P: Lancaster Co 4 Ag
   63
   Gan./Gain   P: (Forks of)
   Brandywine 3 Ja 60, 19 Ja
   69
   Gaven   P: Brandywine 31 Dec 61
   George   P: Fogs Manor 3 Ja
   60; Forks of Brandywine 3 Ja
   60
   Hugh   P: New-Castle Co 3 Ag
   58, 31 Dec 61; Newtown 13
   Oct 63; Whiteclay Creek 12

   Ja 58, 3 Ag 58
   James   P: Bucks Co 8 Jy 62;
   Phila 3 Ja 76, 31 Ja 76,
   1 May 76
   Capt. James   P: Phila 25 Ap
   71
   Jean   P: Phila 25 Jy 65
   John   P: (Forks of)
   Brandywine 3 Ja 60 (2),
   31 Dec 61; Chester Co
   3 Ag 58, 12 Feb 61; Md.
   31 Dec 61; New-Castle
   Co 3 Ja 60, 31 Jy 60,
   31 Dec 61, 18 Mar 62; Pa
   13 Oct 63; Phila 24 Oct
   54, 6 Jy 58, 12 Feb 61,
   31 Dec 61, 15 Mar 64, 10
   Oct 65, 28 Ap 68, 26 Oct
   69, 27 Oct 73
   Josiah   P: Lancaster Co 18
   Ag 57, 2 Sep 62
   Michael   P: Little Elk 31
   Jy 60; New-Castle Co 18
   Mar 62
   Patrick   P: Phila 2 May 65,
   16 Jy 67
   Robert   P: Paxton 19 Ja 69;
   Phila 31 Jy 60, 8 Jy 62,
   5 Ag 62, 30 Ja 66, 10 Ap
   66. T: Bordentown 1 Sep
   68
   Samuel   P: Phila 28 Oct 62,
   4 Ag 63
   Susannah   P: Phila 30 Ap 67
   Tacey   P: Phila 19 Jy 80
   Thomas   P: Pa 13 Oct 63;
   Phila 3 Ja 60
   William   L: Lancaster Co
   20 Ja 73. N: 29 Nov 64.
   P: Baltimore 31 Dec 61;
   Bensalem 27 Oct 73;
   Chester Co 12 Feb 61; Fogs
   Manor 3 Ag 58, 3 Ja 60,
   31 Dec 61; London-Grove
   3 Ja 60; N. Castle Co 26
   Jy 64; Pa 8 Jy 62; Phila
   11 Jy 54, 20 Jy 69
   William or Joseph   L: 14
   May 72
WALLERS
   Benjamin   P: 12 Feb 61
WALLS
   John   C: Goshen 18 Jy 65 (2)
   William   P: Kent Co 3 Sep 61
WALMSLEY
   John   N: 29 Nov 64
WALN
   Robert   P: Phila 13 May 56,
   1 Jy 56, 3 Ag 58, 5 Ag
   62
WALSH
   Christopher   P: Phila-Gaz.
   27 Oct 73
   David   P: Phila 15 Mar 64
   James   P: Phila 19 May 63,

31 Ja 76; Dr. Pa 18 Mar 62
John P: Phila 1 Nov 53, 4
  Feb 68, 20 Oct 68, 2 Ag 70,
  27 Oct 73
Joseph P: Phila-Gaz. 27 Oct
  73
Neal P: Phila-Gaz. 3 Ja 76
Nicholas P: Phila-Gaz. 3 Ja
  76
WALSON
  Andrew P: Pa 15 Mar 64
WALTER/WALTERS
  John P: Phila 3 Ja 65
  Philipa P: Phila 28 Nov 54
  William P: Phila 3 Ja 65, 2
  May 65
WALTHOW
  Edward P: Marcus-Hook 23 Oct
  66
WALTON
  and BOUNEING P: Phila 31 Mar
  63
  John P: Pa 12 Feb 61
  Joshua P: Phila 27 Ja 73
  Mary P: Pa 3 Ag 58
  Roger P: Pennsborough 31 Dec
  61
  William P: Phila 13 Oct 63,
  2 Feb 64, 30 Ap 67
WAME
  John P: Phila 5 Ag 56
WAMSLEY
  Samuel P: Phila 29 Ag 54
WANN
  Richard P: Phila 16 Jy 72
WANNALL
  Henry P: Phila 16 Jy 77
WANSLEY
  George P: Pa 8 Jy 62
WANTON
  Stephen P: Phila 18 Ag 57
WAPPER
  Henry L: Cumberland Co 19
  Dec 71
WARD/WARDE
  Eleanor P: Phila 28 Ap 68
  Esther P: Phila 3 Sep 61
  Ewart P: Phila 19 Ja 69
  Hannah P: N.J. 4 Ag 63
  James P: Phila 19 Ja 69,
  26 Oct 69
  Jeremiah P: Cape May 3 Ag
  58
  John L: Chester Co 29 Jy 72;
  Little Britain 15 Ap 56. P:
  Chester Co 31 Jy 60; Phila
  12 Ja 58, 4 Feb 68, 28 Ap
  68; Salisbury 21 Dec 56
  Joseph P: N. Castle 19 May
  63; N. Castle Co 15 Mar
  64; Phila 13 May 56, 5 Ag
  56
  Josiah P: Pa 2 Feb 64
  Margaret P: Phila 26 Oct 69
  Mary P: Phila 11 Sep 55

Patrick P: Phila 31 Dec 61
Philip W: New-Garden,
  Chester Co 3 Jy 76
Robert P: Phila 31 Ja 76
William P: Bucks Co 1 Nov
  53, 24 Feb 63; Pa 12 Feb
  61; Phila 30 Ja 66, 19
  Ja 69; Capt. Phila 2 Ag 70
  Winiford P: Phila 1 Feb 70
WARDEN
  Joseph P: Phila 24 Feb 63,
  13 Oct 63, 15 Mar 64
WARDS
  James P: Phila 16 Jy 67
WARE
  Gilbert P: Phila 16 Jy 67
  Capt. Richard P: Phila 13
  Ja 63
  William C: at John Hur-
  ford's New-Garden 22 Ja
  67
WARFORD /⁻or WALFOR?⁊
  Sturch⁻ P: Phila 18 Feb 55
WARING
  John P: Phila 5 Ag 62
WARMAN
  John P: Phila 18 Feb 55
WARMER
  Lydia P: Germantown 12 Ja
  58
WARNE
  Frederick P: Phila 15 Mar
  64
WARNELL
  William P: Phila 25 Jy 65
WARNER
  Christopher P: G. Town 28
  Ap 68
  Edith P: Phila 18 Mar 62
  Isaac P: Phila 21 Jy 68;
  Capt. - Blockley 24 Jy
  76
  John P: Phila 4 Ag 63
  John C. P: Phila 5 Ag 62
  Johnson P: Phila 30 Ja 66
  Joseph P: Phila 2 Ag 70;
  Upper Fallowfield, Chest-
  er Co 26 Oct 69
  Phineas P: Phila 30 Ap 77
  Col. Seth Phila 30 Oct 76
  Stephen G. P: Phila-Gaz. 3
  Ja 76
  Thomas P: Phila 20 Oct 68,
  1 Feb 70
  William P: Pa 12 Feb 61
WARNOCK
  John, storekeeper C: East
  Nottingham, Chester Co 28
  Nov 65. P: East Notting-
  ham 26 Jy 64
WARREN/WARRAN
  Edward P: Phila 16 Jy 72
  John P: Phila 20 Oct 68
  Joseph (soldier) 21 Dec 58
  Mary P: Phila 21 Jy 68

Thomas   P: Phila 19 May 63
William   N: Reedy Island 12
   Feb 67
WARRICK
   Alexander   P: Phila-Gaz. 27
      Oct 73
WARRING
   Mr.   P: Phila 30 Ap 67
WARSOP
   Samuel   P: Phila 10 Ap 66
WART
   George   Phila 24 Jy 76
WARTHER
   Thomas   L: Paxton 20 Ja 73
WASBY
   James   P: Pa 12 Feb 61
   William   P: Pa 4 Ag 63
WASON/WASSON
   Archibald   L: 29 Ja 67.   P:
      York Co 13 Oct 63
   John   P: Peach Bottom 24 Oct
      54
WATERBURY
   Sylvanus   P: Phila 3 Ag 58
WATERMAN
   ....   P: Phila 27 Dec 53,
      5 Feb 54
   Capt. John   P: Phila 13 Oct
      63
WATERS
   Catrin   P: Phila 7 Ap 57
   Charles   P: Phila 23 Oct 66
   Edward   P: 12 Feb 61
   Elizabeth   P: Phila 28 Oct 62
   John   P: Phila 5 Ag 56
   Margaret   P: Phila 2 Ag 70
   Rose   P: Phila 21 Jy 68
   Thomas   P: Phila 21 Jy 68
   William   P: Phila 31 Dec 61,
      1 Feb 70, 2 Ag 70
WATERWORTH
   William   P: Pa 24 Feb 63
WATKELL
   John   P: Phila 12 Ja 58
WATKINS
   Benjamin   P: Phila-Gaz. 3 Ja
      76
   Catherine   P: Phila 30 Ja 66,
      10 Ap 66
   Eatborn / or Eathorn?/ P: Phila
      1 Nov 53
   Capt. John   P: in the army 3
      Ag 58
   Richard   P: Phila 11 Sep 55
   Thomas   P: Phila 5 Ag 62,
      26 Jy 64
WATSON/WATTSON
   Alexander   P: Phila 11 Jy 54
   Andrew   P: Pa 2 Feb 64; Phila
      30 Ja 66, 20 Oct 68, 1 Feb
      70, 3 Ja 76
   Arthur   P: Phila 27 Ja 73
   Charles   P: Phila 3 Ja 76
   David   L: 31 Ja 71
   Donald   P: Phila 3 Ja 65;

   Corporal, prob. in Pitts-
      burgh 15 Mar 64
   Elizabeth   P: Phila 27 Ja
      73
   Francis   P: Phila 25 Jy 65
   Henry (soldier)   P: 21 Dec
      58
   James   L: Muddy Run 2 Mar
      74.   P: Pa 12 Feb 61, 31
      Dec 61
   John   P: Pa 3 Sep 61;
      Phila 11 Sep 55, 1 Dec
      58, 3 Ja 60, 31 Jy 60, 3
      Ja 76; Sussex Co 31 Jy 60
   Jos.   P: Pa 31 Dec 61
   Luke   P: Lewistown 31 Dec
      61
   Moses   P: Phila 30 Ja 65
   Nancy   P: Phila 3 May 70
   Robert   P: Phila 3 Sep 61,
      16 Jy 67, 3 May 70, 3
      Ja 76, 30 Oct 76
   Rose   P: Abington 1 Nov 70
   Capt. Samuel   P: Phila 28
      Ap 68
   Thomas   P: Pa 24 Feb 63;
      Phila 21 Dec 58, 5 Ag 62.
      T: Bordentown 31 Ja 71
   William   P: 21 Dec 58,
      (soldier); Phila 12 Ja
      58, 3 Ja 60, 12 Feb 61,
      28 Ap 68; Sussex Co 31
      Dec 61
WATT/WATTS
   Frederick   P: Juniata Creek
      2 Feb 64
   James   P: Phila 3 Ag 58, 3
      Ag 58 (sailor), 27 Ja 73
   John   P: Elk River 12 Ja
      58; Lancaster Co 12 May
      61
   Robert   P: Phila 12 Feb 61
   Samuel   P: 12 Feb 61;
      Phila 20 Oct 68
WATTON
   Robert   Stony-Hill 30 Oct
      76
WAUGH
   John   P: Chester Co 8 Jy
      62; Little Britain 12 Ja
      58; Phila 1 Nov 53
WAY
   Mr.   P: Phila 31 Dec 61
   Elizabeth   P: Wilmington
      30 May 54, 11 Sep 55
   John   P: Wilmington 3 Ja 60
   Joseph   P: Phila 6 Jy 58
   Mary   P: Phila 7 Ap 57
   Samuel   P: Phila 24 Feb 63
   William   P: Wilmington 13
      Oct 63
WAYLEN
   John   P: Phila 4 Feb 68
WAYNE
   Anthony   P: Phila 16 Jy 67,

27 Oct 73
Isaac and Anthony P: Phila-
  27 Oct 73
John   P: Chester Co 12 Ja 58
William   P: Phila 3 Ja 60
WEADE
  Thomas   P: Phila 27 Ja 73
WEAKLEY
  George   P: Phila 26 Jy 64
WEAR
  John   P: Phila 26 Jy 64, 3
    Ja 65
WEARING
  John   P: Bucks Co 7 Ap 57
WEATEN
  Barb.   P: Pa 15 Mar 64
WEATHERBY/WETHERBY
  Adam   P: Salem Co 8 Jy 62
  Edmond, Esq.   P: N.J. 3 Ja 60
  Whitehead   P: Blue Ball,
    Lancaster Road 19 Ja 69
WEATHERSPOON
  David   L: Leacock 2 Mar 74
  John   P: Phila 24 Ag 76
WEAVER
  Margaret   P: Phila 10 Oct 65
  Nicholas   P: Whitemarsh-Gaz.
    27 Oct 73
  Samuel   L: 31 Ja 71
WEBB
  ....   P: Chester Co 11 Sep
    55
  Edith   P: Phila 3 Ag 58
  Elizabeth   P: Phila 16 Jy 67
  Ezekiel   C: 30 Jy 77
  George   P: Phila 9 May 54 (&
    son), 27 Ja 73
  John   P: Phila 21 Dec 58, 3 Ja
    65, 20 Jy 69
  Laetitia   P: Phila-Gaz. 3 Ja
    76
  Leonard   P: Phila 11 Sep 55
  Richard   P: Phila 4 Ap 54
  William   P: Chester Co 22 Nov
    53, 28 Nov 54
WEBBER/WEBER
  Andreas   P: Phila Gaz. 27 Oct
    73
  Benjamin   P: Phila 19 May 63,
    15 Mar 64
  Hannis   P: Phila 23 Oct 66
  John G.   P: Phila-Gaz. 27 Oct
    73
WEBSTER
  Jane   P: Phila 11 Sep 55
  John   P: Abington 5 Ag 56;
    Phila 31 Jy 60, 18 Mar 62
  Patrick   P: Phila 19 May 63
  Sarah   P: Phila 26 Oct 69
  Thomas   P: Phila 2 Feb 64, 20
    Oct 68
WEED
  Elijah   P: Phila 16 Jy 72
  George   P: Haddonfield 27 Dec
    53; Phila 19 May 63 (Dr),

10 Oct 65
WEEKS/WEAKES
  Richard   P: Phila 16 Jy 72
  Robert   P: Phila 19 Jy 80
WEEMS/WEIMS
  William Loch   P: Phila 10
    Oct 65, 25 Jy 65, 30 Ja
    66
WEIDETER
  George   P: Phila 2 Feb 64
WEILER
  Jacob   P: Phila 10 Ap 66
WEILY
  Mary   P: Phila 13 Oct 63
  Peter   L: 14 May 72
WEINKOFF
  Aratus   P: Bucks Co 16 Jy
    72
WEISER
  Col.   P: Tulpahocken 21 Dec
    58
  Conrad   P: Berks 1 Nov 53;
    Esq., Reading 3 Jy 60
  Eve   P: at Henry Kepler's
    Phila 11 Jy 54
WEISS
  George M.   P: Goschehoppen
    5 Feb 54
  Lewis   P: Phila 24 Feb 63
WELAST
  John   P: Phila 3 Ja 65
WELCH
  Hannah   P: Phila 28 Ap 68
  Joseph   P: Phila 26 Jy 64,
    3 Ja 65
  Robert   P: Phila 2 Feb 64
  Sarah   P: Carlisle 12 Feb
    61; Lancaster Co 28 Oct
    62
  Thomas   P: Chester Co 13
    Ja 63
  William   P: Phila 18 Mar
    62, 5 Ag 62; Tanton
    Forge 24 Jy 76
WELDER
  Samuel Stanesby/Samuel
    Stonesby   P: Fredericks
    19 May 63; Md. 24 Feb 63
WELDON
  Benjamin   P: Marcus Hook
    3 Ja 60
WELER
  Nicholas   P: Phila 19 Jy 80
WELL / or WILL? /
  William   P: Chester Co 1
    Nov 53
WELLER
  Mr.   P: Phila-Gaz. 3 Ja 76
WELLMAN
  Francis   P: Phila 31 Dec 61
WELLROY
  William   P: Pa 24 Feb 63
WELLS
  Widow   L: Lancaster 29 Jy
    72

David   P: North Londonderry 27
 Dec 53; West Fallowfield 24
 Oct 54
Edward   P: Phila 20 Ap 69
George   P: Phila 10 Oct 65,
 16 Jy 67, 30 Oct 76
Gideon   P: Phila 3 Ja 65
James   N: near Dover 4 Dec 66
Jed.   P: Phila 24 Feb 63
John   C: Chestnut Level 18
 Jy 65. P: Phila 28 Oct 62
 (Capt)
Joseph   P: Pa 2 Feb 64
Noah   T: near Trenton 10 Ag
 58
Rebecca   P: Phila 1 Nov 53
Richard   P: Dover 31 Mar 63
 (Esq); Kent Co 13 Oct 63;
 Phila 6 Jy 58, 24 Feb 63,
 23 Oct 66, 19 Jy 80
Major Richard   P: in the army
 21 Dec 58; Pa 3 Ag 58
Thomas   P: Dover 31 Mar 63
William   P: Phila 3 Ja 60
WELSH
 Lt. Col.   P: Phila 4 Feb 68
 Ann   P: Chester Co 3 Ag 58
 Dennis   P: Phila 16 Jy 67
 Elizabeth   P: Phila 31 Dec 61
 Capt. J.   P: Phila 31 Dec 61
 James   P: Pa 13 Oct 63, 1 Feb
 70, 3 May 70
 John   P: Kingston 31 Jy 60;
 Phila 19 Ja 69, 1 Feb 70, 1
 Nov 70. W: Christiana
 Bridge 27 Ag 77
 Luke   P: Phila-Gaz. 3 Ja 76
 Miss Margaret   P: Phila 30
 Oct 76
 Neal   P: Phila-Gaz. 27 Oct 73
 Patrick   P: Pa 21 Dec 58, 31
 Ja 76
 Richard   P: Phila 28 Ap 68
 Robert   P: Phila 15 Mar 64
 Thomas   P: Chester Co 12 Ja 58;
 East Marlborough 21 Dec 58
 William   P: Phila 31 Dec 61
WELSON
 George   P: Phila 27 Ja 73
WENBALL
 Thomas   P: Phila 31 Mar 63
WENDELL
 Isaac   P: Phila 19 Jy 80
WENERICH
 Frantz   Reading Town 1 May 76
WENN
 Benjamin   P: Little Creek 1 Nov
 70
WENSTANLEY
 Philip (soldier)   P: in the
 army 21 Dec 58
WERDON
 Gideon   P: Phila 29 Ag 54,
 28 Nov 54
WERE

James (soldier) 21 Dec 58
 Sarah   P: Phila 23 Oct 66
WERLEY
 Elizabeth   P: Phila 10 Ap
 66
WERT
 Peter   P: Phila 5 Ag 56
WESCOTT/WEASCOTT
 George   P: Phila 30 May 54,
 24 Oct 54
WESEN
 John   P: Chester Co 12 Feb
 61
WESSEA
 Francis   P: Dry-Spring 24
 Feb 63
WEST
 Charles   P: Pa 15 Mar 64;
 Phila 15 Mar 64
 David   P: Pa 3 Ja 60
 Esther   P: Sussex Co 13 Oct
 63, 2 Feb 64
 Francis   P: Phila-Gaz. 27
 Oct 73
 Jacob   W: c/o Mr. Humphry
 Carson, merchant, Christ-
 iana Bridge 3 Jy 76
 James   P: Phila 24 Feb 63
 Joel, widow of   P: Phila 2
 Ag 70
 John   P: Phila 28 Ap 68
 Lydia   P: Phila 20 Ap 69
 Capt. Matthew   P: East
 New Jersey 3 Ag 58, 12
 Feb 61
 Richard   P: Phila 15 Mar 64
 Thomas   Charlotte's Valley
 24 Jy 76; Phila 21 Dec
 58, 3 Ja 60
 William   P: Chester Co 1
 Nov 70; Phila 12 Feb 61,
 15 Mar 64
WESTON
 Samuel   P: Reedy Island 30
 May 54, 11 Sep 58
WETHERED
 John   Phila 31 Ja 76
WETHERELL
 Samuel   P: Phila 21 Jy 68
WETHERU
 John   C: 30 Jy 77
WETMAN
 James   P: Pa 19 May 63, 13
 Oct 63
WEYBERG
 Rev.   P: Easton 15 Mar 64
WEYMAN
 Abel   P: Phila 27 Ja 73
WHALDEN
 John   P: Pa 18 Mar 62
WHALE
 Evan   P: Phila 20 Jy 69
WHALEY
 Clary   P: Phila-Gaz. 3 Ja
 76

WHALL
  Hannah   P: Phila 3 Ja 60
WHALON
  James   T: Lomington 4 Nov 72
WHANEY
  Samuel   P: Lancaster Co 28
    Oct 62
WHARRY/WHAREY/WHARY/WHARREY
  Widow   P: Phila 27 Ja 73
  James   C: Nottingham 22 Ja
    67. P: Nottingham 3 Ag
    58, 15 Mar 64
  Samuel   P: Chestnut Level 3 Ja
    60; Pa 13 Ja 63
WHARTON
  Jenny   P: Phila 26 Oct 69
  Sammy   P: Phila 26 Oct 69
WHATZLER
  George   P: Phila 30 Ap 77
WHEALON
  Richard   P: 18th Regt., Phila
    27 Oct 73
WHEAT
  Mrs.   Phila 31 Ja 76
WHEATON/WHETON
  Amos   Phila 31 Ja 76
  Jeffery   P: Phila 16 Jy 67
WHEELER
  Ann   P: Burlington 3 Ja 60
  John   P: Glasgow Iron-Works
    20 Ap 69
WHEELWRIGHT
  Rudy   P: Frankford 4 Ag 63
WHELAN
  Thomas   P: Phila 1 Nov 53
WHELAND
  Levin   P: Phila 16 Jy 72
WHELDON
  John   P: Phila 2 Feb 64
  Mary   P: Phila 18 Ag 57
  William   P: Phila 5 Ag 62
WHELLON
  Godfrey   P: Phila 16 Jy 72
WHERRY
  James   P: Phila 16 Jy 72
WHIANT
  Anna Elizabeth   P: Phila 21
    Dec 58
WHILAN
  Dennis   P: Phila 1 Feb 70
  Thomas   P: Chester Co 4 Ag 63
WHILTON
  James   P: Phila 26 Jy 64
  Judy   P: Pa 3 Sep 61
WHIPPLE
  Daniel Peck   Phila 31 Ja 76
WHITAKER
  Henry   P: Phila 31 Jy 60
WHITALL
  John S.   Phila 16 Jy 77
  Joseph   Phila 30 Ap 77
WHITCRAFT
  James   P: N. London 13 Oct 63
WHITE; see also WHYTE
  ....   P: Caecil Co 11 Jy 54

Col.   P: Phila 4 Feb 68
Mr.   P: Duck Creek 31 Dec
  61; Phila 30 Ap 67, 27
  Ja 73
Abraham   P: Octorara 28 Oct
  62; Phila 2 Sep 62
Agness   P: Pa 12 Feb 61
Andrew   P: Little Britain
  5 Ag 56
Capt. Benjamin   P: Phila 26
  Oct 69
Christopher   P: Phila 21 Jy
  68
Deborah   P: Phila 12 Ja 58
Francis   P: Phila 18 Mar
  62
Garret   P: Phila 19 Ja 69
George   P: Phila 30 Ja 66,
  20 Oct 68, 19 Jy 80
Henry   P: Phila 3 Ag 58,
  10 Oct 65
Hugh   P: Phila 6 Jy 58, 21
  Dec 58
James   L: Lancaster 20 Ja
  73. P: in the army 12
  Ja 58; Christine Bridge
  12 Ja 58; Lancaster Co 13
  Ja 63; Pequea 18 Mar 62;
  Phila 3 Ja 60, 26 Jy 64,
  1 Jy 56, 3 Ag 58 (2), 21
  Dec 58, 9 Ag 59, 28 Oct
  62, 25 Jy 65, 20 Jy 69,
  2 Ag 70, 27 Ja 73, 3 Ja
  76
Jane   P: Phila 11 Sep 55
Joel   P: East Jersey 5 Ag
  62
John   P: 12 Feb 61; Bucks
  Co 30 Ja 66; Chester Co
  24 Feb 63; Forks Brandy-
  wine 27 Dec 53; Phila 18
  Mar 62, 15 Mar 64, 23
  Oct 66, 2 Ag 70, 1 Nov
  70, 27 Ja 73, 27 Oct 73
John Carlos   T: 4 Nov 72
Capt. Joseph   P: Phila 3
  Ja 60
Mary   P: Mount-holly 27 Ja
  73; Phila 31 Dec 61, 8
  Jy 62, 10 Ap 66, 4 Feb 68
Matthew   P: New-Castle Co
  3 Ja 60
Peter   P: Phila 3 May 70
Robert, merchant   N: New-
  Garden 4 Dec 66; merchant
  near N. Castle 12 Feb 67.
  P: Phila 1 Feb 70; Wil-
  mington 2 Feb 64. W:
  Brandywine 27 Ag 77
Samuel   P: Phila 3 Ja 60,
  31 Jy 60. T: near the
  Falls Meeting-house 7 May
  67
Sarah   P: Phila 4 Feb 68
Solomon   P: Germantown 15

Mar 64
Thomas P: Lancaster Co 28
  Oct 62, 13 Ja 63; Phila
  7 Ap 57, 3 Ja 60, 2
  May 65, 16 Jy 67, 2 Ag 70;
  Pilesgrove 1 Feb 70; Potts-
  grove 1 Nov 70
Thomas B. P: Phila 23 Oct 66
Thomas Blanch P: Phila 30 Ap
  67
W.B. P: Phila 13 May 56
William P: Bristol Twp 21
  Dec 58; Chestnut Level 19
  Ja 69; Duck Creek 13 May
  56; Pa 31 Jy 60, 12 Feb 61;
  Phila 30 Ap 67, 16 Jy 67, 27
  Oct 73
William, Jr. P: Phila 30 Ja 66
WHITEACRE
  Samuel L: Cumberland Co 29
  Jy 72
WHITEAR
  William P: Phila 26 Oct 69,
  25 Ap 71
WHITEFIELD
  Margaret P: Pa 3 Sep 61
WHITEHEAD
  James P: Phila 1 Jy 56, 6
  Jy 58, 19 Jy 80
  Matthew P: Phila 26 Oct 69,
  2 Ag 70
  Mercy T: 4 Nov 72
WHITEHILL
  James P: Pequea 11 Jy 54, 7
  Ap 57 (Esq)
WHITEHOUSE
  Solomon, corporal P: Phila
  23 Oct 66
WHITESELL
  Thomas P: Indian Creek 3 Ja
  60
WHITESIDE/WHITESIDES
  Arthur P: Lewis-Town 3 Ja 60
  Phineas P: Pequea 31 Dec 61
  Thomas P: Lancaster Co 12 Ja
  58; Lewis-Town 3 Ja 60
  William P: Wilmington 31 Dec
  61
WHITEWOOD
  Ann P: Phila 21 Dec 58
WHITFORD/WHITEFORD
  John P: Phila 1 Feb 70
  Robert P: Bucks Co 31 Dec 61
WHITHEAR
  George P: Pa 31 Jy 60
WHITLOCK/WHITELOCK
  and DAVIS P: Phila 4 Ag 63
  Isaac P: Lancaster 12 Feb 61,
  8 Ag 62
  J. P: Lancaster 18 Mar 62
  Capt. Thomas P: Phila 31 Mar
  63
WHITMAN
  Charles P: Phila-Gaz. 3 Ja 76
WHITMARSH

Capt. John P: Phila 19 Ja
  69
WHITPAINS
  John P̄: Phila 25 Jy 65
WHITSTONE
  John P: Phila 21 Dec 58
WHITTEN
  John P: Chester Co 12 Feb
  61
WHITTET
  Capt. W. P: Apoquinimy 31
  Mar 63; Phila 8 Jy 62
  William P: Apoquinimy 3
  Ja 60; Noxonton 31 Dec 61
WHITTON
  James P: Phila 3 Ja 65
WHOLLANT
  Daniel P: Chester Co 2 Feb
  64
WHORTER
  Rev. Alexander P: Pa 31
  Jy 60
WHYLOK
  George P: Phila 26 Jy 64
WHYTE
  Alexander P: Phila 31 Jy
  60
  Capt. Rob. P: Phila 1 Nov
  53
WIBLER
  Nicholas P: Phila 20 Ap 69
WICATT
  John Phila 30 Oct 76
WICKERS
  James P: Pa 12 Feb 61
WICKES
  Benjamin P: Phila 25 Ap
  71
  Richard P: Phila 27 Ja 73
WICKHAM
  William P: Phila 20 Jy 69
WIEER
  John L: Chestnut Level 2
  Mar 74
WIELD
  John Peter P: near Phila
  28 Nov 54
WIERE/WIEAR; see also WYER
  David P: Bucks Co 30 Ja
  66
  Frederick P: Phila-Gaz.
  3 Ja 76
  John P: Phila 3 Ja 60
WIGGINS/WIGGANS/WIGGAN
  Thomas, tailor C: in
  Willis Town, Chester Co
  30 Oct 66. P: Phila 31
  Dec 61, 18 Mar 62
WIGHTLY
  Mary P: New-Castle Co 3
  Ja 60
WIGMER/WIGMORE/WIGGMORE
  Daniel P: Pa 18 Mar 62,
  7 Ap 57; Phila 21 Dec
  58, 3 Ja 65, 30 Oct 76

WIGTON/WIGTAN
John P: Bucks Co 4 Feb 68,
    7 Ap 57, 21 Jy 68; Phila
    28 Nov 54
WIKSON
James P: Phila 5 Ag 56
WILBERGER
Mr. P: Pa 31 Dec 61
WILCOCKS/WILCOX
Capt. P: Phila 8 Jy 62
Daniel P: Phila 10 Ap 66
David Fairfield Twp 30
    Oct 76
Elizabeth P: Chester Co 28
    Oct 62; Phila 31 Dec 61, 13
    Ja 63
Robert P: Dover 21 Dec 58
    (Esq); Kent Co 31 Dec 61;
    Phila 1 May 76
Thomas P: Phila 31 Dec 61
William T: at Kingston 21
    Ja 55; at Princetown 21
    Ja 55
WILCOCKSON
William P: Phila 2 Feb 64
WILD
Isaac P: Germantown 21 Jy
    68
Robert P: West Jersey 19 May
    63. T: Bordentown 17 Oct
    54
WILDAY
Grace P: Gloucester Co 21
    Dec 58 (2)
John P: Phila 3 Ja 65
WILEY/WILELY/WILIE/WYLY/WYLE/
WYLLE/WYLLIE
Mr. T: Hanover Forge 31 Ja
    71
Benjamin P: Darby 3 Ja 60
David P: London Grove 18 Ag
    57
Elizabeth P: York Co 13 Oct
    63
Hugh P: New-Castle Co 13 Oct
    63
James P: Pa 21 Dec 58; Phila
    19 May 63
John C: East Fallowfield 30
    Oct 66. P: Pa 18 Mar 62;
    Phila 31 Dec 61
Samuel P: Pa 31 Dec 61, 13
    Ja 63, 24 Feb 63; Phila 3
    Ag 58
Thomas P: Phila 13 Oct 63, 27
    Ja 73
WILKINS/WILKIN
David P: Phila 25 Jy 65.
    W: Whiteclay Creek 3 Jy 76
James L: York Co 19 Dec 71.
    P: Wallace's River 4 Ag 63
John L: Carlsile, see REED,
    Robert
Robert P: New-London 25 Ap
    71; Phila 2 May 65 (2)

Thomas P: Lancaster Co 12
    May 61
William P: Phila 16 Jy 67
WILKINSON/WILKIESON/WILKISON
Mr. P: Darby 8 Jy 62
Capt. Amos P: Phila 19 Jy
    80
Anthony P: Phila 2 Sep 62
Deborah P: Phila 3 Ja 76
Eleanor P: Pa 12 Ja 58
Elizabeth P: Phila-Gaz.
    27 Oct 73
Evan P: Lancaster Co 24
    Feb 63; West Caln 3 Ja 60
Henry P: Pa 3 Ag 58
James P: Phila 18 Mar 62
Jane P: Phila 30 Ap 67
John (soldier) P: 21 Dec
    58; Buckingham 1 Jy 56;
    Bucks Co 29 Ag 54, 18 Mar
    62; Phila 3 Ja 60, 31 Jy
    60, 4 Feb 68, 25 Ap 71
Ro. L: Newberry Twp, York
    Co 31 Ja 71
Robert P: Phila 13 Ja 63
Sarah P: Blockley 16 Jy
    67, 4 Feb 68
Thomas P: Phila 11 Sep 55
William P: 12 Feb 61
WILL
Robert P: Phila 2 Ag 70
William Phila 30 Ap 77
WILLARD
Benjamin P: Phila 24 Jy 76
Thomas P: Gloucester Co 3
    Ag 58; Phila 13 May 56
WILLDRIDGE
Ralph P: Phila 18 Mar 62
Susannah P: Gloucester
    3 Ja 60; Phila 31 Dec 61
WILLES
Thomas P: Phila 2 Ag 70
WILLESON
Thomas L: see CRAIGE,
    Henry &
WILLESTON
George P: Whiteclay Creek
    15 Mar 64
WILLEY/WILLIE/WILLY
Andrew P: Bucks Co 27 Ja
    73; Southampton, B. C. 28
    Ap 68
James L: Cumberland Co
    14 May 72
John P: East Pennsborough
    13 Oct 63; Pa 13 Oct 63
Mary L: Lancaster Co 14
    May 72
Matthew L: Redstone 29
    Jy 72
Robert P: Pa 18 Mar 62
Samuel C: New-London 22 Ja
    67. P: Caecil Co 2 Feb
    64; Mount Pleasant 18 Mar
    62; Pa 15 Mar 64

William   P: Conestogoe 1 Nov
53
WILLIAMS
Abbot   P: Phila 4 Feb 68
Ann   P: Phila-Gaz. 3 Ja 76.
T: Allen-town 17 Oct 54
Benjamin   P: Christeen Creek
1 Nov 53; Lancaster Co 4
Ag 63
Charles   P: Bucks 18 Feb 55;
Phila 1 Nov 53
Daniel   P: near Carlisle 7 Ap
57
Edmund   P: Phila 18 Feb 55
Elizabeth   P: Phila-Gaz. 27
Oct 73
Ellis   P: Chester Co 3 Ag
58
George   P: Hanover Twp 8 Jy
62, 19 May 63
Henry   P: Pa 13 Ja 63; Phila
20 Oct 68, 19 Jy 80
Hezekiah   P: Phila 13 Oct 63
Hugh   P: Phila-Gaz. 3 Ja 76
Isaac   P: Phila 26 Jy 64
Israel   P: Gloucester Co 18
Ag 57
John   L: c/o Dr. Boyd, Lancast-
er 19 Dec 71.   P: Cape May
12 Feb 61; Marlborough 8 Jy
62; Pa 28 Nov 54, 2 Feb 64;
Phila 1 Jy 56, 3 Ja 60, 31 Jy
60, 31 Dec 61, 18 Mar 62,
26 Jy 64, 25 Jy 65, 23 Oct
66 (Capt), 21 Jy 68 (Capt),
20 Oct 68 (34th Regt), 20 Jy
69, 27 Ja 73, 1 May 76, 30
Oct 76; Reading 1 Feb 70.   T:
Trenton 17 Oct 54
Joseph   P: Chester Co 11 Sep
55; Phila 15 Mar 64 (2)
Lewis   P: Chestnut-hill 18
Mar 62
Mary   P: Pa 3 Ag 58; Phila 12 Ja
58, 19 May 63, 26 Oct 69
Michael   P: New-Castle 3 Ag 58
Morris   P: Chester Co 11 Sep 55
Nathaniel   P: Welsh Tract 7 Ap
57
Capt. Nicholas   P: Phila 18 Mar
62
Paul   P: New-Castle Co 3 Sep 61;
Phila 31 Dec 61
Peggy   P: Phila 6 Jy 58
Philip   P: Octorara 7 Ap 57;
Phila 31 Dec 61, 26 Jy 64
Reese   P: Pa 8 Jy 62
Samuel   P: Lancaster Co 15 Mar
64; Phila 28 Oct 62, 26 Oct 69
(Capt); Sadsbury 15 Mar 64
Sarah   P: Mountholly 18 Ag 57;
Va. of Morel. 18 Ag 57
Susannah   P: near Phila 7 Ap 57
Theo.   P: Chester Co 3 Sep 61
Thomas   P: Kent Co 2 Feb 64; Pa

21 Dec 58; Phila 2 May
65, 16 Jy 67
Tobias   P: Phila 18 Mar 62
Walter   P: Chester Co 11
Sep 55
William   P: Darby 1 Jy 56;
North Wales 19 May 63;
Phila 5 Feb 54, 4 Ap 54
(tailor), 30 May 54, 12
Ja 58, 12 Feb 61, 8 Jy
62, 15 Mar 64; Union
Iron Works, West New
Jersey 30 Ap 67.   T:
Union Iron-Works 7 May
67
WILLIAMSON
Alexander   P: Phila 1 Nov
70
Hugh   P: Chester Co 31 Mar
63; Fogs Manor 12 Ja 58;
Phila 10 Ap 66
John   L: 13 Jn 65.   P:
Cumberland Co 26 Jy 64
Mary   P: East Nottingham
3 Ja 60
Robert   P: Nottingham 8 Jy
62
Thomas   P: Lancaster Co
3 Ja 60; Pa 12 Feb 61,
18 Mar 62
Capt. W.   P: Phila 24 Feb
63
William   P: Chester 3 Ja
60 (Capt); Phila 18 Feb
55
WILLIARD
Caspar   P: York Co 18 Mar
62
Thomas   P: Phila 5 Feb 54
WILLING
Charles   L: 13 Jn 65
John   C: London Britain 18
Jy 65
WILLIS
Charles   P: Phila 28 Nov
54
David   P: Lancaster Co 31
Dec 61
Elizabeth   P: Phila 3 Ja
65
Jeremiah   P: Phila 3 Ja 60,
31 Jy 60
John   P: in the army 12 Ja
58
Jonathan   P: N.J. 18 Mar 62;
Pa 26 Jy 64
Joseph   P: Phila 21 Dec 58.
T: Spunktown 6 Dec 64
Mary   P: Pa 2 Feb 64
Robert   P: Phila 30 Ap 67,
28 Ap 68, 21 Jy 68, 20
Oct 68
Capt. Samuel   Phila 24 Jy
76
Solomon   P: Phila 31 Dec 61

WILLMAN
  Samuel P: Phila 13 Ja 63
  William P: Phila 27 Ja 73
WILLOUGHBY/WILLABEY/WILLABEE/
  WILLEBY
  Andrew P: Conecochieg 31 Dec
    61; Elk River 21 Dec 58;
    Pa 31 Dec 61; Phila 18 Ag
    57
  Henry P: Phila 16 Jy 72
  Solomon P: Phila 31 Jy 60
  William P: Phila 2 May 65
WILLROY
  William P: Pa 13 Ja 63
WILLS
  and JACKSON P: Phila 30 Ja 66
  Edward P: Phila 12 Feb 61
  Joseph P: Phila 5 Ag 56, 2
    Feb 64
  Stephen P: Chester Co 12 Ja
    58
  Thomas P: Middleton 3 Ja 60
WILSH
  John P: Carlisle 3 Sep 61
WILSINTEN
  Matthew P: Newgarden 26 Jy
    53
WILSON/WILLSON; see also
  CARMALT & WILSON
  Alexander P: Bucks 28 Nov
    54; Chester Co 3 Ag 58; Pa
    8 Jy 62
  Andrew P: Phila 3 Ja 60
  Asaph P: Frankford 25 Ap 71
  Bella P: Phila 20 Jy 69
  Christopher P: Reading 3 Ja
    60
  David P: Bucks Co 3 Ja 60;
    Middleton 13 May 56
  Elizabeth Mount-Holly 30 Oct
    76; Phila 31 Dec 61
  Francis P: Phila 24 Oct 54
  George L: York Co 19 Dec 71.
    P: Phila 20 Ap 69, 27 Ja 73
  Hugh P: Phila 1 Nov 70
  Isaac P: Phila 23 Oct 66
  Isabella P: Phila 21 Dec 58
  Capt. J. P: Phila 15 Mar 64
  Ja. L: Octerara Creek 31 Ja 71
  Jacob C: London-grove, Chester
    Co 18 Jy 65. P: Pa 8 Jy 62
  James L: Carlisle, see KING,
    Thomas, Carlisle, 20 Ja 73;
    Leacock Twp 2 Mar 74. P:
    Bucks Co 13 Ja 63, 19 May
    63; Chester Co 3 Sep 61, 18
    Mar 62, 26 Jy 64; Lancaster
    Co 12 Feb 61, 18 Mar 62; N.
    Castle Co 15 Mar 64; Noxonton
    31 Dec 61; Pa 3 Sep 61, 31
    Dec 61, 13 Ja 63; Phila 24
    Oct 54, 21 Dec 58, 6 Jy 58,
    3 Ag 58, 24 Feb 63, 19 May
    63, 4 Ag 63, 3 Ja 65, 10 Ap 66,
    23 Oct 66, 30 Ap 67, 28 Ap 68,

20 Oct 68 (2), 19 Ja 69
    (Esq., counseller), 20 Ap
    69, 16 Jy 72, 3 Ja 76,
    19 Jy 80; Reading 26 Oct
    69; Wilmington 31 Dec 61.
    W: Wilmington 27 Ag 77
  Jane, widow C: at Thomas
    Fawset's,Kennet 30 Oct
    66. P: Phila 4 Ap 54
  Jesse P: Phila 30 Ap 67
  John L: Fort Augusta Co
    19 Dec 71; Lancaster 29
    Jy 72. N: 29 Nov 64. P:
    Bucks Co 13 Oct 63, 26
    Oct 69; Chester Co 3 Ja
    60, 13 Ja 63, 24 Feb 63;
    Christine 13 Oct 63;
    Donegal 24 Oct 54, 12 Ja
    58, 3 Ja 60; East Fallow-
    field 13 Ja 63; Great
    Valley 28 Oct 62, 16 Jy
    77; Lancaster Co 3 Ja 60,
    2 Feb 64; Londonderry
    Twp 2 Feb 64; New Britain
    19 May 63; Nottingham 28
    Oct 62; Pa 24 Feb 63;
    Phila 3 Ja 60, 5 Ag 62
    (2), 28 Oct 62, 23 Oct
    66, 1 Feb 70, 3 May 70;
    Pottsgrove 30 Ap 67;
    Wilmington 3 Sep 61. T:
    4 Nov 72; Bethlehem 31 Ja
    71
  Joseph P: N.J. 4 Ag 63;
    Phila 27 Ja 73, 27 Oct 73
  Justice P: Phila 20 Jy 69
  Magnes P: Phila 27 Ja 73
  Margaret P: Abington 2
    Feb 64; Bucks Co 18 Ag
    57; Pa 12 Feb 61, 28 Oct
    62, 13 Ja 63, 13 Oct 63;
    Phila 3 Ja 76
  Mary P: Lancaster Co 27
    Dec 53, 28 Oct 62; Pa 3
    Ag 58
  Matthew/Matt C: 30 Jy 77.
    L: Cumberland Co 14 May
    72. P: Cross-Roads 7 Ap
    57
  Philip P: Phila 30 Ja 66,
    27 Oct 73
  Ralph P: Bucks Co 10 Ap 66
  Rebecca P: Donegall 3 Ja
    60
  Richard P: Phila 16 Jy 77
  Robert L: Cumberland Co
    14 May 72; Shippensburgh
    19 Dec 71. P: Concord
    5 Ag 56; East Jersey 31
    Dec 61; Phila 3 Ag 58,
    18 Mar 62, 5 Ag 62, 19
    May 63, 25 Jy 65, 30 Ja
    66 (carpenter), 30 Ap 67,
    20 Jy 69 (Capt), 1 Nov 70
  Samuel L: Chestnut Level

15 Ap 56. P: Phila 20 Jy
   69, 3 Ja 76
Sarah P: Kensington 19 Ja
   69; Phila 3 Ja 76
Stephen P: Cumberland Co
   19 Ja 69
Thomas P: Carlisle 28 Oct
   62; Chester Co 13 May 56;
   Lancaster Co 3 Ag 58, 15
   Mar 64; Pa 21 Dec 58; Pequea
   4 Ag 63; Phila 24 Oct 54,
   21 Dec 58, 3 Ja 60, 5 Ag
   62, 20 Oct 68. T: Pa 10
   Ag 58)Esq)
William C: carpenter,
   Charlestown, Md. 30 Oct
   66. P: Brandywine 31 Dec
   61; Chester Co 7 Ap 57;
   Cumberland Co 18 Mar 62;
   Kent Co 2 May 65; King-
   ston 26 Jy 64; Pa 3 Sep
   61; Phila 3 Ja 60, 31 Jy
   60, 13 Ja 63, 4 Ag 63, 3
   Ja 76; Sussex Co 31 Dec 61;
   Wilmington 31 Jy 60; York
   Co 18 Mar 62
William Brown T: 4 Nov 72
WILTON
   & RUMSEY/RAMSAY P: Phila 2
   Feb 64, 15 Mar 64, 26 Jy 64
   Mrs. P: Phila 21 Dec 58
   James P: Phila 2 Feb 64, 19
   Ja 69
   Robert P: Phila 28 Oct 62
   William P: Pa 12 Feb 61;
   Phila 30 Ja 66
WILWORTH
   John P: Phila 1 Feb 70
WINCHESTER
   Rev. Elhannan Phila 30 Oct
   76
WIND
   Dr. Somerset Co 24 Jy 76
WINDER
   Edmund/Edmond P: Phila 2 Feb
   64, 30 Oct 76
WINDOWS
   William P: Phila 11 Jy 54
WINDSOR
   Sarah P: Mount-Holly 31 Jy
   60; Phila 31 Jy 60
WINESPERRIER
   Jacob P: Phila 29 Ag 54
WINKELL
   Henry P: Phila 1 May 76
WINTER
   Ann P: Pa 3 Sep 61
   Mat./Matthew P: Phila 28 Oct
   62; smith, prob. in Pitts-
   burgh 15 Mar 64
   Patrick P: Phila 2 Feb 64
   Richard P: Phila 24 Feb 63,
   2 Feb 64, 20 Ap 69
WINTERS
   Daniel P: Phila 31 Mar 63

John P: Phila 5 Ag 62, 26
   Oct 69
WINTHROP
   William Phila 30 Oct 76
WIRE
   Dorothy P: Phila 30 May 54
   Thomas P: Phila 3 May 70
WIRGMAN
   Dr. P: in the army 12 Ja
   58
WIRT
   Mrs. P: Phila 19 Jy 80
WISE
   Anne P: Phila 26 Oct 69
   Engineer P: Phila 18 Ag 57
WISEMAN
   John P: Phila 18 Ag 57
WISHART
   Capt. James P: Phila 19 Jy
   80
WISHER
   Ann P: Phila 21 Dec 58
   Thomas P: Phila 12 Ja 58
WISHURN
   Adam P: Phila 2 May 65
WISSON
   William C: 30 Jy 77
WISTER/WISTAR
   John P: Phila 5 Ag 56
   Sarah P: Phila 9 Ag 59
WITACKER
   Isaac Kent Co 16 Jy 77
WITHERINGTON
   Henry P: Phila 18 Mar 62
WITHERS
   John P: Phila 11 Sep 55
WITHERSPOON; see also
   WEATHERSPOON
   Miss P: Lancaster Co 3 Sep
   61
   David P: near Newcastle 24
   Oct 54, 11 Sep 55; New-
   Castle (Co) 3 Ag 58, 3
   Ja 60 (Esq), 3 Sep 61, 4
   Ag 63 (Esq), 13 Oct 63;
   Pa 12 Feb 61
   Robert P: Pequea 7 Ap 57
   Thomas P: Phila 21 Jy 68
WITHINGTON/WITINGTON
   Evan P: Bucks Co 3 Ag 58
   Peter P: Phila 25 Jy 65;
   Reading 26 Jy 64, 1 Feb
   70
WITHROW/WITHEROW
   John P: Pa 15 Mar 64
   William P: Chester Co 13
   Ja 63, 19 May 62, 4 Ag
   63; Middle Octerara 2 Feb
   64; Pa 31 Dec 61
WITLOE
   Margaret P: Phila 20 Jy 69
WITT
   Dr. P: Germantown 8 Jy 62
WITTERSTROOM
   Capt. C. P: Phila 13 Ja 63

WITTON
  James P: Pa 7 Ap 57
WITTROGEL
  Mr. P: Phila 20 Ap 69
WO..... / illegible /
  Grace P: Phila 7 Ap 57
WOGT
  Henry P: Phila 31 Ja 76
WOLF/WOLFE/WOOLFE
  John P: Phila 26 Jy 64,
    10 Ap 66, 20 Oct 68
  Lion T: Berkshire Co 31
    Ja 71
WOLK
  Phebe P: Phila 13 Oct 63
WOLLARD
  John T: Trenton 6 Dec 64
WOLLASTON
  George P: Whiteclay Creek
    26 Jy 64
WOLLSEN
  Mrs. P: Phila 6 Sep 53
  Matthew P: Phila 26 Jy 53
WOLLSEY
  Capt. George P: 27 Ja 73
WOLSTON
  John P: Bucks Co 18 Ag 57
WONAL
  James P: New-Castle Co 2
    Feb 64
WONDEROM/WONDROM
  James P: Phila 30 May 54,
    3 Ag 58
WOOD
  Edward P: Cohansey 30 Ja 66;
    Cumberland Co 8 Jy 62
  Eleanor P: Chester Co 8 Jy 62
  Elizabeth P: Phila 3 Ja 60
  Emanuel P: Phila 3 Ag 58
  Francis, matross P: Phila 20
    Jy 69
  George P: Cumberland Co 13
    Oct 63; Phila 13 May 56
  Israel T: Amwell 17 Oct 54
  James P: Pa 12 Feb 61
  John P: Pa 12 Ja 58; Phila 18
    Ag 57, 12 Ja 58, 3 May 70,
    27 Ja 73
  Joseph P: Phila 4 Ag 63, 30 Ja
    66
  Joseph, Jr. Phila 30 Oct 76,
    30 Ap 77
  Josiah P: Phila 12 Ja 58
  Mary P: Birmingham, Chester
    Co 16 Jy 67; Phila 3 Ja 60(2)
  Rachel P: Pa 28 Oct 62
  Robert P: Phila 12 Ja 58, 3
    Ag 58, 12 Feb 61, 1 Nov 70
  Sacheveral P: Phila 20 Oct 68
  Samuel P: Salem Co 1 Jy 56
  Thomas C: Chester Twp 30 Oct
    66. P: Chester Co 2 Feb 64;
    Manor of Moreland 13 May 56;
    Phila 27 Oct 73; Summerset
    Co 4 Ag 63

WOODBRIDGE
  Deodat P: Lewes 22 Nov 53;
    Salem 1 Nov 53
  Samuel P: Phila 21 Jy 68,
    16 Jy 72
WOODBURN
  Ja. L: Carlisle 19 Dec 71
  James P: Pa 3 Sep 61
  John P: N. Providence 31
    Dec 61; Pa 3 Sep 61, 18
    Mar 62
WOODBY
  Emanuel P: Phila 12 Feb 61
WOODCOCK
  Mr. P: Phila 3 Ag 58
  Anthony P: Phila 2 Ag 70
WOODERBY
  Benjamin P: Lancaster Co
    15 Mar 64
WOODHOUSE
  Capt. P: Phila 18 Ag 57
  James P: Phila 8 Jy 62
  John P: in the army 12 Ja
    58
  Robert P: Phila 20 Oct 68
WOODING
  James P: N.J. 18 Mar 62
WOODNITT
  Richard P: Salem 31 Jy 60
WOODROW
  Henry P: Phila 3 Ag 58
  John P: Bucks Co 19 Jy 80
  Jos. P: Phila 31 Dec 61
WOODS
  Mr. P: Carlisle 24 Feb 63;
    Phila 12 Feb 61
  Fortunatus P: Phila 18 Nov
    54
  Hugh P: Kent Co, Md. 7 Ap
    57
  Isabella P: Phila 2 May 65,
    25 Jy 65
  James P: Chester Co 12 Feb
    61; Whiteland Twp 3 Ag 58
  Rachel P: Phila 19 May 63
  Samuel P: New-Castle Co 3
    Ag 58
  Thomas P: Bucks Co 12 Ja 58
WOODSIDE
  James P: Mountholly 3 Sep
    61
  John P: Conewago 8 Jy 62;
    Pa 12 Feb 61; Phila 21
    Dec 58, 6 Jy 58, 28 Oct
    62, 13 Oct 63, 19 Jy 80
WOODWARD
  Capt. Henry P: in the army
    3 Ag 58
  Mary P: Phila 23 Oct 66
  Thomas P: Chester Co 3 Ag
    58, 8 Jy 62; East Marl-
    borough 21 Dec 58, 3 Ja
    60; Marlborough 31 Dec 61
  William P: Hollander's
    Creek 13 Ja 63

WOODWORTH
Isaac   P: Phila 12 Feb 61
WOODYEAR
Lumley   P: Phila 26 Oct 69
WOOHAM
Charles   P: Phila 2 May 65
WOOLBRICK
John   P: Pa 3 Sep 61
WOOLMAN
Fanny   P: Phila 3 Ja 65
WOOLRICH
Jacob   P: Phila 31 Dec 61
WOOLS
David   P: Pa 24 Feb 63
WOOLSEY
George   P: Phila 1 Feb 70
(Capt), 30 Ap 77
Henry   P: Pa 4 Ag 63; Phila
31 Jy 60.   T: Hopewell 17
Oct 54
WOOLTE
John   P: Phila 3 Ja 65
WOOLVERTON
Thomas   P: Sussex 13 May 56
WORCOR (tailor)
....   P: Phila 29 Ag 54
WORK
Andrew   P: Lancaster 29 Ag
54; Octorara 31 Dec 61
Capt. Patrick   P: in the
army 3 Ag 58
Robert   P: Phila 3 May 70
WORKMAN
and NAPLETON   P: Phila 6 Jy 58
Daniel   P: near Phila 28 Oct
62; Phila 3 Ja 65
John   L: Chestnut Level 15
Ap 56.   P: Lancaster Co 28
Oct 62
Mark   P: Phila 31 Dec 61, 28
Ap 68
William   P: Phila 3 May 70
WORMLEY
John   P: Phila 21 Dec 58
WORRELL
Dennis   P: Frankford 20 Ap
69; Phila 20 Oct 68
Jacob   P: Phila 1 Nov 53
James   P: Phila 18 Mar 62
John   P: Phila 30 Ja 66
WORSTER
Andrew   P: Phila 25 Ap 71
WORTH
James   P: East New Jersey 5
Ag 56
Joseph   P: Salem 1 Nov 70
Samuel   T: near Princetown
21 Ja 55; Stony Brook 6
Dec 64
Rev. William   New Jersey 31
Ja 76
WORTHY
Lt. John   P: Phila 13 Ja 63
WORTHINGTON
Mary   P: Frankford 19 May 63

WOSDELL
William   P: Phila 3 Ja 60,
31 Jy 60 (Capt)
WOTTON
Dr. T.S.   P: Phila 19 May
63
WRANGELL
Rev. Charles   P: 31 Dec 61
WRENCH
Dr. Robert   P: New-Castle
4 Ag 63
WRICE
Pierce   P: Phila 20 Jy 69
WRIGHT; see also JAMES &
WRIGHT
Mrs.   P: Phila 25 Jy 65
Mr.   P: Phila 2 May 65
Widow   P: Phila 3 Ja 60
Ann   P: Bristol 12 Ja 58
Benjamin   P: Phila 5 Jy 80
-Gaz. 19 Jy
Caspar   P: Phila 25 Jy 65
Charles   P: Phila 27 Ja 73.
T: near Prince Town 15 Jy
56
Elizabeth   P: Pa 18 Mar 62
Israel   P: Phila 3 Ja 65,
20 Ap 69
James   P: Phila 3 Ag 58
Jane   P: Phila 19 Jy 80
John   P: East Jersey 12 Ja
58; N.J. 13 Oct 63;
Passyunk 1 May 76; Pa 3
Ja 60; Phila 28 Nov 54,
10 Oct 65, 30 Ja 66, 20
Ap 69; Phila Co 26 Oct
69; West Jersey 21 Dec
58.   T: Longbridge 15 Jy
56; near Princeton 15 Jy
56
John M'Crakan   P: Phila-Gaz.
3 Ja 76
Patience   P: Phila 2 May 65,
25 Jy 65
Capt. Richard   P: Phila 5
Ag 62, 28 Oct 62
Robert   P: Phila 5 Jy 80-
Gaz. 19 Jy
Capt. Samuel   P: Phila 13
Oct 63, 27 Oct 73
Sarah   P: Phila 11 Sep 55,
21 Dec 58, 26 Jy 64, 3
Ja 65
Sherns   P: Phila 23 Oct 66
Thomas   P: Phila 3 Ja 60;
Plumsted, Bucks Co 27 Ja
73.   T: c/o Archibald
Stewart 31 Ja 71
William   P: Phila 24 Oct
54, 28 Oct 62, 2 Ag 70,
30 Ap 77
WRIGHTSON
Arthur   P: Pa 13 Oct 63
WRITER
Bartle   P: Merion 16 Jy 72

WRONG
  Henry   P: Phila-Gaz. 27 Oct
    73
WUSON
  Robert   L: Antiatem 2 Mar 74
WYATT
  Edward   P: Phila 18 Feb 55
WYER; see also WIER
  William   P: Phila 3 Ag 58
WYLIE & ; see also WILEY
WYNKOOP/WINECOOP/WINCOP
  Benjamin   P: Phila 13 Ja 63
  Catherine   P: Phila 12 Ja 58
  Garret   P: Bucks Co 21 Dec 58
  Nicholas   P: Bucks 1 Nov 53
  Philip   P: Phila 16 Jy 67
WYNN/WINN/WYNNE
  Connelly   P: Phila-Gaz. 3 Ja
    76
  Capt. J.   P: Phila 31 Dec 61
  Jacob   P: Phila 1 Nov 53

YAGER
  John   T: Amwell 6 Dec 64
YARD
  Joseph   P: Phila 8 Jy 62
YARDLEY
  Thomas   P: Bucks Co 12 Ja 58,
    3 Sep 61, 8 Jy 62, 13 Ja
    63; Pa 31 Jy 60; Phila 18
    Mar 62
YARNALL
  Mordecai   P: Phila 3 Ja 65
YARREL and PAYNE
  Mess.   P: Phila 1 Jy 56
YATES/YEATS/YEATES
  Andrew, soldier of the 42d.
    Regt.   P: Phila 23 Oct 66
  Donaldson   P: New-Castle Co
    18 Mar 62
  Eals   P: Phila 13 May 56
  John   P: Phila 11 Sep 55, 7
    Ap 57, 12 Ja 58, 12 Feb 61,
    13 Oct 63, 26 Jy 64
  Thomas   P: East New Jersey 12
    Feb 61
YEARDSLEY
  William   P: Phila 26 Oct 69
YEARWOOD
  Benjamin   P: Phila 1 Jy 56
YEAU
  Thomas   P: Phila 2 May 65, 25
    Jy 65
YERKES/YERKAS
  Silas   P: Moreland 13 Oct 63,
    2 Feb 64
YOCOM
  Abraham   P: Kingsess 30 Oct 76
YORKE
  Capt. Edward   Phila 24 Jy 76
  Richard   P: Phila 27 Ja 73
  William, 34 th Regt.   P: Phila
    20 Oct 68
YORKSON

  Mrs.   Phila 30 Ap 77
  Francis   P: Phila 25 Jy 65
YOULE
  Thomas, sergeant   P: Phila
    23 Oct 66
YOUMANS/YOUMAN
  John   P: Phila 3 Sep 61;
    York Co 24 Feb 63
YOUNG
  Alexander   L: Peter's Twp
    Cumberland Co 19 Dec 71
  Andrew   L: Drummore 31
    Ja 71; Muddy Rùn 15 Ap 56.
    P: Phila 3 Ja 65
  Ann   P: Pa 19 May 63; Phila
    31 Jy 60, 30 Ja 66, 10
    Ap 66
  Archibald   P: New-London
    13 Ja 63; Phila 13 Ja 63,
    20 Jy 69, 2 Ag 70
  David   P: Jersey 20 Oct 68;
    Phila 3 Ag 58, 27 Oct 73
  Edward   P: Phila 3 Sep 61
  Elizabeth   P: Phila 31 Jy
    60
  George   P: Phila 31 Dec 61
  Henry   P: at the Red House,
    close by Schuylkill 20
    Ap 69
  Hugh   P: Londonderry 24
    Feb 63
  James   P: Delaware Forks
    12 Feb 61, 2 Feb 64;
    Phila 3 Ag 58
  John   P: Mill-creek 18 Mar
    62; N. Castle Co 2 Feb 64;
    Phila 29 Ag 54, 1 Jy 56,
    31 Dec 61, 18 Mar 62,
    5 Ag 62, 3 May 70
    (corporal, 18th Regt.),
    27 Oct 73, 19 Jy 80;
    West Caln 13 May 56;
    Wills's Creek 3 Sep 61;
    Capt., Phila 24 Jy 76,
    16 Jy 77,19 Jy 80
  Margaret   P: Phila 31 Dec 61
  Mary   P: Lancaster 8 Jy 62
  Patrick   P: Phila 26 Jy 64,
    3 Ja 65
  Peter   P: Phila 10 Oct 65,
    10 Ap 66
  Philip   P: Cohansey 30 Ap
    67
  Robert   P: Lancaster Co 2
    Feb 64; Nottingham 3 Sep
    61; Phila 5 Feb 54, 9 May
    54, 5 Ag 56, 31 Jy 60, 18
    Mar 62, 10 Oct 65
  Samuel   L: Cumberland Co
    29 Jy 72 (apothecary).
    P: Chester Co 5 Ag 62;
    Mill-Creek 4 Ag 63; Phila
    2 Feb 64, 28 Ap 68 (Capt),
    20 Oct 68, 19 Jy 80.
    See also CROW, James

Thomas P: Phila 26 Jy 64
William L: York Co 20 Ja
   73. P: Forks of
   Delaware 26 Jy 53, 18
   Feb 55; Pa 31 Jy 60, 13
   Oct 63; Phila 30 Ap 77,
   19 Jy 80. T: Bordentown
   1 Sep 69
William, Jr. P: Schuylkill
   1 Nov 70
YOUNGER
  Bryan P: Phila 31 Dec 61,
   26 Jy 64
  Robert P: Phila 31 Dec 61,
   18 Mar 62, 5 Ag 62
YULDALL
  Deborah P: Phila 31 Jy 60
YULE
  Thomas P: Lancaster Co 5 Ag
   62

ZANE
  Jonathan P: Phila 28 Ap
   68, 21 Jy 68
ZANTZINGER
  Adam P: Phila 20 Oct 68
ZUBLEY
  Rev. Dr. John P: Phila-Gaz.
   3 Ja 76
ZUILL
  Matthew P: Chester Town 13
   Oct 63
  Robert P: Phila-Gaz. 27 Oct
   73
ZURHURST
  Henry P: Phila 25 Ap 71

NO SURNAME
  Adam, a Negro man P: Nesha-
   miney-Gaz. 27 Oct 73
  Abraham P: at Mr. Huston's
   Phila 27 Ja 73
  Rachel, Mr. Tilghman's P:
   Phila 21 Jy 68
  OVERSEERS, the, of Callop's
   Island, New Jersey 1 May 76

www.ingramcontent.com/pod-product-compliance
Lightning Source LLC
Chambersburg PA
CBHW070402270326
41926CB00014B/2672